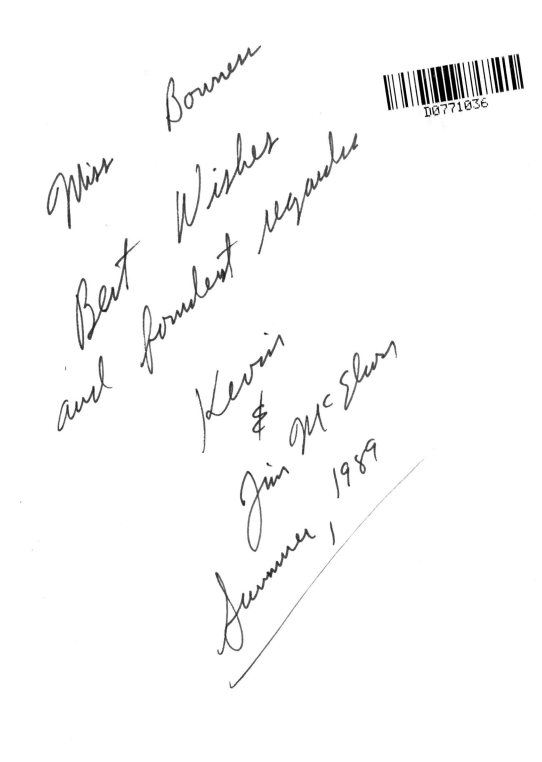

Miss Bowen

Best Wishes
and fondest regards

Kevin
&
Jim McElroy
Summer, 1989

Shit

WORLD WAR II ALMANAC: 1931–1945

WORLD
ALMANAC:

A POLITICAL AND

(OVERLEAF) *An infantryman of the U.S. 3rd Division pauses at the altar of a bomb-damaged church in Acerno, Italy.*

WAR II
1931-1945

MILITARY RECORD

Robert Goralski

BONANZA BOOKS · New York

This 1984 edition is published by Bonanza Books,
distributed by Crown Publishers, Inc. by arrangement
with G.P. Putnam's Sons.

Manufactured in the United States of America

Library of Congress Cataloging in Publication Data

Goralski, Robert.
World War II almanac, 1931-1945.

Bibliography: p.
Includes index.
1. World War, 1939-1945—Chronology.   I. Title.
D743.5.G64   1984   940.53'02'02   84-16844
ISBN: 0-517-44903X

h   g   f   e   d   c

Maps and charts by Robert Goralski
Designed by Barbara Huntley
First Perigee printing, 1982
Printed in the United States of America

PHOTO CREDITS: Armour and Company, 286; Joseph Arens (Captured Enemy Military Documents Collection, U.S. Army), 109; *Bilddokumente von Kampf und Krieg*, 103, 105, 112, 115, 117, 118, 120, 121, 123, 135; Bohlen Collection (U.S. Dept. of State), 293 (bottom); Eva Braun Collection (U.S. Army), 143 (top); Captured Enemy Documents Collection (U.S. Army), 352 (bottom), 355 (top), 365 (bottom), 366 (top and bottom); Captured Enemy Documents Collection (U.S. Navy), 186 (bottom); *Deutschland erwacht, Werden, Kampf und Sieg der NSDAP*, 3, 12 (left and right), 13, 17 (top and bottom), 19, 21, 23, 29, 30 (top); Domei Collection (National Archives), 57, 68; Heinrich Hoffman (Captured Enemy Military Documents Collection, U.S. Army), 77 (bottom); Imperial War Museum, 36, 41 (bottom), 77 (top), 80, 90, 98, 113, 119, 128, 141, 147, 182, 224 (left), 226, 245, 281; Tamura Konosuke (Captured Enemy Documents Collection, U.S. Army), 257; London Fire Brigade, 103 (bottom), 131; McDonnell Douglas, 259, 276, 375; Arai Shori (Captured Enemy Documents Collection, U.S. Army), 262; Susuki Makoto (Captured Enemy Documents Collection, U.S. Army), 352 (top); National Archives, 1 (top), 5, 7 (top and bottom), 9, 25 (top and bottom), 30 (bottom), 41 (top), 49 (top), 59, 61, 126, 178; Nimitz Collection (U.S. Navy), 186 (top), 416 (top), 418 (top); Ribbentrop Collection (U.S. Army), 61 (bottom), 69, 75, 135 (right), 136 (left and right), 137, 138, 139, 173, 180; Miyamoto Saburo (Captured Enemy Documents Collection, U.S. Army), 204, 216; Kobayakawa Tokushiro (Captured Enemy Documents Collection, U.S. Army), 206; U.S. Air Force, 254, 274, 285, 288, 297 (top), 315, 327, 328 (left), 348, 383, 385, 404 (bottom), 415, 418 (bottom); U.S. Army, overleaf, opposite acknowledgments, opposite introduction, 1 (bottom), 174, 195 (bottom), 199, 201, 212, 224 (bottom), 229, 239 (bottom), 246, 251 (bottom), 253, 266, 269, 271, 272, 290, 291 (top), 292, 293 (top), 295, 299 (bottom), 302, 303, 304, 307, 308, 309, 311 (left), 312 (top and bottom), 314 (top and bottom), 317, 318, 323, 324 (left, right and bottom), 325, 328, 329 (top), 330, 331, 333, 338 (right), 339, 341 (top and bottom), 342 (top and bottom), 343, 344, 345, 346 (top left), 347, 349 (top and bottom), 350, 351, 354 (top and bottom), 356, 362, 363 (left and right), 364, 367 (top and bottom), 369 (top), 370, 372, 373, 374 (bottom), 376, 377 (top and bottom), 384, 390, 391, 392, 397, 398, 401, 402, 404 (top), 405 (top and bottom), 406, 412, 413, 419, 420 (bottom); U.S. Coast Guard, 297 (bottom); U.S. Marine Corps, 298, 299 (top), 305, 346 (top right), 380; U.S. Navy, 49 (bottom), 143 (bottom), 161, 186, 190, 195 (top), 213 (left and right), 215, 217, 219, 233, 235, 236, 237, 238 (left and right), 239 (top), 242, 251 (top), 287, 289 (left and right), 291 (bottom), 306, 311 (right), 320 (top and bottom), 321, 322, 326, 329 (bottom), 334 (left and right), 346 (bottom), 353 (all), 355 (bottom), 357 (top and bottom), 358, 360 (bottom), 365 (top), 369 (bottom), 371, 374 (top), 379, 381, 387, 393, 396, 416 (bottom), 420 (top); Ihara Usaburo (Captured Enemy Documents Collection, U.S. Army), 193, 360 (right middle); Lt. W.R. Wilson, U.S. Army, 255; World War II Collection of Seized Enemy Records, National Archives, 160; Diosdado M. Yap, *Bataan Magazine*, 211.

Contents

Acknowledgments   xi

Introduction   xv

1931
Japanese militarism in Manchuria kindles
fires of war.   1

1932
A world in depression is made ripe for dramatic and drastic change.   7

1933
Hitler wins power and Germany accedes to
dictatorial rule.   17

1934
New alignments of power develop of nations
frantically seek security.   25

1935
Hitler rearms Germany; Mussolini conquers
Ethiopia.   31

1936
Spain is engulfed in civil war, and Europe's
will and arms are put to the test.   41

1937
An Axis is forged.   49

1938
Austria and Czechoslovakia fall under the
Nazi jackboot.   61

1939
The peace is shattered in Poland.   77

1940
Germany appears unstoppable until the Battle
of Britain.   103

1941
The mammoth clash of arms begins
in Russia, and Japan slashes through the
Pacific.   143

1942
Japan rules most of east Asia, but the Axis is
halted in North Africa.   195

1943
Allied forces on all fronts turn the tide of
battle.   251

1944
Europe's liberation begins with a Channel
crossing.   299

1945
Peace returns—for a while.   369

Men & Arms   421

Bibliography   457

Index   468

A mule train of the Royal Indian Service Corps slogs through the mud near Crespino, Italy.

Acknowledgments

More people than I can now cite helped in preparing this book. My thanks to each of them. The experience of receiving unstinting and selfless aid from so many will be long remembered.

Above all, my family has been a part of this effort throughout, making writing for us something akin to a cottage industry. Son Douglas assisted in the editorial and photographic process. Daughters Dorothy and Kate were stalwarts in support and bore neglect without ever losing their unsurpassed senses of humor and tolerance. My wife Margaret typed the manuscript, many times, and while that ordeal is deeply appreciated, she contributed more in editing, offering sound suggestions and criticism, counseling patience, and providing encouragement, always. She was truly indispensable.

Bob Trayhern and George Daoust read and edited the manuscript and offered invaluable advice from their political and military backgrounds. Dan Denning, Colonel Tom D'Andrea, and Phyllis Curt contributed many of the documents and materials which will not be found easily elsewhere, if at all. Paddy McLaughlin, Bob Stallings, John and Jo Hicks, Frank Brodziak, Mrs. Frances C. Denning, Karen Jordan, and Jerry Basterache were more helpful than they can imagine.

Many institutions provided facilities and services, including the U.S. Department of Defense, the National Archives, the Library of Congress, the Imperial War Museum, the U.S. Marine Corps Aviation Museum, the Army-Navy Club, the Metropolitan Library of Toronto, the British Information Services, and the London Fire Brigade. Particular thanks are extended to Bettie Sprigg of the Audio-Visual section of the Pentagon, Michael Willis of the Imperial War Museum, Robert A. Carlisle of the U.S. Navy's Department of Information, Harry S. Gann of Douglas Aircraft, Sylvia Danovitch of the National Archives, and Jim O'Sullivan of the London Fire Brigade.

Mention must be made of the dozens of used book dealers who tracked down books long out of print with spirited determination, and incredible success, and those many librarians who unfailingly direct you to the right books and files even with the slimmest of leads and clues.

Any errors, of course, are mine alone. Everyone involved tried very hard to help me avoid them.

A tank leads the advance of U.S. infantrymen on Bougainville.

Introduction

This chronological account of World War II begins in 1931, eight years before the outbreak of hostilities. No one can understand how war began without going back to its origins. It seemed that 1931 was the pivotal year in which events, political and military, began unfolding which led directly to the global conflict.

World War II was mankind's greatest cataclysm. What we did to each other is almost beyond human conception. More than 50 million people were killed. The economic cost can never be fully calculated, but the *conservative* estimates of at least $2 trillion indicate its dimensions. There is hardly a person alive today—whatever the age—who has not felt its impact. For the 85 million men and women who served as combatants and survived, the influence of the war was direct and profound. All others, including today's youngest children, have been touched by the political, economic, and social consequences of the world's first total war. More than twice as many civilians died than did uniformed soldiers, sailors, and airmen. Young and old of all races and religions perished as innocent victims of the juggernaut of war and genocide.

There is an understandable fascination—which is neither macabre nor militaristic—about World War II. Any event approaching its ghastly dimensions would command infinite attention.

The experience is still near enough in time to provide retrospective interest for those who lived through it and to spark intellectual curiosity among those unborn at the time. This book was thus compiled for virtually everyone, and if it encourages objectivity beyond narrow nationalisms, so much the better.

A word on dates and data. It is surprising how often participants and historians disagree on them. Wherever possible, I have tried to go back to original or basic sources where conflicts existed. The dates are those of the area in which the event occurred. Pearl Harbor was attacked December 7, Hawaiian time, and is so recorded in this book, even though it was December 8 in Japan.

As for geographical name confusion, the style was to stick to the spelling of the country which possessed the city or territory when the war began. For example, Brno is the Czech form, used in preference to the German Brühn. When the name differs from today's designation, I have provided wherever possible the present-day name and/or spelling in parentheses. Manchukuo did exist as a Japanese-sponsored state, and as a governmental entity it is referred to as such, but Manchuria was the choice for general references to the region.

PROPHETS AND SINNERS

"I cannot conceive any greater cause of a future war than that the German people should be surrounded by a mob of small states, many of them consisting of peoples who have never previously set up stable governments by themselves, but each of them containing large masses of Germans."
> —David Lloyd George, Former British Prime Minister.

"It is quite a mistake to suppose that Hitler has seized power. All that has happened is that we have given him a job."
> —Franz von Papen, German Vice-Chancellor, 1933.

"Only a madman would consider the possibility of war between the two states [France and Germany], for which, from our point of view, there is no rational or moral ground."
> —Chancellor Adolf Hitler, Oct. 14, 1933.

"One may like or dislike Hitlerism, but every sane person will understand that ideology cannot be destroyed by force. It is therefore not only nonsensical but also criminal to pursue a war 'for the destruction of Hitlerism' under the bogus banner of a 'struggle for democracy'."
> —V.M. Molotov, Soviet Foreign Minister, Oct. 31, 1939.

"Hitler's highly intelligent and therefore would not be prepared to wage a world war."
> —Neville Chamberlain, British Prime Minister, to U.S. Ambassador Kennedy, 1939.

"This war is sheer madness. We have gone to war with a 1918 army against a German army of 1939. It is sheer madness."
> —General Maxime Weygand, Allied ground forces Commander in Chief, 1940.

"The Ruhr will not be subjected to a single bomb. If any enemy bomber reaches the Ruhr, my name is not Hermann Göring: you can call me Meier!"
> —Reichsmarschall Hermann Göring, Aug. 9, 1939.

"Pearl Harbor will never be attacked from the air."
> —Admiral Charles H. McMorris, U.S.N., Dec. 3, 1941.

"The Soviet Union is militarily liquidated with this last gigantic blow we are dealing it. I stake my personal reputation on the accuracy of this."
> —Dr. Otto Dietrich, Reich Press Chief, Oct. 9, 1941.

"It is assumed that there are no enemy carriers in waters adjacent to Midway."
> —Vice Admiral Chuichi Nagumo, Imperial Japanese Navy, on the morning of the Battle of Midway, June 4, 1942.

(*On the atomic bomb*) "That is the biggest fool thing we have ever done. The bomb will never go off, and I speak as an expert in explosives."
> —Admiral William Leahy, Chief of Staff to the Commander in Chief, to President Truman, 1945.

(OPPOSITE, TOP) *Japanese troops attack in China.*

(OPPOSITE, BOTTOM) *Yen Shien, like many towns in China, was laid waste in the war which engulfed that country.*

1931 Japanese militarism in Manchuria kindles fires of war.

Sept. 18–19 Japanese units attacked the Chinese Army's 7th Brigade barracks at Peitaying, near Mukden. The action allegedly resulted from Chinese "sabotage," the dynamiting of a small section (actually less than three feet) of South Manchurian Railway track. The "Manchurian Incident" was all the pretext needed for the assertive Japanese Kwantung Army to embark on its China adventure. (A subsequent League of Nations Commission of Enquiry found the Japanese operations could not "be regarded as measures of legitimate self-defence." Postwar disclosures revealed that elements of the Kwantung Army carefully planned to extend Japan's influence in China through force. The contrived "sabotage" [Japanese soldiers actually blew up the track] triggered a series of aggressive actions which no one felt able or compelled to stop. The commanding general of the Kwantung Army, Honjo Shigeru, insisted up to his suicide in 1945 that his troops were only defending themselves. Firm control over Manchuria was clearly an initial objective of the Japanese military—of key officers in China *and* Tokyo—and the approval or acquiescence of all governmental elements confirmed the basic direction of Japanese policy. Manchuria was seen as a strategic base for possible operations against the Soviet Union. It also offered tremendous resources for the Japanese, who were hard pressed for basic raw materials.

Japanese public opinion avidly supported expansion in Manchuria. General Sadao Araki represented an extreme nationalist element, but his racial views won growing popular support: "Japan must no longer let the impudence of the white peoples go unpunished. It is the duty of Japan . . . to cause China to expel foreign influence from Manchuria, and to follow the way of imperial destiny.")

Sept. 19 Mukden and several towns in south Manchuria were bombed and then occupied by the Japanese. Invoking the need for "the maintenance of the safety of Japanese nationals and the protection of the railway," the Kwantung Army swiftly seized banks, utilities, and municipal administration centers. Tokyo announced Japanese forces were being withdrawn "to the fullest extent possible." The lightning action, completed in less than 24 hours, left 400 Chinese dead. Two Japanese soldiers were killed.

Sept. 21 China appealed to the League of Nations and the United States to "concern" themselves with events in Manchuria. The issue was placed before the Council of the League of Nations.

■ Although the foreign office in Tokyo continued to indicate Japan's intention to localize the Manchurian dispute, the Kwantung Army began occupying the whole of Kirin Province. The Chinese commander was forced to declare Kirin's secession from China with a gun literally pointed at his head.

Sept. 22 U.S. Secretary of State Henry L. Stimson warned the Japanese their actions in Manchuria raised questions of possible violations of international treaties and law.

■ The League of Nations called on China and Japan to withdraw their troops from the disputed area and to refrain from further hostile actions.

Sept. 23 Having been persuaded by Japan's ambassador in Washington, Katsuji Debuchi, that any overreaction by the U.S. would only weaken the influence of civilians in the Tokyo cabinet, Stimson opposed a League of Nations inquiry into the Manchurian Incident.

Sept. 24 Washington called on both the Chinese and the Japanese "to refrain from further hostilities."

Sept. 28 Demonstrations demanding an all-out war against Japan reached a climax as thousands of Chinese stormed the foreign ministry building in Nanking, the capital, and assaulted the foreign minister, C. T. Wang.

Sept. 30 The League Council took official note of Tokyo's intention to withdraw its troops from newly occupied Manchurian territory and its statement that Japan entertained no territorial designs on Manchuria.

Oct. 1 China called for a League observation team to visit Manchuria and insure the promised withdrawal of Japanese troops.

Oct. 8 Japanese planes bombed Chinchow in Liaoning Province, 100 miles southwest of Mukden. The action was significant because the military extremists calculated it would inflame international public opinion and force Tokyo once and for all to support the conquest of Manchuria. It had the effect of dashing all hopes a settlement could be reached.

Oct. 9 Japan refused to withdraw its troops from occupied Manchuria on any fixed schedule but said it would negotiate with the Chinese. Among the key issues was the anti-Japanese boycott in China. Tokyo claimed it was "an instrument of national policy under the direction of the Nationalist party."

■ China sought an immediate meeting of the League Council "in view of the serious information regarding further aggressive military operations upon the part of the Japanese armed forces in Manchuria."

Oct. 10 The U.S. told Japan it was "concerned" about the Japanese bombing of Chinchow. At the same time, Washington called on the Chinese and Japanese to resolve the Manchurian Incident peacefully.

■ Adolf Hitler was received by German President Paul von Hindenburg, the first meeting between the head of the increasingly popular National Socialist German Workers' (Nazi) party and the

A formal portrait of Adolf Hitler, leader of the German Nazi party.

military hero turned statesman. A meeting devoid of substance, it gave Hitler and the Nazis a measure of respectability previously denied them.

Oct. 11 Stimson took a harder line in dealing with the Japanese, saying Tokyo had not honored its pledges to the League on troop withdrawals and that Japan's explanation of the Chinchow bombing was inadequate.

Oct. 13 Japan informed the League Council that its policy in Manchuria was to support the principle of economic equality in China for all nations.

Oct. 17 The Kellogg-Briand Pact (Pact of Paris) of 1928 (specifically the clause "A threat of war, wherever it may arise, is of profound concern to the whole world") was invoked by individual Council members. Identical notes were sent to Japan and China. Most of the major powers joined in the action, including Britain, France, Germany, Italy, and Spain, with the U.S. following suit two days later.

Oct. 24 Invoking Article 10 of the League Covenant, the Council assailed Japan for refusing to set a date for troop withdrawals from Manchuria. It also called on Tokyo to explain "the fundamental principles governing normal relations" which Japan had previously indicated it would discuss with China. Japan was asked to remove its troops by Nov. 16. The Council vote was 13 to 1, Japan casting the only negative vote.

Oct. 27 The British coalition government was overwhelmingly returned to power in national elections. Ramsay MacDonald remained as prime minister.

Oct. 31 Under Secretary of State William Castle told a press conference in Washington the U.S. position on the Sino-Japanese dispute was one of "strict impartiality."

Nov. 4 Fighting erupted in Manchuria again as Japanese and Chinese troops clashed at the Nonni River Bridge. The bridge was strategically and economically important. Japanese officials became edgy about Chinese raids on the bridge while it was being repaired. (The span had been destroyed earlier by retreating Chinese troops.)

Nov. 5 Stimson said the U.S. viewed "with regret and concern" Tokyo's position that basic Sino-Japanese differences must be resolved before Japanese troops could be withdrawn from Man-

churia. He again called on the Japanese to settle the incident along the lines proposed by the League Council.

Nov. 7 A Liaoning provincial government was established by the Japanese. The name was changed to Fengten, as it was called before it accepted union with China in the previous decade.

■ Mao Tse-tung proclaimed the "Chinese Soviet Republic" in the village of Juichin, in the southern area of Kiangsi Province.

No. 12 The Japanese moved to complete their occupation of Heilungkiang Province in Manchuria. Their chief obstacle was General Ma Chan-shan who was served an ultimatum to evacuate his forces from the provincial capital of Tsitsihar in three days.

Nov. 18 Announcing that its actions were "purely defensive," the Japanese occupied Tsitsihar, "aimed at striking a decisive blow against Ma Chan-shan's army."

Nov. 21 Japan proposed the League send a commission to investigate conditions in Manchuria. Tokyo believed the Kwantung Army's actions would be understood and condoned by an impartial inquiry into the "realities" of Manchuria and China. Most of Manchuria was already occupied.

Nov. 24 With reports indicating a Japanese advance on the city of Chinchow, Tokyo responded to American concerns by informing the U.S. State Department that "the Foreign Secretary, the Secretary of War, and the Chief of Staff were all of them agreed there should be no hostile operations toward Chinchow and that military orders to that effect have been issued."

Nov. 25 Japanese army units continued pressing toward Chinchow. China requested the establishment of a neutral zone between the rival forces.

Nov. 26 The League Council agreed to send an observer group to the Chinchow area.

Nov. 27 Tokyo rejected the dispatch of League observers to Chinchow, saying, "the policy which the Japanese Government had so far consistently pursued in the interest of good relations between China and Japan had been not to resort in dispute capable of direct settlement with China, to the interposition of third parties."

■ The concluding ceremonial meeting of the

International Disarmament Congress in Paris was broken up by right wing bullies of veterans and fascist organizations. Thousands in the audience and the distinguished foreign guests were forced out of the auditorium.

Nov. 28 Japanese troops pulled out of the Chinchow area with Tokyo anticipating an early adjournment of the League Council and thus hoping to forestall an international inquiry.

Dec. 10 The League Council voted to establish a Commission of Inquiry to look into the Manchurian affair. It would "contribute towards a final and fundamental solution by the two governments of the questions at issue between them. . . ." Headed by the British Earl of Lytton, the commission included representatives of Italy, France, Germany, and the U.S.

Dec. 11 The Japanese cabinet, which had been trying to resign, was finally able to do so with the League having acted. It was unable to stand as a buffer between the militarists and the League Council. The government was, in fact, incapable of justifying or supporting the army's actions in Manchuria. Public opinion generally regarded the cabinet as too liberal.

Dec. 13 Tsuyoshi Inukai became the new prime minister, and the first act of the new Japanese government was to approve funds for the completion of the occupation of Manchuria.

Dec. 15 Chiang Kai-shek resigned as president of China, saying that "a successful safeguard against foreign invasion depends upon the cessation of civil trouble and the unification of the country." It was an act of petulance, indicating Chiang's disgust with those who insisted on fighting Japan while China was still politically fragmented, and thus too weak to wage war. This view became an obsession of Chiang's and guided him right through World War II and his battles with the Communists.

Dec. 21 The Japanese delivered an ultimatum to the Chinese to force the turnover of Chinchow. At the same time, Japanese army units launched "large scale anti-bandit operations" in the disputed area.

Dec. 24 Paris, London, and Washington protested Chinchow developments.

Dec. 28 A new Chinese government was formed in Nanking.

■ Japanese Prime Minister Inukai said Tokyo would adhere to the principles of the Open Door policy and called on other powers to join with Japan in developing Manchuria economically.

Japanese troops advance in central China, near Nanchang.

THE KWANTUNG ARMY

Although the term "Kwantung Army" was commonly used by the Japanese to describe any overseas unit which operated beyond Tokyo's control, it was the original Imperial force to run amok.

Kwantung was a province at the tip of Liaotung peninsula in southern Manchuria. Japan acquired leaseholds there after winning the Russian-Japanese war in 1905. Dairen and Port Arthur were the main cities of Kwantung and served as economic and military bases.

The Kwantung Army was originally the garrison force protecting Japan's interests in China. Rail operations were vital to the Japanese as requisites for their commercial undertakings. Under concessions granted the Japanese (and other nations), Tokyo was permitted to station troops outside the immediate leaseholds, particularly for the protection of rail traffic.

At the time of the 1931 incident, the Kwantung Army headquarters was in Port Arthur. The army itself was made up of an understrength infantry division and six battalions of the Independent Garrison Unit. The latter had Mukden as its headquarters. In all, the Kwantung Army was a force of only 10,400 men.

Once the Manchurian adventure was launched, the Kwantung Army grew rapidly. The following shows its increased power:

	mid-1931	Dec. 1931	1932
Manpower	10,400	64,900	94,100
Planes	—	30	90

	1933	1934	1935
Manpower	114,100	144,100	164,100
Planes	120	150	180

Eventually, the Kwantung Army was augmented by other units until by the outbreak of the Pacific war in 1941 there were about 700,000 Japanese military personnel in China.

There is little doubt that the Kwantung Army fabricated and escalated the Manchurian Incident. Its contempt and pointed disregard for policies established by the foreign ministry were blatant. The Kwantung Army symbolized the triumph of militarism and the elimination of party government in Japan.

SOURCES ON TROOP STRENGTHS: Saburo Hayashi, *Kogun*.

(OPPOSITE, TOP) *Austrian Democratic Socialists march in a 1932 Vienna May Day rally.*

(OPPOSITE, BOTTOM) *Anti-Semitic demonstrations became common in central Europe.*

1932

A world in depression is made ripe for dramatic and drastic change.

Jan. 3 Citing the continuing danger of "bandits," Japanese troops occupied Chinchow and forced most of the remaining organized Chinese forces, commanded by Marshal Hsueh-liang, out of Manchuria.

Jan. 4 Japanese units completed their occupation of south Manchuria by entering Shanhaikuan.

Jan. 7 Stimson enunciated the Doctrine of Non-recognition. In notes to the Japanese and Chinese governments, the U.S. secretary of state said the U.S. "can not admit the legality of any situation *de facto* nor does it intend to recognize any treaty or agreement entered into between those governments or agents thereof which may impair the treaty rights of the United States or its citizens in China, including those which relate to the sovereignty, the independence, or the territorial and administrative integrity of the Republic of China, or to the international policy relative to China, commonly known as the open-door policy; and that it does not recognize any situation, treaty, or agreement which may be brought about by means contrary to the covenants and obligations of the Pact of Paris of August 27, 1928." The declaration of U.S. policy, which was later adopted by the League of Nations, was the first national act challenging Japan's moves in China.

Jan. 9 A Korean nationalist attempted to assassinate Japanese Emperor Hirohito. Japanese public opinion—enraged by the act itself—turned hostile toward the Chinese when the official newspaper of the ruling Nationalist party (the Kuomintang) expressed regret the emperor was not killed. The Japanese community in Shanghai, 30,000 strong, demanded an official apology.

■ Germany defaulted on its World War reparations payments. Chancellor Heinrich Brüning declared "that any attempt to uphold the system of political debt payments would bring disaster not only on Germany but on the whole world." Under terms of the Treaty of Versailles, Germany was obligated to pay for all damages suffered by its former enemies during the war. In 1921 the Reparations Commission fixed the amount of 132 billion gold marks. Subsequent agreements reduced the amount to at least 660 million marks annually, through 1988 (or a total of $10 billion).

■ Britain declined to endorse the Stimson Doctrine of Nonrecognition, saying it continued to support an Open Door policy which was guaranteed by the Nine-Power Treaty of Washington (1922).

Jan. 18 Five Japanese civilians, two of them monks, were attacked by Chinese factory workers in Shanghai, the first major violence arising from the anti-Japanese boycott and organized civilian resistance to Japanese encroachments in China.

Emperor Hirohito of Japan reviews his troops.

Jan. 20 The consul general of Japan in Shanghai issued demands to the mayor of the city growing out of the Jan. 18 attack on Japanese nationals. Japan sought a formal apology, the arrest of those involved in the incident, indemnification, effective control of the Japanese boycott, and the dissolution of all anti-Japanese organizations. The consul general's demands followed a backlash Japanese riot in Shanghai which included attacks on a Chinese police station, several stabbings, and the burning of buildings.

Jan. 21 Finland and the Soviet Union signed a nonaggression pact. It provided for a conciliation commission in the event of any disputes. Moscow was anxious to settle potential problems along its western frontiers while Japanese militarism in the east was posing a more real threat. The Russians realized that Manchuria under Tokyo's control was a possible menace to the Soviet Union. Japan made clear its strong anticommunist stand at every opportunity.

■ Japanese Rear Admiral Kiochi Shiozawa, military commander of the Shanghai area, threatened to "take necessary steps" unless Japan's demands of Jan. 20 were met immediately.

Jan. 24 In a calculated show of strength, Japan increased its naval force in Shanghai waters to an aircraft carrier, four cruisers, and seven destroyers.

Jan. 27 The Japanese consul general in Shanghai informed the mayor that a deadline of 6 P.M. on the 28th had been set for a reply to Japan's demands.

■ Stimson cabled U.S. Ambassador W. Cameron Forbes in Tokyo and instructed him to inform the Japanese government of Washington's deep concern over the course of events in China. Stimson called the situation serious and noted "that the consular and naval officers of the Japanese Government on the spot are seriously considering the use of force near to or in the International Settlement as an instrument of Japanese policy."

Jan. 28 The Shanghai Municipal Council capitulated and accepted the Japanese demands of Jan. 20. U.S. and British troops moved into prearranged defense positions in the International Settlement at 4 P.M. Seven hours later the Japanese notified the mayor to remove all Chinese troops from the Chapei quarter of the city within 30 minutes.

■ Japan's General Staff approved a plan for the

army to occupy Harbin, a key city in Kirin Province which would facilitate control over northern Manchuria.

Jan. 29 Japanese army and navy units bombed and virtually destroyed Chapei. The first shots were fired at 12:15 A.M. (An eventual force of 70,000 Japanese, including the Kurume Brigade and the 9th, 11th, 14th, and 16th divisions, began moving into the Shanghai area. The battle lasted until Mar. 3. During the fighting, the Chinese offered spirited resistance. Impressive actions by the Communist 19th Route Army and V Corps had a decided psychological effect on the Chinese civilian population which had been clamoring for resistance. In the end, however, the Chinese military was forced to yield to superior Japanese forces. About 4,000 Chinese troops and 8,000 civilians were killed in the fighting.)

CHAPEI AND THE FIRST TERROR BOMBING

Indiscriminate bombing of civilian population centers became a standard practice of Axis and Allied air forces during World War II. The date of the first terror bombing which set the grotesque example was Jan. 29, 1932. Japanese bombers from two aircraft carriers virtually leveled Chapei, a section of northern Shanghai about eight square miles in size. It was bounded on the south and west by the U.S. sector of Shanghai, on the east by the Japanese. North Station, the terminal for trains to Nanking and the coastal area around Woosung, was within Chapei. It was generally referred to as the Chinese quarter of Shanghai and contained mostly ramshackle homes. The devastation of Chapei was observed by the colonies of foreigners who lived nearby. A reporter for the *North China Herald* wrote (in the issue of Feb. 2) of the "terrifying ghastliness" of the bombing: "Opening from a fair height, the Japanese aviators came in lower and lower until at the time they bombed the Railway Station they could have been little more than 300 feet up. They were so low that they leaned over the sides of their machines as they were manoeuvering into position, waved their hands to the watching Volunteers below, then banked, circled, flew over their targets, and could not possibly miss their objectives. Outer Chapei is

ruined. Larger buildings, with few exceptions, last night were bare and gaunt walls, their interiors a seething mass of glowing embers, reflecting against the night sky. Houses by the hundreds are a wreck and a ruin."

No accurate estimate of casualties is possible. Thousands died, but the fearful toll was lost in the superficial interest of the world at the time and the subsequent desensitization to slaughter on any scale.

Jan. 31 A cease-fire and means to settle the fighting were arranged by the British and U.S. consuls in Shanghai, but the agreements quickly evaporated.

February Tokyo figures showed Japan's exports to China had fallen dramatically, the direct result of the massive boycott of Japanese goods by Chinese consumers and merchants. In a year, goods shipped to central China fell 96 percent, south China 97 percent, and 72 percent in trade through Hong Kong.

Feb. 1 A Japanese warship shelled Nanking. Several rounds were fired. Three Japanese cruisers and four destroyers were anchored in Nanking waters, but it subsequently appeared the ship doing the shelling believed it had been shot at and returned the fire. Whatever the cause, the incident added to the deepening concern about an expanding war in China and further inflamed the Chinese population. U.S. citizens began to be evacuated.

Feb. 2 Britain requested the League Council to suspend any action on the Sino-Japanese dispute until the U.S., France, Italy, and Britain were permitted time to deal with the situation directly.

■ The Disarmament Conference was convened in Geneva. This assemblage was required by Article 9 of the League Covenant. Sixty-four nations were invited. Fifty-nine sent delegations, including non-League members the U.S. and the Soviet Union. The opening session was dramatically delayed by reports on the fighting in Shanghai and League Council discussions on events in China. (The conference lasted until Oct. 14, with a notable lack of success. France, Britain, Germany, and Italy did promise "not in any circumstances to attempt to resolve any present or future differences" between them by force. The thorniest issue was how soon Germany would be permitted to rearm, with Berlin demanding the right to possess "defensive weapons" immediately. Germany phrased her demands as "equal status and rights.")

Feb. 5 Latvia and the Soviet Union signed a nonaggression pact.

■ Japan extended its military occupation of Manchuria, including those areas recently dominated by the Soviet Union. Harbin was occupied with Japanese forces taking advantage of an outburst of fighting between rival Chinese armies.

Feb. 8 Bulgaria announced it would make no further reparations payments growing out of its defeat in the World War.

Feb. 9 Former Japanese Finance Minister Junnosuke Inouye was killed by extremists in Tokyo.

Feb. 12 China formally requested intervention by the League in the Sino-Japanese dispute.

■ In unusually harsh words, Stimson criticized the British for not adhering to the Doctrine of Nonrecognition in China. Stimson said, "If the covenants and policies of the Nine-Power Treaty and the Pact of Paris be allowed to be repudiated or repealed, the loss to all nations of the world will be immeasurable."

Feb. 16 League Council members implored Japan "to recognize the very special responsibility for forebearance and restraint which devolves upon it in the present conflict in China." It was noted that the League Covenant would not permit acceptance of Japanese territorial gains through force.

Feb. 17 Means to establish a puppet state of Manchukuo were created by the Japanese. Some prominent Chinese subject to Japanese pressure and controls (and some who were simply opportunists) indicated their desire for the establishment of a new "independent" state. A North Eastern Administrative Committee was set up by the Japanese.

Feb. 18 The North Eastern Administrative Committee issued a "declaration of independence" for a Manchu-Mongolian state, to be known as Manchukuo. Its avowed purpose was "to establish peace within and harmonious relations with the foreign countries promoting industry, agriculture, and commerce, thus bringing prosperity to the people."

■ German Chancellor Brüning called on the dis-

armament negotiators to draw up a plan "on the basis of equal rights and equal security for all peoples," which was a demand for German military "equality" and an abrogation of the Versailles restraints on Germany.

Feb. 19 The Sino-Japanese dispute was referred to the Assembly by the League Council.

Feb. 20 Japanese troops occupied Tunhua in China's Kirin Province.

Feb. 23 Tokyo rejected all appeals to end the fighting in China. Japanese opinion was expressed by the newspaper *Asahi* which editorialized: "The fact should be remembered that China's bad faith brought about the situation."

Feb. 25 Adolf Hitler became a German citizen. He overcame this obstacle to German leadership by getting himself appointed a representative of the Brunswick state government to Berlin.

Feb. 29 The former Manchu emperor of China, Henry Pu-yi, was named the provisional president of Manchukuo by the All-Manchuria convention in Mukden.

■ The U.S. said it would cooperate and participate in a proposed international conference in Shanghai to consider means to halt the fighting.

March 3 The League Assembly was convened to take up the China question.

■ Japanese forces completed their military domination of Shanghai and a cease-fire went into effect.

March 4 The League Assembly passed a resolution calling for an end to the fighting in China and preparations for the withdrawal of Japanese forces. Belgium, Switzerland, and Czechoslovakia led the fight for passage. Britain and France were passive, fearing the consequences to them of military and economic sanctions which might be imposed on the Japanese.

March 5 Japanese industrialist Baron Takuma Dan was murdered by nationalist extremists in Tokyo.

March 9 Manchukuo was officially declared in a ceremony held at Changchun (whose name was changed to Hsinking, meaning "New Capital") under the regency of Henry Pu-yi.

March 11 A resolution was passed by the League Assembly which enunciated the Stimson Doctrine of Nonrecognition in China. A 19-member committee was appointed to report on the Sino-Japanese dispute.

March 12 Washington informed the League it

was gratified "at the action by the Assembly . . . that the nations of the world are united on a policy not to recognize the validity of results attained in violation of the treaties in question (the Pact of Paris and the League Covenant)."

March 13 Hindenburg failed to win a majority of votes in the German presidential election. Hindenburg, the war hero incumbent, polled 18,651,000 votes, to 11,319,000 for Nazi party leader Hitler, and 4,963,000 for the Communist candidate Ernst Thälmann.

MID-MARCH Chiang Kai-shek resumed his involvement in governmental affairs by assuming the position of chairman of the Kuomintang Military Affairs Commission.

(LEFT) *A Nazi party campaign poster urges workers to "Vote for the front-line soldier Hitler" for president, an appeal based on Hitler's record in World War I.* (RIGHT) *A Nazi party campaign poster appeals to the women of Germany.*

April A group of prominent Japanese began organizing the Great East Asian Propaganda Society in Mukden. Its goals were not published until much later, but the purpose agreed upon at the time foretold future events with remarkable accuracy: "The ultimate purpose of Manchukuo . . . is the creation of a foundation so as to successfully serve the unified and friendly Nippon in her struggle against the Anglo-Saxon world, as well as against Comintern aggression. In this holy struggle, all the people of east Asia must join to form the united front of the common fight with the oppressors."

April 10 Hindenburg won the German runoff presidential election, winning 53 percent of the vote. Hitler received 36.8 percent and Thälmann 10.2 percent.

April 13 Chancellor Brüning banned Nazi Storm Troopers (SA), defying the increasingly influential Nazis under Hitler.

Nazi leader Hermann Göring is pictured as the leader of the SA (Sturmabteilung—Storm Troopers).

May 4 Estonia and the Soviet Union signed a nonaggression treaty.

May 5 Japan and China signed an armistice accord, stating that "the cessation of hostilities is rendered definite." A demilitarized zone was established around the International Settlement in Shanghai, and the anti-Japanese boycott was ended.

May 6 A Russian immigrant assassinated President Paul Doumer of France.

May 9 Nations of the Little Entente (Yugoslavia, Czechoslovakia, and Rumania) renewed their treaty of defensive alliance, originally designed to block Austro-Hungarian reassertions of power but now aimed at collective responses to stirrings of German militancy.

May 15 Prime Minister Tsuyoshi Inukai of Japan was assassinated by members of the Young Officers of the Army and Navy and the Farmers Death Band who declared themselves "opposed to weakness and corruption in government and to capitalism."

May 26 Admiral Viscount Makoto Saito became Japan's premier. With the formation of the military-dominated cabinet, democratic party government effectively came to an end in Japan.

May 29 Nazis won control of the Prussian legislature, taking 162 seats to the Socialists' 93.

May 30 Chancellor Brüning of Germany was ousted because of opposition to his government's emergency decrees and East Prussian land settlement policies. Hindenburg felt Brüning lost the support of the army and the general public. His dismissal marked the beginning of a period of confusion in German politics marked by extremist demands for nondemocratic solutions to mounting problems.

May 31 Under terms of the May 5 armistice, Japanese troops completed their withdrawal from Shanghai.

June 2 Franz von Papen was named chancellor of Germany. Papen was considered a centrist, but the term was relative and he loathed the Weimar Republic. No Nazis were included in the cabinet.

■ A deputy in the Prussian legislature, Wilhelm Kube, delivered an anti-Semitic tirade, declaring

April 15 The Chinese Soviet Republic under Mao Tse-tung declared war on Japan, the only such formal act of the China crisis. The Communist regime was not recognized by the international community, and the gesture had no effect on the course of Chinese events except to strengthen a conviction among many that the Communists were more capable, and certainly more willing, than the central government in Nanking to defend China.

April 22 Finland and the Soviet Union signed the Treaty of Conciliation provided for in the Jan. 21 nonaggression pact.

April 30 The League Assembly approved a resolution on a draft armistice agreement between Japan and China and for the eventual withdrawal of Japanese troops.

May 1 Through the good offices of western diplomatic representatives in Shanghai, China and Japan reached tentative agreement to end the fighting.

that "when we clean house the exodus of the Children of Israel will be a child's game in comparison." Kube singled out German-Jewish physicist Albert Einstein for particular attention, saying, "A people that possesses a Kant will not permit an Einstein to be tacked onto it."

June 6 Estonia and the Soviet Union signed a conciliation pact to resolve differences which might arise between them.

June 16 The ban on Nazi Storm Troopers imposed by Brüning two months earlier was lifted, giving new impetus to the Hitler movement. Street clashes broke out almost immediately.

June 18 Latvia and the Soviet Union signed a concilation pact.

June 24 The army and navy seized power in Siam.

July 9 The Lausanne Convention was signed, whereby the problems of reparation payments growing out of the war were simply abolished. The European Allies, however, agreed they would not ratify the terms unless the U.S. was willing to reduce the debts owed to it in return for the European generosity in ending the onerous reparations originally demanded from Germany. Washington, specifically Congress, would not budge and insisted the war debts had to be paid in full. When the payments were due in December, Britain paid in full, Italy, Czechoslovakia, Lithuania, and Finland paid under protest, and France, Belgium, Hungary, Poland, Estonia, and Yugoslavia defaulted. By 1934, every country defaulted, except Finland.

July 20 Martial law was proclaimed in Berlin and Brandenburg to curb the growing violence fomented by Nazi Storm Troopers.

July 22 Germany again demanded equal status at the Geneva Disarmament Conference, saying, "Discriminatory treatment . . . would not be compatible with sentiments of national honor and international justice. It would also be contrary to Germany's contractual rights which she could not renounce. . . ." The demand was Berlin's most forceful call yet for actual rearmament, denied by the victorious Allied powers after the World War.

July 25 Poland and the Soviet Union agreed on terms of a nonaggression pact.

July 26 German Defense Minister Kurt von Schleicher repeated Germany's demand for equal status in defense matters: "We can attain this security if we so organize our armed forces . . . by reorganization, not extension . . . that they would give at least a certain degree of security, and I wish . . . to leave no doubt that we shall take this course if full security and equality of right are further withheld from us. . . ."

July 31 General elections in Germany gave the Nazis 37.8 percent of the vote and the Communists 14.6, thus netting the two parties intent on overthrowing the Weimar Republic a majority in the Reichstag. Neither extremist party would join in a coalition.

Aug. 9 Chiang Kai-shek returned to head the Chinese government.

Aug. 13 Rebuffed by President Hindenburg who would not name him chancellor, Hitler refused to cooperate with him or to permit the Nazi party to participate in the German government.

Aug. 25 Japan announced its intention to recognize Manchukuo. Foreign Minister Count Yusuya Uchida told the Diet the action "will be a notable step towards making Manchuria a happy and peaceful land for natives and foreigners alike, on the basis of the realities of the situation." Uchida declared the Japanese people "were solidly determined not to concede a foot, even if the country turned to scorched earth."

Aug. 27 The Japanese cabinet agreed to replenish its military supplies and to prepare mobilization and emergency economic plans.

Aug. 29 Germany called for a confidential discussion with France on Berlin's claim for equality at the Geneva arms talks, pointing out the need "for the elimination of the existing tension and to the appeasement of the political conditions, which the Germans feel as a humiliation, and which at the same time prevents the establishment of a peaceful equilibrium in Europe."

Aug. 30 Hermann Göring, a World War flying hero and now an ardent Nazi, was elected president of the German Reichstag.

Aug. 31 Defense Minister Schleicher said that unless Germany was given permission to rearm, it would be forced to take unilateral action for the "reorganization" of its security forces.

Sept. 12 Germany walked out of the Geneva Disarmament Conference, saying it "cannot be expected to take part in negotiations with regard to the measures of disarmament to be laid down in the convention until it is established that the solutions which may be found are also to apply to Germany."

■ The German Reichstag was dissolved after an overwhelming vote of no confidence in the Papen government.

Sept. 15 Japan formally "recognized" Manchukuo. General Muto Nobuyoshi was appointed Japanese proconsul in Mukden, with the official title of Special Ambassador, Commander of the Manchukuan Defense Force, as well as Commander of the Kwantung Army.

Oct. 1 Stimson said, "The present crisis in Manchuria is not only a blow to the commercial interests of the United States but a threat to the authority of the great peace treaties which were conceived after the war by the nations of the world in a supreme effort to prevent the recurrence of such a disaster."

Oct. 2 The Lytton Report on the Sino-Japanese dispute was released by the League of Nations in Geneva. Its main point was that Manchuria should remain a part of China and that Japan's claims were unfounded. Japan's special interests, however, were recognized.

Oct. 19 Britain declined to renew its trade agreement with Russia, reflecting London's concerns growing out of Moscow's strident communist propaganda and activism.

Oct. 25 Italian Dictator Benito Mussolini promised he would rule for 30 years. He had been in power for ten years already.

Oct. 28 U.S. Army Chief of Staff General Douglas MacArthur, in an assessment of the world situation, wrote that there was "little likelihood of any belligerent outbreaks which might involve the United States in the Pacific." In Europe, MacArthur thought that "no serious war is likely within any measurable period of time."

Nov. 4 Hitler refused to accept the chancellorship and form a new German government because Hindenburg would not offer him presidential powers as well.

Nov. 6 Elections were held in Germany with the Nazis losing support, garnering two million votes less than they did in the July balloting. Again, however, no party won a majority.

Nov. 8 Franklin Delano Roosevelt was elected president of the U.S. in a landslide.

Nov. 10 London acknowledged the legitimacy of

GERMANY'S ELECTORAL DRIFT TO TOTALITARIANISM (1928–1932)
Deputies (by Party) Elected to the Reichstag

	May 20, 1928		Sept. 14, 1930		July 31, 1932		Nov. 6, 1932	
Nazi	12	(2.4 percent)	107	(18.5 percent)	230	(37.8 percent)	196	(33.6 percent)
National	73	(14.9)	41	(7.1)	37	(6.1)	52	(8.9)
Center	62	(12.6)	68	(11.8)	75	(12.3)	70	(12.0)
Socialist	153	(31.2)	143	(24.8)	133	(21.9)	121	(20.7)
Communist	54	(11.0)	77	(13.3)	89	(14.6)	100	(17.1)
Others°	137	(27.9)	141	(24.4)	44	(7.2)	45	(7.7)
Total	491		577		608		584	

°Including German People's, Bavarian People's, Democratic, State, and miscellaneous minor parties.

Election for Chancellor

March 13, 1932			April 10, 1932		
(82.6 percent of eligible voters participated.)			*(83.5 percent of eligible voters participated.)*		
Hindenburg (incumbent)	18,651,000	(49.6 percent)	Hindenburg	19,325,000	(53.0 percent)
Hitler (Nazi)	11,319,000	(30.1)	Hitler	13,418,000	(36.8)
Thälmann (Communist)	4,963,000	(13.2)	Thälmann	3,719,000	(10.2)
Duesterberg° (Veterans)	2,557,000	(6.8)			
Winter° (splinter party)	112,800	(.3)			

°Duesterberg and Winter dropped out and supported Hindenburg.

German claims to equal status in disarmament talks. France and Italy soon followed.

Nov. 17 Because the Reichstag would not support his plan for a "government of national concentration," Papen resigned as chancellor of Germany.

Nov. 23 Hindenburg again rejected Hitler's bid for the chancellorship on terms which the president feared would give Hitler dictatorial powers.

Nov. 27 Poland and Russia signed their nonaggression treaty.

Nov. 29 France and the Soviet Union signed nonaggression and conciliation pacts. Concern over Germany prompted Paris and Moscow to clear any differences between them and to indicate their common need to deter Berlin from pursuing policies hostile to either. Russia had concluded treaties with as many of the countries on its western borders as possible, establishing a buffer zone between Soviet and German territory.

Dec. 2 Defense Minister Schleicher became the new German chancellor.

Dec. 5 Mathematician Albert Einstein, seeking a visa to visit the U.S., answered charges that he was a communist in an appearance before the American consul in Berlin. The Womens Patriot Corporation had accused Einstein of party membership. Einstein was permitted to enter the U.S.

Dec. 7 A majority of the League Assembly voted to approve the Lytton Report and censure Japan for its actions in China. Japan's League representative, Yosuke Matsuoka, responded by saying, "We are prepared to be crucified, but we do believe, and firmly believe, that in a very few years world opinion will be changed, and that we also shall be understood by the world as Jesus of Nazareth was."

Dec. 9 A Committee of Nineteen was appointed by the League "to study" the Lytton Report on China and to draw up a plan of settlement.

Dec. 11 Germany stated that since its requests for equality had been recognized by Britain, France, and Italy, it would return to the Disarmament Conference.

Dec. 12 Russia and China resumed diplomatic relations.

Dec. 15 Six European nations officially defaulted on their war debt payments to the U.S.

(OPPOSITE, TOP) *Hitler after being named chancellor, with Göring and Rudolf Hess to the extreme right.*

(OPPOSITE, BOTTOM) *Nazi Gestapo leaders pose after gaining power in Germany.*

1933 Hitler wins power and Germany accedes to dictatorial rule.

Jan. 1 Fighting flared anew in China as Japanese and Chinese forces clashed at Shanhaikuan, on the Manchurian–north China boundary, along the rail line between Mukden and Peking. It set the stage for the occupation of Jehol Province.

Jan. 5 Declaring that "no Japanese Cabinet which advocated a compromise of the Manchukuo question could survive," Japanese Ambassador Katsuji Debuchi informed the U.S. that the Manchurian issue was closed. He also said Japan had no territorial ambitions south of the Great Wall.

Jan. 10 President Herbert Hoover called for U.S. Senate ratification of the international convention to suppress international arms trading and to give the president authority to block such exports.

■ Mao Tse-tung, from his remote capital of the Chinese Soviet Republic in Juichin, offered a "united front" to any group willing to fight with his Red Army against the Japanese.

Jan. 28 Under pressure from an antigovernment coalition headed by the Nazis, Schleicher resigned as German chancellor.

Jan. 30 Hitler was named chancellor of Germany. Hindenburg believed the appointment would end the divisiveness which had plagued the country.

Jan. 31 The Geneva Disarmament Conference was reconvened in the hope of implementing a formula granting Germany arms equality while providing other nations adequate security against external attack.

■ Edouard Daladier became premier of France, his first ministry, and the beginning of frequent changes caused by deeply disruptive political, economic, and social controversy.

Feb. 4 Hitler issued a decree, "For the Protection of the German People," which gave the government power to ban political meetings and to suppress any publications deemed harmful to the public interest.

Feb. 9 Reflecting the increasingly pacifist tendencies in Britain, an overwhelming majority of the Oxford Union approved the resolution: "That this House will in no circumstances fight for its King or country."

Feb. 14–16 The powers of the Little Entente (Czechoslovakia, Yugoslavia, and Rumania) met in Geneva to organize formally against what was considered a new threat posed by German and Hungarian stirrings to recover territory lost after the last war.

Feb. 17 Hitler directed German police forces to work cooperatively with the Nazi SS (originally Hitler's personal bodyguard) and SA (Storm Troopers) and in dealing with opposition forces "to make free use of their weapons whenever necessary."

■ The League's Committee of Nineteen report on

Nazi Storm Troopers march through Berlin in mourning for two of their members allegedly shot and killed by Communists.

China was released and broadcast by radio in one of the most dramatic events ever carried by the new medium. It reaffirmed the substance of the Lytton Report but went further in specifying methods to resolve the dispute.

■ Winston Churchill—reflecting a widespread cautionary attitude in the West on developments in Asia—told the Anti-Socialist Union that the League of Nations "with great work to do in Europe" should not involve itself in a squabble with Japan. Churchill indicated some sympathy for Japan's position in China and appreciated Tokyo's concerns about the Soviet Union.

Feb. 22 Göring, newly named minister without portfolio in the Hitler cabinet, established an auxiliary police force of 50,000 men to be drawn primarily from the Nazi SS and SA.

Feb. 23 Japan issued an ultimatum to China demanding Manchukuan sovereignty over Jehol.

Feb. 24 Nanking rejected the ultimatum and Japan moved to occupy Jehol.

■ The Committee of Nineteen report on China was adopted by the League. Japan was thus declared an aggressor. Japan cast the only negative vote (the tally was 42 to 1), and it promptly withdrew from the Assembly. Tokyo said Japan had "reached the limit of endeavors to cooperate with the League." Despite the vote, the League's handling of the Manchurian crisis was deemed inept. Japan retained possession of Manchuria (the League never demanded its withdrawal and even sanctioned continued control, if under nominal Chinese sovereignty). Collective security failed in its first test under the League, a distressing harbinger of things to come.

■ German police raided the headquarters of the Communist party in Berlin and claimed to have seized documents on a planned violent overthrow of the government.

Feb. 27 The Reichstag building in Berlin was set afire, and the Nazis quickly blamed the communists. Nazi Storm Troopers unleashed a campaign

of intimidation against their opponents. About 4,000 persons were arrested, mostly communists and liberals, plus many professionals (doctors and lawyers) who had personally antagonized Nazi leaders. Nazi leaders used the Reichstag fire to inflame the German electorate in opposition to the "Red Peril" and in support of Hitler and his candidates in the March general elections. Hitler witnessed the blaze and led correspondent Sefton Delmer of the London *Daily Express* through police lines with the pronouncement: "This is a God-given signal. If, as I believe, the Communists have done it, you are witnessing the beginning of a great new epoch in German history."

Feb. 28 President Hindenburg signed an emergency decree suspending constitutional guarantees of free speech, a free press, rights of assembly, and privacy. Communist Reichstag members were arrested, as were Communist deputies and civil servants in Prussia. The Weimar Republic was dead.

March 2 In a hate-filled editorial, the Nazi party newspaper *Völkischer Beobachter* attacked Jews and intellectuals for their "pacifist excesses" and "international treason." Specifically named were

Albert Einstein, Thomas Mann, Arnold Zweig and other leading German writers and academics.

March 4 Roosevelt was inaugurated president of the U.S.

■ Jehol City fell to the Japanese. Even though the Chinese force in the area numbered 200,000 men—four times the size of the Japanese force—the defenders were routed.

■ Göring declared in Frankfurt, "My measures will not be hindered by any legal considerations or bureaucracy whatsoever. It is not justice that I have to carry out but annihilation and extermination."

March 5 German elections gave the Nazis and Nationalists a majority. The Communists polled a million votes less than they did in the last election.

March 7 In response to a tide of Naziism and growing political violence, the Austrian government suspended parliament and Chancellor Engelbert Dollfuss assumed semidictatorial powers.

March 10 Einstein declared he would not be returning to Germany: "As long as I have any choice in the matter, I shall live only in a country where civil liberty, tolerance, and equality of all citizens before the law prevail. . . . These conditions do not exist in Germany at the present time."

March 11 The U.S. agreed to participate in a League-sponsored panel to consider the Sino-Japanese dispute. There was still some lingering sentiment to do more than criticize Japan for its actions in China, but no nation was truly interested in even a trade boycott, let alone forcing Tokyo to stand down. U.S. willingness to join in League deliberations was only a slight deviation from the dominant American philosophy—as expressed in a witticism of the time—"of being in the world, but not of it."

March 16 Belgium, fearing the Nazi climb to power in Germany, launched a program of defense, including the construction of fortifications along the Meuse River.

March 18 Hans Frank, the Nazi minister of justice for Bavaria, warned that if Austrian Nazis were threatened, their German counterparts might have to assume responsibility for their security and freedom.

March 23 Hitler was granted dictatorial power for four years by the Reichstag. The Enabling Act also required a two-thirds party majority for future rule, making it more difficult or nearly impossible to oust the incumbents.

March 27 Infuriated by the League censure over China, Japan gave formal notice it intended to withdraw from the League of Nations.

March 28 The German Nazi party began an organized campaign to boycott Jewish stores and shops.

March 31 Because of an alleged antigovernment plot, the Austrian administration disbanded the Socialists' paramilitary organization. Vienna was cracking down on the Left as well as the Right, alienating both sides. The government was isolating itself from the sharply divided elements which were rigidly forming.

April China instituted a program of military training for all male high school and college students. The plan envisaged the addition of 100,000 men each year to the ready reserve force.

April 1 Hitler ordered a nationwide one-day boycott of all Jewish stores, doctors, and lawyers in Germany. Other Nazi leaders began urging the expulsion of Jews from all schools and universitites. The Nazi newspaper *Völkischer Beobachter* said the boycott "is to be regarded merely as a dress rehearsal for a series of measures that will be carried out unless world opinion, which at the moment is against us, definitely changes."

April 7 The Aryan (Civil Service) Law was passed in Germany, barring from public employment anyone with a Jewish grandparent. Anti-Semitic actions of this kind further burdened the Jewish population economically (apart from the deeper psychic wounds). By the end of the year, for example, 31,000 of Berlin's 170,000 Jews were living on charity. Emigration was the escape for most. By 1939, 319,000 German Jews, 64 percent of the total Jewish population, had fled the growing terror.

■ At a secret meeting of his ministers at the Reich Chancellery, Hitler declared that Germany would participate in international disarmament conferences for its own purposes. Hitler explained that "we must for tactical reasons primarily strive for the disarmament of the other nations. This method is more effective than an armaments race." On internal matters, Hitler disclosed that he planned "to eradicate Christianity in Germany, root and branch." Hitler's overall view of religion was that "the churches may take command of the German in the hereafter. The German nation, through its Führer, takes command in this world."

April 11 Göring led a German mission to Rome in an effort to placate the Italian government which feared Nazi intrusions in neighboring Austria. Göring this day was appointed prime minister of Prussia.

May 2 Nazi SS and SA troopers occupied trade union headquarters throughout Germany and the Socialist-led Labor Movement was dissolved. (Unions representing 4,500,000 German workers were no longer a factor in German politics as the Nazis arrested their leaders and confiscated all union holdings. In the future all labor membership was limited to the Nazi-directed German Labor Front.)

May 5 Germany and the Soviet Union extended their treaty of neutrality.

May 7 Japanese troops launched a massive campaign to drive the Chinese out of the Shanhaikuan-Hsifengkow-Luanchow triangle. The Kwantung Army had insisted on permanent withdrawal of Chinese troops from the area. Instead, the Chinese stayed and engaged the Japanese in skirmishes. The campaign was pressed, however, and Chinese resistance ended within three weeks.

May 10 The Nazi government dissolved all socialist parties and confiscated property holdings of the German trade unions and the Social Democratic (Socialist) party. Hitler thus alienated whatever support he may have had from moderates and centrists outside of Germany. He had already overwhelmed those elements within the country.

■ Students of Berlin's Humboldt University and Nazi Storm Troopers burned the books of authors, mostly Jewish and German liberals, considered offensive to the state.

May 12 Vice Chancellor Papen of Germany, revealing his growing drift to extremism, stated that war was an honorable course of action: "The maintenance of eternal life demands the sacrifice of the individual."

■ Nazis in the free city of Danzig (Gdansk) seized the local trade union headquarters in an assumed prelude to a German takeover of the port city.

May 17 Hitler demanded the Treaty of Versailles be revised to grant Germany equality of rights. He declared the pact "did not succeed in solving

President Hindenburg and Chancellor Hitler appear together at the Lustgarten for a traditional May Day Youth Parade celebrating the "Day of Work."

in a clear and reasonable way the questions of the most decisive importance for the future. . . . As it was, through ignorance, passion, and hatred, decisions were taken which, in their injustice and lack of logic, bore the seeds of fresh conflicts." The "equality" issue centered on Germany's right of self-defense. Its army was limited to 100,000 men by the Treaty of Versailles. By comparison, Czechoslovakia had 138,788 men under arms and Poland 265,980.

■ All Germans were denied the right to strike.

May 28 Nazis were elected overwhelmingly to a majority position in the Danzig *Volkstag* (parliament), effectively ending the city's independent status.

May 29 Germany, in an effort to bring down the anti-Nazi government of Austria, imposed a prohibitive 1,000 mark tax on any German visiting Austria. The tax was intended to wreck Austria's tourist trade and cripple the economy. It remained in effect for more than three years but only made the Vienna government more staunchly anti-Nazi.

May 30 The League of Nations condemned Germany's treatment of its Jewish population.

May 31 The Truce of Tangku was signed to end the fighting between China and Japan. China was simply incapable of resisting Japan's military moves. Japanese control of Manchuria and Jehol was thus confirmed. Under terms of the agreement, Chinese military forces were to withdraw from a zone south of the Great Wall. A four-year period of comparative peace in China resulted from the Tangku truce.

June 7 Britain, France, Germany, and Italy agreed to terms of the Four-Power Pact by which each nation pledged to maintain the peace in Europe. Conceived by Mussolini, the pact was in fact an Italian ploy to undercut the League of Nations and place France in untenable relations with Poland, Rumania, Czechoslovakia, and Yugoslavia, all of whom looked to Paris for leadership in preserving the boundaries drawn after the war. As it turned out, the pact was a meaningless mishmash of pious hope and irrelevant posturing.

June 11 Austrian police began a crackdown on Nazi terrorism and arrested numbers of German and Austrian party members, some of whom were deported to Germany.

June 14 Hitler's "Inspector for Austria," Theo Habicht, was expelled from Austria, provoking a new round of terrorist outbursts by the Nazis.

June 19 The German Nazi party was outlawed in Austria. The Vienna government invoked a World War law "to guard against the economic dangers associated with a disturbance of public peace, order and security."

June 22 The German Nazi government officially outlawed the Social Democratic party as part of a coordinated plan to eliminate all political opposition. In rapid order, each of the non-Nazi organizations was dissolved.

June 29 Göring ordered a buildup of the German air force to 32 squadrons (about 320 planes) by October, 1934.

July 5 All German Catholic political parties were dissolved, the final opposition organizations to fall under the Nazi bandwagon.

July 8 A concordat between the Vatican and Germany was initialled in Rome, with Berlin agreeing to respect Catholic rights, practices, and institutions in Germany but limiting any activity which might be construed as political. Even those rights granted Catholics were quickly denied, but the concordat's immediate effect was to thwart the anti-Nazi clerics of Germany who could not expect Vatican support in their losing fight to retain basic freedoms under Hitler. What surprised Hitler was how readily the Vatican abandoned the Catholic Center party and the Catholic trade unions.

July 14 The Nazi party was declared the only legal political party within Germany.

July 15 The Four-Power Pact was signed. (see June 7)

July 26 Reacting to criticism of the concordat with Germany, the Vatican's official newspaper *L'Osservatore Romano* published the first of two articles defending the stance of the Holy See. The articles were written by Eugenio Cardinal Pacelli (who in 1939 became Pope Pius XII), the Vatican State Secretary who was instrumental in drafting the concordat. Pacelli told the British ambassador privately that the Catholic Church "deplored the actions of the German Government at home, their persecution of the Jews, their proceedings against political opponents, the reign of terror to which the whole nation was subjected." But Nazi-Vatican differences were generally not

Hitler turns over the first spadeful of dirt in the construction of the Autobahn in Frankfurt.

aired in public, and the concordat remained a victory for Hitler in the minds of most observers.

Aug. 5 Poland and Danzig agreed on the further use of port facilities and the position of Polish nationals.

Sept. 2 Italy and the Soviet Union signed a pact of friendship, nonaggression, and neutrality, thus extending Mussolini's plan to align all the great powers in a loose alliance to assuage the smaller European nations by protecting the status quo of the continent.

Sept. 3 Hitler renounced war as an instrument of policy, but said an exception must be made in the case of Bolshevism. He said, "By waging war on Bolshevism, Germany . . . is fulfilling a European mission. . . ."

Sept. 18 The Nazi-dominated government of Danzig agreed to guarantee basic rights to Poles living there, while the Polish government established a quota for its imported goods which would flow through Danzig. The port's trade was sharply reduced after the Poles constructed their own facility of Gdynia.

Sept. 23 The Soviet Union charged the Japanese and their "puppets" in Manchuria were planning to seize the Russian-owned Chinese Eastern Railway. The Japanese military mission in Harbin had, in fact, been urging such action.

Oct. 1 Nine senior German generals critical of Hitler were retired, effectively reducing antiregime sentiment within the officer corps.

Oct. 3 An attempt was made on the life of Austrian Chancellor Dollfuss, which was assumed to have been the work of Nazis.

Oct. 10 President Roosevelt opened the way for a resumption of relations between the U.S. and the Soviet Union: "It is most regrettable that these great peoples, between whom a happy tradition of friendship existed for more than a century to their mutual advantage, should now be without a practical method of communication directly with each other."

Oct. 13 At a Berlin policy conference, Hitler decided to "torpedo the Disarmament Conference." He stated, "The path of negotiation is now closed. . . . we shall therefore have to leave both the Disarmament Conference and the League of Nations, since the condition that we be recognized as a nation with equality is not fulfilled."

Oct. 14 Germany formally withdrew from the Disarmament Conference and announced its intention to pull out of the League.

■ Hitler said Germany's relations with France would be harmonious once the Saar issue was resolved.

Oct. 26 A new cabinet was formed in France, but it quickly collapsed in a wave of political instability. Three separate governments were overthrown in as many months.

Nov. 2 U.S. Secretary of State Cordell Hull told German Ambassador Hans Luther in Washington that a general war was likely to begin within the next two to ten years, for "the outlook in Europe at this distance for disarmament or for peace does not appear very encouraging."

Nov. 12 In a national plebiscite, more than 90 percent of the German voters endorsed Hitler's decision to withdraw from the Disarmament Conference and the League of Nations.

Nov. 16 The U.S. recognized the Soviet Union, ending the deep divisions between the two countries flowing from the Russian Revolution. Trade relations were established, and Moscow agreed not to engage in communist propaganda activities within the U.S.

Dec. 18 Germany stated its position on disarmament to the French: "The heavily armed states either have no intention of disarming or do not feel in a position to do so. Germany is entitled to obtain, in one way or another, equality of treatment as regards her own security."

■ Germany defended the Nazi SA and SS as simple organizations whose "sole mission is to organize the political masses of our people so as to make the return of the Communist peril impossible forevermore" and "to immunize the country, intellectually and physically, against the risk of Communist disintegration."

Dec. 26 The United States pledged not to intervene militarily in the Western Hemisphere.

Dec. 28 General Kurt von Hammerstein, chief of the German Army Command, resigned. He was the last of the outspoken anti-Nazi military leaders, and Hitler was now able to manipulate the army as he wished.

Dec. 29 Rumanian Prime Minister Ion Duca, leader of the Liberal party, was assassinated by the Iron Guard, a fascistic, anti-Semitic group dedicated to the establishment of a dictatorship. Martial law was proclaimed and leaders of the Iron Guard were arrested. The government was determined to keep the extremists in line.

(OPPOSITE, TOP) *Hitler presides over the 1934 Nazi rally at Nürnberg.*

(OPPOSITE, BOTTOM) *Five U.S. battleships on maneuvers off Maui, Hawaiian Islands in the mid-1930's.*

1934

New alignments of power develop as nations frantically seek security.

Jan. 1 The German government ordered an aircraft-building program, with the Luftwaffe to be supplied with 4,021 new aircraft by October, 1935. It had already trained thousands of pilots through the Aeronautic Sports Organization (*Deutscher Luftsportverband*), large numbers of men with more professional flying skills in the subsidized commercial airline *Deutsche Lufthansa*, plus those trained secretly in the Soviet Union, particularly at the aircraft experimental center at Lipetzk.

Jan. 22 Foreign Minister Koki Hirota declared that "Japan, serving as the only cornerstone for the edifice of the peace of Eastern Asia, bears the entire burden of responsibility." It was a clear message to all powers not to interfere with Japan's policies in China.

Jan. 26 Germany and Poland signed a 10-year nonaggression pact: ". . . the moment has arrived for inaugurating a new era in Polish-German political relations by means of direct communications between the two countries." It was proposed by Hitler, and Poland never consulted France, its chief ally. Germany was signaling that it had no quarrel with Poland, only with Communist Russia. Warsaw had concluded it could no longer rely on outside support in preserving Poland's independence. The treaty stated that neither signatory would "proceed to use

force in order to settle" disputes. The pact was also significant in that Poland became the first nation to enter into a harmonious relationship with the new Nazi regime. Warsaw was anxious to avoid becoming involved in the quarrels of Poland's neighbors, and the pact accurately reflected a Polish policy of trying to maintain friendly relations with all powers.

Jan. 27 Rightist mobs in Paris, after days of rioting, toppled the government in a final frenzy of destruction. The disruptions were caused by the Stavisky affair, involving the shoddy doings of a well-placed swindler. Using the revelations to attack corruption and the leftist government, the extreme rightists moved to seek greater power.

Jan. 30 Hitler repeated German demands for arms equality: ". . . no threat and no force will ever move the German people to abandon those rights which cannot be denied to a sovereign nation. . . ."

Jan. 31 The British ambassador in Berlin sent an analysis of the German situation to the British Foreign Office in which he commented: "Here it may be said that nothing has so enhanced the prestige of Herr Hitler in Germany as the behavior of the ex-Allies since he took office. All reasonable and cautious opinion in Germany foretold disaster, occupation of the Rhineland, sanctions, perhaps blockade, if Germany reverted to nationalism. The Nazis seized power, and nothing happened. Herr Hitler left the League and still nothing happened. On the contrary, the statesmen of Europe were represented here as having been galvanised into running after Germany. The fear that force may be used against Germany exists, but it is rapidly disappearing, and the man, particularly the young man, in the street thanks Hitler for the removal of a distressing bogey. It is therefore not surprising if the Chancellor pursues methods which hitherto have brought him success."

Feb. The British Air Ministry estimated that Germany possessed or was building a total of 334 military aircraft, a clear violation of the Treaty of Versailles. Britain did not wish to protest since it was then hoping to win an arms control treaty with Hitler which would limit military aircraft production.

Feb. 6 Rightist demonstrations in Paris led to violence and bloodshed. Six people were killed. Hundreds were injured. Disgust with Radical Socialist rule had touched off the outbursts, though the Left saw the rioting as fascist directed for political gain. France henceforth was divided irrevocably between Right and Left.

Feb. 9 The Balkan Pact was signed, with Greece, Turkey, Yugoslavia, and Rumania vowing to maintain "in a spirit of conciliation" the existing territorial order. Bulgaria's absence was its weakness. Bulgaria did not recognize the borders established by the World War peace treaties and now confirmed by the Balkan Pact. Bulgaria would not forget having lost access to the Aegean Sea and other lost territories.

Feb. 12–15 The Austrian government cracked down on the Social Democrats, who had called for a general strike. It outlawed the party, its unions, and social clubs. The actions were enforced violently. As a result, the Dollfuss government lost most working class support and became estranged from a potential ally against the Nazis.

Feb. 17 Britain, France, and Italy declared that Austria's independence and integrity must be maintained.

March 1 Henry Pu-yi, the last of the Manchu emperors, was crowned as Kang Te, emperor of Manchukuo. He had abdicated the throne of Chi-

na in 1912 and was a convenient puppet for the Japanese, who controlled all Manchurian activities through advisers and officials in directly responsible positions.

March 17 The Rome Protocols were adopted, with Italy, Austria, and Hungary agreeing on the pursuit of common policy objectives and closer trade ties. It was a counter to French revival of the Little Entente as a bloc against the Italians.

March 28 Germany rebuffed a Soviet invitation for joint guarantees of peace to the three Baltic nations and Finland.

April 4 The Soviet Union extended its nonaggression treaties with Estonia, Latvia, and Lithuania until 1945.

April 10 The Japanese foreign office announced it was unqualifiedly opposed to any foreign interference in China. Tokyo objected to loans and credits of more than $55 million provided by the U.S. and Britain to the Chinese government, regarding them as "political" in purpose.

April 18 Japan stated its opposition to the shipment of arms or planes and the employment of any military advisers by China. Tokyo, in effect, was beginning to assume responsibility for China's foreign relations.

April 25 Japanese Foreign Minister Hirota said Japan did not seek "special privileges in China," but "various foreign activities have tended to disturb peaceful conditions in China. . . ."

April 26 Foreign Minister Louis Barthou arrived in Prague to renew the alliance between France and Czechoslovakia, another manifestation of the growing common fear of Germany.

April 29 The U.S. again stated it would not recognize territories gained by conquest.

April 30 The Austrian parliament approved a new constitution giving Dollfuss dictatorial rights and then voted itself out of existence.

May 5 Russia and Poland extended their nonaggression pact through 1945. Moscow thus completed the creation of a buffer zone between Russia and Germany, with Poland and the Baltic states pledged not to commit aggression and all to benefit mutually from keeping rivals Germany and Russia apart.

May 19 A coup d'état in Bulgaria established a military dictatorship.

May 29 Jan Masaryk was reelected president of Czechoslovakia.

■ The Disarmament Conference was reconvened. No results were achieved, and it was adjourned on June 11. French inflexibility was regarded as the key divisive element.

June 9 Russia, Poland, and Rumania signed an agreement, with each pledging to honor their common borders.

June 14–15 Hitler visited Venice in what was an unsuccessful effort to establish rapport with Mussolini. In their first face-to-face meeting, the two future allies were unimpressed with each other. (Mussolini whispered to his followers, "I don't like him.") With Austria looming as a menacing sore between them, Hitler told Mussolini he would push for Nazi participation in the Vienna government and Dollfuss would have to be ousted. This led to sharp exchanges. Only on one issue could they agree: neither wanted "regional alliances" in Europe.

June 23 Italian warships steamed into the Albanian port of Durazzo. Mussolini's patience was exhausted by Albanian resistance to Italy's efforts to extend its influence over the small monarchy. The Italian ships were dispatched after Albania closed all Italian schools. With the arrival of the menacing fleet, Albania quickly capitulated and Rome was granted broad concessions.

June 30-July 2 Hitler launched his bloody purge of opposition elements in and out of his party. The Nazi SS murdered Ernst Röhm, leader of the SA. (Polish intelligence had intercepted German military Enigma cipher messages and knew what Hitler was planning, as revealed in this classic intercept: "To all airfields: Bring in Ernst Röhm, dead or alive.") Among the other victims were military leaders and centrist politicians. As many as 200 may have been killed. Hitler admitted the execution of 74 individuals said to be plotting against him. Röhm and many of the Storm Trooper leaders were indeed conspiring to overthrow Hitler, who was believed to be overly willing to make common cause with the army. The Röhm faction had only contempt for the traditional militarists and sought to control the armed forces. Many innocent people were killed, however, in an excess of SS zeal.

July 3 The German government declared the purge murders were legal and necessary for the "self-defense of the state."

July 7 A new government was named in Japan.

Admiral Keisuke Okada became prime minister, and the military's firm control of the country continued.

July 12 Austria decreed the death penalty for terrorists, an action directed at the Nazis whose violent activities had been treated with almost benign tolerance and leniency. The decree infuriated the Nazis.

July 25 Chancellor Dollfuss was assassinated as part of an unsuccessful Nazi Putsch in Austria. Some government buildings and the radio station were seized before the revolt was quelled. Italy quickly mobilized forces at the Brenner Pass to forestall any German ambitions growing out of the Vienna incidents.

July 30 Education Minister Kurt von Schuschnigg was named Dollfuss's successor as Austrian chancellor. He was soon faced with the loss of Italy's full support in resisting Germany's predatory moves. Mussolini told Schuschnigg cryptically, "You must stand on your own feet because we will be busy in East Africa."

■ Stanley Baldwin, lord president of the council, announced sweeping changes in British defense policies. He told Parliament that Britain's favorable stand on disarmament was being abandoned and that Britain had decided to build up the Royal Air Force to a strength equal to any counterpart force within each other's range. The heart of the new policy was contained in Baldwin's words: "The old frontiers are gone. When you think of the defense of England you no longer think of the chalk cliffs of Dover, you think of the Rhine. That is where our frontier lies." Hitler responded by asking, "What would people in Britain say if I, the Führer, declared that the frontiers of German air defense lay on the Thames?"

Aug. 2 Hitler became president of the Reich upon the death of Hindenburg. The revered hero of Germany, who suffered from senility, was a mere figurehead during his last year as president. He died of natural causes at the age of 88. No sooner had Hitler assumed office, than all members of the German armed forces took a new oath of allegiance (which was suggested by the leading generals, not by Hitler, although he readily agreed to the military's act of obeisance): "I swear by God this holy oath, that I will render to

When Hindenburg died, Hitler assumed the title of Führer (leader), combining the offices of president and chancellor.

Adolf Hitler, Führer of the German Reich and People, Supreme Commander of the Armed Forces, unconditional obedience, and that I am ready, as a brave soldier, to risk my life at any time for this oath."

Aug. 19 Hitler was affirmed in his new role as president and chancellor by the German people in a plebiscite. Eighty-eight percent of the voters approved giving Hitler full executive powers.

Aug.–Sept. Chinese Nationalist forces waged a massive military operation to oust Communist troops from the latter's stronghold south of the Yangtze River.

Sept. 12 The Baltic states of Estonia, Latvia, and Lithuania banded together in a treaty of cooperation and coordination in support of League ideals.

Sept. 18 The Soviet Union entered the League of Nations. Moscow's return to international civility was the direct result of events in Germany and Moscow's willingness to forego ideology in the more pragmatic need for collective security.

Sept. 27 Italy, France, and Britain—the former Allies of the World War—jointly announced support for Austrian "independence and integrity" in a move calculated to curb Hitler's menacing actions.

Sept. 29 Italy and Ethiopia jointly announced that neither intended to make war on the other, a reaffirmation of their 1928 treaty of friendship.

Oct. 1 Hitler secretly ordered the creation of a German air force and a rapid expansion of the army and navy. Even then Hitler was bent on rearming, and for more than restoration of Germany's pre-World War position. As Hitler had confided to Danzig Nazi leader Hermann Rauschning: "The struggle against Versailles is the means, but not the end of my policy. I am not the least interested in the frontiers of the Reich. The re-creation of prewar Germany is not a task worthy of our Revolution."

Oct. 5 Socialists, Communists, and Syndicalists launched a general strike throughout Spain and sparked revolutionary turmoil in Madrid, Catalonia, and Asturias.

Oct. 9 A Macedonian revolutionary working with Croatian dissidents in Marseilles assassinated King Alexander I of Yugoslavia and Foreign Minister Barthou of France. (Barthou was succeeded by Pierre Laval, whose own antagonistic attitude toward Russia and Britain was to undo Barthou's policies and push France away from eastern Europe and toward Italy).

Oct. 19 Foreign ministers of the Little Entente (Czechoslovakia, Rumania, and Yugoslavia) and the Balkan Entente (Rumania, Yugoslavia, Greece, and Turkey) met to confer on the situation growing out of the murder of King Alexander of Yugoslavia.

Nov. 22 Yugoslavia claimed the assassinations of King Alexander and Barthou were organized in Hungary and those involved had taken refuge there. The Croatian revolutionary group which was responsible for the killings was based in Hungary.

Nov. 28 Winston Churchill addressed Parliament and warned that the Germans were building a modern air force which would be a menace to Britain.

Dec. 1 Soviet Communist leader Serge Kirov was assassinated. The killing of Dictator Joseph Stalin's close associate triggered off the great purges in which Stalin eliminated opposition to his rule from within the Communist party.

Dec. 5 Fighting broke out between Italian and Ethiopian troops at Wal Wal near the frontier between Ethiopia and Italian Somaliland. The incident which triggered the Italo-Ethiopian war began with the arrival on Nov. 22 of the Anglo-Ethiopian Border Commission and a 600-man military escort at Wal Wal, an oasis 60 miles inside Ethiopia. Emperor Haile Selassie had invited the group there knowing it was occupied by Italy (as it had been for years). He hoped the commission's arrival would force an Italian withdrawal from Wal Wal and their army camp at Wardair (Wardere), 20 miles away. For the next two weeks, Italians and their askaris and Ethiopians faced each other menacingly. Neither would budge. The Ethiopians demanded water and pasturage rights in their own territory, but the Italians insisted they controlled the land. Finally, at 3:30 P.M. on Dec. 5 a shot was fired (by whom, no one could say) and soon a full-scale battle erupted. The Italians sent three airplanes and two armored vehicles from Wardair, routing the Ethiopians in short order. In all, 107 Ethiopians were killed and 45 wounded. All the casualties on the Italian side were native troops, 30 killed and 100 wounded.

■ France and the Soviet Union signed a consultative pact.

■ Yugoslavia began deporting some of the 27,000 Hungarians in Yugoslavia, in retaliation for the allegedly Hungarian-inspired murder of King Alexander.

Dec. 6 Ethiopia charged Italy with occupying Wal Wal and Wardair in Ogaden Province.

Dec. 8 Italy demanded apologies and compensation from Ethiopia, which published extensive details of the clash at Wal Wal.

Dec. 22 International troop contingents arrived in the Saar to oversee the forthcoming plebiscite.

Dec. 29 Japan declared its intention not to adhere to the provisions of the 1922 Washington Naval Treaty which had established imposed limitations on the relative size of each nation's fleet (5;5;3;1.67;1.67 for the U.S., Britain, Japan, Italy, and France, respectively).

Dec. 30 Mussolini issued a secret order to the Italian military for "the destruction of the Abyssinian [Ethiopian] armed forces and the total conquest of Ethiopia."

(OPPOSITE, TOP) *Hitler (with Admiral Erich Raeder) inspects the growing German fleet.*

(OPPOSITE, BOTTOM) *Mussolini reviews Italian troops bound for Ethiopia.*

1935

Hitler rearms Germany; Mussolini conquers Ethiopia.

Jan. 3 Ethiopia appealed to the League for actions "to safeguard peace," which Addis Ababa claimed had been broken by Italy.

Jan. 7 France and Italy signed a treaty in Rome, "desirous of developing in Africa the relations of amity and good neighborliness which exist between the two nations." Italy received a portion of French Somaliland and a share of the Ethiopian railway. France was anxious to use Franco-Italian solidarity as a balance against the menacing actions of Germany. Other nations were invited to join in the Rome agreement. (The immediate consequences of the agreement were to undercut international efforts against Italy for its actions in Ethiopia and the dispatch of large numbers of troops to the Italian colony of Eritrea. Mussolini now assumed he had virtual freedom of action in east Africa. The treaty was the ultimate manifestation of Laval's reoriented foreign policy, friendship with Italy and veering away from the British.)

Jan. 10 Writing in the Carnegie Foundation periodical *International Conciliation*, Mussolini outlined his views on world affairs: "Fascism . . . believes neither in the possibility nor the utility of perpetual peace. It thus repudiates the doctrine of pacifism. . . . War alone brings up to its highest tension all human energy and puts the stamp of nobility upon the peoples who have the courage to meet it."

Jan. 13 A League-supervised plebiscite was held in the Saar, with the voters casting 90.35 percent of their ballots in favor of rejoining Germany. Of the 528,005 participants, only 46,513 voted for a continuation of League rule and 2,124 supported union with France.

Jan. 17 The League of Nations formally awarded the Saar basin to Germany.

Jan. 18 Japanese and their Manchurian troops crossed into the demilitarized zone between the provinces of Chahar and Jehol. Chinese government troops had themselves violated the ill-defined border on several occasions during the past two years.

Jan. 22 Japanese Foreign Minister Hirota said Tokyo hoped China would become stable and that Japan "as China's neighbor and stabilizing force in east Asia . . . [will] try to assist in China in the attainment of this goal."

Jan. 28 In a major speech Russian President V.M. Molotov said the Soviet Union threatened no one: "Not a single country, not even one of the smallest states on the borders of the U.S.S.R., has grounds for entertaining a feeling of unrest in relations to the Soviet Union, which is far from what can be said of certain other big states." The last reference was clearly directed at Germany and Japan.

Feb. 1–3 French officials conferred with their British counterparts in London on Germany's rearmament moves. They invited Berlin to negotiate all outstanding issues. France and Britain felt the highest priority should be given to guarantees on preserving peace in eastern Europe, but the Germans indicated interest only in less vital issues.

Feb. 5 Italy began mobilizing its reserves, calling up troops to place two infantry divisions on a war footing. Shortly thereafter, units began sailing for Ethiopia.

March I The Saar was officially reincorporated as a part of Germany.

March 9 Germany announced to foreign air attachés that the Luftwaffe officially came into being on March 1. Such a force was specifically forbidden by the Treaty of Versailles.

March 13 In an effort to avert further border clashes in the east African area of the Ogaden, Italy and Ethiopia agreed to the establishment of a neutral zone.

March 15 France extended military conscription for two more years in the face of German rearmament measures.

March 16 Hitler formally denounced the Versailles treaty clauses on disarmament. Berlin announced plans to create 36 divisions (550,000 men). Germany ordered compulsory military service, stating, "The German Government considers it impossible still longer to refrain from taking the necessary measures for the security of the Reich or even to hide the knowledge thereof from the other nations." This action, like the earlier creation of the Luftwaffe, violated the Treaty of Versailles. It should be added that the other nations of Europe had agreed to disarm but failed to do so, and Germany witnessed increases in the military strength of its traditional rivals, France and Russia.

March 20 Estonia abolished party government, outlawing all political groupings except the ruling Fatherland party.

March 21 Rome told Berlin it viewed German rearmament as a "particularly grave" development.

March 23 Russia sold the Chinese Eastern Railway to Manchukuo for $40 million, a significant action in that Moscow was thus abandoning Manchuria which had long been in the Russian sphere of influence.

March 25 Lithuania sentenced four German-speaking residents of Memel (Klaipeda) to death. They were charged with "traitorous" activity, seeking a return of the Memel strip to Germany. Eighty-seven other Germans were given prison sentences. Those given death had their sentences commuted, but it marked the onset of extremely strained relations between Germany and Lithuania.

March 30 General Mikhail Tukachevsky, Soviet deputy commissar of war, wrote an article in the party newspaper *Pravda* attacking "Hitler's imperialistic plans." Tukachevsky had been one of the leading figures in Russo-German military exchanges only a few years before. The Kremlin was clearly moving away from its relatively close relationships with Berlin, born of their mutual positions as aggrieved parties of the Versailles treaty.

April 1 Austria reinstituted military conscription, in violation of the Treaty of St. Germain.

April 3 Ethiopia again implored the League to take action on its dispute with Italy, a situation worsened by the construction of roads from the Italian colony of Eritrea to the Ethiopian frontier.

April 9 France complained to the League about Germany's policy of rearmament.

■ Despite worsening Russo-German relations, Berlin and Moscow signed a trade agreement whereby the Soviets were granted 200 million marks for the purchase of German goods. (The following January, Hitler prohibited the sale of military equipment under the agreement.)

April 11–14 The Stresa Conference was held as Britain, France, and Italy considered steps to meet the militant actions of Germany. France called the conference in the belief that joint declarations might deter Germany. By condemning "unilateral repudiation of treaties," the three-nation Stresa front had temporarily isolated Germany diplomatically. Italy's involvement was considered essential, and the hope was that Rome's fear of German encroachments in Austria would bring Italy into an anti-German bloc. Such an effort was negated because of Italy's preoccupation with Ethiopia.

April 12 Germany indicated its willingness to enter into a nonaggression pact with its eastern neighbors at a proper time in the future.

April 14 France and Britain jointly rebuked Germany for the unilateral repudiation of its armament obligations and noted that Germany's "undeclared program" of rearmament was already well in "process of execution."

April 15–17 The League Council considered German rearmament and condemned Berlin for "introducing a disturbing element into the international situation." Germany protested the action.

May 2 France and the Soviet Union signed a five-year treaty of mutual assistance, "looking to the maintenance of national security, territorial integrity, and the political independence of states." Each promised to come to the other's aid if attacked, presumably denying Germany the opportunity of avoiding a two-front war. Both nations felt they had much to gain from a joint anti-German posture. Berlin was incensed by the agreement.

May 12 Marshal Josef Pilsudski died. He was the major driving force in Poland after the war, establishing a benign dictatorship internally and pursuing a tightrope-walking foreign policy, balancing Russia and Germany. Pilsudski's legacy was a strong military and alliances to preserve Poland's oft-lost independence.

May 16 Czechoslovakia and the Soviet Union signed a pact of mutual assistance, with language similar to the Franco-Russian treaty of May 2. A vital feature of the agreement, however, was that Russian aid would only follow French assistance to Czechoslovakia. Germany objected to the pact, claiming the Russians would have access to Czech bases.

May 19 Czechoslovak elections failed to give the coalition government a majority in parliament (parties in the coalition won 149 out of the 300 seats). The German Sudeten party was overwhelmingly supported in the German areas and captured a total of 44 seats, making it the second strongest party in the Chamber.

May 25 Hitler addressed the Reichstag and defended Germany's renunciation of the armaments clauses of the Versailles treaty. He said Germany wanted peace and another world war would be "the most frightful upheaval." He commented on the number of mutual assistance treaties, saying, ". . . the possibility of localizing smaller conflicts has been rendered less and less by an international network of intersecting obligations, and the danger of numerous states and nations being dragged into the struggle becomes all the greater."

May 29 Austrian Chancellor Schuschnigg rejected Naziism and union with Germany.

May 30 Japanese military leaders demanded the Chinese administration in Peking take steps to halt anti-Japanese activities in China.

June 4 The Czech government was reorganized, with the coalition including all parties except the Sudeten Germans and the pro-Nazi Slovak Clericals.

June 7 Pierre Laval was named premier of France.

■ Stanley Baldwin became British prime minister, replacing Ramsay MacDonald. Sir Samuel Hoare was named foreign minister in the coalition government.

June 9 Japan imposed new demands on the Chinese government, including the removal of Chinese Nationalist forces from Peking and Tientsin.

June 10 China capitulated to the Japanese demands, having no resources to resist the anticipated military measures if it refused to yield.

June 11 Chinese bandits or troops in Chahar Province fired on officials of Manchukuo.

June 15 Mao Tse-tung called for a "united peoples front" against Japan, but excepted Chiang Kai-shek "with his terrorist bands of Blue Shirts."

June 18 Germany and Britain signed a naval agreement limiting Germany's fleet to 35 percent of Britain's surface craft and 45 percent of its submarines. It deeply upset the French since Paris doubted Britain's sincerity in an alliance against Germany. France also thought Britain was signaling approval of German rearmament, which it was, of course. The agreement was the first time a European power not only condoned but agreed to an overt violation of the Versailles treaty.

■ Nanking ousted the governor of Chahar because of the June 11 shooting incident.

June 19 With a continuing Italian military build-up in east Africa, Ethiopia said Rome seemed bent on making war "inevitable." Ethiopia requested neutral observers be sent to the disputed region. Italy had now stationed about 240,000 troops and laborers in its east African colonies.

With the rise of Hitler in Germany and anti-Semitism widespread throughout Europe, Jews sought refuge in Palestine.

June 25 Arbitration negotiations between Italy and Ethiopia began at The Hague. (They ended the next month without any indication of breaking the impasse.)

June 28 Germany commissioned *U-1*, the first submarine built there since 1918.

July 4 Austria repealed its antimonarchy laws, reflecting public sentiment for restoration of the Hapsburgs.

July 25 The League of Nations Council voted to investigate the dispute between Italy and Ethiopia beginning Sept. 4. (No such inquiry was ever held.)

Aug. 12 Ethiopia called on the League to lift the embargo member states had imposed on the shipment of arms to Ethiopia and Italy. Addis Ababa was at an obvious disadvantage since it possessed virtually no modern weapons and had to buy them, while Italy had ample material for use against the backward African state.

Aug. 16 At a Paris meeting, France and Britain told Italy that Rome would be permitted wide economic freedom in Ethiopia, provided the government in Addis Ababa agreed to such an arrangement. Italy's rejection underscored the feeling that only total control of the African state would satisfy Mussolini.

Aug. 18 Roosevelt called on Italy to preserve the peace in east Africa. The appeal was in the form of a personal message to Mussolini: An "outbreak of hostilities would be a world calamity, the consequences of which would adversely affect the interests of all nations."

Aug. 20 The Seventh World Congress of the Communist International declared a "Popular Front" strategy. Communists were called upon to create the broadest united front in the struggle for peace and against those who instigated war, against fascism, against militarism and armaments, against chauvinism, and to support the national liberation struggle and wars of national liberation.

Aug. 26 Mussolini said, "It should be realized without possibility of misunderstanding that

JEWISH EMIGRATION TO PALESTINE

Year		Count
1933		(30,327)
1934		(42,359)
1935		(61,854)
1936		(29,727)
1937		(10,536)
1938		(12,868)
1939		(27,561)
1940		(8,398)
1941		(5,886)
1942		(3,733)
1943		(8,507)
1944		(14,464)
1945		(13,121)

10,000   30,000   50,000   70,000

TOTAL: 269,341

SOURCE: LEVIN, THE HOLOCAUST.

whoever applies sanctions against Italy will be met by the armed hostilities of our country."

Aug. 31 The U.S Neutrality Act was signed by Roosevelt. A victory for the American isolationists, it prohibited the export of all "arms, ammunition, and implements of war to belligerent countries." Roosevelt said it was intended "to avoid any action which might involve us in war." He added, however, that the act's "inflexible provisions might drag us into war instead of keeping us out."

■ Italy called up 200,000 more men, raising the size of its army to one million.

Sept. 3 An arbitration commission submitted its report on the Wal Wal incident, concluding that neither Italy nor Ethiopia could be blamed. The border was considered sufficiently ill-defined to create misunderstanding.

■ As an indication of stiffening British public attitudes on the Ethiopian issue, the Trades Union Congress voted 2,962,000 to 177,000 that "all the necessary measures be provided the Government to resist Italy's unjust and rapacious attack."

Sept. 6 A five-member commission was established by the League of Nations "to make a general examination of Italian-Ethiopian relations and to seek a pacific settlement."

Sept. 9 Austria and Hungary signed an agreement to consult with each other on mutual problems, but it made no provision for assistance.

Sept. 10 U.S. Ambassador Breckinridge Long advised the State Department that Italy appeared determined to continue her advances against Ethiopia: ". . . the whole population, both military and civilian, are in complete accord with Mussolini's policies as they have been developed up to now and as they are prospected for the future."

Sept. 11 In an unequivocal speech to the League Assembly, British Foreign Secretary Hoare called for stern action in Ethiopia: "We believe that small nations are entitled to a life of their own

and to such protection as can collectively be afforded to them. . . . we believe that backward nations are, without prejudice to their independence and integrity, entitled to expect that assistance will be afforded them by more advanced nations in the development of their resources and the buildup of their national life."

Sept. 14 Italy's council of ministers rejected a League-inspired compromise solution to its disputes with Ethiopia, noting "the immense efforts and sacrifices made by Italy and after the irrefutable documentation contained in the Italian memorandum presented at Geneva."

Sept. 15 Germany adopted the Nürnberg Laws. Severe anti-Jewish measures were imposed, sharply limiting citizenship for Jews and restricting relations between Aryans and Jews.

■ Hitler charged that Germans in the Lithuanian area of Memel were being tortured and deprived of their rights.

■ The swastika was officially adopted as part of the German national flag.

Sept. 20 In a forceful indication of Britain's strong stand against Italy over Ethiopia, the British ambassador in Rome informed the Italian government that 144 Royal Navy ships—800,000 tons—were cruising in the Mediterranean. Large

Manifesting Nazi-inspired anti-Semitism, the German town of Rosenheim proclaimed, "Jews Not Welcome Here."

elements of the Home Fleet, including the battleships *Hood* and *Renown*, were part of the British naval show of strength.

Sept. 22 A proposed settlement by the League's Committee of Five on the Italian-Ethiopian dispute was turned down by Rome. Italy said the group had not "paid sufficient attention to the fact that Ethiopia was admitted to the League on special and specified conditions, and that she may be regarded as no onger possessing the status of a member of the League. . . ."

Sept. 23 Ethiopia accepted the League's committee proposals on the Italian dispute as a basis for future negotiation.

Sept. 25 Ethiopia again called for neutral observers "to establish the facts in regard to any aggression or other incident that might occur in order to fix the responsibility thereof."

Sept. 26 Saying that efforts of the Committee of Five had failed, the League Council appointed another committee to report on the Italian-Ethiopian dispute. (The Committee of Five—Britain, France, Poland, Spain, and Turkey—had recommended a League protectorate over Ethiopia with Italy gaining outright control over vast desert areas of Ethiopia.) At the same time, the League issued its sternest warning to Italy: "Don't you dare go to war—not for three months." The League felt its new committee could reach a conclusion by then.

Sept. 28 Ethiopia ordered a general mobilization for war and was immediately criticized by Italy for its "warlike and aggressive spirit."

■ Germany imposed governmental control over the Protestant Church. Hans Kerrl was named minister for church affairs with sweeping powers to force conformity with naziism.

Oct. 2 Italy announced general mobilization "because there is an attempt to commit against [us] the blackest of all injustices, to rob [us] of a place in the sun. . . . to us were left only the crumbs from the sumptuous colonial booty of others. . . . With Ethiopia we have been patient for 40 years. Now, enough!"

■ Ethiopia notified the League Council that Italian troops were crossing the frontier in the province of Aussa and that the Italians were advancing through French Somaliland.

Oct. 3 Italy invaded Ethiopia. Italian forces—four Italian divisions and large numbers of native forces—crossed into Ethiopia from Eritrea, allegedly "to repulse the imminent Ethiopian threat." There was no formal declaration of war. Two of Mussolini's sons were pilots in the 14th Bomber Squadron, which was one of the Italian air force units involved in the operation. Defenseless towns were bombed. There was no immediate Ethiopian opposition to the Italians, Haile Selassie having withdrawn his meager, ill-equipped forces.

Oct. 5 Declaring that "a state of war unhappily exists between Ethiopia and the Kingdom of Italy," President Roosevelt embargoed all arms and munitions shipments to the two countries under provisions of the Neutrality Act.

■ Italy declared its actions in Ethiopia were required to protect its African colonies from Ethiopian aggression.

Oct. 6 Italian troops occupied Adowa (Adwa), where in 1896 Ethiopian troops annihilated 12,000 Italian troops, an event which had festered for 39 years in Italy. (A monument was later erected there inscribed: To the Dead of Adowa, Avenged At Last.)

Oct. 7 Italy was declared an aggressor in Ethiopia by the League Council for having caused "a war begun in disregard of the obligations of Article 12 of the Covenant."

Oct. 9 The Export-Import Bank of the U.S. announced no loans or credits would be extended to belligerents.

Oct. 10 The monarchy was reestablished in Greece following a coup d'etat.

Oct. 11 The League Assembly voted arms and economic sanctions against Italy.

Oct. 14 Britain sought French support if Britain were attacked as the result of invoking sanctions against an aggressor state. London desired the backing of Paris to counter possible Italian military counteraction growing out of the Ethiopian war.

Oct. 18 France offered Britain unlimited military backing if the latter were attacked as a consequence of measures taken against a Covenant-breaking state. Britain agreed to take no action without "the full agreement of France."

Oct. 19 British Prime Minister Baldwin denied London's opposition to Italy went beyond Ethiopia: "It is spread about in some places abroad that one of the main objects in the line of action taken up by this country is to fight and to overthrow fascism in Italy. That is a lie of a dangerous kind. What government Italy has is a matter for Italy alone. The day is long past when this country would seek by arms or any other method to overthrow a form of government existing in another country."

Oct. 28 Japanese Foreign Minister Hirota outlined Tokyo's minimum demands in China: a bloc made up of China, Manchukuo, and Japan; an end to anti-Japanese activities in China; and a Sino-Japanese campaign to suppress communism.

Oct. 30 Britain and Italy conferred on a mutual reduction of forces in the Mediterranean, a move intended to indicate that the maritime balance of power was at issue between the two countries, not the Ethiopian war.

Nov. 3 By plebiscite the people of Greece supported restoration of the monarchy.

■ Socialist Léon Blum formed the French Popular Front.

Nov. 6 The League Committee of Eighteen accepted in principle a Canadian proposal to extend embargo measures against peace violators to such items as fuel, iron, and steel.

■ Italian troops took over the Ethiopian fortress of Makallé, an objective it found more formidable than Rome had assumed. In order to reinvigorate the Italian army, Mussolini appointed Marshal Pietro Badoglio to command the expeditionary force.

Nov. 11 Italy protested the imposition of sanctions against it by the League.

■ Roosevelt said the main objective of U.S. foreign policy was to avoid being involved in a war, but he noted that "international confidence in the sacredness of international contracts is on the wane."

Nov. 15 In a resumption of Japanese moves to

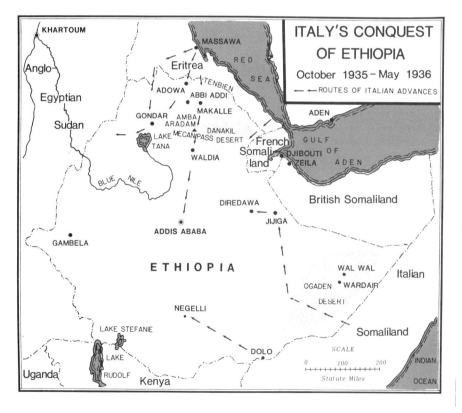

ITALY'S CONQUEST OF ETHIOPIA

October 1935 – May 1936

← ROUTES OF ITALIAN ADVANCES

A skirmish near an ill-defined boundary between Italian Somaliland and Ethiopia sparked a vengeful war against the East African nation. Mussolini's ambitions were briefly satisfied when Italy's superior military forces overwhelmed primitive tribesmen.

gain greater control of China, the pro-Japanese Chinese commissioner of the demilitarized zone, Yin Ju-keng, called for an autonomous north China. A Manchukuo-like administration was envisaged by Tokyo, Japanese domination under nominal Chinese administration.

■ The Philippine Islands received commonwealth status under U.S. rule.

Nov. 18 Arms and economic sanctions against Italy by League members became effective. Several countries, however, attached loopholes in their embargo laws. Oil, significantly, was not on the League-approved list. The net result was a sievelike embargo which was barely a slap in the Italian face.

Nov. 19 Under threat of military occupation, Japanese military authorities demanded "autonomy" for north China.

Nov. 24 Chinese administrator Yin Ju-keng declared eastern Hopei Province to be independent and under the administration of the Anti-Communist Autonomous Council. The Japanese sought economic control over the area which produced coal and the port facilities for its shipment. It was also important as an entry point for goods of Japanese manufacture to be smuggled into China. Hopei also became a key source of narcotics which flowed to countries around the world.

Dec. 1 Chiang Kai-shek became president of the Chinese Executive Yuan in Nanking.

Dec. 5 Secretary of State Hull protested the Japanese-directed autonomy movement in north China.

■ The Soviet Union adopted a liberalized constitution, including the "guarantee" of civil rights. The Communist party, however, remained the only legal party.

■ Finland, wishing to remain neutral and to avoid any involvement in the cauldron of central and eastern Europe, declared a policy of "Scandinavian Orientation," which meant limiting its ties to Sweden, Norway, and Denmark.

Dec. 8 The secretly-arranged Hoare-Laval agreement was signed, giving Italy control over two-thirds of Ethiopia. Laval sought the dual blessing of Italy's actions because he felt France would not go to war against a "desperate" Italy

over the African controversy. The agreement remained secret only a day, and the cynicism of the French agreeing to the Italian territorial gains while deploring them publicly made a mockery of collective security. Hitler, interestingly, disliked the agreement, fearing that Italy would now become allied with France and Britain.

Dec. 9 A naval conference was convened in London and attended by the five major maritime powers. Japan demanded the Washington ratios be scrapped in favor of parity between Japan, Britain, the U.S., France, and Italy.

Dec. 12 Hopei and Chahar, the two provinces bordering Manchuria, were declared autonomous under a Japanese-controlled "Political Council."

■ The League Committee postponed a proposed embargo on oil shipments to Italy because the Council was considering a French and British proposal to end the Italian-Ethiopian war. How unwise the decision was can be seen from Mussolini's comment to Hitler in 1938: "If the League of Nations had followed Eden's advice in the Abyssinian [Ethiopian] dispute and had extended economic sanctions to oil, I would have had to withdraw from Abyssinia within a week. That would have been an incalculable disaster for me."

Dec. 13 Masaryk resigned as Czechoslovak president at the age of 85 and was succeeded by the Foreign Minister, Eduard Benes.

Dec. 22 Anthony Eden replaced Hoare as British foreign secretary because of the latter's attempts to negotiate a settlement of the Ethiopian dispute with France's Laval. The Hoare-Laval plan was thus repudiated.

Dec. 23 Italians began using mustard gas in Ethiopia, dropping cannisters from aircraft on Ethiopian soldiers in Tigre Province on the Takkaze River near Mai Timchet. The responsibility for its use must be placed on the shoulders of Marshal Badoglio, commander-in-chief of the Italian forces in east Africa. Mussolini had approved its use for "supreme defense reasons." Badoglio, however, was intent on speeding up the stalemated Italian offensive by any means, even gas. The material actually used was dichlorodiethyl sulfide, known variously as mustard gas or yperite, although several other forms of less noxious materials were also employed.

■ Commenting on the "China Incident," Japanese diplomat Saburo Kurusu said "foreign people did not understand what it was all about." Japan, he declared, was destined to lead oriental civilization.

(OPPOSITE. TOP) *Spain was convulsed by a tragic civil war.*

(OPPOSITE. BOTTOM) *Civilians greet German troops entering the Rhineland in Hitler's bold remilitarization move.*

1936

Spain is engulfed in civil war, and Europe's will and arms are put to the test.

Jan. 3 Haile Selassie requested the League of Nations appoint a committee to investigate how the war was being fought in Ethiopia. His hope was to reveal Italy's destructive aerial attacks on defenseless villages.

Jan. 8 Japan said it would withdraw from the London Naval Conference unless it won the right to parity in the number of men-of-war it could have in relation to the other powers.

Jan. 10 Molotov delivered a speech in which he suggested rather broadly that Russia wished to improve relations with Germany.

Jan. 15 Japan withdrew from the London Naval Conference, objecting to "the quantitative limitation submitted by the other delegations." (Later, Tokyo announced it would not be bound by the Washington Naval Treaty after Dec. 31, 1936.)

Jan. 17 In a Berlin speech German Propaganda Chief Joseph Goebbels declared: "We can do without butter, but, despite all our love of peace, not without arms. One cannot shoot with butter but with guns."

Jan. 18 Changpeh—40 miles north of Kalgan—was occupied by Inner Mongolians and was immediately incorporated into Manchukuo. While the action was encouraged by the Japanese, the Mongolians detested ruthless Chinese administrative policies and practices.

Jan. 20 Ethiopia asked for financial assistance from the League of Nations and a tighter economic embargo on Italy.

■ Edward VIII acceded to the British throne on the death of George V.

Jan. 22 The Laval government fell in France as the result of opposition to its policies, which reflected approval of Italian expansionism.

Jan. 23 The first battle of Tembien in Ethiopia ended in a stalemate, but the Ethiopians stopped the first major Italian offensive since the inital invasion. The four-day battle ended with 1,100 Italians and 8,000 Ethiopians dead and wounded.

Feb. 10 Italian forces launched a 200,000 man attack against Amba Aradam in northern Ethiopia where the defending forces had concentrated their greatest strength, 60,000 men. Rome described the attack as the Italian "battle of annihilation."

■ A law was enacted making the Gestapo (Secret State Police) a "Supreme Reich Agency," giving Heinrich Himmler, chief of the SS and the Gestapo, absolute control over German internal security.

Feb. 15 The Italians routed the Ethiopian force at Amba Aradam. Two hundred eighty Italian guns fired 23,000 shells, and about 170 planes dropped 396 tons of explosives, killing 6,000 Ethiopians. Italian aircraft pursued the retreating Ethiopian force for four days by dropping mustard gas. Six thousand more Ethiopian troops were killed in this way, and the army of Ras Mulugeta was decimated. (Ras Mulugeta was the Ethiopian war minister. More than 70 years old, he had personally directed the defensive operations in the north. He was killed by a bullet on Feb. 24, while leaning over the body of his son who had just died in the fighting.)

Feb. 16 The Leftist Popular Front won a majority in the Spanish general elections. (Manuel Azaña became premier on the 19th.)

Feb. 25 The British cabinet approved a major rearmament program. In order to increase the output of aircraft and other essential equipment, the government developed a "shadow factory" plan with manufacturers expanding production facilities. It was, as Royal Air Force historians would write, an effort "to catch the electric hare of German rearmament."

Feb. 26 Japanese army extremists attempted to force radical governmental reforms by assassinating the minister of finance, the director-general of military education, and a former prime minister, Makoto Saito. They sought a military-socialistic dictatorship under the emperor and an end to measures pressed by moderates to curb the military's involvement in politics. Prime Minister Keisuke Okada escaped death when his residence was attacked, but the would-be assassins mistook his brother-in-law for Okada. Led by their captains and lieutenants, 1,400 rebellious troops of the Imperial Guard and the 1st Division seized key points in Tokyo, where martial law was imposed. Most military units remained loyal, and the outburst was readily contained. Thirteen officers and four civilian collaborators were later tried and executed.

Feb. 27 Italian troops opened the second battle of Tembien, leading to further devastation of the Ethiopian forces. Bombs and mustard gas left only scattered survivors and the emperor's personal guard to resist the onrushing Italians.

Feb. 29 Roosevelt signed the amended U.S. Neutrality Act which restricted the powers of the president in dealing with foreign belligerents.

March 7 In a cunning gamble German troops marched into the demilitarized left bank of the Rhineland. Three battalions of Germans were ordered in to show Hitler's disregard for the Treaty of Versailles and the Locarno treaties. The French and British did nothing and Hitler's

military finesse worked. Had any immediate resistance been offered, the German troops were under instructions to withdraw promptly. Nations which might have taken immediate counteraction or resisted were preoccupied with Ethiopia, or simply felt incapable of action. General Maurice Gamelin's summary of meetings between the French cabinet and the military leaders reveal why Paris offered only limited reaction to the Rhineland occupation. The generals told the cabinet they were not prepared to undertake offensive action, and they persuaded the civilian leaders that it would be unwise to assemble the large expeditionary force which the generals felt would be required.

March 8 France and Belgium called for League "consideration" of Germany's Rhineland action.

March 9 Poland secretly proposed to France that they jointly attack Germany. Paris declined. Warsaw concluded that regional alliances were useless.

■ British Secretary for Foreign Affairs Anthony Eden condemned Germany for repudiating the Treaty of Versailles and added, "One of the main foundations of the peace of western Europe has been cut away and, if peace is to be secured, there is a manifest duty to rebuild."

■ Foreign Minister Koki Hirota was named Japanese prime minister, and the cabinet was restructured in a manner giving the military even greater power. Hirota himself favored expansion into China and became a prime mover in Japan's membership in the Axis.

March 14 The League Council met to discuss Germany's remilitarization of the Rhineland.

March 20 Noting that the League had done nothing yet, Ethiopia again requested intervention because of "the unquestionable evidence" of Italian aggression.

March 23 Ethiopia called the League's attention to the "atrocities" of the Italians and their use of poison gas.

March 25 The London Naval Agreement was signed, with Britain, France, and the U.S. approving a 35,000-ton limitation on new warships and restricting the size of guns on the vessels. Italy refused to sign the final agreement, and Germany began construction of the 45,000-ton battleships *Bismarck* and *Tirpitz*.

March 29 In a plebiscite on Hitler's foreign policy (which was centered on remilitarization of the

Rhineland and other renunciations of the Versailles treaty), 98.7 percent of the eligible Germans cast ballots of approval.

March 31 Ethiopian troops—including the Imperial Guard—counterattacked Italian positions under the personal command of Haile Selassie. Eight thousand men struck in the Mecan Pass. They were successful in taking some Italian positions at first but quickly withdrew after absorbing heavy casualties and almost running out of ammunition.

April 1 Austria began plans for conscription, whether it was able to rearm or not. Vienna announced that military service was of "social value for physical, moral, and patriotic education." In fact, the Austrian government became fearful of Germany's military muscle-flexing.

April 2 Austria and Czechoslovakia completed a trade treaty, reflecting Vienna's basic desire to establish closer relations with nations seemingly willing to resist Germany's threatening gestures.

April 6 The Little Entente powers (Czechoslovakia, Rumania, and Yugoslavia) protested Austrian conscription. Austria rejected the protest, frustrated that those very countries which should have been sympathetic to Austria's concerns about Germany should rebuff Vienna when it took steps to counter Germany.

April 8 The League's Committee of Thirteen appointed a panel to conduct an inquiry into the use of poison gas by the Italians in Ethiopia.

■ The Soviet Union and Mongolia signed a mutual assistance pact.

April 13 General John Metaxas became prime minister of Greece.

April 17 The Committee of Thirteen said it had failed to conciliate the Italian-Ethiopian dispute.

April 20 The League Council met to discuss Ethiopia and ended up with an appeal to Italy and Ethiopia "for the prompt cessation of hostilities and the restoration of peace." By this time Italy had virtually completed its conquest and there were no Ethiopian troops left to fight.

May 2 Haile Selassie abandoned the Ethiopian capital of Addis Ababa. Two days later he boarded the British cruiser *Enterprise* and sailed for Palestine.

May 5 Marshal Pietro Badoglio's Italian forces entered Addis Ababa. Badoglio became governor general and viceroy of Ethiopia. Like Manchu-

ria, the Ethiopian episode revealed the League of Nations as totally impotent.

May 9 Mussolini staged a victory celebration in Rome, saying, "At last, Italy has her empire . . . a civilizing empire, humanitarian toward all the peoples of Ethiopia." Victor Emmanuel III was proclaimed the new emperor of Ethiopia. The newly conquered nation was grouped with Eritrea and Italian Somaliland into what was designated "Italian East Africa."

May 12 Italy announced its intention to withdraw from the League of Nations, an act of protest against Ethiopia's continuing membership.

June 2 Argentina requested a meeting of the League Assembly to consider Italy's conquest of Ethiopia.

■ Chinese regional military commanders in the southwest demanded Nationalist forces be used to resist the Japanese military buildup in north China rather than be involved in sectional disputes involving only the Chinese. The demand reflected a prevailing attitude and concern about the weak stand of the Nanking government among a growing number of Chinese who were wearied by internal political bickering while the country was being gobbled up by the Japanese.

June 3 Haile Selassie arrived in England on the British passenger ship *Orford*, having been transferred from the Royal Navy cruiser *Capetown* at Gibraltar. The switch from a warship to a civilian liner presumably was to disassociate the British government from his flight from Ethiopia.

June 4 Socialist Léon Blum became premier of France at the head of a Popular Front coalition government. Blum's main opposition came from Pierre Laval, who had badly ruptured French relations with Britain, which Blum sought to repair.

June 18 Australia, Britain, and Canada abandoned sanctions against Italy. Anthony Eden said, "I think it is right that the League should admit that sanctions have not realized their purpose and should face the fact."

June 23 British Prime Minister Stanley Baldwin told the House of Commons that collective security represented a policy of failure, "ultimately because of the reluctance of nearly all the nations in Europe to proceed to what I might call military sanctions . . . the ultimate sanction is always war."

June 30 In a memorable address to the League of

Nations in Geneva, Haile Selassie said, "I ask the 52 nations who have given the Ethiopian people a promise to help them in their resistance to the aggressor: What are they willing to do for Ethiopia? I ask the great Powers, who have promised the guarantee of collective security to small states over whom hangs the threat that they must one day suffer the fate of Ethiopia: What measures do they intend to take?"

■ The French government declared the Fascist party of France illegal.

July 4 The League Council voted to end sanctions against Italy because of its actions in Ethiopia, ending an abortive international attempt to preserve peace and resist aggression. The League had failed again.

July 11 Germany and Austria signed a "gentlemen's agreement" with steps to be taken "for the reestablishment of normal and friendly relations." This paved the way for Rome and Berlin to act in concert in Spain and elsewhere since Italy had been wary of German designs on Austria. Mussolini stated the agreement "would finally remove the last and only mortgage on German-Italian relations." (As a footnote to history, the term "gentlemen's agreement" was used diplomatically for the first time; it was coined by the German ambassador in Vienna, Franz von Papen.)

July 15 Aviators began to be recruited in Italy for service in Spain.

July 17 Civil war erupted in Spain. General Francisco Franco and his legions in Spanish Morocco moved to oust "the ineffectual government" in Madrid. The uprising was triggered by the assassinations of an army officer on the 12th and a rightist politician on the 13th. Within days the army rebellion spread through Spain. It was directed against the policies of President Manuel Azaña and the Spanish Left which had assumed power in May. The "Loyalists" were anticlerical and antimonarchy (King Alfonso XIII went into exile in 1931) and included Republicans, Socialists, Communists, and Syndicalists. Conservatives supported the military insurgents and combined forces under the label of "Nationalists."

July 18 The Spanish government issued orders arming the civilian population to fight the military insurrectionists.

July 19 Chiang Kai-shek established Nationalist control over Kwangtung Province in China

which the Japanese sought to manipulate through their chosen functionaries.

July 20 The Spanish premier of the Loyalist government requested French military aid. In a telegram to Premier Blum, José Giral said Madrid was "surprised by a dangerous military coup. Beg of you to help us immediately with arms and aeroplanes." France did help covertly, while the Russians aided the Loyalist cause openly with arms and men. Italy and Germany supported the Nationalists as openly and even more massively.

July 23 Germany and Italy were invited by France, Britain, and Belgium to join in an agreement guaranteeing peace and preserving Europe's territorial boundaries. Rome and Berlin were not enthusiastic, drawn as they were by their common attitude and actions in Spain and their shared and growing antagonisms toward France and Britain.

July 25 France embargoed arms shipments to Spain, though it practiced tolerance to those shipping material to the Loyalists.

■ General Miguel Cabenallas established a rebel provisional government in Spain at Burgos (which became the Nationalist government).

■ Hitler agreed to a request from Franco to airlift Nationalist troops from Tetuán in Morocco to Spain. (Luftwaffe transport planes flew out the next day.)

■ Germany and China concluded a trade pact covering 100 million marks. The Chinese were to receive arms and manufactured goods in exchange for natural resources, primarily tungsten.

July 28 The Loyalist government confiscated all religious property in Spain.

July 30 Italian aircraft, with crews wearing Spanish uniforms, began operating in support of the Nationalists.

Aug. 2 France called on all governments to agree on a Spanish "nonintervention pact." The French frontier itself, however, remained open for "private" arms shipments to the Loyalists.

Aug. 4 Britain agreed to join in a collective declaration of nonintervention in Spain.

■ General Metaxas, the premier of Greece, abolished constitutional rights and established a dictatorship. Foreign policy remained in harmony with Britain, but Metaxas agreed to trade with Germany and tried to avoid being overly identified with one side or the other.

Aug. 5 Russia accepted the principle of nonintervention and called for an immediate end to all arms shipments to the Nationalists in Spain.

Aug. 7 Hull notified U.S. missions in Spain that while the Neutrality Act did not apply to the Civil War, the United States would "scrupulously refrain from any interference whatsoever in the unfortunate Spanish situation."

Aug. 11 Sweden, Poland, and the Netherlands embargoed arms shipments to Spain.

Aug. 12 A strain of British sentiment on events on the continent was reflected in a letter to the London *Times* by the venerable historian George Macaulay Trevelyan who wrote: "Dictatorship and democracy must live side by side, or civilization is doomed. . . . Englishmen would do well to remember that the Nazi form of government is in large measure the outcome of Allied and British injustice at Versailles in 1919."

Aug. 15 Britain and France agreed on a Spanish nonintervention pledge to become effective when Germany, Italy, Russia, and Portugal offered similar assurances.

■ Premier Hirota—who became increasingly receptive to the views of extremists in the military—outlined Japan's foreign policy goals to the emperor. They included expansion into the Dutch East Indies, Manchurian economic growth, independence for the Philippines, the elimination of white rule in Asia, but all with continued peaceful cooperation with the U.S. and Britain.

Aug. 17 Germany agreed to the nonintervention agreement, provided it applied to individuals as well (as a move against foreign volunteers becoming involved in the Spanish fighting).

Aug. 19 As proof of its good faith, Britain announced a unilateral policy of nonintervention in Spain.

Aug. 20 The U.S.—stating its intention not to intervene in Spain—said it could not participate in any mediation efforts.

Aug. 21 Italy and Portugal joined in the nonintervention pledge.

Aug. 23 The Soviet Union accepted the principle of nonintervention in Spain.

Aug. 24 Germany agreed to an immediate embargo on all arms shipments to Spain.

■ Berlin announced it was increasing the period of compulsory military service from one to two years.

■ A mob in Chengtu, China, killed two Japanese newsmen during a demonstration protesting a Japanese move to reopen its consulate general in the Szechuan capital, which was closed in 1932.

Aug 26 Britain and Egypt concluded a 20-year alliance.

Aug. 27 Portugal enacted legislation to enforce the Spanish arms embargo.

Aug. 28 Russian approval was completed to enforce the Spanish arms embargo.

Aug. 29 Rumanian Foreign Minister Nicolae Titulescu was ousted by rightists who insisted on closer ties with Germany. Foreign policy nonetheless continued to reflect close relations with France and Czechoslovakia.

Aug. 30 Britain announced its biggest naval building program in fifteen years, the construction of 38 warships.

Sept. 1 The director of the German Colonial League of the Reich, General Ritter von Epp, said Germany wished to regain control over those colonies lost after the World War and which were under League of Nations mandates.

Sept. 4 Madrid was threatened by Nationalist forces. The Giral government resigned and was replaced by a coalition of Socialists and Communists headed by Largo Caballero.

Sept. 6 Chiang Kai-shek strengthened his control over China when independent leaders agreed to end autonomous rule and incorporate their forces into the Nationalist army. The key province was Kwangsi, whose officials had been pressing for action against the Japanese.

Sept. 9 The Nonintervention Committee on Spain (representing 25 European nations) met in London. It was clear by then, however, that the Germans, Italians, and Russians had no intention of keeping out of the Spanish Civil War.

■ German Propaganda Minister Goebbels accused Czechoslovakia of permitting Russian military aircraft to use Czech bases.

Sept. 12 In a highly provocative speech, Hitler said the resource-rich Urals area and the Ukraine of the Soviet Union "would swim in plenty" under Nazi rule.

■ Spanish Nationalist forces captured San Sebastián.

Sept. 15 The Loyalist government in Spain protested the shipment of arms to the Nationalists by Germany, Italy, and Portugal.

Sept. 19 Two Japanese consular policemen were killed in Hankow, China.

Sept. 22 Japanese marines landed in Hankow and Pakhoi.

Sept. 23 Japanese naval forces seized control of Hongkew, China, after three sailors were killed.

Oct. 1 General Franco was named commander of the Spanish Nationalist army and chief of the Spanish state (caudillo), resolving internecine disputes over leadership roles among the Nationalists.

■ The Soviet Union agreed to adhere to the terms of the London Naval Agreement, limiting the size of ships and their guns.

Oct. 5 Italy took drastic steps to keep afloat financially. The government devalued the lira and imposed new taxes. The precarious financial position was caused by the Ethiopian war, maintaining a "volunteer" force in Spain, and heavy expenditures for general rearmament.

Oct. 7 Russia protested arms shipments to Spain by some members of the Nonintervention Committee and threatened to withdraw from the group if the violations continued.

Oct. 14 Belgium announced a policy of self-defense and an end to all political and military alliances which, it said, could lead to "becoming entangled in the rivalries of the political and social systems of other states, and of unchaining a keener and more devastating conflagration than that from which we are still suffering." Belgium in fact was repudiating the 1921 French-Belgian military alliance. Belgium feared Germany but wished to avoid war through its connection with the alliance between France and Russia. The action by Brussels was a crushing blow to the French system of interlocking security arrangements.

Oct. 23 As a prelude to recognizing the Franco government, Portugal broke off diplomatic relations with Republican Loyalist Spain.

Oct. 24 Count Galeazzo Ciano, Italy's new 34-year-old foreign minister and Mussolini's son-in-law, visited Hitler at Berchtesgaden and formed the basis for the Axis alliance. Germany recognized Italy's annexation of Ethiopia. Italy, for its part, was prepared to support Germany in all its colonial demands. Both agreed on the need to develop a common front against Bolshevism.

Oct. 25–27 The Rome-Berlin Axis was forged "in the supreme obligation . . . to defend the great institutions of Europe." The agreement covered an Italian-German understanding on Austria, ending that sore point, and put into formal agreement the points covered by the Hitler-Ciano talks.

HOW THE "AXIS" GOT ITS NAME

After Mussolini met with Hitler at Berchtesgaden in October 1936 and reached a secret agreement aligning the foreign policies of the two countries, he returned to Italy to report on the new alliance. In a speech at Milan on Nov. 1, Mussolini said, "this vertical line between Rome and Berlin is not a partition [*diaframma*] but rather an axis [*asse*] round which all European states animated by the will to collaboration and peace can also collaborate." Mussolini had a predilection for the term, having written as far back as 1923 that "the axis of European history" runs through Berlin.

Oct. 28 Russia said it was no more bound to embargo arms to Spain "than those governments who supply the rebels in contravention of the [nonintervention] agreement."

Oct. 29 Russian tanks and planes (with Red Army crews) began operating in Spain on the side of the Republicans. The armored force was commanded by "General Pavlov." The newly arrived tanks underwent their baptism of fire in a successful counterattack against the Nationalist units attacking Madrid. Interestingly, the Russians used massed tank tactics, which formed part of the blitzkrieg ("lightning war") methods developed by the Germans.

■ The siege of Madrid was launched by the Nationalists with a heavy artillery attack.

Nov. 1 Roosevelt was elected overwhelmingly to a second term as U.S. president.

Nov. 2 In an unusually gruff warning to the Baltic states, Soviet Politburo member Andrei Zhdanov told them to "mind only their own business" or "they will not be comfortable if we have to call upon our Red Army to defend our country."

Nov. 6 Germany's "Condor Legion" began to be assembled in Seville to fight on the Nationalist side. It would eventually consist of 6,500 men, equipped with Junkers 52 bombers, Messerschmitt 109 and Heinkel 51 fighters (96 aircraft in all, equally divided between the two types), 32 tanks, and assorted artillery. The Legion was supported by the battleships *Deutschland* and *Scheer*.

■ The Loyalist government fled to Valencia as Madrid was being squeezed by the Nationalists.

Nov. 11 Austria and Hungary recognized Italian control of Ethiopia.

Nov. 13 France signed a treaty with Lebanon providing for the future independence of the Middle East protectorate.

Nov. 14 In contravention of the Versailles treaty, Germany renounced international controls over the Rhine, Elbe, Oder, and Danube rivers, calling the arrangement intolerable. (France, Czechoslovakia, and Yugoslavia protested, to no avail.)

Nov. 18 Germany and Italy formally recognized the Franco government in Spain.

Nov. 25 Germany and Japan signed the Anti-Comintern Pact. The purpose was to block Soviet interference abroad. A secret clause barred either side from making political agreements with the Soviet Union and should Germany or Japan become involved in a war with Russia there would be consultation on joint action.

Nov. 27 The Spanish Republican government appealed to the League against the "armed intervention" of Germany and Italy.

■ Roosevelt—in Rio de Janeiro—called on all the nations of the Americas "to free themselves forever from conflict."

Nov. 28 Poland and Rumania reaffirmed their alliances.

■ Italy recognized Manchukuo, apparently to gain recognition from Japan on Ethiopia.

Dec. 3 Because of a lockout of employees at a Japanese cotton mill in Tsingtao, Japanese marines occupied the Chinese port city.

Dec. 10 Edward VIII abdicated the British throne to marry an American divorcée, Wallis Warfield Simpson.

Dec. 11 George VI acceded to the throne.

Dec. 12–15 In one of the bizarre events of modern history which was to have far-reaching consequences, Chiang Kai-shek was kidnapped in the "Sian Incident." Chiang was poised in Sian with a large army preparing to eliminate the Communists who had holed up in Yenan in Shensi Province after the Long March. Before Chiang could move, he was kidnapped by Chang Hsuehliang, the "Young Marshal," and General Yang Fu-cheng, the warlord in control of northwest China. They preferred Chiang's forces be used to fight the Japanese instead. After Yang almost executed Chiang, Chou En-lai, one of the Communist leaders, negotiated Chiang's release with an agreement that the Nationalists and Communists would fight the Japanese together under Chiang's leadership. Some historians feel Chou was directed by Moscow to free Chiang since Russia wanted a unified China because of the recently concluded Anti-Comintern Pact. Had Chiang not been kidnapped and launched his military drive to eradicate the then very weak Communists under Mao Tse-tung, the course of history might have been greatly altered.

Dec. 18 German troops landed at Cádiz in Spain, a blatant breach of nonintervention.

Dec. 23 The Nonintervention Committee adopted a plan to supervise the Spanish arms embargo.

Dec. 30 China and Japan agreed to settle the Chengtu and Pakhoi incidents.

Dec. 31 The Naval Treaty of London, in effect since Jan. 1, 1931, expired, a meaningless formality since many of the signatory states had no intention of honoring its restraints anyway.

(OPPOSITE, TOP) *Hitler built Germany into a menacing power by 1937.*

(OPPOSITE, BOTTOM) *Crewmen aboard the U.S.S.* Panay *on China's Yangtze River return fire from attacking Japanese aircraft.*

1937 An Axis is forged.

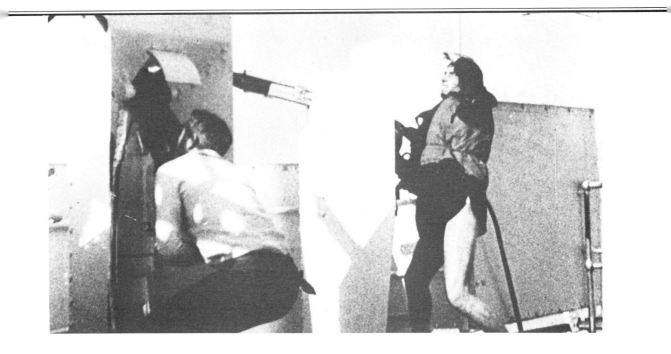

Jan. 2 Great Britain and Italy agreed to respect each other's rights in the Mediterranean and to maintain the status quo of lands bordering the sea. They also committed themselves to uphold Spain's independence. Mussolini, that very day, ordered more troops to Spain, interpreting the British agreement to mean that additional manpower there would help maintain peace in the area.

Jan. 7 Germany and Italy rejected a French-British proposal to halt the flow of foreign volunteers into Spain. They agreed, however, that the matter should go to the Nonintervention Committee which might consider steps for removing volunteers already there.

Jan. 10 Britain invoked an 1870 law to bar Britons from serving as volunteers in Spain.

Jan. 14 The U.S. consul general in Barcelona was instructed by the State Department to discourage Americans from serving as volunteers: ". . . the enlistment of American citizens in either of the opposing forces in Spain is unpatriotically inconsistent with the American Government's policy of the most scrupulous nonintervention in Spanish internal affairs."

Jan. 15 France enacted laws prohibiting Frenchmen from serving in Spain or permitting the transport of any volunteers seeking to reach Spain.

■ In an effort to placate Berlin the Austrian government granted amnesties to Nazis imprisoned in Austria.

Jan. 16 Germany announced that all naval vessels seeking to transit the Kiel Canal would have to request prior authorization from the German Naval High Command.

Jan. 19 Germany's military attaché in London reported that irrefutable evidence had been obtained on advanced plans between Prague and Moscow regarding the use of Czech airfields by the Soviet air force.

Jan. 23 The Hirota cabinet fell in Japan, with the army bickering over policy and creating factions incapable of compromise.

Jan. 24 Bulgaria and Yugoslavia signed a treaty of perpetual friendship, seemingly putting an end to the enmity which had marked relations between the two states.

Jan. 27 Nationalists and Communists reached agreement in China to combine their forces in fighting the Japanese. Overall authority went to Chiang Kai-shek and the Nanking government.

Jan. 30 Hitler demanded a return of all former German colonies, repudiated the war-guilt clause of the Versailles treaty, and ended reparations payments for the management of the Reichsbank and the German railways. He declared that "peace is our dearest treasure" and offered to guarantee the neutrality of Belgium and the Netherlands.

Feb. 4 General Senjuro Hayashi became Japan's premier, but the new government did not command more than token support from any influential group.

Feb. 8 Spanish Nationalist forces, with critical Italian support, captured Málaga. The road from Madrid to Valencia, however, remained open to the Loyalists.

Feb. 13 The Netherlands said its neutrality was axiomatic and not the subject of any agreement with foreign powers, thus turning aside Hitler's gesture of Jan. 30.

Feb. 14 The question of restoring the Hapsburg monarchy in Austria was revived as a political issue when Schuschnigg declared publicly that the issue was his alone to decide. This inflamed the Nazis in Austria and Germany and led to street demonstrations and violence.

Feb. 19 An attempt was made in Addis Ababa to assassinate the Italian viceroy of Ethiopia, General Rodolfo Graziani, who was wounded. Large-scale reprisals, including executions, followed as the Italians vowed to keep the Ethiopians in line.

Feb 20 A ban by the Nonintervention Committee on foreign volunteers serving in Spain went into effect.

■ Portugal announced its willingness to permit British supervision of its land frontiers.

Feb. 23 Hitler declared the "existence of Switzerland answers a European need" and pronounced Germany's intention to respect its neutrality.

Feb. 27 A ministry of defense was created in France. Paris announced plans to extend the Maginot line.

March 2 Germany's ambassador to Britain, Joachim von Ribbentrop, said nations large and small have the right to colonies and "Germany must formally reject every form of argument which seeks to dispute this right with her."

■ Italy's Fascist Grand Council approved further funding for rearmament.

March 5 Hungary uncovered a Nazi subversive plot directed by Ferenc Szalasi, who was arrested with other conspirators. Most of them were eventually given only mild rebukes.

March 8 The Nonintervention Committee approved a plan to supervise land and sea traffic into Spain. Germany indicated it would contribute $46,000 to help meet expenses.

March 16 Mussolini visited Libya and made a sweeping bid for Islamic support, a move which appeared calculated to challenge British and French domination in the Arab world.

March 18 Spanish Loyalist units scored a victory over Italian forces at Brihuega, resulting in a Loyalist change of strategy. Franco's forces, with Axis aid, turned from a thrust against Madrid and concentrated on driving northward toward Bilbao.

March 23 Italy refused to discuss withdrawal of foreign volunteers from Spain. The announcement came immediately after a humiliating defeat of Italian forces at Guadalajara.

March 25 Italy and Yugoslavia signed a treaty with each agreeing to honor the land and sea frontiers of the other and remaining neutral should either be attacked by a third country. Yugoslavia gained broad trade concessions in exchange for the main consideration from Rome's point of view, recognition of Italy's conquest of Ethiopia. The pact appeared to conclude the feud between the two countries going back to the World War. It undercut French influence and marked Yugoslavia as leaning strongly toward the Rome-Berlin Axis.

March 27 Japan turned down a 14-inch naval gun limitation proposal on the grounds that ships of other maritime powers were already equipped with more 15-inch guns than Japan's and Russia had two ships with 16-inch weapons.

March 31 South Africa said it would not even consider returning Southwest Africa to Germany.

April 1 Pacifist Bertrand Russell said the British should treat any German invaders as tourists: "The Nazis would find some interest in our way of living, I think, and the starch would be taken out of them."

April 16 Japan decided to establish an autonomous north China (embracing the provinces of Hopei, Shansi, Shantung, Chahar, and Suiyuan) which would be closely aligned with Manchukuo in pro-Japanese, anti-Soviet policies.

April 20 Patrols began enforcing the Nonintervention Committee's ban on arms shipments and the movement of foreign volunteers to Spain.

April 22 Mussolini met with Schuschnigg in Venice where the Italian said in effect that Rome would not support Austria against Germany. Schuschnigg, as a result, began negotiations to win Little Entente support against Germany.

April 24 Britain and France released Belgium from its obligations under the Locarno treaty (by which collective security guaranteed Belgium's frontiers), but still considered themselves bound to preserve Belgian territorial integrity.

April 27 The Spanish city of Guernica in Vizcaya Province was wantonly destroyed by German planes. Guernica became an antifascist symbol and inspired Pablo Picasso's celebrated painting.

April 29 Belgian Foreign Minister Paul Henri Spaak said no nation would be permitted rights of military passage without the consent of Belgium and the agreement of all her neighbors.

■ Göring ordered a halt in the production of four-engine heavy bombers for the Luftwaffe. (The decision was to prove disastrous for Germany in the war. State Secretary of Aviation Erhard Milch said later, "The great four-engine bombers of Junkers (Ju-89) and Dorniers (Do-19) were not in the construction series despite excellent performance of test models. Thus we had no really adequate aircraft for strategic operations." Without large, dependable bombers, Germany was unable to press its aerial offensive against Britain in 1940, and the U-boat campaign ended in failure when the submarine fleet was denied the air cover it required to sustain operations. The decision to abandon the large bombers was primarily the result of unlimited faith in the twin-engine Ju-88, an aircraft which could be produced in larger quantities than the heavy bombers. It was felt the German aircraft industry could produce only a thousand Ju-89s and Do-19s, but several times that number of Ju-88s would be available. By the end of the war, 10,774 Ju-88s were built, but they were never adequate substitutes for a bigger bomber. Milch said Göring was anxious to impress Hitler with sharp increases in aircraft production figures. Göring was quoted as saying, "The Führer does not ask me *what kind* of bombers I have. He simply wants to know *how many!*")

April 30 The Japanese voted out the Hayashi government, and the Diet was dissolved. It was in part a protest against the military character of the cabinet and the army's control over foreign policy. A lack of social and economic reforms was also a factor. Some of the ultranationalists were themselves disappointed with Hayashi's leadership.

May 1 Roosevelt signed the U.S. Neutrality Act.

May 8 Nazi candidates won a two-thirds majority in the Danzig *Volkstag* (parliament).

May 11 In a move to placate the Germans and to facilitate a policy of appeasement, Germanophile Nevile Henderson was sent to Berlin as the British ambassador.

May 15 In response to criticism of its extremist policies and demands for reorganization, the Republican Caballero government of Spain fell.

May 17 A government under Juan Negrín was formed in Spain with the left-wing Socialists and Anarcho-Syndicalists excluded (but two Communists were included). It vowed to prosecute the war before instituting new social programs.

May 21 Czech Foreign Minister Kamil Krofta challenged Berlin's charges that Prague's foreign policy was "anti-German."

May 28 Neville Chamberlain succeeded Stanley Baldwin as British prime minister.

■ Following the introduction of undisguised Italian army units into Spain, the Loyalist Republican government protested this violation of nonintervention to the League.

May 29 With Britain and France providing visual evidence, the League formally denounced the bombing of open cities and other violations of international law in Spain.

■ The German battleship *Deutschland* was hit in Ibiza harbor by a bomb from a Loyalist plane, killing 32 and wounding 73 crewmen. An Italian warship, *Barletta*, was also bombed. Germany and Italy withdrew from the nonintervention patrol as a result.

May 31 Five German warships bombarded Almería, Spain, in retaliation for the *Deutschland* incident.

June 3 Prince Fumimaro Konoye became Japan's premier. Hirota again took over the foreign ministry. The cabinet was called one of "National Union."

June 11 Eight high-ranking Russian generals were executed for treason. (International public opinion turned against the Soviet Union because of such actions. Russia was also depriving itself of established military leadership, a fact which became readily apparent in the years ahead. The purges continued through 1938. More than 20,000 officers were executed, including 90 percent of the generals and 80 percent of the colonels.)

■ Germany issued the "Racial Violence" decrees.

June 16 France and Britain arranged for the protection of the nonintervention patrol, and Germany and Italy agreed to rejoin the operation.

June 18 Bilbao was occupied by Spanish Nationalist troops, ending a fierce battle lasting several months (with extensive use of German and Italian air power to break Loyalist and Basque resistance).

■ The German cruiser *Leipzig* claimed to have received a glancing blow from a torpedo or had scraped against a submarine in Spanish waters.

June 21 Blum resigned as French premier in a dispute over fiscal policy. He was succeeded by Camille Chautemps, a Radical Socialist.

June 23 Germany and Italy again withdrew from the nonintervention patrol. They also refused to permit French or British patrol activity.

June 25 In his first speech as British prime minister, Chamberlain said Germany had showed "a degree of restraint that we ought to recognize" over the *Leipzig* affair. On Spain generally, Chamberlain declared—to the shocked surprise of most—that nonintervention was working: "Each side is being deprived of supplies of material of which it feels itself in urgent need."

June 30 British observers were pulled off the Portuguese frontier of Spain "in view of the gap in the work of naval observation caused by the withdrawal of Germany and Italy" from the naval patrol.

July 1 Pastor Martin Niemöller was arrested because of his opposition to the German government's control of the Protestant Church. (He was acquitted but rearrested in 1938 and sent to a concentration camp.)

July 7 The British government's study of Palestine—headed by Sir Robert Peel—recommended a partition of the mandated area: "While neither race [Arab nor Jewish] can justly rule all Pales-

AMELIA EARHART

One of the unsolved mysteries of the period was the disappearance of American aviatrix Amelia Earhart. She was the most celebrated woman pilot of the '20s and '30s, the first to solo across the Atlantic. She and her navigator, Fred Noonan, were on the Pacific leg of a round-the-world flight in a Lockheed Electra when they vanished on July 2, 1937, somewhere between New Guinea and Howland Island. No one has provided a satisfactory explanation of what happened. It was widely assumed Earhart and Noonan were on a spy mission for the U.S. government and that the Japanese captured and executed them. Postwar records reveal no such evidence. Others believe they crash-landed in the Marshalls and perished. Many conclude they suffered a navigational breakdown, perhaps in bad weather, and were forced to ditch at sea.

tine, we see no reason why if it were practicable, each race should not rule part of it."

July 7–8 On the pretext that a Japanese soldier was killed, the Japanese army demanded the right to search the Peking suburb of Wanping and touched off the "Marco Polo Bridge Incident." Soldiers (of the Tanake Brigade) were massed in the area for "maneuvers," although there was a questionable legal basis for such a deployment. When local Chinese refused to permit Japanese entry into Wanping, the Japanese launched an infantry and artillery attack. The action was focused on a thrust across the Marco Polo Bridge, which spanned the Hun River at Lukouchiao. The incident triggered the full-scale Sino-Japanese war which continued through 1945.

July 11 China and Japan reached a tentative settlement of the Marco Polo Bridge Incident. By now, however, Japanese Premier Konoye had authorized the movement of massive numbers of troops into China, the Sakai and Suzuki brigades of the Kwantung Army, a division from Korea, and three divisions from Japan itself. In all, 150,000 men were rushed into the area.

MILITARY STRENGTH (JULY 1937)

Japan	China
21 regular divisions (462,000 men)	182 infantry divisions
	46 independent brigades
(Reservists numbered 4,000,000, of whom 60 percent were only partially trained)	9 cavalry divisions
	28 artillery regiments
	(Approximate total number of men in standing army: 2,000,000)
2,800 fighters and bombers	305 fighters and bombers

July 13 Because Portugal imposed a ban on British frontier observers, France barred all international nonintervention personnel from its border with Spain.

July 16 China pointed out the threat of Japan in north China to the signatories of the 1922 Nine-Power Treaty (which guaranteed China's independence and territorial integrity).

■ In a reaffirmation of U.S. foreign policy, Secretary Hull stated, "Any situation in which armed hostilities are in progress or are threatened is a situation wherein rights and interests of all nations either are or may be seriously affected. There can be no serious hostilities anywhere in the world which will not one way or another affect interests or rights or obligations of this country."

July 17 Britain signed naval treaties with Germany and the Soviet Union.

July 20 The Nonintervention Committee on Spain became hopelessly deadlocked. France and Russia insisted on the withdrawal of all volunteers from Spain and reestablishment of border controls. Germany and Italy said those actions could follow only after the granting of belligerent rights.

July 21 Washington informally notified Japan and China the U.S. would be willing to use its good offices in resolving the north China dispute.

July 25 Japanese forces in north China launched a campaign of punitive action against the Chi-

nese. The Japanese 20th Division advanced along on the rail line from Tientsin to Peking, clearing the way by bombing and capturing Langfang. General Kiyoshi Katsuki said the action was directed against Chinese troops "who have been taking acts derogatory to the prestige of the Empire of Japan."

July 27 Japan's army minister, General Hajime Sugiyama, defended the use of force in China and called on the Diet to support the action. Sugiyama said Japanese forces were compelled "to surmount the situation and enhance the prestige of the nation." Sugiyama confided to his colleagues, "We'll send large forces and get the whole thing over with quickly."

July 28 Berlin instructed its embassy in Tokyo to complain about Japanese broadcasts to Germany, "in which they constantly try to represent the war against China as a struggle against Communism and to force at least moral participation upon us. We do not welcome this propaganda."

July 29 China refused to consider a local settlement of the fighting in north China, declaring that relations with Japan were the responsibility of the national government.

■ Chinese garrison militia troops massacred more than 300 Japanese civilians, men and women, in Tungchow. (The next day, the Kwantung Army reduced the city to ruins.)

■ Japanese pilots bombed Tientsin, concentrating on Nankai University. Campus buildings were systematically destroyed because, as explained by Japanese headquarters, they harbored "anti-Japanese elements," by which it meant the students.

July 30 Tientsin fell to the Japanese.

July 31 The Japanese occupied Peking.

Aug. 3 The Japanese bombed a train convoy of Chinese government troops near Nankow.

Aug. 9 Two Japanese soldiers were killed after trying to enter Hungjao airfield near Shanghai during "military maneuvers." The Japanese responded by bringing in two divisions of the Shanghai Expeditionary Force and several cruisers and destroyers, raising their naval strength in Shanghai waters to 30 men-of-war.

Aug. 10 The U.S. repeated its offer of good offices to China and Japan.

Aug. 11 Japanese launched an attack on the Nankow Pass. General Katsuki justified the action by saying the Chinese would inevitably try to reinforce the area, and he preferred to occupy the pass and thus forestall a wider conflict.

Aug. 12 Catalonia, which had been nominally independent under Loyalist rule, was placed back under the control of the collapsing central Republican government.

Aug. 13 Heavy fighting broke out in Shanghai.

Aug. 14 Chinese air force planes—futilely attempting to bomb the Japanese battleship *Isuma* which was tied up in the business district of Shanghai—mistakenly hit a department store and other crowded buildings killing nearly 1,200 people and wounding 1,400.

Aug. 15 Japan said its aims in China were to "eradicate the antiforeign and anti-Japanese movement rampant in China, and completely to eliminate the fundamental causes of unfortunate incidents such as the present one, with a view to bringing about truly harmonious collaboration among Japan, Manchukuo, and China."

Aug. 20 An American cruiser, the *Augusta*, was accidentally struck by a stray shell in Shanghai, killing one seaman and injuring 17.

Aug. 21 China and the Soviet Union concluded a five-year nonaggression pact, "to confirm in a more precise manner the obligations mutually undertaken under the Treaty for the Renunciation of War signed in Paris, Aug. 27, 1928" (Pact of Paris).

Aug. 22 A Gallup poll showed 43 percent of the American public favoring China in the Far East conflict, 2 percent favoring Japan, and 55 percent neither.

Aug. 23 In a move to outflank the Chinese, Japanese troops landed at Woosung, on the coast immediately north of Shanghai.

Aug. 25 Japanese naval forces began blockading Chinese ports, from Shanghai and extending 800 miles southward. Hong Kong and Macao, the British and Portuguese colonies, were not covered.

Aug. 26 Japanese planes damaged the car of the British ambassador during a raid on Shanghai.

Aug. 29 China and the Soviet Union signed a treaty of friendship, which marked the beginning of Moscow's aid program to the Chinese. Moscow wished to prevent Japanese control over Inner Mongolia and ease the Japanese threat along the Russian-Siberian frontier.

■ It was revealed that the *Wichita*, a U.S. government-owned cargo ship, was en route from Balti-more to Hong Kong carrying 19 planes for the Nationalist Chinese. Fear developed that the *Wichita* might be intercepted by blockading Japanese warships and a dangerous confrontation might ensue.

Aug. 30 Moscow informed Rome it would be willing to recognize Italian control over Ethiopia in exchange for a less belligerent attitude toward Russia by the Axis. The Italians rejected the idea out of hand.

Sept. 3 Kalgan, 80 miles northwest of Peking, fell to the Japanese.

Sept. 4 At the instigation of the Japanese, a South Chahar government was established at Kalgan.

Sept. 5 Japanese Foreign Minister Hirota assailed the Chinese government for mobilizing "her vast armies against us," and said that Japan must force China to mend her ways.

■ The Japanese naval blockade of China was extended to all ports, with the exception of Tsingtao and those in leased areas or settlement.

Sept. 6 Moscow charged that a Russian merchant ship had been torpedoed by an Italian submarine in the Adriatic. Numerous incidents of Italian interference with Soviet shipping to Spain through the Mediterranean were a final blow in rupturing relations between the two countries.

Sept. 7 Hitler spelled out Germany's need for living space (Lebensraum): Germany "is too small to guarantee an undisturbed, assured, and permanent food supply. . . . the thought of being permanently dependent on the accident of a good or bad harvest is intolerable. . . . the attitude adopted to this demand by other Powers is simply incomprehensible."

Sept. 11 Japanese forces launched an offensive against Chinese units concentrated south of Peking and Tientsin.

Sept. 12 China repeated its appeals to the League of Nations, invoking Articles 10, 11, and 17 of the Covenant, to "take such action as may be appropriate and necessary for the situation under the said articles."

Sept. 14 Roosevelt banned all vessels owned by the U.S. government from hauling munitions to Japan or China. The move was intended to avoid situations in which Japan might interfere with U.S. vessels operating in east Asian waters.

Sept. 15 China's League delegate, Wellington Koo, told the Council that Tokyo's concept of a "Pax Japonica" in the Far East, "aims not only at the political domination and conquest of China, but also at the elimination of foreign interests wherever the Japanese sword holds sway, and the eventual expulsion of Europe and America from their territorial possessions in Asia."

Sept. 16 The League Council referred China's appeal for aid to the Far East Advisory Committee.

Sept. 19 Japanese aircraft launched a series of attacks on Nanking and Canton. China described the raids as "wanton destruction and terrorization on the part of the Japanese forces, and in utter disregard of all rules on international law." (The air strikes continued through the 25th.)

Sept. 22 Washington protested the Japanese bombing of Nanking.

Sept. 23 Germany declined a League invitation to serve on the Far East Advisory Committee.

Sept. 25 On the grounds that "a just, equitable, and practical solution of the questions concerning Japan and China can be found by the two countries," Tokyo refused to participate on the League's Far East Advisory Committee.

■ Chinese troops won their first military victory over the Japanese at Pinghsingkwan in northern Shansi Province. A Communist division of 9,000 men, commanded by General Lin Piao, ambushed the Japanese 5th Division which lost 3,000 men. Chinese losses were 400 killed and wounded.

Sept. 28 With Britain taking the lead, the League Assembly condemned the Japanese air raids on Chinese cities.

Oct. 5 Roosevelt delivered his "Quarantine" speech in Chicago: "It seems to be unfortunately true that the epidemic of world lawlessness is spreading."

Oct. 6 The League Assembly declared Japan in violation of the Nine-Power Treaty (Feb. 6, 1922), and called on the signatories who had pledged to maintain China's territorial integrity to convene. The Assembly expressed its "moral support for China."

■ The U.S. indicated its approval of the Assembly's actions and issued a statement of general principles to maintain peace.

Oct. 8 Prime Minister Chamberlain endorsed Roosevelt's "Quarantine" speech.

■ Austrian Chancellor Schuschnigg condemned a German policy of Anschluss, the union of Austria with Germany. He said the German-speaking

peoples could remain close "so long as the one is willing to leave the other free and undisturbed to manage his own house."

Oct. 9 Japan denied its actions in China were in violation of existing treaties and said League and U.S. objections "were due to a misunderstanding of Japan's true intentions."

Oct. 10 Four Japanese divisions entered Shihkiachuang, 125 miles southwest of Peking, and continued their pursuit of fleeing Chinese forces.

Oct. 13 Germany pledged to respect Belgium's "invincibility and integrity" and come to its aid if attacked, provided Belgium did not join in military action against Germany.

Oct. 16 The Fascist party of Hungary was organized.

Oct. 17 Japanese troops, aided by Chinese and Mongol mercenaries, captured Paotow, terminus of the Peking-Suiyuan railway.

Oct. 18 Sudeten Germans demanded autonomy for areas of Czechoslovakia with predominantly German-speaking populations.

Oct. 19 As part of its effort to pay for the Ethiopian campaign and finance further rearmament, Italy imposed a 10 percent levy on publicly-owned companies and raised the national sales tax.

Oct. 21 Chamberlain ruled out economic sanctions against Japan by the Nine-Power signatories: "We are here to make peace, not to extend the conflict."

■ Franco's Nationalist forces completed their hold over the whole of northwest Spain by capturing Gijon, which effectively ended all Loyalist opposition in Asturias.

Oct. 23 Japanese planes raided several cities in eastern China.

Oct. 23–24 Danzig erupted in anti-Jewish rioting after local Nazis stepped up their racial propaganda campaign.

Oct. 26 Jehol was declared a federated autonomous government following the Japanese conquest of Suiyuan and the organization of a Peace Maintenance Commission at Kweihua.

Oct. 27 Japan refused to participate in a Brussels conference on the Sino-Japanese conflict called by the Belgian government, citing "China's violent anti-Japanese policy and practices, exemplified particularly in her provocative acts in appealing to force of arms." Tokyo said any international peace-seeking effort "would only serve to complicate the situation still further and to place serious obstacles in the path of a just and proper solution."

Oct. 28 The Spanish Loyalist government moved from Valencia to Barcelona.

Oct. 29 Germany, noting that it was not a signatory to the Nine-Power Treaty, declined to participate in the Brussels conference on China.

Nov. 3 An international conference opened in Brussels "to examine the situation in the Far East and to study peaceable means of hastening the end of the regrettable conflict which prevails there." Nineteen nations participated, but not Japan which repeated that China was "violating the spirit of the [Nine-Power] pact against war." Tokyo insisted direct negotiations between Japan and China would be the best way to solve their differences.

Nov. 5 Hitler met with his top political and military aides at the Reich Chancellery in Berlin and declared Germany's need for Lebensraum (living space) could only be acquired by force. He said Germany could never be self-sufficient within its present borders. Britain and France (Hitler called them "two hate-inspired antagonists") would not permit German expansion, and only by "resort to force with its attendant risks" could Germany achieve its goals. The immediate objectives would be Austria and Czechoslovakia. Hitler said all preparations had to be completed by 1938 at the earliest and 1943–1945 at the latest. From this point forward Germany's political and military leaders were on an irrevocable course of action designed for territorial acquisition and war.

■ Germany and Poland jointly declared mutual observance of minority rights, recognizing "that in both countries the well-being of the minority is better protected when it is certain that the same principles will be observed in the other country."

■ Reflecting the need to prepare civil defense against air attack, an "Air Raid Precautions Bill" was introduced in the British House of Commons.

■ Three Japanese divisions (30,000 men) made an unopposed landing 30 miles south of Shanghai, bringing to 225,000 the number of troops in north China. The Chinese organized surprisingly strong resistance to the superior Japanese force, but the Chinese were compelled to back down to avoid total annihilation.

Nov. 6 Italy joined Germany and Japan in the Anti-Comintern Pact. The signatories noted that "the Communist International continues constantly to endanger the civilized world in the West and East [and] disturbs and destroys its peace and order." (The completion of the anti-Communist triangle ended any hope of isolating any of the three totalitarian states politically or morally. The military implications were alarming. Although the Soviet Union was the avowed target of the pact, the British Empire was threatened in its home waters, the Mediterranean, and the Far East. France and the U.S. were similarly exposed to coordinated global challenge.)

Nov. 7 In Brussels the Nine-Power conferees

A Japanese naval landing unit attacks Shanghai, Nov. 1937.

sought Japanese participation by limiting the number of participants "to throw further light" on Sino-Japanese differences and "to facilitate a settlement of the conflict."

Nov. 8 Chinese resistance in Shanghai ended. It was estimated that more than 100,000 Chinese troops were killed or wounded in the fight for the city, while the Japanese suffered 40,000 casualties. Civilian casualties were estimated at 200,000.

Nov. 12 Japan again refused to participate in the Brussels conference, saying the problem was "one of self-defense forced upon Japan by the challenge of China."

■ A truce was signed to end the 92-day-long battle for Shanghai, and the Japanese completed occupation of the city.

Nov. 13 China's delegate at Brussels, Wellington Koo, called for "concerted action of a moral, material, financial, and economic character" since "the door to conciliation and mediation has been slammed in your face by the latest reply of the Japanese Government."

Nov. 15 The Brussels conferees adopted a joint U.S., French, and British statement naming Japan an aggressor in China, and adding, "the problem appears not in terms simply of relations between the two countries in the Far East but in terms of law, orderly process, world security, and world peace."

Nov. 17 Lord Halifax met with Hitler to help the British assess Germany's intentions in Europe. Halifax proposed peaceful settlements of the Sudeten and other "minority" problems, establishing a pattern of British appeasement. Hitler started off with a diatribe against the democracies, but his attitude changed during the conversation as he sensed the British desire to avoid a military showdown. Hitler concluded the meeting with the observation: "Only a country like Soviet Russia could gain by a general conflict."

Nov. 19 Chinese forces abandoned Süchow.

■ Nazi Sudeten leader Konrad Henlein wrote a pleading letter to Hitler calling for "action" to resolve the problem of German minorities in the Czech border areas.

Nov. 20 The capital of the Chinese Republic was moved from Nanking to Chungking.

Nov. 21 Declaring that "our people's territory is too small," Hitler demanded more living space in colonies for the Germans.

Nov. 24 The Brussels conference adjourned, failing to achieve its goal of mediating or halting the conflict between China and Japan.

Nov. 27 Japan established an autonomous government for northern Honan Province.

■ Tokyo stated it would not relinquish its mandate over South Pacific islands which were formerly German. The announcement was significant because the former German colonies in Asia and the Pacific represented a major area of discord between the two new allies, and Tokyo was standing firm. It confirmed that Germany needed Japan more than the reverse.

■ German Interior Minister Wilhelm Frick rejected the concept of a Greater Germany: "Race and nationality, blood and soil were the principles of National-Socialist thought, and we should be acting in contradiction to them if anywhere we attempted to assimilate a foreign nationality by force."

Nov. 28 Franco declared a Nationalist blockade of the entire Spanish coast. Majorca was to be used as the operational base.

Nov. 29 Sudeten Germans in the Czech parliament walked out of the assembly, claiming they had been attacked by national police.

Nov. 30 France and Britain announced a joint position of neutrality on Germany's demands for colonial territory: ". . . this question was not one that could be considered in isolation and, moreover, would involve a number of other countries. It was agreed that the subject would require much more extended study."

Dec. 1 Japan recognized the Franco government in Spain in return for the Nationalist's recognition of Manchukuo.

■ French Foreign Minister Yvon Delbos launched an intensive campaign to reinvigorate an alliance directed against Germany. He left for Warsaw, Bucharest, Budapest, and Prague, with hopes of effecting a program of collective security. In the end, however, he found the Poles, Rumanians, Yugoslavs and Czechs more inclined to observe developments rather than take assertive action, an indicator of the extent Germany had already intimidated the smaller countries.

Dec. 2 South African Justice Minister Jan Christian Smuts said Southwest Africa became a part of the South African Union as a result of a formal agreement with Germany, and that agreement was binding.

Dec. 3 Indicating Berlin's concern about Germany's economic interests in China, the German ambassador to China offered to serve as a peace intermediary with the Japanese. Germany preferred Japan to concentrate on its anti-Russian policies rather than dissipate its power in a conflict with China.

Dec. 5 A Loyalist counteroffensive was launched in Spain to draw Franco's forces into the northeast.

Dec. 6 Two Japanese army groups—the Shanghai Expeditionary Force and the Japanese X Corps, moving from the east and south—linked up outside Nanking.

Dec. 11 Italy withdrew from the League of Nations, stating, "We had not forgotten, and shall not forget, the opprobrious attempt at economic strangulation of the Italian people perpetrated at Geneva [over Ethiopia]. . . . In these circumstances our presence at the door of Geneva could not be tolerated any longer; it wounded our doctrine, our style, and our martial temperament."

Dec. 12 Japanese aircraft bombed and sank the *Panay*, a U.S. naval gunboat, on the Yangtze River, about 30 miles southwest of Nanking. Six Japanese planes began dropping bombs at 1:38 P.M. while the *Panay* was at anchor, despite clear

U.S. markings carried by the ship. (A U.S. Navy Court of Inquiry later determined the Japanese were "solely and wholly responsible for all the losses which have occurred as a result of this attack." The Japanese eventually paid $2,214,007.36 as "settlement in full" for the *Panay*, the destruction of three small American oil company vessels, three deaths [a civilian captain and two American navy men] and for the injuries suffered by 74 men on the ships attacked. Four British gunboats were also raided, and the Japanese later apologized to London. Seven weeks after the attack on Pearl Harbor, the Japanese government awarded the Kinshi Kinsho Medal to Colonel Kingoro Hashimoto, who was believed to have been primarily responsible for the *Panay* attack.)

■ Germany announced it would never return to the League of Nations, noting that "at no period of its existence has it proved competent to make a useful contribution to the treatment of actual problems of world politics." Few would have disagreed with Berlin's evaluation of the League.

■ Japanese-supported Chinese established a provisional government of the Chinese Republic in Peking.

Panay crewmen abandon their sinking ship.

■ Japan established an autonomous government for Shanshi Province at Taiyuan.

Dec. 13 Nanking fell to the Japanese. The infamous "Rape of Nanking" followed when for two weeks Japanese forces engaged in ruthless criminality. A third of the city was destroyed. More than 200,000 civilians were slaughtered. An estimated 20,000 women were raped, then murdered.

Dec. 14 The Japanese government began cracking down on liberals at home. Police arrested 314 political opponents.

Dec. 15 Units of the Japanese 11th and 13th divisions crossed the Yangtze River.

Dec. 19 The city of Tereul was captured by Spanish Loyalists, one of their few victories in a war they were rapidly losing. It gave the Loyalists a brief respite but did not detract from their constant problem of maintaining adequate supplies.

Dec. 20 Japanese shops and cotton mills in Tsingtao were looted and burned by Chinese mobs.

Dec. 21 Foreign Secretary Eden said the League of Nations could not impose sanctions against Japan because "nobody could contemplate any action of that kind in the Far East unless they are convinced that they have overwhelming force to back their policy."

■ Rumanian elections ended in the ouster of the middle-of-the-road government.

Dec. 22 In an action of far-reaching consequences, the British cabinet overruled the nation's air experts and approved a shift in emphasis from bombers to fighter aircraft. (The dramatic change was the work of Sir Thomas Inskip, minister for the co-ordination of defence, who argued, "The role of our Air Force is not an early knockout blow . . . but to prevent the Germans from knocking us out." The Battle of Britain would never have been won without this decision and England would almost surely have been invaded in 1940.)

Dec. 24 Hangchow was occupied by the Japanese who encountered no resistance.

Dec. 26 Tsingtao was ordered evacuated by the mayor. Public utilities, bridges, and the rail station were ordered destroyed.

Dec. 27 Tsinan fell to the Japanese, without opposition.

Dec. 28 King Carol II of Rumania named an anti-Semitic fascist, Octavian Goga, to head the new government. Goga immediately embarked on a program to establish a dictatorship, extend the power of his party's private army, and restrict and harass Jews.

Dec. 29 Berlin instructed its embassy in Tokyo of its position on the war in China: "The common interest of Germany and Japan directed against the Comintern requires that normal conditions in China be restored as soon as possible, even if all this could be done only by peace terms which did not meet all the Japanese aspirations. The lessons derived from the history of the Treaty of Versailles should be pondered by Japan."

(OPPOSITE, TOP) *Germany quickly established control over Austria.*
(OPPOSITE, BOTTOM) *Hitler greets Göring at the Nazi party rally in Nürnberg, Sept. 1938. Nazi labor leader Robert Ley is to the right.*

1938 Austria and Czechoslovakia fall under the Nazi jackboot.

Jan. 2 Japan communicated a desire to end the war in China through the German ambassador in China. (Japan said China's subsequent reply was not "sincere" and refused further contacts with the government of Chiang Kai-shek.)

Jan. 4 Chancellor Schuschnigg restated Austria's policy of remaining politically independent: ". . . we remain ourselves alone . . . to render great service to the German people as a whole."

Jan. 5 In a crackdown on the Nazis, the Austrians tried and convicted 27 National Socialists for antistate activity.

Jan 7 Italy announced a fleet expansion program, including the addition of battleships.

Jan 10 Japanese forces occupied Tsingtao. There were only about 50,000 Chinese (out of a population of 600,000) left in the city. A naval force of six destroyers and a minesweeper in the harbor provided cover for 1,500 Imperial Marines who landed without opposition.

Jan. 11 A Japanese fleet, consisting of a battle cruiser, carrier, three cruisers, and dozens of smaller ships, sailed into Tsingtao harbor. Ten thousand more troops were put ashore.

■ Roosevelt sent a secret message to Chamberlain proposing an international conference to resolve world problems. (Chamberlain rejected the idea, and many observers have suggested the British leader erred in not accepting Roosevelt's prof-

fered hand to develop a policy of collaboration. Chamberlain, in fact, thought a "staged" conference would be useless—he was probably right—and he could not accept the idea the U.S. might be willing to drop its isolationist attitudes. Said Chamberlain, "It is always best and safest to count on nothing from the Americans but words.")

Jan. 12 Austria and Hungary recognized the Franco regime in Spain.

Jan. 14 The Socialists withdrew from the French cabinet. Chautemps succeeded Blum as premier (but Blum returned in March, only to be ousted again in April).

Jan. 15 Japanese aircraft began systematic bombing raids on Chungking, seat of the Chinese government. (Until Sept. 1941 the city was to be attacked 142 times.)

Jan. 16 Japan cut off further dealings with the Chinese Nationalists who, Tokyo said, ". . . blindly persist in their opposition against Japan, with no consideration either internally for the people in their miserable plight or externally for the peace and tranquility of all Asia." Military operations against Kuomintang (Nationalist) forces would continue until their "complete extermination." Prince Konoye also announced the Japanese "will look forward to the establishment of a new Chinese regime," setting the stage for a puppet administration. Japan now had an army of 540,000 men in China.

Jan. 28 Roosevelt called for a massive rearmament program because the U.S. military force "in the light of the increasing armaments of other nations [is] inadequate for purposes of national security."

■ Austrian Nazi Leopold Tavs was charged with high treason when a raid on the party's headquarters disclosed a plot to overthrow the Vienna government and install Arthur Seyss-Inquart as chancellor.

Jan. 29 Vienna formally protested intensified Nazi activities in Austria to Berlin.

Feb. 2 The League of Nations "deplored" the "deterioration" of the situation in China. It took no action, except to suggest an examination by member states "of the feasibility of any further steps which may contribute to a just settlement of the conflict in the Far East." Japan was unmoved by the rhetoric.

Feb. 4 Hitler rid himself of political and military leaders (primarily Foreign Minister Konstantin von Neurath, War Minister Werner von Blomberg, and Army Chief of Staff Werner von Fritsch) who were deemed insufficiently enthusiastic about his policies and philosophy. Neurath's resignation was accepted after continued efforts to disassociate himself from Hitler's aims. Blomberg was ousted because his wife had been a prostitute, and Fritsch was removed on the fabricated pretext of homosexuality. Hitler appointed Joachim von Ribbentrop as foreign minister and assumed direct control of the military under a newly-formed High Command of the Armed Forces (OKW.). The way was now cleared for compliant military and diplomatic advisers.

Feb. 5 Britain, France, and the U.S. asked Tokyo point-blank if Japan was violating treaty limitations on capital-ship construction.

Feb. 9 Hitler invited Austrian Chancellor Schuschnigg to Berchtesgaden to discuss Austrian-German problems.

Feb. 10 Hull said plans to increase the size of the U.S. fleet were based solely on defense needs since Washington's policy was not to be "drawn into or forced into a war."

■ King Carol of Rumania dismissed Prime Minister Goga whose profascist policies were crippling the country. All political parties were banned,

the constitution was suspended, and a cabinet of former prime ministers was named to run the country. With these actions, which created a dictatorship in Rumania, virtually every nation in central and eastern Europe had abandoned democratic government.

Feb. 12 Schuschnigg met with Hitler at Berchtesgaden and was forced to yield to German demands for Nazi participation in the Vienna government and party freedom of action in Austria. Hitler threatened to invade Austria unless Schuschnigg complied.

■ Japan refused to reveal its naval building plans, saying "mere communication of information concerning the construction of vessels will, in the absence of quantitative limitation, not contribute to any fair and equitable measure of disarmament."

Feb. 14 Britain's Singapore naval base, under construction since 1928, was opened. Its guns were positioned to defend the facility from attack by sea, but not against a land invasion through Malaya.

Feb. 15 Austria's cabinet accepted Hitler's demands, rubber-stamping the Berchtesgaden agreement.

■ Teruel, 140 miles east of Madrid, was recaptured by Spanish Nationalist troops, opening up a near unchallenged route to the Mediterranean.

Feb. 16 Pro-Nazis were installed as ministers of foreign affairs and internal security in the Austrian government. Seyss-Inquart's appointment as interior minister presaged Nazi enforcement of law and order.

Feb. 17 Foreign Secretary Eden said Britain would seek Italian support in blocking Germany's moves in Austria under terms of the 1934 Stresa agreement.

Feb. 18 Italy declared its refusal to get involved in the Austrian dispute, easing Hitler's deepest fear—that Rome would challenge Nazi domination of their mutual neighbor.

Feb. 19 The British cabinet, still clinging to the belief that Italy would check Germany in Austria, rejected Eden's proposal for a withdrawal of Italian troops from Spain.

■ Nazis were permitted to join the ruling party of Austria, the Fatherland Front.

Feb. 20 Eden resigned and was succeeded by Lord Halifax as foreign minister.

■ Hitler, in a Reichstag speech, demanded self-determination for the ten million Germans living in Austria and the Sudetenland: "It is in the long run intolerable for a self-respecting world power to know that fellow countrymen across the frontier are continually undergoing the greatest hardship because of their sympathy, their feeling for union, their common experience, their point of view which they share with the whole people."

■ Hitler recognized Manchukuo and indicated that Japanese expansionism was not abhorrent: ". . . . Even the greatest victory gained by Japan would be infinitely less dangerous for civilization and world peace than any success achieved by Bolshevism. . . . ."

■ Rumania proclaimed a new constitution, granting King Carol his wish for a monarchical dictatorship.

Feb. 21 Austria banned all gatherings and demonstrations of all parties except the government-approved Fatherland Front. The action was designed to suppress Nazi agitation.

Feb. 24 Chancellor Schuschnigg said Austria would resist further German pressures: "For now the will to freedom of the Austrian people and the intrinsic worth of our country stand like a wall."

Feb. 25–27 During extended parliamentary debates, the French government restated its intention to stand with Czechoslovakia and the Soviet Union in resisting Germany.

March 1 Rioting broke out in Graz which soon spread to the province of Styria. The outbreaks placed Austria in a state of near anarchy.

March 2 Chamberlain pointedly disassociated Britain from the French policy of supporting Czechoslovakia against Germany.

March 4 In an unequivocal response to Hitler's demand that Sudeten Germans be given self-determination, the government in Prague said Czechoslovakia would defend itself if attacked. Premier Milan Hodza declared that foreign interference would not be tolerated.

■ Nazi Austrian Minister Seyss-Inquart permitted the Nazi salute to be rendered, pictures of Hitler sold, and "Heil Hitler" voiced in public or private.

March 5 Seyss-Inquart said, "The spiritual German People's Reich (*das geistige volksdeutsche Reich*) is today already a fact. . . ."

March 6 Japanese forces reached the Yellow River in China.

March 9 Schuschnigg announced a plebiscite to be held on the 13th to determine if the Austrian people wanted a "free independent, social Christian and united Austria."

March 10 Hitler vowed to block the Austrian plebiscite, by an invasion if necessary. He felt Schuschnigg, at the urging of Britain and France, was reneging on the Berchtesgaden agreement. The plebiscite was so arranged that a vote against union with Germany was inevitable. German troops were ordered mobilized along the Austrian frontier, and the military was told to prepare for an invasion.

■ With Austrian Nazis rioting in the streets of Vienna, Linz, Graz, and Klagenfurt, Seyss-Inquart called on Schuschnigg to resign over the plebiscite issue.

■ French Socialists refused to support the government in an effort to win public financing for a massive armaments program.

March 11 Hitler demanded the Austrian plebiscite be postponed. Schuschnigg agreed. He was then called upon to resign, which he did. Seyss-Inquart was Hitler's choice to head the Austrian government. The appointment was duly made. Seyss-Inquart was at once told to "request" German troops "to prevent bloodshed" in Austria. Germany closed the frontier to all but its military.

March 12 German army troops crossed into Austria at dawn. They met no resistance and were even embraced by the bulk of the civilian population who displayed pride at the "reunification of the Germanic peoples" (Anschluss). That afternoon, Hitler arrived in his schoolboy home of Linz and announced completion of his mission "to restore my dear homeland to the German Reich." The French and British governments protested the "use of coercion, backed by force, against an independent state in order to create a situation incompatible with its independence." Hitler won the blessing of Mussolini, who said Italy had "declined a French invitation to take part in concerted action, which [we] consider would be groundless and purposeless, and would only result in making the international situation more difficult." By taking Austria, Hitler added nine million people to his domain and acquired vast industrial and natural resources.

March 13 The new Nazi government in Vienna proclaimed Austria "a province of the German

Reich." Austria's army was incorporated into the Wehrmacht (German armed forces) and some Austrian units were immediately sent to Germany. Nazis began anti-Semitic demonstrations with an attack on Zionist headquarters in Vienna.

■ A new French Popular Front cabinet was again formed under Blum.

March 14 Britain declared Anschluss was a fact and "nothing could have arrested this action by Germany unless we and others with us had been prepared to use force to prevent it."

■ Czech President Eduard Benes proposed a meeting of the Little Entente in Bucharest. The idea was immediately squelched when Yugoslavia declared it was unconcerned by the German takeover of Austria.

■ U.S. officials for the first time began criticizing Germany for its actions, but generally the government and the American people did not react negatively. The German ambassador in Washington could cable Berlin: "It was striking that the Congress took no stand on the German action in Austria and that neither representatives nor senators made use of the popular method of expressing their opinions on everything between heaven and earth."

March 15 The Netherlands, fearing an outbreak of war, extended the length of service under conscription.

March 16 Mussolini explained his about-face on Austria (he had previously pledged to support Austrian independence) by saying that "when an event is inevitable, it is better that it should be done with your assent rather than in spite of you or, worse, against you."

■ Sudeten Nazi leader Henlein called on all Germans in Czechoslovakia to join the Nazi party. Henlein was under instructions from Berlin to begin agitating for secession.

March 17 Russia asked the United States, Britain, and France to meet on international developments, declaring that Moscow "is ready as before to participate in collective actions, which would be decided upon jointly with it and which would aim at checking the further development of aggression and at eliminating the increased danger of a new world massacre."

■ Poland issued an ultimatum to Lithuania, demanding normalization of relations between the two countries by the end of the month.

Poland and Lithuania had been negotiating for nearly two decades but could never agree on any plan to establish diplomatic or trade ties or even to open the border between them. Warsaw's apparent motive for acting in so bellicose a manner at this time is open to question, but the Poles seemed convinced of the need to secure their flank along the East Prussian border.

March 19 Hitler announced a plebiscite for April 10 in Germany and Austria on Anschluss.

■ Lithuania capitulated to Polish demands on recognition, declaring it "was obliged to take this decision although it was aware that the entire nation was ready to defend its independence to the last."

March 22 Germany guaranteed its frontier with Hungary after Budapest had recognized Anschluss.

March 24 Britain refused Moscow's call for collective security action, saying Russian proposals would "aggravate the tendency toward the establishment of exclusive groups of nations which must . . . be inimical to the prospects of European peace."

■ Chamberlain told Parliament Britain would not be bound automatically to come to the aid of France if war broke out over Czechoslovakia but "other countries besides those which were parties to the original dispute, would almost immediately be involved." The implication was Britain would join France in fighting Germany over Czechoslovakia but without agreeing to a formal commitment to do so. Chamberlain believed that Russia was "stealthily and cunningly pulling all the strings behind the scene to get us involved in a war with Germany."

March 25 For the first time in the modern era, Japan suffered a major military defeat. The battle of Taierchuang began this date when 3,000 Chinese troops attacked the Japanese garrison holding the walled town on the Grand Canal. For the next two weeks, with each side committing large numbers of troops in escalating combat, the Chinese were able to circle the town completely. Only 2,000 of the 18,000 Japanese survived. The rest were killed. About 15,000 Chinese troops died in the action.

March 26 Japan approved the National Mobilization Bill which authorized the government to assume complete control of the economy.

March 28 Czech Premier Hodza proposed formal

laws protecting the rights of minorities: ". . . because we have not codified them, ill-wishers are able to suggest to the uninformed world at large that our minorities cannot breathe freely. . . . "

■ The Japanese established the "Reformed Government of the Republic of China" in Nanking. A one-time warlord, General Wu Pei-fu, was selected its figurehead, but he courageously said he would accept only when all Japanese troops left China. Instead, the Japanese selected Wang Ching-wei, a more pliable politician who had been vice president of Chiang Kai-shek's Kuomintang.

March 29 Demands for Sudeten autonomy were supported by Hungarian, Polish, and Slovak Clerical members of the Czech parliament.

■ Hitler conferred with Henlein, Nazi leader of the Germans in the Sudetenland. Hitler appointed Henlein his "viceroy" in the territory and promised early action to achieve "justice" for the German minority there. The agreed upon tactic was that "we must always demand so much more that we never can be satisfied."

March 31 Britain, France, and the U.S. invoked the escalator clause of the 1936 Naval Treaty because Japan refused to disclose "information with regard to its present naval construction or its plans for future construction."

April 8 The Blum government fell in France over tax and financial issues.

April 10 In a result which astonished even Hitler, Austrians approved Anschluss overwhelmingly as 99.73 percent of the near total turnout of eligible voters cast affirmative ballots. German approval was equally massive.

■ Daladier, a Radical Socialist, formed a new French cabinet. Blum and the Socialists supported the new government.

April 15 Franco's Nationalists captured the port city of Vinaroz, splitting the Loyalists in Castile from Barcelona and Catalonia.

April 16 Britain and Italy signed an agreement in which London recognized Italian control of Ethiopia in return for the withdrawal from Spain of all Italian "volunteers." London sought to free Britain from possible conflict in the Mediterranean. Rome wanted to ease Italy away from its overly intimate association with Germany.

■ In an effort to appease Germany, Czechoslovakia proclaimed an amnesty for all political prisoners.

April 19 Rumanian Iron Guard leader Corneliu Codreanu was jailed, triggering a massive crackdown on the fascists which, in turn, led to the discovery of a plot to overthrow the monarchy.

April 21 Plans for an invasion of Czechoslovakia, were completed by the German High Command.

April 24 Henlein in Karlsbad outlined eight demands on the Czech government which would result in complete autonomy for the German-speaking areas, including their right to adhere to "the ideology of Germans." Henlein also demanded a complete change in Czech foreign policy which would reflect a pro-Berlin point of view.

April 27 Greece and Turkey concluded a treaty of friendship.

■ The Nazi party newspaper *Völkischer Beobachter* launched a new anti-Semitic campaign: "Jews, abandon all hope! Our net is so fine that there is not a hole through which you can slip."

April 29 Britain and France agreed on joint defense strategy, "not only of their common interests but also those ideals of national and international life which have united their two countries." Chamberlain and Daladier could not agree on much else, with the British leader making it known "the moment was not favorable" for halting the Germans.

April 30 Bulgaria forced the Nazi party to disband, showing Sofia tolerant of German-style fascism abroad but unwilling to accept it at home.

May Japan launched a series of offensives to seize additional territory to the south of areas already occupied in China. Imperial forces met little opposition from the hopelessly outgunned Chinese.

May 3–9 Hitler visited Italy in a display of Axis solidarity. The German leader found more pomp than he cared for and came to regard the Italian monarchy as an intolerable anachronism. Mussolini and Hitler did establish a personal rapport, and a spirit of understanding developed between the two dictators.

May 5 China informed the League of Nations it possessed information that Japanese chemical warfare units had been transferred to northern China. It said it feared the imminent use of poison gas by the Japanese.

■ German army Chief of General Staff Ludwig Beck began circulating criticisms of Hitler's military strategies and policies.

May 6 Czech Foreign Minister Krofta rejected Henlein's demands of greater rights and freedom for Germans in the Sudetenland.

May 7 Britain and France vowed to assist in finding a peaceful solution to the Sudeten problem.

May 11 Driven by German Sudeten successes, Polish minority spokesmen in Czechoslovakia demanded greater autonomy for Poles.

May 12 Under British urging, the League Council passed a resolution permitting member states to recognize Italian rule in Ethiopia.

■ Lord Halifax told the League Assembly that League principles, "the ideal of devotion, unflinching but unpractical," would be secondary to "a practical victory for peace."

■ Britain and France announced increased arms programs.

■ Secretary of State Hull declared it was the intention of the U.S. to continue its policy of neutrality, thus rejecting joint defensive measures proposed by the Russians: ". . . any proposal which at this juncture contemplates a reversal of our policy of strict noninterference . . . would offer a real possibility of complications."

■ Portugal recognized the Franco regime in Spain.

May 13 Béla Imredy became premier of Hungary. He ruled as a strong man, instituting widespread reforms. He also turned to anti-Semitic policies, despite the fact that he had a Jewish great-grandfather.

May 14 The League Council condemned Japan for the introduction of poison gases in China.

May 15 In a series of battles in Honan Province, Chinese forces were routed and ordered to retreat, "in order to avoid a decisive engagement against the enemy under unfavorable circumstances."

May 17 Britain and Turkey signed an amity treaty.

■ Congress completed approval of a bill authorizing a greatly expanded U.S. Navy.

May 18 Lord Halifax told the House of Lords "you have to choose between the impractical devotion to the high purpose that you know you cannot achieve except by a war you do not mean

to have, and the practical victory for peace that you can achieve."

May 19 A 200,000-man Japanese force captured Süchow, junction point on the Lunghai and Tsin-pu rail lines.

May 20 Czechoslovakia ordered a partial mobilization of its armed forces and garrisoned the German border. Clashes occurred between Sudeten Germans and Czech police. The violence was used by the German Sudeten party as justification for ending negotiations with Prague on Henlein's demands.

May 21 Britain informed Germany it might be "forced" to join with France if the French were drawn into a war with Germany over Czechoslovakia. Ribbentrop told the British ambassador war would mean the defeat of France, and Britain and Germany would be left to "fight to the death."

May 25 Stating that Russia did not "want to be isolated in international affairs," the Soviet ambassador to the United States, A. A. Troyanovsky, said Moscow was "ready to defend Czechoslovakia in the event of aggression."

May 26 Britain began plans to stockpile food supplies in the event of war.

■ The Japanese cabinet was reshuffled, with generals and admirals holding six ministries.

May 29 Hitler ordered an expansion of German ground and air forces and completion of the Siegfried line (or West Wall) along the French border ("A great power cannot accept a second time such a mean assault.").

May 30 Hitler confided it was his "unqualified decision" to crush Czechoslovakia.

May 30–June 5 The chief of the Rumanian general staff visited Warsaw. He told the Poles the Russians would not be given rights of passage through Rumania to help the Czechs.

June Fearing Japanese seizure of the vast area between the Yangtze and Yellow rivers, Chiang Kai-shek ordered General Shang Chen to blow up the dikes of the latter. The Chinese XXXII and XXXIX corps evacuated the area and then unleashed the water's full force. While the Japanese advance toward Hankow was halted for a short time, the destruction to the Chinese people was catastrophic. More than two million were left homeless as the torrents swept over portions of Honan, Anhwei, and Kiangsu provinces. Eleven larger cities and towns and 4,000 villages were destroyed. Loss of the crops and washing out of topsoil led to famine for years to come. The precipitate action earned Chiang the contempt of millions of Chinese.

June 1 France announced a plan to strengthen its air force.

June 3 Secretary of State Hull denounced isolation, saying, "There is a desperate need in our country, and in every country, of a strong and united public opinion in support of a renewal and demonstration of faith in the possibility of a world order based on law and international cooperative effort."

June 6 The ancient walled city of Kaifeng fell, but only after the Chinese force of 40,000 men held off a 60,000-man Japanese assault for a week.

June 7 Sudeten Germans called for the virtual dismemberment of Czechoslovakia by demanding autonomy for all minorities under Prague's rule.

June 10 The Japanese Central China Expedition-

Kaifeng, in China's Honan Province, was occupied by Japanese forces on June 6, 1938, after a six-day battle.

ary Force launched a major offensive to crush the Chinese military and impose a settlement. It was the largest drive yet mounted by the Japanese in China. Nearly 400,000 men were thrown into the offensive, aimed at taking Chiang's temporary capital, Hankow.

June 22 Germany began drafting laborers for short-term projects, particularly completion of the western frontier fortifications.

June 30 The U.S., Britain, and France agreed to increase the maximum size of battleships under existing treaties, believing Japan was doing so already.

■ Germany and Britain revised their agreement of July 17, 1937, on naval ship limitations, now permitting construction of men-of-war heavier than 35,000 tons and guns in excess of 16-inches on capital ships.

July 5 France, Britain, Germany, and Italy agreed to plans for the repatriation of "volunteers" in Spain, including their temporary maintenance between withdrawal from combat areas and actual return transport to their countries of origin.

■ Italy and Manchukuo signed a treaty of friendship.

July 6 Russia and Britain signed a new naval treaty permitting larger and more heavily armed ships, citing Japanese naval rearmament.

THE EVIAN CONFERENCE

Jews living under Nazi control faced the dilemma of increasingly difficult existences or fleeing and abandoning their material possessions. Those deciding to emigrate from Germany and Austria found their problem compounded by a lack of nations willing to accept them. At the Evian Conference on Refugees, convened on July 6, 1938, representatives of the Federal Representation of German Jews (who went to Evian with Berlin's blessing) proposed that other countries open up their lands to those Jews seeking a new home. The results were hardly encouraging. The U.S. promised only that it would accept the 27,370 from Germany and Austria permitted under the restrictive immigration quota system. Britain said it possessed no territory suitable for the resettlement of large groups from any country. Australia declared, "As we have no real racial problem, we are not desirous of importing one." New Zealand said the same. Canada, Colombia, Uruguay, and Venezuela agreed to accept only farmers. Nicaragua, Honduras, Costa Rica, and Panama jointly announced they could not accept "traders or intellectuals." Argentina and France said they had reached the saturation point in accepting refugees. Peru commended the U.S. for its policy of "caution and wisdom" in establishing a quota. Only Denmark and the Netherlands showed any sensitivity to the plight of the Jews, agreeing to open their borders without qualification.

July 11 Major fighting broke out between Russian and Japanese forces at Changkufeng, near the juncture of Manchuria, Siberia, and Korea. It lasted for a month, with the Soviets administering an embarrassing slap at the victory-conscious Japanese. It started when a division of the Kwantung Army tried to seize high ground clearly within Soviet territory. The Russians reacted with ferocity and forced the Japanese back into their own areas.

July 11–13 British troops were sent to Palestine to quell an Arab uprising and to control mounting terrorism.

July 12 France stated its guarantees to Czechoslovakia were "indisputable and sacred."

July 19–21 In an effort to promote the Anglo-French alliance, Britain's King George VI and Queen Elizabeth paid a well-publicized state visit to Paris.

July 22 London rejected the proposal of its ambassador in Berlin, Nevile Henderson, for resolving the Sudeten problem through a four-power settlement because of the difficulty of excluding Russia.

July 26 Chamberlain announced that Lord Runciman—at the invitation of the Prague government—would go to Czechoslovakia to mediate the Sudeten dispute.

Hitler and Nazi leaders at the Kiel railroad station in Aug. 1938 await the arrival of Hungarian leader Admiral Miklos Horthy. Foreign Minister Ribbentrop (back to camera) talks to Hitler.

July 31 Bulgaria signed nonaggression agreements with members of the Balkan Entente. In return, Bulgaria was permitted to rearm and fortify its borders with Greece and Turkey.

Aug. German Jews were required to use only Jewish first names. Those with proscribed "Aryan" given names had to substitute Israel or Sara.

Aug. 3 Italy enacted sweeping anti-Semitic laws. Marriages between Italians and non-Aryans were banned. Jewish students and teachers were barred from all schools. Jews who emigrated to Italy within the past 20 years were ordered to leave the country within six months.

Aug. 12 Berlin announced massive military maneuvers and the call-up of 750,000 men for the German military services.

Aug. 15 Germany began "maneuvers" near the Czech border.

Aug. 17 Germany disclosed plans to build up its navy, including the construction of two battleships.

Aug. 18 General Ludwig Beck resigned as chief of the German General Staff in opposition to Hitler's policies, believing they could only lead to a war which Germany would lose.

Aug. 21 Czech government leaders met with Sudeten Germans as part of Lord Runciman's efforts to facilitate a new agreement.

Aug. 27 Chancellor of the Exchequer Sir John Simon warned that Britain might become involved in a war over Czechoslovakia.

Aug. 28 Hitler made a widely-publicized tour of the new German fortifications being built along the western frontier.

Aug. 31 In Berlin Ambassador Henderson restated Britain's position on Czechoslovakia to the Germans, including the possibility of going to war in defense of the Czechs.

■ Germany announced its navy would begin maneuvers in the North Sea, in apparent response to similar moves by Britain.

Sept. 1 Hitler and Henlein conferred on the Sudeten problem.

Sept. 2 Sudeten and Czech government officials began discussing a new minority plan proposed by Prague which was regarded as conciliatory.

Sept. 3 Hitler set Sept. 27 as the date for the invasion of Czechoslovakia.

Sept. 4 Foreign Minister Georges Bonnet reaffirmed France's pledge to maintain the independence and integrity of Czechoslovakia.

Sept. 6 With menacing German moves clearly impending, the Czech government agreed to virtually all of the German Sudeten demands.

■ French newspapers began editorializing—apparently under government inspiration—that the Sudeten issue should not be allowed to spark a general war. Paris appeared to be creating a climate of opinion which might permit France to renege on its promises to Czechoslovakia.

Sept. 7 Sudeten German leaders—who actually felt the Czech proposals met 90 to 95 percent of their demands—nonetheless broke off negotiations on the grounds that Czech police had assaulted a Sudeten deputy in Ostrava.

■ The London *Times* proposed the partition of Czechoslovakia and supported a policy of appeasement.

■ France called up reservists to raise its strength to a million men.

Sept. 9 On the recommendation of the British, the Czechs and Sudetens resumed negotiations.

Sept. 10 Roosevelt told White House reporters it would be "100 percent wrong" to assume the U.S. would join Britain and France in joint action on Czechoslovakia.

Sept. 11 In an effort to stiffen the French, Moscow advised the French government that Russia

intended to honor its mutual defense pact with Czechoslovakia.

■ Rumania said it would continue to permit Russian planes right of transit, including those specifically en route to Czechoslovakia.

■ Prime Minister Chamberlain sought to give substance to British-French mutual defense arrangements by referring to the probability of "going to the assistance of France." The French cabinet, meanwhile, generated the position that France alone might have to stand up to the Germans on the Sudetenland.

Sept. 12 Lord Halifax responded to French clarification of the British position on Czechoslovakia. In answer to the direct question, "Will you march with us?" Halifax said Britain "would never allow the security of France to be threatened, [but] they are unable to make precise statements of the character of their future action, or the time at which it would be taken, in circumstances that they cannot at present foresee."

Sept. 13 In his Nazi Party Day speech at Nürnberg, Hitler vilified Czechoslovakia and threatened unspecified action to aid the Sudeten Germans. Hitler declared "the oppression" of Sudeten Germans must end. He added, ". . . if these tortured creatures cannot obtain rights and assistance by themselves, they can obtain both from us." Rioting broke out almost immediately in the Sudetenland. Czech officials proclaimed martial law and clamped tight restrictions on the Sudetenland to quell the rioting. The Nazis fomented the disturbances hoping German military intervention would follow. Henlein broke off talks with the Czechs.

Sept. 14 Britain ordered its fleet to alert status.

Sept. 15 Chamberlain went to Berchtesgaden to see Hitler. Chamberlain felt he had solid indications the French were actually not prepared to go to war over Czechoslovakia, and he sought to determine Germany's minimum demands. Hitler lectured Chamberlain, who concluded that Germany was determined to annex those parts of Czechoslovakia with a majority German population. Hitler agreed not to begin hostilities (which he acknowledged could lead to a world war) until Chamberlain consulted with the British cabinet.

■ Henlein demanded immediate German accession of the Sudetenland and then fled to Germany to escape arrest.

Sept. 16 Prague was presented new German demands to cede all territory with a German-majority population and to enter into international guarantees on the new boundaries.

■ The French and British cabinets met, with both sharply divided on future action. Both nations' leaders were aware of conflicting attitudes held by their military commanders and strong pacifist opinions among the general public.

■ Russia began massing troops in the Ukraine.

■ Polish newspapers—reflecting the government's position—called for the return of the Czech area of Teschen to Poland.

Sept. 18 Britain and France called on the Czechs to cede German-majority districts to Germany, saying "the maintenance of peace and the safety of Czechoslovakia's vital interests cannot effectively be assured unless these areas are now transferred to the Reich." Premier Daladier and Foreign Minister Bonnet had gone to London to seek agreement on the concessions to Germany.

■ Czech frontier posts were attacked by the Sudeten *Freikorps*.

■ Czechoslovakia declared a state of emergency.

■ Hitler met with his top generals for five hours to discuss the Czech situation. The military leaders tried to dissuade him from attacking, but Hitler remained adamant and finally dismissed them with contempt. General Alfred Jodl noted in his diary: "It is tragic that the Führer should have the whole nation behind him with the single exception of the German Generals."

Sept. 19 Russia told the Czechs it would fight for Czechoslovakia only if France remained "loyal to her obligations." Moscow was hedging, linking Russian involvement to a French guarantee against Germany. Moscow warned Poland not to attack Czechoslovakia.

■ France explained its support for the partition of Czechoslovakia was necessary in the face of Britain's promise to come to the aid of France only if France itself was directly menaced. In other words, France felt it had to have Britain at its side in military action against Germany without qualification, not just in case that action resulted in a German attack on France itself.

■ At the request of China, the League Council invited Japan to meet with its representatives in Geneva to resolve the China issue.

Sept. 20 Prague suggested arbitration with Germany on the basis of the 1925 Locarno treaty, a proposal immediately turned down by London and Paris.

■ Hitler promised Poland and Hungary full German support in their territorial demands on the Czechs.

Sept. 21 Czechoslovakia accepted the German demands. It had no alternative except a German invasion without assured French, British, or Russian support. Paris and London had already told the Czech government leaders that unless the Germans received what they wanted, Prague would be totally isolated. Prague said it was "yielding to unheard-of pressure."

■ Poland and Hungary demanded the same rights for their minorities in Czechoslovakia as were accorded the Germans.

■ Russia called for collective League of Nations action against Germany.

■ In a conversation with the Canadian minister in Washington on the situation in Asia, Secretary of State Hull detailed the U.S. outlook: "I have proceeded here on the theory that Japan definitely contemplates securing domination over as many hundreds of millions of people as possible in eastern Asia and gradually extending her control through the Pacific islands to the Dutch East Indies and elsewhere, thereby dominating in practical effect one-half of the world; and that she is seeking this objective by any and every kind of means; and . . . at the same time I have gone on the theory that Germany is equally bent on becoming the dominating colossus of continental Europe."

Sept. 22 Chamberlain conferred with Hitler at Godesberg and was confronted with new demands from the German leader. Hitler reneged on his earlier promises at Berchtesgaden and outlined broader areas to be turned over to the Reich by Oct. 1. At the same time, the Sudeten *Freikorps* crossed into Czechoslovakia from Germany and began occupying towns and villages.

■ The Czech government fell and was replaced by a "government of national defense" headed by the popular General Jan Sirovy. Strikes and mass protests against capitulation erupted throughout the country. An immediate mobilization was ordered.

■ Polish troops massed along the Czech border.

■ Japan spurned the League invitation on China, objecting to any third-party intervention.

Sept. 23 Moscow informed Warsaw their 1932 nonaggression treaty would be voided if Poland attacked the Czechs. France now feared it might have to fight on Poland's side against Russia and, in effect, be caught in an indirect alignment with Germany.

Sept. 24 Czechoslovakia rejected Hitler's Godesberg demands, calling them "a de facto ultimatum of the sort usually presented to a vanquished nation." Prague said, "Our national and economic independence would automatically disappear with the acceptance of Herr Hitler's plan."

Sept. 25 Hitler declared that once the Sudeten crisis was settled, Germany would have no more territorial claims in Europe.

■ Czechoslovakia agreed to negotiate with Poland on Teschen in order to forestall war, but the Poles refused.

■ France ordered partial mobilization after the cabinet decided to reject Hitler's Godesberg demands.

Sept. 26 Daladier and Bonnet flew to London for further talks with the British.

■ In an emotional Sportspalast speech, Hitler refused to budge on his Godesberg demands and promised to invade Czechoslovakia by Oct. 1 if they were not granted. Hitler screamed, "German patience has come to an end."

Sept. 27 Czechoslovakia again declared its willingness to negotiate or arbitrate the dispute.

■ The British Foreign Office said France was obliged to aid Czechoslovakia if invaded by Germany and in that case Britain and Russia would stand by France. The statement added: "It is still not too late to stop this great tragedy and for the peoples of all nations to insist on a settlement by free negotiation."

■ Chamberlain addressed the British people by radio and said, "How horrible, fantastic, incredible it is that we should be digging trenches and trying on gas masks here because of a quarrel in a far away country between people of whom we know nothing."

■ Roosevelt urged Hitler and Czech President Benes to resolve the Sudeten problem and called on France and Britain to avoid war.

■ The British navy was mobilized.

Sept. 28 Chamberlain repudiated the foreign ministry statement of the previous day, saying,

"We cannot in all circumstances undertake to involve the whole British Empire in war simply on [Czechoslovakia's] account."

■ Chamberlain proposed to Hitler a conference involving Czechoslovakia, France, Italy, Germany, and Britain, saying "I cannot believe that you will take responsibility of starting a world war which may end civilization for the sake of a few days' delay in settling this long-standing problem."

■ On the advice of Mussolini, Hitler postponed his invasion of Czechoslovakia for 24 hours and called a Munich meeting with Chamberlain, Daladier, and Mussolini. The Italian leader had told Hitler, ". . . I feel certain that you can get all the essentials without war and without delay."

Sept. 29–30 The fate of Czechoslovakia was decided in Munich by leaders of Germany, France, Italy, and Britain—but without a single Czech representative. Mussolini, who proposed the eleventh-hour meeting, presented a draft agreement (which was written by the German foreign office). There were a few minor changes in the draft, and Hitler got what he wanted—the Sudetenland became part of Germany and the boundaries were guaranteed by Britain and France. Russia was shocked by Munich, a conference to which it was not invited. Moscow would have been forced to act independently to help Czechoslovakia (and only by crossing Poland or Rumania, who would not give overland transit rights). The word "appeasement" was given a new negative meaning, and Munich became a symbol of capitulation. Munich did spark British armament efforts and raised among other countries as well the need to back up words and promises with military strength, and the will to use it. The fact was, however, that at the time of Munich Hitler had only 13 divisions (with another 44 available under full mobilization). Czechoslovakia possessed 35 divisions, France 85, Russia 260, and Britain's fleet was vastly superior to Germany's. The French ambassador to Germany, André Francois-Poncet, was to say of Munich: "Thus does France treat her only allies who had remained faithful to her."

■ Poland delivered an ultimatum to the Czechs to cede Teschen by Oct. 2. The 419-square-mile area had a population of 240,000, 40 percent of them Poles.

■ The League Council passed a resolution inviting members to invoke individual sanctions against Japan in view of Tokyo's refusal to discuss a settlement in China.

Oct. 1 German troops marched into the Sudetenland, occupying 10,000 square miles of territory with a population of 3,500,000 (including 700,000 Czechs).

■ Alfred Duff Cooper resigned as first lord of the Admiralty in protest against Britain's policy of appeasement.

Oct. 2 Poland occupied Teschen.

■ Hungary agreed to arbitrate its claim on Czech territory populated by Hungarians "in the spirit of the Munich decisions."

Oct. 3 Munich was debated in the British House of Commons. Labor opposition leader Herbert Morrison called the agreement a betrayal of the Czechs. Even some Conservatives opposed it. Churchill said it was "a disaster of the first magnitude." But Chamberlain's action was approved 366 to 144.

■ Commenting on Czechoslovakia, Pope Pius said, "In the past nations had been offered as matrimonial presents; today they are being traded away, animal-like."

■ Japan threatened countermeasures against any nation imposing sanctions as suggested by the League.

Oct. 4 The French Popular Front collapsed when the Communists refused to support the Munich agreement. They alone voted as a bloc against it as the Chamber of Deputies approved Munich 535 to 75. From this point on, France drifted to the right in its domestic politics.

Oct. 5 Benes resigned as Czech president.

Oct. 6 The Slovak Congress formally requested autonomy for the Slovaks within a Czech federal framework.

Oct. 8 Czechoslovakia promised to grant autonomy to Slovakia and Ruthenia.

■ The remaining constitutional pillar in Italy—the Chamber of Deputies—was abolished and replaced by a Chamber of Fasces and Corporations.

Oct. 9 Italy announced that 10,000 Italians would be withdrawn from Spain.

■ Czech and Hungarian officials met to negotiate a territorial realignment.

■ British reinforcements were sent to Palestine as riots continued and civil control over non-Jewish areas collapsed.

Oct. 10 Japanese forces after steady and relent-

Hitler's annexation of the Sudetenland was a prelude to the total absorption of Czechoslovakia by its neighbors. The Munich agreement was to guarantee peace. It only whet Nazidom's appetite for conquest.

less advances up the Yangtze had pushed to within 60 miles of the temporary Chinese capital of Hankow.

Oct. 12 Japanese forces landed at Bias Bay, close to Hong Kong. In addition to serving as a menace to the British colony and naval base, the action served to set the stage for Japanese occupation of southeast China.

Oct. 13 Hungary began mobilizing, saying talks with the Czechs were hopeless.

Oct. 19 U.S. Ambassador Joseph P. Kennedy addressed the Navy League in London and created a furor with this post-Munich observation: "It has long been a theory of mine that it is unproductive for both the democratic and dictator countries to widen the division now existing between them by emphasizing their differences. . . . After all, we have to live together in the same world, whether we like it or not."

Oct. 20 Under German pressure the Czech government outlawed the Communist party.

Oct. 21 Canton was occupied by the Japanese. Seizure of the city cut off the last seaport and the primary rail line for supplies to be shipped to the Chinese armies.

Oct. 24 Ribbentrop informed the Polish ambassador in Berlin that Germany wished to resolve differences between the two countries. He called for German control of Danzig and rail and highway links across the Polish Corridor to join East Prussia and Germany. Ribbentrop proposed that Poland join in the Anti-Comintern Pact and held out the promise of German aid if Poland sought to take the Ukraine from the Soviet Union.

Oct. 25 Hankow fell to the Japanese, who now effectively controlled the Yangtze River from Hankow to the coast. It has been estimated the Chinese military suffered one million casualties and the civilian population two million from the Marco Polo Bridge Incident to this date, about a year. (With the fall of Hankow, the Japanese consolidated their positions and there was virtually no fighting for the next three years. To the Japanese, all that was important in China was now conquered.)

Oct. 28 Thousands of Polish Jews were arrested in Germany and sent back to Poland in retaliation against Polish laws restricting foreign immigration.

Oct. 30 Germany and Italy agreed to serve as arbitrators between Hungary and Czechoslovakia on the rights of minorities in the latter country.

Nov. 2 In the first of the "Vienna Awards" by the Italian and German Arbitration Commission, Hungary was given those districts of Czechoslovakia with predominantly Hungarian populations. In this further dismemberment of the Czech state, Hungary acquired 12,000 square miles of territory, with a population of one million (80 percent Magyar).

■ Japan formally notified the League of Nations it was withdrawing from all specialized agencies, claiming they had been "slandering at every turn Japan's activities in China."

Nov. 3 The Japanese said China had been "a victim of the rivalry between the Powers, whose imperialistic ambitions have constantly imperiled her tranquillity and independence." Tokyo proposed the establishment of a "new order" in east Asia, with Japan, Manchukuo, and China tied together economically and in "a joint defense against communism."

Nov. 4 Japan declared the Nine-Power Treaty—guaranteeing China's independence and territorial integrity—obsolete.

Nov. 7 A German diplomat, Ernst vom Rath, was killed in Paris by Herschel Grynszpan in an act of protest against the deportation of Polish Jews from Germany.

Nov. 9 Britain turned down a plan for the partition of Palestine as impractical.

ORDERS FOR THE "NIGHT OF GLASS"

The following message was issued at 11:55 P.M., Nov. 9, 1938, from Gestapo headquarters:

"Berlin No. 234404   9.11.2355

"To all Gestapo Stations and Gestapo District Stations

"To Officer or Deputy

"This teleprinter message is to be submitted without delay:

"1. At very short notice, *Aktionen* against Jews, especially against their synagogues, will take place throughout the whole of Germany. They are not to be hindered. In conjunction with the police, however, it is to be ensured that looting and other particular excesses can be prevented.

"2. If important archival material is in synagogues, this is to be taken into safekeeping by an immediate measure.

"3. Preparations are to be made for the arrest of about 20,000-30,000 Jews in the Reich. Wealthy Jews in particular are to be selected. More detailed instructions will be issued in the course of the night.

"4. Should, in the forthcoming *Aktionen*, Jews be found in possession of weapons, the most severe measures are to be taken. SS Reserves as well as the General SS can be mobilized in the total *Aktionen*. The direction of the *Aktionen* by the Gestapo is in any case to be assured by appropriate measures.

Gestapo II Müller

"This teleprinter message is secret."

Nazis confiscated the insurance money paid the Jews by imposing a billion mark penalty on them for what Göring called "their abominable crimes."

Nov. 16 Britain accorded formal recognition to the Italian Empire, which now embraced Ethiopia, as the Anglo-Italian pact of April 16 became effective.

Nov. 17 Germany said it would not assume any legal liability for Austria's debts "since they were brought about in order to support the incompetent Austrian State artificially created by the Paris Treaties."

Nov. 19 In appreciation of Mussolini's role in the Czech "settlement," France recognized the Italian Empire.

■ Foreign Minister Hachiro Arita acknowledged that Japan was no longer permitting an open-door economic policy in those parts of China under Japanese influence.

The slain German diplomat Ernst vom Rath was given a hero's burial in Düsseldorf in a service attended by Nazidom's highest leaders, including Hitler (first row, second from right). Rath's murder in Paris triggered "Crystal Night."

Nov. 9-10 The Nazis launched a campaign of terror against the Jews in Germany in retaliation for the Rath murder. "Crystal Night," so-called because of the shattered glass (valued at six million marks) resulting from unbridled window-smashing, marked the vilest form yet of government-supported anti-Semitism. Altogether, 267 synagogues were plundered, 815 shops were wrecked, 36 Jews were killed, and 20,000 were arrested. In one of the grimmest of ironies, the

Nov. 23 The Nazi government in Danzig adopted stern discriminatory laws directed at its Jewish population.

Nov. 24 Poland began issuing decrees for military mobilization.

Nov. 26 Russia and Poland renewed their nonaggression pact. Warsaw's expression of concern over German expansionist policies was shared by Moscow which was again hoping to develop a buffer system against the Nazis.

Nov. 30 Deputies in the Italian chamber launched what was called a "spontaneous" demonstration for the recovery of lost territory, including Tunisia, Corsica, Nice, and Savoy. It was led by the former secretary-general of the Fascist party and triggered a period of tension in Italy's relations with the understandably disturbed—and frightened—French.

■ Emil Hacha was elected president of Czechoslovakia.

■ Rumanian Iron Guard leader Corneliu Codreanu and 13 other imprisoned members of the Nazi organization were shot and killed by their guards, "while attempting to escape." Whether they were actually trying to flee or not has never been established, but the deaths inflamed the Nazis in Germany. Berlin provided agents and funds to foment disorder after the incident.

Dec. 1 Autonomy was granted to Slovakia and Ruthenia. Slovakia created an independent government under Father Joseph Tiso.

Dec. 3 The Italian government formally denied the Nov. 30 demonstration in parliament was officially inspired or that it represented Rome's policy. The statement was far from reassuring to the French.

Dec. 6 Berlin and Paris concluded a friendship treaty, noting that "pacific and neighborly relations between France and Germany constitute one of the essential elements of the consolidation of the situation in Europe and of the preservation of general peace." French interest in the pact was the direct result of Italy's continuing provocations.

■ Mussolini approved a plan to annex Albania, saying he was only concerned about reaction from Yugoslavia.

Dec. 11 Elections in Memel, Lithuania, gave the Nazis more than 90 percent of the vote.

Dec. 12 Prime Minister Chamberlain declared Britain was under no legal obligation to come to the assistance of France if it were attacked by Italy. (The next day Chamberlain "clarified" his remarks by saying Franco-British relations were "so close as to pass beyond mere legal obligations.")

Dec. 15 The French ambassador in Berlin, Robert Coulondre, reported that while Germany had plans for war in the west it was more seriously intent on striking to the east. He quoted Ribbentrop on "zones of influence there and Göring on "an essentially economic penetration in the southeast."

Dec. 16 Bulgarian Prime Minister George Kiosseivanov, with remarkable prescience, said an alliance of Germany and Russia against Poland was a real possibility, with another partition of Poland giving Germany a base for an eastward thrust.

Dec. 17 Italy told France their agreement of 1935 (relating to amicable understandings on African colonial rights) was invalid because the instruments of ratification had not been exchanged. France rejected the spurious argument, but Italy's truculence was again noted with apprehension.

Dec. 19 All Jews in Danzig were ordered to leave by April 1, 1939.

■ Foreign Minister Arita told the Diet that Japan's aim was to help lift China "from its present semicolonial state to the position of a modern state."

Dec. 22 Premier Konoye said extermination of the Kuomintang regime was an essential element of Japan's "new order" in east Asia.

Dec. 23 The Spanish Nationalists of Franco opened their decisive drive in Catalonia. The Loyalists fought back savagely against great odds.

Dec. 26 Chiang said Japan was "dominated by a horde of militarists who know no law and order." He said if they continued in power, "the fate of Japan is doomed."

Dec. 31 The U.S. State Department rejected Japan's "new order," saying, ". . . there is no need or warrant for any one power to take upon itself to prescribe what shall be the terms and conditions of a 'new order' in areas not under its sovereignty and to constitute itself the repository of authority and the agent of destiny. . . ."

(OPPOSITE, TOP) Germany's invasion of Poland launched World War II.

(OPPOSITE, BOTTOM) Stalin confers with the chief of the Soviet General Staff, Boris M. Shaposhnikov, at the signing of the Soviet-German nonaggression pact in Moscow.

1939 The peace is shattered in Poland.

Jan 4 Roosevelt questioned the wisdom of U.S. neutrality laws: "We have learned that when we deliberately try to legislate neutrality, our neutrality laws may operate unevenly and unfairly—may actually give aid to an aggressor and deny it to the victim." He called for a dramatic increase in the U.S. defense budget.

■ Prince Konoye resigned as Japan's premier.

■ Soviet soldiers began taking a new oath to the "Fatherland" instead of to the "proletariat of the world."

Jan 5 Baron Kiichiro Hiranuma was named premier, but Konoye stayed on in the reconstituted Japanese cabinet.

■ Hitler pressed for the return of Danzig to Germany. He told Polish Foreign Minister Joseph Beck that Germany would guarantee Poland's frontiers if a "final settlement" could be reached on all outstanding issues. Hitler stated, "Danzig was German, would always remain German, and sooner or later would return to Germany."

Jan. 10 Chamberlain and Lord Halifax conferred with Mussolini in Rome but received no encouragement on means to reduce tensions.

Jan. 12 Roosevelt outlined a U.S. rearmament program costing $552 million.

Jan. 13 Spanish Nationalists crossed the Ebro River in their drive for Barcelona.

Jan. 15 In a move to appease Italy, British Foreign Secretary Lord Halifax urged the French to offer concessions of rights and transport in Africa to the Italians. Rome had suggested such an arrangement.

Jan. 20 With no nation willing to impose sanctions on Japan, the League of Nations called on member states to undertake unspecified but "effective measures of aid to China." It was the League's final expression of concern on the Sino-Japanese war.

■ Hjalmar Schacht was dismissed as president of the Reichsbank after incurring Hitler's wrath. Schacht had warned him that the German rearmament program would cripple the country's economy.

GERMAN PREWAR MILITARY SPENDING

Fiscal Year	Military Budget (In Billions of Marks)	Total Budget (In Billions of Marks)	Military Percent
1933–1934	1.9	8.1	23.5
1934–1935	1.9	10.4	18.3
1935–1936	4.0	12.8	31.2
1936–1937	5.8	15.8	36.7
1937–1938	8.2	20.1	40.8
1938–1939	18.4	31.8	57.9

SOURCE: *Statistiches Handbuch Des Deutschen Reiches.*

■ Count Ciano began a visit to Yugoslavia to urge improved relations with Italy. Ciano was also seeking to exert Rome's influence to help end the strained relations between Yugoslavia and Hungary.

Jan. 21 Hitler told Czech Foreign Minister Frantisek Chvalkovsky, "Our Jews will be destroyed."

Jan. 24 Göring directed Reinhard Heydrich of the SS to accelerate the emigration and evacuation of Jews from Germany as a solution to the "Jewish problem." (The "final solution" was not enunciated until 1942.)

Jan. 25 Franco's troops reached the suburbs of Barcelona.

■ Ribbentrop visited Warsaw to induce Poland to join the Anti-Comintern Pact. The Poles, though wavering in their attitude toward France, were unwilling to be drawn into an alliance with Germany. Events quickly overtook the Berlin proposals (namely Hitler's decision to invade Poland).

Jan. 26 France stated that if it were threatened militarily, Britain's armed forces would be at the disposal of the French authorities.

■ Barcelona fell to the Spanish Nationalists, backed up by extensive Italian support. With the fall of Catalonia, 200,000 Loyalist troops crossed into France, where they were disarmed.

Jan. 27 Roosevelt approved the sale of military aircraft to Spain.

■ German Agriculture Minister Walther Darré said Germany was ready to risk war in order to achieve its aims, which were identified only generally.

Jan. 30 In a speech widely regarded as conciliatory, Hitler said, "Germany has no territorial claims on England and France, except the return of her colonies."

■ Hitler privately assured Mussolini of German support if any country interfered with Italy's projected conquest of Albania.

Jan. 31 Chamberlain responded to Hitler's speech by calling on the Germans to agree on a constructive step toward peace, such as an arms limitation treaty.

Feb. 4 In a quiet coup Dragisha Cvetkovich replaced Milan Stoyadinovich as premier of Yugoslavia. The ousted leader had been ardently pro-Axis.

Feb. 7 Ribbentrop outlined German policy as an effort to regain lost colonies and to fight communism. He said, "Towards the Soviets, we will remain adamant. We never will come to an understanding with Bolshevist Russia."

Feb. 10 Poland declared it would not permit German road or rail transit across the Corridor.

■ Japanese forces occupied French-occupied Hainan Island in the South China Sea, giving them a base for southern and Chinese operations.

Feb. 15 Premier Imredy of Hungary was forced to resign because of his Jewish ancestry.

Feb. 18 French troops reoccupied east African territory which had been ceded to Italy in 1935, the result of Italy's denunciation of the 1935 agreement.

Feb. 19 A trade agreement was signed between Poland and the Soviet Union. Moscow promoted the pact to bolster Poland as a buffer against Germany.

Feb. 23 Britain and France began naval maneuvers in the Mediterranean in a clear warning to Italy to curb its belligerent posturing.

Feb. 24 Hungary cracked down on the Nazi party, then curiously joined Germany, Italy, and Japan as allies in the Anti-Comintern Pact.

Feb. 27 Britain and France recognized the Franco government in Burgos, Spain, the final death knell of the Loyalist cause.

Feb. 28 Germany informed Britain and France it could not guarantee the frontiers of Czechoslovakia because of conditions within the country and an unsatisfactory state of relations between Berlin and Prague.

■ President Azaña of Loyalist Spain resigned in Paris, where he had taken refuge.

■ Japan told Germany and Italy it wished to transform the Anti-Comintern Pact into an active military alliance.

March 4 Poland and Rumania renewed their defensive alliance, directed against Russia, a further manifestation of Warsaw's hope to defend Poland against Russia and Germany while aligning itself with neither.

March 6 Czech President Hacha ousted pro-Nazis from the Ruthenian cabinet in the face of mounting demands for Ruthenian autonomy.

■ Premier Negrín of Loyalist Spain was stripped of power as a military junta took over in Madrid. The officers pledged to establish "peace with honor." General José Miaja, commander of the

Loyalist forces, broadcast an appeal to end the fighting. Extreme radicals in the Republican cause vowed to keep fighting and actual battles broke out between Loyalist factions. The military junta finally suppressed the Communist-led dissidents.

March 10 Stalin—in a major policy statement—criticized the Western democracies and the fascist nations. He declared there was little to commend either in what he termed the upcoming "Second Imperialistic War." Stalin called for a policy of caution [which would] "not allow Soviet Russia to be drawn into conflicts by warmongers who are accustomed to have others pull the chestnuts out of the fire." At the same time, Stalin castigated those who try "to arouse Soviet anger against Germany, to poison the atmosphere, and to provoke a conflict with Germany without visible reason."

■ Premier Tiso and the Slovak cabinet were dismissed by Czech President Hacha, who proclaimed martial law in certain areas to suppress separatist and autonomous movements.

March 12 Czech troops marched into Bratislava and deposed Father Tiso as premier of Slovakia.

March 13 Father Tiso was summoned to Berlin and told to proclaim Slovak independence. At the same time, Berlin demanded the dismissal of anti-Nazi ministers in the Czech cabinet.

March 14 Under threat of German invasion, Slovakia and Ruthenia declared their independence, dissolving the Czechoslovak state. Military action by the Czechs was beyond question since the mountainous boundary regions, offering natural defense barriers, were now lost. Czech resistance was deemed suicidal. German troops occupied Ostrava and concentrated other units around Bohemia and Moravia.

■ Chamberlain said the British-French guarantee against aggression did not apply in Czechoslovakia since no one had been attacked.

■ Pope Pius XII issued an encyclical "On the condition of the Catholic Church in the German Reich." It was critical of naziism's racist policies and paganlike philosophies and rituals.

March 15 German troops crossed the Czech frontier, and President Hacha signed an agreement making Moravia and Bohemia protectorates of Germany. Former German Foreign Minister Neurath was named "Protector."

■ Hungarian troops crossed into Ruthenia. Budapest demanded the withdrawal of all Czech units from the newly proclaimed state.

■ Chamberlain said the Slovak declaration of independence absolved Britain from any obligations to guarantee the Czech frontiers.

March 16 Slovakia was formally declared a German protectorate.

German troops march into Prague as Czechoslovakia was dismembered and absorbed into the Greater Reich.

March 17 Chamberlain abandoned his policy of appeasement, saying, ". . . no greater mistake could be made than to suppose that, because it believes war to be a senseless and cruel thing, this nation has so lost its fibre that it will not take part to the utmost of its power in resisting such a challenge [domination of the world by force] if it were ever made."

■ At a White House press conference Roosevelt stated the U.S. Neutrality Act had to be revised. He had previously stated privately, "If Germany invades a country and declares war, we'll be on the side of Hitler by invoking the act."

March 18 France, Britain, and Russia protested

Of the 500,000 Jews in Germany when Hitler took power, 319,000 fled. Most who remained became victims of the Holocaust.

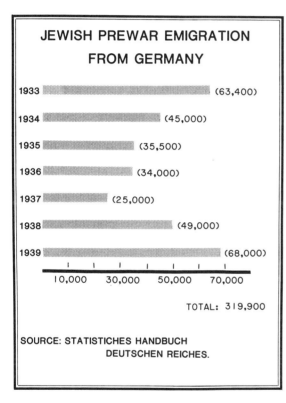

JEWISH PREWAR EMIGRATION
FROM GERMANY

1933 (63,400)
1934 (45,000)
1935 (35,500)
1936 (34,000)
1937 (25,000)
1938 (49,000)
1939 (68,000)

10,000   30,000   50,000   70,000

TOTAL: 319,900

SOURCE: STATISTICHES HANDBUCH
DEUTSCHEN REICHES.

---

the German annexation of Bohemia and Moravia as illegal.

■ Spain and Portugal entered into a nonaggression pact.

March 19 Germany annexed predominantly German-speaking Memel from Lithuania. It was accomplished by the simplest of means, Hitler sending a registered letter announcing the action to the Lithuanian government. An actual treaty was signed subsequently as the Lithuanian foreign minister went to Berlin to give part of his country away. In return for Memel, Lithuania received German guarantees of independence and a flow of trade between the two countries.

■ The French parliament granted the cabinet the right to rule by decree until Nov. 30.

March 20 Washington recalled the U.S. ambassador in Berlin to protest the German actions in Czechoslovakia.

March 21 Germany offered Poland Slovakia in compensation for the return of Danzig and German control of overland routes between Germany and East Prussia.

March 23 Germany signed a treaty with Slovakia guaranteeing the latter's political independence and territorial integrity for 25 years, in effect extending the same kind of control over Slovakia that it had over Bohemia-Moravia (now known as "Czechia"). With this formality completed, Germany maintained hegemony over the entire area of defunct Czechoslovakia.

■ Hitler made a triumphal entry into Memel aboard a German warship.

■ Under German pressure Rumania agreed to permit German participation in the development of Rumania's mineral and agricultural resources.

March 25 For the first time Hitler said the "Polish problem" might have to be settled by military means. He ordered Generals Wilhelm Keitel and Walther von Brauchitsch, his top military advisers, to develop plans for war against Poland. He made clear to his military leaders that he did not want war with Britain.

■ Italy issued an ultimatum to King Zog of Albania in which he was to request a treaty placing his country under Italian protection. Zog requested British aid but was told London would not help. (British policy was to maintain stable relations with Rome.)

March 26 Italy announced its intention to establish control over the Suez Canal, Tunisia, and Djibouti, at the expense of Britain and France.

■ The Franco government committed Spain to the Anti-Comintern Pact.

■ Poland, politely but firmly, rejected Germany's offer on Danzig and the rail and road corridor to East Prussia.

March 28 The Civil War ended in Spain. Madrid was formally surrendered to General Franco.

The collapse of all Loyalist resistance led to a series of tribunals which judged individual leaders of the former government and imposed harsh sentences, including many executions. In all, about 750,000 people were killed in the civil struggle. The Italians had as many as 75,000 "volunteers" involved on the Nationalist side. Germany provided 19,000 men.

March 29 Paris responded to the Italian demands of March 26 for control of African territory held by France, saying it would not cede a foot of land.

■ Chamberlain announced the British Territorial Army would be doubled and placed on a war footing.

■ Poland declared any unilateral action to alter the status of Danzig would be considered an act of war.

March 31 Britain and France offered total and unqualified support to Poland "in the event of any action which clearly threatened Polish independence, and which the Polish Government accordingly considered it vital to resist with their national forces." (The result was to stiffen Warsaw's resistance to Hitler. Not incorrectly, Hitler felt the blank-check commitment permitted the Poles to exercise control over the policies of France and Britain. It also gave impetus to Hitler's thoughts on reaching an agreement with the Russians.)

■ Japan annexed the Spratly Islands in the South China Sea, which had been claimed by France. Tokyo's navy now had a base 700 miles from Singapore, Britain's key defense outpost in Asia, and Japanese submarines soon began operating out of the remote island.

April 1 The U.S. recognized the Franco regime in Spain and lifted its embargo on arms shipments.

■ With Hitler in attendance Germany launched the battleship *Tirpitz*, then the biggest in the world, at Wilhelmshaven. The 42,900-ton giant carried a crew of 2,500, had eight 15-inch guns and 86 antiaircraft weapons. *Tirpitz* was properly called "the most feared ship afloat," altering European naval strategy once war began.

April 2 Japan and the Soviet Union resolved their longstanding dispute over fishing rights in their adjacent waters. Tokyo won equal rights in the auction of fishing areas.

April 3 German military planners drew up plans (code-named WEISS) for a war against Poland to be launched by Sept. 1. Hitler himself drafted the introductory section, on the state of relations between the two nations, which was included in the High Command's "Directive for the Armed Services, 1939–40."

■ Chamberlain repeated the guarantees given Poland on March 31, saying that recent developments have "made every State which lies adjacent to Germany, unhappy, anxious, uncertain, about Germany's future intentions."

■ Italy sent an ultimatum to Albania demanding Italian control over the small Adriatic state.

April 6 Italy assured Britain it had no designs on Albania. London voiced its concern about military movements which appeared directed at Albania.

April 7 Italian forces—on this Good Friday—struck at Albania in what was considered a "rectification" of Italy's claims in the Adriatic. A naval bombardment of coastal centers preceded the troop landings, and the Albanian military was able to offer only token resistance. Hitler had approved of the Italian move generally but was never told when it would happen. The king of Italy questioned Mussolini about the wisdom of an invasion to "grab four rocks." Mussolini's actions can only be understood by his petulance over Germany's successes while Italy's imperial wishes were being frustrated. The official reason given by Rome for the invasion was that "influential persons in Albania had requested Italian intervention on account of the unbearable situation created by King Zog." The occupation was in clear violation of the Anglo-Italian agreement of the previous April, but Britain remained silent.

■ Germany expressed its disappointment over the Polish response on the Danzig proposal, saying, "Poland had obviously not understood the offer."

■ Spain became the fifth signatory in the Anti-Comintern Pact, joining Germany, Italy, Japan and Hungary.

April 9 Italy gave its assurance to Britain that it would respect Albania's independence.

April 11 A modified order was issued to German military planners on a Polish war. It stated such a conflict was to be avoided, but it remained a possibility.

■ Under German pressure, Hungary withdrew from the League of Nations.

April 13 Italy annexed Albania.

■ Britain and France gave guarantees to Greece and Rumania, the same kind of unqualified support for territorial integrity against external threat it had pledged Poland two weeks earlier. London and Paris also sought an identical automatic involvement commitment from Russia covering Poland and Rumania, but Moscow turned down the suggestion. The Russians said they would not be covered in such a manner if the Soviet Union were attacked by Germany or Japan. Moscow also felt the Baltic states and Finland would be unprotected.

April 14 Roosevelt wrote to Hitler and Mussolini seeking assurances Germany and Italy would not "attack or invade" any nation with whom it had issues in dispute. Hitler later termed the appeal a meaningless gesture. Mussolini called it absurd.

■ Britain proposed to Russia that Moscow announce it would respond to requests for aid from any of its neighbors which came under attack.

April 15 Rumania declared it was unwilling to participate in any anti-Nazi alliance.

April 17 Moscow responded to London's proposal of the 14th by counterproposing a detailed five to ten year defensive alliance between Britain, France, and Russia in which each would provide specific military support to the member attacked by a "European neighbor."

April 19 In a further move to deter Hitler, Britain announced it would defend the independence of the Netherlands, Denmark, and Switzerland.

■ The British government created a ministry of supply to coordinate an expanding rearmament program.

April 26 The British government announced that Parliament would be asked to authorize military conscription. Chamberlain declared that "nothing would so impress the world with the determination of this country to offer firm resistance to any attempt at general domination. . . ."

April 27 Berlin renounced the 1935 Anglo-German naval agreement. The Germans said the "British Government is now governed by the opinion that England, in whatever part of Europe Germany might be involved in warlike conflict, must always take up an attitude hostile to Germany, even in a case where English interests are not touched in any way by such a conflict." Britain had by now, of course, given guar-

antees of aid for the first time to countries east of the Rhine.

April 28 In a speech at Wilhelmshaven, Hitler abrogated the German-Polish nonaggression pact of 1934, saying it was incompatible with the "encirclement policy" being directed against Germany. Poland at once told the British it would be willing to join with London and Moscow in a common front against the Germans.

May 3 V.M. Molotov, an old-line Bolshevik, replaced M.M. Litvinov as Soviet foreign minister, signaling a new direction in Moscow's foreign policy. Until now, Moscow had pursued actions within the framework of collective security and cooperation with the League of Nations. Hitler best described the importance of the switch at the Kremlin when he later recalled hearing the news: "Litvinov's dismissal was decisive. It came to me like a cannon shot, like a sign that the attitude of Moscow towards the Western Powers had changed." (Indeed it did, culminating in a few months with the Soviet-German alliance.)

■ Hungary enacted highly restrictive anti-Semitic laws, including the planned expulsion of all Jews within five years.

May 5 Warsaw again turned down Germany's bid for control over Danzig and overland routes through the Polish Corridor.

May 7 The French foreign ministry learned through its embassy in Berlin that the Germans were planning an accommodation with the Soviets on benign neutrality or a possible division of Poland.

■ Russia outlined terms of an alliance with Poland, centering on two routes through Poland to fight the Germans, but Warsaw rejected the idea.

■ Hitler assured Mussolini the Alps would forever form the Italian-German frontier. Rome was concerned about possible German claims on the South Tyrol, regarded as the single obstacle to firm relations between the two countries.

May 8 Britain's ambassador in Moscow told Molotov that Britain—together with Poland and Rumania—were not in favor of Russia's April 17 proposals for a defensive alliance. The British did suggest, however, the Soviets pledge aid to Poland and Rumania once Britain and France were militarily committed, thus creating a firm alliance acceptable to Warsaw and Bucharest.

May 12 Outer Mongolian and Manchurian troops

battled along their border in what became known as the "Nomonhan Incident." It was touched off when 700 Mongol horsemen crossed the Khalka River which the Japanese considered to be the Manchurian-Mongolian border. The Soviets and Mongolians felt the frontier ran twenty miles to the east. (Russian and Japanese troops quickly moved into the dispute between their surrogates, massing troops along the river. Each side accused the other of starting the original fighting, but the issue was lost in the escalation of forces. By September, Japanese forces were to suffer 18,000 casualties. Russian-Mongolian casualties, according to Moscow, were 9,000.)

■ Britain and Turkey agreed to a policy of military cooperation if war broke out in the Mediterranean area "to ensure the establishment of security in the Balkans." Turkey had economic ties with Germany but was concerned about Berlin's ambitions in the Balkans.

■ German agitators began to harass Poles and attack Polish property in Danzig. A campaign began for reunification with Germany.

May 14 In a Turin speech Mussolini said, "According to a cold, objective examination of the situation, there are not at present in Europe problems big enough or acute enough to justify a war that by logical development [would] spread from Europe and become a universal event."

May 17 Britain announced its intention to establish a unified independent Palestine, with Jewish immigration limited to 75,000 over the next five years and none thereafter, unless agreed to by the Arabs.

■ Berlin made the first of several proposals to the Soviets for negotiations on a nonaggression treaty.

May 17–19 Finland, Norway, and Sweden spurned nonaggression treaties with Germany, stating none felt threatened by Germany nor did any intend to join alliances directed against the Germans.

■ Denmark, Estonia, and Latvia accepted Berlin's offer of nonaggression treaties.

May 18 The Japanese 23rd Division, supported by waves of aircraft, attacked the Russians on the Khalka River between Outer Mongolia and Manchuria. Tokyo intended to test Soviet will, knowing Moscow was preoccupied in Europe. Pressing forward, the Japanese secured all territory in dispute.

May 19 General Maurice Gamelin, French commander-in-chief, signed an agreement with Poland promising that if the Germans invaded Poland "France will launch an offensive against Germany with the main bodies of her forces, beginning on the fifteenth day from the first day of Polish general mobilization." (This was never honored, however, and Gamelin explained that neither government had ratified the agreement.)

May 22 The "Pact of Steel" was forged in Berlin, creating a military alliance between Germany and Italy. Each pledged to come to the other's side immediately in case of war. It marked the true creation of the Axis, giving Italy an ally sympathetic to its expansionist policies and Germany the ability to respond to policies of encirclement directed against it. Of later significance was that Mussolini and Foreign Minister Ciano let the Germans know candidly and unequivocally that Italy would not be ready to wage war for several more years.

■ Portugal and Britain reaffirmed their alliance, but Lisbon indicated its desire to remain neutral in the deteriorating European scene.

May 23 Hitler told his military commanders Poland was to be attacked and destroyed. "For us," he said, "it is a matter of expanding our living space in the East and making food supplies secure and also solving the problem of the Baltic States." Poland was to be isolated, and a war with Britain and France was to be avoided. Russia was somehow to become "disinterested" in "the destruction of Poland."

May 27 France and Britain presented new proposals to the Russians on an agreement to act "in concert" in the event one of the signatories was attacked, or if one became involved in a war in the aid of a smaller state under invasion.

■ Secretary of State Hull urged revision of the Neutrality Act to permit the export of arms from the U.S.

May 28 Heavy fighting broke out between Russian and Japanese forces at the Khalka River.

May 30 Molotov objected to the French and British proposal because it failed to take "indirect aggression" into account, citing Czechoslovakia as an example. Russia proposed a tripartite protective umbrella covering the Baltic states, Estonia, Latvia, and Lithuania, if their "independence" were threatened by Germany.

May 31 Germany and Denmark signed a ten-year nonaggression treaty.

■ Molotov, in a speech to the Supreme Soviet, said Russian foreign policy was not rigid and that she was not now committed to any specific course of action. It upset the French and encouraged the Germans.

June 2 Russia again proposed an alliance with Britain and France providing for mutual assistance in the event any of the signatories was attacked by Germany. Moscow also suggested the three nations extend joint guarantees of military support against German aggression to Poland, Belgium, Greece, Turkey, Rumania, Latvia, Estonia, and Finland.

June 6 Under Secretary of State Sumner Welles called for a U.S. military armament program and revision of neutrality laws. Said Welles, "We cannot deny the self-evident truth that the outbreak of a general war in any part of the world will inevitably have grave repercussions upon our national economy, and upon our social well-being, and not improbably upon our national security itself."

June 7 Germany, "earnestly desirous of maintaining peace," signed nonaggression treaties with Estonia and Latvia.

June 14 Following the alleged murder of a Japanese customs officer in Tientsin by four Chinese who took refuge in the International Concessions area, the Japanese launched a program of harassment and mistreatment of British and French residents in the area. Japanese warships blockaded the Concessions. Tokyo demanded Britain end its support of the Nationalist government.

June 15 Germany proposed talks on an economic agreement with Russia. Moscow declined the invitation. The Russians were still more interested in working out a mutual defense alliance with Britain and France.

June 16 China and the Soviet Union signed a trade treaty. (This agreement was the centerpiece of a series of barter arrangements made between 1938 and 1940 involving $300 million.)

June 17 German State Secretary Ernst von Weizsäcker warned Coulondre, the French ambassador in Berlin, not to threaten the Germans with possible Russian involvement, noting that this "method of intimidation produced in us the opposite of what was intended."

June 18 Russian troops tried but failed to force the Japanese out of the disputed areas on the Manchurian-Mongolian border.

June 23 France and Turkey signed a mutual defense treaty. Paris relinquished control over the disputed Hatay (Sanjak of Alexandretta) border area of Syria to Turkey. With this pact and the May treaty with Britain, Turkey clearly aligned itself with the anti-Axis forces.

June 30 German State Secretary Weizsäcker informed the French ambassador, ". . . we are not on the eve of a tremendous eruption, unless it was provoked by Polish excesses. That would certainly mean *Finis Poloniae*." Ambassador Coulondre at the same time told Weizsäcker France would not go to war against Germany if the conflict were started by Poland.

July 4 The French consul general in Hamburg reported to Paris that "if some agreement is not shortly concluded between London, Paris, and Moscow, the Soviet government will be prepared to sign a pact of nonaggression with the Reich for a period of five years."

July 9 Churchill proposed Britain enter into a military alliance with the Soviet Union.

July 17 Marshal Edward Smigly-Rydz declared that Poland would fight alone if necessary should Germany attempt to take Danzig.

July 18 The Danzig Senate offered to resolve all problems with Poland (particularly disputes over Polish custom officials) through the good offices of the League of Nations high commissioner.

July 22 Moscow revealed that "Soviet-German negotiations with regard to trade and credit had been resumed." Skepticism about the possibility of concluding an effective collective defense arrangement against the Germans was prompting Moscow to consider more seriously an accommodation with Hitler.

July 24 Britain agreed to Moscow's insistence that a political agreement between Britain, France, and Russia be completed before entering into a military agreement. The British move was a major concession. It had already been approved by the French, but when the British and French ambassadors informed Molotov of the decision, the Russian inexplicably dismissed the political agreement and asked Paris and London to send military missions to the Soviet Union.

■ Premier Count Paul Teleki wrote to Hitler and Mussolini that although Hungary was loyal to the

Axis cause, it could not take part in a war against Poland.

■ In a statement to satsify the Japanese, Prime Minister Chamberlain announced that British officials and citizens in China were being told not to interfere with Japanese forces which "have special requirements for the purpose of safeguarding their own security and maintaining public order in regions under their control or remove any such acts or causes as will obstruct them or benefit their enemy."

July 26 The U.S. denounced its 1911 commercial treaty with Japan, admitting only that such agreements had been under review to determine "what changes may need to be made toward better serving of the purposes for which such treaties are concluded."

July 27 France and Britain agreed to send military missions to Moscow. (Incredibly, despite the air of crisis, the groups sailed leisurely by ship to get to the Soviet Union. Both delegations were made up of lower-level officers with little authority, thus eliminating any chance of constructive and timely action.)

July 31 The Danzig Senate demanded the withdrawal of all Polish customs officers from the free city. Poland responded by announcing economic reprisals and refusing to pull out the inspectors.

Aug. 2 Ribbentrop—in an almost casual conversation with the Soviet chargé in Berlin—said that "from the Baltic to the Black Sea, there was no problem which could not be solved to our mutual satisfaction." (This was the first firm foundation of the astonishing series of events which were to culminate in the Soviet-German pact and the simultaneous invasion of Poland.)

■ Albert Einstein wrote a letter to Roosevelt alerting him to the potential of creating an atomic bomb. To indicate the power of such a device, Einstein said if the bomb were exploded in a port, it "might destroy the whole port together with some surrounding territory."

Aug. 4 Poland informed the Danzig Senate it would begin arming its customs officers in two days and any interference with their duties would be regarded as an act of violence, to be met accordingly. This came on the heels of rumors that the Danzig-East Prussian frontier would be opened.

■ Franco assumed "absolute authority" in Spain,

saying he was "responsible only to God and to history."

Aug. 7 The Danzig Senate protested the arming of Polish customs officers.

Aug. 8 The German press opened up a propaganda campaign against Poland, citing "criminal war agitation" by the Poles.

Aug. 9 Berlin protested the Polish economic reprisals against Danzig, stating they would result in "serious economic loss to the population of Danzig."

Aug. 10 In a tough note to Berlin, Poland rejected Germany's Danzig protest and said it "cannot perceive any legal foundation justifying Germany to interfere" in Polish-Danzig relations.

Aug. 12 British and French officers held their first formal discussions in Moscow on meeting the German threat militarily.

■ Moscow informed Berlin that Russia was prepared to begin talks on outstanding differences between the two countries.

Aug. 12–13 In conferences with Hitler and Ribbentrop, Count Ciano said Italy, drained militarily from its actions in Albania, Spain, and Ethiopia, would not be ready for war until 1941 at the earliest. Ciano had been told war with Poland was "inevitable," and the Germans were virtually insisting on direct Italian support. Part of Mussolini's concern, as relayed by Ciano, was the fear of Russian intervention, but Hitler assured him that "Russia will not make any move."

Aug. 14 Ribbentrop announced to the Russians that he would be willing to fly to Moscow "to lay the foundation for a final settlement of German-Russian relations."

Aug. 15 France and Britain separately informed Germany that each would go to war "automatically" if a conflict broke out between Germany and Poland.

■ Molotov asked Germany if it were prepared to enter into a nonaggression treaty and use its influence to improve Russo-Japanese relations.

■ Russia broke off military talks with Britain and France, stating that the Soviets could not get Polish approval to grant Moscow transit rights in the event of a German invasion of Poland.

■ Lord Halifax told the Poles he believed Hitler "is still undecided and anxious to avoid war." The Poles, meanwhile, kept refusing to grant transit rights to the Russians. Smigly-Rydz summed up the Polish attitude: "With the Germans we risk losing our freedom, with the Russians we shall lose our soul."

Aug. 17 Germany responded favorably to Soviet suggestions of a nonaggression pact and urged speed in completing it.

■ The Wehrmacht was ordered to supply the SS with 150 Polish army uniforms, which were to be used as "evidence" of Polish "aggression" in a faked border incident.

Aug. 19 Russia signed a trade agreement with Germany.

■ Molotov agreed to have Ribbentrop come to Moscow in a week or so.

Aug. 20 Hitler personally cabled Stalin to request Ribbentrop be received in Moscow as early as possible because of the imminence of war. Stalin at once agreed to Ribbentrop's arrival on the 23rd.

Aug. 20–25 General Georgi K. Zhukov, commander of the Soviet Far Eastern Army, attacked Japanese Kwantung Army positions in Outer Mongolia along the Khalka River. Zhukov's thrust was massive, touching off one of the largest battles since the World War and, until then, the biggest tank fight in history. Zhukov hurled 690 armored vehicles at the Japanese. Nine divisions of infantry and cavalry followed, supported by 15 artillery battalions and 300 aircraft. A total of 150,000 combatants were involved. The Japanese suffered heavy losses, including 18,000 casualties and more than 100 planes. Japanese troops had suffered their worst military setback in modern history.

HITLER'S RETROSPECTIVE AND FUTURE THOUGHTS

Hitler summoned his top generals to Obersalzburg on Aug. 22, 1939. He was in an expansive mood. Germany had just concluded its pact with the Soviets, and Hitler felt he would win everything he wanted. Hitler delivered a lengthy monologue on how he reached his momentous decisions and how he planned to shape history in the future. A transcript was preserved by the International Military Tribunal. One historian has called it "one of the great documents of our great century." Even excerpts reveal Hitler's mind in its fullest cunning and murderous dimensions:

"Since Autumn 1938, and since, I have found out that Japan does not go with us without conditions and that Mussolini is menaced by the weak-headed King and the treacherous scoundrel of a Crown Prince. I have decided to go with Stalin. On the whole, there are only three great statesmen in the world: Stalin, myself, and Mussolini. Mussolini, the weakest, has not been able to break either the power of the crown or that of the church. Stalin and I are the only ones that see only the future. So I shall shake hands with Stalin within a few weeks on the common German-Russian border and undertake with him a new distribution of the world.

". . . History sees only in him a great state leader. What weak Western European civilization thinks about me, does not matter . . . thus for the time being, I have sent to the East only my 'Death's Head Units,' with the order to kill without pity or mercy all men, women and children of the Polish race and language. Only in such a way will we win the vital space that we need. Who still talks nowadays of the extermination of the Armenians?

". . . My pact with Poland was only meant to stall for time. And besides, gentlemen, with Russia will happen just what I have practiced with Poland. After Stalin's death . . . we shall crush the Soviet Union. . . . I saw our enemies at Munich. . . . They were miserable worms.

"The occasion is favorable now as it has never been. I have only one fear and that is that Chamberlain or such another dirty swine comes to me with propositions or a change of mind. He will be thrown downstairs. And even if I must personally kick him in the belly before the eyes of all the photographers.

"No, for this it is too late. The invasion and extermination of Poland begins on Saturday morning. I will have a few companies in Polish uniform attack in Upper Silesia or in the Protectorate. Whether the world believes it doesn't mean a damn to me. The world believes only in success.

"Be hard. . . . Be without mercy. The citizens of Western Europe must quiver in horror."

Aug. 22 Berlin issued a communiqué on the forthcoming Moscow conference and said its purpose was to conclude a nonaggression pact.

■ Moscow stated the talks with the Germans were in "no way incompatible" with the ongoing military discussions with the French and British on "organizing resistance against aggression."

■ Britain announced the proposed Russo-German pact would not change its commitment to Poland. Chamberlain reiterated London's pledge in a letter to Hitler.

Aug. 23 In a move which electrified the world Molotov and Ribbentrop signed the German-Russian nonaggression pact in Moscow. It contained no "escape clause" should either launch a war. It also provided for neutrality by one should the other become involved in a war with "a third Power." Secretly, Germany and Russia carved out spheres of influence in eastern and central Europe, with Russia getting Finland, Estonia, Latvia, eastern Poland, and Bessarabia. Germany received the rest of Poland and Lithuania. Berlin's allies, Italy and Japan, were stunned. They had been left in the dark and the "pact with Satan" could not have fallen harder than in Tokyo and Rome. Japan renounced the Anti-Comintern Pact. Mussolini was partly assuaged by Hitler's agreement to provide Italy with economic aid to prepare for Rome's entry into war. (Mussolini's list of requirements was greedily lengthy and included a variety of scarce raw materials. It was known as the "Molybdenum List.") Hitler felt it was all worthwhile if Britain and France could be kept from interfering with his plans to invade Poland. He was also willing to yield half of Poland to the Russians, but he obviously believed Germany would be getting it all in due time.

■ Hitler responded to Chamberlain's message by saying Germany was fully prepared and determined to go to war with Britain if attacked by her.

■ *Gauleiter* Albert Forster was decreed head of Danzig by the Danzig Senate.

Aug. 24 Roosevelt personally cabled Hitler to avoid war and seek to resolve Germany's differences with Poland by direct negotiation, arbitration, or conciliation. Roosevelt also addressed appeals to President Ignace Moscicki of Poland and Italy's King Victor Emmanuel III.

■ France urged Poland to refrain from military action if Danzig declared itself under German rule, which most observers felt was imminent.

■ Forster was declared Danzig's head of state, an act immediately challenged by Poland.

■ Poland started calling up its military reserves.

Aug. 25 Britain and Poland signed a five-year mutual assistance agreement, an unambiguous declaration of London's intention to fight if Poland were invaded. All such assurances by Britain and France were related to an invasion by Germany in direct language or by implication. Nothing was mentioned about automatic action if, say, Russia invaded Poland.

■ Mussolini told Hitler that Italy could not fight if the Germans became involved in a war with Britain and France. The Italian military, said Mussolini, simply did not have sufficient supplies. The air force had fuel for only three months, and the other services were equally short of vital material. Italy, however, did begin mobilizing. Roosevelt sent a second peace appeal to Hitler.

■ Japan formally protested the Russo-German agreement as a violation of the Anti-Comintern Pact.

■ As a result of the day's developments, Hitler cancelled his orders for an invasion of Poland which had been set for the next morning. At the same time, he told Paris the French borders would not be violated by Germany in the event of a Polish war and assured London the British Empire's status quo would be upheld by Germany.

Aug. 26 France urged direct negotiations between Germany and Poland to avoid war.

■ Poland promised to consult with Britain and France before pursuing any policy which might provoke Germany into military action.

Aug. 27 Hitler wrote to French Premier Daladier that war appeared inevitable: "I see no possibility of persuading Poland, who deems herself safe from attack by virtue of guarantees given to her, to agree to a peaceful solution."

■ Britain proposed Poland attempt to enlist the pope as a peace intermediary and offer Germany neutral observers and a population exchange.

■ British men 20 and 21 years of age were ordered to report for induction into the military. The services were to be built up to a strength of

300,000 men. Arms appropriations were raised to the annual equivalent of $3 billion.

■ The first flight by an aircraft powered by a jet engine was achieved by a German Heinkel 178.

Aug. 28 Poland called up additional reservists.

■ Belgium and the Netherlands offered their good offices to Britain, France, Germany, and Italy "to avert war."

■ A new Japanese cabinet was formed under General Nobuyuki Abe.

Aug. 29 Hitler agreed to begin direct talks with Poland and suggested a Polish delegation be sent to Berlin immediately.

■ German troops completely occupied Slovakia, ostensibly because of a request from Father Tiso who claimed to fear a Polish invasion.

Aug. 30 Poland told the British ambassador in Moscow it would not send a delegation to Berlin. The ambassador cabled that the Poles "would certainly sooner fight and perish rather than submit to such humiliation, especially after the examples of Czecho-Slovakia, Lithuania, and Austria."

■ Britain said it would not encourage the Poles to send anyone to Berlin.

■ Lord Halifax urged Poland not to engage in any violent actions against the German minority and to halt inflammatory anti-German radio propaganda.

THE PREWAR BALANCE OF POWER (1939)

	Population	Per Capita Income (1938)	Standing Army	Combat Aircraft	Major Ships°	Destroyers	Submarines
Allies							
Britain	47,692,000	$498	220,000	1,144	76	201	38
France	41,600,000	248	800,000	735	21	75	59
Poland	34,662,000	92	290,000	390	-	4	5
Axis							
Germany	68,424,000	487	800,000	2,765	11	17	46
Italy	43,779,000	157	800,000	1,500	25	112	104
Japan	70,590,000	81	320,000	1,980	51	104	57
Uncommitted							
U.S.A.	129,825,000	520	190,000	800	57	214	95
U.S.S.R	167,300,000	188	1,700,000	5,000	13	52	150

°battleships, carriers, and cruisers

BALANCE OF POWER (SEPTEMBER 1939)

German and Allied Naval Forces

	German	British	French		German	British	French
Battleships	–	10	3	Bombers	1,180	536	186
Battle cruisers	2	2	2	Dive bombers	366	–	–
Pocket battleships	3	–	–	Attack planes	40	–	–
Aircraft carriers	–	6	1	Fighters	1,179	608	549
Cruisers	6	58	15	Observation aircraft	844	516	377
Destroyers	17	201	75	Total	3,609	1,660°	1,112°
Submarines	46	38	59				
Total	74	315	155				

°Does not include aircraft based outside Britain and France. There were 415 RAF planes overseas. The French had several squadrons of generally obsolescent aircraft in Africa and Indochina.

■ Ribbentrop told the British ambassador Germany had 16 demands to present to the Poles, but he said the issue was academic since Poland was unwilling to send a representative to arrive by midnight.

Aug. 31 Germany announced it considered its demands rejected by Poland: "The Führer and the German Government have now waited for two days in vain for the arrival of an authorized Polish delegate."

■ Germany cut communications with Warsaw.

■ Britain began evacuations from London.

Sept. 1 Germany invaded Poland and touched off World War II. The Germans had arranged a series of elaborate pretexts for launching the attack. Berlin claimed Polish army regulars started firing on Germans along the frontier and that the fire was returned beginning at 4:45 A.M. Hitler addressed the Reichstag, declaring "I am determined to eliminate from the German frontiers the element of insecurity, the atmosphere which permanently resembles that of civil war." German forces slammed into Poland from Silesia, East Prussia, and Slovakia, 1,500,000 men (52 divisions) against a Polish army a third that size. Germany unveiled the blitzkrieg—highly mobile armor and tactical aircraft leading the ground forces through and around the Polish defenses. Large-scale pincers movements were executed to perfection. Britain and France notified Germany that unless all military action ceased, they would have to come to Poland's aid. Britain and France ordered total mobilization. Danzig was proclaimed to be a part of Germany by *Gauleiter* Forster. Italy proclaimed its nonbelligerent status. Norway, Switzerland, and Finland declared their neutrality. Russia mobilized and lowered its draft age from 21 to 19.

TRIGGERING WORLD WAR II

SS Officer Alfred Naujocks gave this sworn affidavit on the incident which triggered the war: "On or about August 10, 1939, [Reinhard] Heydrich personally ordered me to simulate an attack on the radio station near Gleiwitz, near the Polish border, and to make it appear as if the attacking forces consisted of Poles. Heydrich said, 'Practical proof is needed for these attacks of the Poles for the foreign press as well as German propaganda.' I was ordered to go to Gleiwitz with five or six Security Service men and wait until I would receive the code words (CANNED GOODS) for the attack from Heydrich. My instructions were to seize the radio station and to hold it long enough to permit a Polish-speaking German, who would be put at my disposal, to broadcast a speech in Polish." The orders were carried out in every detail.

Sept. 2 Poland called on France and Britain to begin military action against Germany as soon as

Hitler makes his triumphal entry into Danzig after Germany occupied the free city. The banner reads, "Danzig greets its leader!"

possible. France declared it would fulfill its obligations to Poland.

■ Two Polish divisions were destroyed in an attempt to pull back through the Corridor. A Polish cavalry brigade was shattered when mounted lancers attacked German tanks.

■ Italy proposed a conference of the five great powers to discuss the outbreak of war. Britain refused further talks while German troops remained in Poland.

■ Ten British bomber squadrons began deploying to France.

■ Ireland proclaimed its neutrality.

■ Germany told Norway it would respect its neutrality but warned it would not tolerate any abuse of Oslo's position by Britain or France.

Sept. 3 France and Britain issued an ultimatum to Germany demanding the immediate withdrawal of the German forces in Poland. Hitler blamed Britain for encouraging the Poles to pursue a policy of provocation, whereupon Britain, France, India, Australia, and New Zealand declared war on Germany.

■ Some Polish units penetrated East Prussia, but their positions were untenable as German pincers movements cut them off to the south. Czestochowa fell, and the German Tenth Army crossed the Warta River. The Polish air force ceased to exist as an effective fighting element.

■ Belgium declared its neutrality.

■ Britain announced a blockade of Germany. Churchill became first lord of the Admiralty. (Word of Churchill's appointment was flashed to all Royal Navy ships and installations with the simple message: "Winston is back.")

■ British Royal Air Force (RAF) aircraft dropped six million leaflets on cities in northern Germany and the Ruhr, the first of the propaganda raids.

■ Britain completed the three-day evacuation of 1,500,000 civilians from the larger cities to the country.

■ The British passenger liner *Athenia* was torpedoed and sunk west of Scotland en route to Canada. No warning was given by the attacking U-boat commander, contradicting specific orders from Hitler. (Berlin, after initially denying German responsibility, learned later in the month the captain of *U-30* did attack *Athenia*, mistaking it for an armed merchant cruiser. But the Germans did everything possible to cover up the incident and continued to deny responsibility. Of the

1,400 passengers, 118 were killed, including 28 Americans of the 316 aboard.)

POISON GAS

Only Italy and Japan are believed to have used poison gas in the period after World War I. By then the world displayed its unqualified revulsion to the kind of chemical warfare waged in the trenches.

There were numerous cases of the Japanese spreading toxic gases in China prior to Pearl Harbor, including tactical employment in Shansi Province and in Hunan Province around Lake Tungting. The Italians flagrantly used mustard gas against the Ethiopians in 1936.

Once World War II started, however, all belligerents refrained from gas warfare, with one possible exception which was not fatal and probably unintentional (see below). All nations in effect adhered to the Geneva Protocol of 1925 which banned all chemical and bacteriological warfare weapons. Thirty-two nations ratified the agreement, with only Japan among the larger nations failing to commit itself.

That gas was not used during the war is surprising in the light of its previous use and the more desperate positions in which many of the belligerent nations found themselves. Most Allied and Axis armies had prepared for gas warfare; offensive and defensive measures had been taken. The fear of unleashing this kind of ghastly warfare and international condemnation was seemingly a sufficient deterrent to both sides, although the Allies clearly made their repugnance known at early stages of the conflict.

The day Britain declared war, Sept. 3, 1939, London asked the belligerents to state their intention to observe the terms of the Geneva Protocol. Germany, Italy, Bulgaria, Rumania, Finland, and Japan did so. Japan agreed to adhere even though it had not signed the protocol and even though to the Japanese war must have seemed probable.

On June 5, 1942, President Roosevelt threatened Japan with retaliatory gas warfare if it again started using gas in China or anywhere else.

The single case of reported gas warfare was in New Guinea late in the war. U.S. officials believed that a few isolated incidents took place, but there were no resulting deaths among American troops. Japanese officials later admitted the possibility, but denied gas was ever authorized.

Japan did have a chemical warfare school in Narashino and maintained a bacteriological weapons plant at Harbin, Manchuria (which operated for cover purposes as the "Epidemic Prevention and Potable Water Supply Unit").

Germany manufactured three kinds of nerve gases during the war—tabun, sarin, and soman—and 250,000 tons of such material were uncovered in Austria at the very end of the war. Individual units were reported to have received shipments of these gases, but they were never used.

Sept. 4 The Polish Army of Poznan was threatened with encirclement. Government officials were told to prepare to evacuate Warsaw.

■ Advance units of the British Expeditionary Force began landing in France.

FIRST OFFENSIVE OF THE WAR BY THE RAF

The day after Britain's declaration of war against Germany RAF bombers launched the first Allied air offensive. It was a near disaster.

• Twenty-nine Blenheim and Wellington bombers were sent to attack the German navy's North Sea bases at Wilhelmshaven and Brunsbüttel. Here is their record:

• Ten bombers failed to find their targets and returned to their bases without having dropped their bombs.

• One plane bombed Esbjerg, a town in Denmark (then neutral) 110 miles away from the intended targets.

• Three decided to attack British men-of-war in the North Sea until they discovered their mistake and went home.

• Seven were shot down by German antiaircraft batteries.

• Eight of the bombers found the right target areas and made attack runs. Three duds were dropped on the battleship *Scheer*. Several hits were scored on the cruiser *Emden*, but the most severe damage was the result of one of the Blenheims crashing on the ship's forecastle.

SOURCES: RAF Official History, Vol. 1, *The Fight at Odds*, and Martin Middlebrook, *The Nuremberg Raid*.

■ Spain declared its neutrality, but Franco secretly pledged support for the Axis cause.

Sept. 5 German Tenth and Fourteenth army units crossed the Vistula River and occupied Krakow, which the Poles abandoned to avoid entrapment. Hitler visited the front. So far, the German military had lost 150 men killed and 700 wounded in the Polish campaign.

■ Polish rear guards and armed civilians offered determined resistance at Bydgoszcz before yielding to German III Corps units. The invaders found hundreds of German residents of the city massacred by the fleeing Poles. Hitler used these instances of such documented atrocities to justify the invasion.

■ The U.S. declared its neutrality.

■ General Jan Christian Smuts was named prime minister of South Africa after the legislature defeated a proposal that the country declare its neutrality. Many South Africans of Dutch descent were sympathetic to Germany's racial policies and were not disposed to aid the British in any way.

Sept. 6 German troops reached the Warsaw suburb of Ochota but were turned back. Kielce was captured. The Polish government and military command left Warsaw for Brest-Litovsk (Brzesc). Poles capable of fighting, in and out of uniform, were told to cross the Vistula River and join in establishing a new defense line to the east.

■ Britain's first air raid warning turned out to be false. RAF planes sent aloft to intercept the imagined attackers ended up shooting at each other. Spitfires shot down two Hurricanes.

■ South Africa declared war on Germany.

■ Iraq broke off diplomatic relations with Germany.

Sept. 7 Defenders in the Polish enclave of Westerplatte in Danzig surrendered.

■ Hitler, in a meeting with Admiral Erich Raeder, directed the German Navy, "in order not to provoke neutral countries, the United States in particular, it is forbidden to torpedo passenger steamers, even when sailing in convoy. Warfare against French merchant ships, attacks on French warships and mine laying off French ports is prohibited." The order was the result of the *Athenia* sinking, but it also revealed Hitler still thought a peace could be achieved with France at least, and presumably with Britain as well.

Sept. 8 Roosevelt proclaimed a state of "limited national emergency," citing the European war which "imposes on the United States certain duties with respect to the proper observance, safeguarding and enforcement" of its neutral status "and the strengthening of the national defense within the limits of peacetime authorizations." All U.S. military forces were authorized increases in enlisted manpower strength, and the president was allowed to recall reservists to active duty.

■ Sixty thousand Polish soldiers were encircled west of Radom. The German 4th Panzer Division smashed its way to the outskirts of Warsaw. Polish units counterattacked near Kutno on the Bzura River, the beginning of a week of bitter fighting. The attack on Warsaw was temporarily delayed.

■ Declaring that Germany was resorting to unrestricted submarine warfare, Britain announced a long-range blockade, broadening the original blockade announcement of Sept. 3.

Sept. 9 Göring threatened reprisals against Britain if the RAF bombed Germany, but he boasted that Berlin would never be subjected to enemy aerial attack.

■ German tanks were turned back west of Warsaw.

■ French troops advanced into the Warndt Forest across the German border and occupied three square miles of German territory. The actions was more for propaganda than military purposes since "occupied Germany," as the French called it, was a tiny parcel of deserted, heavily mined and booby-trapped land.

■ Molotov prematurely congratulated Berlin on the "entry of German troops into Warsaw" and promised Soviet intervention "within the next few days." Ribbentrop had invited the Russians

to advance to their new common frontier, the Narew, Vistula, and San rivers (the Bug and Pissa would eventually replace the Vistula to avoid a divided Warsaw.)

Sept. 10 Canada declared war on Germany. (Hesitation on Canada's part permitted for a few days the accelerated delivery from the U.S. of large amounts of war goods which were now barred under American neutrality laws.)

■ The main body of British forces began moving to France under the command of Lord Gort.

Sept. 11 Germany announced a counterblockade against Britain, saying that since "economic warfare was forced on her," Germany "is not only able to resist every pressure of blockade and every form of British hunger warfare, but to reply to it with the same methods."

■ The British cabinet decided no further attempt would be made to bomb Germany by air.

■ German ground troops forced their way across the San River line in Poland. The Polish force at Radom was destroyed and 60,000 men captured.

Sept. 12 Polish units pushed the Germans back 12 miles south of Kutno. Lowicz was recaptured. Gdynia was evacuated.

■ A Czech army-in-exile was formed in France.

■ Luftwaffe planes bombed Krzemieniec (Kremenets) in eastern Poland, a declared open village where the diplomatic community from Warsaw had sought refuge.

■ Ribbentrop demanded, on threat of military action, that the Rumanians not give asylum to Polish officials crossing the border.

Sept. 13 The U.S. ambassador in Warsaw, Anthony J. Drexel Biddle, Jr., reported that German bombers were attacking the civilian population. He said "they are releasing the bombs they carry even when they are in no doubt as to the identity of their objectives."

■ The German High Command announced that civilian targets in Poland would be bombed since civilians were involving themselves in the fighting.

Sept. 14 German forces from East Prussia broke into the open when they crossed the Narew River near Modlin and swept around Warsaw to begin encirclement of the Polish capital. Lwow was cut off completely by the Germans. Ukrainians, residents of Poland, began an uprising in Lwow and

Stanislawow (Ivano-Frankovsk), attacking small Polish army units.

■ Moscow unleashed a propaganda campaign to prepare public opinion for Russia's entry into the war. The Communist party newspaper *Pravda* carried a front-page article deploring Poland's treatment of its minorities.

■ The German submarine *U-39* was sunk by Royal Navy destroyers in the Atlantic, the first German naval loss of the war.

Sept. 15 German troops closed in on the encircled Polish Poznan Army at Kutno. Brest-Litovsk, 120 miles east of Warsaw, was surrounded. Warsaw's military commander (Major General Juliusz Rommel of the Polish army) refused to discuss a surrender proposal from the Germans.

■ Anxious to secure its eastern flank, Moscow concluded a cease-fire agreement with Japan, ending the border warfare along the Mongolian-Manchurian border. Tokyo was equally disposed to settle the problem, having suffered fierce Soviet reaction to the frequent forays of the Kwantung Army. Definition of the border was

not concluded until 1941, but both Tokyo and Moscow had resolved an irritant which had been overtaken by more crucial developments.

Sept. 17 Russia invaded Poland. The Red Army struck across Poland's thousand-mile long eastern border with an estimated 40 divisions. Poland had only 25 Frontier Corps battalions left in the east. Many Russian vehicles carried white flags and Red Army soldiers yelled at the Poles, "Don't shoot, we've come to help you against the Germans," confounding and confusing the already overwhelmed defenders. Foreign Minister Molotov announced the reasons for Russia's action: "Events arising out of the Polish-German War have revealed the internal insolvency and obvious impotence of the Polish state. . . . The population of Poland has been abandoned by their ill-starred leaders to their fate. . . . Poland has become a fertile field for any accidental and unexpected contingency that may create a menace to the Soviet Union . . . nor can it be demanded of the Soviet Government that it remain indifferent to the fate of its blood brothers, the Ukrainians and White Russians inhabit-

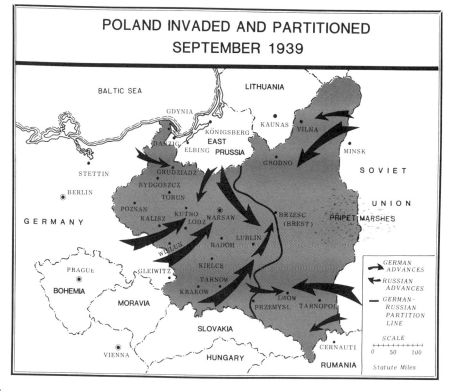

POLAND INVADED AND PARTITIONED SEPTEMBER 1939

With swiftness and assurance, German forces swept through Poland and launched World War II. Russian intervention against Poland came only after Hitler's forces had triumphed.

ing Poland." The Russians were hard pressed to reach their prearranged line dividing Poland with the Germans because of the swiftness of the German advances. By this time Poland had lost all defensive strength it possessed, and the Russian march westward went almost unchallenged.

■ Forty thousand Polish military prisoners were taken at Kutno. Brest-Litovsk was captured by the Germans after a bitter three-day battle. German armies were given a stop line because of the Russian moves in the east.

■ Moscow informed Finland Russia would respect its neutrality.

■ Russia recognized Slovakia as an independent state.

■ Italy assured Athens it would take no military action against Greece even if Italy entered the war.

■ The British fleet carrier *Courageous* was sunk in the Western Approaches, off southwestern Ireland, by a German U-boat while on antisubmarine duty, the first Royal Navy ship lost in the war. More than 500 men were killed. The immediate effect was the British pulling all their fleet carriers out of antisubmarine operations.

■ Warsaw was totally isolated as converging German forces met at Siedlce. Stragglers from the Polish government crossed into Rumania.

Sept. 18 German and Russian troops joined up in Poland, and the two governments quickly implemented plans to divide Poland along the Brest-Litovsk line.

■ The German Third and Tenth armies began attacking Warsaw.

■ In simultaneous announcements, Denmark, Finland, Norway, Sweden, and Iceland declared they intended to continue trading with all belligerents to protect their economic existence.

Sept. 19 Hitler told Britain and France the war could be concluded on the basis of Germany's territorial gains, or it would be fought to its conclusion. He said, "This Germany does not capitulate. We know too well what fate would be in store for Germany. . . . We are determined to carry on and stand this war one way or another."

■ Russian troops occupied Wilno (Vilna) in Poland. To the south, they reached the Ruthenian border near Lawocne.

■ About 30,000 Polish troops reached Warsaw

after fighting their way out of Kutno. German bombers began a continuing assault on Warsaw, initially striking at utilities and other essential public facilities.

Sept. 20 Replying to Hitler, Britain and France vowed to keep fighting. They declared the Allies "will not permit a Hitler victory to condemn the world to slavery and to ruin all moral values and destroy liberty."

■ The first air engagement between the RAF and the Luftwaffe was fought over Aachen when a flight of Me-109s intercepted three RAF Battles patrolling the French-German border. Two Battles and a Messerschmitt were downed.

Sept. 21 Premier Armand Calinescu of Rumania was assassinated by members of the Nazi Iron Guard. The action was in apparent retaliation for Bucharest's tolerant, even sympathetic, attitude toward Poland, such as the acceptance of Polish military and civilian refugees.

■ Roosevelt called a special session of Congress to repeal the arms embargo provision of the U.S. Neutrality Act, saying that by repeal the country "will more probably remain at peace than if the law remains as it stands today."

Sept. 22 Lwow and Bialystok in Poland were taken by the Russians. Hitler visited the front, observing the shelling of Warsaw's suburb of Praga.

Sept. 23 Mussolini restated Italy's intention to remain neutral unless attacked, following a policy to "strengthen our army in preparation for any eventualities and support every possible peace effort while working in silence."

■ Germany declared all organized fighting in Poland had ended. Berlin said: "The Polish Army of a million men has been defeated, captured, or routed. No single Polish active or reserve division, none of their independent brigades, etc., escaped this fate. Only fractions of individual groups were able to avoid immediate destruction by fleeing into the swamps of Eastern Poland. They succumbed there to Soviet Russian troops. Of the entire Polish army only an insignificant remainder still is fighting at hopeless positions in Warsaw, in Modlin, and on the Peninsula of Hela."

Sept. 25 Warsaw was subjected to murderous aerial bombardment as wave after wave of Luftwaffe planes attacked the now defenseless city.

HORSES AT WAR

Despite the commonly held perception of World War II as a highly mechanized conflict, horses formed a key element in the field of transport. It was certainly true in Asia, but few have understood the extensive use of true horse power in Europe. The German army—famed for its panzers and lightning attacks—is a case in point.

When the war began in 1939, only four of the Wehrmacht's 90 infantry divisions were totally motorized. Of the rest, it can be said that without animals they could hardly have moved at all. This is dramatically illustrated by meticulously kept German statistics. The better equipped of the nonmotorized infantry divisions had 394 passenger cars and 615 trucks, but each was also allotted 4,842 horses. The poorest of those divisions had 330 passenger cars and 248 trucks—and 6,030 horses.

The German ground forces possessed well over a half-million horses on Sept. 1, 1939. By the time the war ended, a total of 2,700,000 horses had served the Wehrmacht. That is nearly twice the number used by the Germans in World War I. In that "primitive" war of lesser geographical dimensions, the Germans employed but 1,400,000 horses.

SOURCE: Matthew Cooper, *The German Army, 1933–1945.*

Sept. 26 The German Eighth Army joined in the attack on Warsaw.

■ The French Communist party was dissolved by presidential decree. It became illegal to propagandize themes of the Third International. French Communists at this time were leaders of the antiwar movement, having quickly adapted to the new Moscow-Berlin alliance.

Sept. 27 Warsaw surrendered. More than 140,000 Polish troops laid down their arms. The siege had resulted in the deaths of 2,000 Polish soldiers and 10,000 civilians. An eighth of the city's buildings were destroyed.

■ Hitler told his military commanders that he had decided "to attack in the West as soon as possible since the Franco-British Army is not yet prepared." He set Nov. 12 as the tentative attack date.

Sept. 28 Estonia and Russia signed a 10-year mutual assistance pact, with the Soviets acquiring military rights and access to raw materials. (Moscow was to sign similar pacts with Latvia on Oct. 5 and Lithuania on the 10th, completing Soviet hegemony over the Baltic states.)

Sept. 29 Germany and the Soviet Union signed a boundary and friendship treaty. It formally divided Poland, giving the Germans control over the area generally west of the Bug River. The occupying governments said the partition was necessary "after the disintegration of the former Polish state" and Moscow and Berlin "consider it their task to restore in this region law and order and to insure nationals living there an existence corresponding to their national character." Germany got nearly 73,000 square miles of Polish territory, Russia, 78,000. The Russians were permitted to include all of Lithuania in their sphere of influence. An economic agreement was also signed which extended the previous trade pact. Moscow also promised the Germans the entire oil output of the Dohowicz fields, an action which infuriated the British and French. Russia achieved its gains through an invasion against an overwhelmed Poland and lost only 737 men in the brief conflict.

Sept. 30 Polish President Ignace Moscicki, interned in Rumania, resigned. A Polish provisional government was established in Paris under General Wladyslaw Sikorski.

■ Germany notified Britain its armed merchantmen would be sunk without warning. The action was claimed to be the result of British merchant ships attacking German submarines.

■ The British cabinet authorized poison gas shipments to France for use if the Germans began using chemical warfare weapons.

Oct. 1 The Polish navy surrendered but some ships had been able to escape to Britain and continue fighting with the Royal Navy.

■ Churchill said Russia had "pursued a policy of cold self-interest" in Poland. He added that "we could have wished that the Russian armies should be standing on their present line as the friends and allies of Poland instead of as invaders. But that the Russian armies should stand on this line was clearly necessary for the safety of Russia against the Nazi menace."

■ Japanese XI Corps forces began withdrawing from northern Hunan Province in China, ending an abortive attempt which began in early August to capture Changsha and the Tungting Lake area. Known as the first battle of Changsha, the action was a major victory for Chiang Kai-shek's forces which had previously failed to distinguish themselves in battle.

ENEMY ALIENS IN BRITAIN

At the outbreak of war 75,000 Germans and Austrians lived in Great Britain. Within days about 350 were arrested as dangerous. The more obviously pro-Nazis had already left the country. An estimated 50,000 were refugees and presumed relatively "safe." All Germans and Austrians not arrested, however, were restricted. None could travel more than five miles from home without having official permission or own a plane, boat, car, camera, nautical chart, or large-scale map unless authorized. Tribunals were established to pass on the loyalty of the questionable enemy aliens. Within two months 19,300 cases were reviewed. Of these, 15,140 were released with no further restrictions, 3,920 remained under restrictive security, and 230 were interned.

Oct. 1–2 RAF planes flew over Berlin for the first time in the war, dropping leaflets.

Oct. 2 A "zone of safety" around the Western Hemisphere was proclaimed by the Congress of American Republics in Panama. South of Canada, the zone varied in width from 300 to 1,000 miles, and belligerents were warned to stay clear. The action was objected to by the British and Germans, London on the grounds it would work to the disadvantage of the Royal Navy, and Berlin because it restricted U-boat operations.

■ Germany advised the U.S. all merchant ships in international waters were subject to German navy boardings for search.

Oct. 3 The German Tenth Army was pulled out of Poland and rushed to the western front.

Oct. 5 Hitler flew to Warsaw to inspect the damage inflicted by his forces.

■ Latvia and Russia signed a 10-year mutual assistance treaty. The Soviets were given naval and air bases on the Baltic Sea.

■ Russia, saying that "now that the international situation has altered on account of the war," invited Finland to begin discussions on territorial adjustments.

■ The last of the Polish troops surrendered, in the Radzyn-Kock area. In all, about 694,000 Poles out of an 800,000-man force were captured by the Germans. The remainder were killed, captured, or fled to Rumania and Hungary. German army losses in the campaign were 13,111 killed and missing and 27,278 wounded.

Oct. 6 Hitler delivered a Reichstag speech in which he indicated Germany was now content with its conquests and would agree to peace with the Allies: "Germany has no further claims against France. . . . nowhere have I ever acted contrary to British interest."

Oct. 7 Hitler issued his "Strengthening of Germanhood Decree," providing for "the elimination of the harmful influence of nationally alien populations, which constitute a danger to the Reich and the German community." Poland was to be converted to German "Lebensraum" and Poles were to be evicted or killed.

Oct. 9 Hitler issued a formal directive to put the German army on the offensive in the west: "An offensive will be planned on the northern flank of the West Front, through Luxembourg, Belgium, and Holland." Hitler also said the neutrality of the "Nordic States" (Norway, Denmark, Sweden, and Finland) was to be assumed, and Germany would seek to continue trade relations with them.

■ In the light of Russian demands for talks, regarded by the Finns as aggressive in design, Helsinki ordered mobilization.

■ Thirty-five of the 46 Communist deputies in the French parliament were arrested for agitating against the war.

■ The U.S. cargo ship *City of Flint*, en route from New York to Britain, was captured by the German pocket battleship *Deutschland* on the grounds it was hauling contraband material (tractors, fruit, and grain). (*The City of Flint* incident, which soured relations between the U.S. and Germany, had a more profound effect in swinging American public opinion toward repeal of the Neutrality Act, which was then being debated in Congress.)

Oct. 10 Russia completed its domination of the Baltic states by concluding a 15-year mutual assistance pact with Lithuania. The Soviets, as in the pacts with Estonia and Latvia, received military bases as well as the right to fortify the Lithuanian-German frontier. Lithuania won the right to reoccupy Vilna (Wilno) Province which had been given to Poland after World War I.

■ Hitler repeated his willingness to make peace with Britain and France.

Oct. 11 Fearing war between Russia and Finland, Roosevelt appealed to Soviet President Mikhail I. Kalinin for restraint on Moscow's part and to "make no demands on Finland which are inconsistent with the maintenance and development of amicable and peaceful relations between the two countries, and the independence of each."

■ Finnish delegates met with the Russians in Moscow on demands for Soviet military bases in Finland.

■ Britain's War Office moved to increase the weekly production of mustard gas from 310 to 1,200 tons. Britain now had 158,000 men in France.

Oct. 12 Britain rejected Hitler's peace overtures. Chamberlain warned Germany to choose between permanent security arrangements in Eu-

rope or "war to the utmost of our strength." He added that "past experience has shown that no reliance can be placed upon the promises of the present German Government."

■ Germany began deporting Austrian and Czech Jews to Poland.

■ Russia presented its official demands to Finland, an exchange of territory (2,123 square miles of Russian for 1,042 Finnish) and military bases designed to secure "the safety of Leningrad" and assurances that "Finland will maintain firm, friendly relations with the Soviet Union." Leningrad was 20 miles from the frontier.

Oct. 14 The British battleship *Royal Oak* was sunk at Scapa Flow by a German submarine, and 833 men were lost. The captain of *U-47*, Lieutenant Günther Prien, was acclaimed a national hero for his remarkable feat of penetrating the bay and making two approaches even with several torpedo failures.

■ Finland offered counterproposals to the Soviets, which Moscow rejected because the Russians felt they did not represent even their minimum terms. Stalin was particularly insistent on getting Hangö, west of Helsinki, in the Gulf of Finland, since he said, "The Finnish Gulf must be closed to prevent any nation from entering there."

Oct. 16 German forces pushed the French back to the Maginot line near Saarbrücken.

■ German warships received modified instructions for attacking: "All merchant ships definitely recognized as enemy ones (British or French) can be torpedoed without warning. Passenger steamers *in convoy* can be torpedoed a short while after notice has been given of the intention to do so."

Oct. 17 German planes bombed the British naval base at Scapa Flow. The training ship *Iron Duke* was damaged.

Oct. 18 The president of Finland met with the kings of the Scandinavian nations to consider the threat resulting from the Soviet military demands on the Finns. Hitler had assured the Swedes that Germany would remain neutral in a Russian-Finnish war and strongly advised the Swedes to do the same.

Gas-masked nurses in London carry babies in protective body suits to shelters in an air raid drill.

Oct. 19 Turkey signed 15-year mutual defense pacts with Britain and France. Ankara pledged to aid the European allies if war reached the Mediterranean, but not if such aid could bring Turkey into conflict with the Soviet Union. This and other conditions kept Turkey neutral during the entire conflict. In return, Turkey received control of the disputed Sanjak of Alexandretta from French Syria.

Oct. 26 Hans Frank took over as governor general of Poland.

■ On the eve of a Senate vote on amending the Neutrality Act, Roosevelt delivered a fireside chat: "In and out of Congress we have heard orators and commentators and others beating their breasts proclaiming against sending the boys of American mothers to fight on the battlefields of Europe. That I do not hesitate to label as one of the worst fakes in current history. It is a deliberate setup of an imaginary bogy." (The Senate voted to amend the act, and the House followed suit a week later).

Oct. 27 Hitler again commanded his generals to prepare for the western offensive.

Oct. 29 Reflecting the rising number of Chinese defections to the Japanese, the U.S. military attaché reported there were 100,000 armed Chinese serving as *Huang Hsieh Chun* (Imperial Assisting Troops).

Oct. 31 Molotov—in a speech before the Supreme Soviet—asserted the Russians had a right and duty to adopt strong measures to insure their security and again demanded territorial concessions from Finland.

LIFE IN OCCUPIED POLAND

Under German occupation Poles were barred from:
• riding in taxis,
• carrying briefcases,
• wearing felt hats,
• participating in athletic events,
• walking in public parks,
• calling from phone booths,
• using rail station waiting rooms,
• having their teeth filled with gold.

SOURCE: Nicholas Bethell, *The War Hitler Won*.

■ The death penalty was ordered for all Poles disobeying German authority, with the guilty to be tried in SS courts.

Nov. 1 By decree, Germany formally annexed western Poland.

Nov. 3 Russia incorporated eastern Poland into the Soviet Union following rigged plebiscites in which the majority of the 12 million Poles living in the conquered territory reputedly favored annexation by Moscow.

■ Finland again offered counterproposals to Russia, stating it recognized Soviet security needs but had now gone as far as its "independence, security, and neutrality permit." Helsinki was adamantly opposed to granting the Soviets a military base on Finnish territory.

Nov. 4 Congress repealed the U.S. neutrality law. American policy now permitted "cash and carry" purchases, a move clearly favorable to the British and French. Roosevelt issued new proclamations of neutrality and defined the zones of combat, including the Bay of Biscay, waters adjacent to Britain and Ireland, the English Channel, the North Sea, and the Baltic. All U.S. ships were barred from these waters. The main point was that U.S. manufacturers could now sell arms to belligerents if the material was shipped under the flag of a foreign nation.

Nov. 5 Hitler set Nov. 12 as the date for the attack on France and the Low Countries.

Nov. 7 Hitler delayed the start of the western offensive, the first of many such postponements.

■ Poland's governor general, Hans Frank, established his headquarters in Krakow, which replaced Warsaw as the capital. (His diary entry read, "The Poles will be the slaves of the German Reich.")

Nov. 8 Hitler escaped an assassination attempt. He had left a Munich beer hall 20 minutes before a bomb, concealed in a supporting pillar, exploded. Nine persons were killed.

Nov. 9 Finland again stated it "cannot grant to a foreign power military bases on her territory and within the confines of her frontiers."

■ Chamberlain hailed repeal of the U.S. embargo law as a "momentous event," which, he said, "reopens for the Allies the doors of the greatest storehouse of supplies in the world."

Nov. 13 Negotiations between Finland and Russia were terminated. Stalin ordered plans for an immediate war against Finland.

Nov. 16 An uprising in Prague was quelled. Martial law was imposed and many of the dissidents—including large numbers of students—were killed.

Nov. 18 German magnetic mines accounted for the loss of 60,000 tons of Allied shipping off Britain's east coast during the preceding week.

Nov. 20 Luftwaffe planes began parachuting magnetic mines into the Thames estuary.

Nov. 21 Slovakia was ceded 225 square miles of former Polish territory (which Poland had progressively annexed in 1920, 1924, and 1938) in a treaty signed with Germany.

■ All goods in Britain earmarked for shipment to Germany were confiscated.

■ The Japanese passenger liner *Terukuni Maru* struck a German-laid mine in the Thames estuary, an ironic first casualty of indiscriminate mine warfare.

Nov. 22 The British destroyer *Gipsy* hit a German mine in the Thames estuary. (British experts the next day located one of the German mines in the mud flats near Shoeburyness and soon swept the estuary and began equipping ships with anti-magnetic devices.)

Nov. 23 The German pocket battle cruisers *Scharnhorst* and *Gneisenau* sank the armed British merchantman *Rawalpindi* in the Iceland-Faroes passage.

■ Star of David identification badges were made compulsory for all Jews in occupied Poland.

Nov. 26 Russia charged that Finland had launched artillery barrages on Soviet territory. Moscow also protested "the concentration of Finnish troops in the vicinity of Leningrad," which Moscow described as a "hostile act."

Nov. 27 Finland denied any shelling of Russian territory and said the firing observed the day before near the village of Mainila actually came from the Soviet side of the frontier.

Nov. 28 Britain declared all German exports as contraband.

■ Moscow renounced the Russian-Finnish nonaggression treaty of 1932.

Nov. 29 Russia broke off diplomatic relations with Finland, claiming Finnish troops were continuing attacks on Russian units on the Karelian Isthmus and other points along their frontier.

■ Finland sought conciliation or arbitration in the

dispute with Russia under terms of their nonaggression treaty.

■ The U.S. offered its good offices to Finland and Russia.

■ The German freighter *Idarwild* was sunk by the British warship *Diomede* off the U.S. coast. The American naval ship *Broome* had been following *Idarwild* until the British ship appeared on the scene. *Broome* stood by as the freighter was destroyed. U.S. neutrality practices might have been challenged by Berlin, but they were not.

Nov. 29 Spain ratified its pact of friendship with Germany. Madrid promised the Germans "more than favorable" Spanish neutrality. Secret protocols provided for the use of Spanish ports by the German navy and "cooperative" efforts in police and propaganda matters.

Nov. 30 Russia invaded Finland, launching the Winter War. Red Army forces struck across the border on three fronts. Moscow assumed the action would be the simple military disposition of the "Finnish Problem." Its objectives, seizure of military and naval positions deemed necessary for defense purposes, were to have been completed in 12 days or less. The Russians encountered difficulties from the very beginning, with the Finns resisting fiercely along the Karelian Isthmus, the 90-mile front between the Gulf of Finland and Lake Ladoga. (The war revealed serious deficiencies in the Red Army's leadership, equipment, and morale. Four Soviet Armies, 600,000 men, were involved in the attack from Petsamo in the extreme north to a point 800 miles south in the direction of Viipuri (Vyborg), Finland's second largest city. The Finnish army consisted of about 150,000 men.)

Dec. 1 The Democratic Republic of Finland was established by the Soviets at Terijoki. According to Moscow, "The people already rose in various parts of the country and proclaimed the formation of a democratic republic. Part of the soldiers of Finland's army already have sided with the new government, backed by the people."

Dec. 2 The Finnish Democratic Republic signed a treaty of assistance and friendship with Russia.

Dec. 3 Finland sought intervention by the League of Nations in the war with Russia.

■ British conscription was extended to all men between 19 and 41 years of age, with limited occupational deferments. (Later in the month the upper age was raised to 60 and women between 20 and 30 were required to serve as auxiliaries or in defense jobs.)

BRITAIN'S ANTISUBMARINE BOMBS

Few military weapons developed in peacetime were more disappointing in combat than the British 100-pound antisubmarine bomb. In most cases it was impossible to gauge its effectiveness, but on Dec. 3, 1939, a British submarine was attacked by mistake and the bomb was revealed as almost totally ineffective. H.M.S. *Snapper* received a direct hit at the base of its conning tower from an RAF coastal patrol bomber. Fortunately for the sub crew, the lethal power was limited to four broken light bulbs in the control room. A crash program was then ordered for depth charges to be dropped from aircraft.

Dec. 5 Russia rejected League proposals to settle the war with Finland. Moscow claimed it was no longer at war, having concluded a peace with its puppets. The Soviets said the Finnish Democratic Republic had requested intervention on Dec. 1.

Dec. 7 Russian forces advanced to the main Finnish defense line along the Karelian Isthmus.

Dec. 8 The U.S. protested the British embargo on German exports, stating, "Whatever may be said for or against measures directed by one belligerent against another, they may not rightfully be carried to the point of enlarging the rights of a belligerent over neutral vessels and their cargoes, or otherwise penalizing neutral states or their nationals in connection with their legitimate activities."

Dec. 9 The Soviet news agency TASS carried a report that Germany was sending supplies to the Finns. Actually, Germany was maintaining its neutrality, but Italy was shipping material to Finland through Germany. Moscow-Berlin relations were strained, nonetheless, but the Italians continued to aid the Finns in their "Anti-Bolshevik" war.

Dec. 10 Finland issued a general appeal for aid, stating it had been attacked by Russia "without the slightest cause." Helsinki added that "our

position as the active outpost of western civilization gives us the right to expect the active resistance of other civilized nations."

■ The U.S. granted Finland $10 million credit for agricultural supplies, a gesture largely due to Finland's unique payment of war debts to the United States.

Dec. 11 Finland asked for concrete aid, "not merely words of encouragement," from the League of Nations.

Dec. 12 Russia turned down a League appeal for a cease-fire and mediation on Finland.

■ Adhering to Admiralty instructions to refrain from unrestricted submarine warfare, the British submarine *Salmon* permitted the 52,000-ton German liner *Bremen* to proceed to Germany. The *Bremen* had been intercepted off the Norwegian coast on her return from New York.

Dec. 13–17 The *Graf Spee* was trapped in the Battle of the River Plate. At 6:16 A.M. on the 13th, the British heavy cruiser *Exeter* identified a German pocket battleship in the mouth of the River Plate off the coast of Uruguay. It turned out to be the *Graf Spee*, the warship-raider which had accounted for the sinking of nine Allied ships (50,000 tons) since the beginning of the war. For the rest of the day the *Graf Spee* was engaged in a running battle with *Exeter*, the British light cruiser *Ajax* and the New Zealand light cruiser *Achilles*. *Exeter*, *Ajax*, and *Graf Spee* were heavily damaged, and the German ship was forced to enter Montevideo harbor, where, by international law, she was permitted temporary neutral sanctuary. On instructions from Berlin, the *Graf Spee*'s captain scuttled the ship on the 17th in full view of thousands who had gathered on the Montevideo waterfront. Captain Hans Langsdorff of the *Graf Spee* committed suicide three days later. The incident was significant in that the Royal Navy showed it could still operate throughout the world and take action against marauding German raiders.

Dec. 14 Hitler ordered the German High Command to "investigate how one can take possession of Norway." A former Norwegian war minister, Vidkun Quisling, had met with Hitler the previous summer and encouraged the Germans to occupy Norway as far back as the previous summer. Quisling, a long-time associate of *Reichsleiter* Alfred Rosenberg, had already discussed the seizure of Norwegian ports in collaboration with the German navy three days earlier with the Commander-in-Chief Grand Admiral Erich Raeder.

■ The League of Nations expelled Russia after branding her an aggressor in violation of treaties with Finland, the League Covenant, and the Pact of Paris. Never before had such action been taken against a League member. The League agreed to coordinate international aid programs for the Finns.

Dec. 16 Ciano delivered a violent attack on the Soviet Union in a speech before the Fascist assembly in Rome. The foreign minister's tone had been reflected in the Italian press and radio. It was more than political support. Since the invasion, Italy had sent volunteers to fight with the Finns and large quantities of military equipment.

Dec. 18 Twelve of 24 RAF Wellingtons were shot down by German fighters while attempting to attack naval targets around Wilhelmshaven and Schillig Roads.

■ Hitler met Quisling again and promised him German financial support in return for assistance he would render the German Armed Forces High Command.

Dec. 19 The German passenger liner *Columbus* was scuttled about 450 miles east of Cape May, New Jersey. The *Columbus* had been trailed by the American cruiser *Tuscaloosa* since leaving Vera Cruz, Mexico, with the U.S. ship constantly reporting the German's position by radio for any and all ships to hear. The captain of the *Columbus* felt his position was untenable and he could not avoid seizure or sinking. He concluded scuttling was the only course of action. The *Tuscaloosa*'s actions made the U.S. position of neutrality highly suspect, but Berlin never protested for fear of irritating the U.S. and pushing it into the war.

Dec. 20 The U.S. embargoed the delivery of plans, plants, and technical information required for the production of aviation gasoline to "certain countries" engaged "in unprovoked bombing or machine-gunning of civilian populations from the air." It was the first gesture in what was called a "moral embargo."

Dec. 21 Rumania signed a new economic agreement with Germany.

Dec. 22 The Finns launched an unexpected major counterattack against the Russians.

Dec. 23 Protests were filed with Britain, France, and Germany by 21 Latin American republics over the *Graf Spee* incident, which they claimed violated the neutrality of American waters. British detention and destruction of German merchantmen by British warships were also noted.

Dec. 26 The British began mining the east coast from the Moray Firth to the Thames estuary.

Dec. 27 Washington protested the British seizure of U.S. mail en route to Europe.

■ France and Britain began seeking permission from Sweden for the shipment of "unofficial" aid to Finland through Sweden.

■ Two German army noncommissioned officers were killed by Poles in a Warsaw suburb bar. The bar owner was immediately hanged and 120 Poles selected at random were shot and killed.

■ Indian troops began arriving in France to join the British Expeditionary Force.

Dec. 29 Finnish forces administered a resounding defeat to the Russians at Suommusalmi.

Dec. 30 Hitler vowed to continue the war: ". . . the Jewish reactionary warmongers have awaited this hour for years. They had prepared and were unwilling to cancel their plans for the destruction of Germany. Those warmongers want war. They shall have it."

■ China's revivified air force was dealt a crushing defeat over Liuchow. Forty Chinese fighters challenged 13 Japanese Type-96 planes. In the ensuing air battle 14 of the Chinese planes were shot down without a Japanese loss.

(OPPOSITE, TOP) *German troops march by a knocked out French tank near Sedan.*

(OPPOSITE, BOTTOM) *London became a battleground of war.*

1940

Germany appears unstoppable until the Battle of Britain.

Jan. Chinese military units began mining the Yangtze and Whangpoo rivers to obstruct Japanese shipping. During the next 12 months, the Chinese claimed the mines destroyed 12 Japanese warships, 45 transports, 6 merchant ships, and 66 smaller craft.

Jan. 2 Soviet forces launched major offensive actions against Finnish positions on the Karelian Isthmus.

■ Washington again protested Britain's interference with the U.S. mail, specifically the inspection of postal material on American and other neutral ships and the censorship of mail on ships involuntarily in British ports.

Jan. 3 Roosevelt requested $1.8 billion for national defense in his annual budget request to Congress.

■ Mussolini sent a placating letter to Hitler to help offset Italy's condemnations of Germany's pact with Russia, but the Duce continued to undercut the German move: "The solution of your Lebensraum is in Russia and not elsewhere."

Jan. 4 Göring was given total authority over all German industries involved in the production of war materials.

Jan. 5 Leslie Hore-Belisha was dismissed as British minister of war. He was succeeded by Oliver Stanley.

Jan. 8 The Finns scored a major victory on the Karelian front, wiping out the entire Russian 44th Division.

■ Britain began rationing food. Butter, sugar, bacon, and ham were limited to four ounces per adult each week. German weekly rations then were 32 ounces of all meats and fats, 8 ounces of sugar, two pints of milk, plus restrictions on clothes, soap, shoes, and boots.

Jan. 13 Fearing a German spring offensive, Belgium ordered full-scale mobilization. Holland canceled all army leaves.

Jan. 14 Admiral Mitsumasa Yonai was named to head a new Japanese government.

Jan. 15 Belgium refused a request from Britain and France to grant transit rights across Belgian territory.

Jan. 20 Britain's first lord of the Admiralty, Winston Churchill, warned the uncommitted nations of Europe their best chance of survival was to join the Allies. Churchill said of the neutrals: "Each one hopes that if he feeds the crocodile enough, the crocodile will eat him last. All of them hope that the storm will pass before their turn comes to be devoured."

■ Churchill also condemned Russia's invasion of Finland, increasing fears in Moscow that Britain and France might intervene. *Izvestia* denounced Churchill as "the greatest enemy of the Soviet Union."

General Ernst Busch (at left) inspects German defenses along the Siegfried line.

■ The U.S. protested delays imposed on American ships by British authorities at Gibraltar.

■ Hitler informed his military leaders the invasion of France and the Low Countries would have to be postponed at least until March.

Jan. 21 The British cruiser *Liverpool* stopped the Japanese ship *Asamu Maru* off the coast of Honshu, Japan, and removed twenty-one German male passengers. Tokyo protested the action but subsequently agreed not to transport German military reservists attempting to return home.

Jan. 22 Pope Pius XII condemned German rule in Poland.

Jan. 23 An opposition peace resolution was rejected in the South African legislature by a vote of 81 to 59.

■ Britain and France said their ships would not honor the Pan-American neutrality zone and would attack any German vessel operating in hemispheric waters.

Jan. 24 With recurrent reports of an imminent invasion by Germany, Chamberlain reassured Belgium of Britain's pledge to assist the Belgians if they were attacked.

Jan. 26 The U.S. permitted its 1911 commerical treaty with Japan to lapse. Hull informed Tokyo future trade between the two countries would be conducted on a day-to-day basis.

Jan. 29 Moscow informed the Swedish government that Russia was willing to conclude a settlement with Finland.

Feb. France began receiving shipments of heavy water from the Norsk Hydro plant. The Norwegian facility at Vemork was the only one in the world producing the fluid which served as a "moderator" in atomic research. French officials (security agents, in fact) contracted for Norsk Hydro's entire heavy-water production, which was projected at more than 200 pounds a year, for an atomic pile. Germany was denied the heavy water although it had requested Norsk Hydro's output earlier (through a representative of I. G. Farben, the German industrial giant). Dr. Hans Seuss, one of Germany's leading atomic scientists, had sought heavy water for experiments which could lead to a controlled atomic explosion.

Feb. 1 In a conciliatory speech, Foreign Minister Hachiro Arita said Japan was "anxious to see the development of China's trade with other powers and [would] welcome foreign investments in China as long as they are of a purely economic character."

■ Russian forces launched another attack to break Finnish defenses on the Karelian Isthmus.

Feb. 4 Members of the Balkan Entente (Rumania, Yugoslavia, Greece, and Turkey) declared their neutrality.

Feb. 5 Britain and France decided to send military aid to Finland.

Feb. 9 Roosevelt sent Under Secretary of State Sumner Welles to Britain, France, Germany, and Italy, to report back on "present conditions in Europe." Welles was actually sounding out the prospects for peace but found no interest in any of the Axis or Allied capitals. The omission of Russia from Welles's itinerary was significant. The Soviet Union was a pariah among nations. Its Finnish and Polish invasions were roundly condemned internationally. With Welles visiting the other major combatants, Moscow's suspicions of the West deepened and added to Russia's sense of isolation.

Feb. 10 Germany and the Soviet Union concluded an expanded trade treaty involving increases in material to be exchanged. (By the time Germany invaded Russia, Moscow had delivered 1.5 million tons of grain, a million tons of mineral oil, and vast amounts of chrome and manganese. Germany procrastinated during the 16 months the treaty remained in effect but did provide substantial amounts of raw materials and military goods, including the heavy cruiser *Lützow*.)

Feb. 11 Intense fighting developed between the Russians and Finns on the Karelian front as the Red Army launched what was to become the decisive assault on the Mannerheim line. About 140,000 Russians attacked on a 12-mile front, a massive concentration of seven men each yard.

Feb. 12 The Finnish cabinet authorized moves to end the war against the Russians. It became apparent the Karelian defense line would not hold. At the same time, Finland requested aid from Sweden (which Stockholm rejected).

THE MOLOTOV COCKTAIL

Despite its name, the Molotov cocktail was *not* of Russian origin. It was the term coined by Finnish soldiers fighting the Russians in the Winter War of 1939–1940 and clearly not meant to flatter the Soviet foreign minister.

Bottles filled with gasoline and ignited before tossing were probably first used by infantrymen against tanks in the Spanish Civil War. The Finns perfected the crude but effective weapon when they found themselves woefully short of any kinds of guns to stop the onrushing Russian armor.

At the onset of the Winter War the Finnish state liquor board thoughtfully provided the army with fifths (empty, it is assumed). The bottles were filled with a combination of gasoline, kerosene, and tar. Ignition was achieved by wrapping a soaked rag around the neck or by attaching an ampul of sulfuric acid to the bottle.

It is estimated that about 70,000 Molotov cocktails were hurled at the invading Russian tanks during the war. Given the fact that 2,300 of the tanks were lost in less than four months of fighting, the Molotov cocktails must have been successful. The more credible evidence of their effectiveness, however, is that the Russians turned the weapon used against them on the Germans just a short time later.

■ The first contingent of ANZAC (Australian and New Zealand) troops arrived in Egypt.

Feb. 14 Britain began arming its merchant ships operating in the North Sea.

Feb. 15 Germany declared any armed British merchant ship would be treated as a combatant.

Feb. 16 British raiders freed naval prisoners of war in Norwegian waters in the *Altmark* episode. *Altmark* was one of the German ships most sought after by the Royal Navy at this time. The tanker and supply ship had served the now scuttled *Graf Spee*. To the British it was a prison ship, for *Altmark* was known to have aboard hundreds of merchant seamen rescued from the nine ships destroyed by the *Graf Spee*. After a hemispheric search the *Altmark* was located at Trondheim, Norway, a neutral port. The British destroyer *Cossack* followed her out of Trondheim on the morning of the 16th when *Altmark* tried to break out, but she sought refuge in the Jössing Fjord on the southwest tip of Norway when pursued. *Cossack* entered the fjord with five other men-of-war and demanded release of the prisoners. The Germans refused, and the Norwegian authorities insisted *Altmark* was unarmed and had been searched. Captain Philip Vian, commander of the Fourth Flotilla Group, ordered an armed party from *Cossack* to board *Altmark*. The Germans were overpowered after a brief skirmish. The British found—and freed—299 British prisoners and quickly steamed to Britain, leaving *Altmark* intact. What the British did may have been a violation of international law, but German and Norwegian protests were ignored. Hitler felt the incident was proof the British would not respect Norwegian neutrality and ordered accelerated planning for the occupation of Norway.

Feb. 17 Finnish forces began pulling back from the Karelian defense line. The Russians now had assembled 35 divisions (organized under General

Semyon Timoshenko), and the Finns, with 15 depleted divisions, were on the defensive.

■ Britain announced that 400,000 more children would be evacuated from the larger cities and sent to the safer countryside.

Feb. 19 Hull extended the U.S. moral embargo to the Soviet Union.

Feb. 20 Moscow offered new peace terms to Finland.

Feb. 22 Russian forces gained control of the islands in the Gulf of Finland.

Feb. 23 Helsinki requested Sweden and Norway to grant transit rights for foreign troops to enter Finland.

Feb. 24 Germany and Italy signed a trade agreement, with the Italians to receive substantial quantities of coal.

■ German military planners completed details for the offensive into France and the Low Countries.

Feb. 27 Churchill claimed (erroneously) that the Allies had sunk half of Germany's U-boat fleet.

■ Sweden and Norway refused Finland's request for transit rights.

Feb. 28 Finnish forces began pulling back from their positions around Viipuri.

■ Germany warned Sweden not to aid Finland directly or indirectly.

March The U.S. Congress, reluctant to authorize funds beyond "absolute defense needs," began pruning the military budget during the month, killing, among other things, $12 million for Alaskan defense and permitting the purchase of only 57 planes as replacements for the entire Air Corps.

March 1 Hitler issued a formal directive to the German military for the invasion of Norway and Denmark.

March 2 France and Britain formally requested Swedish and Norwegian approval to send Allied troops to Finland through the Scandinavian countries. (Units were to begin arriving by the 20th. Daladier was planning on a force of 50,000 French "volunteers" and 150 aircraft. Britain planned a force which would reach an eventual level of 100,000 men.) The request was rejected. Paris and London were primarily interested in occupying the Swedish iron ore fields and denying their strategic output to Germany.

March 5 Finland agreed to discuss Soviet proposals for ending the war.

March 6 France and Italy concluded a trade agreement providing for an increase in the volume of trade between the two countries.

■ Finnish peace negotiators left for Moscow.

March 9 Britain and France told the Finns troops and planes would be sent to fight the Russians if Helsinki would request such aid.

■ Admiral Raeder told Hitler the British and French might occupy Norway and Sweden under the pretext of aiding the Finns and encouraged an invasion of Norway at the earliest time.

LAW AT WAR

The situation in 1940—of temporary alliances and insecure positions—gave rise to complex issues of international law (a loose generic term since no law seemed to exist in Europe at this time). One of the more fascinating was the dispute over the nickel mines at Petsamo, Finland. They were owned by the Canadian Nickel Company, with the Göring Works of Germany holding a minority interest. Canada and Germany, of course, were at war. The Finns, just defeated by the Russians, were neutral and hoped everyone would just go away. Moscow, however, wanted the Petsamo nickel production. Helsinki said no laws existed to permit cancellation of the concession, so the Russians told the Finns to enact a law permitting abrogations. Finland would not do it. Britain and Canada had no wish for the Germans or the Russians to get the nickel and, since there was no way to transport it to the west, supported the Finns to sit on it. Like many disputes of the time, it was settled in military fashion when Finland aligned itself with Germany and invaded Russia.

March 12 The Russo-Finnish war ended with an agreement signed in Moscow. Russia got an area of about 16,000 square miles, including the Karelian Isthmus, the naval base at Hangö, and the city of Viipuri. Two hundred thousand Finns in the ceded areas were to be sent to Finland. The campaign cost Russia a dear price. More than 68,000 men were killed in action, and 1,600 tanks and 700 aircraft were lost. Finland suffered 24,923 military dead.

March 14 Only three of 30 Chinese fighters escaped destruction when they engaged a flight of 12 Japanese Zeros over Chengtu. The Japanese suffered no losses.

March 18 Hitler and Mussolini conferred at the Brenner Pass. The Duce agreed to join in the war. Italy's choice was to attack either France or Yugoslavia, and Mussolini chose the former because its share of the plunder would be greater.

March 19 Chamberlain defended Britain's lack of assistance to Finland. He said only once did Field Marshal Mannerheim request troop assistance, in January, for 30,000 men to arrive in May. But Chamberlain claimed that while "Germany publicly professed her neutrality," it "made every effort to prevent others from saving Finland." According to Chamberlain, "It was fear of Germany which prevented Norway and Sweden from giving us permission to pass our troops through their countries, the fear of Germany which prevented her (Finland) from making her appeal to us for help."

■ Fifty RAF bombers struck Hörnum, the German seaplane base on the island of Sylt. Photo reconnaissance found no evidence of any damage inflicted.

March 20 Daladier resigned as French premier and was succeeded by Paul Reynaud, who promised a vigorous prosecution of the war.

■ Moscow stated its strong opposition to a proposed Finnish, Norwegian, and Swedish alliance because it would "be directed against the Soviet Union" and run counter to the Russo-Finnish peace treaty.

March 22 Russian forces assumed control over Hangö.

March 28 The Supreme War Council of the Allies agreed neither France nor Britain would enter into separate peace arrangements. A study was ordered "for the bombing of the Russian oil area of the Caucasus," a reflection of concern that the Germans would be fueled by Soviet oil. The council also ordered the mining of Norwegian waters.

March 29 Foreign Minister Molotov declared the Soviet Union would remain neutral in the European war.

March 30 A pro-Japanese government for all of China was proclaimed in Nanking to be headed by Wang Ching-wei. Tokyo stated, "A renascent China has just set out on the road to progress; a new defence is about to commence in East Asia."

■ The U.S. refused to recognize the Japanese puppet Chinese government: "In the light of what has been happening in various parts of China since 1931, the setting up of a new regime at Nanking has the appearance of a further step in a program of one country by armed force to impose its will upon a neighboring country and to block off a large area of the world from normal political and economic relationships with the rest of the world."

■ Hitler decreed that "so far as necessary" arms shipments to Russia would receive priority over deliveries to the German army. This remained in effect until April 14, when he ordered "punctual delivery to Russia only till the spring of 1941."

March 31 Mussolini told his king that Italy must inevitably go to war, but he said it would be "a war parallel to that of Germany to obtain our objectives, which can be summed up in this phrase: Liberty on the seas; a window on the ocean."

April 2 The U.S. fleet sailed from west-coast ports for Pacific maneuvers in the area of Hawaii.

April 4 Churchill was given overall defense responsibilities in Britain.

April 8 British and French ships mined the waters of neutral Norway because "Germany obtains from Norway facilities which place the Allies at a dangerous disadvantage." The Norwegian government protested.

■ The Polish submarine *Orzel* sank the German troop transport *Rio de Janeiro*, one of the invasion-fleet ships, off the south coast of Norway. A few of the troops survived, reached shore, and told the Norwegians they were bound for Narvik to help fight the British. German secrecy was preserved.

■ The British destroyer *Glowworm* was sunk off Norway by the German cruiser *Hipper* after separating from her group to search for a man overboard. *Glowworm* went down quickly, with few survivors, but not before she rammed and seriously damaged *Hipper*.

April 9 Germany invaded Denmark and Norway. In a swift series of land, sea, and air strikes, Germany extended the war, claiming it possessed

Hitler commissioned Joseph Arens, a German artist, to portray the German military in action. This is one of his pen sketch lithographs, captured by U.S. forces.

"documentary proof that England and France had jointly decided, if necessary, to carry out their action through the territory of the Northern States against the will of the latter. . . . Germany has thus preserved the Scandinavian countries and peoples from destruction, and will until the end of the war defend true neutrality in the North." German occupation forces were embraced by Norwegian pro-Nazis led by Vidkun Quisling, whose name henceforth became synonymous with traitor. Quisling proclaimed himself prime minister, though he was as surprised as any Norwegian by the swift German action. Denmark submitted to Germany under protests, but its military forces were directed to offer no resistance. About 10,000 German troops—hidden aboard merchant vessels—stormed ashore at Oslo, Bergen, Kristiansand, Trondheim, and Narvik, while paratroopers seized the airfields of Oslo and Stavanger. The invasion caught the Norwegians completely by surprise. Germany's only major loss was the new heavy cruiser *Blücher*, which was sunk by shore units at the entrance to Oslo. A thousand sailors and soldiers were lost when the ship rolled over after being hit repeatedly. The British Royal Navy reacted too late to block a naval operation it thought the Germans incapable of launching. King Haakon VII and most of the cabinet and parliament (together with the country's gold reserves) escaped by train to Hamar, 70 miles north of Oslo. With the action against Norway and Denmark, Hitler abandoned whatever hopes remained that he could negotiate a peace with France and Britain. The "Phoney War" was over.

■ Denmark's government capitulated when German forces gained all their objectives within four hours. Resistance was almost nonexistent. The Danish army suffered 13 dead and 23 wounded. German casualties were 20. Copenhagen authorities issued the following statement by afternoon: "The government have acted in the honest conviction that we have saved the country from an even worse fate. It will be our continued endea-

vor to protect our country and its people from the disasters of war, and we shall rely on the people's cooperation."

■ The German cruiser *Karlsruhe* was torpedoed and sunk in the Skagerrak south of Kristiansand, Norway.

■ Soviet Foreign Minister Molotov told the German amabassador in Moscow, "We wish Germany complete success in her defensive measures [against Norway and Denmark]."

April 10 Iceland ended Denmark's royal control over the island, and said it would act as an independent state.

■ Norwegian and Danish funds in the U.S. were frozen by Washington. The U.S. also extended its maritime danger zone to include all waters surrounding the Scandinavian countries.

■ Belgium went to a military alert but reaffirmed its neutrality. Brussels rejected an offer of "preventive aid" by Britain and France because it said acceptance would mean abandonment of Belgium's policy of neutrality.

■ The First Battle of Narvik was fought off the Norwegian coast. German and British naval forces suffered equally in this initial full-scale duel, each side losing two destroyers. But five other German destroyers were disabled or severely damaged and would fall easy prey to the pursuing British force.

■ Pilots of the British Fleet Air Arm, flying Blackburn Skuas, sank the German cruiser *Königsberg*, which was docked in Bergen harbor. This was the first sinking of a major warship by aircraft in history. *Königsberg* had been damaged by Norwegian shore batteries during the invasion and could not defend herself against the dive bombing Skuas which scored two fatal bomb hits.

NORWAY AND THE SAPPING OF GERMAN NAVAL STRENGTH

Even though the conquest of Norway was unquestionably a psychological triumph for Germany, its main effect on the future course of the war was how the campaign decimated the already small German fleet. During the Norwegian operation three of Germany's eight cruisers and ten of her twenty destroyers were sunk. The German navy could no longer be considered a major surface force. Only its U-boats remained a strategic element to worry the Allies. Britain's naval effort in Norway was thus significant. The Royal Navy did lose two cruisers and ten destroyers and sloops during the Norwegian campaign, but it was a small price to pay. Although the British did not maintain mastery of the sea, they achieved greater gains by making the German navy impotent for the rest of the war. As a prime example, the Germans were incapable of acting during the Dunkirk evacuation which followed within two months. It would have been difficult if not impossible for the British to have withdrawn the large force from the Continent had the German navy been able to offer an effective challenge across the narrow English Channel.

April 11 King Haakon called on all Norwegians to resist the Germans.
■ The Netherlands moved toward a war footing by approving measures to complete a defense network.

Hitler sent his forces into Norway and Denmark to prevent the Allies from using Scandinavia as an operational base.

April 11–13 In the Second Battle of Narvik, ten British warships—led by the battleship *Warspite*—sank seven German destroyers.

April 15 Japanese Foreign Minister Arita said Tokyo wished to maintain the status quo in the Dutch East Indies, noting that should "the hostilities in Europe be extended to the Netherlands and produce repercussions in the Dutch East Indies, it would . . . interfere with the maintenance and furtherance of . . . economic independence and co-existence and co-prosperity."
■ A combined British, French, and Polish force landed near Narvik. It was essentially a diversionary effort, with the hope of maintaining a toehold in Norway. (Within three days a total of four battalions were ashore in northern Norway, but they were quickly rendered helpless by German aircraft which had established mastery of the skies.)
■ Quisling was removed as Norway's prime min-

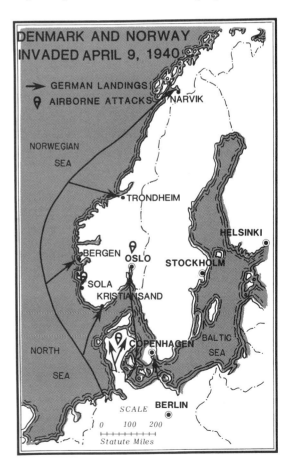

ister by the Germans who felt no need then for even an obsequious puppet.

April 16 Iceland requested recognition and formal relations with the U.S.

■ British forces occupied the Faeroe Islands. They also landed at Andalsnes and Namsos, about a hundred miles south and north of Trondheim, the rail center leading over the mountains of central Norway into Sweden.

April 17 The U.S. said any change in the status of the Dutch East Indies "would be prejudicial to the cause of stability, peace, and security."

April 18 German forces pressed their advances in Norway, breaking out of the Oslo area and advancing toward Hamar to the north.

April 19 The Netherlands declared a state of siege and reaffirmed its desire to remain neutral. A statement said it "shuns" all assistance, "whether offered or actually forced on us."

■ Yugoslavia announced it had smashed a Nazi plot to overthrow the Belgrade government.

■ Two thousand French mountain troops landed in central Norway, but the operation was a logisitics nightmare. The units operated without most of their heavy weapons and equipment.

April 20 Denmark's army was demobilized by the Germans.

■ Germany and Rumania signed a trade agreement, with the latter to receive Czech-made arms and aircraft.

April 24 Germany assumed administrative control over occupied Norway after King Haakon refused to negotiate with the invasion force. Hitler decreed the action "in order to safeguard public order and public life in those parts of Norwegian territory which are under the protection of German troops. . . ."

■ British and French forces failed in a drive to advance toward Trondheim.

THE REINDEER AIRFIELD

Pilots of the Norwegian air force at Vaernes, in central Norway near Trondheim, were faced with a double dilemma. They ran out of fuel and more than two feet of snow had covered their airstrip, making it impossible to take off and escape from the advancing Germans. The second problem was solved when a herd of 3,000 trained white reindeer miraculously

appeared. They were being led by their Lapp keeper in the yearly spring trek from the valleys to the mountains. Bribed by some pure alcohol provided by a medical officer, the herdsman used his reindeer to trample a strip of snow down to a hard surface six inches thick, adequate for aircraft to take off. The Norwegian fliers had no similar good fortune in locating fuel and were forced to abandon their planes.

April 25 Rumania declared a political amnesty, setting the Nazi Iron Guard free to function again.

April 26 Under increasing German pressure, Allied units in northern Norway began retreating.

April 27 Himmler issued orders for the construction of a concentration camp at Auschwitz in occupied Poland. Unlike other such camps, this was to be the central "extermination" facility.

April 30 German units advancing northward from Oslo linked up with the Germans fighting around Trondheim. The important rail center of Dombas was captured.

■ The first enclosed and guarded ghetto in Poland was established by the Germans in Lodz.

May 1 Mussolini told the U.S. ambassador in Rome, William Phillips, that Germany could not be defeated militarily. He said, "Fifteen countries can now be called upon by Germany for every kind of supplies. . . . the blockade of the Allies was therefore completely ineffective."

■ Roosevelt appealed to Italy to refrain from entering the war.

■ The Norwegian force at Lillehammer surrendered.

■ Japanese forces resumed offensive operations with broad attacks in western Hupei Province aimed at extending control over the Yangtze River and adding to the pressures on Chungking, the seat of Chiang Kai-shek's government.

May 2 Mussolini wrote to Roosevelt suggesting "reciprocity," continued recognition of the Monroe Doctrine by Italy in exchange for a U.S. pledge not to interfere in the affairs of Europe.

■ Namsos in Norway was evacuated by the Allies.

May 3 All British troops in central and southern Norway were evacuated, leaving only a small force at Narvik.

■ Greenland appealed to the U.S. for protection.

May 4 The Netherlands cracked down on antigovernment elements, arresting suspected saboteurs and Nazi fifth columnists.

May 5 German troops began pressing north from Trondheim.

■ The 13th Demi-Brigade of the French Foreign Legion landed at Narvik.

May 6 Italy promised to respect the neutrality of Greece and the Balkan countries if Britain and Italy went to war, provided the British did not establish bases there.

May 7 The Netherlands completed its defense mobilization program.

■ Roosevelt ordered the U.S. fleet to remain in Hawaiian waters indefinitely.

May 8 Marshal Timoshenko was named Soviet defense commissar.

May 9 Mussolini made his final decision to bring Italy into the war. It was a personal choice, made without consultation or comment from his staff or advisers.

May 10 Germany invaded the Low Countries. Claiming the British and French were preparing to attack Germany through Belgium, the Netherlands, and Luxembourg, the Germans marched into the countries which had repeatedly stated their desire to remain neutral. Berlin claimed to be "in possession of irrefutable evidence" of Allied invasion plans. Belgium and the Netherlands were said to be conspiring directly with the Allies on action which would threaten Germany itself. The German invasion was aimed primarily at France and a quick knockout blow at the Allied forces in the west.

■ Chamberlain resigned and Winston Churchill became Britain's new prime minister. Chamberlain declared "some new and drastic action must be taken if confidence was to be restored to the House of Commons and the war carried on with the vigor and energy which are essential to victory." A new coalition government was formed with Conservative, Labor, and Liberal participation.

■ Belgium protested Germany's violation of its neutrality, saying, "All the facts and all the documents in the possession of the Belgian govern-

ment prove that the aggression was premeditated."

■ The U.S. froze all assets of the Low Countries and applied the Neutrality Act to the three countries.

■ British troops occupied Iceland to assume defense responsibilities for the strategically-located island. Hitler had considered taking Iceland, but actual plans never advanced beyond preliminaries. (Canadian forces later joined the British garrison, but both nation's units were later withdrawn and replaced by U.S. troops. Iceland had resented the British-Canadian presence but did not object to the neutral Americans.)

May 10–11 Britain launched the first of its strategic bombing raids on Germany. Eight Whitley bombers attacked communication targets in the areas of Geldern, Goch, Aldekerk, Rees, and Wesel in an effort to impede German troop and supply movements.

The Phony War, or Sitzkrieg, ended swiftly May 10, 1940, with the German assault on France and the Low Countries.

THE START OF RETALIATORY AIR RAIDS

A continuing argument is whether the RAF or the Luftwaffe started the raids on civilian population centers which led to unrestricted aerial warfare. The first of these raids is often attributed to the RAF in an attack on Freiburg, Germany, May 10, 1940. Even so distinguished a military historian as British Major General J.F.C. Fuller concluded the Freiburg attack was the raid which touched it off. He held Churchill personally responsible for the attack. Freiburg was bombed. Twenty-four civilians were killed, among them thirteen children playing in a park. But it was the *Germans* who bombed Freiburg. Three Luftwaffe planes planning to attack French targets at Dijon ran into overcast weather. Mistakenly believing they were over Dijon, the pilots dropped their bombs on Freiburg in the kind of sloppy navigation common to all sides at this stage of the war. It was an incredible 140-mile error. Actually, the first British civilian casualties in a raid were killed in the Orkneys on March 16. The British undersecretary of state for air conceded in 1942 that the RAF "began attacks on military lines of communication in western Germany on 11 May, 1940, and on the following nights and days." Whatever one concluded, it was not Freiburg.

May 11 German troops advanced rapidly into the Low Countries, easily reaching one of their key initial objectives—the Albert Canal. Belgian units had failed to demolish many important bridges in their hurried retreat, facilitating the German armor and infantry advance. Fort Eben Emael fell. It was one of the supposedly solid outer defense points to protect Liège.

■ British and French troops landed at Aruba and Curaçao, in the Dutch West Indies. The occupation was described as an effort "to prevent possible German attempts at sabotage in the important oil refineries of these islands."

■ Japan demanded the maintenance of the political and economic status quo in the Dutch East Indies.

May 11–12 The German city of Mönchenglad-

bach, near Düsseldorf, was attacked by 18 Whitley and 18 Hampden bombers of the RAF. The night raid was directed against roads and rail facilities and was considered the first major attack by either side against a "population center." Three of the RAF bombers were lost.

May 12 General Heinz Guderian's XIX Panzer Corps reached the Meuse River.

May 13 Churchill declared in the House of Commons that Britain would prosecute the war at all costs, "for without victory there is no survival." But he added, "I have nothing to offer but blood, toil, tears, and sweat."

Winston Churchill became prime minister in Britain's darkest hour. He is pictured at work as his train rolls through the Kentish countryside.

■ German paratroopers landed in northeast France. Liège fell. The 7th Panzer division under General Erwin Rommel crossed the Meuse River at Huy, driving a wedge into the thinly held front of the French Ninth Army. General George-Hans Reinhardt's XLI Panzer Corps crossed the Meuse at Monthermé against feeble

Ninth Army resistance. Guderian's XIX Panzer Corps established bridgeheads south of the Meuse at Sedan, overpowering the French 55th and 71st divisions, which fell back in panic. Many French Rightists assumed the Paris-based troops of the two routed divisions were mostly communists adhering to the antiwar party line, an erroneous conclusion but one which reflected the growing atmosphere of recrimination.

■ Dutch fortifications were outflanked by the rapidly advancing Germans. Tanks reached the Meuse valley between Dinant and Sedan.

May 14 The government of the Netherlands fled to Britain, saying it "wanted to prevent ever being placed in such a position that it would have to capitulate." All Dutch resistance in the Netherlands ceased. The commander of Dutch forces, General Henri Winkelman, surrendered, saying it was necessary "to prevent annihilation." German Stuka bombers attacked Rotterdam in a brutal raid, the most devastating until then, killing 980 people and destroying 20,000 buildings.

■ The greatest losses ever suffered by the RAF until then occurred when 45 Battles and Blenheims out of a force of 109 planes were shot down while attacking German troop concentrations in the Sedan bridgehead.

■ Roosevelt again wrote to Mussolini, saying, "Reports reaching me from many sources, to the effect that you may be contemplating early entry into the war, have given me great concern." Roosevelt said a further outbreak of war could lead to the "destruction of millions of lives and the best of what we call liberty and culture of civilization."

■ French attempts to counterattack near Sedan broke down in confusion. Guderian's tanks smashed through the French defenses and wheeled to the west in an effort to isolate the Allied forces in Belgium.

May 15 In a disastrous climax to a futile three days of combat, the RAF lost more of its French-based bombers, bringing the total to 100. Half the force was lost in 72 hours.

■ German U-boats resumed patrolling the Western Approaches to the North Atlantic after a three-month diversion caused by the Norwegian campaign.

■ Churchill wrote his first message to Roosevelt as prime minister in continuation of their "inti-

mate private correspondence" which had started when Churchill became first sea lord eight months earlier. Churchill outlined his "immediate needs from the U.S., a loan of up to 50 older destroyers, several hundred late-model aircraft, antiaircraft guns and ammunition, steel, a 'prolonged' visit to Irish ports by U.S. Navy ships, and American use of Singapore 'in any way convenient' to 'keep the Japanese quiet in the Pacific.'"

May 15-16 The largest raid thus far in the RAF's strategic air offensive was launched against oil and steel facilities in the Ruhr. A total of 99 bombers was involved but results were negligible.

May 16 Roosevelt called for sharply increased military spending and modernization of the U.S. Army and Navy. The largest expenditures were for an unprecedented production schedule of 50,000 planes a year. In all, $1.2 billion more was requested in new funds.

■ German units penetrated the northwest extension of the Maginot line.

■ British forces began retreating west of Brussels in an attempt to avoid entrapment.

May 17 The U.S. Navy was ordered to recommission 35 destroyers.

May 18 German forces in Belgium broke through toward the coast, capturing Antwerp. In France, they reached Amiens. A fifty-mile-wide gap in the French line was quickly flooded with the advancing Germans who moved 45,000 vehicles in columns at a rate of 30 miles a day. Cambrai and St.-Quentin were captured.

■ Mussolini abandoned all public pretense of staying out of the war: "Italy is and intends to remain allied with Germany and . . . Italy cannot remain absent at a moment in which the fate of Europe is at stake."

■ Hitler decreed the reincorporation of Eupen, Malmédy, and Moresnet into the German state.

■ Marshal Henri Philippe Pétain was named vice-premier of France.

May 19 General Maxime Weygand was designated commander-in-chief of Allied forces, replacing Gamelin.

■ The French 4th Armored Division under General Charles de Gaulle launched a counteroffensive against the Germans at Laon but was repulsed.

THE KATYN MASSACRE

About 180,000 Polish prisoners of war were transported to the Soviet Union after Poland's collapse. As many as 10,000 were officers, who were imprisoned in camps at Kozielsk, Starobelsk, and Ostashkov. Those at Kozielsk (about 4,000) were removed by the NKVD (the Russian secret police) in March 1940 and sent to the small forest of Katyn, near Smolensk. During April and May they were bound and summarily executed by pistol shots in the base of their skulls (as determined by subsequent exhumation). Stacked corpses in a mass grave were covered with dirt and young trees were planted to obscure the site. Why? According to a postwar apparently sanctioned account given by a Russian official attached to the embassy in London, Stalin had been pressed by the NKVD on what to do with the officers. He wrote the single word "liquidate" as instructions. Some give Stalin the benefit of the doubt and claim he only wished the prison camps removed and that the NKVD took him too literally. Others feel Stalin, as was his wont in the past, simply wished to rid himself of potential trouble by resorting to a simple murderous solution. No one knows what happened to the other 6,000 Polish officer POW's.

SOURCES: James E. McSherry, *Stalin, Hitler, and Europe, 1939–1941*; J.K. Zawodny, *Death in the Forest*; and Stanislaw Mikolajczyk, *The Pattern of Soviet Domination.*

May 20 General Paul von Kleist's panzers reached the English Channel west of Abbeville in France, cutting off all Allied forces to the north.

■ Arthur Seyss-Inquart, minister without portfolio in the German cabinet, was appointed *Reichskommissar* for the Netherlands. He had formerly been governor (*Reichs Stattlalter*) of Austria.

May 21 Berlin claimed the annihilation of the French Ninth Army.

■ Rommel's 7th Division halted a counterthrust by the British Expeditionary Force south of Arras designed to isolate Guderian's Panzer Corps to the west. The Allies were now forced to retreat westward to the Lys River. No further major offensive action was initiated by Allied forces.

May 22 Churchill was granted absolute power over Britain's manpower, financial, and industrial resources to mobilize its war capacity to full power under the Emergency Powers Act.

■ Rumania began to call up all its military reservists.

May 23 Boulogne, Amiens, and Arras were occupied by the Germans.

May 24 Hitler ordered German armored units to halt mop-up operations and to continue toward Paris. If the panzers had continued they would have wiped out the Allied troops caught in ever-smaller pockets. Hitler overruled his commanders on the scene because he was sticking to the original plan of a southward thrust after the breakthrough to the English Channel. The largest concentration, about 380,000 Allied troops, were encircled by German forces around Dunkirk. They were trapped in an area of about 60 square miles, but the main German movement was away from Dunkirk.

Bridges destroyed by the retreating Allies only temporarily delayed the Germans advancing into France and the Low Countries.

■ French leaders concluded the war was lost.

May 26 The evacuation of Allied troops at Dunkirk began. In one of the most dramatic withdrawals in military history, a hastily assembled fleet of 861 ships and boats began pulling what was left of the trapped Allied armies off the beaches of Dunkirk. In a week, 224,585 British and 112,546 French and Belgians were taken to safety. About 40,000 Frenchmen were left behind. A total of 231 of the rescue vessels were sunk, mostly by the Luftwaffe, but German air strikes were restricted by bad weather and the tenacious fighters of the RAF. For all the glory that accompanied the gallant retreat, Dunkirk represented the nadir of the war for Britain.

■ Hitler, after a crucial two-day delay, ordered German troops to attack Dunkirk. The first units could not advance until late in the day, but the main force could not be organized until the following day. "By then," said General Guderian, "it was too late to achieve a great victory."

May 27 The port of Calais on the English Channel—a mere 26 miles from Dover, England—fell to the Germans after determined resistance by the trapped Allied defenders.

May 27–30 RAF fighters fought off German planes attempting to impede the Allied evacuation from Dunkirk. The British downed 179 Luftwaffe aircraft while losing only 29.

May 28 The Belgian army of nearly a half-million men surrendered under orders from King Leopold III, but the government (which had moved to France) repudiated the action. Leopold was ordered deposed.

■ Allied forces, under French General Béthouart, occupied the port of Narvik in Norway.

■ Rumania's Crown Council decided to abandon its policy of straddling the fence between the Germans and the Russians and opted for a policy of collaboration with Berlin. Russia had been demanding southern Bessarabia and frontier clashes between Soviet and Rumanian troops were becoming more common.

May 29 Germany occupied Ypres, Ostend, and Lille.

■ Rumania concluded a trade treaty with Germany, exchanging its oil for German arms.

May 30 Mussolini informed Hitler that Italy would enter the war against France within ten days.

May 31 Roosevelt called on Congress to expand military preparedness "as measured in both machines and men." In addition to the $3 billion already requested until then, Roosevelt called for further authorizations of $1.3 billion.

June 1 The U.S.S. *Washington* was launched at Philadelphia, the first battleship to be added to the American fleet since 1921.

June 3 Norway sued for peace, agreeing on partition of the country: ". . . the Government was bound more and more to come to see that it would not be practically possible to regain for Norwegian control the whole of the rest of Norway in the immediate future."

■ German forces renewed their assault on the Maginot line.

■ Paris was bombed by German aircraft.

■ The U.S. released surplus or outdated stocks of weapons, ammunition, and planes to the British. (June transfers amounted to $43 million.)

June 4 The Dunkirk evacuation was completed. British aircraft losses during the operation totaled 180. Nine British and six French ships were sunk or severely damaged. When the last boat had left, the British had left behind 11,000 machine guns, 1,200 artillery pieces, 1,250 antiaircraft and anti-tank guns, 6,400 antitank rifles, and 75,000 vehicles.

■ Churchill, in Britain's bleakest hour, told the House of Commons: "We shall not flag or fail. We shall fight on the beaches, we shall fight on the landing ground, we shall fight in the fields and in the streets, we shall fight in the hills. We shall never surrender."

CHURCHILL'S BROADCAST DOUBLE

Those present in the House of Commons on June 4, 1940, heard Churchill himself deliver his memorable post-Dunkirk speech, but radio listeners around the world heard the same words later in the day voiced by a 37-year-old actor impersonating the prime minister. The idea was Churchill's. He told the BBC, "I'm rather busy. Get some actor to do it." Norman Shelley of the BBC repertory staff was chosen. He told the London *Daily Mail* in 1979: "I was a fan of Winnie. I had imitated his voice around the BBC. Someone must have remembered this, because they summoned me to the old Transcription Service Studios near Regent's Park, gave me a copy of his speech, sat me down and told me to get on with it. It was just another job. As I recall, I did it in a couple of takes." Churchill approved Shelley's reading before it was broadcast, saying, "Very nice. He's even got my teeth right."

By the time the Germans entered Dunkirk, which was almost totally destroyed, nearly 340,000 Allied troops had escaped capture or death.

June 5 German forces launched their attack on France proper. The French now possessed only 37 divisions, and as General Weygand said, they were nothing but "a line of troops without depth or organization." German troops occupied Dunkirk.

June 6 French Premier Reynaud assumed control of foreign affairs, dropping Daladier as for-

eign minister. General Charles de Gaulle was appointed under secretary of war.

June 7 The Norwegian government fled to Britain and established an administration in exile.

■ British and French troops began withdrawing from Narvik.

By early June the French army of 60 divisions was totally defeated and surrendering en masse.

■ Italy ordered its ships at sea to sail to neutral ports, a further indication of its intention to enter the conflict.

■ French bombers attacked Berlin.

June 8 Rumania accelerated its mobilization, adding five more reserve classes to its call-up.

■ While aiding in the evacuation of Narvik, the British aircraft carrier *Glorious* was sunk by the German warships *Scharnhorst*, *Gneisenau*, and *Hipper*. Inexplicably, the planes on *Glorious* were not flying scouting missions, and the ship was caught totally surprised by the attack. Two destroyers accompanying *Glorious* were also lost.

Of the 1,561 men aboard the three stricken British ships, only 46 survived.

June 9 Norway's High Command ordered the army to stop fighting at midnight: ". . . . it is impossible to continue in this country against a superior power as formidable as Germany. Our defensive forces, which fought two months with spirit and courage, are without necessary war materials, particularly ammunition and fighter planes, and no longer are able to obtain them."

■ British and French forces completed their withdrawal from Narvik. Twenty-five thousand men were brought out under air cover, ending the Allied effort to challenge the Germans on Norwegian soil.

■ German casualties in the Norwegian campaign were 1,317 killed, 1,604 wounded, and 2,375 missing or lost at sea. The Allied dead included 4,400 British, 1,335 Norwegian, and 530 French and Polish. Hitler called the campaign "not only bold, but one of the sauciest undertakings in the history of modern warfare."

■ The French Tenth Army was encircled as a panzer division crossed the Somme River and pressed westward. German infantry pushed across the Oise River east of Paris and established bridgeheads for panzers to charge through to the Marne. German Army Group A launched its offensive to break through to the south over the Aisne. Here, French resistance was determined.

June 10 Italy entered the war. Italian forces invaded France and declared war on France and Britain. Mussolini announced: "We take the field against the plutocratic and reactionary democracies who always have blocked the march and frequently plotted against the existence of the Italian people. . . . We are taking up arms, after having solved the problem of our continental frontiers, to solve our maritime frontiers. We want to break the territorial and military chains that confine us in our sea, because a country of 45 million souls is not truly free if it has not free access to the ocean." Italy's entry into war brought the conflict to the Mediterranean and Africa. Until now it had been confined to central and northern Europe. (Italy was ill-equipped to enter the war. Its army was halted at the border town of Menton, leading Mussolini to delare, "It is the material I need. Even Michelangelo had need of marble to make statues. If he had only clay, he would have become a potter.")

■ Canada delcared war on Italy. Belgium broke relations with Italy.

■ German troops reached the suburbs of Rouen.

■ French reserve forces counterattacked from Juniville and won an initial victory over the Germans trying to break across the Aisne but were eventually driven back in a fierce two-hour battle.

■ France made an urgent plea to the U.S. for help "before it is too late." Officials began fleeing Paris to establish a temporary French seat of government in Tours.

Narvik, in Norway, after a Royal Navy force entered the harbor shortly after it was seized by the Germans.

■ Roosevelt promised to "extend to the opponents of force the material resources of this nation and, at the same time, we will harness and speed up the use of those resources in order that we ourselves in America may have equipment and training equal to the task of any emergency and every defense." He referred to the Italian invasion of France as ". . . the hand that held the dagger has struck it into the back of its neighbor."

■ Three Japanese divisions attacked the Yangtze River port of Ichang, between Hankow and Chungking. The Chinese defenders fell back into the city itself after the Japanese quickly advanced to within five miles of it.

June 11 Roosevelt extended provisions of the U.S. Neutrality Act to include the Mediterranean and the mouth of the Red Sea.

■ Australia, New Zealand, and South Africa declared war on Italy.

■ Panzer units under Kleist and Guderian smashed through Champagne and drove toward Troyes and St.-Dizier. The French pulled back across the Marne at Soissons.

■ Italian aircraft bombed French military bases in Tunisia and Corsica.

■ Premier Reynaud asked Churchill to release France from its pledge not to sign a separate peace arrangement. Churchill rejected the request.

June 11–12 The RAF directed its first raid against Italy. Refueling in the Channel Islands, 36 Whitley bombers were dispatched. Of these, 23 aborted because of the extremely bad weather, 10 dropped their bombs on Turin's Fiat works or alternate targets in the city, two struck Genoa, and one failed to return.

June 12 Britain ordered a total blockade of Italy, which, London charged, "made herself a party to the method of waging war adopted by Germany."

■ Churchill conferred with Reynaud and Weygand in France.

■ German units advanced to within 12 miles of Paris. Reims and Rouen were occupied by the Germans. The British 51st Highland Division was trapped at St.-Valéry.

■ Egypt broke diplomatic relations with Italy.

■ Japan and Thailand signed a nonaggression treaty.

■ Moscow accused Lithuania of conspiring in a military alliance directed against the Soviet Union.

■ Spain declared its neutrality.

■ The U.S. ordered the construction of 22 new warships.

June 13 Paris was declared an open city. Reynaud appealed to President Roosevelt to send "clouds of war planes . . . to crush the evil force that dominates Europe." Pétain told the cabinet, "An armistice is, in my view, the necessary condition for the survival of eternal France."

■ The French cabinet met at the Loire chateau of Cagne. Weygand reported that communists had seized control of Paris.

■ British General Sir Alan Brooke arrived at Rennes to regroup French and British remnants which had escaped capture in the Channel pockets and continue fighting from a "Breton redoubt." German troops crossed the Marne at Château-Thierry.

■ An Italian submarine torpedoed and sank the British light cruiser *Calypso* in the Mediterranean.

Two carefree drunken French soldiers surrender to the advancing Germans.

■ The German raider *Orion* laid a mine field on the approaches to Auckland, New Zealand. (Six days later the steamer *Niagara* struck two of the mines and was sunk.)

June 14 German troops marched into Paris. The Maginot line was breached by the German First Army south of Saarbrücken. With air and artillery support, the Germans easily cracked the supposedly impregnable line, mostly by blindside attacks with flame throwers and grenades.

■ The French government implored the U.S. for aid. "Our divisions are decimated. Generals are commanding battalions. The *Reichswehr* has just entered Paris. We are going to attempt to withdraw our exhausted forces in order to fight new battles. . . . France can continue the struggle only if American intervention reverses the situation by making an Allied victory certain."

■ Russian troops invaded Lithuania on the pretext of anti-Soviet activity by the Lithuanians (a pro-Communist government was established two days later).

■ Spanish troops occupied the Tangier International Zone in Morocco to "guarantee" its neutrality. At the same time the Madrid government told the Germans it was willing to enter the war on the Axis side in exchange for control of Gibraltar, French Morocco, the province of Oran in Algeria, and parts of French West Africa.

■ The pro-Japanese Nanking government of China demanded the withdrawal of all British, French, and Italian troops from China "in order to maintain peace and order and protect the lives and property of the Chinese in the areas concerned."

■ British desert forces surprised and routed the Italian garrison at Fort Capuzzo, an important frontier outpost just inside the Libyan border. Outnumbered overall in North Africa, however, the British chose to abandon the fort and retain mobility.

■ Roosevelt signed the "11 percent Naval Expansion Act," increasing U.S. ship strength by 142,000 tons.

June 15 Verdun—the French city which had been defended so valiantly by Allied troops in World War I—was captured by the Germans. French forces began pulling out of the Maginot line.

■ Churchill urgently requested Roosevelt to turn over overage U.S. destroyers to Britain. With the Royal Navy reduced to only 68 destroyers in fit condition to face a German invasion (compared to the 433 operating in 1918), Churchill said, "We must ask therefore as a matter of life or death, to be reinforced with these destroyers." The proposal was not well received by the U.S. military or Congress. To the contrary, it was even suggested that, given its dire position, Britain should surrender. The chairman of the Senate Forcign Relations Committee, Key Pittman of Nevada—a nominal interventionist—proposed Britain dispatch its remaining ships to North America and then capitulate: "It is no secret that

German troops entering Paris parade past the Arc de Triomphe.

After taking Verdun, German troops goosestep past the French World War I memorial.

government of the Third Republic was formed at Bordeaux for the purpose of negotiating an end to the war. Reynaud proposed Pétain as his successor, and President Albert Lebrun agreed.

June 17 France sued for peace. Pétain asked the Germans for armistice terms but indicated "peace with honor" was an essential condition. In a speech over French radio shortly after noon, Pétain said, "With a heavy heart, I tell you today that it is necessary to stop the fighting."

■ German forces poured through the Maginot line and reached Belfort. French units in Alsace and Lorraine were completely enveloped by panzer units.

■ Britain announced it would carry on the fight against Germany alone: "What has happened in France makes no difference to British faith and purpose. We have become the sole champions now in arms to defend the world cause."

■ A belated shipment of 150 U.S. aircraft left Halifax bound for France.

■ The U.S. Senate passed a resolution which precluded the recognition of territory in the Western Hemisphere transferred from one non-American power to another.

■ Moscow announced that Estonia and Latvia, like Lithuania, would come under Soviet domination. Russian troops would have free rights of passage and new friendly governments would be formed. The pretext was that the Baltic states were planning joint military defense measures against Russia, and Moscow "considers that such a situation cannot be tolerated any longer." Russian troops immediately moved to occupy the two countries.

■ Two Chinese army corps counterattacked in the Ichang area and reentered the ancient city which had been abandoned the week before. Japanese losses were heavy, but the Chinese decided to pull out again. In six weeks of fighting in Hupei Province the Japanese had suffered about 20,000 casualties, to 50,000 for the Chinese. Another lull in the fighting now developed.

■ The U.S. Navy requested an appropriation of $4 billion to construct a "two-ocean navy."

Great Britain is totally unprepared for defense and that nothing the United States has to give can do more than delay the result. . . . It is to be hoped that this plan [withdrawal of the British fleet] will not be too long delayed by futile encouragement to fight on. It is conclusively evident that Congress will not authorize intervention in the European war."

June 15–16 Russia delivered ultimatums to Latvia and Estonia "to achieve the honest and loyal execution" of their mutual assistance treaties, which would put the Baltic states under Moscow's rule. (Pro-Moscow governments were in place in Latvia on the 20th and Estonia by the 22nd.)

June 16 In a desperate bid to bolster France, Britain offered a union of their empires. Reynaud resigned as premier—because he refused to issue a cease-fire order—and was succeeded by Marshal Pétain.

■ German forces reached the Swiss border at Pontarlier.

June 16–17 At midnight, the last constitutional

American strategy until now had always centered on a Pacific fleet.

June 18 General de Gaulle, broadcasting from London, called on Frenchmen to join him in continuing the fight: "Whatever happens, the flame of French resistance must not be extinguished." The then largely unknown officer said, "France has lost a battle. But France has not lost the war."

■ The French army was in full retreat. The last of the RAF squadrons was evacuated from France.

■ Churchill delivered his memorable speech in the face of adversity: "Let us brace ourselves to our duties, and so bear ourselves that if the British Empire and its Commonwealth last for a thousand years, men will say, 'This was their finest hour'."

■ General Auguste Noguès, commander of French forces in North Africa, cabled Weygand that his forces were "burning" to fight. Noguès was expecting new Dewoitine D520 fighter planes, the still-intact French navy, and large shipments of U.S. equipment.

■ France assured the U.S. its fleet would not be turned over to the Germans. Instead, "it might be sent overseas or it might be sunk."

■ Hitler and Mussolini conferred in Munich on dividing up the spoils of their conquest of France. The Duce was disappointed that Italy's colonial empire was not to be expanded as Hitler permitted the French to retain far more territory and independence than Mussolini desired. Hitler suggested to Mussolini that Madagascar could be converted into a "State of Israel."

■ Molotov extended "the warmest congratulations of the Soviet Government on the splendid success of the German Armed Forces."

■ The U.S. told Germany and Italy it would not recognize or acquiesce in any attempt to transfer "any geographic region of the Western Hemisphere from one non-American power to another non-American power."

■ Bulgaria demanded the area of Dobruja from Rumania.

June 19 Lyon fell to the Germans.

■ General de Gaulle called on Frenchmen in France's colonies and possessions abroad to continue the fight: "Every Frenchman who still bears arms has the absolute duty to continue resistance."

■ The Polish and Belgian governments-in-exile were moved to London from France.

■ Tokyo announced it would object to any change in the status of French Indochina because of Japan's geographic proximity and special economic interests in the Asian colony.

June 20 France asked Italy for its surrender terms.

■ A Japanese military mission arrived in Vietnam with the permission of French authorities in Indochina. The area of Tonkin—adjacent to China—was opened to Japanese military control. At the same time Tokyo called for an embargo on all arms shipments to China from French Indochina.

June 21 France surrendered to Germany. The agreement was signed at Compiègne in the same railway car in which Germany had surrendered 22 years before. Hitler personally witnessed the humiliation of the French. For him and the German people it was sweet revenge. Just before he led his generals to the ceremony, Hitler noted the granite monument which the French had built after their victory. It carried the inscription: "Here on the eleventh of November 1918 succumbed the criminal pride of the German people." Pétain explained his country's loss: "Too few children, too few arms, too few allies, these are the causes of our defeat." Hitler now expected an early end to the conflict. He told Jodl, "The British have lost the war, but they don't know it. One must give them time, and they will come round."

■ Italian troops drove into France along the entire frontier between Mt. Blanc and the Mediterranean.

■ King Carol II of Rumania assumed dictatorial powers "to guide the moral and material life of the nation."

■ National defense taxes of $994 million per year were voted by the U.S. Congress.

■ Prince Konoye formed a new Japanese cabinet with General Hideki Tojo as minister of war.

June 22 Polish officials and remnants of the Polish army which had fought in France sailed for England from St.-Jean-de-Luz aboard the Polish liner *Batory*, the last ship to escape from France.

June 23 Laval was named vice premier of France. Weygand formally ousted de Gaulle from the government.

By June 20, 1940, a cease-fire was declared in France and German troops marched to occupy the remainder of the fallen country at will.

CASUALTIES OF THE LIGHTNING WAR

The six weeks of fighting which ended in the fall of France and the Low Countries was achieved with relatively light losses on the German side, only a third of the number of their men lost in the Battle of Verdun in 1916.

German Casualties		Allied Casualties	
Killed	27,074	Killed	90,000
Wounded	111,034	Wounded	200,000
Missing	18,384	Prisoners and	
		Missing	1,900,000

(Total British casualties - 68,111)
(Total Belgian casualties - 23,350)
(Total Dutch casualties - 9,779)

AIRCRAFT LOSSES

Luftwaffe	1,284	
RAF	931	(477 fighters)
French	560	(225 on the ground)

■ German troops advanced at will along the entire French Atlantic coast area.

June 24 France signed the formal surrender document with Italy.

■ Admiral Jean Darlan ordered all French naval captains to keep their ships from falling under German control.

■ French troops holding out in the Vosges Mountains laid down their arms. The surrender at Le Donon netted the Germans 22,000 prisoners.

■ The Pétain government declared it would remain in France and exercise domestic control: "The government considered that it was its duty to remain in France and share the fate of all Frenchmen and that France could recover only through reflection of order and labor."

■ France yielded control of its sector in Shanghai to the Japanese.

■ Tokyo called on the British to halt the shipment of war goods to China through Burma and Hong Kong.

June 24–25 One hundred fifteen British Commandos staged their first operation of the war near Boulogne in France in an attempt to obtain information on German defenses and bring back prisoners. Two German sentries were killed, one commando was slightly wounded, and little was learned.

June 25 All fighting ended in France.

■ Churchill said Britain had agreed to the French armistice but only on condition the "French fleet is dispatched to British ports and remains there while the negotiations are conducted." But, Churchill stated, the French had agreed that French warships, except those needed to protect France's colonial interests, "shall be collected in ports to be specified and there demobilized and disarmed under German or Italian control."

■ The Italian ambassador in Berlin issued a peace feeler to London through the U.S. embassy which was immediately communicated to—and rejected by—the British.

June 26 Russia issued an ultimatum to Rumania to cede Bessarabia and the Ukrainian-majority area of Bukovina to the Soviet Union within 48 hours.

■ Hitler urged Mussolini to launch an offensive from Libya toward the Suez Canal. "Any such strike," he said, "would be a great gain." The Italians had a 215,000-man force in Libya, while the British had only 36,000 troops in Egypt, plus a 30,000-man Egyptian army which was not trained for combat. British Middle East forces were also faced with a severe supply problem. With the Mediterranean insecure at best, ships had to haul war goods 12,000 miles from Britain to Egypt around the Cape of Good Hope, a six-week trip.

■ A new strict set of rules for workers was established by the Soviet Union as part of a campaign to boost industrial output, including the manufacture of war materiel. Among other things, Russians were now required to work eight hours a day instead of the seven which was the maximum established by the constitution.

June 27 German troops reached the French-Spanish frontier.

■ The British war cabinet decided that French ships in North African ports would not be permitted to return to France, no matter what action or aggravation that might entail. France then had a substantial task force in Alexandria, six cruisers in Algiers, and four battleships and a cruiser at Mers-el-Kebir.

■ The French army commander in Syria accepted terms of the surrender to Germany.

■ Roosevelt declared a "national emergency."

■ Moscow decreed all factories begin seven-day workweeks, the first indication of Russia going to a full war footing.

June 28 Britain recognized the Free French government of de Gaulle.

■ The Germans told the French government that French naval ships would be interned in French-retained territory and would not have to proceed to Nazi-occupied bases. Without knowing this, the British organized a task force at Gibraltar to destroy the French ships if necessary to deny them to the Germans.

■ The Channel Islands were evacuated and demilitarized by the British.

■ Churchill turned down an unofficial peace feeler received from the Germans through the papal nuncio in Switzerland.

■ Rumania capitulated to Moscow's ultimatum and transferred Bessarabia and northern Bukovina to Soviet control, losing 17 percent of its territory (19,300 square miles) and a population estimated at 3,500,000.

■ As a move to control possible subversion, the U.S. Alien Restoration Act became law, making it illegal to advocate overthrow of the government. It also required the registration and fingerprinting of all aliens.

■ Italo Balbo, Italy's celebrated aviator and at the time governor general of Libya, was killed when his plane was accidentally shot down by Italian antiaircraft fire over Tobruk.

June 29 Japan declared the South Seas as an area where it had a special interest, broadening its assumed sphere of influence. Foreign Minister Arita said, "The countries of East Asia and the regions of the South Seas are geographically, historically, racially, and economically very closely related. . . . The uniting of all those regions in a single sphere on a basis of common existence, insuring thereby the stability of that sphere, is a national conclusion."

June 30 The Channel Island of Guernsey was occupied by German forces.

July 1 Sir Stafford Cripps, Britain's ambassador to Russia, carried a personal letter from Churchill to Stalin in which the British leader called for consultation between them in the face of Germany's intention to dominate all of Europe. Stalin responded candidly, saying that Moscow's policy was to avoid conflict with Germany. He did predict, however, that Hitler might decide to attack the Soviet Union in the spring of 1941 if Britain should lose the war by then. (Interestingly, Stalin turned over a copy of Russia's minutes of the meeting to the Germans two weeks later.)

■ A one-ton bomb was dropped on the town of Kiel by the RAF. It was the largest weapon delivered thus far in the war. The Hampden bomber had tried to hit German warships in the harbor and failed on six runs. The bomb was finally dropped in a nonmilitary area because of the defect in the release mechanism.

■ Rome threatened to take military action against Greece, claiming to have proof "that British warships were using Greek territorial waters for the purpose of attack against the naval forces of Italy. This is an intolerable state of things. . . ."

■ Germany rejected the U.S. note on nonrecognition of any territorial transfer in the Americas to another European power. Berlin said the Monroe Doctrine was "legally valid only on condition that the American nations for their part do not interfere in the affairs of the European Continent."

■ Germany called on the United States to withdraw its diplomatic missions from Norway, Belgium, the Netherlands, and Luxembourg by July 15 since Berlin would handle the foreign relations of those occupied countries.

■ Former Prime Minister Chamberlain, after talking to his long-time friend, the American ambassador, wrote in his diary: "Saw Joe Kennedy who says everyone in USA thinks we shall be beaten before the end of the month."

■ At the request of Germany, Rumania renounced the British guarantee of Rumanian territorial integrity.

■ The French government was moved to Vichy.

■ Britain said it would not permit the occupation of Syria by the Axis.

■ German troops landed on the Channel Island of Jersey.

July 2 Hitler issued orders for the invasion of Britain (Operation SEALION).

■ Rumania embraced naziism in announcing a "new orientation." In addition to the menacing posture of Russia, Hungary and Bulgaria were becoming bellicose. Bucharest wanted to impress Berlin with its unqualified commitment. Nazi Iron Guards were released from prison and one of its leaders was named to the cabinet. British employees were expelled from the oil fields. Allied ships were harassed on the Danube.

■ The U.S. Congress gave the president discretionary authority to prohibit export of any war materiel "in the interest of national defense."

July 3 British naval units sank or seized the ships of the French fleet in the Algerian ports of Oran and Mers-el-Kebir. London explained to the French, "It is impossible for us now to allow your fine ships to fall into the power of our German or Italian enemies." The battleships *Bretagne, Provence,* and *Dunkerque* were sunk or disabled and several submarines and auxiliaries were sytematically destroyed. Although the French had planned to resist if attacked by the British, they had no time. French casualties were heavy; 1,267 men were killed. The battle cruiser *Strasbourg* escaped to Toulon. At the same time, all French warships in British ports were taken over by the

Royal Navy, although the uncompleted and unarmed *Jean Bart* remained under Vichy control in Casablanca,

■ Vichy declared de Gaulle a "stalking horse" for "British imperial interests."

July 4 The Pétain government of France broke off diplomatic relations with Britain because of the Royal Navy's attacks on the French fleet. Pétain, Laval, and Darlan urged a declaration of war against Britain and discussed military action which might be initiated, including an attack, with the Italians, against Alexandria to free the French ships there. War was not declared, primarily because of the arguments of Foreign Minister Paul Baudouin that war with Britain would worsen France's already pitiful condition. Laval was most insistent on a declaration of war, as he was to state later: "France has never had, and will never have, a more relentless enemy than Great Britain. All our history attests to it."

■ Churchill said, "I have never in my experience seen discussed in a Cabinet so grim and somber a question as to what we were to do about the French Fleet."

■ King Carol appointed a pro-Axis government in Rumania.

July 5 Rumania proclaimed its friendship with Germany and Italy.

■ French aircraft from Morocco attacked Gibraltar but caused negligible damage. The action was taken by Vichy because of the Royal Navy's destruction of the French ships in North Africa.

■ Unarmed German soldiers were granted rail transit rights across Sweden by Stockholm.

■ Roosevelt banned the shipment, without license, of strategic minerals, chemicals, aircraft parts and engines to Japan. It marked the beginning of the limited embargo against Japan.

July 8 Royal Navy aircraft from the carrier *Hermes* torpedoed and immobilized the French battleship *Richelieu* at Dakar, French West Africa.

July 9 French warships in the Egyptian port of Alexandria were demilitarized by their crews under pressure from the British.

■ Rumania was declared to be under the military protection of Germany.

■ British and Italian naval units fought an inconclusive sea battle in the Mediterranean.

July 10 German bombers attacked Swansea and

Falmouth as well as convoys in the English Channel.

■ The French parliament voted itself out of existence, giving Marshal Pétain dictatorial powers.

■ Roosevelt again asked Congress to increase the U.S. military budget, including funds for 15,000 new planes and a 1,200,000-man army. He outlined plans for an eventual 2,000,000-man force.

July 11 Pétain was named "Chief of the French State." He immediately decreed new basic laws for France and outlined the policies which Vichy would pursue: "France stands alone, attacked today by England for whom she consented to many severe sacrifices. . . . International capitalism and socialism exploited and degraded France. Both participated in preliminaries of the war. We must create a new order in which we no longer admit them."

■ The Luftwaffe assured General Franz Halder, chief of the German army General Staff, that it could eliminate the RAF within a month or less.

■ Rumania announced its withdrawal from the League of Nations, a meaningless gesture but one which appeased the vocal Nazi minority and Germany.

■ A British Commando force was badly mauled in an attack on Guernsey.

July 15 The German General Staff directed that plans be completed to invade southern England some time after August 15. The force was to land along a 200-mile front, from Ramsgate to Lyme Bay.

■ Vichy refused a German request to use French military bases in North Africa, an act of considerable courage which Hitler, surprisingly, accepted.

July 16 The Japanese cabinet resigned after Minister of War General Shunroku Hata forced its hand by stepping down and demanding sweeping governmental changes. Prince Konoye again became prime minister.

July 18 Britain complied with Japan's demand of June 24 to stop shipments of war materiel to China through Burma and Hong Kong. This action ended all traffic on the Burma Road and cut off vital seaborne shipments through the last major port available to the Chinese government. Only the difficult Siberian routes remained open. Britain tried to placate the Japanese by the Burma-Hong Kong closings and was in no position to rebuff Tokyo. The British said they "were bound to have regard for the present world situation, nor could they ignore the dominant fact that we ourselves are engaged in a life or death struggle."

July 19 Hitler lamely offered a vague peace to

Emperor Hirohito and his minister of war, Lieutenant General Hideki Tojo, in a Tokyo ceremony. By now the military had almost complete control over the Japanese government.

Britain in a Reichstag speech: "Mr. Churchill, or perhaps others, for once believe me when I predict a great empire will be destroyed, an empire that it was never my intention to destroy or even to harm. I do realize that this struggle, if it continues, can end only with the complete annihilation of one or the other of the two adversaries. Mr. Churchill may believe this will be Germany. I know that it will be Britain."

■ The Australian light cruiser *Sydney* sank the Italian cruiser *Bartolomeo Colleoni* in a running fight off the north coast of Crete.

■ Denmark withdrew from the League of Nations.

■ Roosevelt signed the Naval Expansion Act, adding 1,425,000 tons to the Navy—a 70 percent increase—and 15,000 planes.

July 21 Estonia, Latvia, and Lithuania formally "asked" to be incorporated into the Soviet Union, following resolutions of the Communist-dominated parliaments in each of the Baltic states.

■ Hitler directed the German army to begin planning an invasion of the Soviet Union. He assumed Britain would either choose to end the war or Germany would overwhelm Britain in the projected invasion, after which German military might would be directed to the east.

July 22 Britain rejected Hitler's peace offer. Lord Halifax said Hitler made "no suggestion that peace must be based on justice, no word of recognition that the other nations of Europe had any right to self-determination, the principle which he has so often invoked for Germans. His only appeal was to the base instinct of fear, and his only arguments were threats. . . . His picture of Europe is one of Germany lording it over those peoples, whom he has one by one deprived of freedom."

July 24 On the pretext that improper data was presented, the Rumanian government seized British oil interests in the country.

July 26 The U.S. government extended its licensing on war goods for Japan, controlling the shipment of aviation fuel and specific categories of iron and steel scrap. It was not a strict embargo, however, and initally exports of the commodities were not that seriously affected.

July 27 Japanese secret police began arresting foreign nationals on various charges vaguely associated with alleged spying activities.

■ Foreign Minister Yosuke Matsuoka informed the British ambassador in Tokyo that Japan "was determined, and in fact, compelled by circumstances, to step up a new order in the Far East," while London was "resisting these tendencies with every means. . . . It was therefore difficult to see how [a] fundamental clash of interests and purpose could be avoided."

■ A Rumanian mission arrived in Rome, its members attired in their new Nazi-styled uniforms, to pay obsequious tribute to their new Axis partners. The Italians were less than impressed. Ciano wrote, "They are simply disgusting." The king said the Rumanians looked like a bunch of hotel porters. Mussolini advised the visitors to rid Rumania of all Jewish influence.

July 29 Hitler told his military leaders it was his "intention" but not yet his "decision" to attack the Soviet Union.

■ German bombers attacked Dover harbor.

■ After a meeting with Laval, U.S. diplomat Robert D. Murphy reported to Washington that Laval "hoped ardently that the English would be defeated."

July 30 Delegates to the Inter-America Conference in Havana adopted a plan for the joint trusteeship of European possessions in the Western Hemisphere which appeared likely to be transferred to Germany.

July 31 Hitler told his assembled military leaders: "The sooner we smash Russia the better. The operation makes sense only if the Russian state is shattered in one blow. A gain of territory is not enough. To have to halt during the winter is questionable business. Therefore it is better to wait [until 1941], but the decision to dispose of Russia is definite."

■ All aviation fuel destined for use outside the Western Hemisphere was embargoed by the U.S.

■ Secretary of War Stimson called for military conscription in the U.S. He said, "Today we are face to face with a potential enemy which not only has been conscripting and training its own forces for the past six years but which today is putting conscription into effect upon its victims in Poland and France, and in Norway, Denmark, and Holland, in order that its own war supplies may be more ample." Privately, Stimson felt Britain would fall within a month.

Aug. 1–6 All the Baltic states were occupied by

the Red Army and incorporated into the Soviet Union.

Aug. 1 Foreign Minister Matsuoka defined Tokyo's policy for "Greater East Asia": ". . . the mission of Japan is to proclaim and demonstrate the imperial way throughout the world. Viewed from the standpoint of international relations, this amounts to enabling all nations and races to find each its proper place in the world. Accordingly, the immediate aim of our foreign policy at present is to establish a great East Asian chain of common prosperity with the Japan-Manchukuo-China group as one of the links. We shall thus be able to demonstrate the imperial way in the most effective manner and pave the way towards the establishment of world peace."

■ Molotov reaffirmed Russia's adherence to its alliance with Germany and denounced Britain and the U.S.

■ Italy heightened its anti-Greek propaganda campaign, centering on Athens' pro-British position.

Aug. 3 Japan protested the U.S. embargo on aviation fuel.

■ Italian forces invaded British Somaliland in east Africa. About 200,000 Italians and 150,000 African levies, under the command of the duke of Aosta, were garrisoned in Ethiopia and Eritrea, while British strength in the whole of east Africa and Aden was about 21,500.

Aug. 5 Hitler and Mussolini met in Rome for a review of strategy now that France had been defeated. Mussolini promised to launch a major offensive toward Cairo and the Suez Canal from Libya.

Aug. 6 Secretary of State Hull declared the only way for the U.S. to avoid being drawn into war was to "continue to arm, and to arm to such an extent that the forces of conquest and ruin will not dare make an attack on us or any part of this hemisphere."

Aug. 8 In an admitted move to increase India's "contribution to the war," Britain promised a new constitution and partnership with India after the war.

■ American aircraft production reached a rate of 500 per month.

■ RAF fighter pilot James B. Nicholson won the only Victoria Cross awarded during the year's aerial battle over Britain. The flight lieutenant attacked a German squadron over the New Forest while his own aircraft was being consumed in flames. The medal was awarded posthumously.

Aug. 9 Britain pulled its military forces out of Shanghai and north China because of the pressing manpower needs elsewhere.

Aug. 10 Laval informed the Germans that the French World War I ace, Colonel René Fonck, had organized 200 pilots to join in the fight against Britain.

Aug. 11 Italians attacked the Tug Argan Pass in British Somaliland. (A four-day battle ensued for control of the key approach to Berbera, capital of the territory. Outnumbered British and South African troops were forced to yield the pass.)

Aug. 14 Germany suspended the constitution of Luxembourg on the grounds the regent and government had fled the country. German laws were applied to the occupied nation.

Aug. 15 German planes launched a massive

Sikh troops of the British army behind a Bren-gun carrier clear a village in the east African campaign.

offensive to cripple the RAF. Hitler had signaled the Luftwaffe on Aug. 8: "Operation *ADLER* [EAGLE]. Within a short period you will wipe the British Air Force from the sky. Heil Hitler." Eagle Day (*Adlertag*) saw 1,786 sorties flown by the Luftwaffe. It was directed at RAF operational bases in the hope of enticing British fighters into combat and destroying them. This would give the Germans mastery of the skies and permit the planned invasion of Britain. (Instead, Eagle Day ended with the loss of 75 Luftwaffe aircraft. Only 32 of the 700 RAF fighters were downed. The Germans were less able to absorb their losses, and Göring was forced to limit the use of aircraft and restrict the number of trained pilots and crewmen committed to combat at any one time. Eagle Day helped turn the tide against Germany in the Battle of Britain. One of the key factors which determined the outcome was the ability of the British to read Luftwaffe radio dispatches covering operational plans transmitted by Enigma code. These were quickly intercepted and utilized through Ultra decipher.)

■ The Greek cruiser *Helle* was torpedoed and sunk (by an Italian submarine) while anchored at the Island of Tenos. Fearing the Italians, Athens made no protest though proof of the aggressive act was irrefutable.

■ Franco wrote to Mussolini that Spain was "preparing herself to take her place in the strife against our common enemies. . . ."

Aug. 16 Turin and Milan were attacked by RAF bombers.

■ Southern England was subjected to heavy raids involving 1,720 Luftwaffe aircraft.

Aug. 17 Germany declared a "total blockade" of Britain. Berlin announced that "the naval war in the waters around the British Isles is in full progress. The whole area has been mined. German planes attack every vessel. Any neutral ship which in the future enters these waters is liable to be destroyed."

■ Berlin privately advised Italy not to launch a war against Greece until Britain was vanquished.

Aug. 18 Canada, which was at war with Germany, and the U.S., which was not, established coordinated military planning procedures through a binational joint defense board, which would "consider in the broad sense the defense of the northern half of the Western Hemisphere."

Aug. 19 Italian forces occupied Berbera, the capital of British Somaliland, which had been evacuated by a numerically inferior Commonwealth force.

Aug. 20 Churchill offered to lease British bases in Newfoundland and the West Indies to the U.S., an idea which had originally been proposed by Roosevelt.

■ Churchill saluted the RAF: "Never before in the field of human conflict was so much owed by so many to so few."

■ Italy announced the imposition of a total blockade of British ports in the Mediterranean and Africa.

Aug. 20–21 British troops were withdrawn from all of British Somaliland in east Africa.

Aug. 21 Leon Trotsky, Stalin's one-time rival, was assassinated in Mexico City by a Spanish communist, Ramón Mercader. Moscow denied any responsibility.

■ The southern portion of Dobruja was ceded to Bulgaria by Rumania.

Aug. 23–24 The Luftwaffe began raiding RAF installations in the London area. Portsmouth was also attacked. Through error, ten Luftwaffe night bombers attacked the heart of London. The aircraft were to bomb oil storage facilities at Thameshaven, just east of the city. Making a navigational mistake in approaching the target, the bombers instead dropped their bombs on the city itself, destroying many old buildings, including St. Giles Church, Cripplegate.

Aug. 25 Estonia, Latvia, and Lithuania signed formal documents making them part of the Soviet Union.

Aug. 25–26 RAF bombers retaliating for the London bombing attacked Berlin for the first time, striking at industrial targets. Eighty-one Wellingtons, Whitleys, and Hampdens flew the missions with poor results. Twenty-nine claimed to have hit Berlin, 27 could not locate their targets, 18 bombed alternate targets, 7 aborted, and 5 did not return. This and subsequent RAF raids on Berlin provoked Hitler into ordering the Luftwaffe to switch its effort from RAF airfields to London, a major strategic blunder. Efforts expended on the destruction of civilian targets denied the Germans the opportunity to reduce British air strength to a level of impotence.

Aug. 26 The French African territory of Chad

declared its loyalty to de Gaulle and Free France.

Aug. 27 Congress authorized the induction of National Guard units into the U.S. military for a one-year period.

Aug. 30 The foreign ministers of Germany and Italy awarded half of Rumanian Transylvania to Hungary, an area of 17,370 square miles.

■ French authorities agreed to permit Japanese occupation of all ports, airfields, and railroads in northern Indochina.

Aug. 31 National Guard units began to be federalized and incorporated into the U.S. Army. Sixty thousand men were included in the first induction.

■ Molotov protested the award of Transylvania to Hungary because Russia had not been consulted. Moscow correctly interpreted it as anti-Russian. Italy and Germany agreed to guarantee Rumania's new frontier, and Russia still coveted Rumanian territory.

ALASKAN COLD

The U.S. air base landing strip at Fairbanks, Alaska, had to be built to withstand temperatures down to minus 60° F. By the time it was completed in September 1940, more concrete was used in its construction than had been used previously for *all* streets and sidewalks in the entire history of Alaska.

Sept. 3 An agreement for the transfer of 50 aging American destroyers for rights to British air and naval bases in Newfoundland, Bermuda, the Caribbean and British Guiana was announced in Washington and London. The leases were to run for 99 years. It was a masterstroke of permissible emergency aid to the hard-pressed British, giving them necessary—though antiquated—ships to serve as convoy escorts while relieving them of responsibility for defending their American bases.

■ RAF Fighter Command was reduced to 840 available pilots, from the 1,438 flying when the Battle of Britain began.

■ The German invasion of Britain was fixed for Sept. 21 at the earliest.

GERMAN CAMOUFLAGE

With the RAF bringing the war to Germany itself, the Germans attempted to foil the bombers through extensive camouflage of the main target areas. Lake Lietzen, which was presumed to be an aid to navigators on flights over Berlin, was completely covered with gauze to prevent its reflection by moonlight. At least five "dummy" Berlins were built around the German capital, flimsy but giant representations of Berlin to confuse the British airmen. They were located at Nauen to the west, Pausin to the northwest, Schönlinde to the northeast, and two others, in the eastern and southern suburbs. Several fake Hamburgs were created, as well as duplicates of the marshaling yards at Hamm and the Leuna Chemical Works.

SOURCE: Frederick Oechsner, et al., *This Is the Enemy.*

Sept. 4 Hitler promised reprisals against Britain for the RAF attack on Berlin. He said: "The British drop their bombs indiscriminately and without plan on civilian residential quarters and farms and villages. For three months I did not reply because I believed they would stop, but in this Mr. Churchill saw a sign of weakness. The British will know that we are now giving our answer night after night. We shall stop the handiwork of these night pilots."

■ Hull advised Japan the U.S. would disapprove of any aggressive moves against French Indochina.

Sept. 5 Vichy France broke relations with Belgium, Holland, Luxembourg, and Norway.

■ The German navy gave up its base at Murmansk which had been granted them in the early days of Russian-German military cooperation.

Sept. 6 King Carol II of Rumania abdicated the throne in favor of his son, Michael. General Ion Antonescu became dictator and declared the Nazi Iron Guard as the only recognized political party. There was widespread public dissatisfaction with the Axis-imposed loss of northern Transylvania, but Antonescu was determined to stand on the side of Germany and Italy.

■ The U.S. said it would use the newly-acquired

British bases "for the common defense of the Hemisphere." The first eight of the 50 destroyers were transferred to the Royal Navy.

Sept. 7 The Germans began their most destructive raids on London. A force of 625 bombers was directed against the British capital in the initial blitz. (Until Nov. 13, with only 10 days excepted, between 150 and 300 Luftwaffe bombers dropped at least 100 tons of explosives on London each and every night. About a million incendiary bombs fell. Initially, the air defenses were totally inadequate and improved only barely. Berlin claimed only 81 German aircraft were downed during the period, a figure which, even if understated, represents a small percentage of the 12,000 night sorties flown by the Germans.)

■ The signal was flashed in southern England to alert Britons that an invasion was "imminent."

■ Southern Dobruja (about 3,000 square miles) was formally ceded to Bulgaria by Rumania in the Treaty of Craiova.

Sept. 9 Germany issued a warning that any ship, of any nationality, in any war zone was subject to attack.

■ U.S. destroyers began operating with the Royal Navy in the North Atlantic.

■ In the largest naval procurement order in history, the U.S. Navy awarded contracts for the construction of 210 ships, including 12 carriers and 7 battleships.

Sept. 11 Buckingham Palace and St. Paul's Cathedral in London were damaged in the blitz.

Sept. 12 U.S. Ambassador Joseph C. Grew in Tokyo warned Secretary Hull that the Japanese might retaliate in the face of U.S. embargoed oil shipments to Japan.

■ Finland signed an agreement with Germany permitting its troops transit rights. The privilege was used immediately to transport Wehrmacht units to Norway through the port of Vaasa.

■ Foreign correspondents in Berlin were told by a high-ranking officer from the air ministry that the "RAF will not be able to hold out for more than two weeks."

Sept. 13 Five Italian divisions crossed into Egypt from Libya in the first major offensive of the North African war, attacking the British frontier post at Sollum (Salum). The badly outnumbered British did not seriously contest the Italians. The first major defense position, at Mersa Matruh, was 120 miles east of the frontier. The Italians quickly advanced 50 miles to Sidi Barrani, but the cautious Marshal Rodolfo Graziani ordered a halt to the offensive and established a series of fortified camps.

■ In a further test of its combat capabilities, thirteen Zeros encountered 27 Chinese fighters over Chungking. Every Chinese plane was shot down without a loss to the Zeros.

London firefighters battle blazes caused by the German bombing.

Sept. 15 Luftwaffe planes launched a climactic daylight attack on London, designed to crush Fighter Command and clear the way for an unobstructed invasion of England. Instead RAF pilots downed nearly 60 German planes, while 26 British aircraft were downed. The result was a decisive swing in the attrition rate against the Germans. The date has been celebrated by the British ever since as "Battle of Britain Day." The Luftwaffe's failure to eliminate the British fighter force prompted Hitler to postpone Operation SEALION, set for Sept. 21, first by days and then indefinitely. Germany soon switched to the night bombing of London and daylight attacks on provincial targets.

Sept. 16 The U.S. moved to begin a military draft as Congress completed approval of the Selective Training and Service Act. It was the first peacetime conscription program in U.S. history. All men between 21 and 35 were to be registered with 1,200,000 men (plus 800,000 reservists) to be given 12 months of training.

Sept. 17 The German military officially postponed for an indefinite period the launching of the invasion of England.

■ In one of the fiercest raids of the blitz 10,000 Britons were killed or wounded. (During the first half of the month, 2,000 people had lost their lives.)

Sept. 18 Sidi Barrani in Egypt was occupied by Italian forces.

Sept. 20 Field Marshal Wilhelm Keitel, chief of the Armed Forces High Command, issued a memo to German field commanders explaining that Wehrmacht troops were being sent to Rumania "in case a war with Soviet Russia is forced upon us."

Sept. 22 Japan was formally granted air bases and the right to maintain troops in French Indochina under terms of a treaty signed in Hanoi. The governor general of Indochina, General Georges Catroux, sought Allied aid to fight the Japanese, but Britain (and the United States) said it was not possible to consider military action in Asia.

■ Uruguay arrested eight Nazi leaders on charges of conspiring against the state.

Sept. 23–25 Free French forces with British support attempted to occupy Dakar in French West Africa. Secrecy had been compromised, and the local units—loyal to Vichy—anticipated the operation and resisted. Nothing went right for the Allies, who, among other things, couldn't find their objectives because of heavy fog. Three French cruisers and three destroyers—which had slipped through the Strait of Gibraltar—were in Dakar and resisted the occupation effort. The British battleship *Resolution* was heavily damaged. The entire operation was abandoned.

Sept. 24–25 French planes dropped 600 tons of bombs in an attack on British military installations at Gibraltar.

Sept. 25 U.S. intelligence was able to decode for the first time a complete Japanese message transmitted in the Purple supersecret diplomatic code used by Tokyo. Henceforth, most messages of extreme sensitivity to the Japanese could be read by Washington. The major breakthrough came when, after three frustrating years and without any knowledge of what the original looked like or its operational principles, the encoding and decoding machine was duplicated. Even so, the proper cryptographic sequences had to be solved. Colonel William Friedman, a U.S. Army intelligence officer, was finally able to unlock all its secrets. The painstaking decipherment was, with the breaking of the German Enigma code, the greatest intelligence coup of the war.

■ Washington announced a loan of $25 million to shore up the Chiang Kai-shek government in Chungking.

■ Allied forces were withdrawn from Dakar. London said it had never been its intention "to enter into serious warlike operations against those Frenchmen who felt it their duty to obey the commands of the Vichy government."

■ All political parties were dissolved in Norway, except Quisling's pro-Nazi National Union Party.

Sept. 26 Scrap iron and steel were barred from export to Japan by Roosevelt.

■ Britain protested Finland's grant of transit rights to Germany.

Sept. 27 Germany, Italy, and Japan entered into a 10-year military and economic agreement. The Tripartite Pact was signed in Berlin. Its declared "prime purpose" was "to establish and maintain a new order of things calculated to promote the mutual prosperity and welfare of the peoples concerned." The pact was the formalization of the Axis partnership, and the unmistakable targets of the strengthened alliance were the United States and the Soviet Union.

■ Fifty-five Luftwaffe planes were downed over Britain.

■ In a highly pessimistic assessment of the situation in Britain, U.S. Ambassador Joseph P. Kennedy cabled the State Department: "I was delighted to see that the President said he was not going to enter the war, because to enter this war, imagining for a minute that the English have anything to offer in the line of leadership or productive capacity in industry that could be of the slightest value to us, would be a complete misapprehension. . . . It breaks my heart to draw these conclusions about a people that I sincerely hoped might be victorious, but I cannot get myself to the point where I believe they can be of any assistance to the cause in which they are involved."

Sept. 28 Under Secretary of State Sumner Welles outlined U.S. policy in Asia toward Japan. He said Tokyo's intention to create a new order in Asia had resulted in Japan's reliance "upon the instrumentality of armed force, and it has made it very clear that it intends that it alone shall decide to what extent the historic interests of the United States and the treaty rights of American citizens in the Far East are to be observed." Welles called for "complete respect" for U.S. rights, "equality of opportunity for the trade of all nations," and "respect" for all treaties and international agreements to which the U.S. had agreed. "Modifications" through "peaceful negotiations" would be considered.

■ The first of the 50 destroyers which the U.S. turned over to Britain reached England.

Sept. 29 Luxembourg was incorporated into Greater Germany. Berlin stated, "Luxembourg derives from the German race and the population therefore must be treated as though it was already German."

■ The pro-Vichy government on Madagascar rejected a British ultimatum that it repudiate Marshal Pétain's rule.

Sept. 30 British civilian casualties for the month as a result of the German bombing were 6,954 killed, 10,615 injured.

Oct. Italian bombers began flying long-range raids, a short-lived attempt to extend the operational base of the *Regia Aeronautica* (Royal Air Force). During the month, aircraft from Eritrea

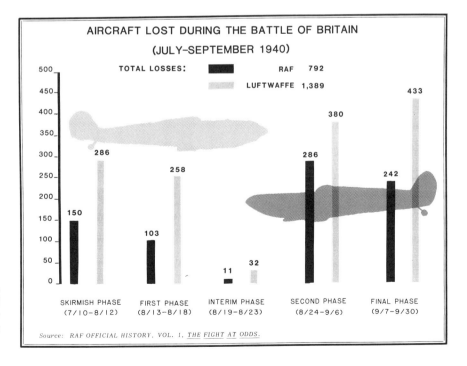

The Battle of Britain became a contest of wills, and of attrition. Germany's air arm never recovered from its losses.

AIRCRAFT LOST DURING THE BATTLE OF BRITAIN
(JULY–SEPTEMBER 1940)

TOTAL LOSSES: RAF   792   LUFTWAFFE   1,389

Phase	RAF	Luftwaffe
SKIRMISH PHASE (7/10–8/12)	150	286
FIRST PHASE (8/13–8/18)	103	258
INTERIM PHASE (8/19–8/23)	11	32
SECOND PHASE (8/24–9/6)	286	380
FINAL PHASE (9/7–9/30)	242	433

Source: RAF OFFICIAL HISTORY, VOL. 1, THE FIGHT AT ODDS.

attempted to bomb British oil installations at Bahrein on the Persian Gulf, a prodigious feat of navigation over the wastes of the Arabian Peninsula. The aircraft reached the gulf but missed their targets. Slight damage was done, however, to the neighboring oil field in neutral Saudi Arabia, 25 miles from Bahrein.

Oct. 1 Weihaiwei in China was occupied by the Japanese.

Oct. 4 Hitler and Mussolini conferred at the Brenner Pass. With the planned invasion of Britain becoming more questionable, Hitler sought Italian help in fighting the British on other fronts. Spain, said Hitler, would join in the action. Hitler assured Mussolini he did not trust Stalin either.

HITLER'S PLOT TO KIDNAP
THE DUKE OF WINDSOR

Hitler ordered the SS to kidnap the duke of Windsor, who as Edward VIII had abdicated the English throne to marry Wallis Warfield Simpson, in the hope of eventually luring him with money to take up the Axis cause.

According to SS Intelligence Chief Walter Schellenburg, Hitler believed the duke was pro-German and only needed to be spirited away from the British authorities. The plan was to kidnap the duke, then in neutral Portugal but preparing for a hunting trip to pro-Axis Spain. While in Spain, he would be lured with money. Foreign Minister Ribbentrop told Schellenburg, "We would declare ourselves willing to give him a 20-year *appenage* [income] of 50 million Swiss francs."

Schellenburg went to Portugal to plan for the enticement but felt it would be too difficult. Ribbentrop cabled him to proceed anyway, saying, "The Führer orders a kidnap operation now."

Anxious to remove the duke from harm's way and possible embarrassments of just this kind, the British government had already prepared to remove the duke to the more secure and benign Bahamas to spend the rest of the war.

SOURCE: Schellenburg Memoirs, *Welt am Sonntag*.

■ Churchill again asked Roosevelt to send U.S. naval ships to Singapore. (The U.S. rejected the plea. Hull told the British ambassador: "It will not be wise, even from a British viewpoint, for two wars to be raging at the same time, one in the East and the other in the West. If this country should enter any war, this would immediately result in greatly cutting off supplies to Great Britain.").

Oct. 5 Prime Minister Konoye said a war between Japan and the U.S. was inevitable if the U.S. saw the Axis alliance as "hostile."

Oct. 7 Japan protested the U.S. embargo on aviation fuel and machine tools, and the ban on the exports of iron and steel scraps. Ambassador Kensuke Horinouchi said the actions "cannot fail to be regarded as directed against Japan, and, as such, to be an unfriendly act."

■ German troops entered Rumania, ostensibly to defend the oil fields and help train the Rumanian army.

Oct. 8 U.S. citizens were advised by Washington to leave the Far East "in view of abnormal conditions in those areas."

Oct. 12 Hitler reset the date for the German invasion of Britain. It was now scheduled for April 1941.

■ Roosevelt said the U.S. was arming only to defend the Western Hemisphere: "We are building a total defense on land and sea and in the air sufficient to repel total attack from any part of the world. . . . The people of the United States, the people of the Americas, reject the doctrine of appeasement. They recognize it for what it is—a major weapon of the aggressor nations."

Oct. 13 Ribbentrop wrote to Stalin proposing the Soviets join Germany, Italy, and Japan in a virtual division of the world. Stalin replied that he favored such an arrangement and sent Molotov to Berlin to begin negotiations.

■ Japan invited the U.S. and others to join the Tripartite alliance. Foreign Minister Matsuoka said: "The new world order envisaged by the three powers is one in which economic barriers will be broken down and the natural geographic divisions of the earth established in complementary fashion which will make for the prosperity of all peoples. . . . We three nations, Japan, Germany, and Italy, will be very glad to welcome other powers into our alliance, whether it

German Heinkel 111 bombers on their way to blitz Britain.

be the United States or any other nation, should they desire to join in the spirit of the new order."

Oct. 15 A shipment of military aircraft destined for Sweden was blocked by the U.S. government. The planes were then requisitioned for use by the Army Air Corps.

Oct. 16 A total of 16,400,000 American men were registered for the draft.

■ U.S. iron and steel scrap exports were barred to all countries except Britain and the nations of the Western Hemisphere "with a view to conserving the available supply to meet the rapidly expanding requirements of the defense program in this country."

Oct. 18 Britain reopened the Burma Road, again giving China access to the outside world over an overland route.

■ Germany and Italy issued demands upon Greece, including the transfer of land to Italy and Bulgaria, use of air bases by the Axis, and a new, sympathetic government in Athens.

■ Göring congratulated Luftwaffe crews on their attacks on Britain, which, he said, "caused the British world-enemy disastrous losses by uninterrupted, destructive blows. Your indefatigable, courageous attacks on the heart of the British Empire, the city of London with its 8½ million inhabitants, have reduced British plutocracy to fear and terror. The losses which you have inflicted on the much vaunted Royal Air Force in determined fighter engagements are irreplaceable."

Oct. 21 Churchill called on the people of France not to block British war efforts against Germany. He said, "Remember, we shall never stop, never weary, and never give in. . . . We seek to beat the life and soul out of Hitler and Hitlerism—that alone, that all the time, that to the end." He also taunted Hitler: "We are waiting for the long-promised invasion. So are the fishes."

Oct. 22 Hitler met with Laval in Montoire in occupied France to discuss France's future in the new order of Europe.

■ Jews began to be deported from Alsace-Lorraine and the Rhineland.

Pierre Laval meets with Hitler on the Führer's special train.

Oct. 23 Hitler met Franco at the French resort town of Hendaye on the Spanish border. Germany wanted a joint attack on Gibraltar, but Hitler was unwilling to grant Franco's wishes for large

Hitler and Franco meet at Hendaye, on the Spanish-French border, Oct. 23, 1940.

areas of French North and West Africa in exchange for Spain's participation in the war. Without these territorial concessions, Franco declined to go ahead with the Gibraltar plan and began hedging on his promise to go to war.

Oct. 24 Hitler conferred with Marshal Pétain at Montoire and came to an agreement on French cooperation with Germany, essentially that German attitudes and actions would be improved in direct relationship to the degree of French collaboration.

■ The U.S. warned of any transfer of French naval ships to the Axis. Washington said the Vichy government claimed to be under duress, but it did not alter the fact that such a move "would most definitely wreck the traditional friendship between the French and American peoples, would permanently remove any chance that this Government would be disposed to give any assistance to the French people in their distress, and would create a wave of bitter indignation against France on the part of American public opinion."

Hitler confers with Marshal Pétain, Oct. 24, 1940.

Oct. 26 Italy claimed Greek-inspired attacks had taken place on the Greek-Albanian frontier. By now, Italy had massed a force of 162,000 men along the border. Greece had only 75,000 men to counter an invasion along this front.

Oct. 27 De Gaulle formally proclaimed the Free French government, with powers of the state to reside in himself and a council of defense.

Oct. 28 Italy invaded Greece. At 3:00 A.M Premier Metaxas of Greece was presented a list of demands by the Italian minister in Athens. The Greeks were given three hours to comply. Because of alleged assistance to British naval and intelligence units, the Italians demanded "the right to occupy with their military forces, for the duration of the present conflict with Great Britain, certain strategic points in Greek territory" and the right of military passage. Metaxas said the demand amounted to a declaration of war and that "Greece will resist the Italian invasion with all her forces." Italian forces launched a four-pronged attack from Albania at 5:30, a half-hour before the deadline expired. General Sebastiano Visconti-Prasca, the Italian commander in Albania, employed the Ninth and Eleventh armies (consisting of seven divisions, about 87,500 men) as the invasion force. The Greek army under General Alexander Papagos totalled 150,000, but it was initially widely dispersed. Rome planned on a quick and easy victory. One strategic effect of the action was to drain off Italian strength from North Africa where an advance to the Suez Canal was highly probable.

■ Mussolini and Hitler met in Florence, but a delay in the invasion of Greece which Hitler had planned to request was academic.

■ Laval was named foreign minister in the Vichy government.

Oct. 29 British troops landed on the Greek island of Crete.

Oct. 30 Campaigning for reelection in Boston, Roosevelt declared, "I have said this before, but I shall say it again and again and again: your boys are not going to be sent into any foreign wars."

■ British naval ships mined Greek waters.

■ Russia sent 134 fighter planes to aid in the defense of Greece.

Oct. 31 British civilian casualties for the month as a result of the German bombing were 6,334 killed and 8,695 injured.

GERMAN AND BRITISH AIR STRENGTH ON THE EVE OF THE BATTLE OF BRITAIN

RAF	Luftwaffe°	
Hurricanes, Spitfires, and Boulton Paul Defiants 609	Me-109 fighters	809
	Me-110 fighter-bombers	280
	Ju-87 dive bombers	316
	Various long-range bombers	1,198

°The figures cover fighters based only in France and other aircraft in France and the Low Countries.

Between July 10 and Oct. 31, 1940, a total of 1,733 German aircraft of all types were destroyed (the British at the time claimed 2,698), while 915 RAF planes of all types were downed (the Germans had claimed 3,058).

Nov. 1 Marshal Pétain assured Roosevelt the "French Government has declared that the French fleet would never be surrendered and nothing can justify questioning today that solemn undertaking."

■ Italian forces reached the Kalamas (Thiamis) River in Greece.

Mussolini and Ribbentrop in Florence, Italy, discuss future Axis policies, Oct. 28, 1940.

■ Royal Navy ships mined the Bay of Biscay.

Nov. 3 The first British troops and RAF units began arriving in Greece to aid in the fight against the Italians. Interestingly, the Germans lodged no objections to the Greek government, although the German minister in Athens pointedly warned against the stationing of RAF planes in northern Greece, where they would be a threat to the Rumanian oil fields.

Nov. 4 Spain incorporated the International Zone of Tangier into its offical area of control.

Nov. 5 Roosevelt was elected president of the U.S. for an unprecedented third term.

■ The British armed merchant cruiser *Jervis Bay* was sunk while on Atlantic convoy patrol by the German pocket battleship *Admiral Scheer*.

Nov. 6 RAF bombers began flying combat missions out of Greece. Their initial raid was directed against the airfield at Valona in Albania.

Nov. 7 The Krupp factory at Essen was bombed by the RAF.

Nov. 8 Hitler had to stop speaking to a Munich gathering when British bombers began raiding the city.

■ The Italians suffered a major defeat in Greece when 5,000 men of the 3rd Alpine Division were captured in the Pindus gorges. General Visconti-Prasca was dismissed as commander of Italian forces in the campaign and replaced by General Ubaldo Soddu, an admission of the campaign's failure. Greek forces stiffened their resistance as the fighting flowed into the Pindus Mountains. The momentum of the campaign now passed to the Greeks.

■ Heavy earthquakes damaged the oil-producing facilities in Rumania.

■ The first U.S. merchant vessel to be lost in the war, the S.S. *City of Rayville*, went under after striking a mine off Cape Otway in the Bass Strait of Australia.

Nov. 10 Neville Chamberlain died at his Hampshire home.

Nov. 11 In one of its few raids on Britain, the Italian air force lost 13 aircraft.

■ Twenty British torpedo planes from the carrier *Illustrious* attacked the Italian naval base at Taranto, inflicting heavy losses. Only two of the seemingly out-of-date Royal Navy Swordfish biplanes were downed, but the battleships *Conte di Cavour*, *Littorio*, and *Duilio* were all sufficiently crippled to keep them out of action for most of the war. Nearly half the Italian battle fleet was thus incapacitated by a handful of near obsolete planes. The attacking aircraft, making their bombing runs at under 35 feet, used special torpedoes which carried under the harbor's defensive nets. It was the first successful attack on ships by planes launched from carriers.

Nov. 12–14 Soviet Foreign Minister Molotov visited Berlin and conferred with Hitler and other German leaders. The talks revealed the widely differing outlooks of two uneasy allies. Hitler regarded the Soviet views as "parochial," as Molotov insisted on keeping the discussions centered on the Balkans and Finland. Agreement was reached, however, on the broad objectives of each member of the new four-power alliance. German aspirations in the "Central African region" were recognized. Italy was to extend its empire in north and northeast Africa. Japan's interests were defined as "south of the Japanese home islands and Manchukuo." Russia's expansion plans were acknowledged "in the direction

Soviet Foreign Minister Molotov arrives in Berlin for conferences with German leaders, Nov. 1940.

of the Indian Ocean," plus a base on the Bosporus or the Dardanelles. All this was subject to Italian and Japanese approval.

Nov. 13 Germany started moving troops to Italy to salvage the bogged-down Italian invasion of Greece.

Molotov and Hitler with their interpreter confer in Berlin.

Nov. 14 The cathedral city of Coventry was mercilessly bombed by 449 German bombers personally led by General Albert Kesselring, who commanded the Luftwaffe's Second Air Fleet. As many as 30,000 incendiaries, plus 503 tons of high explosives, were dropped. Historic St. Michael's Cathedral was destroyed, 554 people were killed and 865 wounded. The raid was in retaliation for the Nov. 8 RAF raid on Munich. It should be noted that Coventry was also a munitions and military construction center, but the bombers were notoriously indiscriminate in their targeting. Sixty thousand buildings were destroyed or damaged. Most of them were private residences, with 75 percent of the residential area of Coventry smashed by the raid. Much has been written to the effect that Churchill knew, through Ultra, that Coventry was to be attacked but did not act in order to protect the flow of information gleaned from the intercepts of German military messages. Evidence suggests otherwise, that Coventry was not definitely known to be a target prior to this particular date. By the time full information was available, the attack

had begun and defensive measures or evacuation were impossible.

■ Vichy France protested the expulsion of French-speaking residents from Lorraine, telling the Germans "no measure of this kind was ever under discussion at the Franco-German meetings."

■ Greek troops pushed the Italians back into Albania, the jumping off point for their astonishingly embarrassing adventure in Greece.

Nov. 15 Jews of the Warsaw ghetto were prohibited from leaving the sealed-off area.

THE FUTURE POPE AS A FUGITIVE

Karol Wojtyla was a 19-year-old student when the Germans invaded his native Poland. In the early days of the occupation he worked as a laborer in the stone quarries of Zielonki near Krakow. He was also active in helping Polish Jews escape arrest and imprisonment. The Gestapo placed him on an execution list, but Wojtyla found refuge, along with other wanted Poles, in the residence of the archbishop of Krakow, Stefan Cardinal Sapieha. Here, he began his studies for the priesthood in what became an underground seminary. Wojtyla later lived with a poor tailor, Jan Tyranowski, in the Krakow suburb of Dzbuiki, while continuing his studies, still a fugitive from the Nazis. By the time the Russians occupied Krakow, he had completed most of his training and was ordained Nov. 1, 1946. Thirty-two years later he became Pope John Paul II.

Nov. 18 Mussolini said Italy struck at Greece because "since May Greece had offered the French and English all her air and naval bases. It was necessary to bring an end to this situation." He added, "We have enough men and means to annihilate all Greek resistance."

■ Erseke in Albania fell to the Greeks.

Nov. 19 Switzerland banned the Swiss Nazi party, saying that "this movement was working for the transformation of public institutions by other than constitutional means." The action was particularly noteworthy because the Swiss were totally surrounded by Axis allies who had shown no respect for the neutrality declared by other nations.

■ Luftwaffe bombers attacked Birmingham.

Nov. 20 Hungary formally joined the Axis by becoming a signatory to the Tripartite Pact.

■ Hitler offered to send German troops to help the Italians provided they would be released by May 1, 1941, for the invasion of Russia.

■ The Skoda munitions works in Czechoslovakia were bombed by the RAF.

■ Chinese Communist forces launched large-scale guerrilla operations against Japanese military units and communications lines in southern Shansi and northwest Hopei provinces. Called "The 100 Regiment Offensive," forces of the Eighth Route Army inflicted losses which prompted rapid and vengeful retaliation by the Japanese against Chinese villages known to be assisting the Communists.

Nov. 22 The Italian Ninth Army was routed by the Greeks who captured Koritsa (Korce), the Albanian town about 15 miles from the frontier. It was a major tactical victory for the Greeks, who also seized the Koritsa airfield, the only advanced base available to the Italians. Koritsa was also a road juncture, permitting pursuit to the north and northwest. The Greeks captured enough small arms and ammunition to equip two divisions.

Nov. 23 Rumania joined the Axis by adhering to the Tripartite Pact.

Nov. 24 Slovakia formally joined the Axis.

Nov. 25 Bulgaria rejected membership in the Axis by refusing to sign the Tripartite Pact. Strong pan-Slavic feelings inclined the Bulgarians toward Russia, and they had no particular affinity for the Germans or their political philosophy.

Nov. 26 The Belgian Congo declared war on Italy.

Nov. 27 A reign of terror was unleashed in Rumania in a series of political assassinations. Sixty-four former officials identified with the King Carol government were executed by the Iron Guard.

Nov. 28 The port city of Liverpool suffered extensive damage in a heavy raid by German bombers.

Nov. 29 The German High Command completed its plans for the projected invasion of Russia.

Nov. 30 Germany annexed Lorraine and said it had "righted a political wrong. The century-long battle for the Rhine has now been ended. Within this territory the complete economical and political union of Lorraine and Saarpfalz will be effected."

■ The U.S. granted another $100 million in loans and credits to China.

■ Japan and the pro-Japanese Chinese government of Wang Ching-wei in Nanking concluded a peace treaty.

■ British air raid civilian casualties for the month were 4,588 killed, 6,202 injured.

Dec. 1 Greek forces continued forcing back the Italians.

Dec. 2 Athens announced the capture of 5,000 more Italian troops.

Dec. 4 Greek forces forced the Italians out of

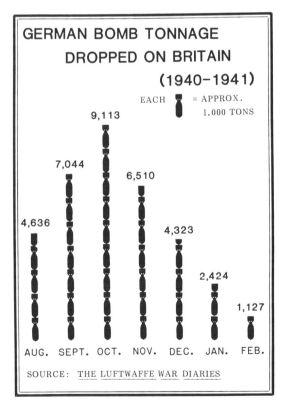

GERMAN BOMB TONNAGE
DROPPED ON BRITAIN
(1940–1941)

EACH = APPROX. 1,000 TONS

9,113
7,044
6,510
4,636
4,323
2,424
1,127

AUG. SEPT. OCT. NOV. DEC. JAN. FEB.

SOURCE: THE LUFTWAFFE WAR DIARIES

German bombers rained down a blitz on Britain, but the Luftwaffe could not sustain this kind of aerial warfare.

Permet. A total of 28,000 Italians were claimed to have been captured.

Dec. 6 A humiliated and frustrated Marshal Pietro Badoglio resigned as chief of staff of the Italian army in the wake of the military disaster in Greece. He was succeeded by Ugo Cavallero.

■ Sarande (or Porto Edda) on the Adriatic fell to the Greeks who continued to press northward into Albania.

■ Japan and Thailand concluded a treaty of friendship, the result of a Thai initiative.

Dec. 7 The German raider *Passat* mined the Tasmanian coast and the Bass Strait between Tasmania and Victoria, Australia.

Dec. 8 Italy requested German military intervention in the Greek war.

■ Franco told Admiral Wilhelm Canaris that Spain was not ready to join the Axis and start fighting, reaffirming what Franco told Hitler.

■ The chief of the Italian navy, Admiral Domenico Cavagnari, resigned and was succeeded by Admiral Arturo Riccardi.

Dec. 9 Japanese Foreign Minister Matsuoka said war with the United States was not inevitable: "We have no difference that cannot be surmounted if we keep our heads cool and mind our own business. . . . We do not pass judgment on what the United States does in the West, and we try to confine ourselves to this part of the world."

■ Greek forces advanced to Pogradec on Lake Ohrid in Albania, more than 40 miles from the Greek frontier.

■ The British launched their first offensive in North Africa, outflanking the Italian forces to the south and cutting them off at Sidi Barrani. With a 31,000-man strong Western Desert Force, Lieutenant General Sir Richard O'Connor attacked the Italian army of 80,000 from the rear and achieved total surprise. Two thousand Italian prisoners were taken in the first hours of fighting.

Dec. 10 Britain provided China $40 million in loans.

Dec. 11 Sidi Barrani in Egypt was recaptured by the British. The Italian 4th Blackshirt and the 1st and 2nd Libyan divisions surrendered. Two other divisions were decimated. A total of 38,000 Italians and Libyan levies were captured. British losses were 624 killed, wounded, or missing.

Dec. 12 Germany informed Franco that Gibraltar would be attacked on January 10, and Spain was asked to join in the action. Franco adamantly refused, saying Britain would promptly occupy the Spanish and Portuguese islands in the east Atlantic. Rebuffed by Franco, Hitler abandoned the Gibraltar operation.

■ Yugoslavia and Hungary signed a treaty of "perpetual friendship." Both nations apparently did not wish to be associated with German and Italian policy too closely and hoped to establish a neutral bloc when the Italian-Greek war ended.

■ Sheffield was hit hard by Luftwaffe bombers.

Living through the blitz, Londoners gather in an underground station converted into an air raid shelter.

Dec. 13 Laval was ousted from the Vichy government. Pétain said the action was taken "for high reasons of interior policy."

■ Germany began planning for a drive toward Greece and Turkey, through Bulgaria.

Dec. 16 RAF bombers carried out a War Cabinet directive to launch a massive "area bombing" of a German city (Operation ABIGAIL). Three cities (Bremen, Düsseldorf, and Mannheim) were preselected, with the final choice made at the last minute based on most favorable weather conditions at that time. Mannheim was the selection, and 134 bombers were sent to inflict maximum damage. Of those which took off, 103 actually made their way to Mannheim and in six hours dropped 89 tons of high-explosive bombs and 14,000 incendiaries. Ten aircraft were lost. The main target was to have been a plant producing submarine engines, but German records show the damage was inflicted elsewhere. Five industrial plants were hit (only one was seriously damaged), but the heaviest destruction was in the residential area. Casualties, considering the weapon quantities, were light: 23 killed and 80 injured.

Dec. 17 Roosevelt, for the first time, publicly suggested direct arms aid to Britain. He told a press conference that "it is important from the selfish viewpoint of American defense that we should do everything to help the British Empire defend itself."

■ The British pushed their western advance in Egypt and reached Sollum, near the Libyan border.

Dec. 18 Hitler decided to proceed with the invasion of Russia even though Britain had not been knocked out of the war, and the armed forces were directed to begin planning for the effort. With incredible foresight and brilliant timing, the U.S. naval attaché in Berlin, Commander A.E. Schrader, on this same day warned Washington that Germany would now attack the Soviet Union and annex the Ukraine and the Caucasus region.

Dec. 21 Germany deplored the pro-British position of the United States. Berlin said its policy toward the U.S. was one of "restraint onto self-effacement" while Washington's was "from morn until night of pinpricks, injury, insult, challenge, and moral aggression."

Dec. 23 Anthony Eden again became Britain's foreign secretary, succeeding Lord Halifax, who was named ambassador to the U.S.

■ Greek troops captured Himare, the Albanian seacoast town 45 miles north of the frontier. Italian resistance began to stiffen at this point.

Dec. 28 To stretch out its petroleum supplies the Japanese embarked on a substitute fuel program to power private automobiles. Charcoal was the prime replacement to be used instead of gasoline.

Dec. 29 Roosevelt called for a direct arms aid program to Britain: "The Nazi masters of Germany have made it clear that they intend not only to dominate all life and thought in their own country, but also to enslave the whole of Europe, and then to use the resources of Europe to dominate the rest of the world. . . . The people of Europe who are defending themselves do not ask us to do their fighting. They ask us for the implements of war, the planes, the tanks, the guns, the freighters which will enable them to fight for their liberty and our security."

■ Incendiary bombs were dropped in massive quantities on London. Fifteen hundred fires were started.

Dec. 31 Hitler wrote to Mussolini and said he regretted Franco's decision not to join the fighting on the side of the Axis.

■ The British civilian air raid casualty toll for the month: 3,793 killed, 5,244 injured.

(OPPOSITE. TOP) *Hitler directing his war.*
(OPPOSITE. BOTTOM) *The Naval Air Station at Pearl Harbor during the Japanese attack.*

1941

The mammoth clash of arms begins in Russia, and Japan slashes through the Pacific.

Jan. 1–2 British naval and air forces pounded Bardia continuously to soften the Italian defense position in extreme northwest Libya for a ground assault.

Jan. 3 The recently-arrived Australian 6th Division broke through the Bardia defenses and captured the city. Italian losses were 10,000 killed or wounded, and 30,000 prisoners were taken. Italy had now lost eight divisions since the British offensive began. British Commonwealth casualties in taking Bardia were fewer than 500 men.

■ Italian forces launched a counteroffensive in Albania. Units of the Luftwaffe began arriving in Albania to assist the Italians.

■ British bombers attacked the German port city of Bremen.

Jan. 6 Roosevelt outlined the lend-lease program and enunciated the "Four Freedoms" principle. He asked Congress for approval to extend arms credits "to those nations which are now in actual war with aggressor nations. Our most useful and immediate role is to act as an arsenal for them as well as for ourselves. They do not need man power, but they do need billions of dollars worth of weapons of defense. The time is near when they will not be able to pay for them all in ready cash. . . . For what we send abroad, we shall be repaid within a reasonable time following the close of hostilities, in similar materials, or at our option, in other goods of many kinds, which they can produce, and which we need."

■ Four British merchant ships steamed out of Gibraltar with vital supplies for Malta. It was the first convoy to make the dangerous Mediterranean run since November. The Royal Navy assigned Force H, comprised of capital ships, to escort the cargo ships in and to provide support for their return. A number of merchantmen which had been in the November convoy were also stuck at Malta, and they, too, would be escorted out by Force H. Malta at this time had only 15 RAF Hurricane fighters for its myriad defense responsibilities.

■ Thai troops began attacking Cambodia and seized disputed border areas.

Jan. 8 Roosevelt's budget message to Congress requested a defense appropriation of $10,811,000,000 for fiscal 1942.

Jan. 10 The British carrier *Illustrious* was put out of action after being attacked by German and Italian aircraft about sixty miles west of Malta. She had been leading the escort force for the Malta convoy when 40 Luftwaffe Ju-87s and Ju-88s led the attack and scored six hits. More than 200 *Illustrious* crewmen were killed or wounded. She limped into Malta and eventually had to be sent to the U.S. for repairs, a heavy loss to the British at a time of great need for carrier cover in the Mediterranean. The additional loss of a cruiser and a destroyer in the Axis aerial attack further aggravated the British problem. From this day Britain no longer commanded the central Mediterranean, and the Germans were able to supply the Axis forces in North Africa with the equipment needed for the eventual drive into Egypt. Malta was nearly defenseless and was subjected to incessant aerial attack.

■ Germany and the Soviet Union concluded agreements on increased trade ("an amount of mutual deliveries considerably exceeding the level of the first year of operation of the agreement") and a settlement of the new frontier in Lithuania. The land adjustment was actually a sale. Germany received $7,500,000 in gold, and the Russians acquired a small strip of southern Lithuania around Kalvarija.

■ A bill to provide lend-lease was introduced in the U.S. Congress.

■ The U.S. issued directives requiring export licenses for the shipment of copper, brass, bronze, zinc, nickel, potash and semimanufactured products made from those materials. The action gave Washington further control over trade with Japan.

■ Klisura in Albania, 22 miles from the Greek border, fell to Greek troops.

Jan. 11 Hitler declared that Germany would dispatch aid to Libya, which, he said, must be saved on "strategic, political, and psychological grounds."

■ The British cruiser *Southampton* was sunk by German aircraft based in Sicily. She had been escorting 14 merchantmen out of Malta (all of which made the convoy run safely). *Southampton* was set afire by the Luftwaffe planes, became totally incapacitated, and finally had to be sent to the bottom by British ships.

Jan. 13 The Greek government turned down a British offer to send troops to Greece.

■ General Ugo Cavallero, Chief of the Italian General Staff, relieved General Soddu of command in Albania. It marked the beginning of the Axis counteroffensive.

Jan. 14 Germany called on Rumania to enter the war on the side of the Axis.

Jan. 16 Roosevelt asked Congress to appropriate $350 million for the construction of 200 merchant ships.

Jan. 19 British troops launched a counteroffensive in east Africa. They moved into the Italian colony of Eritrea and Ethiopia with a force made up of the 4th and 5th Indian divisions and the Sudan Defense Force under the command of Lieutenant General Sir William Platt. Attacking from the Sudan, the British units encountered little resistance as the Italians retreated to better defense positions.

Jan. 19–20 Hitler and Mussolini conferred at Berchtesgaden. Hitler actually summoned the now chastened Duce to discuss the problems of Libya and Albania and how the Germans might help the Italians. It was agreed two German divisions were to be sent to Africa at the earliest time and assistance in Greece would begin by April.

Jan. 19–21 Civil war erupted in Rumania. The Iron Guard, with extensive popular support, attempted to seize power and was ruthlessly put down by Antonescu's forces. Iron Guard leaders who could not flee the country were imprisoned.

Jan. 20 Roosevelt was inaugurated for his third term as president of the United States, an unprecedented event in American political history.

Jan. 21 The U.S. ended its prohibition on exports to Russia which had been imposed as part of the "moral embargo."

■ British and Australian units broke through the Italian Tobruk defenses in Libya.

■ In an address to the Diet, Foreign Minister Yosuke Matsuoka warned the U.S. against interfering in Asian affairs.

Jan. 22 Tobruk fell. British and Australian forces captured 25,000 Italians and 87 tanks at a cost of fewer than 400 casualties, mostly Australians.

Jan. 23 British forces advanced to the Biskia railhead in Eritrea.

Jan. 26 Matsuoka repeated Japan's determination to impose a "new order" in Asia.

Jan. 27 Ambassador Grew advised Washington of reports circulating in Tokyo of a Japanese attack on Pearl Harbor being planned by the Japanese military in case of "trouble" with the U.S. Grew wrote that "the attack would involve the use of all the Japanese military facilities. My colleague (a member of the U.S. embassy and the source of the reports) said that he was prompted to pass this on because it had come to him from many sources, although the plan seemed fantastic."

■ Matsuoka told a budget committee of the Japanese Diet that Japan must "dominate" the western Pacific if it were to achieve its goals: "My use of the word 'dominate' may seem extreme and while we have no such designs, still in a sense we do wish to dominate and there is no need to hide the fact. Has America any right to object if Japan does dominate the western Pacific? As Minister of Foreign Affairs, I hate to make such an assertion, but I wish to declare that if America does not understand Japan's rightful claims and actions, then there is not the slightest hope of improvement of Japanese-American relations."

Jan. 29 American and British military staff planners began conferring in Washington on a common strategy in the event the U.S. entered the war.

■ General Metaxas, the Greek dictator, died. For all his authoritarianism, Metaxas had rallied his country against the Italians. His death deprived Greece of a powerful leader in time of crisis.

Jan. 30 Derna in Libya was occupied by the advancing British Army columns, which then began pushing toward Benghazi.

■ Germany warned that ships of any nation carrying aid to Britain would be torpedoed.

Jan. 31 Churchill asked Turkey to grant permission to station ten RAF squadrons on Turkish territory. (Ankara eventually refused, saying it would break its neutrality and join the Allies only if attacked by the Germans.)

February German authorities began rounding up Polish Jews for transfer to the ghetto in Warsaw. (About 72,000 were transferred from all parts of German-occupied Poland through April 1941.)

Feb. 1 The U.S. Navy created the Atlantic Fleet, to be commanded by Rear Admiral Ernest J. King. Its work, essentially, would be convoy escort.

■ Italian forces in Albania launched a series of counterattacks against Greek positions along the entire front.

■ Agordat in Eritrea was captured by British forces who continued their advance to the Red Sea in pursuit of the retreating Italian forces.

Feb. 3 The German pocket battleships *Gneisen-*

au and *Scharnhorst* maneuvered through the Skagerrak and broke into the North Sea.

■ The battle of Keren began in Eritrea as the Italians consolidated their defense positions.

■ British forces pressed their Libyan offensive. In the Battle of Beda Fomm, the Italian Tenth Army was completely destroyed, and Benghazi was encircled.

Feb. 6 Erwin Rommel was named to command two German divisions—the Afrika Korps—to help rescue the Italians in North Africa. It was a token force which grew into a legend.

■ British and Australian forces swept into Benghazi.

THE AFRIKA KORPS

Few military formations have been more misunderstood than the Afrika Korps. It was not the entire German force in North Africa, but in fact was made up only of the German 5th Light (later redesignated the 21st Panzer) and the 15th Panzer divisions. Rommel's own *Wehrpass*, his official record, does not even list him as commander of the Afrika Korps. He was, according to that register of commands, listed as leading the *Deutschen Truppen in Libyen* from Feb. 15 to Aug. 14, 1941, and then successively as *Kommando der Panzergruppe Afrika, Oberkommando der Panzer Armee Afrika, Oberkommando der Deutsch. Ital. Panzerarmee,* and, finally, *Oberkommando der Heeresgruppe Afrika.* Rommel's command at its fullest embraced the two divisions of the Afrika Korps, the German 90th Light Division, and six Italian Divisions—Ariete, Trieste, Pavia, Bologna, Brescia, and Savona.

Feb. 7 The British completed the occupation of Cyrenaica with the total collapse of the Italians. Since the British offensive was launched two months ago, the Italian army had lost 380 tanks, more than 1,000 artillery pieces, 241 planes, and 130,000 men as prisoners. British Commonwealth losses were 500 killed, 1,373 wounded, and 55 missing.

Feb. 8 The first of the German forces for North

Africa, the 5th Panzer Regiment, left Naples by sea transport.

■ The British intercepted the Japanese merchant ship *Yamafuji* at the entrance to the Persian Gulf and confiscated all the mail it was carrying. Protests were filed with the British. (The British were also examining all mail on vessels calling at Hong Kong, which also embittered the Japanese.)

Feb. 9 British warships attacked targets on the northern Italian mainland. Force H, operating out of Gibraltar, steamed into the Gulf of Genoa and bombarded factories and port facilities in the city of Genoa, hit the oil refinery at Leghorn, and *Ark Royal* aircraft mined La Spezia. The British force returned to Gibraltar without suffering damage of any kind.

■ El Agheila was occupied by the British, who had now penetrated about 500 miles into Libya.

The advance was halted at this point as London decided to pull out many of the units and send them to Greece.

■ In a radio broadcast to the United States, Churchill pleaded for arms support: "Give us the tools, and we will finish the job." (The House of Representatives had voted approval the day before of the Lend-Lease bill—260 to 165—but the Senate had yet to act.)

Feb. 10 Britain broke off diplomatic relations with Rumania because its territory was "being used by Germany as a military base in furtherance of her plans for prosecuting the war. These measures are being taken without a word of dissent from the Rumanian Government." About 680,000 German troops were soon to be stationed in Rumania.

■ British forces under the command of Lieutenant General Sir Alan Cunningham began advanc-

British desert forces advance past a fallen enemy in a bayonet charge against a German strong point in North Africa.

ing into Italian Somaliland and Ethiopia from Kenya. A force made up of the South African 1st Division and two African divisions struck out for the Indian Ocean port of Kismayu.

Feb. 11 Five merchant ships in a British convoy off the Azores were sunk by Luftwaffe bombers.

Feb. 12 German troops began landing in Tripoli.

■ Rommel flew to Tripoli to assume command of the German forces in North Africa.

■ German planes attacked Benghazi, the first action in Africa for the Luftwaffe.

Feb. 14 Hitler issued a virtual ultimatum to the Yugoslav ministers he had summoned to Berchtesgaden, demanding Yugoslavia's participation in the Axis, rights of transit for German troops and arms, economic cooperation, and "passivity" to the German occupation of Bulgaria. Roosevelt, at the same time, sent a personal message to the Yugoslav regent, Prince Paul, warning against Yugoslav participation in the Axis.

■ The first German ground units landed at Tripoli.

■ The new Japanese ambassador to the United States, Admiral Kichisaburo Nomura, presented his credentials to President Roosevelt.

Feb. 16 Britain mined the waters of Singapore.

■ Kismayu in Italian Somaliland fell to the South African force from Kenya.

■ Turkey and Bulgaria signed a nonaggression pact, insuring Sofia a neutral Turkey in the projected campaign against Greece.

Feb. 17 The U.S. Senate began debating the lend-lease bill.

Feb. 19 The 8th Australian Division landed in Singapore.

■ Ambassador Nomura said there would be a war between Japan and the United States only if the United States wanted it.

Feb. 22 Rommel began moving his German units into position for an offensive in Libya.

■ Foreign Secretary Eden and Sir John Dill met with Greek officials in Athens to discuss specifics of British military assistance to Greece.

Feb. 23 German Foreign Minister Ribbentrop advised the Japanese ambassador in Berlin that Japan should enter the war against Britain "as soon as possible—in its own interest."

■ British statistics showed the fighting in North

Africa to date had resulted in British Commonwealth losses of 604 killed and 2,362 wounded or missing, while the Italians had suffered 20,000 dead or wounded and 180,000 captured.

■ Free French forces landed in Eritrea.

■ Mussolini assured the Italian people of victory despite the setbacks in Africa and Albania. He also denied Italy and Germany had any designs on the U.S.: "The lie is that the Axis powers, after they finish Great Britain, want to attack America. . . . In all cases it is more likely that the United States, before it is attacked by Axis soldiers, will be attacked by the not well-known but very warlike inhabitants of the planet Mars, who will descend from the stratosphere in unimaginable flying fortresses." (A measure of the studied concern about the content of this particular speech is that Mussolini read it from a prepared text. It was only the second speech of his career which was not extemporaneous. His only previous speech delivered from text was after the German occupation of Austria.)

Feb. 24 Admiral Darlan was named head of the Vichy government in France.

■ The British War Cabinet agreed to send troops to aid the Greeks, though it could not possibly provide the many divisions and support forces which Athens thought necessary.

■ Hitler claimed the German military had sunk 215,000 tons of British shipping in two days.

■ The Italian cruiser *Armando Diaz* was sunk by a British submarine in the Mediterranean.

Feb. 25 Foreign Minister Matsuoka of Japan said the white race must cede Oceania to Asians: "This region has sufficient natural resources to support from 600,000,000 to 800,000,000 people. I believe we have a natural right to migrate there."

■ Foreign Minister Ribbentrop met Japanese Ambassador Hiroshi Oshima near Salzburg. Ribbentrop said Germany would "crush" Britain, which was hard pressed for supplies. According to Ribbentrop, Britain was receiving one-third of its needs from the U.S. He said the only Americans wishing to enter the war were "Roosevelt, the Jews who surround him, and a group of financiers."

■ Nigerian troops of the British army occupied Mogadishu, the capital of Italian Somaliland. They had advanced 275 miles in just three days after the Italians had abandoned any pretense of defending the east African colony.

Feb. 26 Blaming Jews for attacks on Germans in northern Holland, occupation officials proclaimed martial law in that part of the country.

■ Franco formally reneged on his promise to join Germany in the fighting, telling Berlin previous agreements were "outmoded."

Feb. 27 British and German forces engaged each other for the first time in North Africa.

Feb. 28 Bridges near Giurgiu were destroyed by the Bulgarians to forestall any German attack through Rumania.

■ The British civilian air raid casualties for the past two months were 2,289 killed and 3,080 injured.

March 1 Chiang Kai-shek told the opening meeting of the Peoples Political Council that China would never reach a compromise with Japan. He also said any Japanese advance into the South Seas would further menace China.

■ Bulgaria joined the Axis, "upon the invitation of the German government." King Boris III (who was married to the daughter of the king of Italy) could not withstand the internal and external pressures. Moscow had told Sofia not to expect Soviet aid if attacked by Germany.

■ The first U.S. force for the protection of convoys in the North Atlantic was established. It consisted of destroyers and patrol aircraft.

March 2 The German Twelfth Army crossed the Danube and marched into Bulgaria, effectively controlling the country through occupation. Remaining resistance to German domination henceforth was ruthlessly squelched. The move was explained to the Russians, with whom the Bulgarians had a close affinity, as a "precautionary measure to prevent the British from gaining a foothold in Greece." The Russians protested anyway.

■ Eden conferred with Greek officials in Athens to complete plans for the introduction of British troops into Greece. The Greek government had hesitated to permit the landing of Commonwealth forces until the Germans crossed the Danube. With German forces in Bulgaria, the British quickly issued orders for the rapid deployment of their forces.

■ Hitler met with Prince Paul, told the Yugoslav leader that Germany planned to attack Russia and called for Yugoslav friendship when war started. Hitler also hoped the Yugoslavs would cooperate in Greece and promised Paul Salonika in return. The British, meanwhile, were urging Yugoslavia to attack the Italians in Albania.

■ Turkey imposed tighter controls on traffic through the Dardanelles, allowing ship transits by permit only.

March 3 The Greek-Albanian front was stabilized with the Greeks having pushed the numerically superior Italian forces completely out of Greece. Greek units had advanced to the Shkumbi River, occupied about a third of Albania, and were within 25 miles of the Albanian capital of Tirana.

March 4 British Commandos raided the Lofoten Islands off the extreme northern coast of Norway. The first raid of its kind during the war, it yielded considerable successes. Many German prisoners were captured, hundreds of Norwegians were evacuated for future military operations, all targets ashore were destroyed, and a 10,000-ton German fish factory ship was sunk.

■ The first of the British Commonwealth forces for Greece, including the 6th Australian Division, the 2nd New Zealand Division, and a Polish brigade, set sail from Egypt. (A total of 56,657 men would be sent to Greece as a counter to German moves and take up positions west of the Vardar River.)

March 5 Britain broke off diplomatic relations with Bulgaria noting that "from the nature of the German military movements in Bulgaria it is clear that the German aim is to menace and, if necessary, attack Great Britain's ally, Greece."

■ Hitler called on the Japanese to become active participants in a Far East war.

■ General Weygand announced that French territory in Africa would be defended.

March 6 Churchill issued his "Battle of the Atlantic Directive," giving highest priority to measures for knocking out German U-boats and bombers blocking shipments to Britain.

■ German aircraft began dropping acoustic magnetic mines in the Suez Canal, further impeding the flow of British supplies to Greece and North Africa. The initial mine-laying operation had the immediate effect of blocking the vital waterway for three weeks while the waters were cleared.

March 7 British troops began disembarking at Greek ports.

March 8 The U.S. Senate voted to approve lend-lease by a margin of 60 to 31.

March 10 Japan resolved a number of outstanding disputes in Southeast Asia by winning a French cession of Cambodian territory to Thailand and receiving a monopoly on the production of all the rice produced in Indochina. French authorities in Indochina also granted Japan full use of the Saigon airport. Previously, Japan had sought military rights only in the northern section of Vietnam.

March 11 U.S. lend-lease arms trade was permitted under provisions of an amendment to the Neutrality Act signed into law by President Roosevelt, who said, "This decision is the end of any attempt at appeasement in our land; the end of urging us to get along with the dictators; the end of compromise with tyranny and the forces of oppression."

March 12 Roosevelt requested $7 billion in military credits to Britain under the new land-lease law. Churchill expressed British thanks for the measure, hailing it as a "new Magna Charta."

■ Italian forces in Albania launched another offensive along the 130-mile-long front in an effort to throw the Greek forces back to their own territory.

March 13 Germany repeated its demand that Yugoslavia join the Axis. It became increasingly apparent to Berlin that German troops would be needed in Greece and access through Yugoslavia was essential.

March 16 Hitler predicted the war would be won by the Axis by the end of the year.

■ Berbera in British Somaliland was retaken by a small British landing force from Aden.

March 17 The Italian defense of Keren in Eritrea began to collapse when British Commonwealth reinforcements entered the assault on the fortress.

■ Jijiga in Ethiopia fell to British forces which had started off from Kenya and pressed through Italian Somaliland. The British now had reached a point about a thousand miles from the Kenyan border in just five weeks.

March 18 Rommel was denied permission to launch a German counteroffensive in North Africa by the end of May.

■ The Italian offensive in Albania was halted with only insignificant gains made in a week of fighting.

March 19 Hitler issued an ultimatum to Yugoslavia to accept German terms which would place the Yugoslavs under virtual total control of Berlin.

■ Admiral Raeder met with the Japanese ambassador in Berlin and "expressed his desire for a Japanese attack on Singapore."

March 20 Under Secretary of State Welles told Soviet Ambassador Constantine A. Oumansky that the U.S. had confirmed information Germany would shortly attack the Soviet Union. (The knowledge was acquired by methods which could not be revealed to the Russians. U.S. Signal Intelligence Service analysts had predicted "a German attack on the U.S.S.R. within two months." The estimate came from a reading of top secret Japanese diplomatic messages, primarily the dispatches to Tokyo from Baron Oshima, the Japanese ambassador in Berlin.)

■ Four members of the Yugoslav cabinet resigned rather than face capitulation to the German demands. British agents kidnapped the pro-German leader Milan Stoyadinovich and spirited him away to Greece to eliminate his influence in the political turmoil of Belgrade.

■ Hargeisa in British Somaliland was retaken by British forces who continued their advance westward into Ethiopia.

March 22 Two U.S. grain-carrying ships were permitted to pass through the British blockade and deliver their cargoes to Vichy France.

March 23 A small British relief convoy reached Malta, but two of the ships were bombed by German planes while unloading. The quantity of supplies actually delivered to the island's defenders was meager.

■ A total of 59,141 tons of British shipping was lost the previous week, primarily in the North Atlantic where German U-boats were marauding at will.

■ RAF bombers raided Berlin.

March 24 Turkey and the Soviet Union signed a neutrality treaty, each pledging to remain neutral if the other were attacked.

■ German forces in North Africa under Rommel mounted their first major offensive operation and reached El Agheila, which fell without offering resistance.

■ Allied forces ousted the last of the Italian troops from British Somaliland.

March 25 Yugoslavia yielded to German pressures and joined the Axis by adhering to the Tripartite Pact. The Belgrade government said it had no alternative save military occupation by Germany. Hitler did agree that somehow Yugoslav "neutrality" would be observed.

■ Germany announced its blockade of Britain would extend to within three miles of Greenland.

March 27 American and British staff officers concluded their conferences in Washington on a common strategy if the U.S. entered the war.

■ Britain and the U.S. reached an agreement for the transfer of British naval and air bases in Newfoundland, Bermuda, Jamaica, St. Lucia, Antigua, Trinidad, British Guiana, and the Bahamas to the U.S.

■ Congress approved an appropriation of $7 billion for the U.S. lend-lease program.

■ Seventeen-year-old King Peter II assumed power in Yugoslavia after army and air force officers overthrew the government which had been forced to bring the country into the Axis. Churchill immediately promised British aid, but the new Belgrade government under General Dusan Simovich vowed to remain neutral. Hitler, upon hearing of the coup, said to his military leaders, "Destroy Yugoslavia as a national unit . . . with unmerciful harshness." (The decision forced a crucial month-long delay in the German invasion of Russia.)

■ British forces captured the fortress of Keren in Eritrea. It was the main defense bastion for the Italians, who fought fiercely for seven weeks to keep it. The British overpowered the garrison but lost 4,000 men. The Italians suffered 3,000 losses. With Keren gone, all of Eritrea was open to the British.

March 28 The Italians suffered a crushing defeat in the Battle of Cape Matapan off the southern tip of Greece. Most of the Italian fleet was concentrated in these waters, but the British nonetheless challenged the large enemy force with aircraft and surface forces. The cruisers *Pola*, *Zara*, and *Fiume*, and two destroyers were sunk by British gunfire. More than 2,400 Italians were

lost aboard the five ships. The only British loss was a Swordfish torpedo bomber aircraft.

■ Total British air raid civilian casualties to date were 28,859 killed and 40,166 injured.

March 30 The U.S. government seized all German, Italian, and Danish ships in American ports.

■ RAF planes failed to damage the German battle cruisers *Scharnhorst* and *Gneisenau* which were attacked while in port at Brest, France.

March 31 British naval and air forces had sunk one-fifth of the German submarine fleet during the month. The losses were particularly damaging to the German effort since many of their experienced commanders were among those lost.

■ British civilian air raid casualties for March were 4,259 killed and 5,557 injured.

April 1 Japanese Foreign Minister Matsuoka began talks in Rome with Italian officials. He met with the king and told him Japan was in complete sympathy with Italy's war aims.

■ Asmara in Eritrea fell to Commonwealth troops.

■ The first 4,000-pound bombs were dropped by RAF Wellingtons, on Emden, Germany.

April 2 British units began falling back in North Africa, abandoning Mersa Brega in the face of heavy German attacks.

■ Mussolini told Matsuoka the U.S. was deliberately provoking war. Matsuoka also visited the Vatican and reported to Tokyo: "The Pope took an utterly detached attitude, free of any favoritism regarding the European war, and approached the question from the point of view of a general peace throughout the world."

April 2-3 German troops crossed into Hungary while the Budapest government was still considering a grant of transit rights. Germany had demanded them in order to use Hungary as a military jumping-off point. Prime Minister Count Teleki committed suicide to dramatize Hungary's plight.

April 3 Yugoslavia ordered full military mobilization.

■ A pro-Axis Arab officer faction in Iraq, led by Rashid Ali Gailani, seized power in Baghdad. Rashid Ali had assurances from the Vichy officials in neighboring French Syria that German aircraft would operate out of Syrian bases in attacking the British in Iraq and that other German support would be forthcoming.

■ Stalin was personally told by the British ambassador in Moscow, Sir Stafford Cripps, that German units were being deployed along their eastern frontier for an attack on the Soviet Union.

April 3–4 German U-boats sank 10 ships out of a 22-vessel convoy in the North Atlantic. These losses prompted U.S. naval leaders to bring American ships operating in the area under convoy protection.

April 4 German and Italian troops wrested control of Benghazi. Rommel's forces then moved out swiftly along the coast and directly across the Cyrenaican desert.

■ Addis Ababa was abandoned by the Italians.

■ Hitler conferred with Matsuoka in Berlin. The German leader had previously told his guest, "England has already lost the war. It is only a matter of having the intelligence to admit it." At this meeting Hitler again urged the Japanese to attack the British and other Allies in Asia. Hitler denigrated the United States, apparently to ease Japan's fears about possible U.S. entry into a Pacific war. The minutes indicate Hitler's arguments: "Germany had made her preparations so that no American could land in Europe. Germany would wage a vigorous war against Americans with U-boats and the Luftwaffe, and with her greater experience . . . would be more than a match for America, entirely apart from the fact that German soldiers were, obviously, far superior to the Americans." In the end Hitler assured Japan that Germany would fight against the United States if Japan got into a war with the U.S.

■ The United States rejected German and Italian protests of the March 30 ship seizures, and requested withdrawal of the Italian naval attaché.

April 5 Russia and Yugoslavia signed a treaty of friendship and nonaggression, which the Germans condemned. The pact marked a crucial point in the rupture between Germany and Russia.

■ Japan declared it would control all rubber exports from Thailand, Indochina, and the Dutch East Indies through a Japanese association of rubber dealers. Japan was reduced to a month's supply of rubber stocks.

April 6 German troops launched coordinated attacks against Yugoslavia from Bulgaria, Rumania, Austria, and Hungary. Spearheading the invasion were 33 German divisions, supported by 1,200 planes of the Luftwaffe. Hitler said he had "tried to convince Yugoslav statesmen of the absolute necessity for their cooperation with the German Reich for restoration of lasting peace and order within Yugoslavia." Yugoslavia had 28 divisions to defend its long borders and could never offer concentrated or coordinated resistance. The Germans drove for Zagreb and Belgrade in the north, while other units were to occupy southern Yugoslavia and break through to Greece. Belgrade was subjected to intense aerial bombardment, primarily from Stukas, and was reduced to near rubble by the 13th.

■ German forces invaded Greece. Units of the XXX Corps swept into Thrace and the XVIII Corps into Macedonia from Bulgaria. Greek defenses in the northeast part of the country were arrayed along the Metaxas line, which was attacked frontally. As Yugoslav defenses collapsed, the German 2nd Panzer Division swung south and moved behind the Metaxas line toward Salonika.

■ The capital of Ethiopia, Addis Ababa, was occupied by the South African 1st Division.

■ Six British generals, including Sir Richard O'Connor and Sir Philip Neame, were captured by a German patrol in Libya. They had become lost in a sandstorm. (O'Connor later escaped from captivity and ended up commanding the VIII Corps in the Normandy invasion.)

April 7 Advance elements of a German panzer division reached Skoplje, having fought their way 60 miles in 32 hours through incredibly difficult terrain. German planes had effectively neutralized Yugoslavia's rail system by knocking out key junctions. The Yugoslavs found it impossible to strengthen faltering defense points. With transportation so decisive a factor, those Yugoslav troops which had penetrated into northern Albania were forced to withdraw.

■ Claiming that Hungary had become "a base of operations" against the Allies, Britain severed diplomatic relations with Budapest.

■ RAF bombers raided Sofia.

■ Derna in Libya was occupied by the advancing Germans and Italians. The British evacuated Benghazi.

■ A 12,000-ton ship laden with TNT exploded in Piraeus, Greece, severly crippling port facilities. Six merchant ships and 60 lighters were lost in the blast. An ammunition train was ignited on shore. The accident created a logistical hardship for the British in the crucial days ahead.

■ The first British jet plane, a Gloster E28/39, was test flown successfully.

■ British forces and French Foreign Legionnaires occupied Massawa, the main Italian naval base in east Africa. Ten thousand Italians were captured. The Red Sea was now cleared of all Italian naval activity, which allowed for unobstructed runs through the Indian Ocean to the Suez Canal. The fall of Massawa also permitted President Roosevelt to declare the Red Sea was no longer a combat zone and opened the way for U.S. merchant ships to use the route.

■ German troops took the Skoplje Gap and the Rupel Pass, opening the way into Serbia and northern Greece.

■ Axis forces in Libya overwhelmed the badly-decimated British 2nd Armored Division and the 3rd Indian Brigade at Mechili.

■ Chiang Kai-shek told the Executive Yuan that the Kuomintang would pursue a policy of cooperating with the Chinese Communists: "These border embroglios [territorial disputes with the Communists] are mere secondary questions. We can't worry too much over such trivialities. As the international situation improves, they will automatically be settled. Let's wait at least until we get a definite assurance from England and the United States before we clamp down on the Communists."

April 9 The United States acquired full military defense rights in Greenland. The agreement affirmed Greenland's loyalty to Denmark and agreed on the need for protection "against attack by a non-American power." German reconnaissance flights had been made over Greenland, causing concern that Berlin might be able to establish bases on the island to be used in attacking North America. The Danish minister in Washington arranged the agreement, but his action was disavowed by the government in Copenhagen.

■ Rommel's forces swept into Bardia.

■ German 2nd Panzer Division tanks smashed into Salonika, Greece. Nish in eastern Yugoslavia fell to the Germans, opening the southern "back door" to Belgrade. Djevdjeliya (Gevgelija) was taken, cutting the last land link between Yugoslavia and Greece.

■ A Croatian national government was proclaimed in Zagreb as German troops reached the outskirts of the city. The Croats were generally favorably disposed to the Germans, a fact recognized by the Germans who spared all cities in Croatia from air attack.

April 9–10 British bombers hit Berlin in an attack which brought the war home with devastating impact. The Wellingtons gutted the State Opera House and caused extensive damage along Unter den Linden.

April 10 The first American "shot in anger" against Germany was fired by a U.S. destroyer south of Iceland. After picking up survivors from a torpedoed Dutch freighter, the U.S.S. *Niblack* detected a submarine in the area, assumed it was attacking, and dropped depth charges on it. The German submarine, which was indeed there, left the scene, apparently undamaged.

■ Hungary and Italy joined in the attack on Yugoslavia. The Italian Second Army crossed the Julian Alps and proceeded to drive down the Adriatic coast. Hungary occupied Yugoslav territory north of the Danube which it had lost after the last war.

■ The German Second Army occupied Skoplje in Yugoslavia. All of southern Serbia was under control of the German Twelfth Army.

■ Allied defenders held off the German XL Corps which was sweeping down from Yugoslavia along the Aliakmon River.

■ In North Africa, the 9th Australian Division pulled back into Tobruk.

■ The U.S. proclaimed that the Red Sea and Gulf of Aden were no longer areas of combat, thereby opening these waters to American ships.

■ Military and conservative factions in Japan gained greater influence in a cabinet reshuffle. Musatsume Ogura, Admiral Teijiro Toyoda, and Lieutenant General Teichi Suzuki, all considered proexpansion, were added to the cabinet. In another move strengthening the "war hawk" point of view, Admiral Osami Nagano replaced Prince Hiroyasu Fushimi as chief of the Naval General Staff.

April 12 Belgrade, the capital of Yugoslavia, fell to the Germans as armored columns of the XLVI Panzer Corps stormed in from three sides. Even before the tanks entered, a young German captain and nine enlisted men bluffed their way into the city, and virtually the entire defense garrison surrendered. Zagreb was occupied, and the Germans were greeted enthusiastically by the Croatian population.

■ Allied forces formed a defense line centering on Mount Olympus in Greece. Outnumbered Australian troops at Vevi, in the Monastir gap just south of the Yugoslav border, fought a bitter defensive battle with a panzer division but finally had to yield.

■ RAF bombers flew daylight missions against targets on the continent.

■ South Greenland's governor informed the American consul at Godthaab that he would not recognize the agreement concluded by the Danish minister in Washington giving the U.S. military base rights in Greenland. He said he would resist any such move until "faced with the fait accompli." (The U.S. presented him with the fait accompli when it sent a contingent of U.S. Marines and three Coast Guard cutters to Greenland.)

April 13 Japan and the Soviet Union signed a five-year neutrality pact in Moscow. Stalin thoroughly feared Germany's intentions and needed Russia's Asian flank protected; German control of the Balkans and information that Berlin was already thinking of invading the Soviet Union dictated a peaceful resolution of relations with Japan. Tokyo, for its part, was increasingly determined to move south and wished to protect its northern flank. It was a marriage of convenience. Stalin's parting words to Foreign Minister Matsuoka were interesting in understanding Stalin's

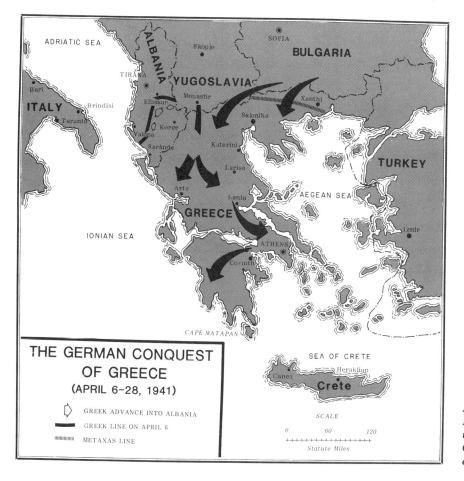

THE GERMAN CONQUEST OF GREECE
(APRIL 6–28, 1941)

▷ GREEK ADVANCE INTO ALBANIA
▬ GREEK LINE ON APRIL 6
▥ METAXAS LINE

SCALE

0   60   120

Statute Miles

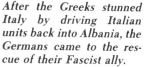

After the Greeks stunned Italy by driving Italian units back into Albania, the Germans came to the rescue of their Fascist ally.

desperation. Stalin said he "was a convinced adherent of the Axis and a foe of England and the United States."

■ Rommel's forces encircled Tobruk and recaptured Bardia, placing the Afrika Korps at the Egyptian border. Churchill assured Roosevelt the British would not abandon North Africa but said U.S. supplies could be crucial to the outcome.

■ Malta was pounded by Axis bombers.

■ RAF bombers attacked Sofia, Bulgaria.

■ Veroia and Katerini, points on the original British defense line in Greece, fell to the Germans.

April 14 Tobruk's defenders beat back a determined assault by the German 5th Light Division on the encircled city.

■ Yugoslavia sued for peace, seeking to negotiate a surrender.

■ German troops reached the Aliakmon River in Greece.

April 15 Bulgaria broke diplomatic relations with Yugoslavia. Its troops began marching into Macedonia.

April 16 Roosevelt outlined four essential points as a foundation for relations between nations: 1) territorial integrity; 2) noninterference in the affairs of other countries; 3) equal commercial opportunity; and 4) a status quo in the Pacific. The points were made as talks began in Washington between U.S. and Japanese officials.

■ St. Paul's Cathedral in London was bombed and damaged in the blitz.

■ Four British destroyers destroyed an entire Italian convoy (totaling 14,000 tons) en route to Libya with supplies for Axis forces in North Africa.

■ Rommel deployed the full 15th Panzer Division for the first time in North Africa to launch another assault on Tobruk.

■ German panzers from Macedonia reached the Pindus Mountain passes and cut off the escape routes of Greek troops in Albania. German Second Army units began attacking Allied positions at the Servia Pass, with the plain of Thessaly lying open beyond it.

April 17 German forces took the Servia pass.

■ A large RAF bombing force struck Berlin.

■ Royal Navy units bombarded the old Italian fortress of Fort Capuzzo in Libya.

■ A German raider sank the Egyptian steamship *Zamza* in the South Atlantic. About 150 Americans were among the rescued.

April 18 Admiral Ernest J. King, commander in chief, U.S. Atlantic Fleet, ordered U.S. ships and planes to attack any Axis ship within 25 miles of the Western Hemisphere on the assumption it was hostile.

■ British troops in Greece began withdrawing to Thermopylae.

April 19 British troops were sent to Iraq to quell the pro-Axis rebellion under terms of the 1930 Anglo-Iraqi treaty: "The aid of the King of Iraq in the event of war or imminent menace of war will consist in furnishing to His Britannic Majesty, on Iraq territory, all facilities and assistance in his power, including the use of roads, rivers, ports, airdromes, and means of communications." A force of British and Indian troops—originally earmarked for Malaya—was landed at Basra and Shaibah.

■ Greek Premier Alexander Korizis committed suicide. The impending military defeat and the great suffering endured by Greece during the war left Korizis in a state of deep depression.

■ Admiral Darlan informed the League of Nations that Vichy was withdrawing French membership in the moribund international organization.

April 20 Greece was forced to capitulate. The government in Athens advised the British that further resistance in Greece was useless: "You have done your best to save us. We are finished. But the war is not lost. Therefore save what you can of your Army to help win elsewhere." Greek forces in Macedonia and Epirus were cut off by the Germans.

■ The encirclement of Tobruk was tightened, but resistance continued, aided by British naval and air support.

April 21 Greece submitted to an armistice agreement dictated by Germany.

■ Tripoli in Libya was bombarded by British warships. Only one Axis ship was sunk and unloading at the docks was barely disrupted. The British felt that only by finding and destroying ships at sea could the flow of supplies to the Italian and German armies in North Africa be properly disrupted. Prospects for effective defense along the coastal land route appeared increasingly bleak.

■ Japanese army forces occupied Foochow in China.

April 22 Two thousand U.S. Army reinforcements were sent to the Philippines.

■ Emmanuel Tsouderos was named premier of Greece.

April 23 Greece formally surrendered to Germany and Italy. King George II escaped to Crete. The British fought a battle to permit evacuation, falling back to a line across the peninsula at Thebes. Air cover was important, but the British had only 100 planes to the German force of 1,000.

■ Bulgarian troops occupied Thrace in northern Greece.

■ Japan began a six-day ceremony to "deify" 14,976 soldiers and sailors "who sacrificed themselves in the China affair."

■ Athens severed diplomatic relations with Bulgaria.

■ Chiang complained to Ambassador Nelson T. Johnson in Chungking that promised U.S. aid to China was not forthcoming.

■ The America First Committee held its first mass rally. Thirty thousand people attended the New York gathering and heard keynote speaker Charles A. Lindbergh say: "The British government has one last desperate plan: . . . to persuade us to send another American Expeditionary Force to Europe and to share with England militarily, as well as financially, the fiasco of this war." Lindbergh added that Britain was guilty of having "encouraged the smaller nations of Europe to fight against hopeless odds."

April 24 British forces began evacuating all their positions in Greece and proceeded to the southern beaches for transport. (The weather turned out to be a savior for the British. Even though the Luftwaffe completely dominated the air, the British were able to avoid the expected interdiction and evacuated 40,000 men out of an original force of 62,500. They were transported to Crete and Egypt. The moon remained largely obscured by heavy cloud cover through the 29th, when the evacuation was completed. Two destroyers and four transports were sunk during the evacuation operation. For the entire abortive Greek campaign, the RAF lost 207 aircraft and the British Expeditionary Ground Forces lost or abandoned more than 8,000 vehicles of all types.)

■ Bulgaria declared war on Greece and Yugoslavia. Bulgarian troops began occupying territory in western Thrace, which was already under German control.

■ Australian reinforcements reached Singapore to aid in land and sea defense preparations.

■ U.S. naval units began patrolling the Atlantic eastward to 26° east longitude and southward to 20° north latitude.

April 25 The German naval attaché in Moscow cabled Berlin that rumors were rife on a German-Russian war. He quoted the British ambassador as stating that it would begin on June 22 (which it did).

■ Roosevelt criticized Lindbergh for his New York speech, calling him defeatist and an appeaser.

■ Rommel's forces in Egypt took the Halfaya Pass and pushed the British forces back to Mersa Matruh.

■ Hitler issued orders for an airborne invasion of Crete.

April 26 German paratroopers seized Corinth in Greece. The bridge over the canal was blown up by a British rear guard, which inflicted heavy losses on the Germans.

April 27 Athens was occupied by the Germans. Motorcycle troops raised the German flag over the Acropolis at 8:35 A.M.

■ American, British and Dutch military representatives—meeting in Singapore—agreed on common action in the Pacific if Japan entered the war.

■ Rashid Ali advised the British he would not permit any more troops to be brought into Iraq.

April 28 German units took Sollum in Egypt.

Lindbergh resigned his commission as a colonel in the U.S. Army Air Corps Reserve.

April 29 The last of the main British forces were evacuated from Greece.

■ Two shiploads of British reinforcements arrived at Basra to aid in what was building up to a military confrontation with the new pro-Axis Iraqi government. Rashid Ali proposed British women and children be evacuated out of Baghdad to the RAF base at Habbaniyah, 50 miles to the west, for "their protection."

April 30 German troops completed their occupation of Greece.

■ Rommel's forces continued pouring into Egypt and advanced six miles beyond the frontier.

■ Nine thousand Iraqi troops with twenty-eight pieces of artillery surrounded the RAF base at Habbaniyah. The 230 British women and children who had taken refuge at the base were declared to be hostages. There were 6,000 civilians at Habbaniyah, with a military force of 2,200. The oil pipelines out of Iraq were blocked.

JEWS IN THE THIRD REICH

For those Jews remaining in Germany (mostly because they held critical jobs), life was rigidly proscribed. They were forbidden to:

• leave their residences without a police permit,
• buy clothes,
• shop except between 4 and 5 P.M. (when most stores were out of basic provisions),
• smoke tobacco,
• use public telephones,
• ride on public transport unless all Aryan passengers were seated,
• keep pets,
• have their hair cut by an Aryan barber,
• own any electric appliances, record players, typewriters, or bicycles.

May Himmler outlined educational policies for eastern territories seized by Germany: "There must not be a more advanced education for the non-German population of the east than four years of primary school. This primary education has the following objective only: doing simple arithmetic to 500; writing one's name, learning that it was God's command that the Germans must be obeyed, and that one has to be honest, diligent, and obedient. I don't consider reading skills necessary. Except for this school, no other kind of school must be allowed in the east."

May 1 German bombers hit Liverpool in the first raid of a week-long attack.

■ German attacks on Tobruk were again repulsed.

May 2 British troops occupied Basra and several of the oil fields of Iraq. Fighting broke out in several areas. The pro-Axis government demanded the withdrawal of all British troops and requested German military aid. At Habbaniyah, meanwhile, the British used antiquated training planes and two World War I artillery pieces to attack the Iraqis encircling them. This action permitted evacuation of the women and children.

May 3 Germany and Italy split up Slovenia and each annexed its share of the former Yugoslav territory.

■ Revolutionary Iraqi forces occupied Rutba and other oil fields.

■ Hamburg was bombed by the RAF.

■ Heavy fighting broke out at Amba Alagi in Ethiopia as British forces closed the ring on Italian forces under the command of the Italian viceroy, Amadeus, Duke of Aosta.

May 4 Hitler said the entire Balkan campaign had cost the Germans only 5,500 casualties.

May 5 Tokyo advised the Japanese ambassador in Washington, "According to a fairly reliable source of information, it appears almost certain that the United States Government is reading your code messages." (The information was correct, but subsequent investigations in Tokyo and Washington led the Japanese to conclude their Purple diplomatic code was not compromised. No effort was made to change it. The source of Tokyo's concern, "the fairly reliable source of information," was probably the German ambassador in Washington who had been confronted by the Russian ambassador who had knowledge of an impending German attack on the Soviet Union. These reports may have been given the Russian by U.S. Under Secretary of State Sumner Welles, who had access to the Magic intercepts of the Purple code, and was anxious to rupture Soviet-German relations. Some have suggested they may have originated with a German agent working at the Soviet embassy.)

■ Iraqi troops abandoned the heights around Habbaniyah.

■ Emperor Haile Selassie was returned to his Ethiopian throne. He made his triumphal return to Addis Ababa five years to the day after Italian troops had conquered his capital.

May 6 Secretary of War Stimson proposed the use

of U.S. Navy ships to protect British-bound convoys.

■ The Soviet military attaché in Berlin, Captain Voronstov, advised Moscow: ". . . according to a statement of a certain German officer from Hitler's headquarters, Germany is preparing to invade the USSR on May 14 through Finland, the Baltic countries and Latvia. At the same time Moscow and Leningrad will be heavily raided and paratroopers landed in border cities. . . ."

May 7 Stalin assumed the premiership of the Soviet Union.

■ A boarding party from the Royal Navy destroyer *Somali* found an intact German naval Enigma coding machine and cipher book when it captured the weather ship *München* in the North Atlantic. The cryptographic equipment proved useful in breaking the German naval code through Ultra intercepts.

■ Churchill won a vote of confidence, 447–3, two Labor members and a Communist opposing him.

May 8–10 German planes arrived at the airfield at Mosul in Iraq to begin operations against the British. About fifty fighters were based at the Iraqi base.

May 8 The first of the German raiders (converted merchantmen) were sunk. *Pinguin* was caught in the Indian Ocean by the British cruiser *Cornwall* whose 8-inch shells exploded 130 mines being carried by the raider.

May 9 In a move to conciliate Germany, the Soviet Union withdrew its recognition of Belgium, Norway, and Yugoslavia.

■ Representatives of Thailand and French Indochina concluded a peace treaty in Tokyo.

■ The Royal Navy's *Bulldog* and *Broadway* captured the submarine *U-110* in the North Atlantic, the first German underwater craft to fall into Allied hands. Although the U-boat sank the next day, crewmen from the British destroyer and sloop were able to remove an Enigma machine, cipher books, and the rotor settings then in use. It was even more valuable a find than the equipment recovered from *München* two days earlier. The combination of the two captured cryptographic prizes were crucially important in breaking German U-boat codes and ultimately in winning the Battle of the North Atlantic.

May 10 Rudolf Hess, the number three-ranked German behind Hitler and Göring, flew to Scotland alone in a fighter plane and dropped by parachute on the estate of the Duke of Hamilton. It stunned the Allies and Axis alike. Hess apparently believed he could conclude a peace treaty with Britain. His mental condition was thought to have been a key factor in the famous flight, but Hess's notions of concluding the conflict reflected the belief of many Germans that the real struggle was not between them and the British and a peace should be concluded. At no time did the British authorities take him seriously (although the Russians could never accept that fact and always assumed Hess was being kept available for an eventual separate peace). (After the war, Hess was tried as a war criminal, but the flight probably spared him his life. He received a life sentence instead of being executed.)

■ A German experimental jet-powered fighter plane, the Me-163, was flown at 621 miles per hour. (Work on this jet and another, the Me-262, was never accelerated despite the revolutionary qualities of the aircraft and the tremendous advantages the Luftwaffe would have enjoyed in defending Germany's cities and production facilities against Allied bombers in the years ahead.)

■ British units began advancing toward Baghdad. Arab Legion forces from Transjordan, meanwhile, forced Iraqi troops out of Rutba.

■ Benghazi was shelled by British warships.

May 10–11 German bombers directed their heaviest and deadliest raid of the war on London. Casualties were 1,436 killed and 1,792 injured. Among the historic buildings hit in the raid were Westminster Abbey, the House of Commons, and the British Museum. It was to be the last raid on London for ten weeks.

May 11 Former President Hoover said only by staying out of the war could the U.S. aid Britain. He thought "America is as yet unprepared even for adequate defense; that our people are not united." Hoover predicted an invasion of Europe would require 5 million U.S. soldiers.

May 12 Japan proposed a general settlement of all its disputes with the U.S. Ambassador Nomura said the proposals would lead to a "just peace in the Pacific."

■ Darlan met with Hitler at Berchtesgaden to discuss expanded cooperation between Vichy France and Germany in economic and military matters. Hitler sought the use of French bases in North Africa and Syria.

■ In a further move to placate Germany, Moscow recognized the pro-Nazi government in Iraq.

■ German aircraft began operating out of Iraqi and Syrian bases.

■ A British convoy reached Alexandria with 238 desperately needed tanks for the Western Desert Force.

May 13 Australian Prime Minister Robert G. Menzies said U.S. involvement in the war was essential, "for parliamentary liberty and the ordered rights of self-government are our joint and several heritage."

■ The U.S. War Department said labor strikes were seriously delaying military procurement. Firms with army orders had lost 1.7 million man-days of production since the first of the year because of shutdowns.

■ Martin Bormann was named German Nazi party chancellor, succeeding Hess.

May 14 Germany declared the northern part of the Red Sea a combat zone.

■ A German delegation arrived in Baghdad to arrange for a formal request from the Rashid Ali government for German troop intervention in Iraq. (The situation in Baghdad was far from stable, however, and the forthcoming invasion of Crete—with its large manpower commitment—precluded any immediate direct involvement in Iraq.)

■ RAF aircraft attacked Palmyra (Tadmor) and other airfields in Syria which were being used by the Germans to attack British troops in Jordan and Iraq. This was the first British action against Vichy-controlled Syria.

■ More troop reinforcements landed at Singapore.

■ The Gestapo arrested 3,600 Jews in Paris.

May 15 In a broadcast to the people of France, Roosevelt criticized the Vichy government for its collaborationist policies toward Germany: "The people of the United States can hardly believe that the present Government of France could be brought to lend itself to a plan of voluntary alliance, implied or otherwise, which would apparently deliver up France and its colonial empire, including French African colonies and their Atlantic coasts, with the menace which that involves to the peace and safety of the Western

Hemisphere." Pétain, at almost the same time, was announcing a policy of closer collaboration with Germany in Europe and Africa.

■ Roosevelt ordered American guards aboard eleven French ships (including the luxury passenger liner *Normandie*) which were in U.S. ports, placing them under U.S. jurisdiction.

■ British Commonwealth armor and infantry counterattacked from Egypt, retaking the Halfaya Pass. (The British force was now reduced to about 25,000 men, Britons, Australians, Indians, and South Africans. A major offensive could not be sustained, and the Allies soon withdrew.)

■ Crete came under heavy German aerial attack.

May 16 Iceland formally severed its ties to Denmark and became an independent nation.

■ Britain banned all shipments of rubber to Japan from Malaya.

■ Three Luftwaffe bombers attacked the RAF base at Habbaniyah in Iraq.

■ Berlin ordered Rommel to leave Tobruk to the Italians and employ his German force in the Sollum area.

May 18 Italy took the Dalmatian coast and the former Yugoslav Adriatic islands. Rome also effectively annexed Croatia and placed the territory under the "protection" of the Italian throne. The Duke of Spoleto, a nephew of the king of Italy, was proclaimed monarch as King Tomislav I.

■ The German warships *Bismarck* and *Prinz Eugen* left the Baltic port of Gdynia.

■ Vichy France declared it would resist any British moves in Syria.

■ Cordell Hull outlined a program of reconstruction for the postwar world.

May 19 One hundred thousand French POW's were released by the Germans. French costs for maintaining the German army of occupation were reduced to 240 million francs per day. The gestures were Germany's response to increased collaboration by Vichy France.

■ Because of heavy losses of their aircraft on Crete by Luftwaffe raids, the British decided to withdraw their few outnumbered planes from the island. The airfields themselves, however, were not rendered inoperable.

May 20 Germany invaded Crete. The most spectacular air assault of the war was launched at dawn as 22,750 German paratroopers and glider-borne units landed along the northwestern coast of the island. It was the first time in history an entire invasion force was moved by air. To defend the island, which was strategically important to the Allies and the Axis, the British had committed 28,000 troops, augmented by two weak Greek divisions of 14,500 men. Crete is 335 miles from Alexandria, 450 from the Suez Canal. The Germans suffered heavy casualties during the first day of fighting. Part of the pressure was relieved after the second wave landed much later in the day to the east around Heraklion and Retimo. (Within ten days, the Germans won the island, but they suffered 6,000 dead. German aircraft losses totaled 250. Allied casualties were great, too. Only 15,000 Allied soldiers were evacuated. Three times that number were left behind, dead or to be captured. Crete, in terms of impact, led the German command to conclude that airborne operations were not worth the cost, and no further such assaults were attempted. Hitler, two months after the invasion, said, "The day of the parachutist is over." Britain's problems after Crete were immediate. In addition to the losses in manpower, the RAF had lost 46 aircraft, and the Royal Navy had one aircraft carrier, three cruisers, and six destroyers sunk, making Britain's position in the eastern Mediterranean precarious.

■ Soviet spy Richard Sorge in Tokyo advised Moscow that Germany was preparing to invade Russia with a force of between 170 and 190 divisions, which was being massed in Poland. Sorge anticipated the invasion would take place on June 20 (missing the actual date by two days).

■ Germany completed its positioning of forces for the invasion of Russia, massing 120 divisions along the Soviet border.

■ Ambassador Nomura informed Tokyo the U.S. was reading coded Japanese diplomatic messages. (The embassy in Washington was told to have only one person handle sensitive cipher messages.)

May 20–21 Twenty-five small vessels transporting German troops to Greece were attacked by an overwhelming British force of three cruisers and four destroyers off the coast of Crete. Most of the transports were sunk, and 2,300 German troops killed.

May 21 A German submarine torpedoed and sank the American freighter S.S. *Robin Moore* in the South Atlantic. The ship was en route to South Africa.

■ Declaring Paris "an extended zone of operations," the Germans requested all foreign diplomats leave the city by June 10.

■ German forces captured the Maleme airfield on Crete. A British counterattack failed.

May 22 Britain warned the Pétain government of the consequences of collaboration: "If the Vichy government, in pursuance of their declared policy of collaboration with the enemy, take action or permit action detrimental to our conduct of the war . . . we shall no longer feel bound to

A German antitank gun prepares to cover advancing infantrymen on Crete.

draw any distinction between occupied land and unoccupied territory in the execution of our military plans."

■ Soviet Deputy Military Attaché Khlopov, in Berlin, advised Moscow that ". . . the attack of the German Army is reportedly scheduled for June 15, but it is possible that it may begin in the first days of June."

■ Roosevelt ordered the U.S. military to make plans for the immediate occupation of the Azores to forestall German seizure of the Portuguese islands.

■ The British navy suffered heavy losses in action around Crete. Two cruisers, *Gloucester* and *Fiji*, were sunk, and the battleships *Warspite* and *Valiant* were damaged.

May 23 Royal Navy ships bombarded the Maleme airfield on Crete.

■ British ships remaining in operation around Crete were given permission to return to their base at Alexandria.

■ Admiral Darlan said France was compelled to collaborate with Germany because to ameliorate the "consequences of defeat and of the conditions of the armistice," it was "necessary for her to choose between life and death. The Marshal [Pétain] and the Government have chosen life." Darlan also declared the Vichy government would not surrender its colonies or fleet to anyone.

■ Hitler issued a directive barring any major military effort in Iraq—or any place else in the Middle East—until after Russia was conquered, which Hitler believed could be done in two months.

May 24 In a classic naval duel involving giant men-of-war, the Germans destroyed the British battle cruiser *Hood*. The action took place in the early morning hours in the Denmark Strait, between Iceland and Greenland. The German battleship *Bismarck* and the cruiser *Prinz Eugen* were en route from Bergen, Norway, to the Atlantic for forays against merchantmen supplying the British. The *Hood* and the brand-new battleship *Prince of Wales* intercepted the Ger-

man ships but did not take them by surprise, having lost them briefly just before the engagement. The four ships opened up on each other at 26,000 yards and kept firing for 20 minutes, the British with their total broadside of eight 15-inch and ten 10-inch weapons. The *Hood* was struck two or three times. The after magazines exploded and she went down in four minutes. Only three of the 1,419 crew survived. The *Prince of Wales* was severely damaged, having received seven hits, and withdrew, but she had hit *Bismarck* causing an oil leak which left a slick which permitted British aircraft to find her eventually. The German ships gave up their Atlantic raiding plans as a result of the action and started to make their way to Brest, France, instead.

■ The 18,000-ton Italian liner and troop transport *Conte Rosso* was sunk by a British submarine in the Mediterranean.

May 25 The *Bismarck* eluded a British force sent to engage her.

May 26 An obsolete torpedo bomber, a Swordfish from the carrier *Ark Royal*, disabled *Bismarck*. The torpedo struck aft, jamming the rudder and damaging the propellers.

■ Stuka dive bombers damaged the British carrier *Formidable* off Crete.

May 27 Roosevelt proclaimed an unlimited national emergency in the U.S. He said: ". . . what started as a European war has developed, as the Nazis always intended it should develop, into a world war for world domination. . . . The war is approaching the brink of the Western Hemisphere itself. It is coming very close to home." The Neutrality Patrol was

The German battleship Bismarck *is shown in action against the British battleship* Prince of Wales *in the North Atlantic. The* Bismarck *was crippled by fire from the British ship and later sank.*

extended, with several ships to be transferred from the Pacific to the Atlantic Fleet. Roosevelt also said if the Azores or the Cape Verde Islands were seized by Germany, the U.S. would regard its security directly threatened.

■ The *Bismarck* was sunk 500 miles west of Brest by the British battleships *Rodney* and *King George V.* Only 110 of the 2,000-man crew survived. *Bismarck*'s sinking considerably eased fears of Allied shipping losses in the Atlantic. *Bismarck* was Germany's newest and most feared warship.

■ The protocols of Paris were signed, outlining Vichy's cooperation with the Germans in French possessions and protectorates. Vichy agreed to open Syrian and Lebanese air and naval bases to Germany for use against the British in Iraq, the transfer of munitions stored in Syria for Iraq, and German military rights in north and west Africa, including a submarine base at Dakar. By these protocols, Vichy came within a whisper of actually fighting on the side of Germany.

■ New Zealand Major General Bernard Freyberg was given permission to evacuate all British Commonwealth forces from Crete.

■ An Italian force landed at Sitia Bay in eastern Crete.

■ The strategic Halfaya Pass was again captured by the Afrika Korps.

May 28 Heraklion was evacuated by British troops on Crete.

May 29 The U.S. agreed to train British pilots who would fly American planes exported under lend-lease.

■ British troops on Crete fell back to positions east of Suda Bay.

■ Eden stated Great Britain's postwar aims.

May 30 Iraq's pro-Axis government collapsed. British troops reached Baghdad and Rashid Ali and dozens of his followers (dubbed "Ali and the Forty Thieves") fled to Iran.

May 31 An armistice was signed in Baghdad with the British reestablishing control over the Iraqi government. The cease-fire would take effect when assurances were received "that the complete independence of the country and the honor of the Army will be guaranteed."

■ The last of the British forces on Crete were evacuated from Sfakion.

■ British civilian air raid casualties for April and May totaled 11,459 killed and 12,107 injured.

June The month was marked by the culmination of violent attacks by Croatian extremists against Serbs in the new state of Croatia. Killings were widespread. Whole villages were decimated. It reached a point where the Germans had to call on the Zagreb government to stop the atrocities.

June 1 Apparently incensed over the British reoccupation of Baghdad, Arab mobs swept through the city's Jewish quarter and killed 600 Jews and injured 850.

■ The Royal Navy cruiser *Calcutta* was sunk while en route to Crete from Alexandria to aid in the evacuation.

■ *Prinz Eugen* reached Brest.

June 2 Hitler and Mussolini conferred at the Brenner Pass. The Axis leaders discussed control over Greece and Croatia. The Duce was thoroughly misled over Russia, Hitler never mentioning the forthcoming invasion. Ribbentrop said talk of an invasion was "excessively premature."

June 3 Gurkhas of the British army occupied the city of Mosul in Iraq.

■ Vichy announced it would resist any Allied attempt to move into Syria or Tunisia. Germany said it would extend "full cooperation" to Vichy in any such action.

June 4 A pro-Allied government was restored in Iraq.

■ The former kaiser, Wilhelm II, died at Doorn in Nazi-occupied Holland, where he had lived in exile since Germany's loss in World War I. (The kaiser always despised Hitler as an uncouth politician, but he finally congratulated Hitler in a telegram after the fall of France. One of the kaiser's sons, known as "Auwi," was an SS general during World War II, a dedicated Nazi.)

June 6 Washington authorized the acquisition of all idle foreign merchant ships in U.S. waters "for urgent needs of commerce and national defense."

■ Luftwaffe units in Syria were withdrawn.

■ Hitler advised the Japanese ambassador, in Berchtesgaden, that Germany might go to war with Russia. He did not refer to an invasion, but said troop reinforcements were being sent east. "Under such circumstances," he confided, "war might be unavoidable between us."

June 7 RAF bombers pounded Brest in the beginning of a five-day attack.

June 8 Australian, Indian, and Free French troops under the command of General Sir Henry Maitland Wilson invaded Syria and Lebanon for the announced purpose of "eliminating German personnel and influence from certain areas in which they are securing a dominating position through continued infiltration." The campaign was launched from Palestine and Transjordan. Vichy forces were numerically superior. They numbered 55,000, mostly Tunisians, Algerians, and Senegalese under French officers. Fighting was bitter and Allied hopes of rallying the French in the area to the Gaullist side quickly vanished.

■ German troops began arriving in Finland to position themselves for the Russian invasion.

June 9 Allied troops occupied Tyre in Lebanon.

June 10 Vichy French resistance along the Litani River in Lebanon collapsed as the Allies continued their drive northward.

June 11 Japan and Russia agreed to expand their trade under terms of a new treaty of commerce.

June 12 Fourteen Allied nations (including governments in exile) pledged to conclude no separate treaties with the Axis: "There can be no settled peace and prosperity so long as free peoples are coerced by violence into submission to domination by Germany. . . ."

■ Free French units advanced to within twelve miles of Damascus.

■ Members of the U.S. Naval Reserve were called to active duty.

June 13 TASS, the Soviet news agency, denied a split between Berlin and Moscow: "These rumors are a clumsy propaganda maneuver of the forces arrayed against the Soviet Union and Germany, which are interested in a spread and intensification of the war."

June 14 The U.S. froze all German and Italian funds under authority given the president by the declaration of an unlimited national emergency.

■ Molotov rejected intelligence reports of an imminent German attack, saying "only a fool would attack Russia."

June 15 British Commonwealth forces went on the offensive in the Western Desert. While the objective was to recapture Cyrenaica and its vital airfields, Operation BATTLEAXE miscarried

because of muddles and skilled German countermoves. (By the 17th of June the British were back to their starting point, having lost 91 tanks in the abortive effort.)

■ Vichy France issued a decree limiting the rights of Jews.

■ German warships were authorized to engage in the "annihilation of Russian submarines without any trace, including their crews," in waters south of the Aland Islands. Actual incidents were to be covered up as attacks on presumed British submarines operating in the Baltic.

June 16 All German and Italian consular, information, and tourist officers and staff personnel were ordered to be withdrawn from the U.S. by July 10. The State Department said they had engaged in activities of "an improper and unwarranted character."

June 17 Canada and the U.S. established joint economic committees to effect "a more efficient and more coordinated utilization of the combined resources of the two countries in the production of defense requirements" and to plan on postwar economic recovery.

June 18 The Soviet embassy in London cabled Moscow: "As of now Cripps [the British ambassador to Moscow who had returned to London] is deeply convinced of the inevitability of armed conflict between Germany and the USSR, which will begin not later than the middle of June. According to Cripps, the Germans have now concentrated 147 divisions (including air force and service units) along the Soviet borders. . . ."

■ Germany and Turkey signed a ten-year treaty of friendship in Ankara. Each agreed "to respect the inviolability and integrity of their territories and abstain from all actions directed directly or indirectly against one of the contracting parties." Turkey was now truly neutralized, already having signed pacts with Britain and France.

■ Japan broke off trade talks with the Dutch East Indies government because the Dutch insisted on unilateral rights to decrease the export of goods which were deemed essential by the Japanese.

June 19 Germany and Italy ordered U.S. consular staffs withdrawn from their countries by July 15 in retaliation for the similar U.S. action.

■ Vichy French forces temporarily halted the Allied advance in Syria and recaptured Mezze, just outside Damascus.

■ The U.S. State Department said it would not

grant visas to aliens who had a close relative living in German-controlled areas.

June 20 Roosevelt denounced the sinking of the *Robin Moore* by Germany, calling it "the act of an international outlaw."

■ German U-boat *203* tried to attack the battleship *Texas* between Newfoundland and Greenland, but the U.S. ship outran it. The German captain assumed *Texas* was a British lend-lease vessel.

■ The Allies resumed offensive actions and hurled Vichy forces back in Syria and Lebanon and advanced toward Damascus.

June 21 Australian forces occupied Damascus in sharp fighting. Commonwealth units began moving into Syria from Iraq, advancing toward Palmyra.

■ General Sir Claude Auchinleck succeeded General Sir Archibald Wavell as Commander in Chief, Middle East.

June 22 In the greatest military attack in history, Germany and its Axis partners invaded the Soviet Union along a 1,800-mile front from the Arctic to the Black Sea. More than 3 million troops, 600,000 vehicles, 750,000 horses, 3,580 tanks, and 1,830 planes were hurled against the Russians. The defenders were 4,500,000 strong along the frontier but were caught totally unprepared. There were no elaborate deception plans as in Poland. At 3 A.M. when the guard was changed at the International Bridge at Brest-Litovsk, the German sentries simply gunned down their Russian counterparts instead of saluting them. Hitler hoped to score a quick victory and drive to the Ural Mountains before winter. The immediate objectives were Leningrad, Moscow, and Kiev, with an army group directed at each of the key cities. Germany claimed widespread frontier violations as a pretext for the attack. ("Waiting would be a crime against Germany.") It was, however, the delayed fulfillment of Hitler's plan to win Lebensraum for Germany and to crush the Communist giant to the east. Italy, Rumania, Slovakia, and Croatia declared war on Russia, and Rumanian and Finnish troops also crossed into Soviet territory. Churchill promptly promised British help to Russia: "Any man or State who fights against Naziism will have our aid. Any man or State who marches with Hitler is our foe."

■ Mussolini was told of the invasion only after it had started. Hitler told Mussolini: "The partnership with the Soviet Union, in spite of the complete sincerity of the efforts to bring about a final conciliation, was nevertheless often very irksome to me, for in some way or other, it seemed to me a break with my whole origin, my concepts and my former obligations. I am happy now to be relieved of these mental agonies."

■ Heartened by the news that Vichy was dispatching air aid to Syria (including German help from Greece), pro-Pétain units stiffened their resistance to the Allies. At Palmyra, on the pipeline from Iraq, 150 Foreign Legionnaires stopped a 3,500-man Commonwealth force advancing from the east.

June 23 German forces in Russia drove across the Bug River, using rubber dinghies until a bridge could be built. XVII Corps made nine miles in the first day of fighting. German Army Group North advanced through Lithuania along the Baltic coast and reached Latvia.

■ The Russians lost more than 500 planes while destroying only a dozen or so German aircraft, leading to the suicide of Lieutenant General Kopets, commander of the Russian bomber group.

■ Hungary declared war on the Soviet Union.

■ British troops battled their way through Vichy French units and advanced to Palmyra in Syria.

June 24 Roosevelt promised to aid the Soviet Union and ordered the release of all Russian credits in the U.S.

■ Vilna and Kaunas in Lithuania fell to the Germans. The Russians introduced their giant Klim Voroshilov tanks into action near Raseiniai (Raseynyay). Models weighing 43 and 52 tons surprised the Germans who found the KVs nearly unstoppable. One of these Russian tanks took 70 direct hits but none penetrated its armor.

■ About 2,000 Soviet planes had now been destroyed. In just seventy-two hours the largest air force in the world had been reduced to an ineffectual remnant.

June 25 Sweden permitted the passage of a German division from Norway to Finland, explaining that "our chief interest is to maintain our liberty and stay outside of the conflict, and the government came to the conclusion that the only way to do so was to accept the German-Finnish demand."

■ Finland declared war on Russia.

■ Russian air force planes bombed Finland, but the prepared Finns shot down 26 of the attacking aircraft.

■ In order to keep the port of Vladivostok open for arms shipments to Russia, Roosevelt refused to apply the neutrality statute to the Soviet Union.

■ Churchill revealed that staggering shipping losses had been suffered by Britain in the North Atlantic. Members of Parliament were told of the U-boat toll in a secret session of the House of Commons.

■ Japan abandoned plans it was developing for the occupation of Portuguese Macao.

June 26 German forces began an all-out assault on Brest-Litovsk. The fight for the citadel was marked by stiff resistance for four days. In the north, the Germans had pushed 190 miles. Hitler ordered General Fritz von Manstein's panzer corps to halt while the infantry moved up, missing an opportunity to strike directly at Leningrad. Manstein was idled for six days.

June 27-29 Panzer Groups Two and Three under Guderian and General Hermann Hoth began a drive to link up near Minsk, in an effort to trap three Russian armies which constituted the bulk of the western defenses.

June 27 A British mission, headed by Sir Stafford Cripps, arrived in Moscow for talks on military and economic aid with the Russians.

June 28 German forces captured Minsk, the capital of Byelorussia, 200 miles inside Russia proper. Finnish troops began crossing into Russia.

■ The Italian protectorate of Albania declared war on Russia.

■ Japanese leaders decided not to attack the Soviet Union, feeling they could not spare forces from the Pacific and China.

■ A pogrom in Kaunas, Lithuania, resulted in the deaths of 3,800 Jews.

June 29 The Soviet Union formed an overall defense committee consisting of Stalin, Georgi Malenkov, Marshal Kliment Voroshilov, and Lavrenti Beria. Rumormongering, spreading panic, and cowardice were decreed to be crimes punishable by death.

■ German forces from Norway advanced on the vital Russian port of Murmansk but were halted along the Litsa River, 35 miles to the west.

■ Finnish forces under Field Marshal Carl Gustav Mannerheim began attacks on the Karelian Isthmus, hoping to link up with German Army Group North in the Leningrad area.

June 30 Vichy France broke diplomatic relations with the Soviet Union, claiming that "diplomatic and consular agents of the Soviet Union in France were exercising influence affecting the security of the State."

■ Lwow (Lvov) in what was once Poland fell to the advancing Germans. Brest-Litovsk was cleared by the Germans who took 7,000 prisoners. Through the end of June the Germans had lost 8,886 men in Russia.

■ Stalin summoned General D. G. Pavlov, commander of the West Front, his chief of staff, and other top aides to Moscow. (Pavlov and an unknown number of the front staff were court-martialed and executed for the disastrous collapse of the Russian forces primarily responsible for defending the central region.)

July Parisians were limited to one pound of meat per week (if available) and one pound of bread per day.

July 1 Germany, Italy, and the other Axis nations recognized the pro-Japanese government of Wang Ching-wei in China.

■ Russia proposed an alliance with the Chinese government of Chiang Kai-shek.

■ Panzer units under Guderian crossed the Berezina River on the central Russian front while German forces in the north captured Riga in Latvia.

■ Timoshenko was named commander of the newly designated Russian West Front.

■ U.S. Army troop strength reached a level of 1,400,000 men, an eightfold increase in little more than a year.

July 1-2 The *Prinz Eugen* was hit by RAF bombers at Brest. Fifty-one crewmen were killed, and the cruiser was forced to undergo extensive repairs.

July 2 Japan called up a million men for military service. The action followed an imperial conference in which it was decided to advance into Indochina and Siam even at the risk of war with the U.S. and Britain. In a rebuff to pro-Axis Foreign Minister Yosuke Matsuoka, Tokyo's leaders chose not to attack Russia immediately but to wait until Germany had achieved a thorough military victory. In anticipation of eventual war against the Soviet Union, the Japanese decided to raise the strength of the Kwantung Army from 400,000 to 700,000 men.

■ All Japanese merchant ships in the Atlantic were ordered to return to their home ports.

July 2–3 About 7,000 Jews were murdered by German *Einsatzgruppen* units in newly occupied Lwow.

July 3 Stalin ordered the Red Army to engage in a "scorched earth" defense policy.

■ In a view which reflected the optimism within the German High Command, General Franz Halder, chief of the Army General Staff, recorded in his diary: "It is . . . not an exaggeration when I assert that the Russian campaign will be won within 14 days. Naturally, that will not constitute its end. Because of the size of the territory and the resistance, pursued obstinately

and with every means at hand, we will still require many weeks."

■ Vichy French troops yielded Palmyra in Syria to the Allies.

■ Japan complained to Germany about what Tokyo considered to be pro-Chinese, anti-Japanese German officials in China. The Japanese asked for the "discharge of these superannuated officials and replace them with new blood which is more imbued with the spirit of National Socialism."

July 4 Tito (Josip Broz), general secretary of the Yugoslav Communist party, announced a Communist resistance movement in Yugoslavia, the Partisans (the first use of that term, which became common during the war).

■ A Peoples Military Reserve was formed in Moscow, with 270,000 men organized into 25 divisions for defense of the capital. German forces in the north reached the 1939 Soviet-Polish border.

July 6 Münster was pounded by the RAF, the

The greatest clash of arms in history stretched from the Baltic to the Black Sea with Hitler's invasion of Russia. Germany planned to deliver a quick knockout blow, but the Russians retreated and eventually held.

first of three nights of consecutive bombing which destroyed a quarter of the city.

July 7 U.S. Marines occupied Iceland, Trinidad, and British Guiana "to supplement, and eventually to replace, the British forces." The U.S. added that the move was to prevent "the occupation by Germany of strategic outposts in the Atlantic to be used as air or naval bases for eventual attack against the Western Hemisphere."

■ Churchill sent his first personal message to Stalin, seeking to forge a partnership against Germany.

July 8 Japan informed the U.S. it hoped to maintain good relations with the Soviet Union.

■ A Soviet military mission arrived in London.

■ Yugoslavia was carved up between Germany and Italy.

■ B-17s were flown in combat for the first time, by the RAF in an attack on Wilhelmshaven. (The Fortresses were a near disaster for the British who suffered severe operational losses and experienced high altitude difficulties, plus the streaming of telltale contrails.)

■ All Jews in the Baltic states were ordered to wear Stars of David.

July 9 The Minsk pocket and Vitebsk were overrun by the Germans. A total of 290,000 Russians surrendered. About 2,500 Soviet tanks were lost, plus 1,500 artillery pieces.

■ Beirut was isolated as Australian units occupied Damur.

July 10 Stalin assumed the role of commander-in-chief of the Red Army, removing Marshal Timoshenko who was given command of the forces on the western approaches to Moscow.

■ Finnish forces smashed across the Karelian defenses and penetrated into Soviet territory.

■ German panzers of Army Group Center crossed the Dnieper River. Tanks advanced to within ten miles of Kiev.

■ Berlin called upon the Japanese to enter the war against the Soviet Union at the earliest time, but Tokyo had already decided against such a move and so informed the Germans.

July 12 Britain and the Soviet Union signed a mutual assistance treaty in Moscow, formalizing previously given oral agreements from London to aid the Russians.

■ Vichy France failed to win Turkish approval for sending military supplies to its forces in Syria.

Turkey was intent on maintaining its absolute neutrality.

■ Vichy French forces sought a truce in Syria. They had suffered about 6,000 losses (double the Allied casualties).

■ An "independent" Montenegro under Italian protection was proclaimed at Cetinje.

July 14 An armistice was signed at St.-Jean-d'Acre (Acre) in Palestine, ending the fighting in Syria and Lebanon. The agreement left the two Arab states under British and Free French control. About 20,000 of the 26,000 Vichy French forces were permitted to leave, among them 600 Germans of the Foreign Legion.

■ German forces pressed toward Leningrad, reaching the Luga River.

■ All Christian Science churches in Germany were closed and their property was confiscated.

July 16 Russian special units near Smolensk tested the Katyusha in combat for the first time. The highly effective rocket mortar was to play a significant part in the battles ahead. Area weapons, they could be mounted on any kind of vehicle and shower dozens of solid-fueled rockets on the enemy more than three miles away.

RUSSIA'S MOVING MIRACLE

In an unprecedented relocation of industry, the Soviet Union physically moved its production strength out of the combat areas almost as fast as the German panzers could strike eastward. Beginning in July 1941 the Russians employed their vast manpower and sorely strained transport system to haul industrial cargoes on the equivalent of a million-and-a-half rail freight cars to safer areas stretching to the farther reaches of the Soviet Union. By Nov. a total of 1,523 complete factories had been relocated. Most importantly, 1,360 of these were major facilities directly involved in arms production. The number of plants placed back in operation were relocated in the following places:

Volga area	226
Urals	667
Western Siberia	244
Eastern Siberia	78
Central Asia and Kazakhstan	308

SOURCE: Alexander Werth, *Russia at War, 1941-1945.*

■ Smolensk fell to the Germans. About 600,000 Russians were trapped. It was a military disaster, but Soviet resistance now began to stiffen for the first time since the invasion. (Shortly thereafter Hitler ordered a temporary halt in the drive toward Moscow, more than 200 miles away, and sent panzer units to help Army Group South in its efforts to defeat the Russian forces in the Ukraine under Marshl Semyon Budenny.

■ Finnish forces reached Lake Ladoga, splitting the Russian defense line and imperiling units on the Karelian Isthmus.

■ General Weygand was appointed governor general of Algeria.

■ The Japanese government resigned, with Foreign Minister Matsuoka holding out for a hardline position in dealing with the U.S. and a break in talks with Washington.

■ Free French and British troops marched into Beirut.

July 17 Spain's Franco warned the U.S. to stay out of the war or face a "catastrophe." He added, "The Allies have lost. . . . German arms are leading the battle . . . in which the blood of our youth is going to be mingled with that of our comrades of the Axis, as a living expression of our solidarity." (In September 14,000 Spaniards of the Blue Legion were sent to the Leningrad front in Germany as "volunteers" to fight the Russians.)

■ In another pincers operations, Hoth and Guderian's panzer armies trapped more than 300,000 Russian troops east of Smolensk.

■ Stalin called on the British to open up a "Second Front" as a means of easing the pressures on the beleaguered Russian forces on the eastern front.

July 18 Prince Konoye formed a new but basically identical Japanese government with Vice Admiral Soemu Toyoda succeeding Matsuoka as foreign minister in the only actual shift.

July 19 The U.S. Navy was ordered to escort the shipping of any nation to and from Iceland.

■ Japan issued a virtual ultimatum to French authorities in Indochina which would give the Japanese full military control over the Vichy colony.

July 21 Japan occupied military bases in French Indochina. The Vichy government, which was in no position to resist Tokyo's demand, stated that

France "sees no inconvenience in permitting Japan temporarily to occupy military bases in Indochina on the condition there is no menace to Indochinese integrity and French sovereignty. Japan has made no territorial demands. We merely want to protect Indochina." Japan's ambassador in the U.S. explained that Tokyo wished to insure the uninterrupted flow of food and raw materials from Indochina, and there was a need to guarantee military security in the light of alleged Free French and Chinese "agitation."

■ Moscow was bombed by German aircraft. Hitler goaded Göring into ordering the raid by disparaging the Luftwaffe for its failure to attack the Russian capital. A total of 127 Ju-88s and He-111s dropped 100 tons of high-explosive bombs and 45,000 incendiaries. (Raids of diminishing intensity continued though the rest of 1941, but German losses were heavy as the Russians assembled the most powerful antiaircraft defenses of the war.)

■ Shipping through the Panama Canal was curtailed, ostensibly for "repairs," but the action had the effect of preventing the passage of several Japanese ships.

July 22 For the first time in their Russian offensive, German forces came to a temporary halt, exhausted by their ceaseless drive. The German forces in the north had advanced to Lake Ilmen, more than 400 miles from their starting point. A month after the start of the campaign, the combined German and Axis armies had conquered about 720,000 square miles of Russian territory.

July 23 Under Secretary of State Welles told Ambassador Nomura the U.S. felt there was no reason to continue talks with Japan since the Indochinese actions showed the "Japanese Government intended to pursue the policy of force and of conquest."

July 24 Vichy agreed to permit the Japanese full use of military bases in Indochina. The heavist of pressure was applied by Tokyo. Roosevelt offered Japan guarantees of free access to Indochinese materials in return for Tokyo's promise to maintain Indochina's neutrality.

■ Fifteen RAF Halifax bombers scored five direct hits on the *Scharnhorst* which was en route from Brest to La Pallice, a German naval base on the Bay of Biscay. Having drawn 3,000 tons of water, the battle cruiser was forced to return to Brest for repairs. Five of the aircraft which attacked her were downed.

July 25 Foreign Minister Toyoda told U.S. Ambassador Grew that Japan was being encircled by hostile forces in southeast Asia, and he compared Japan's moves in Indochina to the British occupation of Syria.

July 26 All Japanese assets in the U.S. were frozen "to prevent the use of financial facilities of the United States in trade . . . in ways harmful to national defense and American interests, to prevent the liquidation in the United States of assets obtained by duress or conquest, and to curb subversive activities in the United States." (Japanese assets in the U.S. amounted to $138 million; U.S. assets in Japan were $110 million.) At the same time, the U.S. froze all Chinese assets, at the request of the Chiang Kai-shek government, "with a view to strengthening the foreign trade and exchange position of the Chinese Government."

■ Britain froze all Japanese assets in the United Kingdom and the dominions and denounced all commercial agreements.

■ Malta received a British convoy which had undergone almost continuous attack for the past two days.

■ Italian E-boats (small surface craft) attacked Malta's main port of Valetta.

■ General Douglas MacArthur was returned to active duty with the U.S. Army. Roosevelt nationalized the armed forces of the Philippines for the duration of the emergency.

July 27 After a hiatus of ten weeks, German bombers renewed their attacks on London.

■ The Netherlands froze all Japanese assets.

July 28 Japanese troops began landing in Indochina.

■ Japan froze all American, British, and Dutch assets.

July 29 Japan and Vichy France concluded an agreement which recognized "that should the security of French Indochina be menaced, Japan would have reason to consider the general tranquillity in East Asia and its own security endangered."

■ Washington denounced Japan's military build-up in Indochina, saying Tokyo sought bases there "for purposes of further and more obvious move-

ments of conquest in adjacent areas." The U.S. also noted that Japan's moves "tend to jeopardize the procurement by the United States of essential materials such as tin and rubber which are necessary for the normal economy of this country and the consummation to them of our defense program."

■ Roosevelt proposed a Japanese troop withdrawal from Indochina in exchange for its neutralization.

■ Japanese troops occupied the naval facilities at Camranh Bay in French Indochina.

July 30 In a fateful decision, Hitler ordered Field Marshal Fedor von Bock's Army Group Center to halt the drive to Moscow. The German strategy was to concentrate on the Ukraine and the capture of Leningrad.

■ Harry Hopkins, representing President Roosevelt, arrived in Moscow. (The visit proved important because Hopkins concluded at the end of his stay that Russia could somehow survive the German onslaught, a view not widely held by observers who saw the Red Army on the brink of collapse. He reported his optimism to Roosevelt who henceforth came to the same conclusion.)

■ The U.S. Navy river gunboat *Tutuila* was bombed by Japanese naval planes at Chungking. A single bomb hit the vessel from one of the 26 aircraft attacking the Chinese capital. The Japanese said it was accidental.

July 31 Göring issued the first known written order for the elimination of Jews living under Nazi rule. In a memorandum to Reinhard Heydrich, Göring said, ". . . I instruct you further to submit to me as soon as possible a general plan showing the measures for organization and for action necessary to carry out the desired final solution (*endlosung*) of the Jewish question."

■ Bulgarian troops occupied parts of southern and eastern Yugoslavia and announced that these areas would be incorporated into Bulgaria. The action was taken with the permission "of German military authorities."

■ RAF bombers attacked German and Finnish ships in Petsamo harbor in northern Finland.

■ British civilian air raid casualties for the month were 900 killed and 908 injured.

■ Japan apologized for the bombing of *Tutuila*.

Aug. 1 In "the interest of national defense," the U.S. embargoed the export of all aviation fuel.

■ Japan halted the export of silk to the U.S.

■ Finland broke off relations with Britain.

■ Thailand recognized Manchukuo, a gesture to appease the Japanese in order to maintain Tokyo's recognition of Thailand's neutrality and independence.

Aug. 2 Washington and Moscow reached agreement on an aid program which would dramatically increase Russia's ability to replace war weapons lost thus far in the war.

■ The British naval blockade was extended to Finland.

Aug. 3–4 Large numbers of Russians were enveloped around Uman by German Army Group South.

Aug. 4 Vichy France indicated it would not permit the Axis powers to use its military bases in North Africa.

Aug. 5 The siege of Odessa began (it was to last for 73 days).

■ German units crushed all resistance in the Smolensk pocket.

Aug. 6 Japan proposed negotiations with the U.S. to consider a counterproposal on Indochina.

■ Britain and the U.S. warned Japan against attacking Thailand.

■ Britain announced that 459,000 tons of its shipping had been sunk or damaged during July.

■ Gen. Wladyslaw Anders was appointed commander of Polish forces in Russia.

Aug. 8 Berlin was earmarked for attack for the first time by Russian aircraft. Five Ilyushin Il-4s took off from Estonia. Two were shot down en route. Two failed to find Berlin. The last dropped its light bomb load on a stretch of railroad tracks outside the city.

■ Ambassador Nomura proposed a meeting in Honolulu between Roosevelt and Konoye.

■ The Russian Twenty-eighth Army was smashed fighting its way out of Kazaki, 110 miles south of Moscow. An estimated 38,000 prisoners and 200 tanks were taken by the Germans.

Aug. 9 In their first of many meetings, President Roosevelt and Prime Minister Churchill conferred in Placentia Bay at Argentia, Newfoundland. While the Atlantic Charter was the announced result of the conference, its real significance was the firm commitment by Roosevelt to have the U.S. play as large a role as possible in the war against Germany.

Aug. 10 German subversive plots in Argentina, Chile, and Cuba were uncovered by local authorities with heavy direction from the American FBI.

Aug. 12 Roosevelt and Churchill enunciated the Atlantic Charter. Its eight points were: The U.S. and U.K. sought no new territories, no territorial changes without consent of the people involved, the right of self-determination, free trade, joint economic development, "freedom from fear and want," freedom of the seas, and the abandonment of the use of force.

■ Britain and Russia declared they would come to Turkey's aid if it were attacked by any European power.

■ Hitler continued redirecting his armies away from Moscow, sending Guderian's panzer army to the Ukraine and Hoth's toward Leningrad.

■ Pétain announced that Vichy France would collaborate fully with Germany. He said, "Our relations with Germany have been defined by an armistice convention, the character of which could only be provisional. Dragging out this situation makes it that much harder to support in so far as it governs relations between two great nations."

Aug. 14 An attempt was made on the life of the Japanese vice-premier.

■ The Germans calculated they had lost 30,000 dead in the first six weeks of the campaign in Russia.

Aug. 15 Britain and the U.S. requested approval from the Soviet Union to send delegations to Moscow "to arrive at speedy decisions as to the apportionment of our joint resources."

Aug. 16 Stalin accepted the proposal of the U.S. and Britain for an urgent conference.

■ German units of Army Group North reached Novgorod and advanced beyond the Volkhov River.

Aug. 17 The Germans cleared Novgorod and hardly paused as they pushed forward to the October Railway which led to Moscow.

■ Roosevelt agreed to renew informal discussions with Japan "to ascertain whether there existed a basis for negotiations relative to a peaceful settlement covering the entire Pacific situation." The President conferred with the Japanese ambassador to determine whether direct talks with Konoye could be productive.

ARCTIC CONVOYS TO RUSSIA

The first of the convoys to the Arctic ports of the Soviet Union in August 1941 marked the beginning of a four-year effort to supply Russia under the most difficult of conditions. German surface ships, submarines, and aircraft posed constant threats. Appalling weather conditions prevailed much of the time, making navigation and simple existence difficult in the extreme. A total of 1,528 ships sailed in convoys in and out of the Arctic ports. Of the 811 going to Archangel and Murmansk, 720 arrived safely. Thirty-three (4.1 percent) were forced to turn back and 58 (7.2 percent) were sunk. (The loss rate on the North Atlantic convoys to Britain was 22.6 percent, 654 ships sunk of the 2,889 involved.) The Arctic convoys carried a total of four million tons of equipment and supplies to Russia, of which 300,000 tons were lost (including 5,000 tanks and 7,000 aircraft).

SOURCE: S. W. Roskill, *White Ensign: The British Navy at War, 1939–1945.*

■ Britain and Russia demanded that Iran order Germans out of the country on the grounds many were involved in subversive activity which menaced the Allied cause. There were about 3,200 Germans in the country, mostly technical experts brought in by the shah who wished to industrialize the country without being swallowed up by the Russians or British. The shah, personally, was demonstrably pro-German.

■ RAF bombers attacked Syracuse, in Sicily.

■ Kiev and Dnepropetrovsk fell to the Germans whose push into the Ukraine remained unstoppable.

Aug. 18 Russia proposed a settlement with Finland in which the Finns would be granted territorial concessions after an armistice.

■ German troops occupied Nikolayev and Kingisepp. Fighting was heavy around Novgorod.

■ The U.S. announced that Pan American Airways was ferrying combat planes from the U.S. to the Middle East by way of Brazil and West Africa. It was a means to speed up delivery of aircraft to the hard-pressed British.

■ Two Italian troop transports were sunk en route to North Africa.

Aug. 19 Polish forces began arriving at Tobruk to relieve the Australian and Indian forces.

Aug. 21 Hitler, after slowing down the Russian drive, issued a strategic and important directive: "The most important objective to be achieved before the onset of winter is not the capture of Moscow but the seizure of the Crimea. . . ." Hitler felt the need for Crimean wheat and the industrial facilities of the Donets Basin were more important.

■ Marshal Voroshilov called on the defenders of Leningrad to fight to the death. The Germans pressed their encirclement of the Russian city.

■ A German naval cadet named Moser was shot and killed in the subway station of Barbès-Rochechouart in Paris, the first German military casualty in France since the armistice.

Aug. 23 Vichy France began cracking down on anti-Nazi activity.

■ The Italian Second Army occupied the Adriatic coast of Yugoslavia.

Aug. 24 Russian defenders at Viipuri were completely surrounded by Finnish units.

■ The Russians counterattacked at Gomel. Rumanian units suffered heavy casualties at Odessa.

Aug. 25 British and Russian troops invaded Iran. They said Iran failed to respond satisfactorily to their note of the 17th and, consequently, they were forced to move militarily. In order to make sure Iranian warships around Abadan did not shell the oil facilities, a British cruiser sank two of the shah's sloops.

■ British Commandos landed on the Norwegian island of Spitzbergen.

■ Hitler and Mussolini conferred in East Prussia for a general discussion of the war. Hitler asked Italy to provide replacement troops wherever possible to free more Germans for combat in Russia.

Aug. 26 The U.S. announced it would send a military mission to Nationalist China to study "the needs of the Chinese Government for materiel and materials" in the light of the military situation there.

■ The Great Dam on the Dnieper River was blown up by the retreating Russians.

■ Japan protested the shipment of U.S. materials to the Soviet Union through Vladivostok.

■ British forces entered Abadan and Tabriz in Iran.

■ The German legation in Göteborg, Sweden, began recruiting Swedes for service in the German army.

Aug. 27 Prince Konoye personally invited Roosevelt to meet with him "to discuss from a broad standpoint all important problems between Japan and America covering the entire Pacific area, and to explore the possibility of saving the situation."

■ Laval was shot and wounded at a ceremony for the first French volunteers to be inducted into German service to fight the Russians. A 21-year-old former French sailor intended to kill a leading collaborator at the Versailles function, with-

---

THE CAPTURE OF *U-570*

The German submarine *U-570* was on its first combat patrol when, on Aug. 27, 1941, it had the misfortune to surface directly under an RAF Hudson patrol bomber operating out of Iceland. Within minutes, the submarine surrendered. *U-570's* presence in the area had been detected by another Hudson an hour earlier, but the sub crash-dived and escaped. The second Hudson caught the vessel just as it broke through the surface, but a second crash dive came too late. Straddled by four depth charges, *U-570* lost her lights and chlorine gas began seeping through the compartments. The inexperienced crew demanded that the ship surrender. Twelve of them came out on deck when it surfaced and one waved a white shirt at the plane. Others held up a large white board to indicate surrender. *U-570's* captain, also on his first operational mission, lost control of his men and agreed not to fight. The Hudson fired several bursts of machine-gun fire to keep the crew off deck and then circled until relieved by a Catalina flying boat. By the following afternoon a destroyer and several trawlers had arrived on the scene to remove the German crew and send sailors aboard to return the ship to port intact. *U-570* eventually became H.M.S. *Graph.*

---

out knowing Laval would be present and would become the primary target.

■ The Iranian government resigned.

Aug. 28 Japan delivered a note to the U.S. "to give broad assurances of its peaceful intent, including a comprehensive assurance that the Japanese government has no intention of using without provocation military force against any neighboring nation."

■ Iran's new premier, Ali Furanghi, ordered the army to end all resistance to Russian and British forces. A cease-fire followed.

■ All Russian forces were evacuated from the Karelian Isthmus.

Aug. 29 A Nazi puppet government, under General Milan Nedic, was established in Serbia, completing the partition of Yugoslavia.

Aug. 30 Leningrad's last rail outlet, at Mga, was captured by the Germans.

Aug. 31 Soviet and British forces linked up in Kazvin, completing the military occupation of Iran.

Sept. Luftwaffe Stukas launched a series of almost daily attacks on the Red Fleet base at Kronshlot (Kronstadt). They sank the battleship *Marat* and the cruiser *Kirov* and seriously damaged the battleship *October Revolution.*

Sept. 1 Roosevelt pledged every effort to defeat Germany because fundamental rights "are threatened by Hitler's violent attempt to rule the world."

■ A 60-ton Japanese fishing boat was sunk after hitting a Russian mine near Vladivostok, touching off a bitter exchange between the Soviet Union and Japan. Tokyo demanded guarantees of safety for its ships. Moscow told the Japanese to stay clear and refused to pay an indemnity.

■ The U.S. Navy extended convoy protection in the North Atlantic to cover all ships from Newfoundland to Iceland.

■ General Timoshenko's forces launched a counterattack in the Gomel area.

Sept. 2 German units advanced to within 20 miles of Leningrad.

Sept. 3 The Germans used poison gas for the "extermination" of prisoners at Auschwitz, apparently the first case of this particular form of Nazi criminality. Russian POW's were the first victims.

■ All Russian men born in 1922 were called up

Hitler bids farewell (Sept. 1941) to Admiral Miklos Horthy, who brought Hungary into the Axis and united his country with the Germans against the Soviet Union.

for military service and all previous deferments were canceled.

■ A German noncommissioned officer named Hoffman was shot and killed at the Gare de l'Est in Paris, leading to new mass reprisal executions.

Sept. 4 The American destroyer *Greer* was attacked by a German submarine 175 miles southwest of Iceland but suffered no damage. *Greer* had been tracking the U-boat.

■ Finnish forces advanced to Finland's pre-Winter War boundary with the Soviet Union.

■ The last of five futile Soviet air raids on Berlin was attempted but again with no real damage inflicted. Evacuation of the Estonian bases precluded further attacks.

Sept. 5 The occupation of Estonia was completed by the Germans.

■ Children under 12 in Moscow were ordered evacuated.

Sept. 6 Emperor Hirohito was told the risks of going to war against the U.S. An imperial conference, attended by Japan's leading military and civilian leaders, concluded that, "although America's total defeat is judged utterly impossible, it is not inconceivable that a shift in American public

opinion due to our victories in southeast Asia or to England's surrender might bring the war to an end." Konoye was permitted six weeks to effect a diplomatic settlement of all outstanding issues with the U.S.

Sept. 7 Guderian's Second Panzer Group reached Lokhvista, about 100 miles east of Kiev. With the First Panzer Group under Kleist wheeling up from the south, the Russians defending Kiev were faced with encirclement.

■ The U.S. merchant ship *Steel Seafarer* was sunk in the Gulf of Suez by German aircraft.

■ Two RAF squadrons arrived at Murmansk. The Hurricanes were flown by British pilots for five weeks (they shot down 16 German planes for one loss) before turning them over to the Russians.

Sept. 7–8 About 200 RAF bombers swept over Berlin at low levels for four hours during the moonlit night in the biggest raid on the capital yet. Among the areas hit were the residential district of Hochmeisterplatz, the zoo, and the Eden Hotel.

Sept. 8 German tank columns completed the land encirclement of Leningrad by seizing Petrokrepost (Schlüsselburg).

■ German forces at Vyazma were 150 rail miles

A Russian antitank crew knocks out an attacking German tank.

from Moscow. Heavy fighting took place at Vyazma and Bryansk.

■ Elnya, near Smolensk, was retaken by the Russians.

■ Finnish forces cut the Murmansk rail line at Lodeynoye Pole, about 25 miles east of Lake Ladoga.

Sept. 9 Iran accepted terms of an armistice imposed by Britain and Russia, including provisions for the ouster of German and Italian diplomatic personnel and "tourists" who were assumed to be Axis agents.

Sept. 10 With the Norwegian trade unions threatening a general strike, German occupation authorities imposed martial law in Oslo.

Sept. 11 The U.S. Navy was ordered to shoot on sight if any ship or convoy was threatened. Roosevelt said, "It is the Nazi design to abolish the freedom of the seas and to acquire absolute control and domination of the seas for themselves."

■ Russia warned Bulgaria against the use of its territory by Germany or Italy for attacking the Soviet Union.

■ Lindbergh, at a Des Moines rally, accused "the British, the Jewish, and the Roosevelt administration" as being "the three most important groups who have been pressing this country toward war."

Sept. 12 "King Winter" made its entry into the Russian-German war as an early snow began falling along most of the front. The immediate effect was an appreciable slowdown of the German advance as mechanized forces were burdened by the weather.

■ The U.S. Coast Guard cutter *Northland* seized the German trawler *Buskoe* in Mackenzie Bay, Greenland. The German ship had been sent to the area to serve as a weather monitoring and reporting station for the German military.

Sept. 13 Iran ordered the expulsion of all Axis diplomats.

Sept. 15 The Second and First German Panzer groups directed by Generals Guderian and Kleist joined up at Lokhvista, near Kiev on the southwest front, trapping four Russian armies.

■ Leningrad came under full siege by German Army Group North.

■ Stalin asked Churchill for 25 to 30 British divisions to fight in Russia.

■ The Star of David was decreed to be worn by all Jews six years of age or older in the Greater Reich.

Sept. 16 In the single greatest capitulation of the war, more than a half million Russians in the area of Kiev surrendered to the Germans. (The precise figure is disputed. German records put the number at 665,000. The Russians admitted to the 527,000 men captured and wounded during the previous week's fighting. By Moscow's account a total of 677,085 Red Army troops were committed on the entire southwest front. However, large numbers of the "Peoples Army," an inferior militia-type force pressed into service in desperation, were involved in the Kiev fighting, and, together with armed civilians, lend credence to the higher German figure.) Collapse of the Kiev front represented the nadir of the war for the Russians.

■ Syria was proclaimed independent by the Free French government.

■ Reza Khan, the shah of Iran, abdicated the Persian throne in favor of his son, Mohammed Reza Pahlevi. (The ousted shah was exiled to the island of Mauritius and then South Africa, where he died in July 1944 at the age of 66.)

■ General Keitel responded to growing Russian partisan warfare by ordering the execution of as many as 100 hostages for every German soldier killed by the civilian irregulars.

■ U.S. ships began formal convoy operations, escorting Allied ships as far east as Iceland at which point the Royal Navy assumed responsibility.

Sept. 17 The Russian Army High Command (STAVKA) ordered the withdrawal of its forces from Kiev, but the action came too late as the badly mauled defenders were already encircled and had no escape route.

■ British planes went into action for the first time on the Russian front.

■ Teheran was occupied by Russian and British troops.

■ U.S. Navy ships escorted a British-bound convoy for the first time.

■ The Second Battle of Changsha was launched by 125,000 Japanese XI Corps troops under General Tadaki Anan. Tokyo planned to eliminate the main obstacle to an advance in Hunan Province, the formidable forces of General Hseuh Yuan, commander of the Chinese Ninth War Area. The Chinese were concentrated around Changsha, about 350 miles east of Chungking. General Anan mustered a force of about 125,000 men, supported by 100 aircraft, to drive on Changsha from the north.

Sept. 18 Orders were issued to the Japanese army to prepare for offensive operations in southeast Asia and the South Pacific.

■ The Italian troop transports *Neptunia* and *Oceania* were sunk in the Mediterranean, the second and third largest such vessels torpedoed by the famous Royal Navy submarine *Upholder*. The German command in Italy viewed losses of transports on this scale as "catastrophic."

■ The German army began annihilating Russian forces trapped in the Kiev pocket.

Sept. 19 Kiev fell to the Germans. The battle for the city was disastrous to the Russians who suffered 350,000 casualties and lost 3,718 guns and 884 armored vehicles. Five armies were eliminated. Stalin had ordered a "stand and die" defense.

Sept. 21 German forces reached the Sea of Azov and cut off the Crimea.

Sept. 22 Britain told Finland to conclude a peace treaty with Russia or risk being regarded as a belligerent.

■ German troops cut off Leningrad from the rest of the Soviet Union by reaching the southern shore of Lake Ladoga.

Sept. 23 Japan repeated its call for a Roosevelt-Konoye meeting.

■ Free France officially came into being. The government-in-exile would "exercise, in fact, as well as provisionally, the normal attributes of public power," with Charles de Gaulle heading the National Committee.

Sept. 25 In order to secure its Adriatic flank, Italy reoccupied the demilitarized zone in Croatia.

■ Leningrad was attacked frontally.

■ German paratroopers were landed behind Russian lines in the Crimea.

■ Berlin acknowledged that "irregular" troops were engaging Axis forces in Serbia.

Sept. 26 Hitler ordered a halt in the offensive directed at Moscow. He had refused his generals permission to concentrate their drive against the Russian capital preferring to take the Ukraine with all its resources. Hitler disparaged their thinking, saying, "My generals know nothing about the economic aspects of war."

■ The German drive east of Kiev was halted by seasonal rainstorms, the *Rasputitsa*.

■ U.S. merchant ships operating in "defense waters" were directed to report any sightings of Axis planes or ships and to attack them if possible.

Sept. 27 Reinhard Heydrich was named protector of Bohemia, replacing Neurath.

■ Japanese units penetrated into Changsha. Paratroopers were dropped behind the Chinese lines. These forces were eliminated, and the Chinese turned the battle around by moving 11 divisions north of the city in a maneuver which cut off the Japanese troops attempting to fight their way into Changsha. About 100,000 Japanese were left with no escape route.

■ The first U.S. Liberty Ship, the S.S. *Patrick Henry*, was launched in Baltimore. (A total of 2,742 of these vessels was to be delivered by the end of the war. Roosevelt dubbed them "Ugly Ducklings" but the ungainly ships were the backbone of the merchant fleet. They were built at a cost of $1.5 million each, with bonuses to the builders for earlier-than-scheduled deliveries.)

SHIPBUILDING MIRACLE

U.S. Liberty Ships were constructed in record numbers in record time. The first of the cargo vessels were built in six months. Within a short period, the time was reduced to two months, and finally shipyards were turning them out in just one month. The record was set by the Kaiser Corporation, just under five days. The S.S. *Robert E. Peary*'s hull was assembled from 250-ton prefabricated sections on Nov. 8. Its upper deck was finished on the following day. Masts and fittings were in place on the third day. On the 11th all final detail work was completed, and it was launched. A week to the day from the initial work, *Robert E. Peary* was at sea with a full cargo.

Sept. 28 The first British convoy for Russia left Iceland.

■ Syria was declared independent by Vichy France.

■ Citing "irresponsible elements" with acts antagonistic to the Reich, Germany declared a state of emergency in Bohemia and Moravia.

Sept. 28–29 SS troops massacred nearly 34,000 Jews from the Kiev area in the nearby Babi Yar ravine. In its official report, *Einsatzgruppe C* related: "The Jewish population was invited by poster to present themselves for resettlement. Although initially we had only counted on 5,000-6,000 Jews reporting, more than 30,000 Jews appeared; by a remarkably efficient piece of organization they were led to believe in the resettlement story until shortly before their exe-

cution." It had been suggested the Jews were killed in reprisal for the bombing of a Kiev hotel used as a German headquarters, but the SS had been systematically killing Jews in Russia in the wake of the advancing Wehrmacht. Babi Yar stands as perhaps the most horrible single example of vengeful genocide.

Sept. 29 American and British delegations (headed by Averell Harriman and Lord Beaverbrook) began meeting with Russian officials in Moscow to determine Soviet defense needs.

■ Japan for the fourth time called for a Roosevelt-Konoye meeting.

Sept. 30 The Second Panzer Army began an offensive directed at Orel and Bryansk, southwest approaches to Moscow. First Panzer Group reached the Dnieper River in the Ukraine.

■ Japanese forces outside Changsha began fighting their way out of their encircled positions. (The Chinese failed to press their advantage and most of the Japanese escaped, though badly mauled in retreating to their original positions around Yoochow. It was, nonetheless, a major victory for the Chinese. According to the Chinese, the Japanese suffered 40,000 casualties.)

■ British air raid civilian casualties for Aug. and Sept. totalled 386 dead and 405 injured.

Oct. Germany and Italy began pressuring Japan to inform the United States that anti-Axis actions must be stopped or Berlin and Rome would invoke the Tripartite Pact. If this were done, Japan would, at the least, have to break off talks with the U.S. or, at the extreme, be compelled to join in a war against America.

Oct. 1 An agreement on U.S. and British arms in exchange for Russian raw materials was negotiated in Moscow.

Oct. 2 The U.S. sought clarification from Japan on whether it planned to withdraw troops from China and Indochina. Roosevelt, on the advice of Hull, turned down the idea of a direct meeting with Prince Konoye. Failure to arrange the high-level conference led to Konoye's downfall.

■ The Third and Fourth Panzer groups launched a massive offensive directed toward Vyazma. The Germans enjoyed a two-to-one advantage in men and tanks over the beleaguered Russian defenders astride the Moscow highway.

■ Gestapo troops began destroying the synagogues of Paris.

Oct. 3 In a speech at the Sportspalast, Hitler reviewed the war against Russia and said, "This opponent is already broken and will never rise again."

Oct. 4 Britain and the U.S. agreed to send the following to the Russians each month: 400 aircraft, 500 tanks, 200 gun carriers, 22,000 tons of rubber, 41,000 tons of aluminum, 3,860 tons of machine tools, and substantial quantities of food, medical supplies, and other raw materials.

THE RELATIVE COSTS OF PLANES AND TANKS

Production of war weapons in the United States during the war was the ultimate in assembly technique. Because of the massive numbers produced and the generally simple ancillary equipment, costs were, by today's standards, incredibly low. Today's machines of war, of course, are equipped with electronic gear and other sophisticated devices which make the old planes and tanks appear crude in the extreme. Inflation has been an obvious factor, too. But the following comparisons show what has happened to costs for equipping the military in a 40-year period.

WW II Aircraft Costs
(1940–1941 Figures)

SBD-2 Navy attack plane	$ 59,814
B-17 bomber	200,000
B-26 bomber	131,000
OS2U Navy observation plane	49,195

1980 U.S. Aircraft Costs

F-14 Navy fighter	$27,754,166
F-15 Air Force fighter	16,491,666
P-3 Navy surveillance plane	35,850,000

1941 U.S. Army Tank Costs
M-3 $33,500

1980 U.S. Army Tank Costs
XMI $2,020,000

Oct. 6 The entire staff of the Russian Ninth Army, except for the commanding officer who had been evacuated by air, was captured by the SS Adolf Hitler Division near the Sea of Azov.

The Russian Ninth and Tenth armies suffered heavy casualties and more than 100,000 men were captured in Ukrainian pockets.

■ Rumania said its forces in Russia had accounted for 70,000 dead, 100,000 wounded, and 60,000 Russian prisoners while Rumanian forces suffered 20,000 dead and 15,000 missing.

Oct. 7 Finland refused to end its war with Russia: "Finland wages her defensive war free from all political obligations, but grateful that she need not fight alone this time."

■ Large numbers of Russian troops were trapped around Vyazma and Bryansk as German armored columns pinched in around the Russian cities.

Oct. 8 Heavy rains made most of the Russian front a quagmire. The Germans captured Orel.

■ Italy, which felt Japan was not carrying its weight in the Tripartite Pact, called on the Japanese to go to war against Britain. Rome felt that it was unnecessary for Japan to attack Russia and that the U.S. would not come to Britain's aid. The Italians said, ". . . if Japan fails to fight now, no matter which side wins the loss to be sustained by Japan will be great."

Oct. 9 Roosevelt asked Congress to permit the arming of U.S. merchant ships engaged in international trade. Neutrality Act prohibitions, he said, "have no realism in the light of unscrupulous ambitions of madmen."

■ Germany and Turkey signed a 200-million-mark trade pact, with Germany to supply manufactured goods for Turkish raw materials.

Oct. 10 Moscow factories began to be disassembled for evacuation to the east. Priority went to facilities engaged in war production. Equipment of all kinds was crated to be shipped out of the immediate war zone as fast as possible.

Oct. 11 Russian T-34 tanks went into action against the XXIV Panzer Corps, inflicting severe losses on the Germans. With the introduction of the highly mobile and powerfully equipped new tanks, the Russians began to achieve armored superiority over the Germans.

Oct. 12 Women and children began being evacuated from Moscow.

Oct. 13 German forces entered Kaluga, 100 miles southwest of Moscow.

Oct. 14 All resistance ended in the Vyazma pocket, between Smolensk and Moscow. Panzer units captured Kalinin, 93 miles northwest of Moscow, cut the Moscow-Leningrad rail line, and captured a bridge intact across the Volga River. Advance units reached a point 60 miles from Moscow.

Oct. 16 The Soviet government left Moscow for Kuibyshev, 525 miles to the east. Stalin was the only high official who remained in Moscow. A condition approaching panic developed in the city when it was learned that Lenin's coffin had been removed from Red Square. Odessa fell to the Germans.

■ Under the supervision of Russian and Japanese advisers, talks were concluded at Harbin to set the border between Manchukuo and Outer Mongolia.

■ Richard Sorge, a correspondent for the *Frankfurter Zeitung*, was arrested by the Japanese as a Soviet spy, ending the career of perhaps the most successful espionage agent of the war. (He was hanged three years later.)

■ Prince Konoye resigned as prime minister of Japan. He lost the support of War Minister Hideki Tojo who had called for a new government to show a firmer policy. It became apparent to Tokyo's military leaders that talks with the U.S. were hopelessly deadlocked. A thoroughly mili-

tary-dominated government was inevitable since the Konoye cabinet represented the final civilian effort to resolve the impasse with Washington, and Konoye had to acknowledge failure. Konoye and others in the cabinet had argued for a withdrawal of Japanese troops from China, the key issue which split the government.

■ Russia suffered another military disaster as the battles of Bryansk and Vyazma ended with overwhelming German victories. Nine armies (up to eighty divisions) were destroyed. The Germans took 663,000 prisoners and knocked out or captured 1,242 tanks and 5,412 artillery pieces.

■ More than a half million children, women, and old men working day and night completed the defenses around Moscow, 60 miles of antitank ditches, 5,000 miles of troop trenches, and 177 miles of barbed wire.

Oct 17 The U.S. destroyer *Kearney* was torpedoed and damaged southwest of Iceland while on convoy escort duty. Eleven men were killed, the first American military casualties of the war.

■ The U.S. Navy ordered all American merchant ships in Asian waters to put into friendly ports.

■ General Hideki Tojo was named prime minister of Japan.

Oct. 18 Rumania incorporated Odessa and a large area east of the Dniester River. The conquered Russian territory became Transdniestria.

Oct. 19 Siberian and Far Eastern forces began arriving on the front against Germany. Moscow apparently felt able to rush the troops from the east in part because of information from Soviet spy Richard Sorge in Tokyo that Japan would remain neutral in the German-Russian war.

■ Complying with the demands of Britain and Russia, Afghanistan expelled citizens of the Axis nations.

■ The American merchant ship *Lehigh* was torpedoed and sunk by a German submarine off the west coast of Africa.

Oct. 20 A state of siege was proclaimed in Moscow. German forces were 60 miles from the capital after having won a victory over the Russians at Borodino, where Napoleon won a Pyrrhic victory in 1812.

■ The Germans occupied Stalino (Donetsk).

Japanese Premier Hideki Tojo.

■ The ranking German officer in Nantes was killed. (Forty-eight French hostages were executed two days later.)

Oct. 21 General Georgi Zhukov was named commander of all Russian forces defending Moscow.

■ About 6,000 Serbians from the town of Kragujevac were murdered by the Germans in reprisal for partisan attacks on the occupying army. Several hundred children were among the victims.

Oct. 22 In order to recover a ceded portion of Transylvania, Rumania renounced the 1940 Vienna agreement with Hungary. Italy and Germany had pushed for the territorial transfer to lure Hungary into the Axis.

Oct. 24 Kharkov, the industrial center of the Ukraine, fell to the Germans.

Oct. 25 Churchill and Roosevelt condemned reprisal killings by the Germans in occupied territories.

■ The German advance on Moscow became stalled, in part by stiffer resistance by the Russians, but more by mud and rain.

Oct. 26 The Australians were relieved at Tobruk by the British 70th Division, the Polish Carpathian Brigade, and British tank elements.

Oct. 27 Russian forces launched a counterattack from Moscow.

Oct. 29 German forces broke through Russian lines in the Crimea.

Oct. 30 Roosevelt offered the Soviet Union a one billion dollar interest-free loan for the purchase of lend-lease equipment. Repayment was to begin five years after the end of the war and be completed in ten years.

■ German Army Group Center launched an assault on Moscow from the northwest. The closest German forces were concentrated within 50 miles of the Russian capital.

■ The siege of Sevastopol began (it was to last for nine months).

■ The U.S. Navy oiler *Salinas* was torpedoed 700 miles east of Newfoundland but made it to port with no casualties.

Oct. 31 The American destroyer *Reuben James* was torpedoed and sunk off the west coast of Iceland, while escorting a British convoy from Halifax. One hundred and fifteen men were killed. It was the first U.S. combat vessel lost through hostile action in World War II.

Nov 1 The German First Panzer Group began a major attack aimed at Rostov and the Caucasus.

Nov. 2 Rival anti-Nazi Yugoslav guerrilla forces—the Chetniks and Tito's Partisans—began fighting each other in a clash outside of Uzice in western Serbia.

Nov. 3 U.S. Ambassador Grew cabled from Tokyo to Washington that Japan "might resort with dangerous and dramatic suddenness to measures which might make inevitable war with the United States." He said that "it would be shortsighted for American policy to be based upon the belief that Japanese preparations are no more than saber rattling, merely intended to give moral support to the high pressure diplomacy of Japan."

■ Admiral Isoroku Yamamoto's plan to attack Pearl Harbor was approved by the Japanese command.

■ The Germans captured Kursk.

■ Secretary of State Hull said the German government had informed the U.S. it would not offer compensation for the loss of the *Robin Moore*.

■ American women and children were evacuated from Guam, Wake, and Midway islands.

Nov. 5 Secret instructions (Combined Fleet Ultrasecret Operation Order I) were issued to the Japanese navy for the attack on Pearl Harbor. An imperial conference resulted in agreement to continue negotiations with the U.S. but to go to war if they failed to produce a settlement. The military was thus ordered to prepare for the worst.

■ The U.S. Congress voted to stay in session indefinitely because of the deteriorating state of relations with Japan.

Nov. 6 Moscow announced that since the German invasion in June, Russian losses were 350,000 killed, 1,020,000 wounded, and 378,000 missing.

■ The one billion dollar American loan to the Soviets was approved by Congress.

■ The Japanese Southern Army was ordered to prepare for attacks on the Philippines, Malaya, Thailand, and the East Indies.

■ The German blockade runner *Odenwald*, which was disguised as a U.S. flag ship (it was called the *Willmoto*), was captured by the American cruiser *Omaha* and destroyer *Somers* in the South Atlantic.

■ A committee of the U.S. National Academy of

Ribbentrop meets with Hitler at the Führer's forward headquarters in East Prussia. The dog is Hitler's pet wire-haired terrier.

Sciences recommended immediate construction of an atomic bomb.

Nov. 7 Stalin delivered his famous "Mother Russia" speech from the Kremlin. He rallied the Russian people against the Germans by invoking the long list of heroes from the past.

■ Russian defenders stalled the Finnish offensive.

■ Secretary of State Hull informed the U.S. cabinet that a critical stage had been reached in relations with Japan. American military leaders began working on the assumption that the Pacific constituted a combat area.

■ Japanese naval units were informed that Dec. 7 had been set for the planned Pearl Harbor attack.

Nov. 8 Hitler announced that German forces had inflicted between eight and ten million casualties on the Russians.

Nov. 9 The Tikhvin railhead fell to the Germans, tightening the noose around Leningrad. Yalta in the Crimea was occupied by the Germans.

■ Two Italian convoys in the Mediterranean were devastated by the Royal Navy which had received precise intelligence data through Ultra intercepts.

Nov. 10 Churchill restated British policy to declare war on Japan "within the hour" if Japan and the U.S. became involved in a conflict. The prime minister also said Britain had achieved equality of air power with the Luftwaffe.

■ A division of British troops (22,000 men) sailed from Halifax for the Far East aboard U.S. ships protected by the U.S. Navy. The convoy was made up of the carrier *Ranger*, two cruisers and seven destroyers, together with the six transports, an impressive force for a still neutral nation.

Nov. 11 U.S. lend-lease aid was extended to the Free French.

Nov. 12 Finland again rejected U.S. efforts to bring an end to the Russian-Finnish war.

■ Tula was recaptured by the Russians.

■ The British carrier *Ark Royal* was torpedoed by German submarine *U-81* off Gibraltar but managed to stay afloat.

■ Allied shipping losses for the months of July through October totaled 750,000 tons.

Nov. 13 Roosevelt called on Congress to repeal the key sections of the Neutrality Act. He said the U.S. "position in the struggle against aggression would be definitely weakened, not only in Europe and Asia, but also among our sister republics in the Americas."

■ Halder, chief of the German army General

Staff, summoned the chiefs of staff of all the major units in Russia at Orsha for a secret conference. With the temperature at minus 20° centigrade, they decided to resume the offensive against Moscow. (The winter was to be the coldest in 140 years.)

■ China requested British aircraft to fly cover over the Burma Road.

Nov. 14 Red Army forces attempted a counterattack to relieve the pressures on Moscow.

■ The Soviet air force began a concerted campaign to airlift essential supplies into Leningrad. (Through the 28th a total of 1,200 tons were delivered.)

■ *Ark Royal* sank after a valiant two-day effort by the crew to keep her afloat. Only one casualty resulted from the carrier's loss.

■ All U.S. Marines were ordered out of China. (Of the 750 Marines involved, 183 were held up by transportation delays and eventually imprisoned by the Japanese once the war started.)

■ U Maung Saw, premier of Burma, left London after failing to win a promise of independence from the British. (Returning to Rangoon by way of New York, the premier contacted Japanese representatives in the U.S. and asked them to arrange a meeting with "prominent Japanese," apparently to seek their aid against the British.)

Nov. 15 A Canadian army contingent of about 1,000 men arrived in Hong Kong to beef up the defense garrison in the British colony.

Nov. 17 Congress further repealed sections of the U.S. Neutrality Act, as requested by Roosevelt. It was now possible for merchant ships to be armed and enter combat zones.

■ Foreign Minister Shigenori Togo said a U.S.-Japanese understanding was still possible if Washington would "understand Japan's national requirements and her position in East Asia and consider the situation as it exists there in the light of realities." At the same time, he said any threat would be met with resolve: "There is naturally a limit to our conciliatory attitude."

■ Ambassador Grew cabled Washington: "I take into account the probability of the Japanese exploiting every possible tactical advantage, such as surprise and initiative."

■ General Ernst Udet, World War I flying hero and one of the organizers of the Luftwaffe, committed suicide. He was in despair and frustrated over the secondary roles given him in the war.

(Udet's death was not announced until the following January and then as the result of an airplane crash.)

Nov. 18 The newly formed British Eighth Army launched its first counteroffensive in North Africa (Operation CRUSADER). Seven British divisions were pitted against three German and seven Italian divisions. Axis tank strength was only half the Allies, 395 to 748, but the German armor was qualitatively superior.

■ The Japanese Diet approved a "resolution of hostility" directed against the U.S.

Nov. 19 German troops launched "The Autumn Offensive," which was directed at Moscow.

■ The Australian cruiser *Sydney* was apparently sunk by the German raider *Kormoran* off the west coast of Australia. The *Sydney* had pulled to within a mile of the raider, which was disguised as a Dutch merchantman, when the German ship fired torpedoes and all her guns at the cruiser. Fully aflame, the *Sydney* steamed away but was never seen again and no crewmen were ever rescued. Before breaking contact, the cruiser had fired at the *Kormoran*, which was badly damaged and finally scuttled.

■ The Germans advanced to Rostov.

■ British Commandos failed to kill Rommel in a raid on his headquarters at Beda Littoria, in Libya.

■ Commonwealth forces advanced to Sidi Rezegh in Libya, touching off the biggest battle of the Western Desert thus far. It lasted four days but it did halt the Allied advance. So confused was the fighting at times that Rommel one night slept in the desert behind the British line and only a short distance from an Allied command headquarters.

Nov. 20 Japan offered new and "final" proposals to the U.S. in response to the American note of Oct. 2. The Japanese ambassador stressed that Japan "never pledged itself to a policy of expansion," but the tone of the proposals were really an ultimatum by which the U.S. would not aid the Chinese and give the Japanese a free hand in China and Indochina.

■ President Roosevelt drafted his own compromise plan to break the deadlock with Japan. He was willing to resume oil shipments to Japan and have the U.S. participate in direct negotiations between Japan and China. Japan, in return, would send no more troops overseas and not comply with terms of the Tripartite Pact, even if the U.S. became involved in the European war. China opposed these proposals and was supported by Churchill, and they were withdrawn. Instead, the U.S. substituted proposals outlined by Secretary of State Hull which were submitted to Tokyo. They were far more severe and considered to constitute a counterultimatum to the Japanese.

Nov. 21 New Zealand forces crossed the Egyptian-Libyan frontier and took Fort Capuzzo.

Nov. 22 Secretary Hull told the Japanese that the U.S. and other governments with interests in the Pacific felt the general differences with Tokyo "could all be settled if the Japanese could give us some satisfactory evidences that their intentions were peaceful."

■ The British North African offensive was blocked by tanks commanded by General Rommel.

■ The German raider *Atlantis* was sunk in the

southern Atlantic by the British cruiser *Devonshire*. The *Atlantis* had claimed 22 merchant ships (146,000 tons) in its 20 months of raiding.

Nov. 23 The 5th South African Brigade was virtually annihilated in a ferocious battle in North Africa. Rommel issued orders for his forces to "dash to the wire," a reference to the Egyptian-Libyan border.

■ Officers and men of the Japanese strike force to attack Pearl Harbor were told of their mission for the first time. The force was then assembled at Tankan Bay, an anchorage at Etorofu Island in the Kuriles.

■ U.S. forces occupied Dutch Guiana (Surinam) with the approval of the Dutch and Brazilian governments. Surinam provided more than 60 percent of the bauxite needed for the defense-related aluminum industry of the U.S.

■ Rostov was captured by Kleist's First Panzer Army. (The Russians quickly counterattacked and inflicted heavy casualties on the Germans in the city.)

■ Germany told the Danes they must join the Anti-Comintern Pact: "If not, Germany will cancel the agreement of the 9th of April 1940, and Denmark will be regarded as an enemy country and must face the unavoidable circumstances."

Nov. 24 In an action to discourage Vichy French collaboration with Germany, the U.S. revoked all export licenses to French North Africa, Spain and Tangier.

■ U.S. lend-lease aid was approved for the Free French.

■ Russian forces launched a counterattack around Rostov.

■ The British battleship *Barham* was sunk in the Mediterranean by a German submarine with heavy loss of life.

■ General Auchinleck directed the Eighth Army to "attack and pursue. All out everywhere."

■ Admiral N. Suetsugu, who represented Japan's military extremists, told the Associated Press, "Consciously or not, America seems inspired by the inhuman motive of holding us down in a subordinate position to herself and seeks to justify

German Ju-87 dive bombers attack British tanks at Ghobi in the Western Desert of Egypt.

such a policy by the specious plea of defending the American ideal of peace and democracy."

■ U.S. Navy commanders in the Pacific were warned that talks with the Japanese were unlikely to produce results and Tokyo's forces were preparing for military action. Washington advised the officers of the possibility of "a surprise aggressive movement in any direction, including [an] attack on Philippines or Guam." Japanese transports had been observed en route to the Malayan Peninsula from Formosa.

Nov. 25 The Anti-Comintern Pact was renewed for five years. Signing the Axis agreement were Germany, Italy, Japan, Hungary, Spain, Bulgaria, Croatia, Denmark, Finland, Rumania, Slovakia, Manchukuo, and the Chinese government in Nanking.

■ Demonstrations broke out in Copenhagen to protest Denmark's forced adherence to the Anti-Comintern Pact.

■ German forces opened up an all-out attack on Moscow.

Nov. 26 Washington rejected the Japanese proposals of Nov. 20 because they "contain some features which, in the opinion of this Government, conflict with the fundamental principles which form a part of the general settlement under consideration and to which each Government declared that it is committed." The U.S. did suggest, however, "that further effort be made to resolve our divergencies of view in regard to the practical application of the fundamental principles. . . ." The rejection marked the end of the long efforts to negotiate a settlement.

■ The Japanese Pearl Harbor Attack Force, under Vice Admiral Chuichi Nagumo, completed its rendezvous and sailed from isolated Tankan Bay in the Kuriles.

■ Lieutenant General Sir Neil Ritchie assumed command of the British forces in North Africa.

■ Free France proclaimed the independence of Lebanon.

Nov. 27 All U.S. military forces were placed on a "final alert" status with Pacific units receiving a "war warning." Washington said "an aggressive move by Japan is expected within the next few days."

■ Third Panzer Group tanks advanced to within 19 miles of Moscow, where they were stopped.

■ Gondar, the last outpost still occupied by the Italians in east Africa, capitulated. With the fall of the Ethiopian city, the war for control over the Gulf of Aden and the Red Sea was over. In less than a year the Italian force of 350,000 men was totally defeated by a combined Allied force of 21,500.

Nov. 28 For the second time Hull warned the U.S. military of a possible imminent attack by Japan.

■ The Japanese foreign ministry advised its embassies throughout the world that relations with the U.S. and Britain had reached an extremely critical stage.

■ *Waffen* (combat) SS units were within 20 miles of the Kremlin as the temperature dropped to minus 32° centigrade.

Nov. 29 The U.S. warned Britain of an impending Japanese attack in the Asia-Pacific area.

■ Tojo restated Japan's leadership role in east Asia: "Nothing can be permitted to interfere with this sphere because this sphere was decreed by Providence."

■ The Russians recaptured Rostov, forcing the Seventh Panzer Army out of the "Gateway to the Caucasus." It was the first setback for the Germans on the Soviet front. Hitler ordered his troops to stand firm. Field Marshal Gerd von Runstedt, commander of Army Group South, resigned rather than pass on the order.

■ Finland restored its former border with the Soviet Union, reincorporating the territories retaken by its military actions.

Nov. 30 Japanese Foreign Minister Shigenori Togo informed the ambassador in Berlin that "war may suddenly break out between the Anglo-Saxon nations and Japan . . . quicker than anyone dreams." The Germans were not informed.

■ Heavy fighting resumed between Tobruk and Sidi Rezegh.

■ The thousandth air raid alert of the war was sounded on Malta.

■ British air raid casualties for October and November were 351 killed and 516 injured.

■ Eleven thousand Russians starved to death in Leningrad during the month.

Dec. 1 Japan made its irrevocable decision to go to war. A council meeting in the imperial presence ended with a unanimous vote to begin hostilities. The minutes of the meeting read: "Our negotiations with the United States regarding the

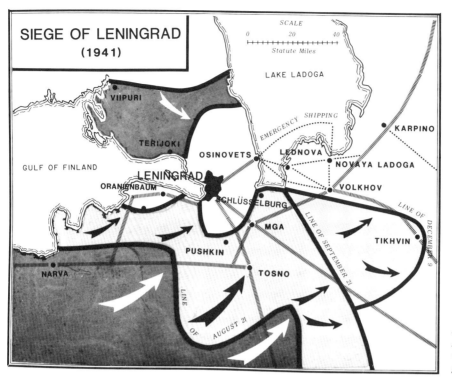

SIEGE OF LENINGRAD
(1941)

SCALE
0   20   40
Statute Miles

LAKE LADOGA

VIIPURI

EMERGENCY SHIPPING

KARPINO

TERIJOKI

OSINOVETS

LEDNOVA

NOVAYA LADOGA

GULF OF FINLAND

LENINGRAD

VOLKHOV

ORANIENBAUM

SCHLÜSSELBURG

LINE OF DECEMBER 9

MGA

LINE OF SEPTEMBER 21

TIKHVIN

PUSHKIN

NARVA

TOSNO

LINE OF AUGUST 21

One of the longest, and certainly the deadliest, sieges in history began as the Germans virtually isolated Leningrad. The city survived after enduring unspeakable hardships.

execution of our national policy, adopted November 5, have finally failed. Japan will open hostilities against the United States, Great Britain and the Netherlands." Tojo led the meeting. Emperor Hirohito did not speak at all.

■ German tanks were positioned within nine miles of the Kremlin. It was possible to see the spires.

Dec. 2 Roosevelt—in a personal note to the Japanese envoys in Washington—asked Tokyo for an explanation of the Japanese troop build-up in Indochina. The President said, "The stationing of these increased Japanese forces in Indochina would seem to imply the utilization of these forces by Japan for purposes of further aggression, since no such number of forces could possibly be required for the policing of that region. . . ."

■ Japan's cabinet was reshuffled because of "the deteriorating international situation." The new cabinet affirmed the final decision to attack Pearl Harbor, and the code message to proceed, "Climb Mount Niitaka," was flashed to the naval attack force the next day.

■ The Japanese embassy in Washington was ordered to destroy all but its most secret coding facilities. Similar orders went to Japanese missions in British, Dutch, and Canadian cities, Cuba, the Philippines, and the South Pacific.

■ London announced the formation of a new and expanded Eastern Fleet. Britain in the past had maintained a cruiser squadron, but its naval presence in Asia would now be led by more powerful men-of-war. The battleship *Prince of Wales* and the battle cruiser *Repulse* arrived in Singapore this date. This announced action indicated the concern of Britain as it viewed Japan's southward penetration.

■ Soviet troops evacuated the last areas of Finland occupied since the 1939–40 war.

■ U.S. Navy gunners reported aboard the American merchantman S.S. *Dunboyne*, the first such ship to be under armed guard.

Dec. 3 The first organized military resistance in Axis-held territory began with Yugoslav Partisan attacks on German units.

■ Stalin approved the movement of the reconstituted Polish army to Iran and Iraq for eventual inclusion with British forces, preferring to see them fight in the West even though Russia was in need of all the help it could get.

■ The U.S. merchantman *Sagadahoc* was torpedoed and sunk in the South Atlantic.

■ German units—some suffering 40 percent frostbite casualties—began pulling back from the suburbs of Moscow. High winds from the Arctic coupled with minus 38° centigrade temperatures reduced some battalions to fewer than 100 men.

Dec. 4 The Japanese ambassador in Berlin asked what the German government's position would be if Japan initiated war against the Allies. Such a possibility was not covered under the Tripartite Pact. Hitler had never been advised of the planned attacks in the Pacific.

■ Japan declared the Netherlands an enemy power and said it would treat the Dutch as if a state of war existed between them.

■ The Japanese Twenty-fifth Army began leaving Hainan Island for the invasion of Malaya and Thailand.

Dec. 5 U.S. naval offices and facilities in Tokyo, Bangkok, Peking, Tientsin, Shanghai, Guam, and Wake were ordered to destroy all but absolutely essential communication codes and secret documents.

■ Hitler ordered a halt to German offensive operations aimed at Moscow. Of the 3,500,000 men committed to Russia by the Axis, 750,000 were killed, wounded, or missing by this date.

■ Japan told Roosevelt it was reinforcing its army units in Indochina because "Chinese troops have recently shown frequent signs of movement along the northern frontier of French Indochina bordering on China."

■ Thailand sought assurances from Britain that if the Thais were attacked by the Japanese London would declare war on Japan immediately. (Churchill the next day suggested the Thais defend themselves if attacked and that British aid would be forthcoming. Roosevelt was advised of Churchill's offer and agreed to supply U.S. assistance as well, but neither agreed on an automatic declaration of war.)

Dec. 6 Roosevelt sent a message to Emperor Hirohito calling on Japan to withdraw its troops from Indochina. He said the large military force there created "a reasonable doubt on the part of

U.S. WAR PLANS PUBLISHED

Readers of the *Washington Times–Herald*, the *New York Daily News*, and the *Chicago Tribune* read on Dec. 5, 1941, of U.S. plans to mobilize for war. *Tribune* correspondent Chesly Manly's bylined story said: "Confidential report prepared by the Joint Army and Navy high command calls for American expeditionary forces aggregating five million men for a final land offensive against Germany and her satellites. It contemplates total armed forces of 10,045,658 men. It is a blueprint for total war on a scale unprecedented in at least two oceans and three continents, Europe, Africa, and Asia." It went into highly specific details of how the plan was to be implemented. The revelation was, in the words of the plan's principal author, General Albert C. Wedemeyer, "irrefutable evidence that American intervention in the war was planned and imminent, and that President Roosevelt's promises to keep us out of war were only campaign oratory" *(Wedemeyer Reports!*, p. 16). Isolationists pounced upon the disclosures as proof of White House perfidy. It produced an electric political effect. An Army captain who was isolationist himself (like Wedemeyer) stole the secret document from the War Plans Division, passed it on to Senator Burton K. Wheeler, who in turn gave it to correspondent Manly. To the German High Command, which received cabled summaries of the Manly story immediately from the embassy in Washington, the information was pure gold. With this material Hitler's military planners, at the direction of Chief of Staff Alfred Jodl, reexamined their own policies "in the light of the incontrovertible intelligence that had become available."

White House Press Secretary Stephen T. Early told newsmen no action would be taken as a result of the publication of secret material: "Your right to print the news is, I think, unchallenged and unquestioned. It depends entirely on the decision of the publisher and editor whether publication is patriotic or treasonable."

other nations that this continuing concentration in Indochina is not defensive in its character. . . . the people of the Philippines, of the hundreds of islands of the East Indies, of Malaya, and of Thailand itself are asking themselves whether these forces of Japan are preparing or intending to make attack in one or more of these many directions."

■ Russian forces under General Zhukov began their counteroffensive from Moscow. Three fresh Soviet armies (made up of more than a million men) were thrown against the now exhausted and overextended German forces, who were caught by surprise. Zhukov's counteraction was the salvation of Moscow.

■ Finnish forces captured Medvezhyegorsk, on the Murmansk rail line just north of Lake Onega. It marked their easternmost advance into the Soviet Union.

■ Britain declared war on Finland, Hungary, and Rumania.

■ Roosevelt approved research funds for an atomic bomb and a promise of "enormous" resources if the project showed promise.

Dec. 7 Japanese forces attacked Pearl Harbor and other U.S. and British territories and possessions in the Pacific, launching the Pacific war. The major force was directed at the Hawaiian naval base in the hope of delivering a devastating knockout blow to the U.S. Pacific Fleet. U.S. carriers—which would play the major role in the forthcoming battles—were not in port because of a fortuitous decision which was not related to intelligence gained from breaking of the Japanese radio codes. U.S. losses at Pearl Harbor were staggering, but the American fleet was not destroyed. Four battleships were lost. All told, 92 navy and 96 army planes were destroyed, 2,334

Japanese military planners had a miniature mock-up of Pearl Harbor constructed to assist pilots involved in the attack.

A view of the damage inflicted at Pearl Harbor was photographed by one of the attacking Japanese aircraft.

American servicemen were killed, and 1,347 were wounded. The Japanese lost 28 aircraft, 5 midget submarines, and fewer than 100 men. In a note delivered to Hull at 2:15 P.M. (Eastern Standard Time), the Japanese said, "Obviously it is the intention of the American Government to conspire with Great Britain and other countries to obstruct Japan's efforts toward the establishment of peace through the creation of a new order in East Asia, and especially to preserve Anglo-American rights and interest by keeping Japan and China at war."

THE JAPANESE PEARL HARBOR STRIKE FORCE

Attack Force (Vice Admiral Chuichi Nagumo)
Carriers: *Akagi, Kaga, Soryu, Hiryu, Zuikaku, Shokaku*

Support Force (Vice Admiral Gunichi Mikawa)
Battleships: *Hiei, Kirishima*
Heavy cruisers: *Tone, Chikuma*

Scouting Force (Rear Admiral Sentaro Omori)
Light cruiser: *Abukuma*
Destroyers: *Tanikaze, Hamakaze, Urakaze, Asakaze, Kasumi, Arare, Kagero, Shiranuhi, Akigumo*

Attack Aircraft
First Wave: 51 bombers, 89 torpedo planes, 43 fighters
Second Wave: 78 bombers, 54 torpedo planes, 35 fighters

THE ADMIRAL KILLED MANNING HIS MACHINE GUN

The highest ranking U.S. naval officer killed during the war lost his life on the first day of American involvement. Rear Admiral Isaac C. Kidd was aboard the *Arizona*, his flagship as commander of Battleship Division One. When the Japanese attacked, Kidd manned a machine gun and was last seen firing at the attacking aircraft. Shortly thereafter, *Arizona*'s magazine blew up and the ship exploded and sank in the harbor. His body was presumed to

have been entombed in the hull of the stricken vessel, which is today a memorial to the dead. A total of 1,103 men were killed aboard the battleship.

U.S. NAVAL LOSSES AT PEARL HARBOR

Sunk:
Battleships: *Arizona, California, Oklahoma, West Virginia*
Minelayer: *Oglala*
Target ship: *Utah*

Damaged:
Battleships: *Maryland, Nevada, Pennsylvania, Tennessee*
Light cruisers: *Raleigh, Honolulu, Helena*
Destroyers: *Cassin, Shaw, Downes*
Seaplane tender: *Curtis*
Repair ship: *Vestal*

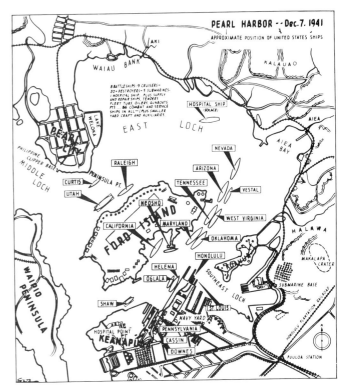

The battleships West Virginia *and* Tennessee *burn during the Pearl Harbor attack.*

■ Hitler issued an order (known as the "Night and Fog Decree") directing German authorities in western European occupation areas to eliminate those individuals "endangering German security." They were to be disposed of in a discreet manner, to "disappear" into the night and fog so that even their relatives would never know what happened to them.

■ Costa Rica declared war on Japan.

Dec. 8 The U.S., Britain, Canada, New Zealand, Free France, the Netherlands, the Netherlands East Indies, the Dominican Republic, El Salvador, Guatemala, Haiti, Honduras, and Panama declared war on Japan. Colombia broke diplomatic relations with Japan.

■ An estimated 60 million Americans heard Roosevelt's call for Congressional declarations of war against the Axis powers. The president's reference to the previous day as one "that will live in infamy" was a clarion call to action, but recruiters were already straining to accommodate the volunteers seeking to enlist. A thousand men were turned away by the navy in New York City for lack of facilities.

■ Japanese aircraft attacked the Philippines. The heaviest strikes were directed against Clark Field. Half the bombers of the U.S. Far East Air Force were destroyed.

■ Japanese forces landed in Malaya and Thailand. Singapore and Hong Kong were bombed. Guam, Midway, and Wake were attacked. The International Settlement in Shanghai was occupied by the Japanese.

■ Japan requested Germany to declare war on the U.S.

■ Axis troops began withdrawing toward Gazala, pursued by the British Eighth Army.

■ The German High Command issued a communiqué, saying, "The continuation of operations and the manner of the war's conduct in the East from now on will be dictated by Winter."

■ German troops started pulling back from the Moscow area. The Russians reoccupied Tikhvin on the Leningrad rail line as German Army Group North pulled out of the city.

■ Thailand signed an agreement with Japan granting Japanese troops right of passage. The Bangkok government felt it could not offer resistance to the overwhelming Japanese forces. In order not to be beholden to Japan, however, it did reject a proposal from Tokyo which would have returned disputed Thai-Cambodian territory to Thailand.

■ Phony air raid alerts were sounded across the United States. Three were sounded in San Francisco alone as 30 hostile planes were reported over the city. Confusion and panic were fanned by statements by Lieutenant General John L. DeWitt, head of the Western Defense Command: "Death and destruction are likely to come to this city at any moment. These planes were over our community for a definite period. They were enemy planes. I mean Japanese planes. They were tracked out to sea. Why bombs were not dropped, I do not know." There were no Japanese aircraft, of course, but the pattern of hysteria was set.

■ A blood bath in Riga, Latvia, claimed the lives of 27,000 Jews.

Dec. 9 Japanese forces occupied Bangkok, Thailand, without opposition and invaded Tarawa and Makin in the Gilbert Islands.

■ Dutch aircraft from the East Indies arrived in Singapore to bolster British defenses.

■ China declared war on Japan (even though war had been raging for years), Germany, and Italy. Cuba and South Africa declared war on Japan. Argentina and Uruguay announced they would consider the U.S. a "belligerent" in the war against Japan.

Dec. 10 The British battleship *Prince of Wales* and the battle cruiser *Repulse* were sunk off Kuantan, Malaya. They were attacked by 99 Saigon-based aircraft of the Japanese navy's First Air Group. In 90 minutes the Japanese had won the first battle in history between planes and capital ships on the high seas (Taranto and Pearl Harbor were not in the same category, since the ships were in harbors, not under way). *Repulse* was hit by 14 torpedoes, *Prince of Wales* by four. Of the total of 2,921 men on the two British ships, 2,081 were rescued by destroyers. The Eastern Fleet commander, Admiral Sir Tom Phillips, was among the victims. The Japanese lost only four aircraft. The action dramatically ended the dominant role of the battleship in modern naval warfare.

■ The pro-Japanese Burma Independence Army (BIA) of 2,300 men marched into Burma from Thailand where it had been secretly organized and trained by the Japanese. Aung San, a Bur-

mese nationalist officer, led the BIA in the fight to oust the British. The BIA was the creation of a Colonel Suzuki of the Japanese army who posed as a news correspondent in Rangoon.

■ Guam surrendered to a 6,000-man Japanese invasion force. There were a little more than 500 U.S. servicemen on the island who had nothing heavier than .30 caliber machine guns for defending themselves.

■ The U.S. naval base at Cavite in the Philippines was heavily damaged by 50 Japanese bombers. Most of the base was destroyed, and the entire reserve stock of torpedoes for the U.S. Far East Fleet was lost. Four thousand Japanese troops from Formosa landed on northwestern Luzon without encountering any resistance. (The relatively small Japanese force was rapidly and mightily reinforced and was eventually able to overwhelm the Philippines, which were defended by 19,000 U.S. Army troops, 12,000 Philippine Scouts, and 100,000 newly mobilized but ill-equipped members of the Philippine army.)

■ The 242-day-long siege of Tobruk ended. Commonwealth troops broke out of the city and joined up with British Eighth Army units at nearby Acroma. During the siege the Allied garrison survived by being supplied with 34,113 fresh troops, 72 tanks, 92 heavy guns and 34,000 tons of supplies. To get the men and material to Tobruk, the Royal Navy lost 25 warships. Another 5 merchant ships were destroyed.

■ The Japanese battleship *Haruna* was erroneously reported as sunk. Captain Colin Kelly became the first American hero of the war when it was believed his bomber hit the battleship in Philippine waters, but later investigation revealed no Japanese warships of that size were in the area. (The *Haruna* actually survived until the very end of the war when it finally foundered in Kure harbor in July of 1945.)

Dec. 11 A Japanese landing party, backed by nine men-of-war, attempted to capture Wake Island. Its defenses were meager, consisting of a Marine fighter squadron with 6 Grumman Wildcats (16 others were lost on the ground in the Dec. 8 raid), a 388-man detachment of the 1st Marine Defense Battalion, equipped with 3-inch and .50 caliber antiaircraft guns and .30 caliber machine guns, plus 75 unarmed army and navy personnel. There were 70 civilian employees of

Pan American Airways and about 1,200 construction workers. Despite the superiority of the invading force, the Marines drove them back. Shore batteries sank the destroyer *Hayate*, and Marine aircraft destroyed the destroyer *Kisaragi*. Three other destroyers were damaged.

■ Germany and Italy declared war on the U.S. Washington declared war on them.

■ Germany, Italy, and Japan concluded an agreement, pledging that none would conclude a separate peace.

■ Nicaragua and the Polish and Dutch governments-in-exile declared war on Japan.

■ The Dominican Republic, Guatemala, and Nicaragua declared war on Germany and Italy. Mexico broke diplomatic relations with the Axis powers.

■ RAF bombers in Malaya were restricted to night missions because of a shortage of fighter aircraft for protection during daylight operations. The fighters were primarily employed in the defense of Singapore.

■ Japanese aircraft attacked the Tavoy airdrome in southern Burma preliminary to a ground offensive into Burma.

Dec. 12 A Japanese force of 2,500 men landed unopposed at Legaspi in southern Luzon.

■ Small numbers of Japanese troops began infiltrating into Burma from Thailand. An American Flying Tigers squadron—made up of American volunteers and commanded by Colonel Claire L. Chennault—flew into Burma from China to aid in the defense.

■ British troops began withdrawing from the mainland territories of Hong Kong.

■ French ships in American ports were seized by the U.S. government.

■ Finnish forces completed the destruction of two Russian divisions south of Medvezhyegorsk in Soviet Karelia. (Henceforth, the Finns remained on the defensive and effectively withdrew from the war. The campaign against Russia cost the Finns 25,000 dead and 50,000 wounded. Russia's losses were several times greater but Moscow never disclosed casualty figures.)

■ General Auchinleck was told forces intended for North Africa would be diverted to Asia.

■ Rumania and Hungary declared war on the U.S. (Not until June 5, 1942, did the U.S. Senate "accept" the declarations and then only under Russian pressure on the American government.)

■ Ireland announced it would continue its policy of absolute neutrality.

■ Slovakia declared war on the U.S. and Britain (Washington never "accepted" the declaration, as it refused a Croat declaration on the 14th.)

A Japanese midget submarine—part of the Pearl Harbor attack force—failed to penetrate the naval base and ended up beached on a nearby Oahu strand.

■ Haiti, Honduras, and Panama declared war on Germany and Italy.

Dec. 13 Japanese aircraft attacked U.S. naval and air bases in the Philippines, virtually eliminating what was left of American aircraft available for defense of the islands.

■ The small Indian detachment left in the Brunei-Sarawak area withdrew after destroying the oil fields and production facilities.

■ Both sides suffered heavy losses as the British tried to break through the Gazala line of Rommel's Panzer Group Africa.

■ Bulgaria declared war on the U.S. (King Boris had refused to declare war on Russia because of historical sympathies between the two countries.)

■ The U.S. Department of Justice had interned 595 Japanese and 187 German alien residents of the Far Western states.

JAPANESE-AMERICANS DECLARED U.S. ENEMIES

Lieutenant General John L. DeWitt, commander of the Western Defense Command, recommended to the secretary of war that 112,000 Japanese-Americans, two-thirds of whom were U.S. citizens, be moved from the states bordering the Pacific. General DeWitt requested they be removed from their homes to "relocation centers." He believed they were bent on sabotage: "The very fact that no sabotage has taken place to date is a disturbing and confirming indication that such action will be taken." He added: "In the war in which we are now engaged, racial infinities [sic] are not severed by migration. The Japanese race is an enemy race and while many second and third generation Japanese born on American soil, possessed of U.S. citizenship, have become 'Americanized,' the racial strains are undiluted." The general's recommendations were approved by the War Department on the basis of military necessity. The relocation, called "our worst wartime mistake" by Eugene V. Rostow, was endorsed right up the chain of command, with no one willing to assume the responsibility of challenging DeWitt's recommendations. The military, the Congress, the

president, and the courts permitted those Japanese-Americans to be stripped of their property and confined in concentration camps "on a record which wouldn't support a conviction for stealing a dog."

SOURCE: *Harper's*, Sept. 1945.

Dec. 14 Japan and Thailand entered into an alliance, with Bangkok retaining a measure of independence but the Japanese exercising whatever control necessary to operate in Thailand.

Dec. 15 Russian forces continued to advance in the north, capturing Klin and Istra.

■ British forces were driven back in Malaya, Burma, and Hong Kong. All U.S. B-17 bombers were flown to Australia from the Philippines.

■ After further British attacks on his positions near Gazala, Rommel decided to pull his forces out of Cyrenaica.

■ The British cruiser *Galatea* was sunk off the Egyptian coast by a German submarine.

■ The Japanese merchant ship *Atsutasan Maru* was sunk by the American submarine *Swordfish*, the first shipping loss of the war for Japan.

Dec. 16 Japanese forces invaded British Borneo.

■ Johnston Island in the Pacific was shelled by a Japanese submarine.

■ Tojo warned the Japanese people the war would be a long one.

■ Continuing to push the Germans back from Moscow, Russian forces recaptured Kalinin.

Dec. 17 Red Army forces launched strong counteroffensives along a broad front, while the German Army Group South opened a new drive toward Sevastopol in the Crimea.

■ The British pulled back to the Perak River in Malaya.

■ Albania declared war on the U.S.

■ Top U.S. military commanders were replaced in the Pacific. Admiral Chester W. Nimitz was named commander of the U.S. Pacific Fleet. Lieutenant General Delos C. Emmons became commanding general of the Hawaiian Department.

Dec. 18 Germany announced all its forces had been withdrawn from Finland.

Dec. 19 Hitler assumed personal command of the German army, replacing the ousted Field

Marshal Brauchitsch who felt Moscow could not be taken and that the Germans should go on the defensive.

■ Three Italian "human torpedo" teams—led by Prince Borghese—entered Alexandria harbor in Egypt and seriously disabled the British battleships *Queen Elizabeth* and *Valiant*. The underwater demolition crews attached delayed-action mines to the hulls of the warships.

■ The British cruiser *Neptune* struck four mines off Malta and sank immediately with only one survivor. With the successful attack on the ships in Alexandria, British naval strength in the Mediterranean reached its low point.

■ Japanese troops crossed over to Hong Kong proper from Kowloon.

■ British troops were evacuated from Penang (Pinang) in Malaya.

■ Derna and Mechili in Libya were recaptured by the British.

■ Colombia broke off diplomatic relations with Germany and Italy.

Dec. 20 Japanese troops landed at Davao, Mindanao, in the Philippines.

■ The Flying Tigers entered combat for the first time, successfully challenging Japanese aircraft over Kunming.

■ Nicaragua declared war on Rumania, Hungary, and Bulgaria.

Dec. 21 Japanese troops began massive landing operations at points along the coast of the Lingayen Gulf in the Philippines, about 135 miles north of Manila.

■ Churchill cabled Governor Sir Mark Young of Hong Kong: "Every day that you are able to maintain your resistance you help the Allied cause all over the world, and by a prolonged resistance you and your men can win the lasting honour which we are sure will be your lasting due."

Dec. 22 The first American troops arrived in Australia.

■ Japan's Fourteenth Army, under Lieutenant General Masaharu Homma, was put ashore at Lingayen Gulf. This was the main force (about 40,000 men) of the Japanese offensive which took the Philippines.

■ Chiang Kai-shek offered two Chinese armies to help the British defend Burma. General Wavell accepted a division with a regiment to be held in reserve.

■ More than 32,000 Jews were murdered by German *Einsatzgruppen* execution squads in Vilna, Lithuania. (*Einsatzgruppen A* would report a total of 229,052 Jews killed in the Baltic states during the first six months of German occupation.)

Dec. 23 Wake Island fell to the Japanese. A U.S. relief force from Hawaii was 425 miles away when it was told to turn back. The Japanese naval landing force of 1,500 men took eleven hours to overcome the outnumbered American defenders. With the loss of Wake, there was no U.S. base left between Hawaii and the Philippines.

■ The first meeting of the U.S. and British War Council was held in Washington.

■ Japan achieved total air and naval superiority in the Philippines.

■ General MacArthur decided to evacuate Luzon and make a last stand on Bataan. (By this action, 75,000 troops were permitted to prolong the fighting in the Philippines for four months and tie up sizeable numbers of Japanese who might have been used in offensive operations elsewhere in the southwest Pacific.)

■ Japanese forces began landing at Kuching, Sarawak, in Borneo.

■ Rangoon was bombed as the Japanese moved to establish air supremacy over Burma.

■ Palmyra Island in the Pacific was shelled by a Japanese submarine.

■ Supply problems forced the Eighth Army to halt its westward drive in North Africa.

■ Mexico broke diplomatic relations with Bulgaria, Hungary, and Rumania.

Dec. 24 Benghazi was reoccupied by the British after the Germans were found to have abandoned the Cyrenaican city.

■ A 7,000-man Japanese force landed at Lamon Bay on Luzon in the Philippines.

■ Jolo Island in the Sulu Archipelago was occupied by the Japanese. The president of the Philippines, Manuel L. Quezon, and Filipino and American officials abandoned Manila and fled to Corregidor.

■ The ARCADIA conference opened in Washington with President Roosevelt and Prime Minister Churchill conferring with their top military leaders to plan Allied strategy. Out of the meeting developed the Combined Chiefs of Staff which shaped strategy throughout the war.

■ Despite U.S. objections, three corvettes and a submarine of the Free French navy under the command of Vice Admiral Emile Muselier seized control of Saint Pierre and Miquelon islands off the Newfoundland coast. Washington had wanted Canadian control over the French possessions rather than either Gaullist or Vichy administration. The U.S. still recognized the Pétain government, and the Free French action complicated American diplomacy.

Dec. 25 Russian forces began pushing forward in the Crimea.

■ About 3,700 Russians died of starvation in Leningrad. In a grim irony, it was the day the bread ration had been increased because of new supplies reaching the city.

■ Hong Kong's garrison surrendered to the Japanese. The colony was never considered defendable, and the Commonwealth forces, with volunteer defenders, could not do more than delay the conquest. Commonwealth combatant losses in defending Hong Kong amounted to 11,848.

Countless civilians were also killed and wounded. Japanese casualties were 675 killed and 2,079 wounded.

■ The Chinese announced they would no longer cooperate with the British and all Chinese troops in Burma would be withdrawn. Chiang Kai-shek's ire was aroused when the British failed to release preciously short ammunition aboard the American ship *Tulsa* which was in the Rangoon harbor. China insisted on delivery since the munitions were shipped for Chinese use, but the situation in Burma prompted reconsideration.

Dec. 26 Russian forces landed on the Kerch Peninsula in an effort to relieve Sevastopol.

■ The Japanese broke through the Perak River defense line in Malaya and pushed through to Ipoh, which was evacuated by the defending Indian division.

■ Manila was declared an open city. All troops were removed and military supplies destroyed. Japanese bombings continued.

Dec. 27 British Commando raids were made on Vaagso and the Lofoten Islands of Norway.

Dec. 28 German and British tank forces inflicted

Hong Kong Governor Sir Mark Young surrenders to Japanese Lieutenant General T. Sakai on Christmas Day, 1941, as portrayed by Japanese artist Ihara Usaburo.

heavy losses on each other as the Eighth Army resumed offensive action and drove toward Agedabia.

■ Manila was bombed by Japanese planes.

Dec. 29 Kerch and Feodosiya were recaptured by Russian amphibious forces in the Crimea. The Germans, however, maintained their drive toward Sevastopol. On the central front the Germans continued withdrawing from the Moscow area.

■ Corregidor Island in Manila Bay was attacked for the first time by Japanese aircraft.

Dec. 30 U.S. and Filipino forces abandoned their defense line on Luzon and began pulling back to their final positions before Bataan.

■ The British halted their drive for Agedabia in Libya after losing still more tanks to what were now concluded to be superior German armored vehicles.

Dec. 30 Kaluga, 90 miles southwest of Moscow, was recaptured by the Russians.

Dec. 31 With Japanese forces 30 miles away, Manila was evacuated.

■ The isolated Axis garrison at Bardia was assualted by South African and British troops.

■ The Germans eased their pressure on Sevastopol and moved to halt the Russian forces advancing from Kerch and Feodosiya.

(OPPOSITE, TOP) *A Japanese soldier with fixed bayonet guards Americans and Filipinos on the Bataan Death March.*

(OPPOSITE, BOTTOM) *British Eighth Army infantrymen, advancing in the Western Desert, take cover behind a disabled German tank.*

1942 Japan rules most of Asia, but the Axis is halted in North Africa.

Jan. 1 The United Nations was conceived in Washington with 26 signatories vowing to employ their "full resources, military or economic, against those members of the Tripartite Pact and its adherents." They agreed "not to make a separate armistice or peace with the enemies."

■ U.S. and Filipino forces in southern Luzon retreated after blowing up bridges across the Pampanga River. The South Luzon Force was disbanded.

■ Sarawak was abandoned by the British after the oil field facilities were destroyed.

■ British units assaulted Bardia in a night attack.

■ The Germans executed 23 Czech workers as saboteurs.

Jan. 2 The Japanese occupied Manila and the naval base at Cavite in the Philippines. Corregidor came under daily air attack.

■ Chinese troops began arriving in Burma to aid in defense of the British territory.

■ Japanese planes caused widespread destruction in raids on Singapore.

■ British and South African troops recaptured Bardia, taking 7,000 prisoners.

Jan. 3 Roosevelt and Churchill announced a unified command for the southwest Pacific, with General Sir Archibald P. Wavell as supreme commander of Allied forces. Wavell was directed to hold a line from Malaya through Sumatra,

Java, and northern Australia. Chiang Kai-shek was given command of the China theater of operations.

■ Japanese troops invaded Labuan Island in Brunei Bay and met no opposition.

■ The British chiefs of staff directed the Home Forces to begin planning operations for a second front in western Europe. (It was the genesis of what would be the Normandy invasion 29 months later.)

Jan. 3–12 Chinese troops routed a Japanese force estimated at 70,000 men in a major battle in the Hunan provincial capital of Changsha.

Jan. 4 Japanese forces bombed Rabaul for the first time. The air offensive signaled Tokyo's intention of seizing the strategic air and naval base in the Bismarck Archipelago.

■ The Russians recaptured Borovsk.

■ Indian leaders promised to support the Allied war effort if Britain granted India dominion status.

Jan. 5 Stalin directed Russian units to launch an all-out offensive along the entire front.

■ Reinforcements were landed on the Crimean coast as the Red Army tried to break the siege of Sevastopol. They encountered heavy German resistance.

■ British forces assaulted the German defenses in the Halfaya Pass in Libya.

■ Japanese reinforcements for Malaya landed on

the west coast of the peninsula. British forces withdrew to new defensive positions.

■ U.S. and Filipino troops established the Layac line, a holding operation to permit evacuation through Layac junction through which all roads to Bataan passed.

Jan. 6 In his State of the Union message, Roosevelt said cooperative military planning would dictate strategy during the war: "We shall not fight isolated wars, each nation going its own way. . . . The militarists of Berlin and Tokyo started this war, but the massed, angered forces of common humanity will finish it."

■ Washington announced U.S. troops would be stationed in Britain.

■ The British ground offensive in Libya was temporarily halted east of El Agheila. Eighth Army's first offensive was nonetheless successful in inflicting a severe defeat on Rommel's Panzer Group Africa which suffered 38,000 killed, wounded, and missing. It was the first British victory over German troops in World War II.

THE LEGEND OF ROMMEL

For sheer panache, few generals of the war equaled Erwin Rommel. When he arrived in North Africa—at the age of 49—the Italian army was in retreat and the British Western Desert Force was rolling westward as fast as its logistics would permit. Rommel changed all that. In a little more than two months, he turned the situation around and soon stood at the frontier of Egypt. He became a legend.

The British, oddly enough, helped create the legend. Churchill discussed his feats in the House of Commons: "We have a daring and skillful opponent against us, and, may I say across the havoc of war, a great general."

The British Commander in Chief, Middle East—General Sir Claude Auchinleck—delivered the ultimate accolade in Jan. of 1942 when he issued this directive to commanders of the Eighth Army:

"There exists a real danger that our friend Rommel is becoming a kind of magician or bogeyman to our troops, who are talking far too much about him. He is by no means a superman, although he is undoubtedly very energetic and able. Even if he were a superman, it would still be highly undesirable that our men should credit him with supernatural powers.

"I wish you to dispel by all possible means the idea that Rommel represents something more than an ordinary German general. The important thing now is to see that we do not always keep harping on Rommel.

"Please ensure that this order is put into immediate effect, and impress upon all Commanders that, from a psychological point of view, it is a matter of the highest importance."

■ A Japanese amphibious force was landed and occupied Brunei Bay in Borneo. Units in Malaya continued advancing down the west coast.

■ U.S. and Filipino forces began pulling back from the Layac line.

■ A typhus outbreak reached epidemic proportions in Lithuania.

Jan. 7 Bataan came under seige.

■ The central Malayan defense line of the British was cracked by the Japanese. The 11th Indian Division was no longer considered an organized fighting unit, the latest losses in this action coming atop its previous setbacks. Wavell arrived in Singapore.

■ Japanese forces in Sarawak reached the border of Dutch West Borneo.

■ German troops were found to have pulled out of Agedabia, Libya. The British moved in unchallenged.

Jan. 8 Jesselton (Kota Kinabalu) in British North Borneo (Sabah) was taken by the Japanese.

■ Kuala Lumpur's outer defense lines were penetrated by the Japanese in Malaya.

■ The seige of Sevastopol was lifted by Red Army forces.

Jan. 9 Russian forces cracked German defenses and reentered Smolensk Province.

■ British forces in Malaya were ordered to pull back to Johore for a final stand in defense of Singapore.

■ Three Japanese regimental combat teams launched the Bataan offensive in simultaneous midafternoon attacks.

Jan. 10 The Japanese began dropping leaflets over U.S. and Filipino positions calling on the troops to surrender.

■ Japanese aircraft launched daytime air strikes on Singapore's airfields. Kuala Lumpur and Port Swettenham were abandoned by British and Indian troops.

Jan. 11 Japan formally declared war on the Netherlands.

■ Japanese forces invaded the Celebes in the Dutch East Indies. There was only token resistance by the small defending garrisons.

■ Kuala Lumpur was captured by the Japanese 5th Division. Japanese troops were 150 miles from Singapore.

■ The U.S. carrier *Saratoga* was hit by a torpedo from a Japanese submarine about 500 miles southwest of Oahu but suffered no major damage.

■ The rail line between Rzhev and Bryansk was cut as Soviet forces continued their westward push on the Orel front.

■ A Japanese attempt to outflank the Bataan defense line failed. U.S. and Filipino forces on Bataan were put on half rations. Efforts to resupply were frustrated by the Japanese blockade. Fifteen blockade runners, totaling 40,000 tons, were sunk trying to carry in supplies from Cebu.

Jan. 11–17 British forces completed the recapture of Sollum and the Halfaya Pass, eliminating the last Axis strongholds in Egypt. Rommel fell back to the natural defense position at El Agheila.

Jan. 12 Field Marshal Walther von Reichenau, commander of Army Group South, died of a stroke on the Russian front. He was an ardent Nazi even before Hitler's rise to power, and his death deprived Hitler of a senior field commander he could trust.

■ Leaders of nine occupied European nations and China issued a resolution to try Axis officials for war crimes "whether they have ordered them, perpetrated them or in any way participated in them." (The principle of postwar war crimes trials was established by this action of the Inter-Allied Conference in London.)

Jan. 13 Russian forces captured Kirov on the central front, driving a deep wedge between the Second Panzer and Fourth German armies. Red Army units attacked Mozhaisk, 65 miles west of Moscow.

■ A badly needed convoy reached Singapore with antiaircraft weapons and 50 Hurricane

fighters. The British prepared to abandon Johore.

Jan. 14 The ARCADIA conference ended in Washington with the top-level U.S. and British strategists agreeing on a policy of defeating the Germans before embarking on an all-out war against Japan. It was decided to launch an operation (GYMNAST) to occupy French North Africa because German use of the navy and air bases would constitute an unacceptable threat to Allied shipping in the Atlantic.

■ The U.S. blacklisted 1,800 European companies, making it illegal for any American to engage in a business transaction with them.

■ Singapore and Rangoon were bombed by Japanese aircraft.

■ The German battleship *Tirpitz* was assigned to anticonvoy duty in the North Atlantic and was moved to Trondheim in Norway.

■ German U-boats began attacking ships off the American east coast. The Panamanian tanker *Norness* was torpedoed off Cape Hatteras.

Jan. 15 Japanese troops pushed vigorously across the entire Bataan front.

■ Jawaharlal Nehru succeeded Mohandas K. Gandhi as leader of the Congress party of India.

Jan. 16 Burma was invaded by Japanese forces from Thailand. Units of the Fifteenth Army met no resistance until they reached Myitta, about 30 miles inside lower Burma.

■ Bataan's defenses were seriously imperiled when the Japanese broke through the western flank.

■ Remaining RAF aircraft in Singapore were evacuated to Sumatra with the Japanese attacking the island's airfields relentlessly.

Jan. 17 Effective resistance ended in eastern Cyrenaica, Libya, as the remaining Axis forces in the territory surrendered to the British. The surrender of the Halfaya garrison came as the Free French were about to assault the position.

■ The South African parliament turned down a move to declare the country a republic and disassociate itself from Britain and the war.

■ Filipino forces made little headway in attempting to restore the western flank on Bataan.

Jan. 18 Germany, Italy, and Japan signed a military convention in Berlin, laying down "guidelines for common operations against the common enemies."

■ Russian forces under General Timoshenko launched a fresh offensive against the Germans on the central front. The southern front was marked by strong gains by the Red Army in the Ukraine.
■ Burma's Premier U Saw was "detained" by the British for allegedly being in communication with the Japanese.
Jan. 19 Moscow was freed from immediate peril when Russian forces recaptured Mozhaisk, the last German stronghold near the Soviet capital. In the Crimea, the Germans recaptured Feodosiya.
■ British North Borneo was formally surrendered to the Japanese at Sandakan.
■ Japanese troops crossed the Muar River in Malaya, placing them within 80 miles of Singapore.
■ British commanders were told their objective in North Africa was to capture Tripoli in Libya.
■ U.S. air units arrived in Aruba and Curaçao in the Dutch West Indies.
Jan. 20 The infamous Wannsee Conference was held, with the SS outlining Germany's "Final Solution to the Jewish Problem." Meeting, ironically, in the Berlin suburb offices of the International Criminal Police Commission, the SS, police, and officials of other Axis nations were told by Reinhard Heydrich that some Jews would be sent to work projects and many "will fall out through natural diminution." He then added, "The remnant that is able finally to survive all this, since this unquestionably is the part with the strongest resistance, must be given treatment accordingly, because these people, representing a natural selection, are to be regarded as the germ-cell of a new Jewish development should they be allowed to go free." It was cryptic but clear. Shortly, genocide became the order of the day.
Jan. 21 *I-22*, a Japanese mine-laying submarine, was sunk by the U.S.S. *Edsall* and Australian minesweepers at Darwin, Australia.
■ British forces in Malaya began a withdrawal to Singapore.

A German gunner mans his weapon in defense of the captured Russian port of Feodosiya in the Crimea.

■ The Japanese began a drive toward Moulmein in Burma.
■ In a dramatic (and to the British, surprising) move, Rommel turned his Afrika Korps around and began an offensive in Libya. Three Axis columns, with powerful air cover, began advancing eastward along the coastal road. The British were ordered to pull back to Agedabia.
■ Allied positions on New Guinea came under Japanese air attack. The aerial offensive was launched in a 50-plane raid directed primarily against Lae and Salamaua.
Jan. 22 Rommel recaptured Agedabia in Cyrenaica.
■ U.S. forces began another withdrawal on Bataan. Japan sent reinforcements ashore at Subic Bay.

■ Mussau Island, north of New Ireland, was occupied by the Japanese.

■ The British fell back toward Moulmein in Burma.

Jan. 23 Japan invaded New Britain, New Ireland, Dutch Borneo, and the Solomon Islands, bringing the war to less than a thousand miles from northeast Australia. Landings were made at Rabaul, Kavieng, and Balikpapan. New Guinea was dangerously exposed.

■ Australia requested emergency military assistance from the U.S. and Britain.

■ In a major breakthrough the Russians advanced along a 250-mile-wide front between Smolensk and Lake Ilmen.

Jan. 24 A special court of inquiry, headed by Supreme Court Justice Owen J. Roberts, submitted its report on the attack at Pearl Harbor. It placed the major blame on Rear Admiral Husband E. Kimmel and Lieutenant General Walter C. Short, the navy and army commanders, for neglecting to heed warnings of an imminent attack, for not consulting each other on necessary precautions, and for taking only minimum and inadequate defense measures.

■ Japanese ships en route to the oil center of Balikpapan, Borneo, for a landing were intercepted by four U.S. destroyers. In the ensuing Battle of Makassar Strait, four of the Japanese transports were sunk with heavy casualties. It was the first major naval engagement of the Pacific war.

■ Balikpapan was secured by the Japanese. (Capture of the Borneo oil field center was critical for the Japanese who eventually produced 70,000 barrels a day from there, or 90 percent of their total petroleum consumption.)

■ Australian forces evacuated Lae and Salamaua in New Guinea.

■ Peru severed diplomatic relations with Germany, Italy, and Japan.

■ Soviet troops smashed through German positions in the Ukraine. Barvenkova was recaptured.

Jan. 25 Thailand declared war on the U.S. and Britain. Its forces immediately joined in the invasion of Burma.

■ South Africa and New Zealand declared war on Thailand.

■ Uruguay severed diplomatic relations with Germany, Italy, and Japan.

■ Japanese forces landed at Lae in New Guinea.

■ A Japanese submarine shelled Midway Island.

■ British forces attempted a counterattack on Msus in Libya which had just been overrun by Rommel's forces. The British 1st Armored Division was routed as the Germans captured 96 tanks, 12 aircraft, 38 guns, and 190 trucks.

Jan. 26 Rabaul on the island of New Britain fell to the Japanese, giving them a major strategically located air and naval base.

■ The defenders on Luzon fell back to their final defense line on Bataan.

■ Japanese reinforcements landed in eastern Malaya, at Endau, 90 air miles north of Singapore.

■ The first contingent of American forces to reach Europe arrived in Northern Ireland. Headquarters for the U.S. armed forces in Britain was established in London.

Jan. 27 The British began their retreat to Singapore across the causeway from Johore Baharu.

■ The U.S. submarine *Seawolf* arrived at Corregidor, delivering ammunition and evacuating all available pilots.

■ Soviet forces captured the rail center of Lozovaya on the Donets front.

■ Free France agreed to open French possessions in the Pacific as Allied military bases.

Jan. 28 German forces reoccupied Benghazi as the British withdrew to new defense lines.

■ Rossel Island off Papua (southeastern New Guinea) was occupied by the Japanese.

■ Brazil and Paraguay broke relations with Germany, Italy, and Japan.

Jan.29 Britain, Russia, and Iran concluded a treaty of alliance. Iranian independence was to be respected, and the two powers agreed to withdraw their troops six months after the end of the war.

■ Ecuador severed diplomatic relations with Germany, Italy, and Japan.

■ Despite British military setbacks, Churchill was given his most overwhelming vote of confidence in the House of Commons, 464 to 1.

■ U.S. troops began arriving in the Fiji Islands.

Jan. 30 British forces were driven from the mainland of Malaya and withdrew to Singapore after destroying the connecting causeway.

■ A bitter fight developed for control of Moulmein in Burma. Japanese forces seized the city's airport.

■ Japanese forces invaded Amboina Island in the Dutch East Indies which controlled the southern approaches to the Molucca passage. Allied air and naval units had already pulled out under the pressure of air attacks.

■ Hitler spoke menacingly of ridding Europe of all Jews in a Berlin speech marking the ninth anniversary of Nazi rule in Germany: "They [the Jews] rightfully hate us, just as much as we hate them. . . . We are well aware that this war could eventually end [and] that they be uprooted from Europe or that they disappear."

■ The Irish Republic protested the arrival of U.S. troops in Northern Ireland as a violation of its neutrality.

Jan. 31 Japanese aircraft began a steady series of raids on Singapore's Kalang air base and dock facilities.

■ Moulmein was evacuated by the British who were forced back over the Salween River.

Feb. 1 U.S. warships attacked Japanese air and naval bases in the Gilbert and Marshall islands. The force of two carriers, five cruisers, and ten destroyers was the largest to go on the offensive. The American ships and planes inflicted severe damage. It was the first air attack of the war against Japanese positions.

■ In Libya British forces pulled back to a Gazala-Bir Hacheim defense line.

■ Vidkun Quisling was proclaimed minister pres-ident of Norway. The appointment was made by the Reich commissar for the occupied country, Josef Terboven. Quisling proclaimed, "Hitler's victory is Norway's victory." (A month later, when he failed utterly to win support, Quisling said, "There's no use appealing to the Norwegian people's intelligence. In Norway it has become necessary to impose the new order by force."

Feb. 2 Major General Joseph W. Stilwell was named chief of staff to Chiang Kai-shek and instruced "to increase the effectiveness of United States assistance to the Chinese Government for the prosecution of the war and to assist in improving the combat efficiency of the Chinese Army."

■ Feodosiya on the Black Sea was reoccupied by the Russians.

■ British forces were ordered to hold Tobruk as a supply center for future offensive operations by the Eighth Army.

Feb. 3 German troops in Libya fought their way back into Derna.

■ Japanese aircraft attacked Port Moresby and the Dutch naval base at Surabaya on Java.

■ Chiang Kai-shek and the British agreed on the deployment of Chinese troops in the defense of Burma.

Feb. 4 The Japanese demanded the unconditional surrender of the British forces on Singapore.

■ Allied and Axis forces halted their fighting

A Japanese soldier administers the coup de grâce to captured Sikhs of the British army who had already been shot by a firing squad.

along a line between Gazala and Mechili, regrouping and planning for the next round of action.

■ In order to forestall the appointment of an Egyptian government which was anti-British and leaned toward the Axis, the British ambassador in Cairo, Sir Miles Lampson, demanded King Farouk's abdication or the appointment of a pro-Allied prime minister. The 22-year-old king capitulated after a small British force seized the royal palace. Farouk and his advisers had been hoping to welcome Rommel's forces in Cairo and name Ali Mahir as prime minister. From September 1939 at the latest Ali Mahir Pasha had been suspected of being on the German payroll.

Feb. 5 British reinforcements and supplies began arriving in Singapore. Air attacks, however, interfered with the effort. The *Empress of Asia* was sunk before reaching Singapore.

Feb. 6 Britain and the U.S. established the Combined Chiefs of Staff, the highest level of Allied joint command, "to insure complete coordination of the war effort of Great Britain and the United States, including the production and distribution of war supplies, and to provide for full British and American collaboration with the United Nations."

■ Borneo's oil facilities at Samarinda were captured by the Japanese.

Feb. 7 Roosevelt approved a Congressional resolution authorizing up to $500 million in financial aid to China.

■ Japanese forces began a diversionary landing on the extreme eastern end of Singapore. The British commander, Lieutenant General A.E. Percival, declared the island would not surrender.

■ Defending troops launched a counterattack on Luzon. Japanese forces were forced to withdraw from the southwest coast.

Feb. 8 The main attack on Singapore was launched after dark as three Japanese divisions crossed the narrow waters between Johore and the island on small landing craft. A bridgehead was established without difficulty, and the Japanese set out for Tengah airfield, their immediate major objective.

■ Lieutenant General Masaharu Homma ordered

Nazi Germany's most heinous crimes were committed in the network of concentration camps which spanned the Greater Reich and occupied territories. Millions of "undesirables" were tortured and murdered.

a general pullback for all Japanese forces on the Bataan front. The Japanese were exhausted at this point and badly needed fresh troops before a final drive could be started.

Feb. 9 Tengah airfield on Singapore fell to the Japanese. Its capture permitted the quick resupply of the invading force and, if there was any remaining doubt on the outcome, sealed the fall of Singapore. Percival ordered all defenses be concentrated in the southern sector of the island, around the city of Singapore.

■ Japanese forces suffered heavy casualties in Luzon.

■ Chiang Kai-shek began a visit to India. He conferred with British officials and urged Indian nationalist leaders—particularly Jawaharlal Nehru—to lay aside political differences and join in the military effort against Japan.

■ Roosevelt called on the Vichy French government to reaffirm its position of neutrality. He noted reports of supplies being sent from France to Axis forces in North Africa.

Feb. 10 The 82,423-ton liner *Normandie*, which had been taken over by the U.S., burned and turned over on its side in New York, the apparent result of a welder's carelessness. Berlin implied it was the result of Axis sabotage.

■ Wavell visited Singapore and ordered the island to be held at all costs. All remaining RAF personnel, however, were ordered evacuated.

■ French-Canadian M.P. Pierre Gauthier spoke out against a Canadian $1 billion grant to Britain, saying "so-called patriots" supporting such aid would "throw this country into the arms of the United States sooner than we expect."

Feb. 11 French-Canadians in Montreal protested military conscription which was proposed by the government. Demonstrations flared into full-scale rioting in Montreal. Shouting "A bas la conscription," a thousand people, mostly students, smashed windows, attacked streetcars, and battled police, 12 of whom were injured. The issue of French-Canadians serving as draftees festered throughout the war.

■ London claimed that during December and January 5,500 tons of gasoline and aviation fuel had been sent from France to German forces in Libya.

■ More Japanese forces crossed the Salween River in Burma.

■ The Japanese issued an ultimatum for Singapore's surrender.

■ Japanese planes bombed Samarai Island, 380 miles north of Australia. The Australian government called up all married men up to 35 years old, unmarrieds up to 40.

■ The U.S. granted China a $500 million loan.

Feb. 12 The German battle cruisers *Scharnhorst* and *Gneisenau* and the cruiser *Prinz Eugen* ran the English Channel and the Dover Strait and broke into the North Sea from Brest.

■ A three-ship British convoy for Malta from Alexandria was attacked and all ships were sunk.

■ Japanese forces continued pulling back in Luzon.

■ The Japanese began occupying Bandjarmasin, the capital of Borneo, and Makassar, capital of the Celebes.

Feb. 13 The Russian Army reentered Byelorussia. As the forward elements moved west, German defenses were strengthened.

■ Japanese forces began tightening their circle around the defenders of Singapore. The British began requisitioning even the smallest boats.

■ Premier Antonescu met with Hitler, who called for more Rumanian troops for service in Russia.

Feb. 14-16 The Japanese invaded the island of Sumatra and quickly seized the oil-refining area of Palembang. About 360 paratroopers were used in taking the area.

Feb. 15 Singapore and its garrison fell to the Japanese. A total of 64,000 British, Indian, and Australian defenders on the island surrendered after 9,000 had been killed in combat. General Percival had been directed to fight as long as possible but was given discretion in determining when further resistance was futile. Faced with an impossible military situation and a critical water shortage, Percival elected to surrender. He personally met with General Tomoyuki Yamashita, commanding the Japanese Twenty-fifth Army, and the armistice was signed at 6:10 P.M. Singapore fell in 70 days. The Japanese thought it would take a hundred when the campaign was being planned. Total Allied casualties in the entire Malayan campaign were 67,340 Indian, 38,496 British, 18,490 Australian, and 14,382 local volunteer troops (of this total of 138,708

Lieutenant General Arthur Percival surrenders Singapore to General Tomoyuki Yamashita, as portrayed by Japanese artist Miyamoto Saburo.

about 130,000 were prisoners). Japanese casualties were 9,824.

■ All Allied shipping in the Mediterranean was halted because of the severe losses.

■ Allied forces on Sumatra were ordered to the west coast for evacuation.

Feb. 16 German U-boats shelled oil-refining facilities on Aruba and Curaçao, off the coast of Venezuela.

■ Hitler named Martin Bormann to replace Hess as second in line, behind Göring, in the Nazi line of succession.

Feb. 17 Auchinleck was ordered to release two more divisions for Far East duty. (Subsequently only one, the British 70th, actually left the Middle East.)

Feb. 18 The Japanese crossed the Bilin River in Burma, and the situation on all sectors began to deteriorate. British authorities ordered mass evacuations from Rangoon.

Feb. 19 About 150 carrier-based Japanese naval aircraft attacked the Australian city of Darwin, killing 240 people and injuring 150. Without adequate defenses, the Australians absorbed decisive material losses, including the sinking of 11 transports, an American destroyer, several supply ships, and vast quantities of stores. The result was the certain loss of Java which could no longer be supplied.

■ Japanese troops landed on the Portuguese island of Timor in the East Indies. Tokyo said the action was taken in self-defense and that its forces would withdraw when the area was secure. The neutral Portuguese accepted the occupation.

■ Bali was invaded by the Japanese.

■ Mandalay came under aerial attack for the first time. Defending forces were ordered to fall back from the Bilin River.

■ The British war cabinet was reformed (additional changes were made on the 22nd).

■ Canada's Parliament voted to begin military conscription.

■ The Supreme Court of Vichy France began trials in Riom to establish responsibility for the military defeat and national disaster of 1940.

Feb. 19–20 Dutch and American warships attempted to block the buildup of the Japanese force invading Bali. The attack failed in a confused battle, marked by two Japanese destroyers firing at each other. All the Allies could do was inflict minor damage on a few of the invasion ships, and the Japanese landed their force without difficulty.

Feb. 20 The U.S. provided the Soviet Union with a $1 billion loan.

■ Hitler received a report on the staggering number of German casualties suffered thus far in the Russian campaign: 199,448 dead, 708,351 wounded, 112,627 cases of severe frostbite, and

44,342 missing. He was nonetheless optimistic, saying, "Now that January and February are past, our enemies can give up the hope of our suffering the fate of Napoleon. . . . Now we're about to switch over to squaring the account. What a relief!"

■ All civilians were ordered evacuated from Rangoon.

■ Japanese planes intercepted a U.S. Navy task force en route to Rabaul. The American ships were forced to turn back, but Japanese losses were extremely heavy and plans for operations against New Guinea had to be delayed.

■ Bali and Timor were occupied by the Japanese.

■ U.S. Navy Lieutenant Edward ("Butch") O'Hare shot down five Japanese bombers in five minutes. (The first navy ace of the war, O'Hare was later honored by having Chicago's airport named for him.)

Feb. 21 British forces began pulling back behind the Sittang River in Burma. A brigade from the Middle East arrived in Rangoon.

■ In a farewell message to the people of India, Chiang Kai-shek called for their wholehearted support in the war and indicated Britain "without waiting for any demands on the part of the people of India, will as speedily as possible give them real political power."

Feb. 22 President Roosevelt ordered MacArthur to leave the Philippines. The general was named commander of Allied forces in Australia.

■ B-24s of the U.S. Tenth Air Force dropped 40 British magnetic mines in the mouth of the Rangoon River in Burma, the beginning of a campaign to interfere with Japanese shipping in occupied areas.

Feb. 23 In the first direct attack on the U.S. mainland, a Japanese submarine shelled an oil refinery near Santa Barbara, California.

THE FIRST SHELLING OF THE U.S. MAINLAND

Japanese submarine *I-17* shelled the Elwood oil field west of Santa Barbara, California, in the early evening hours of Feb. 23, 1942. About 25 shells were fired by the craft, most of which exploded close but harmlessly among the derricks and storage facilities. One rig was hit,

causing $500 in damages. There were no casualties. Why was this particular facility attacked? A history of the Richfield Oil Corporation, *From the Rio Grande to the Arctic* by Charles S. Jones, says the shelling was an act of revenge by the submarines's captain, Kizo Nishino. In the late 1930s, Nishino commanded a Japanese tanker which picked up a cargo of crude oil at Elwood. He and the crew were received by company and local government officials in a formal ceremony. Captain Nishino slipped while climbing a path from the beach and fell into a cluster of cactus. The American party was as embarrassed as the Japanese captain, but a group of workers at a nearby rig could not contain their laughter as cactus spines were being removed from Captain Nishino's backside. The uproarious behavior irritated the captain, and he vowed never to forget the incident. He returned with his submarine in 1942 to remind the Americans of it.

■ Russian forces recaptured Dorogobuzh on the Dnieper River.

■ In the battle of the Sittang River, the 17th Indian Division was virtually destroyed. The bridge across the river was blown up with some of the Allied troops trapped on the other side. They made their way across by swimming or by small boats.

■ U.S. B-17s attacked Rabaul, the first Allied raid on the newly established Japanese base.

■ Stalin said the war against Germany had turned in favor of the Soviet Union: "Now the Germans no longer possess the military advantage which they had in the first months of the war by virtue of their treacherous and sudden attack. The momentum of unexpectedness and suddenness which constituted the reserve strength of the German fascist troops has been fully spent."

Feb. 24 The German II Corps was encircled southeast of Staraya Russa on the northern front.

■ Orders were issued to prepare for the withdrawal of Allied forces from Java.

■ An American naval task force attacked Wake Island.

■ Vichy France responded to Roosevelt's note of

the 9th, stating its desire to remain neutral and not assist belligerents in any theater of operations.

Feb. 25 The rail line between Rangoon and Mandalay was threatened as the Japanese broke through a wide gap in the British defense line at Pegu.

Feb. 26 Soviet leaders forcibly pressed the British and Americans to launch a "second front" against Germany.

■ The American carrier *Langley*, with 32 fighters bound for Java, was sunk by Japanese planes.

Feb. 27 Indian territory was attacked for the first time as the Japanese raided the Andaman Islands in the Bay of Bengal, south of Burma.

Feb. 27–March 1 Allied ships suffered their worst naval defeat of the war in the Battle of the Java Sea. The Japanese navy dominated the ill-coordinated defense of the area by U.S., British, and Dutch men-of-war. Japanese ships were able to take control of the southwest Pacific in the first major surface-to-surface naval combat of the Pacific war. Using their superior oxygen torpedo (the Type-91 with a range of 25 miles or five times that of American or British models), the Japanese on the night of the 27th quickly sank the Dutch cruisers *De Ruyter* and *Java*, the Dutch destroyer *Kortenauer*, and the British destroyer *Electra*. On the 28th, Japanese cruisers and destroyers outgunned another Allied force,

sinking two cruisers, the American *Houston* and Australian *Perth*, and the Dutch destroyer *Evertsen*. On the 1st, three British ships, the cruiser *Exeter* and destroyers *Pope* and *Encounter*, were sunk by Japanese gunfire. Only a handful of Allied vessels slipped through the Bali Strait, all that remained of what only three months before had been a formidable force. Now, the Japanese could move with virtual impunity throughout the southwest Pacific area.

Feb. 28 The Japanese Sixteenth Army was landed on the north coast of Java, with the main force striking for Batavia (Djakarta), capital of the Dutch East Indies. The landing was met with Allied aerial attacks.

■ The U.S. military announced the army and navy commanders in Hawaii at the time of the Pearl Harbor attack would be court-martialed "when such time as the public interest and safety would permit." In the meantime Lieutenant General Walter C. Short and Rear Admiral Husband E. Kimmel were permitted to retire.

■ British civilian air raid casualties for the month were 22 killed and 21 injured.

Feb. 28–March 1 A mixed Allied naval force sank four invasion transports in the Sunda Strait.

March Allied merchant shipping losses during March were the heaviest of the war. In all, 273 ships were lost, a total of 834,164 tons. Ninety-five were sunk in the North Atlantic, 98 in the

Japanese artist Kobayakawa Tokushiro's portrayal of the sinking of the U.S. cruiser Houston *in the Battle of the Java Sea.*

Far East. The safest of the convoy routes was to Murmansk, where only one of 110 ships hauling material to Russia had been lost in 1941 and through March 1942. It was at this juncture, however, that the Germans began shifting their naval and air strength to Norway and began scoring dramatic successes on the northern convoys.

■ Germany began collecting church bells to be melted down. The bronze and copper were needed for airplane engine production. By now, all one and two pfennig copper coins had been collected. Copper, chromium, tungsten, and vanadium were the metals in shortest supply.

March 1 Russian forces initiated another offensive in the Crimea. The Germans were still unable to extricate the trapped II Corps near Staraya Russa.

■ During two months of fighting on Luzon, the Japanese had lost 2,700 men killed in action and nearly 7,000 wounded.

March 2 Japanese forces landed on Mindanao in the Philippines.

■ Batavia was ordered to be evacuated. The Dutch government moved to Bandung.

■ The U.S. recognized Free French authority over all French possessions and said it would cooperate in their defense: "In its relations with the local French authorities in French territories the United States has and will continue to be governed by the manifest effectiveness with which those authorities endeavor to protect their territories from domination and control by the common enemy."

■ All persons of Japanese ancestry (including U.S. citizens) were barred from Pacific coastal areas by the U.S. government.

■ Australia declared war on Thailand.

March 3 The Dutch continued their withdrawals on Java in the face of continuing pressure by numerically superior Japanese troops.

■ RAF bombers struck the Renault works in the suburbs of Paris. Many of the bombs landed on workers' homes, killing 623 French and injuring 1,500.

■ Two Japanese "Emily" bombers from the Marshalls (refueled by submarines) attacked Hawaii. The nighttime attack was unsuccessful, hampered in part by cloud conditions. Pearl Harbor was again the target, but one plane missed the

naval base by six miles and dropped its four bombs on Mount Tantalus. The other plane's four bombs fell harmlessly in the Pacific.

March 4 Marcus Island in the central Pacific was attacked by American carrier-based aircraft in a predawn raid causing extensive damage.

■ Japanese Zeros destroyed 23 Allied planes in an attack on Broome, Australia, the refueling station on flights from Perth to Java.

March 5 Martial law was proclaimed in southern Burma as Lieutenant General Sir Harold Alexander assumed command of British forces in the area. Japanese troops entered Pegu.

■ Moscow announced the capture of Yukhnov on the central front.

March 6 All installations in Rangoon which might be useful to the Japanese were ordered destroyed.

■ Batavia fell to the Japanese.

March 7 Japanese forces landed unopposed at Lae and Salamaua on New Guinea.

■ British troops began moving out of Rangoon, but their withdrawal to Prome in the north was obstructed by the Japanese who blocked the road at Taukkyan.

■ Communication was lost with the last defenders in Java as the Japanese completed their occupation of the island.

March 8 Rangoon fell to the Japanese. Loss of the Burmese capital was particularly serious to the Allied cause because it cut off the last port through which supplies could be funneled over the Burma Road to China. British forces cleared the roadblock at Taukkyan to permit the retreat northward.

■ The naval base at Surabaya in Java was occupied by the Japanese.

March 9 The Dutch formally surrendered Java to the Japanese.

March 10 All Allied forces in the Dutch East Indies surrendered unconditionally.

■ The port of Finschhafen in northeast New Guinea was taken by the Japanese.

■ More than a hundred U.S. carrier-based planes attacked Japanese shipping and troop concentrations on New Guinea.

March 11 General MacArthur, his wife, and small child left Corregidor on a PT boat for Mindanao. MacArthur told the Filipinos in a final message, "I shall return."

■ Burmese defenses were reorganized to halt the Japanese in the upper part of the country.

■ Tojo said one of Japan's war aims was to free India from Anglo-Saxon rule and influence.

■ Brazil confiscated up to 30 percent of funds held by Axis nationals, the total amount to match the loss of Brazilian ships which had been sunk in the Atlantic.

■ Churchill announced that Sir Stafford Cripps, lord privy seal, would undertake a mission to India to win approval of terms for self-government from Indian leaders. Churchill said the British wished to avoid "fierce constitutional and communal disputes at a moment when the enemy is at the gates of India."

March 12 A U.S. Army force of 17,500 men landed at Nouméa in New Caledonia.

■ The Japanese Imperial Guards Division was landed without opposition in northern Sumatra.

■ The British garrison on the Andaman Islands in the Bay of Bengal was evacuated because the seaplane base could no longer be defended with the loss of southern Burma.

■ Under Japanese auspices King Norodom Sihanouk proclaimed Cambodia's independence.

THE CHANNEL DASH: A GERMAN STRATEGIC ERROR

Three of Germany's most formidable warships—the *Scharnhorst*, the *Gneisenau*, and the *Prinz Eugen*—were ready to join in the North Atlantic convoy attacks by March of 1942. They had been bottled up in Brest, being repaired and replenished after their previous encounters. In order to break through the narrows of the English Channel, the most feasible way of reaching their North Sea home bases, the ships risked a hazardous dash, herewith chronicled:

MARCH 11 10:45 P.M. Accompanied by a protective force of six destroyers and an array of smaller ships, the Germans departed Brest.

MARCH 12 6:00 A.M. The column was still undetected as it passed Cap de la Hague at the northern tip of the Cherbourg peninsula.

■ **10:30 A.M.** RAF Spitfires identified the German armada but maintained radio silence and thus did not report their findings until landing, wasting precious time.

■ **12:28 P.M.** RAF Swordfish torpedo bombers took off to attack.

■ **12:30 P.M.** Five Royal Navy torpedo boats failed to penetrate the destroyer escort screen protecting the larger German ships and did not even engage the ships.

■ **1:00 P.M.** All of the attacking Swordfish aircraft were shot down and none of the torpedoes hit.

■ **2:31 P.M.** The *Scharnhorst* hit a mine and suffered minor damage.

■ **3:30 P.M.** Six Royal Navy destroyers from Harwich attacked the Germans but inflicted no damage at all.

■ **4:00 P.M.** About 25 of the 240 RAF bombers sent aloft were able to locate the Germans and started their attacks in poor visibility. They scored no significant hits, nor did they impair the progress of the German ships.

■ **7:55 P.M.** The *Gneisenau* struck a mine off the Dutch island of Terschelling but no major damage resulted.

■ **9:25 P.M.** The *Scharnhorst* hit a second mine but suffered only minor damage.

MARCH 13 EARLY A.M. The *Scharnhorst* reached Wilhelmshaven and the *Gneisenau* and the *Prinz Eugen* put into Brunsbüttel.

The Channel dash was a resounding psychological victory for the Germans and triggered off a howl of protest in Britain. Poor communications and a lack of coordination were blamed for permitting all that floating firepower from escaping virtual entrapment. In fact, it turned out to be a blessing in disguise. The Germans later felt they had blundered by moving the ships out of Brest, where they posed a far greater threat to the flank of the main Allied north-south convoy route supplying North Africa and the Mediterranean. It is likely the Allies would have experienced tremendous difficulties in mounting the North African and subsequent Italian invasions with the three German marauders interfering with vital shipments in the crucial months which followed. Admiral Raeder correctly called the Channel dash an "outright retreat."

March 13 U.S. Air Force personnel began arriving in Karachi, the first American detachment to reach the China-Burma-India (CBI) theater.

They were originally to be deployed in the defense of Java.

March 14 The U.S. Joint Chiefs of Staff decided to continue a defensive policy in the Pacific while building up American strength in Britain for offensive operations against Germany.

■ The first U.S. troops arrived in Australia.

■ MacArthur reached Mindanao.

■ Pétain renamed Laval as premier of Vichy France.

March 15 Hitler confidently predicted the early destruction of the Russian army: "The Bolshevist masses which were not able to conquer the German and allied soldier in the winter, will be beaten in every direction in the summer."

■ The Japanese began heavy artillery attacks on the fortified islands of Manila Bay.

March 16 The Soviet ambassador in London called on the British to begin diversionary military operations on the European continent to draw off German strength from the Russian front.

■ Australian-based U.S. bombers attacked Japanese positions in the Philippines.

March 17 General MacArthur arrived in Darwin, Australia, to take up his new duties as supreme commander of Allied forces in the southwest Pacific theater.

■ Three U.S. fighter squadrons began operating out of Darwin. The Kittyhawks were instrumental in reducing the Japanese air threat.

■ Roosevelt recalled the U.S. ambassador to Vichy France, Admiral William D. Leahy.

March 18 Admiral Lord Louis Mountbatten was named chief of Combined Operations.

March 19 The Germans renewed their campaign to break through to the besieged II Corps in the area of Staraya Russa.

■ Stilwell assumed command of the Chinese Fifth and Sixth armies operating with British forces in Burma, the first time in history Chinese troops had ever been led by a foreigner. Lieutenant General William Slim arrived in Burma and became commander of Imperial troops in the country.

■ Japanese forces completed their occupation of Sumatra and Timor.

■ President Ismet Inonu of Turkey vowed the country would remain neutral and that "we will maintain our contractual relations with the belligerents, and we mean to carry on those rela-

tions . . . with a straight heart and with royalty."

March 20 Chinese troops entered the fighting in Burma, engaging Japanese troops along the Sittang River.

■ British Eighth Army raiding groups attacked Derna and Benghazi as a means to divert the Axis from action against a convoy bound for Malta which was desperately in need of resupply.

March 21 China and the U.S. completed arrangements for the $500 million in aid to the Chungking government.

■ The American defense of the Philippines was reduced to Corregidor in Manila Bay. General Jonathan Wainwright moved his headquarters to the heavily fortified island as a further stand on Bataan would have been futile without real hope of reinforcements or resupply.

■ The depleted air defenses of Burma were further weakened when the Japanese attacked the air base at Magwe. A ferry command was activated in CBI with 25 Pan-American transports being pressed into airlift service.

■ Some German aircraft were drawn off the Malta convoy, but the Allied ships came under attack despite the diversionary raids by the British in Libya.

March 22 Magwe airfield in Burma was evacuated by British and American flight units, leaving the retreating British without any close air support.

■ U.S. forces on Bataan were issued a surrender ultimatum by the Japanese.

March 23 The Andaman Islands in the Bay of Bengal were occupied by the Japanese.

March 24 The Japanese opened up their final drive to occupy the Bataan Peninsula. Corregidor came under heavy air attack.

■ Chinese and Burmese troops were badly mauled by the Japanese, isolating Toungoo and pushing the defenders back to the Irrawaddy River.

March 25 Japanese troops inflicted heavy losses on the Chinese 200th Division around Toungoo.

March 26 For reasons not readily apparent to most people at the time, Churchill declared, "It now seems very likely that we and our Allies cannot lose this war . . . except through our own fault."

■ Roosevelt ordered a speedup in the shipment of supplies to the Soviet Union.

■ Admiral Ernest J. King was named chief of Naval Operations, succeeding Harold R. Stark as the ranking U.S. naval officer. The army command was totally overhauled under General George C. Marshall.

■ The Japanese occupied most of Toungoo.

March 27 The U.S. issued plans for a limited cross-Channel attack in the fall of 1942 as a means of aiding the Russians if the Red Army showed signs of collapsing. But the main invasion of northwest Europe was set for the spring of 1943.

■ Chinese defenders rallied and held off the Japanese attack on Toungoo.

March 27–28 British forces raided the St.-Nazaire naval facility in France. The German battleship *Tirpitz* was in Norway, but the British feared it would break out to menace Atlantic convoys. If it did, it could only be docked at the St.-Nazaire lock which in peacetime had accommodated the French luxury liner *Normandie*. British Commandos were, therefore, given the task of destroying the huge lock. In the early morning hours of the 28th a force of 260 men aboard a former American destroyer (*Campbeltown*) loaded with explosives tried to ram the lock. Eighteen coastal craft went in with her. The operation succeeded but only after the force was severely mauled. All but two of the small ships were sunk, stranding many of the Commandos. In all, 170 of the men were killed or captured. But the old American destroyer, with its delayed action fuses, blew up around noon before the Germans could disarm her, and *Tirpitz* was deprived of its base to prey on convoys.

March 28 Bataan's defense garrison was beginning to experience severe problems as further efforts to break the Japanese blockade failed. Horses and mules were by now being slaughtered for food.

■ The Vatican established diplomatic relations with Japan.

■ The first trainload of Jews from Paris began being shipped to Auschwitz. Six thousand were earmarked for imprisonment.

March 28–29 Lübeck was subjected to a devastating raid by the RAF, the opening of Bomber Command's main offensive against Germany.

March 29 In an achievement which buoyed Allied hopes, a convoy reached the Soviet Arctic port of Murmansk by evading German ships and

planes. The Murmansk run remained the most dangerous of the war.

■ The Chinese withdrew from Toungoo, and the Japanese moved forward toward Prome.

■ Philippine guerrillas were organized as the Anti-Japanese Peoples Army (the Hukbalahaps) under communist leader Luis Taruc.

■ Britain offered India independence after the war.

March 30 Japanese troops broke through the outer defenses of Prome.

March 31 For the previous four months, British air raid civilian casualties were 189 killed and 149 injured.

■ The Congress party demanded immediate independence for India, rejecting a plan submitted by Sir Stafford Cripps for dominion status after the end of the war.

April An infusion of new forces from Germany's partners was introduced into combat in Russia during the month in an effort to recapture the offensive. Additions of fifty-one divisions (more than a half million men) were made to the Axis armies. They came from Italy, Hungary, Rumania, and Slovakia, while Spain added a volunteer division.

■ German housewives were asked to work full- or part-time as clerks in grocery stores to help fill the manpower shortage. Food rationing became more severe, with some areas limited on vegetable consumption.

April 1 Japanese forces began landing on Dutch New Guinea.

■ Forced mass evacuation of Japanese-Americans from the Pacific Coast states was begun by the U.S. Army.

■ A relative stalemate developed along the entire Russian front, with the Germans concentrating on aiding the II Corps to escape from the pocket at Staraya Russa.

April 2 U.S. Tenth Air Force planes flew their first missions in the CBI theater, bombing Japanese fleet units in the Andaman Islands.

■ Prome was abandoned by the British.

April 3 About 2,000 people were killed in a destructive Japanese air raid on Mandalay, Burma.

■ Japanese forces, reinforced by a fresh division, began their final assault on the last American defense line on Bataan. The U.S. units were sub-

Japanese soldiers are triumphant after overwhelming U.S. forces in April 1942 near Orion in their final drive to take the Bataan Peninsula in the Philippines.

jected to a five hour air and artillery bombardment.

April 4–8 A marauding Japanese naval surface squadron and submarines roamed the Bay of Bengal sinking merchantmen almost at will. The British had cleared Calcutta harbor, fearing an air attack, and the ships at sea were picked off at an alarming rate. During this five day period the Japanese sank twenty-eight ships, totaling 144,400 tons.

April 4 U.S. and Filipino defenders were forced to yield ground on Bataan.

April 5 Japanese naval forces moved to complete their dominance of the Indian Ocean with an attack on Colombo, Ceylon. The carriers *Akagi* and *Kaga*, which had been involved at Pearl Harbor, launched 127 planes which inflicted only light damage on the port but which caught two British cruisers trying to escape to open water. *Dorsetshire* and *Cornwall* were sunk by dive bombers in attacks of remarkable accuracy.

April 6 Red Army units advanced in the area of Smolensk.

■ Japanese troops landed in the Admiralty Islands.

■ A Japanese naval force under Vice Admiral Jisaburo Ozawa sank 92,000 tons of merchant shipping along the east coast of India.

■ Vizagapatam (Vishakhapatnam) and Cocanada (Kakinada), Indian cities on the Bay of Bengal, were bombed by Japanese aircraft.

■ Chiang Kai-shek promised another division to help defend Burma. More Japanese troops arrived in Rangoon.

■ Axis planes bombed Alexandria, Egypt.

April 7 Russian forces were able to open a rail line to Leningrad.

■ Malta sounded its 2,000th air-raid alert of the war.

■ The Japanese pressed steadily forward all along the Bataan front, piercing the final American defense positions.

April 8 About 2,000 of the force of 78,000 men defending Bataan escaped to Corregidor as defense efforts collapsed.

■ U.S. Air Ferry Command began flights over the Himalayas to China. Traffic over the Hump played the key role in supplying China.

April 9 Bataan fell to the Japanese. General Edward P. King, Jr., signed the surrender document at 12:30 P.M. About 35,000 American and Filipino troops fell into Japanese hands. Almost immediately, the prisoners began the forced "Bataan Death March" from Balanga to San Fernando. Japanese air and artillery units were moved in to concentrate on Corregidor.

■ Japanese naval aircraft attacked the Ceylonese port of Trincomalee. The British had anticipated the attack and cleared the harbor, but the planes located the British carrier *Hermes*, a destroyer, a corvette, and two tankers in nearby waters and sank them.

■ A strong attack by the Russians in the Crimea

gained little ground. German defense positions were overrun around Orel.

■ General Mikhail G. Yefremov, commander of the Russian Thirty-third Army, committed suicide near Vyazma rather than surrender to the Germans. Yefremov was one of the heroes of the Red Army in the defense of Moscow.

■ Vichy protested the establishment of an American consulate in Brazzaville in the French Congo.

April 10 Japanese units landed on Cebu and Billiton in the Philippines.

April 10–11 An RAF Halifax dropped an 8,000-pound bomb for the first time, in a raid on Essen.

April 11 Red Army reinforcements landed in the Crimea near Eupatoria (Yevpatoriya) but encountered extremely heavy German resistance.

German mortar men fire in the fight for the Kerch Peninsula in the Soviet Union.

■ Sir Stafford Cripps announced that Indian leaders had rejected Britain's offer of postwar independence.

April 12 Japanese units began occupying Migyaungye and exposed the entire British western front in Burma.

■ Iran broke off diplomatic relations with Japan. The Japanese legation in Tehran was reported to have served as a propaganda center in Iran.

April 13 Moscow issued a stern warning to Tokyo to continue observing the Russian-Japanese neu-

trality pact: "It is necessary that the Japanese military and Fascist cliques whose heads have been turned by military successes realize that their prattle about an annexationist war in the north may cause damage . . . to Japan herself."

■ The oil fields of central Burma lay exposed to the Japanese as a British defense line collapsed.

April 14 Marshal Pétain became Vichy French chief of state, and Laval became chief of government. Laval thus assumed actual direction of the Vichy administration, and the aging Pétain remained to perform an essentially ceremonial function.

■ British forces began destroying the Yenangyaung oil fields in Burma as the Japanese pressed their drive northward.

April 15 French resistance forces attacked German headquarters at Arras.

■ U.S. bombers conducted a daylight attack on the occupied French port of Cherbourg.

April 16 In one of the most unusual awards of the war, the British government presented Malta—the whole island—the George Cross. The medal, like the Victoria Cross, was given only for the most gallant of deeds. (Later in the war, King George VI himself was to visit Malta, whose survival was an important element in sustaining the Mediterranean war.)

■ More than 4,000 Japanese troops were put ashore on Panay in the Philippines, with an immediate withdrawal by the 7,000-man American and Filipino defense force into the mountains to operate as guerrillas.

April 18 Japan was bombed by American warplanes. Sixteen B-25 bombers under the command of Lieutenant Colonel James H. Doolittle took off from the carrier *Hornet* to carry the war to Japan for the first time. The first attacking aircraft was launched at 8:18 A.M., about ten hours ahead of schedule because the naval convoy had been spotted by a Japanese vessel. The range to Tokyo was thus increased to 800 statute miles instead of the planned 650, which was considered the maximum to achieve success. Some of the planes reached Tokyo during a practice air alert, and most Japanese were first confused, then startled when actual bombs started falling. Yokohama, Kobe, and Nagoya were also struck. Only one plane was hit by antiaircraft fire, suffering only minor damage. Eight of the aircraft bombed their primary targets. Five others had to select secondary objectives. Only one failed to drop its bombs on Japan. Favored by an uncommon tail wind, the planes continued westward, most of them to China and safety. One landed near Vladivostok, and the crew was interned by the Russians. Two crews came down in Japanese-occupied China (three of the men were executed by the Japanese; five were made prisoners, and four of them were freed at the end of the war). Little damage was inflicted on the Japanese cities, but the Doolittle raid gave Japanese military leaders pause and was a factor in their decision to consolidate their vast holdings rather than expand even further. For the Allies, the attack was an antidote for the painful doses of defeat.

■ MacArthur formally assumed his position as supreme commander, southwest Pacific Area, Australian Vice Admiral Herbert F. Leary as Allied Naval Force commander, and U.S. General George H. Brett as commander of Allied air forces.

■ The road to the key transportation center of Lashio in Burma was threatened when the Chinese 55th Division collapsed under heavy Japanese pressure.

■ Field Marshal Wilhelm Ritter von Leeb was relieved of his command of German forces in the northern sector of Russia. Leeb was frustrated by Hitler's direction of the war, and Hitler was equally frustrated by the marshal's inability to occupy Leningrad.

April 19 Cebu Island in the Philippines was declared under total Japanese control. Small guerrilla bands remained the only forces of resistance.

April 20 Japanese forces completed their conquest of Visayan Island in the Philippines.

■ Laval warned the French people of the dangers which would befall Europe if Russia won the war and called for a national "reconciliation" with Germany.

■ French resistance forces unsuccessfully tried to kill Jacques Doriot, leader of the French Fascist party.

April 21 President Roosevelt ordered the seizure of all patents controlled or owned by nations at war with the U.S. The action was aimed at Germany which technically could hinder American

(ABOVE) *One of Doolittle's B-25 bombers takes off from the carrier* Hornet *to attack Japan.*

(RIGHT) *Major General Doolittle, Captain Marc A. Mitscher, commanding officer of the U.S.S.* Hornet, *and the crews of the B-25s before their raid on Japan.*

war production through patent arrangements with U.S. companies.

■ French General Henri Giraud, a German prisoner since May of 1940, escaped from occupied France. (He eventually made his way to North Africa to join the Allies.)

■ Spain pledged a million men if necessary to help defeat the Soviet Union. Spanish Foreign Minister Rámon Serrano Suñer said Madrid hoped the Axis powers would win the war because "a victory for the Allies would be tantamount to a victory of Bolshevism."

April 22–23 Fourteen German U-boats were refueled and resupplied 500 miles from Bermuda, giving the Germans a total of eighteen submarines to operate almost unmolested from Nova Scotia to Florida.

April 22 A joint U.S.-New Zealand Naval Command was established.

■ Yenangyaung in Burma was evacuated by British forces.

■ Washington announced that U.S. forces had arrived in India.

■ Fifteen French hostages were executed by the Germans in Paris.

April 23 Luftwaffe bombers began a series of retaliatory air strikes directed at British cathedral cities. The initial raid was launched this date on Exeter.

■ Rostock was the target of an intensive raid by the RAF.

■ South Africa broke off diplomatic relations with Vichy France.

April 24 Jews were barred from using all forms of public transportation in Germany.

■ Japanese forces captured the Burmese town of Taunggyi from Chinese troops defending it.

April 25 U. S. troops landed in New Caledonia which was under Free French control.

■ The Chinese recaptured Taunggyi.

April 26 General Alexander decided to defend India rather than concentrate his waning strength to hold Burma.

■ Declaring that German people understand "the nation is not there for them, but they for the nation," Hitler asked the Reichstag to grant him "the positive assurance that I possess the legal authority to see to it that every individual performs his duty and that I may condemn such cases which in my opinion do not fulfill their duties to be imprisoned or to be deprived of their

office . . . no matter who they be or what rights they may have acquired." Hitler was given such personal absolute authority.

April 27 The American economy was placed on a full war footing by Roosevelt.

■ The All-India National Congress rejected a policy of nonviolence directed at both the British and Japanese as proposed by Gandhi.

April 28 Forces defending Mandalay were ordered moved to help defend Lashio which was under immediate threat.

■ Chiang Kai-shek told the U.S. government that as a result of the Doolittle raid, Japanese troops attacked the coastal areas of China where the U.S. crews had landed. According to Chiang, the Japanese "slaughtered every man, woman, and child. . . ." in some of the villages which had assisted the American pilots.

■ In a national plebiscite Canadians voted by a 129,000 plurality to free the government from its pledge not to send draftees overseas.

April 29 Hitler and Mussolini met at Berchtesgaden. One of the key issues was the rupture between Axis partners Hungary and Rumania who were close to fighting each other over continuing territorial disputes.

■ Lashio in Burma fell to the Japanese, closing the Burma Road into China. The Japanese had covered 300 miles in only 18 days. That pace was maintained in a race with monsoon weather. Had the rains not been delayed the Japanese would have been bogged down in mud and water.

■ Japanese forces from Cebu were moved to Mindanao in an effort to secure the island. Heavy air and artillery attacks were launched against Corregidor.

April 30 British civilian air raid casualties for the month were 938 killed and 998 injured, a reflection of the intensification of Luftwaffe attacks on British cities.

■ All of central Burma fell to the Japanese as the defending forces fell back across the Irrawaddy River.

May 1 Mandalay fell to the Japanese as British forces found their left flank totally exposed.

May 2 The British cruiser *Edinburgh* was sunk while returning with a convoy from Russia.

May 3 Tulagi in the central Solomons was occupied by the Japanese, the first phase of what Tokyo had planned as an operation leading to the invasion of Australia.

May 4–8 The Battle of the Coral Sea was fought, the first naval battle in which the participants never saw the enemy (carrier aircraft were solely involved in the attacks). The Japanese suffered their first setback of the war. Even though the Japanese won a numerical victory, their losses were sufficient to cancel the planned invasion of Australia through Port Moresby in New Guinea. U.S. Navy losses were the carrier *Lexington*, the destroyer *Sims*, and the oiler *Neosho*. The carrier *Yorktown* was damaged. U.S. Navy pilots from the carriers *Lexington* and *Yorktown* sank the light carrier *Shoho*, the first Japanese ship larger than a destroyer to be sunk in the war. The Japanese also lost the destroyer *Kikuzuki* and three auxiliaries. A squadron leader, Lieutenant Commander Robert Dixon, radioed the sinking of *Shoho* with a message which became memorable: "Scratch one flattop. Dixon to carrier. Scratch one flattop!" Each side lost about 30 planes in the battle.

Survivors from the U.S.S. Lexington *are picked up by another American warship after the Battle of the Coral Sea.*

May 4 British forces landed on the north coast of Madagascar, encountering only light Vichy French opposition.

■ RAF bombers attacked the Skoda munitions facility in Pilsen (Plzen), Czechoslovakia.

■ The American Flying Tigers abandoned Burma and reestablished their base at Kunming, China. Bhamo fell to the Japanese. British forces evacuated Akyab (Sittwe).

May 5 Japanese forces landed on the only remaining U.S. outpost in the Philippines, the island of Corregidor. They established a beachhead at Cavalry Point, several miles east of where they were supposed to be put ashore.

■ Red Army units began assaults directed at Kharkov and Kursk.

■ The U.S. backed up the British action on Madagascar and said American military units would use the island as a base if it were felt necessary to do so.

■ Karl Oberg arrived in Paris to assume the position of "Supreme Head of the SS and Police." A vicious anti-Semite, Oberg once dismissed a complaint on the abduction of Jewish orphans in unoccupied France by saying, "A Jew is not a human being."

■ Marshal Pétain called on the governor general of Madagascar and all French units on the island to resist the British: "I am at the side of the military commander in this tragic trial in which he is defending the honor of France."

■ Vichy France delivered a protest note to the U.S. on Madagascar, saying Roosevelt would have "to judge what part of the responsibility he has in the consequences which may result from this aggression."

■ Imperial General Headquarters ordered the Japanese Navy to seize Midway Island and key points in the western Aleutians and "to destroy all enemy forces that may oppose the invasion."

May 6 Corregidor surrendered. About 16,000 Filipinos and Americans were captured by the Japanese. On this last day of fighting, 350 defenders were killed. The force had resisted fiercely, but the notion (common in the U.S.) that Corregidor might hold out until large numbers of reinforcements could arrive was widespread. In a letter written just before the surrender, General Wainwright wrote: "As I write this we are subjected to terrific air and artillery bombardment and it is

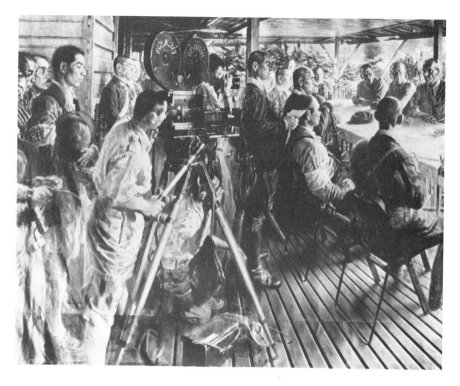

Japanese artist Miyamoto Saburo depicted the Bataan surrender meeting between generals Jonathan Wainwright and Masaharu Homma.

unreasonable to expect that we can hold out for long. We have done our best, both here and on Bataan, and although beaten we are still unashamed." Actually the dogged resistance did have an impact on the Pacific war. One Japanese division (the 4th) was so badly mauled in fighting for control of the island that its remnants were returned home. That division had been earmarked for the fighting in New Guinea and the Solomons. Other forces, involved in cleaning up in the Philippines, might also have been freed for crucial battles ahead, including Guadalcanal.

■ Chinese troops in Burma recaptured Maymyo.

■ U.S. forces began arriving in Liberia.

May 7 Churchill told Parliament that Diégo-Suarez (Antsiranana) on Madagascar had surrendered to British forces and ships of the Royal Navy were entering the harbor. He regretted the need to fight French troops, who, he said, fought with gallantry. Churchill said, "We trust that the French nation in time will come to regard this episode as a recognizable step in the liberation of their country, including Alsace-Lorraine, from the German yoke."

■ Spitfire reinforcements were flown into Malta from the carriers *Wasp* and *Eagle*.

May 8 German forces in the Crimea launched preparations for their summer offensive. Initial action was directed against Kerch. The ultimate objectives were the oil fields of the Caucasus.

■ Japan's hope to exploit the capture of the Dutch East Indies oil fields received a jolt when a U.S. submarine sank a transport carrying 900 Japanese supervisors and skilled workers en route to the production areas. Loss of the men seriously affected Japan's fuel supplies for a time.

■ Myitkyina in the north of Burma fell.

■ The Japanese launched new attacks on Mindanao. Captive General Wainwright called on the remaining defenders to surrender.

■ The British Foreign Office announced that British commanders in Madagascar had assured French authorities there that the island would remain French and revert to French sovereignty after the war. These assurances were given "in return for their cooperation and in order to avoid bloodshed."

May 9 Russia launched a major offensive from

216

the Donets bridgehead in an effort to push the Germans back to Kharkov.

■ The U.S. issued an ultimatum to Admiral Georges Robert, high commissioner in the French West Indies, to yield military and communications control to American authorities because "the French possessions might become bases for aggression on the part of the Axis." (Vichy rejected the demands and protested "this interference by the American Government in French internal politics.")

May 10 Churchill warned the Germans that if they introduced poison gas in the Russian campaign the British would retaliate in kind: ". . . if we are satisfied that this new outrage has been committed by Hitler we will use our great and growing air superiority in the West on the largest possible scale far and wide against military objectives in Germany."

■ U.S. and Filipino forces were told to give up their arms, but formal resistance did not end for another month.

May 11 A German U-boat penetrated the St. Lawrence River in Canada and torpedoed a transport.

■ U.S. submarine *S-42* torpedoed and sank the 4,400-ton Japanese minelayer *Okinoshima* in the Solomon Islands.

■ In retaliation for the Doolittle raid, the Japanese launched an offensive in China's Chekiang province.

■ German troops went back on the attack in the Crimea, recapturing Feodosiya.

■ German planes sank three British destroyers attempting to disrupt a North Africa-bound convoy in the Mediterranean.

May 12 The first major contingent of the U.S. Eighth Air Force arrived in England.

■ German forces renewed their offensive in the eastern Crimea.

May 13 Admiral Robert agreed to the immobilization of French ships in ports under his jurisdiction in West Indies ports.

May 14 An area off St. John's, Newfoundland, was mined by a German submarine. (The mines were not discovered until late the following year.)

■ The U.S. Women's Army Auxiliary Corps (WAAC) was established by legislation. ("Auxiliary" was dropped in 1943 and it became WAC, an integral part of the army.)

■ The French high commissioner for Martinique and Guadeloupe agreed to immobilize three French warships, accommodating the U.S. which did not want them to end up in German hands and conforming to Vichy's obligations under the armistice not to turn them over to the U.S.

May 15 Japan completed the conquest of Burma as remaining British forces crossed into India and the Chinese were pushed back into their own territory along the Burma Road.

■ German forces under Manstein retook Kerch,

American and Filipino prisoners on the Bataan Death March rest briefly before being taken to the Cabanatuan prison camp.

eliminating the Russians from the Crimea, except for Sevastopol in the southwest corner of the peninsula. The Russian Crimean front suffered 176,000 casualties and most of its armor in the disastrous action. Stalin's reaction was, "You see, that's where going on the defensive gets you."

May 16 Roosevelt ordered the release of U.S. Communist party leader Earl Browder from federal prison. Browder had served fourteen months of a sentence for passport irregularities, which the Russians insisted was a trumped-up charge. Moscow had been calling for his release since the Soviets became allies of the U.S.

May 17 The Russian drive toward Kharkov was halted, and the Germans began a slow, costly effort which eventually pushed the front eastward 25 miles.

May 19 German troops completed capture of the Kerch Peninsula in the Crimea, taking 100,000 Russian prisoners.

May 20 Having intercepted Japanese coded messages and knowing Tokyo's plans to attack Midway and the Aleutians, U.S. forces were ordered deployed to meet the threats, concentrating on Midway and not on the diversion to the north.

May 21 Hitler called off plans to invade Malta. He decided to wait until Egypt fell to the Axis.

May 23 Russian forces were trapped in the Izyum salient west of the Donets River as the German counteroffensive halted the Red Army advance toward Kharkov.

■ A defeated General Stilwell arrived in Dimapur, India, with a 400-man force after a 140-mile retreat through the Burmese jungle. He said the Allies took "a hell of a beating" from the Japanese, and it was necessary to regroup and "throw them out."

May 26 The Soviet Union and Britain signed a 20-year mutual aid agreement. Foreign Minister Molotov, who was in London, signed the pact for the Soviet Union. Molotov pressed for a second front. Churchill would not commit Britain to such an effort until it was "sound and sensible," adding, "Wars are not won by unsuccessful operations."

■ After a month-long lull, Rommel's Panzer Army Africa launched an attack on the Eighth Army's Gazala Line, a series of mine fields and field fortifications stretching from Gazala to Bir Hacheim. Rommel's plan was to make a feint attack with Italian infantry on the Gazala defenses while swinging his armor around Bir Hacheim, cutting across the British rear to the sea. The Axis forces were inferior in tanks, 560 to 849 for the Allies, but they had a substantial advantage in aircraft, 704 to 320.

May 27 Japanese Prime Minister Tojo called on Indians to revolt against the Allies; "The people should be inspired with courage and destroy, wipe out the British and American forces."

May 28 British units halted the German drive to swing around the Gazala defenders.

■ Germany scored a victory by knocking out the Russian force threatening Kharkov.

■ U.S. forces began arriving at Espiritu Santo in the New Hebrides.

■ Chinese forces abandoned Kinhwa as the Japanese pressed forward in Chekiang Province.

May 29 SS Commander for Czechoslovakia Reinhard Heydrich was severely wounded by partisans in an assassination attempt near Prague. His car was hit by a grenade as Heydrich was being driven to his country residence at Penenske Brezany. The blast severed Heydrich's spine.

■ A Japanese midget submarine entered Diego-Suarez harbor in Madagascar and heavily damaged the British battleship *Ramillies* and sank a tanker with its torpedoes.

■ Rommel withdrew his forces into a bridgehead on the eastern side of the Gazala line, covering supply corridors through the mine fields back to their bases.

■ The Royal Australian Air Force opened bombing operations against Tulagi in the Solomons.

■ Molotov arrived in Washington to discuss U.S. arms aid to Russia and to review U.S.-British planning for a second European front in 1942.

May 30–31 RAF bombers launched a devastating night raid on the German cathedral city of Cologne in the first thousand bomber raid of the war. A total of 1,046 aircraft (Wellingtons, Stirlings, Whitleys, Manchesters, Halifaxes, and Hampdens) plus 50 aircraft attacking German fighter bases took off from 52 fields in Britain. Of that number, 898 actually attacked Cologne, dropping 1,455 tons of bombs (two-thirds of them incendiaries). More than 12,000 fires were started, 1,700 of them major conflagrations. The crews returning home could see Cologne burning when they were 150 miles away. German records showed the following results: 486 people killed, 5,027 injured, 59,100 made homeless, 18,432 buildings of all kinds destroyed, 9,516 heavily damaged, 31,070 slightly damaged, 328 industrial plants destroyed or damaged (larger factories halted their production from three to nine months), and half the city's power supply eliminated. Forty-two British planes were downed, 12 were damaged so badly they could not fly again, and 104 were damaged and returned to duty.

May 31 Chiang Kai-shek pleaded with the U.S. to speed up military aid to China.

■ Japanese midget submarines entered Sydney harbor in Australia, sinking a small boat.

■ Mosquito aircraft flew their first operational missions—bombing runs and photo reconnaissance over Cologne.

■ British civilian air raid casualties for the month were 399 killed and 425 injured.

June 1 In reprisal for the RAF raid on Cologne, German bombers attacked the English cathedral city of Canterbury.

■ Japanese forces opened large-scale attacks in China to clear the rail line between Canton and Hankow.

■ Mexico declared war on Germany, Italy, and Japan.

■ German tanks smashed two British brigades in fierce fighting at Sidi Muftah in Libya. Rommel halted the offensive and ordered his unit to regroup.

■ All Jews in France and Holland were order to wear Star of David identification badges.

June 2 German artillery began a five day pounding of the Russian positions on the approaches to Sevastopol.

■ The Krupp works at Essen were bombed by the RAF. Other targets in the Ruhr were also attacked.

■ The Germans executed 131 Czechs in reprisal for the attack on Heydrich.

June 3 British Commandos raided the Boulogne-La Touquet area on the coast of France.

June 3–4 Japanese carrier-based aircraft bombed Dutch Harbor and Fort Mears in Alaska, part of Tokyo's diversion plan to draw the U.S. fleet from Midway.

June 4 Hitler visited Field Marshal Mannerheim in Finland.

June 4–6 The decisive Battle of Midway was fought, marking a turning point in the war in the Pacific. Admiral Chester W. Nimitz knew a month before that the Japanese were planning to invade Midway and to launch a diversionary assault on the Aleutians. Intercepts of secret Japanese radio messages gave the commander of the U.S. Pacific Fleet as much knowledge of Japanese intentions as was known by the Japanese planners themselves. Nimitz was ready, and the Japanese were administered a resounding defeat which altered the course of the Pacific war. Four Japanese carriers—*Kaga, Soryu, Akagi,* and *Hiryu*—were lost, in addition to a heavy cruiser (the *Mikuma*). The U.S. carrier *Yorktown* and a destroyer, the *Hammann,* were sunk. American air losses were 147 planes, compared to the Japanese total of 332. Henceforth, Japan was no longer affected by the "victory disease," which had marked the first six months of the war, and the Allies shortly went over to the offensive.

U.S.S. Yorktown *crewmen fight fires during the Battle of Midway.*

June 4 Heydrich died of wounds inflicted by the Czech partisan assassination team near Prague.

■ A counterattack was launched by the British in Libya.

June 5 The British counterattack in Libya collapsed after the loss of two infantry brigades and four artillery regiments.

■ The U.S. declared war on Bulgaria, Hungary, and Rumania. In calling for the actions, Roosevelt said they had declared war first, but "I realize that the three Governments took this action not upon their own initiative or in response to the wishes of their own people but as the instruments of Hitler."

■ Roosevelt said "authoritative" reports indicated the Japanese were using poison gases in China. "If Japan persists in this inhuman form of warfare," he said, "retaliation in kind and in full will be meted out."

■ German forces smashed Russia's outer defenses at Sevastopol.

■ An explosion at an ordnance plant in Elmwood, Illinois, killed 49 civilian war workers.

June 6 Fighting was intense around Bir Hacheim as the Germans threatened to break through to Tobruk. A Free French brigade and a battalion of Palestine Jews bore the brunt of the defense. Only 45 of the 1,000 Jews survived the fighting in the next month.

■ German troops opened up a massive assault and bombardment of Sevastopol.

June 7 Japan invaded the Aleutian Islands. In the only actual Axis occupation of North American territory, Japanese forces landed on Attu and Kiska in the western Aleutians. A force of 1,800 men was put ashore and was unopposed.

■ Chuhsien in Chekiang Province was attacked by the Japanese, beginning four days of fierce fighting.

■ Japanese submarines shelled the naval base at Sydney.

■ The State Department warned Helsinki the U.S. would break relations with Finland if it continued a policy of collaboration with Germany.

July 8 Free French forces defending Bir Hacheim in Libya faced severe resupply problems and began pulling back.

June 9 On the direct orders of Hitler (who delivered the eulogy at Heydrich's funeral) Nazi troops took revenge for the SS leader's murder on the Czech mining village of Lidice. All the men of Lidice—199—were killed outright. The 195 women residents were imprisoned in concentration camps and the 98 children were sent to other penal camps.

■ Germany launched a new offensive on the Kharkov front.

■ All formal resistance in the Philippines ended. In all, 140,000 U.S. and Filipino personnel were killed, wounded, or missing in trying to defend the islands.

■ Fierce ground and air attacks were launched against the Free French at Bir Hacheim, with the British unable to send in reinforcements.

June 10 Germany launched a limited offensive northeast of Kharkov to aid in the stalled drive toward Sevastopol.

■ Free French forces withdrew from Bir Hacheim.

■ Chuhsien fell to the Japanese.

June 11 The U.S. and Britain concluded a mutual aid agreement with Russia. Allied lend-lease could now be repaid by Moscow in goods instead of cash.

■ American aircraft began attacking Japanese positions on Kiska in the Aleutians.

■ Rommel's forces hammered through Allied positions at Bir Hacheim and reached the approaches to Tobruk.

■ German submarines began mining U.S. waters. U-87 planted 10 mines off Boston harbor. (No damage was ever recorded as a result, and U.S. authorities never knew Boston had been mined until captured German naval files were studied after the war.) U-373 dropped 15 mines off Delaware Bay. The German mines generally were set with devices which rendered them harmless after 80 days to permit submarines to return to those areas and plant additional devices without fear of being blown up themselves.

June 12 U-373 proceeded to the waters off the Chesapeake capes and planted 15 mines. (Three ships were sunk soon thereafter, severely disrupting coastal traffic.)

■ U.S. planes based in Egypt began long-range bombing missions, the first target being the Ploesti oil fields in Rumania.

■ In fierce fighting near "Knightsbridge" behind the Gazala line, Rommel's forces inflicted severe losses on British armor units.

■ Chinese forces abandoned Kiangshan.

Japan's "new order"—the Greater East Asia Co-prosperity Sphere—became a reality as Imperial forces won claim to a vast Pacific domain. With its expanded empire, Japan hoped to achieve economic self-sufficiency.

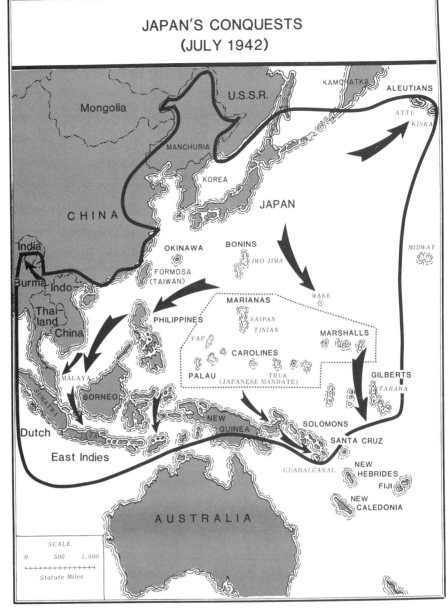

JAPAN'S CONQUESTS (JULY 1942)

■ Canada and Russia agreed to resume diplomatic relations after a break of six years.

June 13 In a staggering defeat, which opened the floodgates to Rommel, the British Eighth Army was shorn of most of its armor in what was known as "Black Saturday." Despite Ultra knowledge that Rommel was primed for defense against an attack, Lieutenant General Sir Neil Ritchie ordered about 300 of his tanks headlong into an ambush near El Adem. The Germans were waiting with 88-mm cannon and within a few hours had destroyed 230 of the helpless British armored vehicles. (Rommel followed through by capturing Tobruk and advancing all the way to El Alamein. Ritchie was discredited and later relieved of his command. From "Black Saturday" until Rommel's thrust was halted the Eighth Army was to suffer 75,000 casualties.)

■ Four German agents were landed by submarine near Amagansett, Long Island.

■ U.S. ships operating off the American east coast were warned: "Recent information indicates that enemy submarines, before proceeding to United States, are loading mines." Navy intelligence had also learned that the Germans had secretly advised the government of Chile to keep its ships away from New York since Germany intended to mine the harbor. (Two U-boats carrying 66 mines to be floated in New York waters were sunk in the North Atlantic while en route.)

June 14 British forces in North Africa recovered sufficiently from the beating of the day before to delay the advance of Rommel's numerically superior forces. Auchinleck ordered Ritchie to hold a line between Tobruk and El Adem.

■ Advance units of the 1st U.S. Marine Division landed in New Zealand.

June 15 Gazala was abandoned, with the 1st South African and British 50th Divisions ordered to withdraw.

■ The first U.S. ship was lost as a result of German mines dropped by U-boats off the east coast. The S.S. *Robert C. Tuttle*, an 11,000-ton tanker en route to Philadelphia from Key West, hit a mine, exploded, and was run ashore at Virginia Beach.

June 16 A British convoy from Gibraltar reached Malta, but another from Alexandria bringing supplies to Malta and Tobruk was forced to return to the Egyptian port because of Axis attacks.

June 17 Under cover of night the British pulled back from El Adem and Sidi Rezegh in Libya. The Germans gained control of the coastal road to Bardia, isolating Tobruk.

■ Four German agents were landed by submarine at Ponte Vedra Beach, Florida.

■ A U.S. ship carrying 11,000 tons of coal was sunk by a German mine outside Hampton Roads, Virginia. Three crewmen of the S.S. *Santore* were killed.

June 18 Churchill arrived in the U.S. for conferences with Roosevelt with emphasis on opening a second front.

■ Tobruk and its garrison of the 2nd South African Division, 201st Guards Brigade, 11th Indian Infantry Brigade, and 32nd Army Tank Brigade, under the command of General H.B. Klopper, was now isolated and besieged. German forces also captured the Gambut air field, denying the Tobruk garrison the aid of immediate close air support.

■ German forces—after 12 days of intense fighting—knocked out all but one of the 13 fortifications defending Sevastopol.

■ Bernard Robinson was commissioned an ensign in the U.S. Naval Reserve, the first black to become an officer in the navy.

June 20 Rommel launched his attack on Tobruk, directing the main effort at the now largely derelict southeast sector perimeter defense. The Germans penetrated deep into Tobruk proper. A British relief force failed to get through to the besieged garrison.

■ Churchill and Roosevelt agreed on an invasion of northwest Africa.

■ A Japanese submarine shelled a wireless station on Vancouver Island, the first action to take place on Canadian territory.

■ German forces reached the north shore of Sevastopol.

June 21 Tobruk fell as Rommel led his forces into the fortress city. The Germans took 33,000 Allied prisoners and captured vast amounts of supplies. According to the official South African history of the campaign: "The capture of Tobruk crowned what was probably the most spectacular series of victories ever gained over a British Army." Rommel immediately pushed eastward, an action approved by Hitler over the objections of the German staff which felt Malta had to be neutralized first.

■ In a broadcast to the French people, Laval stated his hope that Germany would win the war.

June 22 In the first attack on a U.S. continental military base since the War of 1812, a Japanese submarine shelled Fort Stevens, Oregon. There were no casualties or damage.

■ The last of the Russian fortifications around Sevastopol was knocked out by the Germans.

■ The German 90th Light Division crossed into Egypt.

June 24 Rommel's forces advanced to Sidi Barrani in Egypt.

■ German troops secured their positions east of

the Donets River and established a new line on the Oskol River.

■ Major General Dwight D. Eisenhower assumed command of U.S. forces in the European theater.

June 25 General Sir Claude Auchinleck took over personal command of the British Eighth Army, replacing Lieutenant General Sir Neil Ritchie. Axis forces had penetrated 50 miles into Egypt.

■ More than 1,300 planes attacked Bremen.

June 26 As a reward for his victories in North Africa, Rommel was promoted to field marshal.

■ Rommel's forces broke through the mine fields south of Mersa Matruh.

■ Germany announced it would begin unrestricted submarine warfare off the east coast of the United States.

June 27 The German offensive surrounded British forces in Mersa Matruh.

■ The FBI announced the arrest of the eight German saboteurs who had been landed by submarines on Long Island and the Florida coast.

■ Britain provided a credit of $100 million to the Soviets for the purchase of British arms.

June 28 German forces launched their summer offensive and touched off the largest-scale battle of the war on any front, the Battle of Kursk. The drive was directed toward the Don River and was designed to cut off the Russians in the salient around Kursk.

■ The British X Corps broke out of Mersa Matruh. Two days of heavy fighting resulted in the capture of 8,000 Allied troops. All British forces were ordered to pull back to El Alamein, only 70 miles from Alexandria, Egypt.

■ The code used by the U.S. military attaché in Cairo was changed. It was a blow to Rommel since German intelligence was routinely decoding his highly informational reports being transmitted to Washington. The new code could not be broken immediately, denying Rommel his best source of intelligence.

June 29 Rommel's forces reached a point 15 miles from El Alamein.

■ Mussolini flew to Tripoli in preparation for the assumed Axis victory parade in Cairo.

June 30 Axis troops reached El Alamein and Alexandria was bombed by Axis planes.

■ Intoxicated by his military triumphs, Hitler issued a directive for a linkup in Egypt of German North African forces and those sweeping through eastern Europe. The plan was for Rommel to press for a decisive victory from the west and the Germans in Bulgaria would march through Turkey (whether Ankara agreed or not) and the Levant, to complete the destruction of the British position in the Middle East.

■ The Germans threw more men into the Kursk offensive. All Russian resistance ended west of Volkhov on the northern front.

■ British civilian air raid casualties for the month were 300 killed and 337 injured.

July 1 Intense fighting developed around El Alamein as the British Eighth Army began to stiffen. Rommel was frustrated in a two-pronged thrust to break through Auchinleck's mobile defense. The Germans actually achieved their deepest penetration into Egypt on this date with the capture of a fortified position at Deir el-Shein, just south of El Alamein. The Germans lost 18 of their 55 tanks, but Rommel's plans were thrown off by the delay. The 1st South African Division stopped the German 90th Light Infantry Division, and the 18th Indian Infantry Brigade blocked the Afrika Korps.

■ Axis forces now arrayed on the Russian front for what was planned to be the knockout punch included 178 German divisions, 31 Rumanian, 17 Hungarian, 10 Italian, 2 Slovak, and 1 Spanish.

■ Axis planes bombed Haifa, Palestine.

July 2 Churchill won a vote of confidence in the House of Commons on his handling of the war, 476 to 25.

■ The British began counterattacking in Egypt, with the XIII Corps sweeping around Rommel from the south.

■ The British occupied Mayotte Island at the north end of the Mozambique Channel. It was subsequently used as a seaplane base.

■ Sevastopol fell to the Germans after a protracted and costly battle which began the previous October.

July 3 Voronezh was taken by the German Fourth Panzer Army which then wheeled southward along the Don.

■ Anti-British leaders of the Egyptian Liberation Movement conferred with Rommel at his field headquarters to prepare for the German entry into Cairo.

July 4 U.S.-manned bombers flew their first missions in Europe. Six A-20s joined in an RAF attack on four German air bases in Holland. Only two of the planes reached their targets. Two were shot down, and one was damaged.

■ German forces advanced along a broad front in southern Russia, securing a solid base on the Don River.

■ Australia's 9th Division arrived on the Egyptian front.

■ The Panzer Army Africa was reduced to a mere 36 tanks and an exhausted and depleted group of men suffering from severe ammunition shortages. Rommel began to regroup, withdrawing his remaining German armor and putting Italian units into the front line. The British Eighth Army failed to take advantage of the German plight even though Auchinleck had been urging his field commanders to initiate offensive operations. Their troops, too, were equally drained of will and resources.

■ The Flying Tigers in China were incorporated into the U.S. Army Air Corps as the 23rd Pursuit Group.

July 5 The Crimea was occupied totally by German forces as all Russian resistance ended.

■ A Russian-bound convoy from Iceland (PQ-17) came under heavy attack by German aircraft and U-boats in the Barents Sea. The convoy was ordered to scatter when *Tirpitz* and other German warships were believed heading from Norwegian ports to intercept the Allied ships. Without benefit of escorts once the vessels dispersed and proceeded independently, they were easy prey for about 200 Luftwaffe planes and subs operating in the area. Of the 22 American and 11 British merchantmen, 23 were sunk, most by aircraft and U-boats but some by mines as well. (The severe losses forced the British Admiralty to suspend convoys for Russia "at least till the northern ice packs melted and receded and until perpetual daylight passed." This in turn drew the wrath of Stalin and seriously exacerbated inter-Allied relations.)

July 6 Voronezh along the southern Russian front fell to the Germans.

An Allied convoy under attack.

■ Argentina reaffirmed its neutrality.

■ Japanese troops cleared the rail line between Hangchow and Nancheng.

July 7 The German Sixth Army joined up with the Fourth Panzer Army northeast of Valuyki. German units began their drive to take the Caucasus.

■ The Canadian House of Commons voted 158-14 to begin sending draftees overseas.

July 8 The Russians abandoned Stary Oskol, southwest of Voronezh.

■ Orders were issued by Admiral Nimitz for the invasion of Guadalcanal.

July 9 German and Axis forces in southern Russia were redirected, with one army group ordered to drive toward Rostov and into the Caucasus, and the other to occupy Stalingrad (Volgagrad) and thence to Astrakhan.

July 10 Making use of detailed knowledge of Rommel's troop dispositions through Ultra intercepts of German Enigma ciphers, Auchinleck began a new strategy of hitting Italian units under Rommel's command. Rommel was forced to employ his own German strike forces to plug up holes in the front, sapping German strength as a result. In the first such attack the 9th Australian Division, preceded by a heavy preparatory bombardment, routed the Italian Sabratha Division on the northern sector of the Alamein front.

July 11 Futou Island near Foochow was occupied by Chinese troops.

■ Lisichansk, on the Donets River, fell to the Germans driving toward Rostov.

■ Australian troops inflicted heavy casualties on the Italians near El Alamein. Significantly, from this action on, the Germans felt the Italians could not be relied upon to maintain their defensive positions.

July 12 An Australian force reached Kokoda. The small unit trekked five days over a difficult trail across the Owen Stanley Range from Port Moresby.

■ Vichy French officials in Indochina ceded a disputed border region of Cambodia to Thailand.

July 14 The Fourth Panzer Army joined in the German drive toward Rostov, while other Axis forces continued smashing toward Stalingrad.

■ Limited gains were made by the British in Egypt.

■ Free French forces were officially redesignated "Fighting French."

July 15 Two German armies reached Kamensk on the Donets.

■ Auchinleck's forces routed the Italian Brescia and Pavia divisions south of El Alamein. As a result, Rommel was forced to send German troops to stabilize the front and upset plans for Axis offensive actions. German troops did capture part of the ground lost around the Ruweisat ridge.

July 16 British forces advanced to a point three miles west of El Alamein in a day of confused fighting.

■ The U.S. broke off diplomatic relations with Finland.

■ Tojo said Japan had received reassurances of Russian neutrality from the Soviet Union.

July 17 Top U.S. military leaders arrived in London to press the British for a limited cross-Channel invasion in 1942.

■ Churchill informed Stalin the British would no longer sail convoys along the northern route to Murmansk and Archangel because of the heavy losses suffered by PQ-17. Churchill told the Soviet leader a continuation of the shipping effort "would bring no benefit to you and would only involve dead loss to the common cause." (Stalin protested the cancellation of the shipping.)

July 18 Russian forces were routed along a broad front in the south as the Germans captured Voroshilovgrad, a coal and coke center in the Donets Basin.

July 19 SS Chief Oberg issued "The Family Hostage Law" in occupied France. If any identified French "terrorist" did not surrender within ten days of his crime, all his adult male relatives would be executed, females would be sent to "work camps," and children under 17 would be sent to reform schools.

July 20 Mussolini returned to Rome from Libya after giving up his plan for a triumphal entry into Cairo.

July 21 Three Japanese submarines were sunk off the Aleutians.

■ Infantrymen cleared the passage for British tanks as the British opened a direct attack on German positions in Egypt.

■ Admiral William D. Leahy, ambassador to

Vichy France, was named chief of staff to President Roosevelt.

July 22 German forces opened an all-out attack on Rostov.

■ Auchinleck's attacks on the Ruweisat ridge and the area south of El Alamein collapsed in confusion.

■ The British refused to launch a limited cross-Channel attack in 1942, preferring to build up forces for a major effort later.

■ The Treblinka concentration camp was opened by the Germans.

■ The Germans began the resettlement of Jews from Warsaw. By Oct. 3, a total of 310,322 were transferred to work or concentration camps.

July 22–23 Japanese Eighteenth Army troops landed at Buna on the northern coast of Papua. Within two weeks 13,500 troops had been put ashore. They occupied Buna and Gona and moved over the Owen Stanley Range with Port Moresby as the ultimate objective.

July 23 Rostov fell to the Germans after bitter fighting. The Germans took 240,000 Russian prisoners. The Germans then split their forces, with eventual disastrous results. One group headed for Stalingrad, the other for the Caucasus.

■ The main approaches to the Mississippi River were mined by a German submarine.

July 25 The Germans captured Novocherkassk, northeast of Rostov.

July 26 Under cover of darkness the British conducted a major attack on the northern sector of Rommel's position, hoping to force a withdrawal of the Axis forces. The effort failed because of poor coordination between infantry and armor units.

■ Sir Stafford Cripps attacked Gandhi's position on immediate Indian independence: "We cannot allow the actions of a visionary, however distinguished in his fight for freedom in the past, to thwart the United Nations' drive for victory in the East." Gandhi had previously rejected any compromise, saying, "Anarchy is the only way. Someone asked me if there would be anarchy after British rule. Yes, it will be there. But I tell the British to give us chaos."

July 27 Speaking in Osaka, Tojo called on Australia to surrender: "At this time Australia, which has been orphaned, is showing a pitiful existence earnestly requesting aid from America. There is no need for me to mention that the Imperial Government [of Japan] will not hold any hesitation if the leaders of Australia still do not recognize the existing situation and continue to offer a profitless resistance."

■ About 600 RAF bombers attacked Hamburg.

July 28 Japanese forces were ordered to advance on Milne Bay and Port Moresby in New Guinea.

■ Soviet forces began mass withdrawals from the lower Don River area.

■ Roosevelt announced that four million Americans were now in the U.S. military services.

July 29 Kokoda in New Guinea was captured by the Japanese, but two of their transports with reinforcements were turned back in an attempted amphibious landing on the north coast by Allied planes. The Australians fell back to Deniki.

■ Chinese units regained areas along the Hangchow-Nancheng rail line.

July 30 Stalin issued orders to all Russian units

German troops clear Rostov in house-to-house fighting to capture the "Gateway to the Caucasus."

prohibiting "another step back." No further retreats would be tolerated. The Germans were within 80 miles of Stalingrad and advancing through the Caucasus.

■ Auchinleck halted offensive operations in Egypt until more troops arrived. He had nonetheless stopped Rommel in the July fighting (which became known as the first battle of El Alamein).

■ The U.S. Women's Naval Reserve (WAVES) was established (WAVES stood for Women Appointed for Voluntary Emergency Service).

July 31 German 4th Panzer Division troops launched an offensive directed toward the Don River. On the central front near Rzhev, Red Army troops launched offensive actions.

■ Japanese units pushed over the Owen Stanley Mountains from Buna and Gona toward Port Moresby in New Guinea.

■ A German submarine laid mines off Charleston, South Carolina.

■ British civilian air raid casualties for June and July were 711 killed and 1,208 injured.

Aug. 1 The rail center of Salsk, on the Stalingrad rail line, fell to the Germans. Other units reached the Kuban River.

■ Cairo was bombed by Axis planes.

■ RAF planes attacked Düsseldorf.

Aug. 2 Rumania declared war on Nicaragua and Haiti.

■ Allied planes struck at Axis communication and supply lines in North Africa.

Aug. 3 Voroshilovsk was captured by the Germans who moved southward to establish a bridgehead on the other side of the Kuban which would expose the Maikop oil fields.

■ German planes bombed Iceland.

Aug. 5 Russian forces suffered heavy losses near Stalingrad. Kotelnikovo was occupied. German troops moved across the Kuban River.

Aug. 6 A campaign of civil disobedience was threatened in India if the British did not make India "free and independent," at the earliest possible time, not after the war.

Aug. 7 U.S. forces in the Pacific took the offensive for the first time in the war with the invasion of Guadalcanal and the Solomon Islands. Naval and air support aided the 1st Marine Division which put ashore on Guadalcanal and four other islands in the Solomons group. Benefiting from bad weather, the invasion force of 11,000

Marines landed on Guadalcanal without initial opposition. Soon, however, the Japanese offered stiff resistance, and the campaign for the island lasted six months.

■ Churchill visited the Egyptian front.

■ Britain announced formation of the Palestine Regiment.

■ U.S. naval forces bombarded Japanese-held Kiska Island in the Aleutians (bad weather delayed the attack for almost three weeks).

Aug. 8 Tulagi in the Solomons was secured by U.S. Marines.

■ U.S. planes attacked Japanese installations in Canton, China.

■ Six German agents, arrested after landing by submarine on the U.S. east coast, were electrocuted. Eight saboteurs had been put ashore on Long Island and Florida but were quickly apprehended by the FBI. The two others were given life sentences instead of being executed because they cooperated with the government.

■ A dozen mines were laid near the St. John's Lightship off Jacksonville, Florida, by a German submarine. (They were discovered three days later and destroyed.)

■ British Lieutenant General W.H.E. Gott was killed when his plane was attacked by German fighters. Gott had been scheduled to take command of the Eighth Army. The post was now given to Lieutenant General Bernard Montgomery. General Alexander was named to succeed Auchinleck as Commander in Chief, Middle East.

Aug. 9 Allied naval forces suffered one of their most severe losses of the Pacific in the Battle of Savo Island, a one-sided two-hour duel of major ships. The American cruisers *Astoria*, *Quincy*, and *Vincennes* and the Australian cruiser *Canberra* were sunk, and the U.S. cruiser *Chicago* and the destroyers *Ralph Talbot* and *Patterson* were damaged. Japanese losses were negligible. After this battle, the waters between Guadalcanal and Florida islands became known as "Ironbottom Bay."

■ The Germans captured Krasnodar and Maikop, key oil-producing areas.

■ Gandhi and other Congress party leaders were arrested for resisting the war effort in India. Serious rioting broke out in Bombay and other cities. Troops were called in to preserve order. Several people died in the ensuing clashes.

Aug. 10 Alexander was ordered to destroy the Axis forces in Egypt and Libya.

■ German forces reached Pyatigorsk in the foothills of the Caucasus.

■ RAF planes raided Osnabrück and military targets in Belgium and Holland.

Aug. 11 The British carrier *Eagle* was sunk by Axis while escorting a convoy to Malta.

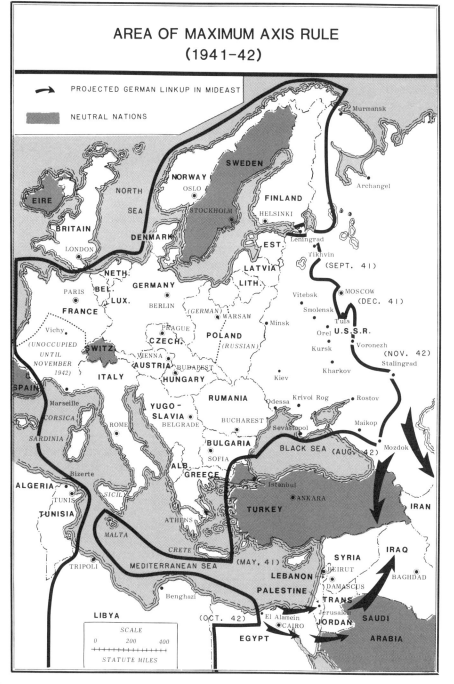

AREA OF MAXIMUM AXIS RULE
(1941–42)

PROJECTED GERMAN LINKUP IN MIDEAST

NEUTRAL NATIONS

At the height of his military successes, Hitler ruled supreme in Europe and threatened the entire Middle East and beyond. A linkup of his forces in Russia and North Africa would have opened the way to a meeting with the Japanese in Asia.

■ Stalingrad was imperiled as the Russian Fourth Tank Army suffered heavy losses in the bend of the Don River near Kalach. German units began crossing into Circassia and drove toward the Grozny oil fields.

■ Mainz was bombed by the RAF.

■ Laval declared, "The hour of liberation for France is the hour when Germany wins the war."

■ U.S. planes attacked Canton, Hankow, and Yoochow in China.

Aug. 12 Churchill arrived in Moscow for a four-day visit in which the second front was the main issue.

■ Soviet attacks near Rzhev were repulsed after making only small gains.

■ Himmler was given responsibilities for maintaining order in Denmark, Norway, Belgium, and Holland.

Aug. 13 Anti-British rioting continued in India. Several factories involved in the production of military materiel were closed because of strikes.

■ U.S. planes bombed Formosa.

■ Japanese forces took control of the Buna-Kokoda trail in New Guinea, taking the main pass over the Owen Stanley Range. An additional 3,000 construction troops were landed near Gona.

Aug. 15 The German Sixth and Fourth Panzer armies opened their major offensive toward Stalingrad.

■ The first U.S. resupply ships reached Guadalcanal as Marine rations were cut.

■ Alexander officially succeeded Auchinleck as Commander in Chief, Middle East. Montgomery assumed command of the Eighth Army.

■ German reconnaissance forces suffered heavy losses but continued their push toward Astrakhan.

Aug. 16 U.S. Army Air Corps planes went into action in North Africa for the first time, attacking German positions on the Egyptian front.

Aug. 17 U.S. Marine Raiders, led by Lieutenant Colonel Evans E. Carlson, were landed on Makin Island in the Gilbert Islands by two Navy submarines. The 221-man force destroyed all installations, including the newly completed seaplane base, on the Japanese-held island and killed the entire Japanese garrison of about 90 men. The Japanese commander's last radio message was "All men are dying serenely in battle." "Carl-son's Raiders" lost 30 men and 14 were wounded.

■ The Germans established several bridgeheads across the Kuban River.

■ American Eighth Air Force bombers launched their first independent air raids on the continent, attacking the rail center of Rouen, France. RAF Spitfires provided fighter escort.

Aug. 18 A large Japanese landing force went ashore unopposed near Basabua in New Guinea.

Aug. 19 Canadian and British raiding forces landed at Dieppe on the coast of France but were repulsed. About 6,000 troops stayed ashore for nine hours and suffered 50 percent casualties without achieving any military objective.

Although the Dieppe raid was a tactical failure, the Allies netted a number of German prisoners.

■ The P-51 Mustang fighter, which was to play such a decisive role in the war, made its debut in combat over Dieppe. An RAF Mustang was credited with downing a German fighter in this initial foray.

■ General Friedrich von Paulus, commander of the German Sixth Army, ordered his forces to take Stalingrad despite their great losses. Russian troops evacuated Krasnodar.

■ Advance units of the Australian 7th Division arrived at Port Moresby.

■ Alexander directed Montgomery to hold the line at El Alamein and to delay offensive operations until the manpower buildup was completed.

Aug. 20 The first U.S. planes landed at Henderson Field on Guadalcanal.

■ German forces crossed the Don River around Kletskaya.

■ Five hundred RAF and U.S. bombers attacked Rouen.

Aug. 21 The Japanese launched a counterattack on U.S. Marine positions on Guadalcanal but were driven back, suffering 800 casualties to 110 for the Marines.

■ Krymsk, near the east coast of the Black Sea, fell to the Germans.

■ Roosevelt restated the principle of holding the occupying power officials responsible for war crimes against civilian populations: "It seems only fair that they should have this warning that the time will come when they shall have to stand in courts of law in the very countries which they are now oppressing and answer for their acts."

Aug. 22 U.S. Army planes began arriving on Guadalcanal.

■ German paratroopers landed behind Russian lines near Stalingrad and were badly mauled.

■ Australian Major General Cyril A. Clowes took over command of the Milne force in New Guinea, which consisted of 8,133 Australians and 1,365 Americans and faced a Japanese contingent of more than 11,000.

■ Brazil declared war against Germany and Italy. The loss of five of its ships to U-boats triggered the action. Brazil's entry into the war facilitated Allied air transport, opening up the safer and shorter South Atlantic by way of Ascension Island.

Aug. 23 The Russians launched a major offensive south of Lake Ladoga. On the Stalingrad front, German units reached the Volga River. Stalingrad was bombed by 200 Luftwaffe planes. The town of Elbrus on the east coast of the Black Sea fell to the Germans.

Aug. 24–25 In the battle of the eastern Solomons, the Japanese failed in their attempt to reinforce units on Guadalcanal. A regiment was to land under naval escort, but the force was intercepted by U.S. Task Force 61, commanded by Vice

Admiral Jack Fletcher. The American carrier *Enterprise* and battleship *North Carolina* were damaged, but the Japanese lost the carrier *Ryujo*, a cruiser, and a destroyer. Ninety Japanese planes were downed to 20 U.S. More importantly, the battle again demonstrated to Tokyo that Guadalcanal could not be easily defended.

Aug. 24 Air action intensified over Guadalcanal as the Japanese lost 21 planes to 3 for the Marines.

■ A 1,500-man Japanese force sailed from New Ireland and Buna for Milne Bay in New Guinea.

Aug. 25 U.S. Marine and Army planes disrupted a Japanese force on its way to Guadalcanal, sinking a destroyer and transport and forcing the Japanese to withdraw.

■ The Japanese landed at Milne Bay, but the force was weakened when their landing craft were intercepted by American fighters.

■ German troops opened up a drive for the Grozny oil fields.

■ The Duke of Kent was killed. The 39-year-old brother of King George VI had waived his honorary rank of RAF marshal and was an air commodore who served as chief welfare officer of the RAF Home Command. He was en route from England to Iceland in bad weather when his flying boat crashed in Scotland.

■ The Swedish ship S.S. *Gripsholm* arrived in New York with 287 Allied officials and their families who had been exchanged for Japanese diplomats at Lourenço Marques in Portuguese East Africa (Mozambique).

Aug. 26 The Battle of Stalingrad intensified with an estimated million German troops attacking the Russian defenders. The Red Army attempted to ease the pressures on Stalingrad by launching diversionary attacks in the areas of Rzhev and Vyazma.

■ The Japanese beachhead at Milne Bay was pounded by Allied aircraft. Most of their supplies were destroyed, but the Japanese nonetheless forced the Australians to withdraw.

■ A training center for Chinese troops was opened at Ramgarh, India.

Aug. 27 The battle for Stalingrad continued to increase in intensity.

■ U.S. B-17s bombed the harbor facilities at Rotterdam.

■ Japanese forces pressed their attack on Australian forces defending the overland route to Port Moresby.

■ Units of the Japanese force on Attu began to be evacuated to Kiska.

■ Rioting and sabotage swept India in the campaign to win independence from the British.

Aug. 28 Novorossiysk on the Black Sea came under German attack.

Aug. 29 Another 775 Japanese were landed at Milne Bay.

Aug. 30 The southern sector of the El Alamein line was assaulted by Axis forces, with the main effort swinging north against the Alam el Halfa ridge. It was an effort to reach the coast behind the Eighth Army. Three German divisions were to break for the Nile if the maneuver succeeded.

■ Adak in the Aleutians was reoccupied by U.S. troops who encountered no opposition.

■ German and Russian forces continued battling in a costly stalemate at Stalingrad.

■ Soviet planes bombed Berlin, Danzig, Stettin, and Königsberg.

■ Thirty more U.S. aircraft landed on Guadalcanal.

Aug. 31 Rommel's forces were halted after bitter fighting southwest of the Alam el Halfa ridge. Axis losses were heavy, and the Germans were beginning to realize severe supply shortages. Most crushing was the sinking of a large tanker carrying vitally needed gasoline by a British submarine outside Tobruk's harbor.

■ Australian forces attacked the demoralized Japanese at Milne Bay, and the Japanese on the Owen Stanley Range were told to go on the defensive when they reached the coast.

■ German Army Group B established positions across the Terek River near Mozdok, although Russian resistance began to stiffen.

Sept. Soviet air force planes launched a series of small raids during the month on Budapest, Bucharest, and Vienna. They were more for psychological purposes than military value.

Sept. 1 British Eighth Army troops repulsed another German attack on the Alam el Halfa ridge.

■ German forces pounded the Stalingrad defense perimeter with the heaviest fighting taking place northwest and southwest of the smashed city.

■ Premier Tojo assumed the functions of foreign minister after the resignation of Shigenori Togo.

The Japanese also created a "Ministry of Greater East Asia" to centralize controls over the occupied areas.

Sept. 2 German and Rumanian troops crossed the Kerch Strait from the Crimea and linked up with other Axis units, adding to the threat to Novorossiysk.

■ Soviet planes bombed Warsaw.

■ Rommel issued orders for a staged withdrawal of his main offensive forces.

■ A thousand Japanese reinforcements were landed at Basabua in New Guinea, adding to the pressures on Port Moresby.

Sept. 3 A furious nighttime battle was waged in the desert as New Zealand troops tried to cut Rommel's withdrawal from Alam el Halfa. Allied aircraft pounded the retreating Axis forces, especially supply transport.

■ German elements penetrated into the western suburbs of Stalingrad.

■ Spanish Foreign Minister Serrano Suñer was requested to resign from the Spanish cabinet.

Sept. 4 Heavy fighting took place near El Alamein as Rommel completed his retreat to positions just east of the old British mine fields.

■ Australian troops pressed the Japanese at Milne Bay, who began evacuating their wounded.

■ Lanchi in China was recaptured by Japan.

■ The U.S. destroyer-transports *Little* and *Gregory* were sunk by Japanese warships in Sealark Channel in the Solomons.

■ Lend-lease agreements were signed between the U.S. and Britain, Australia, New Zealand, and the Free French.

Sept. 5 German troops "entered" Novorossiysk on the Black Sea which had served as the base of the Soviet fleet in those waters since the fall of Sevastopol.

■ Russian planes bombed Budapest, Vienna, and Breslau.

■ U.S. aircraft attacked Le Havre.

■ Japanese forces were withdrawn from Milne Bay under cover of darkness. Of the original 1,900-man force, 1,300 were evacuated.

■ U.S. and British military planners named Algiers and Oran in Algeria and Casablanca, Morocco, as landing sites for the TORCH invasion.

Sept. 6 Violent fighting continued at Stalingrad. German troops completed the occupation of the Black Sea port of Novorossiysk.

■ British forces made small gains against Rommel's forces in Egypt.

Sept. 7 All organized Japanese resistance ended at Milne Bay, but the Japanese continued their advance toward Port Moresby over the Owen Stanley Range.

■ U.S. forces took over control of military installations on the Ecuadorian coast and in the Galápagos Islands.

■ A lull developed in the El Alamein area as both sides regrouped. The Germans had gained about five miles on the southern flank.

■ Roosevelt proposed an antiinflation program in the U.S., including a ceiling of a $25,000 annual wage for all Americans.

■ Laval protested the bombing of Le Havre and Rouen by U.S. planes. He was told the U.S. regretted any suffering by the people of France "but that military plants operated by or for Germany and other German military properties in France will be bombed at every opportunity in the future."

Sept. 8 Two Australian battalions were trapped in the Owen Stanley Range.

■ U.S. Marine raiders and paratroopers attacked the Japanese base near Taivu Point on Guadalcanal.

Sept. 9 In the only air attack on the continental U.S. during the war, a Japanese submarine-based plane dropped incendiary bombs in a forest near Brookings, Oregon. A small fire was the only damage.

■ RAF bombers dropped the first "heavy" incendiaries of the war on Düsseldorf.

■ British forces renewed their offensive on Madagascar to secure control of the Mozambique Channel.

■ German forces advanced on a broad front in the Caucasus.

■ Iran declared war on Germany.

■ Military conscription was instituted by the Germans in Alsace-Lorraine.

Sept. 10 Russian forces fell back in the western suburbs of Stalingrad.

■ Churchill announced in the House of Commons that troop reinforcements had arrived in India and that "firm but tempered measures" were being taken against "the revolutionary" action of the Congress party.

■ German U-boat *69* planted 12 mines off the

Chesapeake capes. The channel was cleared by minesweepers within two days. It was the last mine threat of the war off the Virginia coast.

Sept. 11 The Japanese thrust in the Owen Stanley Range was beginning to meet resistance by Australian forces at Ioribaiwa, 32 miles from Port Moresby. The encircled Australian forces broke out of their trap and joined in the defense. MacArthur ordered U.S. and Australian reinforcements to clear New Guinea of the Japanese.

■ RAF bombers attacked Japanese targets in Rangoon, Mandalay, and Prome.

Sept. 12 A German U-boat torpedoed and sank the 19,695-ton British transport *Laconia*. Only when the submarine captain started picking up survivors did he realize the ship was carrying 1,800 Italians captured in North Africa. Five hundred of the POW's were killed instantly. The U-boat had crammed 200 survivors aboard when it sent out an uncoded message to ships of any flag to join in the rescue effort, guaranteeing not to attack any Allied vessels. A tragedy of errors over the next four days compounded the original horror. French ships were en route from west Africa when an American plane out of Ascension attacked the German sub even though it had displayed a giant Red Cross flag. The attack was ordered even though it was known *Laconia* survivors might be killed. Two other U-boats were also in the area in the rescue effort, and the three submarines eventually turned over the survivors to the French. Of the original 2,732 people aboard (including 80 women and children) 1,111 survived. Both sides were embittered by the losses. For the Germans the incident resulted in the "*Laconia* Order," by which the U-boat captains were prohibited from picking up any survivors except prisoners of war who might possess special military intelligence.

Sept. 13 Eisenhower took over command of TORCH planning with headquarters in London.

■ Two British raids on Axis supply bases at Tobruk and Benghazi resulted in heavy casualties and little destruction.

■ East African troops spearheaded the Allied drive toward Tananarive on Madagascar.

■ U.S. Marines held off a determined Japanese force of two battalions which attempted to take

Henderson Field on Guadalcanal. The Japanese suffered 1,200 casualties.

■ Vichy France ordered compulsory labor for all men between 18 and 50 and single women between 20 and 35.

Sept. 14 Heavy fighting on Bloody Ridge on Guadalcanal left 600 Japanese dead and 143 U.S. Marine casualties.

■ British naval forces were badly mauled in an attack on Tobruk.

Sept. 15 The U.S. carrier *Wasp* was torpedoed and sunk by a Japanese submarine near Espiritu Santo. Damage to the battleship *North Carolina* forced its return to Pearl Harbor for repairs.

The U.S.S. Wasp is hit by Japanese submarine torpedoes. American destroyers later sank the mortally stricken carrier.

■ Units of the U.S. 32nd Division landed at Port Moresby, the first American infantrymen to arrive in New Guinea. The other units were primarily engineering and antiaircraft.

Sept. 16 German troops smashed their way to the northwest suburbs of Stalingrad.

■ The French governor general of Madagascar requested peace terms.

■ Japanese forces were finally halted in their drive toward Port Moresby over the Owen Stanley Range. Australian troops prepared to go on the offensive.

■ All Japanese forces were secretly withdrawn from Attu to Kiska.

Sept. 17 French authorities on Madagascar rejected the Allied peace terms.

■ Heavy fighting developed in the streets of Stalingrad.

Sept. 18 Tokyo instructed its New Guinea forces to hold their positions as long as possible, though acknowledging the severe supply and manpower shortages facing them.

■ U.S. troops on Guadalcanal were given full food rations for the first time in about a month. More than 4,000 Marine reinforcements were landed.

■ An East African brigade landed on the east coast of Madagascar unopposed. Another brigade drove down the west coast toward Tananarive, the capital.

■ Canadian and British planes bombed Tobruk.

■ A German submarine mined the channel leading into Charleston, South Carolina. (No damage was ever recorded as a result of the dozen mines sown, although only four were ever rendered harmless.)

■ Rumania and Turkey signed a trade agreement, with the Rumanians trading lubricating oil for Turkish cotton.

Sept. 20 House-to-house fighting broke out in Stalingrad.

■ November 8 was established as the date for the Allied invasion of North Africa.

Sept. 21 In the first offensive by the British in southeast Asia, Commonwealth forces struck southward along the Arakan coast in Burma.

■ All women and children were evacuated from Stalingrad.

Sept. 22 Plans were approved for shipping U.S. war supplies to the Russians through Iran.

■ Vichy announced the execution of 70 hostages in Bordeaux in reprisal for acts of sabotage, bringing the number to 186 for the week.

Sept. 23 Incredibly stiff Russian resistance slowed the Germans to a virtual halt at Stalingrad.

■ U.S. Marines at Guadalcanal began clearing the Japanese from all positions from which they could attack Henderson Field.

233

■ East African forces entered Tananarive, which had been declared an open city.

■ Wendell Willkie, a personal representative of Roosevelt, conferred with Stalin at the Kremlin.

■ Marshal Antonescu was given absolute authority to rule in Rumania: "The 1936 Constitution is but a reflection of the regime that was overthrown. The present Government, therefore, has empowered Marshal Antonescu to create general constitutional laws, at the same time the law creator is above the law."

Sept. 24 Benghazi was attacked by British bombers.

SOVIET WOMEN IN COMBAT

Olga Yamschchikova of the Red Air Force shot down a Ju-88 twin-engine German bomber over Stalingrad on Sept. 24, 1942. She became the first woman night fighter pilot to score an aerial victory. While many nations are still debating whether women can perform combat functions, the Soviets proved how effective they can be during World War II. Miss Yamschchikova was a member of an all-woman unit, the 586th Fighter Aviation Regiment of the 122nd Air Division which saw action from Stalingrad through the end of the war. During that period, the women pilots flew 4,419 combat missions and were credited with having downed 38 enemy aircraft.

Sept. 25 Australian forces went on the offensive in New Guinea, pushing the Japanese back along the Kokoda trail.

■ Britain announced it had placed Madagascar under military jurisdiction "in order to ensure law and order and to provide for the administration pending the establishment of a friendly regime." Two East African brigades linked up in the central part of the island.

Sept. 26 Stalin called for a British-U.S. second front in western Europe as soon as possible.

Sept. 27 Japanese forces began a full retreat from Ioribaiwa in New Guinea.

■ U.S. Marines were hurled back in four separate attempts to secure better positions on Guadalcanal.

■ Japan's new foreign minister, Masayuki Tani, vowed to continue a policy of nonaggression toward the Soviet Union.

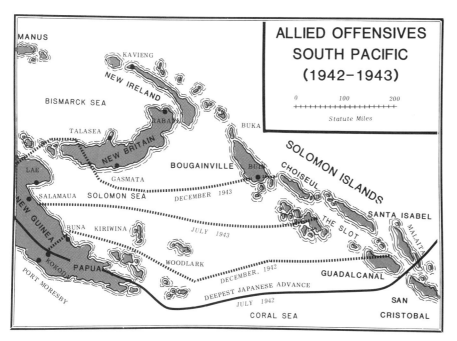

ALLIED OFFENSIVES SOUTH PACIFIC (1942–1943)

With the U.S. landing on Guadalcanal, the Allies turned to the offensive after months of whirlwind advances by the Japanese. The South Pacific turnaround was slow and costly to both sides.

Photographed from the battleship Tirpitz, *the heavy cruiser* Admiral Hipper, *pocket battleship* Admiral Scheer, *and escorting destroyers of the German fleet leave their Norwegian fjord base.*

Sept. 28 The main force of the U.S. 32nd Infantry Division reached Port Moresby and was ordered to join the drive on Wairopi.

Sept. 29 Americans of the three Eagle Squadrons of the RAF were transferred to U.S. command.

■ A small South African force landed on the southwest coast of Madagascar while East African troops struck out of Tananarive to the south.

■ Chinese troops inflicted heavy losses on Japanese units attacking from Kinhwa.

Sept. 30 Turkey signed a trade agreement with Germany, exchanging chrome for armaments.

■ Hitler vowed that Stalingrad would be taken. He publicly ridiculed U.S.-British military leaders planning a second front in western Europe: "If I had an opponent of stature, of military stature, then I could calculate pretty closely where he would attack. But when one faces military idiots, one cannot know, one cannot know where they will attack. It may be the craziest sort of undertaking, and that is one unpleasant thing—the fact that in the case of these mentally sick or perpetually drunk persons one never knows what they are really up to."

Oct. The German offensive in Russia bogged down during this month. Its forces were suffering extremely heavy casualties and fuel shortages were becoming critical. The Red Army was also fighting valiantly at Stalingrad and around the vital Grozny oil fields, but suffering incredible casualties.

Oct. 1 The first U.S. jet plane, a Bell XP-59, was flown at Muroc, in the Mojave Desert of California.

Oct. 2 The 81,235-ton *Queen Mary* knifed through its sole escort ship, the British cruiser *Curaçao*, 20 miles off the Irish coast in perfect weather. The *Queen Mary* was carrying 10,000 U.S. troops to Britain at a speed of 28½ knots on a zigzag course. It made a turn to maintain such a course and, incredibly, did not communicate to the *Curaçao*. The cruiser was sliced in two, her halves separated by 100 yards after the *Queen Mary*'s high speed maneuver. A total of 338 men aboard the curiser were killed and 101 were saved, no thanks to the *Queen Mary* which feared U-boats in the area and never so much as paused to find out what happened. (A court decision in 1947 held the *Curaçao* at fault for failing, as an escort, to stay clear of the ship overtaking it.)

Oct. 3 Stalin, in a written response to the Associated Press, said Allied aid to the Soviet Union had been of little military value compared to the impact the Russians were having in drawing to themselves the main German forces. "In order to amplify and improve this aid," said Stalin, "one thing is required: that the Allies fulfill their obligations fully and on time."

■ The Germans captured Elkhotovo in the Caucasus, only seven miles from Drag Kokh.

■ U.S. troops occupied the Andreanof Islands in the Aleutians.

Oct. 4 Göring declared that the people of the occupied territories, not the Germans, would suffer from the Allied naval blockade. He said, "The German people come before all other peoples for food."

■ A small British force raided Sark Island in the English Channel.

Oct. 5 U.S. planes in the Aleutians bombed Japanese installations on Kiska Island.

Oct. 6 Montgomery issued orders for a major offensive directed at El Alamein.

■ The city of Malgobek, in the oil producing region of the Soviet Union, fell to the Germans.

■ The U.S. signed a second protocol with the Soviet Union which formalized a massive aid program to the Russians consisting of military equipment, munitions, and raw materials. Through July 1, 1943, the Russians were to receive 3.3 million tons of supplies.

Oct. 7 U.S. Marines launched a new offensive to extend the defense perimeter around Henderson Field on Guadalcanal.

■ Germany threatened to chain POW's captured at Dieppe

An American B-17 in a bombing run over Gizo Island in the Solomons.

■ Roosevelt pledged there would be no mass reprisals against former enemies after the war but "ringleaders responsible for the organized murder of thousands of innocent persons and the commission of atrocities which have violated every tenet of Christian faith" would receive just punishment. A war crimes commission would be established to investigate individual cases.

Oct. 8 The German High Command announced it would level Stalingrad by heavy artillery, thereby abandoning its policy of frontal assaults on the Russian city. According to Berlin, the decision was taken to avoid the "unnecessary sacrifice" of German soldiers.

■ Britain threatened to retaliate and place German POW's under chains if Germany carried out its threat to chain the Dieppe prisoners.

■ Chennault submitted a letter to Roosevelt asking for a significant increase in U.S. air power in China for eventual attacks on the Japanese homeland which he claimed would end the war.

Oct. 9 About 60 U.S. B-17 bombers launched the heaviest daylight raid of the war, attacking industrial targets at Lille, France. RAF and U.S. fighter protection was effective, with more than 100 German planes destroyed or damaged.

■ The U.S. renounced extraterritorial rights in China, the first nation to abandon the principle of special rights for foreigners living in China. A new treaty outlining new ties—without the humiliating abuse of sovereignty—was proposed to the Chinese.

■ Ethiopia joined the United Nations.

Oct. 10 The Soviet Presidium abolished the political commissar system in the Red Army. Henceforth military commanders were to be freed from the sometimes repressive measures of the commissars which adversely affected combat operations.

■ Attorney General Francis Biddle announced that 600,000 Italian citizens living in the U.S. would no longer be regarded as enemy aliens. Biddle said the action was the result of "the splendid showing the Italians in America have made in meeting the test [of loyalty]."

■ Mass strikes and demonstrations marked Gandhi's birthday in India.

Oct. 11–12 The midnight Battle of Cape Esperance in the Solomons ended in a victory for U.S. naval forces against the Japanese. The heavy cruiser *Furutaka* and three destroyers were sunk,

while the heavy cruiser *Aoba* was seriously damaged. (The force commander, Rear Admiral Aritomo Goto, aboard *Aoba*, was killed.) One U.S. destroyer, the *Duncan*, was lost. With these additional losses, the Japanese were hard pressed to block further reinforcement of U.S. forces on Guadalcanal.

Oct. 12 Roosevelt recommended the induction of 18- and 19-year-old men into the U.S. military.

Oct. 13–14 Japanese naval and air units unleashed heavy attacks on Guadalcanal. The battleships *Kongo* and *Haruna* bombarded U.S. positions on the island for 90 minutes with 16-inch guns and inflicted great damage. Henderson Field was knocked out temporarily. Only 42 aircraft were left operational, and aviation fuel was down to critical levels.

Oct. 13 A regiment of the America Division reached Guadalcanal, the first U.S. Army unit to reach the island.

Oct. 14 Hitler ordered a temporary halt in offensive operations on the Russian front.

■ Moscow called for the immediate trial and punishment of Rudolf Hess and all other German leaders already in Allied custody.

Oct. 15 Japanese reinforcements (about 4,000 men) landed at Tassafaronga Point on Guadalcanal. U.S. supplies also reached the island, mostly aboard transport planes.

■ American planes bombed Lashio, Burma.

Oct. 16 Thirty-two U.S. aircraft landed at Guadalcanal, giving the Marines a total of 66.

■ A cyclone in the Bay of Bengal killed about 40,000 people, most of them in the area south of Calcutta. The destructive force severely crippled transportation and logistics for the Burma front.

■ U.S. submarines began mining the Gulf of Siam, on the approaches to Bangkok.

Oct. 17 Stiff fighting developed at Eora Creek along the Kokoda trail. Japanese reinforcements were sent in to stop the Australian advance.

■ Ships for the North African invasion forces began being assembled at the Firth of Clyde.

Oct. 18 Hitler ordered the execution of all British Commandos taken prisoner.

Oct. 19 Washington agreed to train and equip another 30 Chinese divisions.

■ British East African troops overcame French resistance and continued their southward drive on Madagascar.

■ Laval told French laborers they might be called upon to work in Germany.

Oct. 20 Allied aircraft began a four-day operation to establish air superiority over El Alamein, a requirement for the planned ground offensive.

■ German forces were repulsed in a massive attack on Stalingrad.

■ The cabinet of Chile resigned after widespread agitation against what most Chileans considered a pro-Axis government policy.

Oct. 21 Roosevelt signed a $9 billion tax bill, the largest in U.S. history.

Oct. 22 Australian forces landed on Goodenough Island off New Guinea to secure the northeast coast. A Japanese force of 353 men had been stranded on Goodenough since Aug. 25.

■ Britain lowered its draft age to 18.

■ U.S. General Mark Clark arrived in Algiers by submarine for a secret meeting with pro-Allied French officers to facilitate the forthcoming North African invasion. The first of the cargo ships left British ports.

■ President Juan Antonio Rios of Chile announced a policy aligning the country in the pro-Allied hemispheric alliance.

Oct. 23 The desert war reached a turnaround point with the beginning of the second battle of El Alamein. More than a thousand British guns pounded the Axis batteries for 20 minutes before XXX Corps began its drive on the northern end of the battle line.

The architects of the British victory in the Western Desert, General Bernard Montgomery and Air Vice Marshal Arthur Coningham.

■ Genoa and Turin were bombed by the RAF.

■ Japanese forces attempted to cross the Mataniko River on Guadalcanal. After an intense artillery barrage (the heaviest in the fighting) the Japanese scored some initial success but lost an estimated 600 men. The Marines suffered 25 dead.

■ Radio Berlin announced that Britain would not be a member of the postwar "European Charter" because "she had estranged herself from Europe more and more under Churchill's regime."

■ Admiral Darlan arrived in Rabat, Morocco, and called for unity and defense of the Vichy-controlled area.

■ U.S. forces sailed from Hampton Roads, Virginia, for the invasion of North Africa.

■ Mrs. Eleanor Roosevelt arrived in London as a guest of King George VI and Queen Elizabeth.

Oct. 24 Four British Commonwealth divisions broke into the Axis defenses at El Alamein, but failed to penetrate as far as planned.

■ RAF Lancasters raided Milan in the first daylight raid on Italy from British bases. The planes covered 2,800 miles.

■ Roosevelt personally directed the emergency dispatch of reinforcements to Guadalcanal.

■ Vice Admiral William F. Halsey assumed command of U.S. naval forces in the South Pacific, succeeding Vice Admiral Robert L. Ghormley.

Oct. 25 German counterattacks at El Alamein were turned back as Montgomery continued pressing his own local attacks.

Oct. 26 In still another attempt to control the area around Guadalcanal, the Japanese engaged an American naval force in the battle of Santa Cruz Islands. Although the U.S. carrier *Hornet* and destroyer *Porter* were sunk, the outcome gave the U.S. more time to reinforce Guadalcanal. The loss of 100 Japanese aircraft further impaired their defenses. It was the last time carrier-based aircraft were used by the Japanese in the Guadalcanal campaign.

A Japanese torpedo bomber passes over U.S. ships while searching for a target in the Battle of Santa Cruz.

Japanese torpedo planes and dive bombers attack the already fatally crippled U.S. carrier Hornet *in the Battle of Santa Cruz.*

Heavy flak fills the sky over U.S. ships undergoing Japanese aerial attacks in the Battle of Santa Cruz.

■ Only 29 U.S. planes were left in operation on Guadalcanal.

■ Japanese planes bombed British bases in Bengal and Assam, disrupting efforts to resupply forces in Burma.

■ Small gains were made by the Eighth Army at El Alamein. RAF planes made German counter-action difficult.

■ Troop convoys for the North African invasion left British ports.

Oct. 27–28 RAF aircraft scored successes in routing concentrations of German armor south of El Alamein. German counterattacks were turned back.

Oct. 28 The "Tokyo Express," the American name for the Japanese resupply effort, began

Abandoned German vehicles litter the Egyptian desert as British Eighth Army troops advance westward.

landing troops on Guadalcanal from Kokumbona to Cape Esperance.

Oct. 29 Knowing Axis plans through Ultra intercepts, Montgomery changed his offensive plans and decided to direct his next attack to the south against the Italians rather than hit the newly reinforced Germans astride the coastal roads. Australian forces held the Germans in a counterattack on the northern flank.

■ Because of heavy losses, the Japanese began pulling back to Koli Point and Kokumbona on Guadalcanal.

■ Attu Island in the Aleutians was reoccupied by the Japanese.

■ The Alaska Military Highway was opened.

Oct. 30 U.S. Army Chief of Staff General Marshall disclosed that 800,000 Americans were in service overseas.

Oct. 30–31 The British Eighth Army launched a major attack, trapping large numbers of Axis troops when the Australian 9th Division reached the sea. (Most of the Germans later escaped when armor reopened a line along the east-west route.)

Oct. 31 Canterbury was bombed by German planes.

Nov. 1 The Russian Sixty-second and Sixty-fourth armies withstood the most deadly attacks on Stalingrad and continued to hold their ground. German efforts to take the Grozny oil fields were repulsed by the Russians.

■ By German count, 5,150,000 Russians had been taken prisoner since the invasion was launched 16 months before. There were only the roughest estimates of killed and disabled, but the Red Army had suffered near incomprehensible losses. Still, from the point of view of the German High Command, the Russian casualties were submerged by the fact that the Soviets were not defeated and were somehow continuing to resist.

■ U.S. Marines staged a new push to drive the Japanese back to Poha River on Guadalcanal.

Nov. 2 The British massed their strength and launched Operation SUPERCHARGE against Axis positions. It was intended to be the decisive break through Rommel's positions at El Alamein. New Zealand's 2nd Division led the attack, and the 9th Armored Brigade poured through the corridor.

■ Japanese reinforcements arrived on Guadalcanal. Fifteen hundred more men were landed east of Koli Point with instructions to build an airfield. At Point Cruz, U.S. Marines trapped a Japanese force. Army and Marine 155-mm artillery units arrived at Lunga Point.

■ Australian troops seized Kokoda and its airfield on New Guinea, permitting resupply in the difficult area.

Nov. 3 The British 9th Armored Brigade maintained a bridgehead west of the German mine fields at El Alamein although suffering 75 percent casualties. Tanks of X Corps began moving through the corridor, but were immediately stopped by strong German resistance. Montgomery began deploying forces to outflank the Germans. Some German units were already starting to retreat.

Nov. 4 Rommel's forces were in full retreat from El Alamein. The British delayed in their pursuit, however, but the Germans and Italians were subjected to intense air attacks.

■ The 8th Marine Regiment was landed at Aola Bay on Guadalcanal to construct an airfield, but no suitable site could be found.

■ Australian forces faced stiff resistance at Oivi on New Guinea.

■ Madagascar's governor general again sought peace terms.

Nov. 5 Montgomery announced that British forces had won a complete and absolute victory in Egypt and that the German Afrika Korps was in full retreat. General Ritter von Thoma, Rommel's second in command, was captured. A total of 10,000 Germans and 20,000 Italians were taken prisoner. About 450 Axis tanks and 1,000 heavy guns were destroyed or captured. The Eighth Army broke through the Axis fall-back defense line at Fuka.

■ Fighting ended on Madagascar at 2 P.M.

■ Eisenhower established headquarters on Gibraltar for the North African invasion.

■ The State Department ordered a ban on all U.S. food shipments to the French West Indies, which was still controlled by Vichy France.

■ General Giraud, who escaped from the Germans, was picked up on the French coast by the British submarine *Seraph*.

Nov. 6 MacArthur arrived at Port Moresby to direct New Guinea operations.

■ Heavy rains slowed down the British in their pursuit of the retreating Axis forces in Egypt.

For the first time in weeks the fighting at Stalingrad began to slow down.

Stalin again deplored the lack of a second front. He said the Russians were facing 240 Axis divisions (179 German, 22 Rumanian, 14 Finnish, 13 Hungarian, 10 Italian, one Slovak, and one Spanish) while the Allied forces were facing only 15 German and Italian divisions in North Africa.

Nov. 7 Four German and eight Italian divisions were effectively smashed on the five days of fighting in Egypt. The British had captured 30,000 men, including nine generals.

■ Giraud arrived at Gibraltar from France to meet with Eisenhower and his staff on the North African invasion.

■ A U.S. troop transport on its way to North

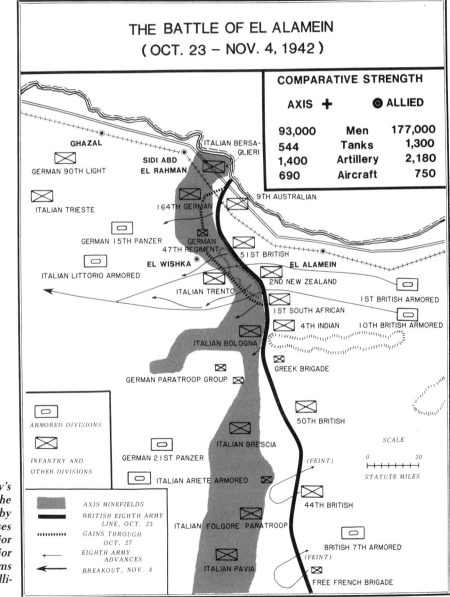

General Montgomery's Eighth Army turned the tide in North Africa by breaching the Axis defenses at El Alamein. The major victory was due to superior numbers of men and arms and skilled use of intelligence.

THE BATTLE OF EL ALAMEIN
(OCT. 23 – NOV. 4, 1942)

COMPARATIVE STRENGTH

AXIS +		⊙ ALLIED
93,000	Men	177,000
544	Tanks	1,300
1,400	Artillery	2,180
690	Aircraft	750

GHAZAL
ITALIAN BERSAGLIERI
GERMAN 90TH LIGHT
SIDI ABD EL RAHMAN
ITALIAN TRIESTE
164TH GERMAN
9TH AUSTRALIAN
GERMAN 15TH PANZER
GERMAN 47TH REGIMENT
EL WISHKA
51ST BRITISH
ITALIAN LITTORIO ARMORED
EL ALAMEIN
ITALIAN TRENTO
2ND NEW ZEALAND
1ST BRITISH ARMORED
1ST SOUTH AFRICAN
4TH INDIAN
10TH BRITISH ARMORED
ITALIAN BOLOGNA
GREEK BRIGADE
GERMAN PARATROOP GROUP
50TH BRITISH

ARMORED DIVISIONS

INFANTRY AND OTHER DIVISIONS
GERMAN 21ST PANZER
ITALIAN BRESCIA
ITALIAN ARIETE ARMORED
(FEINT)
44TH BRITISH
ITALIAN FOLGORE PARATROOP
BRITISH 7TH ARMORED
(FEINT)
ITALIAN PAVIA
FREE FRENCH BRIGADE

SCALE
0   20
STATUTE MILES

AXIS MINEFIELDS
BRITISH EIGHTH ARMY LINE, OCT. 23
GAINS THROUGH OCT. 27
EIGHTH ARMY ADVANCES
BREAKOUT, NOV. 4

Africa, the *Thomas Stone*, was torpedoed off the southeast coast of Spain. It stayed afloat and the troops were taken aboard landing craft.

Nov. 8 Allied forces landed on the Algerian and Moroccan coasts, with Casablanca, Algiers, and Oran as their main objectives. Strategically, the decision was based on the need to deny Germany control of the west coast of Africa and to give the Allies a base for eventual operations against southern Europe. Algiers was taken by nightfall. French resistance at Oran was stiff. One force destined for Casablanca lost 64 percent of its landing ships (242 boats) but managed to establish a solid beachhead. General de Gaulle called on all Frenchmen in North Africa to aid the Allies: "Our Algeria, our Morocco, our Tunisia, are to be made the jumping-off ground for the liberation of France." A joint U.S.-British declaration said the North African action was only a first step in the ouster of Germany from France: "The hour of national uprising has not sounded. We have already promised you that we will warn you when this hour shall have come. Today, that moment is closer." Vichy France broke off diplomatic relations with the U.S. Pétain told Roosevelt: "It is with stupor and sadness that I learned tonight of the aggression of your troops against North Africa. . . . France and her honor are at stake. We are attacked; we shall defend ourselves; this is the order I am giving."

FIREWORKS AT WAR

Among the weapons carried ashore by the U.S. Regimental Combat Team in the landing at Oran in the North African campaign were mortars which fired Fourth of July-like fireworks.

Egg-shaped bombs were shot about 200 feet into the air where they exploded into a pyrotechnic display of the Stars and Stripes, a hundred feet wide.

The reason was strictly identification. Americans were assumed to be more welcome by the French than the British (and since the British had only recently bombed the French fleet in Oran, it was a fair assumption) and quick recognition by the French that Americans were coming ashore was important. At the same time, GI's carried loudspeakers for the French-speakers among them. They shouted, "Ne tirez pas! Vive la France!" under the fireworks displays which covered the landing beach.

■ Hitler stated he still intended German forces to take Stalingrad despite the staggering losses. He said the city was of immense strategic value: "There, 30 million tons of traffic (on the Volga) can be cut off, including 9 million of oil shipments. There, all the wheat pours in from those

The French battleship Jean Bart *in Casablanca after an air attack during the Allied invasion of North Africa.*

enormous territories of the Ukraine, of the Kuban territory, there to be transported to the north. There, the manganese ore was forwarded. A gigantic terminal was there. I wanted to take it."

Nov. 9 Forces attempting to outflank Oran encountered heavy French resistance, but the airport at La Senia was captured. In Morocco the French fought bitterly to deny Port Lyautey (Kenitra) to the Allies.

■ Germany invaded Tunisia. Forces were landed by air at Tunis. There was no French opposition.

■ Clear weather brought a renewal of the British offensive in Egypt.

■ U.S. Marines surrounded a Japanese force at Gavaga Creek on Guadalcanal.

Nov. 10 German forces began pulling out of Sidi Barrani as the British broke through the Halfaya Pass.

■ Commenting on British successes in Egypt, Churchill said, "This is not the end. It is not even the beginning of the end. But it is, perhaps, the end of the beginning." During the same speech at the Mansion House, Churchill also declared, "I have not become the King's First Minister to preside over the liquidation of the British Empire."

■ Admiral Darlan in Algiers called on all French forces in North Africa to lay down their arms.

■ U.S. troops entered Oran. Port Lyautey was occupied.

■ Vichy Premier Laval met in conference with Hitler and Mussolini on the new situation growing out of the Allied landings in North Africa.

■ Oivi in New Guinea was cleared of Japanese forces.

■ The approaches to New York harbor were mined by a German U-boat. Ten mines were planted about five miles east of Ambrose Light. (Some were discovered three days later, and all traffic in and out of New York was halted for 48 hours while the channel was swept. Only five of the mines were located.)

Nov. 11 German troops marched into all the unoccupied areas of France except the Mediterranean coast. Hitler informed Pétain that Germany could no longer preserve the armistice and that all measures had to be taken to "arrest the continuation of the Anglo-British aggression,"

and to "protect France." Pétain responded by protesting the German action, saying it was "incompatible" with the armistice agreement. Vichy created an autonomous defense zone around the Toulon naval base, which contained the main units of the French fleet.

■ All French resistance in North Africa ended at 7 A.M.

■ Casablanca was occupied by the Allies. A British brigade was landed at Bougie (Bejaïa), 110 miles east of Algiers.

■ Bardia in Libya was seized by the British Eighth Army after all Axis forces were ousted from Egypt.

■ Churchill used the term "soft underbelly of the Axis" in a report on the war situation in the House of Commons. It was the first reference by Churchill to an attack through the Balkans, which he considered vulnerable and a politically advantageous area of operations.

Nov. 12–15 In a major naval engagement off Guadalcanal, Japanese and American ships inflicted severe losses on each other. The U.S. cruisers *Atlanta* and *Juneau* and seven destroyers were sunk, while the Japanese lost the battleships *Hiei* and *Kirishima*, three destroyers and 11 transports. With their losses the Japanese could no longer effectively resupply units on Guadalcanal. The garrison there was now virtually isolated. What had been a statemate now turned into an American victory.

Nov. 12 The British First Army occupied Bône (Annaba), 260 miles east of Algiers.

■ Japanese forces were withdrawn across the Kumusi River in New Guinea. U.S. 32nd Division troops reached Bofu and Pongani and moved toward Natunga.

■ U.S. Marines closed the Gavaga Creek pocket on Guadalcanal, having killed 450 Japanese. American reinforcements began pouring in from New Caledonia and New Hebrides. Six thousand men were landed, including Army Americal Division troops.

Nov. 13 British troops reached Tobruk.

■ Eisenhower flew to Algiers and met with Darlan.

Nov. 15 Four Japanese transports which survived the Guadalcanal battle were sunk off Tassafaronga Point on Guadalcanal and all the supplies they had unloaded were destroyed on the beach.

■ Five Sullivan brothers were killed when the cruiser *Juneau* was sunk off Guadalcanal. They had enlisted together in Waterloo, Iowa, only eleven months before. *The Sullivans*, a destroyer, was named in their honor in April, 1943.

■ British troops reached Tunisia at Takarka, 80 miles west of Tunis.

Nov. 16 Darlan assumed the position of protector of French interests in North Africa, and he appointed Giraud as commander of French forces in the area. The moves were denounced by Pétain, who stripped Darlan of his Vichy posts, and by de Gaulle, who disassociated the Free French from Darlan.

■ The British pushed out in Tunisia. First actions in Tunisia were reported by French forces encountering German units.

■ Australian and U.S. forces trying to seize the Buna-Gona beachhead on New Guinea were hard hit by Japanese forces.

Nov. 17 The British 78th Division met with German resistance 70 miles west of Tunis, the first encounter in Tunisia.

Nov. 19 Premier Laval was given total authority in Vichy France, including the power to make laws and issue decrees on his signature alone. Pétain granted Laval the extraordinary powers "to deal speedily at any hour and in all places with the difficulties through which France is passing."

■ The British entered Cyrene (Shahat) in Libya.

■ Germans went on the offensive in Tunisia, but were turned back at Djebel Abiod by the British and by the French at Medjez el Bab.

Nov. 19 The winter offensive was launched by Russian forces, with relief of the Stalingrad defenders as the immediate objective. With the temperature minus 30° centigrade artillery boomed across the Don front for nearly eight hours before 60 Red Army divisions went on the attack. The Rumanian Third and Fourth armies bore the brunt of the assault and soon retreated in full flight. Only the intervention of the German 22nd Panzer Division saved the Rumanians from annihilation.

■ French forces refused to surrender Medjez el Bab in Tunisia. The XIX Corps under General Georges Barré withstood heavy German artillery and air assaults.

■ A 34-man Norwegian-British sabotage team tried but failed to land in Norway to destroy the Norsk Hydro heavy-water facility at Vemork. Some were killed when their glider crashed. Sur-

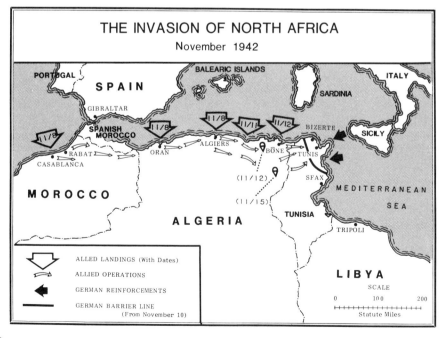

THE INVASION OF NORTH AFRICA
November 1942

PORTUGAL · SPAIN · BALEARIC ISLANDS · ITALY · SARDINIA · GIBRALTAR · SPANISH MOROCCO · BIZERTE · SICILY · RABAT · ORAN · ALGIERS · BONE · TUNIS · CASABLANCA · (11/12) · SFAX · MOROCCO · MEDITERRANEAN SEA · ALGERIA · (11/15) · TUNISIA · TRIPOLI · LIBYA

SCALE
0   100   200
Statute Miles

ALLED LANDINGS (With Dates)
ALLIED OPERATIONS
GERMAN REINFORCEMENTS
GERMAN BARRIER LINE
(From November 10)

The Axis was caught by surprise when Allied forces launched their invasion of North Africa with ground, naval, and air assaults.

vivors were executed after being captured along the Norwegian coast.

Nov. 20 Soviet forces forged through German positions south of Stalingrad.

■ Benghazi was captured by the British.

■ Medjez el Bab in Tunisia was evacuated by the Allies.

■ Turin was bombed by the RAF in the most devastating raid on Italy of the war.

■ Laval vowed to collaborate even more closely with Germany. He said Britain and the U.S. were "tearing France limb from limb. . . . The entente with Germany is the sole guarantee of peace in Europe." Darlan repeated his commitment to the Allies in a radio broadcast to all French: "I confirm to you my previous orders to fight at the side of the American and Allied forces for defense and liberation of our territories and integral restoration of French sovereignty."

Nov. 21 Tripoli harbor was bombed by U.S. B-24s operating out of Gambut in Libya.

Nov. 22 Soviet forces scored major breakthroughs in their counteroffensive in the Stalingrad area. The German Sixth Army (270,000 men) was surrounded as Red Army units from the Don and Stalingrad fronts linked up at Kalach, 50 miles west of Stalingrad.

Nov. 23 Hitler issued orders for the German forces at Stalingrad to "dig in and await relief."

■ Allied forces occupied Dakar in Senegal without opposition.

■ Secretary of State Hull said U.S. troops would not be needed to occupy Martinique or other French possessions in the West Indies because of an agreement concluded with local French authorities.

■ A total of 84 U.S. and New Zealand planes were now operating on Guadalcanal.

■ The U.S. Women's Coast Guard Reserve (SPARS) was established. (SPARS stood for Semper PARatus—always prepared—the motto of the U.S. Coast Guard.)

Nov. 24 Russian forces made further gains around Stalingrad. On the central front the Red Army went on the offensive near Velikiye Luki and Rzhev.

■ The British First Army was ordered to advance on Tunis.

■ Australian troops were turned back in an effort to take Buna on New Guinea.

Nov. 25 Medjez el Bab in Tunisia was recaptured by the Allies.

■ A stalemate developed on New Guinea.

Nov. 26 British forces pressed forward toward Tunis with an armored battle south of Mateur.

Nov. 27 Hitler dissolved the Vichy army, citing what he called the "betrayal" of French officers who elected to fight with the Allies in Tunisia. He told Pétain he could no longer "trust French admirals and generals."

■ Germans occupied Toulon, and the French immediately scuttled the navy ships harbored there under orders from Vichy.

■ British troops advanced to within 20 miles of Tunis.

Nov. 28 British and U.S. troops reached a point 15 miles from Tunis.

■ A third of the French garrison at Vichy-

German infantrymen move into Stalingrad under cover of mortar fire.

controlled Djibouti in French Somaliland crossed into British Somaliland and declared for the Allies.

■ The Vichy admiralty said the scuttling of the French fleet at Toulon was taken "in accordance with the standing instruction dating from the time of the Franco-German armistice, which had ordered the fleet to scuttle rather than be taken over by a foreign power." According to Vichy, when it was informed of the German decision to occupy Toulon it tried unsuccessfully to order naval authorities there not to adhere to the armistice terms.

■ Red Army units scored advances near Velikiye Luki and Rzhev.

Nov. 29 Red Army troops went on the offensive in the Caucasus, attacking the Terek bridgehead.

■ British paratroopers failed to take the airfield at Ovnda, south of Tunis, denying the Allies that approach to the city. Allied forces to the west were also stalled.

■ Churchill declared that northern Italian cities were being subjected to greater aerial bombardment than Britain was in 1940. He said 300,000 Italians, including 100 generals, were being held as prisoners by the Allies.

Nov. 30 A major naval battle off Tassafaronga Point developed when nine U.S. ships intercepted eight Japanese destroyers heading to Guadalcanal with reinforcements. The Japanese displayed masterful night-fighting tactics and their torpedoes struck and sank the cruiser *Northampton* and crippled the cruisers *New*

Orleans and *Minneapolis*, while losing one destroyer. The Japanese won a major tactical victory but no reinforcements were landed.

■ Tunisian action turned against the Allies, with 15,500 Axis troops fighting desperate battles to avoid being thrown into the sea.

TROOP STRENGTH ON GUADALCANAL (1942)

	Japanese	U.S.
Aug. 7	2,200	10,000
Aug. 20	3,600	10,000
Sept. 10	6,000	11,000
Oct. 23	22,000	23,000
Nov. 12	30,000	29,000
Dec. 9	25,000	40,000

Dec. 1 Darlan assumed leadership of the Imperial Council of France, saying Pétain was no longer able to exercise any power because of his virtual prisoner status under the Germans.

■ Ethiopia declared war on Germany, Italy, and Japan.

Dec. 2 The first nuclear chain reaction (fission of uranium isotope U-235) was achieved at an abandoned football stadium on the campus of the University of Chicago. Under the direction of physicists Arthur Compton and Enrico Fermi, an antifascist Italian who had fled his native country, the United States had produced the scientific breakthrough for the creation of an atomic bomb.

■ A Japanese force of 800 men was landed north of Gona in New Guinea.

■ Mussolini reported on Italian casualties in the 30 months of war:

	Army	Navy	Air Force	Total
Killed in action	36,619	2,178	1,422	40,219
Wounded	30,745	3,599	1,620	35,964
Prisoners	215,512	12,284	5,982	233,778
Missing	25,923	10,390	2,200	38,513

Red Army troops advance to the bank of the Don River in the first phase of the Soviet counteroffensive.

Allied prisoners of war held by the Italians were listed by Mussolini:

	British	Other Allied	Total
Generals	21	8	29
Other Officers	2,441	1,782	4,223
Enlisted	39,089	30,088	69,177

Dec. 3 U.S. and French forces captured the Faid Pass south of Tunis.

■ Russian troops broke through German positions west of Rzhev.

Dec. 4 The British were forced to evacuate Tebourba in Tunisia after suffering heavy losses.

■ B-24s attacked Naples harbor, the first American air attack on Italy.

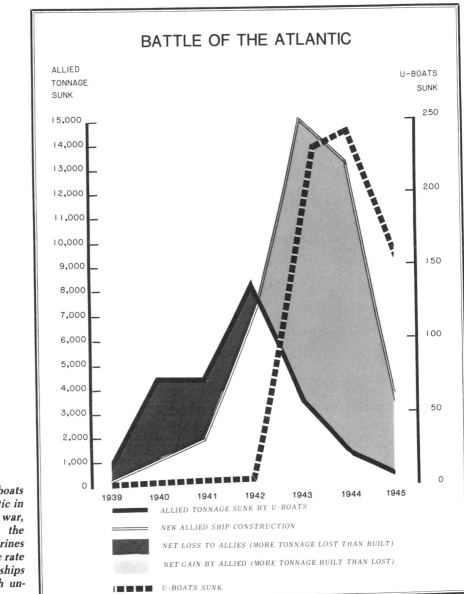

BATTLE OF THE ATLANTIC

ALLIED TONNAGE SUNK

U-BOATS SUNK

ALLIED TONNAGE SUNK BY U-BOATS

NEW ALLIED SHIP CONSTRUCTION

NET LOSS TO ALLIES (MORE TONNAGE LOST THAN BUILT)

NET GAIN BY ALLIED (MORE TONNAGE BUILT THAN LOST)

U-BOATS SUNK

While German U-boats commanded the Atlantic in the early years of the war, the battle swung to the Allies in 1943. Submarines were sunk at a dramtic rate while new Allied ships were constructed with unprecedented speed.

■ Carlson's Raiders completed a month's trek from Aola Bay to Lunga Point on Guadalcanal, losing 17 Marines while accounting for 400 Japanese dead.

Dec. 5 Allied forces reached Buna on New Guinea but suffered heavy losses in the actual fighting and to heat prostration and malaria.

■ The German hospital ship *Graz* was torpedoed and sunk off the Libyan coast.

Dec. 6 Germans attacked U.S. positions at El Guessa in Tunisia.

■ Queen Wilhelmina promised domestic autonomy within the Dutch Commonwealth to the Indonesians after the war.

Dec. 7 British Marine Commandos used canoes to attack the Gironde River estuary in France.

Dec. 8 The British First Army was given permission to withdraw to better defense positions and regroup for a resumption of the offensive in Tunisia.

■ Allied planes turned back a Japanese convoy from Rabaul attempting to reinforce positions on New Guinea.

■ U.S. Navy PT boats intercepted Japanese destroyers attempting to resupply Guadalcanal and turned them back.

Dec. 9 Australian forces captured Gona on New Guinea in brutal hand-to-hand fighting.

Dec. 10 The Fourth Panzer Army, with the aid of seven German divisions drawn from the Caucasus and Orel fronts, began an offensive to relieve the Germans trapped around Stalingrad.

■ A German tank attack was turned back at Medjez el Bab in Tunisia.

■ London announced that Axis POW's would be unchained in 48 hours.

■ General Kurt Zeitzler was named chief of staff of the German army.

Dec. 11 Russian forces made small gains around Stalingrad. Heavy pressure was applied by the Red Army along the entire front, plus holding off the German counterattacks.

■ Another German attack at Medjez el Bab was repulsed.

■ U.S. forces began arriving in Iran and Iraq.

Dec. 12 Hitler refused to permit a withdrawal of the Sixth Army at Stalingrad, saying such a move would destroy "the whole meaning of the campaign."

■ British Commandos attached limpet mines to merchant ships in Bordeaux harbor.

■ The Japanese navy recommended that Guadalcanal be evacuated because of heavy shipping losses incurred in bringing in reinforcements and supplies.

Dec. 13 Panzer Army Africa forces withdrew from El Agheila in Libya.

■ Dutch Nazi Anton Mussert was appointed führer in the Netherlands, although supreme authority continued to be held by Seyss-Inquart, chief of German occupation.

Dec. 14 British and New Zealand troops pursued German forces fleeing to the west in Libya.

■ The Fourth Panzer Army made headway in its efforts to reach Stalingrad.

■ Japanese reinforcements (800 men) were landed at the mouth of the Mambare River in New Guinea.

■ Free French and British authorities agreed on a plan to turn over control of Madagascar to Gaullist officials.

Dec. 15 The 2nd New Zealand Division moved to outflank the retreating Germans in Libya.

Dec. 16 Russian forces advanced on the Don River front, inflicting heavy losses on the Italian Eighth Army which was forced to withdraw. An attempt to aid the trapped German Sixth Army was abandoned after the Fourth Panzer Army reached a point 40 miles from Stalingrad.

■ The 14th Indian Division launched an overland offensive to capture Akyab on the Arakan coast of Burma. Maungdaw was occupied immediately when it was found the Japanese had abandoned the city.

Dec. 17 Foreign Secretary Eden told the House of Commons that Germany was "now carrying into effect Hitler's oft-repeated intention to exterminate the Jewish people in Europe." He revealed Jews from the occupied nations were being sent to eastern Europe where they were "worked to death in labor camps" or "deliberately slaughtered in mass executions." It was the first public statement by any official on the campaign of genocide being waged against European Jewry.

■ Admiral Darlan declared that French ships in Dakar and other North African ports would join the Allied side: "French Africa, with the Allies, must make the maximum military effort for the defeat of Germany and Italy. . . ."

■ Russian units advanced to points 70 miles west of Stalingrad.

■ The U.N. announced that crimes against the Jews would be avenged.

■ Buthidaung in Burma was taken over by Indian troops.

Dec. 18 Heavy fighting broke out in New Guinea with U.S. and Australian forces launching tank-led attacks at several points.

Dec. 19 Red Army troops reached Kantemirovka on the Voronezh-Rostov rail line.

■ Australian troops gained ground at Sanananda Point on New Guinea.

Dec. 20 Spain and Portugal announced the creation of a neutral Iberian bloc.

■ An 8,000-ton Japanese cargo ship hit a U.S.-planted mine and sank off Cape Inubo, due east of Tokyo. It was the first Japanese ship lost in home waters after American submarines began mining the coast.

Dec. 21 British Eighth Army troops reached Sirte in Libya before halting.

Dec. 22 Soviet forces made new attacks in the Caucasus, striking southeast of Nalchik as the Germans started to pull back.

■ The British First Army renewed its drive for Tunis.

Dec. 23 Heavy rain curtailed action in Tunisia.

■ A stalemate developed at Sanananda Point on New Guinea.

■ Russian forces in the Don area continued advancing, having gained up to 103 miles in the past eight days.

Dec. 24 Darlan was assassinated by a French monarchist in Algiers. Giraud succeeded him as high commissioner of French Africa.

■ Eisenhower decided to abandon the attack for Tunis until the rainy season ended.

Dec. 26 More Allied troops and tanks were landed in New Guinea at Oro Bay.

■ Free French forces met no opposition in occupying French Somaliland. They secured the rail line from Djibouti to Addis Ababa.

By the winter of 1942 the Russians had regained their strength and began pushing back the German invaders. Progress was slow in brutal battles.

■ Soviet troops advanced to within 105 miles of Rostov.

Dec. 27 Indian forces reached the tip of Mayu peninsula in Burma. The drive for Akyab continued unopposed.

Dec. 28 Hitler approved the withdrawal of Army Group A from the Caucasus.

Dec. 29 Kotelnikovo, southwest of Stalingrad, was recaptured by the Russians.

Dec. 31 The Japanese decided to evacuate Guadalcanal and establish a new defense line in New Georgia.

■ An outnumbered Royal Navy force engaged the German pocket battleship *Lützow*, cruiser *Hipper*, and six destroyers while escorting a convoy to Russia. A British destroyer and minesweeper were sunk, but a German destroyer was lost and *Hipper* badly damaged. Hitler was infuriated by the outcome (which he learned about from a BBC broadcast). (It resulted in the resignation of Raeder as commander in chief of the German navy and almost led to the scrapping of Germany's larger ships, which Hitler originally ordered. Raeder's successor, Karl Dönitz, talked Hitler out of turning what was left of German naval power into scrap.)

■ Free French troops from Chad advanced into the southern Fezzan of Libya.

■ British civilian air raid casualties for the last five months were 743 killed and 986 wounded.

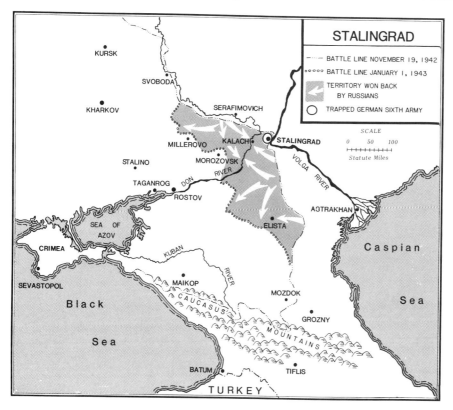

Stalingrad was the war's most critical battle. Hitler doggedly determined to take the city and paid an enormous price in men and weapons which would undermine his entire effort in the east.

(OPPOSITE, TOP) *A U.S. Navy SBD dive bomber circles Japanese-held Wake Island before dropping its half-ton weapon.*

(OPPOSITE, BOTTOM) *Lieutenant General George S. Patton, Jr., arrives ashore at Gela, Sicily, to take command of U.S. forces clearing the Italian island.*

1943

Allied forces on all fronts turn the tide of battle.

Jan. 1 Red Army troops continued to reduce the pocket in which the German Sixth Army was trapped around Stalingrad. The Germans were compressed into an area of only 25 by 40 miles. Air resupply efforts were far from sufficient. During the first part of January, the Luftwaffe never delivered more than 120 tons daily, less than a third of the Germans' minimum requirements.

■ The key rail center of Velikiye Luki, about 250 miles west of Moscow, was taken by the Russians. The town had been under German occupation since August 1941 and was strategically important in supplying forces involved in trying to take the Russian capital.

■ In order to avoid encirclement Kleist's Army Group A began falling back toward Rostov from the Caucasus, pursued by the Russian Thirty-ninth Army under General Ivan I. Maslennikov.

■ German U-boat operational strength reached 212, its peak of the war. They were assigned as follows:

Atlantic	164	Arctic	21
Mediterranean	24	Black Sea	3

■ A law limiting all Americans to a maximum annual salary of $25,000 went into effect. (It was repealed before the end of the year as a well-intentioned but impractical method of fighting inflation.)

Jan. 2 resistance ended at Buna in Papua. About 2,800 Japanese were killed in the campaign. U.S. and Australian casualties were 620 dead, 2,065 wounded, and 132 missing. The overland threat to Port Moresby was now ended, and Japan could no longer count on establishing a southern flank anchored on New Guinea or freely impeding Allied naval and air movements north of Australia.

Jan. 3 Red Army troops pursued the retreating German armies northward from the Caucasus, occupying Mozdok and Malgobek.

Jan. 5 Eighteen Allied nations signed a formal declaration which would have the effect of nullifying Axis plundering in occupied Europe. The governments reserved all rights to invalidate all transfers and dealings of properties, rights, and interests in all territories seized by Germany and Italy.

■ Morozovsk, the major German air base supplying Stalingrad, fell to the Russians.

Jan. 6 A stalemate developed on the Arakan front in Burma as the Japanese dug in at Donbaik and Rathedaung.

Jan. 8 General Konstantin K. Rokossovsky sent a surrender ultimatum to Paulus at Stalingrad.

Jan. 9 The puppet Chinese government in Nanking declared war on the U.S. and Britain.

■ Japan and the Nanking regime signed an agreement abolishing all extraterritorial rights in China and providing for the return of all concessions and settlements to Chinese control.

Jan. 10 Paulus refused to surrender, and Red Army forces launched the final offensive at Stalingrad, with seven armies of 281,000 men closing the ring around the trapped Germans.

■ The U.S. 25th Division began the final offensive to clear Guadalcanal.

Jan. 11 Great Britain and the U.S. signed treaties with the Nationalist Chinese. The western powers relinquished all extraterritorial rights in China.

■ Roosevelt submitted a budget of $100 billion to Congress.

■ Russian troops occupied large chunks of territory in the Caucasus evacuated by the Germans.

■ An offensive was launched by the Russians to relieve Leningrad. It was concentrated against positions held by the Hungarian Second Army and Italian and Rumanian forces.

Jan. 12 U.S. forces landed unopposed on Am-chitka Island in the Aleutians. Only 69 miles east of Japanese-held Kiska, the island gave the U.S. an advanced fighter base to begin offensive operations against Kiska and Attu.

■ German fighter protection within Stalingrad was lost when the Russians captured the airstrip at Pitomnik.

Jan. 14–23 Roosevelt, Churchill, and the Combined Chiefs of Staff met at Casablanca to plan future Allied strategy. The American Chiefs of Staff pushed for a 1943 cross-Channel attack, but Churchill argued for a more limited operation against Sicily, which was agreed upon in the end. The buildup for the invasion of France was to continue. Agreement was reached on a vigorous campaign in Burma and the opening of a land route into China. French problems were papered over as de Gaulle and Giraud formed a committee of liberation, which underscored the rivalries rather than cooperation. Roosevelt surprised almost everyone at the conference by enunciating a policy of unconditional surrender, which in the end probably prolonged the war by stiffening Axis resistance since there was no alternative except to fight to the end.

Roosevelt and Churchill pose with their top military advisers during the Casablanca strategy conference.

An 88-mm antiaircraft shell has just hit this B-26 bomber of the U.S. Twelfth Air Force, which was attacking Toulon in southern France.

Jan. 15 British forces began their drive to take Tripoli and assaulted the Buerat defense line. Little resistance was encountered.

■ Red Army troops crashed through the defenses of the Second Hungarian Army south of Voronezh, opening up a 175-mile gap in the Axis defenses.

■ Hitler ordered the Luftwaffe to airlift 300 tons of supplies daily to the Sixth Army at Stalingrad. (The impossible requirement was never attained, although German efforts were speeded up under the most adverse of conditions. For the two months the Sixth Army was under siege, Luftwaffe airlift deliveries averaged 94 tons daily.)

Jan. 16 The Buerat line was pierced by the British who penetrated main Axis positions all along the barrier.

■ Italian forces were routed by the Russians west of the Don as the Red Army launched a major offensive across the upper reaches of the river.

■ RAF bombers raided Berlin, the first attack on the German capital in more than two months.

■ Iraq declared war on Germany, Italy, and Japan.

Jan. 18 Moscow announced that the 900-day-long siege of Leningrad had been lifted. A corridor ten miles wide was opened south of Lake Ladoga. Leningrad's population was now dying at the rate of 20,000 a day. Had the city not been relieved, the rest of the winter would have been cataclysmic beyond imagination.

■ New Mark VI Tiger tanks were used by the Germans for the first time, in Tunisia. They were employed in a major counteroffensive to recover the approaches to Tunis. Colonel General Jürgen von Arnim assumed command of Axis forces in Tunisia.

■ Armed resistance took place for the first time in the Warsaw ghetto. The Jews began to fight back with the resumption of deportations, which they now realized meant certain death.

Jan. 19 Novgorod, south of Leningrad, was occupied by the Russian Fifty-ninth Army, forcing the German Army Group North to fall back or risk entrapment east of Lake Peipus (Chudskoye).

■ Red Army forces pressed forward in massive waves along the central and southern fronts. Valuyki and Kamensk were liberated.

■ Homs was occupied by the British in Libya.

■ The Japanese pulled out of Sanananda Point in New Guinea, but Australian and U.S. forces continued to face stubborn rear-guard resistance. Other Japanese units landed at Wewak, New Guinea.

Jan. 20 The Germans pressed their way down the Rebaa and Ousseltia valleys in Tunisia. Allied forces on the southern flank went to defensive positions.

■ With the German Sixth Army now destroyed or about to be captured, Russian forces began to move out from the Stalingrad front to the mouth of the Donets River.

■ Chile broke relations with the Axis nations.

Jan. 21 The U.S. 1st Armored Division began a drive to push the Germans out of the Ousseltia Valley of Tunisia.

■ Using Ultra intercept knowledge, Montgomery changed his plans and ordered the drive for Tripoli be directed along the coastal road rather than to the south.

■ Mopping up operations near Sanananda Point, New Guinea, left 500 Japanese dead.

Algiers illuminated by antiaircraft fire during a German air raid.

Jan. 22 Red Army forces launched an offensive to retake Voronezh. Paulus radioed Hitler from Stalingrad: "Rations exhausted. Over 12,000 wounded unattended in the pocket." Hitler responded: "Surrender is out of the question."

■ The British Eighth Army advanced to within 17 miles of Tripoli.

■ The Papuan campaign on New Guinea ended with the Allies scoring their first land victory against the Japanese. About 16,000 Japanese participated in the fight and at least 7,000 were killed. Australian casualties were about 5,700, U.S. 2,788. By clearing Papua, the Allies had eliminated the most pressing threat to Australia. -The Battle of the Coral Sea ended an amphibious invasion attempt and now the overland challenge had been turned back as well. With Papua in Japanese hands, Australia would have been subjected to air and naval attack across a narrow span of water. -

■ Stiff Japanese resistance on Guadalcanal slowed the final drive to clear the island.

Jan. 23 British forces entered Tripoli to receive the surrender of the city and the province.

■ Russian troops recaptured Armavir, a key rail

junction in the Maikop oil fields. Advance elements moved into Voronezh. Stalingrad's Gumrak airfield fell to the Russians, cutting the Sixth Army's last link to the outside. The Germans now had only 495 operational tanks left on the entire Russian front. Since the invasion the Germans had lost 7,800. In two weeks of fighting on the Don front, Axis losses included 50,000 dead.

■ All Japanese resistance ended on Guadalcanal's Mount Austen.

Jan. 25 Voronezh was totally reoccupied by the Russians, who took 52,000 prisoners.

■ British Eighth Army units pressed westward from Tripoli to drive the Axis forces into Tunisia.

Jan. 26 The Stalingrad pocket was reduced substantially as Russian forces split it in half.

■ French troops began moving forward in the Ousseltia Valley of Tunisia.

Jan. 27 The rail line to Leningrad from Moscow was cleared, permitting delivery of supplies to the only partially recovered population of Leningrad. Moscow announced the capture of 86,000 Axis troops, mostly Hungarians, on the Voronezh front near Alekseyevka.

■ U.S. bombers conducted their first all-American raid on Germany, hitting the port facilities at Wilhelmshaven.

■ Axis troops fought a determined rear-guard action near Zwara in Libya.

Jan. 28 After more than three years of war Germany finally went to a wartime footing, ordering full mobilization of the labor force.

■ Red Army units captured Kasternoe on the Kursk-Voronezh rail line.

Jan. 29 Kropotkin on the Baku-Rostov rail line fell to the Russians.

Jan. 30 Soviet forces reoccupied the oil center of Maikop. German Army Group A was cut off as the Russians captured the rail center of Tikhoretsk. German Army Group Don was no longer an effective force. The Stalingrad pocket was narrowed to a 300-yard defense perimeter.

■ Counterattacking German troops overran the Faid Pass in Tunisia.

■ The RAF launched its first daylight attack of the war on Berlin. Mosquitos bombed the German capital in the midst of ceremonies marking the 10th anniversary of Hitler's accession to power.

■ RAF bombers began using H2S, in a raid on Hamburg. The device was a simple radar set which displayed a rough picture of the ground below. It served primarily as an all-weather bombing aid but was also used for navigational purposes. The early models were notoriously unreliable.

■ The U.S. cruiser *Chicago* was sunk off the Solomons after being hit by an airborne torpedo.

Jan. 31 Paulus, promoted to field marshal the day before, surrendered at Stalingrad. When told of the surrender, Hitler said, "Paulus did an about-face on the threshold of immortality."

■ British troops cleared Zwara in Libya and pressed toward the Tunisian frontier.

■ Indecisive but heavy fighting continued in Tunisia as the Allies attempted to retake the Faid Pass.

■ Dönitz replaced Raeder as commander in chief of the German navy.

Feb. 1 Svatovo, southeast of Kharkov, fell to the Russians, cutting the rail line from Kharkov to the Donets Basin.

■ Allied area commanders met in New Delhi and decided to launch a major campaign to retake all of Burma beginning in November. The ultimate objective was to clear the way into China which would be used as a base for direct action against Japan.

Feb. 2 All resistance at Stalingrad ended. About

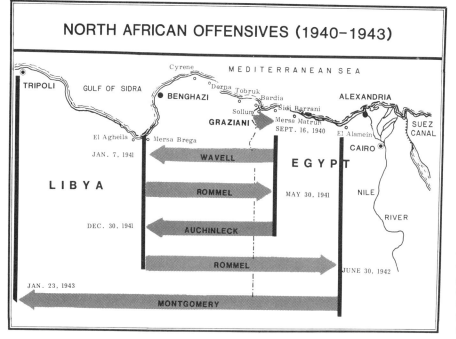

NORTH AFRICAN OFFENSIVES (1940–1943)

For two and a half years the North African campaign was a seesaw of advances and retreats. Victory in North Africa permitted the Allies strategic freedom in the Mediterranean.

147,200 Germans were killed in the extended and abortive campaign for the city, and another 91,000 surrendered, including 24 generals. Only 34,000 men ever made it out on the airlift. A thousand Luftwaffe crewmen and 488 transport planes were lost in the resupply and evacuation effort.

■ The first group of Japanese troops was evacuated from Guadalcanal.

Japanese artist Tamura Konosuke's combat painting of the Guadalcanal campaign, Suicide Unit Bidding Farewell to Commander in Jungle.

Feb. 3 Berlin acknowledged the end of the fighting at Stalingrad, saying that "the sacrifices of the Army, bulwark of a historical European mission, were not in vain." Germany began a three-day period of national mourning. Soviet forces advanced on all fronts in Russia.

Feb. 4 All nonessential businesses were ordered to close in Germany.

■ Advance elements of the British Eighth Army crossed the frontier into Tunisia from Libya.

■ Eisenhower was given command of all Allied forces in North Africa.

■ Soviet Commandos landed on the Black Sea coast near Novorossiysk to destroy the trapped vestiges of German Army Group A.

Feb. 5 Mussolini assumed control of the Italian ministry of foreign affairs, ousting his son-in-law

Ciano. It thus gave him, as Rome announced, "the entire burden for the conduct of political and military operations in this delicate phase of the conflict."

Feb. 6 The noose around German Army Group A was further tightened as the Red Army reached the Sea of Azov at Yeysk. Russian forces advanced to within five miles of Rostov.

Feb. 7 Moscow announced that the Red Army had established complete control over the south bank of the Don River. Azov was recaptured. The main highway between Orel and Kursk was cut.

■ Japanese destroyers began their final attempt to evacuate forces from Guadalcanal.

Feb. 8 Kursk, held by the Germans since Nov. 11, 1941, was reoccupied by Soviet troops. It had served as a key German base.

■ Finland, through the U.S., offered to negotiate an end to its war with Russia. (Contacts continued through April when they foundered on details of an armistice.)

■ Major General Orde Wingate's first Chindit group (named after a figure in Hindu mythology), made up of the 77th Indian Brigade, set off from Imphal to conduct irregular warfare behind Japanese lines in Burma. Supplied by air drops, the British, Indian, and Ghurka troops trekked through the impossible jungle to cut Japanese communications.

■ Japanese rear-guard units were evacuated from Guadalcanal. A total of 10,652 men were removed from the island in a week, a remarkable feat in view of the American air and naval presence in the area.

Feb. 9 All organized Japanese resistance on Guadalcanal ended. The Americans were completely unaware of the pullout and were surprised when they realized late in the afternoon that no Japanese were left.

■ Belgorod was recaptured by the Russians, cutting the rail line to Kharkov.

Feb. 10 Russian troops advancing toward Kharkov took Chuguev and Volchansk.

Feb. 12 The escape route for the Germans from Rostov was narrowed as the Russians cut the main rail line at Krasnoarmeisk. Red Army units threatened encirclement of the German corps defending Kharkov.

Feb. 13 Russian control was established over the entire rail line between Rostov and Voronezh.

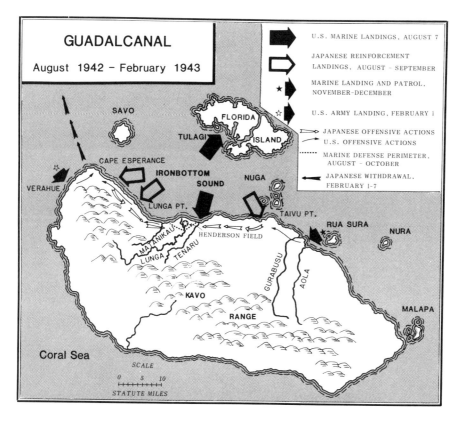

GUADALCANAL

August 1942 – February 1943

U.S. MARINE LANDINGS, AUGUST 7

JAPANESE REINFORCEMENT LANDINGS, AUGUST – SEPTEMBER

MARINE LANDING AND PATROL, NOVEMBER–DECEMBER

U.S. ARMY LANDING, FEBRUARY 1

JAPANESE OFFENSIVE ACTIONS

U.S. OFFENSIVE ACTIONS

MARINE DEFENSE PERIMETER, AUGUST – OCTOBER

JAPANESE WITHDRAWAL, FEBRUARY 1–7

SAVO

FLORIDA

TULAGI   ISLAND

CAPE ESPERANCE

IRONBOTTOM SOUND

VERAHUE

NUGA

LUNGA PT.

TAIVU PT.

MATANIKAU   HENDERSON FIELD

RUA SURA

NURA

LUNGA   TENARU

GURABUSU

AOLA

KAVO

RANGE

MALAPA

Coral Sea

SCALE

0   5   10

STATUTE MILES

The long and bitter Guadalcanal campaign showed that U.S. Marines were as adept at jungle warfare as the Japanese. It also revealed critical logistical deficiencies in the Imperial forces.

Feb. 14 Red Army troops recaptured Rostov, the main outlet for the Germans retreating from the Caucasus. Kleist's Army Group A had to withdraw to the Taman Peninsula between the Sea of Azov and the Black Sea. The First Panzer Army was the only force to get through to the north before Rostov fell. By retaking Rostov, the Russians eliminated the threat to the Caucasus and its oil riches.

■ German forces launched a powerful counteroffensive from the Faid Pass in Tunisia and broke through to the Kasserine Pass. Allied forces began pulling back to the west toward Sbeitla.

Feb. 15 Vichy France began drafting laborers for work duties.

■ Contrary to Hitler's orders to stand and fight, the II SS Panzer Corps withdrew from Kharkov.

Feb. 16 Kharkov was reoccupied by the Russian Fortieth and Third Tank armies. Hitler equated the loss of Kharkov to Stalingrad and vowed to retake Russia's fourth largest city. The Russians

had now advanced 375 miles west of Stalingrad.

■ U.S. and British forces suffered heavy losses in Tunisia, with the Germans advancing 25 miles northwestward from Gafsa and to the southwest toward Feriana.

■ British Eighth Army troops attacked the Mareth defense line in Tunisia at Ben Gardane.

Feb. 17 British forces captured Medenine in Tunisia, but U.S. and British units began falling back on the other fronts in the face of heavy German armor attacks. The Mark VI tanks were proving effective for the Germans since their introduction into combat.

Feb. 18 Convoy ON 166 was intercepted by U-boats in the North Atlantic. (Over the next week, 15 of the Allied ships were picked off and sunk.)

■ Tatahouine in Tunisia was occupied by the British.

■ German units of the German Sixteenth Army began pulling back along the northern Russian

Allied ground units in Burma are resupplied by air drop.

front. Soviet tanks were 36 miles east of Zaporozhye.

■ Madame Chiang Kai-shek addressed a joint meeting of the U.S. House and Senate.

■ British Chindits, the long-range penetration forces of General Orde Wingate, crossed the Chindwin River in Burma and eventually cut the Mandalay-Myitkyina rail line well behind Japanese lines.

Feb. 19 Allied defenses in Tunisia were restructured in the face of a deteriorating situation. The Germans and Italians began frontal assaults on American positions in the Kasserine Pass.

■ German Army Group South opened a counteroffensive toward Kharkov and Belgorod.

Feb. 20 Axis forces cleared the Kasserine Pass. The U.S. II Corps fell back to avoid being totally routed. The Germans and Italians swung out and started driving northward toward Thala and westward to Tebessa.

Feb. 21–22 British Commandos raided Akyab in Burma and withdrew after attacking Japanese positions.

Feb. 21 Churchill tanks were put into action in Tunisia as the Allies groped to stop the Axis offensive. Fighting was intense in several sectors as the three-pronged German drive reached a point 21 miles beyond the Kasserine Pass and

threatened the entire Allied force in central Tunisia.

■ The U.S. 43rd Division and a Marine force occupied the Russell Islands in the Solomons. Occupation of the islands provided the Allies with a fighter airstrip 60 miles northwest of Guadalcanal.

MALARIA IN THE SOUTH PACIFIC

Perhaps the highest incidence of malaria was at Milne Bay, New Guinea, during the Papua campaign of early 1943. At one point the U.S. malarial rate of incidence was 2,236 per 1,000 men. In other words, each soldier could expect to contract the disease which was endemic to the area 2.2 times.

Feb. 22 Rommel ordered a halt in the Axis drive before his forces reached El Kef. They pulled back to the Kasserine Pass.

■ *Régiment Normandie*, an anti-Vichy French flight group, went into action for the first time on the Russian front. (Formed in Syria in 1942, the 72-man French contingent flew fighters with remarkable success, downing 117 German planes to 25 losses by the end of the year.)

Feb. 23 Rommel was appointed to command the newly formed Army Group Africa. The Italian General Giovanni Messe replaced him as commander of the First Italian Army.

Feb. 24 Ribbentrop conferred with Mussolini in Rome.

■ General Josef "Sepp" Dietrich's Sixth SS Army counterattacked south of Rzhev. (The badly mauled Russians withdrew along a broad front during the next two weeks.)

Feb. 25 U.S. troops of II Corps reoccupied the Kasserine Pass, encountering only mines and booby traps.

Feb. 26 The German Fifth Panzer Army launched a strong offensive in Tunisia making rapid progress around El Aroussa. Beja and Medjez el Bab were threatened.

Feb. 27 Stiff resistance by the British First Army halted the German advance near Beja.

Feb. 27–28 Norwegian Commandos destroyed the Norsk Hydro heavy-water facilities at Vemork. Nine men parachuted into Norway from Britain, demolished the heavy-water tanks, and let 2,000 pounds of the material spill uselessly in the area. Piping and tubes used in its production were also destroyed. (Germany's heavy-water program was delayed for only four months, however, as German and Norwegian engineers returned the facility to full production in June.)

Feb. 28 German forces were contained in Tunisia. Their counteroffensive was costly to the inexperienced American troops of II Corps who suffered heavy casualties, 6,500. Total Allied casualties in the Kasserine fighting were 10,000 to 2,000 for the Axis troops.

■ Counterattacks by the Germans in the Donets area were accelerated as the temperatures began to climb above freezing. German planners feared an early thaw would bog down their offensive.

March 1 Moscow told the Polish government-in-exile it would claim eastern Poland, the lands seized in 1939, as Russian territory.

March 2–5 Tokyo's attempts to strengthen Japanese units resulted in the Battle of the Bismarck Sea. American and Australian planes initiated the action by intercepting a 16-ship Japanese convoy en route to Lae, New Guinea. Four destroyers

were sunk by the Allied aircraft which were then joined by PT boats, resulting in the destruction of eight transports. It was the last attempt by the Japanese to reinforce positions in that sector of New Guinea. About 3,000 Japanese were killed, most of them aboard the troop ships. More than 20 Japanese planes were downed, to five U.S.

March 2 Rzhev, the strongly fortified German base, was evacuated by German Army Group Center.

■ RAF bombers delivered their most devastating raid of the war to date on Berlin.

■ German tank units forced Allied groups to fall back to Sedjenane in Tunisia.

March 3 Russian forces reoccupied Rzhev. In the south, German panzer units reached the Don River and recaptured Slavyansk and Lisichansk.

March 5 RAF bombers used the OBOE navigational aid for the first time, in a raid on Essen. The attack marked the beginning of the air battle of the Ruhr to destroy German industry in the area.

March 6 Rommel fought his last battle in Africa, directing an offensive against British positions at Medenine. The Germans were routed, losing 50 tanks before retiring. Coincidentally, General George S. Patton at the very same time took command of the U.S. II Army Corps.

■ Allied convoy SC 121 in the North Atlantic came under U-boat attack. (Thirteen of the 56 ships were eventually lost.)

■ Japan again told Berlin it could not enter the war against the Russians.

March 8 Japanese forces crossed the Yangtze River between Ichang and Yoyang.

■ British First Army forces fell back near Tamera in Tunisia.

■ The U.S. ambassador in Moscow—Admiral William Standley—said the Soviet government was suppressing news of American aid: "It is not fair to mislead Americans into giving millions from their pockets, thinking that they are aiding the Russian people, without the Russian people knowing it."

March 9 Arnim succeeded Rommel as commander of Axis forces in Africa. Rommel left Africa for the last time.

■ The Russian people were told for the first time, in a radio broadcast, that the Soviet Union was receiving supplies from Britain and the U.S.

■ SS panzer corps units reached the western outskirts of Kharkov.

■ British Chindits in Burma began operations east of the Irrawaddy River.

■ A German submarine, *U-510*, sank nine ships off the coast of Brazil.

March 10 Sharp fighting took place at Tamera and Ksar Rhilane in Tunisia.

March 11 German forces reached Kharkov in their counterattack and violent fighting in the streets ensued. The German thrust was a brilliant tactical move by Manstein. Russian units held a seven-to-one manpower advantage, but the Germans were able to secure a solid line along the Donets River.

March 13 The first of two attempts to kill Hitler within the span of a few days failed. General Henning von Tresckow, who was Field Marshal Hans Günther von Kluge's chief of staff, and an aide planted a bomb aboard Hitler's private plane. The device, made of plastic explosives, was contained in a package supposedly containing two bottles of brandy for delivery to a member of Hitler's staff at *Wolfsschanze* (wolf's lair), Hitler's military headquarters in East Prussia. The detonator failed, as the conspirators discovered when they recovered the bomb.

■ Chinese troops hurled the Japanese back across the Yangtze River.

March 14 Two German SS divisions recaptured Kharkov. Russian resistance west of the Donets River collapsed.

March 16–19 Nazi U-boat destruction reached its height in a running battle between 38 of the German underwater craft and two Allied convoys and their escorts in the North Atlantic. The official Royal Navy history of the war called the outcome a "serious disaster to the Allied cause." The action occurred along the east coast of Newfoundland when a fast eastbound (HX 229) convoy overtook a slower-moving one (SC 122). Together they formed a mass of ships concentrated in a small area, which also happened to be along the patrol line of three U-boat groups. In the end, 21 of the Allied merchant ships were sunk, a loss of 141,000 tons. A naval escort ship was also lost. Only one of the U-boats was destroyed when it came under aerial attack. The entire convoy concept was now in jeopardy and the British Admiralty questioned whether the

war itself could be properly prosecuted. (What turned the tide was the introduction of long-range aircraft, carrier escorts, and the development of ship and aircraft shortwave radar which pinpointed the presence and location of submarines.)

WEAPONS OF FEAR

More than 700 U.S. Army enlisted men wounded in North Africa were questioned by the U.S. Army's Research Branch on which weapons they considered most frightening and the most dangerous. The results showed there was a strong relationship between the two, but there were distinctions between the ones feared and those considered most deadly (as shown in percentages given by the men who had personally been subjected to each weapon).

	Most Frightening	Most Dangerous
88-mm artillery gun	48	62
Dive bomber	20	4
Mortar	13	17
Horizontal bomber	12	5
Light machine gun	7	6
Strafing attack	5	4
Land mines	2	2
Rifle fire	0	0
Miscellaneous (including booby traps, tanks, heavy machine guns, etc.)	4	2

SOURCE: Samuel A. Stouffer, et al., *The American Soldier, Combat and Its Aftermath.*

March 17 Patton's II Corps went on the offensive in Tunisia, making good progress despite heavy rains.

■ Japanese forces launched an offensive on the Arakan front in Burma. British forces were outflanked and had to withdraw.

March 18 U.S. units occupied El Guettar in Tunisia as the Axis forces fell back.

■ French Guiana formally disassociated itself from Vichy and declared the territory on the side of the Free French.

■ British units were hurled back on the Arakan front in Burma. Chindits behind Japanese lines began filtering back to India after extreme hardships which forced them to abandon plans for cutting the Mandalay-Lashio rail line.

March 20 For the second time in a week, anti-Hitler military officers tried and failed to kill him. Kluge's chief of intelligence, Colonel Rudolf von Gertsdorff, carried a concealed bomb which he would detonate by acid while close to Hitler at the Zeughaus in Berlin, blowing both of them to bits. Hitler left the exhibit hall before the acid could act, and Gertsdorff flushed the fuse down a toilet in the men's room.

■ The British Eighth Army unleashed a strong attack on the Mareth line while American troops opened new assaults directed toward Maknassy, in what was the start of the last phase of the battle of Tunisia.

■ Belgorod was recaptured by the Germans, clearing the area north of Kharkov.

March 21 U.S. II Corps forces made strong gains in Tunisia. An encirclement operation at Djebel el Ank netted 700 Axis prisoners.

■ Mud caused by the spring thaw slowed action along the entire Russian front. Both sides were already drained by the intense and costly winter action and welcomed the spring respite. Russia found the forthcoming two-month long lull advantageous because its military might was being replenished in part through U.S. and Brit-ish aid, while Germany could not match the mounting strength of its rivals.

March 23 Allied and Axis forces suffered heavy losses in hard fighting around El Guettar and Djebel Naemia.

March 24 Wingate's Chindits were ordered to leave their operational area in northern Burma. In seven weeks the group had endured extreme hardships and one of three men ended up as a casualty. The most notable success was in disrupting traffic along the Mandalay-Myitkyina rail line which was cut at 75 points.

March 26 In one of the major misreadings of history Mussolini wrote to Hitler that Russia was so weakened after Stalingrad "she cannot hope, at any rate for a long time to come, to constitute a serious menance."

■ New Zealand troops assaulted the western flank of the Mareth line under intense RAF close air support. The defense line fell apart and the Axis forces began retreating.

■ A Japanese naval force en route to the Aleutians was turned back by U.S. ships. In the battle of the Komandorski Islands, the Japanese were unable to reinforce their Attu garrison even though they possessed numerical combat ship superiority. Only one Japanese cruiser was damaged (to a damaged U.S. cruiser and destroyer), but the task force had to return to Japan without putting men or material ashore.

March 28 The British Eighth Army completed

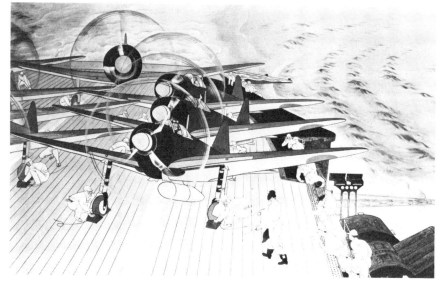

Japanese artist Arai Shori's painting of launch operations aboard a carrier of the Imperial Navy.

occupying the main positions on the Mareth line. Patton's II Corps opened up an offensive directed at Gabès. French colonial camel corps troops of the Southeast Algerian Command completed the capture of a string of towns to the south.

March 29 Montgomery's forces pressed northward through Gabès and El Hamma.

March 30 U.S. units were blocked in trying to reach the Fondouk gap in Tunisia.

■ Stalin was told the Allied convoys to Murmansk were being suspended because of heavy losses. Increasingly suspicious of Washington and London, Stalin assumed the suspension was motivated by political rather than military considerations.

March 31 Cap Serrat in Tunisia was occupied by the British.

■ British civilian air raid casualties for the first three months of the year were 973 killed and 1,191 wounded.

April 2 A stalemate developed in Tunisia with both sides battered and unable to dislodge the opposing forces.

April 5 Japanese forces overran British brigade headquarters on the Mayu peninsula in Burma.

■ A concerted Allied air campaign was begun to destroy Axis shipping and air facilities in Tunisia and Sicily, making it virtually impossible to resupply the Germans and Italians left in North Africa.

April 6 The British army resumed offensive operations, attacking Wadi Akarit in Tunisia.

April 7 Mussolini met with Hitler at Klessheim Castle near Salzburg. Although the Duce had been urged by his advisers to press Hitler to end the war in Russia, the subject never came up and Mussolini was nothing more than a passive participant. Hitler did all the talking, mostly about a new German offensive in Russia. Hitler was concerned about Mussolini's physical condition and told Dönitz he wondered whether the Duce had the will "to carry on to the end."

■ Japanese planes hammered Guadalcanal. A total of 188 aircraft were involved in the attack in which three Allied ships were sunk.

■ Bolivia declared war on the Axis Powers.

■ U.S. 9th Division troops from Gafsa linked up with British Eighth Army units in Tunisia, 20 miles from the coast.

April 8 A predawn attack on the Fondouk line in Tunisia was launched by Allied forces. Heavy

fighting resulted with the Axis troops offering a strong defense.

April 10 Sfax in Tunisia was occupied by the British Eighth Army.

April 11 Two wings of the Allied forces in Tunisia linked up near Kairouan. The Faid Pass was retaken, generally restoring the positions which existed two months before.

April 12 Germany announced its forces had uncovered a mass grave of thousands of Polish army officers killed by the Russians at Katyn, near Smolensk.

■ Sousse, the last supply port on the Tunisian east coast, was taken by the British.

April 13 British troops reached the Enfidaville Line in Tunisia, the final Axis defense position, but to breach the positions required additional beefing up of the Eighth Army.

April 15 General Omar Bradley assumed command of the U.S. II Corps from Patton who was assigned to plan the invasion of Sicily.

April 16 The Polish government in London announced it was requesting the International Red Cross to investigate the Katyn massacre.

■ By order of the Vichy government children in the shore areas of Cherbourg, Dieppe, St.-Malo, and Le Havre were evacuated inland.

April 18 Admiral Isoroku Yamamoto, commander-in-chief of the Japanese Combined Fleet, was killed when his plane was shot down just before landing at Kahili airfield at the southern tip of Bougainville. P-38s from Guadalcanal had been sent up to "get Yamamoto" after the U.S. had intercepted coded radio messages informing the appropriate Japanese military authorities of his arrival. It was surprising the Japanese did not consider the possibility that the code was compromised, for this was another instance of clear intelligence data begin used by the Allied forces. No effort was made to change the code. The loss of the respected naval officer was a shock to the Japanese people and is said to have demoralized everyone. For Americans, Yamamoto was the Japanese who ordered the attack on Pearl Harbor. What was not known then is that Yamamoto opposed the war, feeling it could not be won.

■ In what became known as the "Palm Sunday Massacre," 51 Luftwaffe transports and 16 escorting fighters were shot down in about ten minutes while attempting to ferry supplies from Europe to the hard-pressed Army Group Africa.

Seventy U.S. and British fighters (directed to the proper intercept point from Ultra intercepts) had little trouble pouncing on the slow, trimotor Junker 52 aircraft. Seven of the Allied planes were lost.

■ Moscow accused the Germans of the massacre of Polish officers at Katyn: "The hand of the Gestapo can easily be traced in this hideous frame-up."

■ Australian Prime Minister John Curtin was critical of the Allied "Europe first" policy, which denied supplies to Australia which was rapidly exhausting its resources: ". . . the Australian Government accepts the global strategy . . . but it does not accept a flow of war material, notably aircraft, that does not measure up to the requirements of a holding war."

■ Germany and Turkey signed a trade agreement with the Germans to receive cotton, tobacco, and dried fruits in exchange for heavy industrial machinery, locomotives, trucks, and chemicals. The agreement is noteworthy in that Germany was more interested in consumer products than in potential war material, even in the fourth year of the war.

April 19 Jews in the Warsaw ghetto began a heroic but suicidal battle against the Germans. One of the Jewish commanders wrote of the uprising: "Jewish self-defense has become a fact. Jewish resistance and revenge have become realities." Poorly armed Jews fought 2,000 tank-supported SS troops who were stunned by the ferocity of the Jewish fighters. The Germans withdrew from the ghetto after suffering 200 casualties. (Fighting continued through May 10, with few Jews surviving. The ghetto was eventually reduced to "one huge cemetery.")

April 20 Roosevelt met with Mexican President Manuel Ávila Camacho in Monterrey, Mexico, as the two "good neighbors" discussed cooperative wartime efforts and made plans for postwar reconstruction.

■ U.S. II Corps forces smashed through the mountains north of Medjez el Bab, opening the way for the tanks to advance into the Tine River valley of Tunisia.

April 21 With credible indications from neutral sources and American intelligence that American prisoners of war were being executed by the Japanese, President Roosevelt issued a statement

on criminal responsibility: "This Government has vigorously condemned this act of barbarity in a formal communication sent to the Japanese Government. In that communication this Government has informed the Japanese Government that the American Government will hold personally and officially responsible for these diabolical crimes all of those officers of the Japanese Government who have participated therein and will in due course bring those officers to justice." This set the course for the postwar trial of war criminals in Japan.

■ Orders were issued to U.S. forces for the recapture of Attu Island in the Aleutians.

MOST IMAGINATIVE DISPATCH OF THE WAR
(Alliteration Department)

U.S. Army Air Force pilot Capt. Fred M. Smith sent this report after sinking a Japanese destroyer-mine sweeper with his P-38 during the Aleutians campaign:

SAW STEAMER, STRAFED SAME, SANK SAME, SOME SIGHT, SIGNED SMITH.

April 22 Allied forces in Tunisia began the final phase of the North African campaign. The main thrust was directed at the capture of Tunis and Bizerte.

April 23 Hitler ordered "utmost severity" in coping with the uprising in the Jewish ghetto of Warsaw.

■ The Union of South Africa severed relations with France.

April 24 U.S. Army invasion forces for the reoccupation of Attu set sail from San Francisco for Cold Harbor, Alaska.

April 26 Moscow broke off relations with the London-based Polish government because of its request for an investigation into the Katyn massacre and Moscow's claim the Poles were in contact with the Germans.

April 27 Premier Antonio Salazar restated that Portugal would not act to damage British interests.

April 28 Sweden protested the mining of its territorial waters by Germany.

April 28–30 In what turned out to be the last

German armored attack in North Africa, panzer units captured Djebel Bou-Aoukaz.

April 28–May 6 In a turning point of the battle of the Atlantic, new antisubmarine measures began achieving results. A running battle between 51 U-boats and westbound convoy ONS 5, made up of 42 ships and 9 escorts, resulted in a reversal of the usual pattern of surface ship destruction when confronted by wolf packs. Although 13 merchantmen were sunk, the Allies were able to sink seven of the submarines, two of them by land-based Catalina patrol craft.

April 29 German submarine *U-515* sank five ships in a 24-hour period along the west African coast off Freetown.

■ Goebbels, reflecting growing concern about an Allied strategy directed toward the Balkans, wrote in his diary: "If an invasion were to take place in the southeast, there would be cause to fear that large parts of the population would immediately desert us. The Balkans are still the powder barrel of Europe. It is to be hoped that the English and Americans are not aware of the chances beckoning them there." (Churchill, alone among the western Allied leaders, was aware of the vulnerability of the Balkans and the area's strategic and political potential, but he was constantly refused such operations.)

April 30 New antisubmarine strategies were formally adopted by the Royal Navy, centering on carrier-based aircraft cover and long-range patrol planes. They were immediately employed in the Bay of Biscay, where in the following month 38 U-boats were sunk. The key to the program was catching the submarines while they were leaving or returning from their bases on the French coast. Ultra messages were invaluable in giving British ships and planes specific times and locations for intercepting the submarines.

May During the month a total of 41 German U-boats—a third of the submarines on station— failed to return to their bases. Twenty-eight of the submarines were lost in mid-Atlantic convoy areas. It was known as "Black May" in the German navy. As a result of the losses, Dönitz ordered all U-boats to pull out of the North Atlantic and position themselves southwest of the Azores. The battle of the North Atlantic was effectively and decisively ended in favor of the Allies.

May 1 German troops in Tunisia began withdrawing from positions opposite the U.S. II Corps.

May 2 Darwin, Australia, was bombed by Japanese aircraft operating from Salamaua, New Guinea.

May 3 Red Army troops halted a German counteroffensive in the Kuban area.

■ The U.S. 1st Armored Division occupied Mateur after it was abandoned by the Germans. Allied units were now only 20 air miles from Bizerte.

May 5 Djebel Bou-Aoukaz in Tunisia was recaptured by the British in bitter and deadly fighting. The left flank was now secure for the attack on Tunis.

■ Krymsk fell to the Russians.

May 6 Allied forces launched the final offensive against Axis positions in Tunisia. The defenses were breached by the British First Army, and two armored divisions pushed on to Massicault, halfway to Tunis.

■ Russian aircraft began a series of tactical air strikes against German positions on the central front.

May 7 Tunis and Bizerte were occupied by Allied forces. The main body of Axis forces under Arnim retreated into the Cape Bon peninsula, but 41,000 Germans were captured at Bizerte alone.

May 8 The Hungarian parliament was dissolved.

May 9 German forces facing the U.S. II Corps in Tunisia surrendered. Six generals were among the prisoners.

May 10 Allied forces cut off all escape routes for the Germans on the Cape Bon peninsula.

■ Lieutenant General Jacob L. Devers took over as commander of the European Theater of Operations, succeeding Lieutenant General Frank M. Andrews who was killed in a plane crash.

May 11 The U.S. 7th Division landed on the Aleutian island of Attu, achieving total tactical surprise. Dense fog aided the landings.

■ Churchill arrived in Washington for meetings with Roosevelt and their respective military staffs.

May 12 General Jürgen von Arnim surrendered all Axis forces in North Africa. A total of 238,243 German and Italian prisoners were taken. Africa

Japanese troops fought to the death before U.S. and Canadian troops could regain control of the Aleutians.

was now cleared of Axis troops. For Montgomery and the British Eighth Army it was a grueling 1,500 miles from El Alamein to Tunis. A final message was sent by General Gustav Fehn, last commander of the Afrika Korps: "Ammunition exhausted. Equipment destroyed. In accordance with orders received, the Afrika Korps has fought to the last man. The Afrika Korps must be reborn. *Heia Safari.*"

■ The first Arakan campaign in Burma ended in failure. Maungdaw was evacuated, and the Allied force was back where it started.

■ Franco of Spain offered to mediate a peace between Germany and the U.S. and Britain if the Allies severed their ties with the Soviet Union.

May 13 British Deputy Prime Minister Clement Attlee formally announced the end of the campaign in North Africa.

■ The island of Pantelleria in the Strait of Sicily came under Allied naval and air attack. Allied strategy was to bomb it into submission, then attack Sicily.

■ Japan's powerful lord keeper of the privy seal, Marquis Koichi Kido, confided to the foreign minister, Mamoru Shigemitsu, that the war could be ended only by the royal family's assistance in bringing the military under control. Shigemitsu had joined the Tojo cabinet in an effort to conclude a peace in China honorable to the Chinese

and to avert what was increasingly perceived as a disastrous military outlook in the war against the U.S. Kido, Sigemitsu, and other Japanese leaders, however, could never overcome the destructive momentum of the military's actions until it was too late. The emperor was by no means the ultimate decision-maker.

May 14 Pantelleria was blockaded.

■ A Japanese submarine torpedoed the Australian hospital ship *Centaur*.

May 15 The bey of Tunis was ousted.

May 16–17 RAF Lancaster bombers breached the Eder and Möhne dams in the Ruhr. They were two of Germany's largest dams and strategically important as suppliers of power for munitions plants.

May 16 The Attu campaign which had progressed too slowly for the Americans despite a powerful numerical superiority in troops suddenly turned when the Japanese unexpectedly withdrew to Chichagof Harbor for a final stand.

May 17 For the first time since Italy entered the war, an Allied convoy passed through the Strait of Gibraltar and steamed across the length of the Mediterranean without meeting any Axis opposition. Possession of the North African littoral permitted safe and free passage for the movement of troops and supplies.

May 18 Japanese forces opened a new offensive

across the Yangtze River in China. Its ultimate objective was the Chinese capital of Chungking.

■ The air bombardment of Pantelleria was intensified as the Allies concentrated on two airfields on the island. (Heavy raids would continue through June 5.)

May 19 Churchill addressed a joint meeting of the U.S. House and Senate.

■ Pantelleria was again subjected to heavy bombing.

May 21 The neutralized French fleet in Alexandria elected to join in the Allied war effort.

May 22 The Soviet Union formally dissolved the Communist International (Comintern): ". . . long before the war, it became more and more clear that, with increasing complications in internal and international relations of various countries, any sort of international center would encounter obstacles in solving the problems facing the movement in each separate country."

May 23 In the heaviest raid of the war to date, the RAF dropped 2,000 tons of bombs on Dortmund.

May 25 Roosevelt and Churchill concluded their Washington (TRIDENT) conference after having selected May 1, 1944, as the date for the invasion of France. It was also agreed to knock Italy out of the war after the capture of Sicily, to increase aid to China, and to step up the tempo of the war against Japan by island-hopping through the central Pacific. Churchill's calls for a strike through the Balkans, the "soft underbelly," were rejected.

May 27 The first of the British liaison groups was dropped into Yugoslavia to aid Tito's Partisans.

■ All contractors involved in the production of U.S. war materials were barred from practicing racial discrimination.

May 28 Leaflets were dropped on the surrounded Japanese troops on Attu to surrender.

May 29 Chinese Nationalist troops in the Ichang area halted the Japanese advance on Chungking. They promptly went on the offensive.

■ The remaining Japanese on Attu staged a final counteroffensive, but it was quickly repelled.

May 30 U.S. forces secured Attu Island. Only a handful of the original 2,350 Japanese forces survived. U.S. losses were 512.

■ Vichy announced that the previously immobil-

ized French naval squadron in Alexandria harbor had gone over to the Allies. According to the Laval government, the French ships had been subjected to incessant pressure from the British, including the withholding of pay.

■ Churchill and de Gaulle arrived in Algiers.

May 31 Admiral Réne Godfroy, commander of the French naval units in Alexandria, formally announced that his ships would join the Allied military effort.

■ General Guderian tried to talk Hitler out of a summer offensive on the Russian front. Hitler replied, "You're quite right. Every time I think of this attack my stomach turns." (In the end, however, he approved Operation CITADEL, which turned into the disastrous Battle of Kursk.)

June 1 The Allied air offensive against Pantelleria was intensified, while the Royal Navy maintained its heavy bombardment.

June 2 Pope Pius appealed to the combatants to apply the "laws of humanity" in air warfare. The British particularly were stung by the inference that its large-scale attacks against German population centers were immoral.

June 3 Competing anti-Vichy French military and political elements were united in a Committee of National Liberation at Algiers. It was to serve as a provisional government for the French Empire.

■ Japan seized all shipping on the upper Yangtze in Hupei Province.

■ Waters off Halifax, Nova Scotia, were mined by a German submarine. The field was discovered immediately, but only after the 2,000-ton Panamanian cargo ship *Halma* was sunk.

June 6 The attacks on Pantelleria were concentrated on shore defenses and gun emplacements.

June 7 Japanese planes resumed their attacks on Guadalcanal, losing 23 aircraft to 9 for the U.S.

June 8 Kiska was ordered abandoned by Tokyo. The Aleutian island was subject to a naval blockade and air attacks whenever the weather permitted.

June 10 In an appreciation of the military situation, the German High Command expected the Allies to land in Sardinia and Corsica. It discounted the possibility of a Sicilian operation and a prolonged campaign up the Italian peninsula.

June 11 Pantelleria surrendered to Allied forces. The British 1st Division landed and met very little opposition. Submission by bombing, particularly through air attacks, was thus achieved for the first time. For about a month Allied planes had flown 5,285 sorties and dropped 6,200 tons of bombs on the island.

■ Himmler ordered the liquidation of all the Polish ghettos.

June 12 Britain's King George VI arrived in North Africa.

■ Lampedusa Island in the Strait of Sicily surrendered to the Allies. Like Pantelleria, it was bombarded into submission.

June 13 Allied bombers encountered their stiffest opposition yet in attacking Germany. Luftwaffe aircraft destroyed 22 of the 60 U.S. B-17s attempting to bomb Kiel. Another attack on Bremen by 102 B-17s was only lightly opposed.

DAY OF WAR

Perhaps the most unusual film produced during the war was the Russian documentary *Day of War*. The concept of director Mikhail Slutsky was to show the conflict in all its dimensions during a 24-hour period. Only two days before the date selected by Slutsky, June 13, 1943, were the 240 cameramen notified. Posted at 140 "filming points" throughout the Soviet Union, the cameramen documented what they saw. "We asked the cameramen," said Slutsky, "to strive for outward effect, in preference to inner significance or film dramatizations." The result was a gripping eight-reel film which was shown to vast audiences in the Soviet Union, as well as in Britain and the United States. It is not known if there were any casualties among the cameramen, but it would not be surprising. More than 100 Soviet combat cameramen were killed during the war. The most famous was Vladimir Sushinsky, whose footage was edited into a documentary, *Cameramen at the Front*. Sushinsky was shot while filming combat, and his camera recorded the blurred aftermath. The film ends with another cameraman filming Sushinsky's death. That cameraman was also killed.

June 14 Tojo conferred in Tokyo with Subhas Chandra Bose. The pro-Axis Indian leader had fled India in 1941 while awaiting trial and worked his way to Germany. He arrived in Tokyo after an 18-week trip from Kiel on German and Japanese submarines. Tojo encouraged Bose to form a provisional government which could take control of Indian territory which the Japanese planned to occupy.

June 15 Turkey reconfirmed its policy of strict neutrality. It reaffirmed both its friendship with the Soviet Union and the German-Turkish 1941 treaty of amity.

June 16 Tojo told the Japanese Diet the war situation had reached a critical stage.

■ A total of 107 Japanese planes (out of a force of 120) were downed in a massive attack on Guadalcanal. Only six U.S. planes were lost. The Japanese were only able to beach two ships and damage another.

June 18 Targets in Sicily were pounded by Allied bombers in preparation for the forthcoming invasion.

■ Prime Minister Curtin announced that Australia was no longer in danger of being invaded.

■ Field Marshal Sir Archibald Wavell was appointed viceroy of India and was succeeded as commander in chief in India by General Sir Claude Auchinleck.

June 19 Goebbels boasted that Berlin was now "free of Jews."

June 20 In anticipation of an Allied landing the Italian government ordered the evacuation of Naples and all cities and towns in Sicily.

■ RAF Lancasters flew the first shuttle bombing mission, from Britain to North Africa, attacking Friedrichshafen on the way out and La Spezia, Italy, returning. The attack on the former zeppelin facilities at Friedrichshafen was designed to impair the production of radar components manufactured there, but the results were only partly successful.

June 21 Himmler ordered the liquidation of Jewish ghettos in German-occupied Russia. Simultaneously, German execution teams began carrying out the murder of Jews in the Lwow ghetto. Through the 27th 20,000 Jews were killed.

June 22 In the first major daylight raid on the Ruhr, U.S. bombers attacked the synthetic rub-

The vaunted German U-boat fleet was slowly depleted through Allied attacks and countermeasures. By war's end, it had absorbed perhaps the heaviest unit losses of the war.

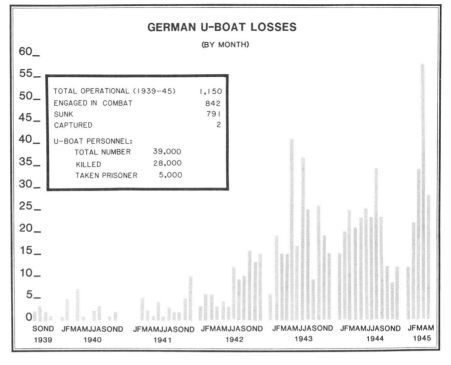

GERMAN U-BOAT LOSSES

(BY MONTH)

TOTAL OPERATIONAL (1939-45)	1,150
ENGAGED IN COMBAT	842
SUNK	791
CAPTURED	2
U-BOAT PERSONNEL:	
TOTAL NUMBER	39,000
KILLED	28,000
TAKEN PRISONER	5,000

SOND 1939 | JFMAMJJASOND 1940 | JFMAMJJASOND 1941 | JFMAMJJASOND 1942 | JFMAMJJASOND 1943 | JFMAMJJASOND 1944 | JFMAM 1945

ber plant at Huels, putting the facility out of operation temporarily.

June 24 In a broadcast from Tokyo, Bose made an appeal for an armed uprising by Indians against the British: "Civil disobedience must develop into armed struggle. And only when the Indian people receive the baptism of fire on a large scale will they qualify for their freedom."

June 25 Messina, Sicily, was attacked by Allied planes which dropped 300 tons of bombs on the important transport and communications center.

■ Jews in the ghetto of Czestochowa in Poland began an uprising. The ghetto was immediately reduced to rubble with an unknown number killed.

June 30 Allied forces launched amphibious operations against Japanese-held islands in the southwest Pacific (Operation CARTWHEEL) aimed at Rabaul. The islands included New Georgia, Sasavele, Baraulu, Vangunu, Trobriand, Rendova, and New Guinea. Nassau Bay was denied to the Japanese, isolating Lae and Salamaua.

■ The U.S. ended the fiscal year having expended

U.S. forces huddle for cover after coming ashore on Rendova Island in the Solomons.

$71 billion on direct war expenditures. That represented 93 percent of all government outlays in a record spending year. Total receipts for the period were only a little more than $21 billion.

■ Vichy's high commissioner in the French West Indies, Admiral Georges Robert, in Martinique, asked the U.S. to send a "plenipotentiary to fix the terms for a change of French authority . . . to avoid bloodshed." Robert had previously kept the island and other French possessions in the Caribbean loyal to Pétain. Fighting had broken out, however, between military units, some of which were insisting on aligning the islands with de Gaulle.

July 1 U.S. Marines completed the capture of Viru harbor on New Georgia.

■ More than 1,000 U.S. heavy bombers were now operating out of British bases.

July 2 Japanese aircraft attacked newly established Allied positions at Rendova in the Solomons in a destructive raid.

■ U.S. 43rd and 37th Division units landed at Munda on New Georgia.

July 4 General Wladislaw Sikorski and other leading Polish leaders in exile were killed in an air crash near Gibraltar.

■ British Commandos attacked German military air bases on Crete and withdrew safely.

■ A Yugoslav draftee in the German army who deserted to the Russians told his questioners the Germans were planning a huge attack around Kursk at dawn on the 5th. Russian forces were alerted and moved into stronger defense positions.

GEOGRAPHICAL DISTRIBUTION OF GERMAN ARMY

Divisions in	June 16, 1942	July 1, 1943
Soviet Union	167	175
France/Low Countries	26	38
Norway/Denmark	12	12
Balkans	5	14
Finland	5	7
Africa	3	–
Italy	–	6
Total	218	252

July 5 German forces launched a major offensive against the Kursk salient which turned out to be their last such effort on the central front. The battle was decisive since the initiative passed to the Russians. Three armies were involved in the push from Orel and Belgorod. They met with some success in the south at first but were quickly blocked by the strength and depth of the Russian defenses. The Soviets managed to establish a comfortable superiority of numbers in armor and manpower. Kursk, like Stalingrad, was a major turning point in the Russian war.

July 5–6 The Battle of Kula Gulf was fought as the Japanese tried to land troops and supplies to Kolombangara in the Solomons. Three U.S. cruisers and four destroyers engaged 10 Japanese destroyers in the night fight. The U.S. cruiser *Helena* was lost, while two Japanese destroyers were sunk. Despite the fierce fighting, 850 Japanese troops were able to land.

July 6 Kiska was bombarded by a U.S. naval force. It was the first attack on the Japanese-held island in 11 months.

July 7 Russian forces began counterattacking at Kursk.

■ London announced that Malta would be given its independence at the end of the war.

July 9 U.S. and British airborne troops began being dropped in Sicily as a prelude to the full-scale invasion. Bad weather and errors, however, placed the men 30 to 50 miles away from the airfields which they were assigned to neutralize.

■ Russian forces in fierce fighting withstood German attacks north and south of Kursk.

July 10 Sicily was invaded. First elements of the U.S. Seventh and the British Eighth armies (about 12 divisions altogether) began landing at 2:45 A.M. on the southeast coast of Sicily. The occupation of the island was regarded as a necessary prelude to an attack on Italy itself. The landings caught the ten Italian and three German divisions (350,000 men in all) by surprise, and there was very little initial resistance. In the first day about 160,000 Allied soldiers were put ashore, along with 1,000 artillery pieces and 600 tanks.

■ German forces north of the Kursk salient were blocked, having gained only a little more than

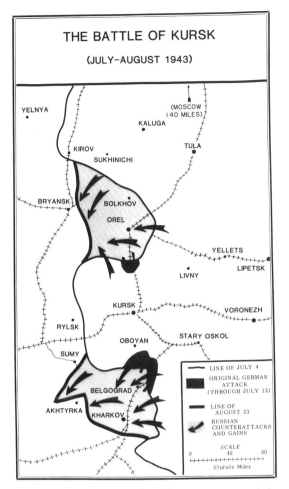

THE BATTLE OF KURSK

(JULY–AUGUST 1943)

YELNYA

(MOSCOW 140 MILES)

KALUGA

KIROV
SUKHINICHI

TULA

BRYANSK

BOLKHOV

OREL

YELLETS

LIPETSK

LIVNY

KURSK

VORONEZH

RYLSK

OBOYAN

STARY OSKOL

SUMY

BELGOGRAD

AKHTYRKA   KHARKOV

LINE OF JULY 4

ORIGINAL GERMAN ATTACK (THROUGH JULY 13)

LINE OF AUGUST 23

RUSSIAN COUNTERATTACKS AND GAINS

SCALE
0   40   80
Statute Miles

German forces tried to close the pincers around the Russians at Kursk, but were instead defeated in the greatest land battle in history.

Russian snipers advance to forward positions as the Red Army continued its westward path.

five miles while losing 25,000 killed, 200 tanks destroyed, and 200 planes downed.

July 11 Despite the beginnings of some spirited resistance, Allied forces fanned out from the beachheads on Sicily and achieved their early objectives.

July 12 Russian troops began their massive counteroffensive around the Kursk salient. The largest tank battle in history was fought near the village of Prochorovka. The Germans alone lost more than 400 tanks. About 3,000 tanks were deployed by the two sides in this vicious clash of armor.

■ British and U.S. forces joined up at Ragusa on Sicily. Six airfields had been captured. U.S. 1st Infantry forces hurled back a German counterattack spearheaded by 100 tanks. The port of Syracuse was taken by the British.

■ The Japanese landed 1,200 more men on Kolombangara, as a U.S. naval force failed to stop the operation. A Japanese cruiser was lost in the fighting.

July 13 Hitler ordered a halt to German offensive operations around Kursk and began pulling troops out for redeployment to Italy because of the invasion of Sicily.

■ Allied fighter aircraft began operating out of Pachino airfield on Sicily, further establishing Allied control of the air.

■ British Commandos and paratroopers landed on the Sicilian east coast to capture key bridges on the highway between Syracuse and Catania.

July 14 Messina was hit by 212 Allied bombers which dropped 800 tons of bombs. The Sicilian city was the funnel for Axis reinforcements and supplies from the Italian mainland.

July 15 Red Army units stepped up their offensive near Orel.

■ In an overwhelming defeat of Japanese air units in the central Solomons, U.S. aircraft downed 45 out of 75 planes while losing only three. Japanese daylight attacks were now sharply curtailed.

July 16 Roosevelt and Churchill addressed a joint message to the Italian people: "If you continue to tolerate the Fascist regime, which serves the evil power of the Nazis, you must suffer the consequences of your own choice. . . . We are determined to destroy the false leaders and their doctrines which have brought Italy to her present position." They concluded that Italians will have to decide whether to "die for Mussolini and Hitler—or live for Italy and for civilization."

■ The Canadian 1st Division captured Caltagirone, while U.S. forces took Barrafranca and Porto Empedocle on Sicily. About a quarter of the island was now in Allied hands.

July 17 General Alexander was appointed Allied military governor of Sicily, and "benevolent" control of the island was to be established by non-Fascist Italians under the Military Government of Occupied Territory.

■ Hitler ordered the reinforcement of German units in the Balkans, believing the Allies' next landing would be there.

■ Allied forces began pushing toward Salamaua in New Guinea, but the main effort was to secure the Huon Peninsula and the Markham valley.

■ Japanese forces launched their only counterattack at Munda on New Georgia but were repulsed.

July 18 The only U.S. lighter-than-air craft lost during the war was shot down off the Florida Keys. Airship *K-74* spotted German submarine *U-134*, tried to attack it, but was brought down by gunfire.

THE BOMBING OF BOISE CITY, OKLAHOMA

Only one city on the American mainland was bombed during the war. Boise City, Oklahoma, was "attacked" in July 1943 by a single U.S. Army Air Force plane on a bombing training mission. The aircraft—operating out of Dalhart, Texas—was to drop six 100-pound practice bombs (each carried four pounds of explosives) on a desolate bombing range. Instead, the pilot delivered his load on Boise City, 45 miles away from the range. The bombs hit the Baptist Church and a garage. There were no casualties.

July 19 U.S. Nineteenth Air Force bombers struck airfields and the rail marshaling yards in Rome. More than 500 planes participated in the raid, dropping 1,000 tons of bombs.

■ Hitler and Mussolini conferred at Feltre in the Italian Dolomites. In this, their thirteenth meeting, the Axis leaders discussed German aid to Italy. Mussolini had been urged by his advisers to tell Hitler that Italy was faltering badly and might not be able to continue, but the Duce did not do so. He was convinced Hitler would never permit the Italians any "freedom of action."

■ Patton's army in Sicily made rapid progress in striking to the northern part of the island.

Troops of the U.S. 45th Division advance through Caltanissetta, Sicily.

July 19-21 Luftwaffe planes of the 1st Air Division conducted a campaign to stem the advance of the Russians near Orel. Red Army tanks incurred some of the heaviest losses ever suffered from the air by armored units.

July 20 Russian forces captured Mtsensk as the German Army Group North pulled back toward Orel.

July 21 An anti-Hitler National Committee of Free Germany was formed in the Soviet Union.

July 22 Sicily's chief city of Palermo fell to General Patton's forces. A planned final assault was found to be unnecessary when all resistance in the city ended.

July 23 All German forces involved in the Kursk offensive had been pushed back beyond their starting positions 18 days before.

■ Mopping up operations in western Sicily were begun by Patton's forces. Montgomery's army encountered strong resistance near Leonforte.

July 24 "Window" decoy tinfoil to confuse German radar was used for the first time by RAF aircraft in the Hamburg raid. Only 12 of 740 bombers were downed, testament to its initial success.

July 24-25 The first in a series of massive RAF and U.S. Air Force raids on Hamburg began as 740 British planes dropped 2,396 tons of bombs. Hamburg was of vital strategic importance with its 3,000 industrial plants, almost all of them involved in war production.

July 25 Mussolini was overthrown. The 60-year-old dictator had been in power since the early 1920s. With the Allies poised to invade the Italian mainland, Italian generals and politicians moved to oust Mussolini. In a meeting of the Fascist Grand Council the vote was 19 to 7 to give King Victor Emmanuel III command of the armed forces. Mussolini met with the monarch and was then placed under arrest in the palace grounds. He was first exiled to the island of Ponza and then transferred to a hotel in the Abruzzi mountains. The immediate effect of Mussolini's ouster was large-scale defections by the Italian military. Many units tried to establish contact with the Allies, while some began collaborating with anti-Axis guerrillas in Yugoslavia, Greece, and Albania.

■ The American destroyer escort *Harmon* was launched. It was the first U.S. Navy ship ever named for a black, Leonard Roy Harmon, a mess attendant killed while saving a shipmate's life during the fight for Guadalcanal. He received the Navy Cross posthumously. The ship was christened by his mother.

■ Hitler dispatched Rommel, his "favorite general," to command German forces in Greece. Hitler still believed the Allied landings in Sicily were a deception prior to the main operation which would be in Greece.

July 25-26 Essen was attacked by 627 RAF bombers which dropped 2,032 tons of bombs. Twenty-six of the planes were lost, but the damage inflicted prompted Goebbels to write in his diary: "The last raid on Essen caused a complete stoppage of production in the Krupp works. Speer is much concerned and worried." A total of 340 Germans were killed.

July 26 A new Italian government under Pietro Badoglio proclaimed martial law throughout the country, dissolved the Fascist party, and banned all political meetings.

July 27-28 In the deadliest RAF raid of the war, 739 bombers attacked Hamburg, killing about 20,000 and wounding 60,000. A total of 2,417 tons of bombs were dropped, including large numbers of incendiaries which touched off firestorms with temperatures close to 1,000 degrees centigrade and winds of more than 150 miles an hour.

AERIAL INCENDIARIES

Incendiary bombs "probably caused as much death and destruction as any other weapon used in World War II," according to the official U.S. Army history of the war.

Aerial incendiaries were generally dropped behind enemy lines, unlike the fire bombs (or napalm) which were tactical weapons.

The RAF did most of the early experimenting with incendiaries and concluded that when properly used they were more effective against strategic targets than high-explosive bombs.

The series of devastating raids against Hamburg in July and Aug. 1943 seemed to prove the point. During that period RAF and U.S. Eighth Air Force bombers dropped nearly a million-and-a-half incendiaries on Hamburg. According to Hamburg civil defense officials, "Exact figures could not be obtained out of a layer of human ashes."

Japan was more vulnerable to Allied incendiary attack than was Germany. In the latter, 95 percent of the construction was brick and stone, while 80 per cent of Japanese construction was wood and paper.

July 28 Allied surrender terms were broadcast to the Italians by Roosevelt.

■ Japanese forces were secretly evacuated from Kiska, in the Aleutians. The U.S. was totally unaware of their removal and was proceeding with plans for an armed invasion.

July 30 Axis forces pulled back into a pocket on the northeastern tip of Sicily, the only major resistance remaining.

Aug. 1 U.S. bombers from Libya—flying at low levels—attacked the Ploesti oil complex in Rumania. A force of 178 B-24s was employed on the mission; 41 were downed by the heavy defenses and another 13 were lost for other rea-

A low-flying B-24 bomber makes its bombing run through towering smoke in a U.S. raid against the Astra Romana oil refinery at Ploesti, Rumania.

sons. Damage to the refineries was severe though they were eventually repaired. Rumania supplied about 21 million barrels a year to the Axis forces, almost half their needs.

■ German and Italian troops were ordered to begin pulling back to Messina for evacuation to the Italian mainland.

■ German divisions under the command of Rommel began infiltrating into northern Italy, part of a plan to take control of the area from the Italians.

■ Italian troops on Crete were disarmed by the Germans.

■ De Gaulle became head of the French Committee of National Defense. Giraud was given command of Free French forces.

■ The Allies warned neutral nations not to give sanctuary to Axis war criminals.

■ Japan declared Burma's independence. The government in Rangoon under Dr. Ba Maw immediately declared war on Britain and the U.S. The title of the new president was "Adipadi," the Pali word for Führer.

THE PATTON SLAPPING INCIDENTS

General Patton's combat prowess was as renowned as his flamboyance and ill temper were deplored. The most notorious of his actions involved slapping three hospitalized American enlisted men.

On Aug. 1, 1943, while visiting the 15th Evacuation Hospital near Nicosia, Sicily, Patton cursed and slapped a private of Company L, 26th Infantry Regiment. The GI, diagnosed as suffering from a moderately severe case of psychoneurotic anxiety, told Patton, "I guess I can't take it." Patton exploded and hit the private in the face with his gloves, unleashed a torrent of abuse on him, and physically threw him out of the tent.

Ten days later Patton was at the 93rd Evacuation Hospital near the north coast of Sicily. Here, Patton slapped two men, Sergeants Paul Bennett and Charles H. Kuhl, both from the 17th Field Artillery Regiment. Bennett was down with malaria, Kuhl suffered from a severe case of shell shock. Patton slapped Bennett three times, accusing him of malingering. Kuhl was quivering on his cot when Patton pulled a pistol on him and slapped him with his free hand, saying, "You ought to be lined up against a wall and shot." As the general left the hospital he told the medical commander, Colonel D. E. Currier, "I won't have those cowardly bastards hanging around our hospitals. We'll probably have to shoot them sometime anyway, or we'll raise a breed of morons."

Patton later apologized for the incidents, but he was reprimanded by Eisenhower. One newsman reported there were 50,000 American GIs on Sicily who would have killed Patton if given the chance. Yet when the general addressed his troops at an assembly in early September he was cheered lustily when he said, "I thought I'd stand here and let you fellows see if I am as big a son of a bitch as you think I am."

Aug. 2 The Italian ambassador to Portugal opened negotiations for peace with the Allies.

■ An Allied broadcast from Algiers warned the Italian people of an imminent invasion.

■ The U.S. turned over 150 merchant ships to Britain for the duration of the war.

■ Kiska was bombarded by a U.S. naval force of two battleships, five cruisers, and nine destroyers, the beginning of a series of heavy attacks against the Aleutian outpost, which was already abandoned.

■ U.S.S. *PT-109*, commanded by Lieutenant John F. Kennedy, was sunk after it was rammed by a Japanese destroyer in Blackett Strait in the Solomons. Eleven of the 13 crewmen survived and a week later were returned to their base at Rendova after harrowing and heroic efforts to elude the Japanese. (The official report on *PT-109*'s loss was cowritten by the flotilla's intelligence officer, Lieutenant (j.g.) Byron R. White, a 1962 appointee to the U.S. Supreme Court by President John F. Kennedy.)

■ Allied air units completed a week-long bombardment of Hamburg. While industrial facilities were heavily damaged, the raids took a large toll in civilian casualties.

Aug. 3 Red Army forces broadened their offensive as they opened a drive toward Kharkov in the northern Ukraine and closed in on Orel from three sides.

THE DEVASTATION OF HAMBURG

From July 24 through Aug. 2, 1943, the RAF and the U.S. Air Force staged six raids on Hamburg and its immediate suburbs. More than 2,600 bombers were involved (87 British planes were downed). Goebbels wrote of the raids in his diary: ". . . a catastrophe, the extent of which simply staggers the imagination." The police president of Hamburg calculated the losses:

Casualties

41,800 killed instantly	37,439 injured (an undetermined number died)

Property Destruction

40,385	homes	83	banks
275,000	apartments	12	bridges
580	factories	1	zoo (the once famous Hagenbeck, which was totally destroyed in the first attack)
2,632	shops		
24	hospitals		
277	schools		
58	churches		

■ The British Eighth Army in Sicily pushed toward Catania after meeting stiff German resistance.

■ A wave of labor unrest began sweeping the northern Italian industrial cities of Genoa, Turin, and Milan. (Strikes were called during the next month until Badoglio revoked martial law and agreed to release political prisoners. Badoglio was walking a political tightrope between the Germans, who had lost all confidence in the Italians, and the people who wanted out of the war as soon as possible.)

Aug. 4 Russian troops pierced the defenses of the German LII Infantry Corps and recaptured Belgorod.

Aug. 5 Sweden canceled its agreement with Berlin whereby unarmed German soldiers and goods were permitted passage across Sweden to and from Norway and which permitted the Germans to ship war materiel across Sweden.

■ The Soviets captured Orel and Belgorod. The German Second Panzer Army was almost destroyed at Orel. Hitler ordered a withdrawal to the Desna River in order to free more troops for redeployment to Italy.

■ Munda's airfield on New Georgia was captured by U.S. forces, ending six weeks of hard ground fighting and air combat which resulted in the loss of 350 Japanese and 93 American planes.

Allied paratroopers descend from their low-flying transports in an attack behind Japanese lines in New Guinea.

Aug. 6 Germany began a partial evacuation of Berlin because of the destructive air raids.

■ Fearing a complete defection by Italy, German troops started pouring into the country to assume complete control of its defense.

Aug. 6–7 Four Japanese destroyers bringing troops and supplies to Kolombangara in the Solomons were intercepted by six U.S. destroyers in Vella Gulf. Three of the Japanese ships were sunk. The other was damaged. None of the American destroyers was hit.

Aug. 9 Hungary and Britain reached a secret agreement in Ankara. RAF and American bombers on missions from Italy would not be fired on while overflying Hungary. In return the Allies promised not to bomb Hungarian targets.

Aug. 10 Churchill arrived in Canada for the QUADRANT conference in Québec.

Aug. 12 German forces began being evacuated from Sicily.

■ Marshall advised Eisenhower that seven divisions would be withdrawn from Italy beginning in November. They would be employed in an invasion of southern France. (It was a decision which prolonged the Italian campaign at the expense of an operation which contributed very little to the end of the war.)

■ The Russians recaptured Chuguyev and the final drive for Kharkov got underway.

CASUALTIES OF THE CAMPAIGN IN SICILY

Axis

32,100 Germans and 131,900 Italians killed, wounded, or captured

1,500 aircraft, 78 tanks and armored cars, and 287 artillery pieces captured or destroyed

Allied

2,721 British Commonwealth troops killed in action

1,233 U.S. troops killed in action

7,939 British Commonwealth troops wounded

4,695 U.S. troops wounded

2,183 British Commonwealth troops missing

968 U.S. troops missing

Aug. 13 Rome's rail yards were hit by 274 Allied aircraft which dropped about 500 tons of bombs. Heavy damage resulted. U.S. Twelfth Air Force planes bombed Messerschmitt factories near Vienna.

■ U.S. bombers from Italy attacked the manufacturing center of Wiener Neustadt in Austria, the first flight over Hungary under the Aug. 9 agreement.

Aug. 14 Rome was proclaimed an open city.

■ Russian units reached the Donets River and the suburbs of Kharkov.

Aug. 14–24 The QUADRANT conference was held in Québec. Several key decisions were made on the future course of the war. The cross-Channel invasion was confirmed for May 1, 1944, but Churchill pushed for some qualifications, among them the elimination of the Luftwaffe over the landing beaches, more secure beachhead conditions, and the prospect of not having to face more than 12 German reserve divisions. Pacific action was to be directed along two routes leading to

Japan, one through the Gilberts and Marshalls and the other over a route leading through the Philippines. A landing near Naples was approved, with a subsequent drive into France.

Aug. 15 U.S. and Canadian forces (34,000 men) landed at Quisling Cove on the west coast of Kiska in the Aleutians which had been occupied by the Japanese since June 12, 1942. What the Allies did not know was that the Japanese had already withdrawn.

■ U.S. Army and Marine units landed on Vella Lavella in the Solomons, bypassing the Japanese on Kolombangara.

■ The Italian government began negotiations for peace in Madrid. General Giuseppe Castellano met with Allied representatives at the British embassy. Italy offered its forces to fight on the Allied side when the invasion of Italy began.

■ Allied aircraft pounded Axis forces fleeing Sicily.

■ After more than two weeks of work engineers were able to construct only three miles of the Ledo Road, the projected land route from Burma to China.

Aug. 16 Only Axis rear guards remained on Sicily. More than 60,000 Germans had been evacuated to the Italian mainland. All organized resistance on the island ceased.

Aug. 17 The battle for Sicily ended as U.S. troops entered Messina at 10 A.M., and British units shortly thereafter. The islands of Stromboli and Lipari, north of Sicily, surrendered to an American destroyer and PT boats. The conquest of Sicily made it easier to invade Italy and to step up the air campaign against Italian mainland targets. Axis casualties in the 39-day Sicilian campaign were 167,000, including 37,000 German. It was viewed as a "major military disaster" for the Axis, having delayed the invasion of Italy by only five weeks. Allied casualties were 25,000.

■ Allied bombers began hitting German V-bomb experimental bases with a nighttime attack against Peenemünde, on the Baltic. A total of 571 planes dropped 1,937 tons of bombs on the research and construction sites. U.S. planes hit German aircraft plants at Schweinfurt and Regensburg. Of the 315 planes involved in the daylight raid, 60 were downed, and the future of dawn to dark attacks was debated by British and American planners.

CODE NAMES

Britain's Public Record Office estimated the Allies assigned more than 10,000 code names to operations, places, and people. Some became famous because they designated historic events, most notably OVERLORD, the Normandy landings. Indeed, most of the code names were applied to military actions. Less known (with the exception of Roosevelt's and Churchill's) are those assigned to individuals or groups. The following were listed among the operational code names contained in *The Second World War: A Guide to Documents in the Public Record Office.*

ADMIRAL Q	President Roosevelt (also VICTOR)
ALI BABA	The Russians
BRAID	General Marshall (for Casablanca Conference)
CELESTES	Chiang Kai-shek (for Cairo Conference)
COLLODON	Secretary of State Stettinius
COMPOST	Foreign Secretary Eden
DESTINY	The U.S. Army
DUCKPIN	General Eisenhower
ECUADOR	The Greeks
FORMER NAVAL PERSON	Prime Minister Churchill (also COLONEL WARDEN)
GLYPTIC	Stalin
GOLLIWOG	The Free French
ICEBLINK	Secretary of State James F. Byrnes
JULIAN	Soviet Ambassador to London Ivan Maisky
KILTING	President Truman
KINGPIN	General Henri Giraud
LAUNDRESS	Vichy French
MOSS BANK	Pierre Laval
PEANUT	Chiang Kai-shek°
PETER	Soviet Foreign Minister V. M. Molotov (also DUNKER)
SINBAD	Secretary of State Cordell Hull

°This appears to be an official code name, not the term of contempt given the Chinese leader by General Joseph Stilwell. The term gained notoriety when Stilwell's diary was published, but it appears the general was only using the term assigned to Chiang by the British and Americans.

■ Portugal agreed to British use of bases in the Azores.

■ The Japanese established a base at Horaniu, Vella Lavella, to be used in evacuating their troops from Kolombangara by barges which were towed to the area.

Aug. 18 Eisenhower was authorized to send representatives to Lisbon to discuss an armistice with Italy.

■ China's Foreign Minister T.V. Soong complained to Hull that China was being excluded from Allied top-level strategy conferences. He said matters of "utmost concern" to Chiang were being decided by others. Soong said, "Even when given a hearing by the Combined Chiefs of Staff, Chinese spokesmen had not been allowed to share in the agreements and the making of decisions." China, in fact, wanted to share policy and status as a Big Four ally, which had really been extended only in propaganda.

■ General Hans Jeschonnek, chief of the Luftwaffe General Staff, committed suicide, apparently because of blame and abuse heaped upon him by Hitler for the increasingly intense Allied air campaign against Germany, and especially the raid on Peenemünde. Jeschonnek remained loyal to Hitler to the end, however, blaming Göring for the state of the Luftwaffe. His suicide note read: "I can no longer work together with the *Reichsmarschall*. Long live the Führer!" When the Germans announced his death, Jeschonnek was said to have died of a stomach hemorrhage lest the Allies and German people infer it was related to the growing inability of the Luftwaffe to defend Germany.

■ Zmiev, south of Kharkov, was captured by the Russians.

Aug. 22 Allied forces completed their sweep through Kiska in the Aleutians and learned there were no Japanese on the island. Some casualties were suffered, the result of nervous, trigger-happy troops firing on friendly units.

■ German troops pulled out of Kharkov with most of the city in ruin.

Aug. 23 Kharkov was reoccupied for the second time by the Russians.

■ Japanese aircraft bombed Chungking.

Aug. 24 Hitler appointed SS Chief Heinrich Himmler as Reichminister of the Interior.

Aug. 25 Lord Louis Mountbatten was appointed Supreme Allied Commander, Southeast Asia.

■ U.S. Army troops secured New Georgia Island in the Solomons. Japanese troops withdrew to Kolombangara and Arundel.

■ Roosevelt addressed the Canadian Parliament in Québec.

Aug. 26 A campaign to drive the Germans out of the eastern Ukraine was launched by the Russians.

■ Allied nations recognized the French Committee of National Liberation.

Aug. 27 A German division occupied Ljubljana, the capital of Italian-controlled Slovenia, and began fighting the Italian XV Corps. The Italians refused to withdraw from the city. Croatian troops joined the Germans in attacking them.

■ Sevsk, south of Bryansk, was captured by the Russians.

■ British reconnaissance teams landed on the toe of Italy.

■ Arundel Island in the Solomons was occupied by the U.S. Army. Marines landed on Nukufetau in the Ellice Islands.

Aug. 28 King Boris III of Bulgaria died under peculiar circumstances after visiting Hitler. Boris was never firmly in the Axis camp and resisted German pressures but had no choice but to yield. It appeared he died a natural death, but there are many who were convinced that he was assassinated.

■ Germany announced a state of emergency in Denmark, including a ban on meetings involving more than five people, press censorship, the closing of all places of entertainment, the death penalty for sabotage, and the surrender of all arms. The small military was disarmed. King Christian X threatened to abdicate. The Danish government said the people could not accept the terms and resigned.

■ U.S. Marines occupied Nanumea in the Ellice Islands.

Aug. 29 The U.S. issued a warning to Germany on crimes against civilians. Washington said it had received "trustworthy information" on atrocities committed by "the German invaders against the population of Poland." The U.S. government would, said the statement, take such "crimes into account against the time of the final settlement with Germany."

■ The Danish king was seized by the Germans. In retaliation for the German crackdown, the Danes scuttled their fleet. Twenty-nine ships were destroyed. Only 13 small craft were taken intact by the Germans.

Aug. 30 Red Army troops smashed the southern end of the German line, capturing Taganrog and launching the campaign to cut off German forces in the Crimea. Other elements pushed toward Smolensk.

Aug. 31 General Castellano met with Allied officers in Sicily and told them the Badoglio government could not accept proposed surrender terms until guarantees were given on sufficient numbers of Anglo-American troops landing in Italy to protect the Italians from German reprisals.

Sept. A catastrophic famine swept Bengal in India. More than a million people died of starvation. The 1942–43 rice crop produced disastrously poor yields of the vital food, and a lack of transportation facilities made it impossible to distribute emergency supplies on a timely basis. The British chiefs of staff felt "that unless the necessary steps are taken to rectify this situation, the efficient prosecution of the war against Japan by forces based in India will be gravely jeopardised and may well prove impossible."

Sept. 1 Russian troops ousted the Germans from Dorogobuzh on the Smolensk front.

■ The Calabrian coast of Italy was bombed by ships and planes in a preinvasion attack.

■ U.S. Navy planes attacked Marcus Island, causing heavy damage to the Japanese base, 1,185 miles southeast of Tokyo. The F6F Hellcat fighter was used in combat for the first time in this action. Baker Island was occupied by U.S. Army troops.

Sept. 2 Five Russian armies bore down on the Germans on a broad front. The Bryansk-Kiev rail line was cut 150 miles from Kiev.

Sept. 3 A secret armistice was signed, ending Italy's participation in the war as a member of the Axis. There were actually two surrender documents. The one signed this date (by General Castellano for Italy) at Cassibile, Sicily, and which was not made public lest the Germans move to seize control of Italy, made no reference to unconditional surrender. When the second document was signed five days later, it covered capitulation without qualification. It was, however, not the kind of surrender outlined at the

Italy, invaded by the Allies, capitulated and switched sides, but German troops occupied the country and offered fierce resistance.

THE INVASION OF ITALY (1943)

Scale

0   50   100

Statute Miles

Casablanca conference. The British Eighth Army landed at Reggio di Calabria on the Italian toe, which was to draw the Germans down from the area south of Naples. Field Marshal Albert Kesselring did not take the bait, correctly assuming the main Allied force would land around Salerno.

Sept. 4 The last rail outlet out of Kharkov was blocked by the Russians who captured Merefa.

■ British forces were delayed in advancing in Calabria by rear-guard demolition activity.

■ Australian and U.S. forces on New Guinea began attacking Lae, the main objective of the campaign. Other Australian units landed on the Huon Peninsula, near Lae.

Sept. 5 Russian troops moved to encircle the Germans at Orel.

■ Most of Calabria was cleared by the British Eighth Army.

Sept. 6 Allied shipping began operating in the Strait of Messina in Italy.

■ U.S. bombers suffered heavy losses—45 out of 407 aircraft—in attacks on German cities.

■ General Stilwell proposed the use of both Chinese Nationalist and Communist troops to defend airfields to be used in attacking Japan's home islands. Stilwell's notion of employing Communist troops was heresy to Chiang Kai-shek, whose own units were largely employed in containing the Communists.

Sept. 7 Berlin announced that Stalino (Donetsk), had been abandoned.

■ Italian units were in full retreat in southern Italy.

Sept. 8 The Italian surrender was made public. Eisenhower announced the capitulation at 6:30 P.M. Marshal Badoglio confirmed the action by broadcast an hour and fifteen minutes later. Italian ships and planes moved to predesignated points to surrender. An American airborne drop on Rome was canceled at the last minute since the Germans had concentrated troops there.

■ Berlin reported the Italian surrender as a treacherous and cowardly act. One official said, "Mussolini was too great a person for a nation like that."

MUSSOLINI'S SECRET DIARY

When Mussolini was exiled to Ponza, he was permitted to keep a diary. It eventually consisted of about 75 short notes, epigrams, observations, reflections, and recollections. His writings reflected a mood of loneliness, resignation, and despair. The Duce saw his life occurring in seven-year cycles: his expulsion from Austria (1908) (it was actually 1909); "intervention" (presumably Italy's entry in the war) (1915); the march on Rome (1922); reconciliation of church and state (1929); founding the empire (1936); fall from power (1943); and "death at last" (which Mussolini believed would come in 1950).

Mussolini wrote of his "anxious and despairing" efforts to save the peace in 1939. He believed the Germans and British were equally responsible for the conflict, Britain because of its unqualified guarantees to Poland, and Germany, "having a mighty military machine ready to strike, could not resist the temptation of setting it in motion."

The Duce recalled his July meeting at Feltre with Hitler, during his "week of suffering." Hitler, wrote Mussolini, was friendly but reserved and at one point delivered a two-hour monologue. When Hitler departed, Mussolini recalled telling Field Marshal Keitel, "Give us at once everything we need, especially air protection for Rome; after all, we're both in the same boat."

SOURCE: German foreign ministry files (marked "Duce-Documents") captured by U.S. forces. Photostat copies were made of the diary and translated into German. The papers were impounded by the Germans after Otto Skorzeny rescued Mussolini from Gran Sasso. Mussolini in 1944 asked Skorzeny if he might have them back, and Skorzeny returned them to the Duce in 1944. The originals have never been found.

■ An armed civilian uprising began on Corsica with attacks on the 115,000 German and Italian garrison troops on the island.

■ The Italian Acqui Division in the Ionian Islands disarmed German contingents. A call was made for Allied assistance and when none came the Germans sent in reinforcements and imprisoned the Italians.

■ Hitler belatedly approved a withdrawal from the Ukraine. The decimated German forces were permitted to fall back to the Dnieper River, the final natural buffer before the Carpathian Mountains.

Sept. 9 The U.S. Fifth Army (made up of the

German troops, with a self-propelled antiaircraft artillery piece, proceed cautiously during the fighting in Italy.

British X and U.S. VI Corps) began landing south of Salerno at 3:30 A.M. A beachhead was quickly established against the defending 16th Panzer Division. Only on the right flank was there any significant resistance. A British airborne division was also landed at Taranto, on the Italian heel.

■ A German Dornier 217, using radio-controlled bombs, sank the Italian battleship *Roma* off Corsica as it was attempting to surrender to the Allies at Malta.

■ Red Army units took Bakhmach on the rail line to Kiev and reached the rail outlet south of Bryansk.

Sept. 10 German troops marched into Rome and seized control of the Italian capital. Italian soldiers in northern Italy were disarmed by the Germans. (Subsequently, Italian units were disbanded in the Balkans and France as well. The Germans neutralized a total of 43 Italian divisions.)

■ British forces landed on the Dodecanese Islands, in the Aegean.

Sept. 11 Brindisi fell to the British, completing occupation of the heel of Italy without any real opposition. Sardinia was evacuated by the Germans. The Salerno beachhead was expanded. The bulk of the Italian fleet which escaped to

Malta surrendered to the British, although the Germans seized 10 cruisers, 10 destroyers, and several submarines. In all, the Italians surrendered 6 battleships, 8 cruisers, 28 destroyers, and 19 submarines.

■ German SS troops began raiding the homes and properties of Jews in Nice.

■ Yugoslav Partisans occupied the port of Split.

■ Japanese forces began pulling back from Salamaua to Lae, pursued by Australian and U.S. troops.

■ A German submarine laid mines off Charleston, South Carolina, but no damage was ever reported.

Sept. 12 In a daring action 90 German gliderborne troops under Colonel Otto Skorzeny rescued Mussolini from imprisonment at the Hotel Camp Imperatore in Abruzzi. The 250-man Italian force guarding Mussolini surrendered within minutes. (The success of the mission prompted the Germans to develop plans to kidnap Tito and Pétain.)

■ The U.S. Fifth Army at Salerno came under heavy counterattack. Kesselring's XIV Panzer Corps came within a whisper of cutting the beachhead in two.

Sept. 13 The Salerno beachhead was still seriously imperiled, but heavy artillery began holding the aggressive German divisions attempting to push the Allied forces into the sea. They came within three miles of doing so at one point.

■ Chiang Kai-shek was named president of China for a three-year term, succeeding Lin Sen who died on Aug. 7. Chiang thus assumed even greater authority in Nationalist territory.

Sept. 14 The 5th Australian Division occupied Salamaua, and the Japanese began pulling out of Lae.

Sept. 15 Mussolini reconstituted the Italian Fascist party and formed a government of the phantom Salò Republic. (Salò was the town on Lake Garda in northern Italy near Mussolini's new residence.) After his rescue Mussolini met with Hitler to determine how best to keep Italy even remotely in the war on the Axis side.

■ A pause developed on the Salerno beachhead. German forces had spent much of their force by now and were subjected to heavy air and naval bombardment.

■ The Soviets opened up a final offensive to retake Smolensk.

■ Chiang Kai-shek and the Chinese Nationalists began urging Roosevelt to recall Stilwell from China. The Chinese leaders regarded the caustic American general as an obstacle who did not understand the "realities" of China.

Sept. 16 Red Army troops recaptured Novorossiysk and other cities and towns along a broad front. Bryansk was abandoned by the Germans.

■ Americans at Salerno began pushing out from their beachhead. Units of the U.S. Fifth Army and the British Eighth Army met 40 miles southeast of Salerno, uniting the Fifteenth Army Group under General Alexander in a single front. This critical phase of the Italian front was now considered over.

■ British forces occupied Samos Island in the Aegean.

■ Lae was occupied by the 9th Australian Division.

Sept. 17 German troops began pulling back from Salerno.

■ Bryansk was occupied by the Red Army.

Sept. 18 U.S. Fifth Army troops began pushing out from Salerno. The 3rd Division was landed to bolster the force.

■ Sardinia surrendered to a small British force which landed aboard two motor torpedo boats. German troops had abandoned the island.

Sept. 19 German units began pulling back to the Dnieper River. Red Army troops rolled toward Smolensk.

■ Tarawa in the Gilbert Islands was attacked by U.S. Navy and Army planes.

■ The Salerno plain was secured by the American Fifth Army.

Sept. 20 U.S. and British units linked up at Eboli in Italy, completing the consolidation of a solid Allied line.

Sept. 21 Arundel Island in the Solomons was secured by U.S. Army forces. The Japanese lost 600 men in the fight. Tokyo decided to abandon the central Solomons.

Russia's massive military might was now harnessed for the great push westward.

Sept. 22 Poltava fell to the Russians. Red Army forces established bridgeheads on the west bank of the Dnieper River.

■ Australian forces made an amphibious landing six miles north of Finschhafen in New Guinea.

■ Two British X-craft midget submarines (out of the six which started the mission) penetrated Altenfjord in Norway and attached eight tons of explosives under the German battleship *Tirpitz*, causing crippling damage. (Structural repairs would have to be completed in Germany if *Tirpitz* could ever operate in open sea again, and Hitler and Dönitz decided to keep it in Norway as a floating battery.)

Sept. 23 Mussolini publicly announced the creation of the Salò Republic, embracing an ill-defined portion of Italy where the Germans were in control.

■ Free French troops occupied Bonifacio on Corsica.

Sept. 24 Berlin announced the evacuation of Smolensk and Roslavl.

■ The airfield at Vella Lavella in the Solomons became operational for the Allies.

■ Japanese aircraft bombed Allied ships attempting to resupply the Australians near Finschhafen.

Sept. 25 Smolensk and Roslavl were reoccupied by the Russians.

■ Mussolini declared the central portion of Italy as a neutral zone for civilians.

Sept. 26 Japanese troops failed to drive the Australians out of the Finschhafen area.

■ The German force on Corfu surrendered.

■ U.S. naval forces began operating out of Natal, Brazil.

Sept. 27 Foggia, the major objective of the British Eighth Army, was abandoned by the Germans. (The large airfields there were important for future Allied operations.)

■ U.S. P-47s provided protection for Eighth Air Force bombers all the way to Germany in an attack on Emden. The fighters carried belly tanks to make the long trip possible.

■ Mussolini convened the first cabinet meeting of the Salò Republic at his residence at La Rocca delle Caminate, near Gargnano on Lake Garda. The rump Italian government sought to let Italians continue jurisdiction over civil affairs under German military authority, but Hitler had totally lost faith in his Italian allies by now.

■ Russian troops forged a bridgehead across the Dnieper near Pereyaslav, 60 miles southeast of Kiev. Two panzer divisions failed to oust the Russians.

Sept. 28 The evacuation of Kolombangara in the Solomons was begun by the Japanese. (It continued through Oct. 3 with Allied forces attempting to block their removal. In the end 9,400 Japanese were removed.)

Sept. 29 Eisenhower and Badoglio signed the final Italian surrender document aboard the British battleship *Nelson*, off Malta.

Sept. 30 British troops surrounded Mount Vesuvius near Naples.

■ British civilian air raid casualties for the month reached a low since the bombing began, 5 killed, 11 wounded. Since April the total was 1,237 killed and 1,607 wounded.

July–Sept. In one of the failings of the U.S. Selective Service System, the army found itself sorely short of men. During this three month period, the army had requested a draft of 585,000 men but only 447,000 were inducted, a 24 percent shortage. This was to have a direct impact on the Italian front during the 1943–44 winter. The deputy Allied commander, General Devers, reported, "Replacements allocated to this theater are not adequate to sustain operations in Italy on the present scale." The U.S. Fifth Army was then short by 13,000 officers and men.

MINE WARFARE IN AMERICAN WATERS

By Oct. 1943 the threat of German submarine-laid mines along the American east coast had passed. U-boats were no longer available for this kind of warfare. In two years the subs had laid 338 mines in U.S. and Canadian waters. They accounted for seven Allied ship sinkings. Three others were damaged. The threat of German mines, however, had tied up ships and men for long periods of time. At the height of the war, 125 U.S. mine sweepers were occupied with clearing the mines. Shipping was also slowed down, with New York, Wilmington, Jacksonville, Savannah, Charleston, and Chesapeake Bay ports all closed down at one time or another until their channels were cleared.

SOURCE: Arnold S. Lott, *Most Dangerous Sea*.

Oct. 1 Naples was occupied by the British army's King's Dragoon Guards. The port was heavily damaged but repairs began at once to put it back in operation.

■ Averell Harriman was appointed U.S. ambassador to Moscow.

Oct. 2 British Commandos landed at Termoli and shortly linked up with the Eighth Army. U.S. troops advanced to Benevento and moved to establish a line on the Volturno River, where the Germans were ordered to delay the Allied advance as long as possible.

■ Finschhafen in New Guinea was captured by Australian forces.

■ U.S. submarines began mining the waters off the Celebes to cut traffic through the Makassar Strait.

■ German infantry divisions were reformed to include only 10,708 men each, including 2,000 Russian POW's who had volunteered for noncombat duty. (They were known as "Hiwis," short for *Hilfswilliger*.)

Oct. 3 Japanese troops opened up offensive operations on a broad front in central China.

■ All Japanese forces were evacuated from Kolombangara in the Solomons.

■ Kos Island was occupied by German forces. It was the only Allied air base in the Aegean, and its loss endangered Samos and Leros.

Oct. 4 French partisans, Moroccan Goums, and American OSS agents completed the occupation of Corsica, which was now totally abandoned by the Germans.

■ Admiral Sir Andrew Cunningham was named Britain's first sea lord, succeeding Sir Dudley Pound who had resigned because of ill health and who died shortly thereafter.

■ Frankfurt was bombed in round-the-clock attacks. Casualties included 529 dead.

Oct. 5 Germany annexed Trieste, Istria, and the South Tyrol.

■ Churchill announced the surrender of additional Italian ships at Malta.

■ U.S. ships and planes began bombarding Wake Island. The initial bombardment was conducted by 6 carriers, 7 cruisers, and 24 destroyers.

Oct. 6 U.S. Fifth Army troops reached the south bank of the Volturno River about 15 miles northwest of Naples. A brief lull developed as the Allies prepared for an assault on the German Gustav Line.

■ American troops were landed on Kolombangara Island which had been abandoned by the Japanese. It closed the battle for the central Solomons. U.S. losses in the campaign totaled 1,094 dead to over 2,500 Japanese. Four airfields were now in Allied hands, all within range of the next major objective, Bougainville.

Oct. 7 The frontwide Russian offensive slowed down in the face of stiffening German resistance.

■ All Japanese troops were evacuated from Vella Lavella.

Oct. 8 Tojo assumed control over the Japanese ministries of commerce and industry.

■ Pro- and anti-Communist guerrillas began a series of violent clashes in Greece, the beginning of the civil war in that country which was to last for six years.

Oct. 9 Russian forces reoccupied the entire Taman peninsula.

Oct. 10 The Atlantic entrance to the Panama Canal was mined by a German submarine.

Oct. 12 Portugal agreed to permit the Allies use of the Azores as a base for the protection of convoys.

■ U.S. Fifth Air Force planes opened an offensive to isolate Rabaul and neutralize the Bismarck Archipelago. About 350 bombers inflicted heavy damage, but lost only four planes.

Oct. 13 Italy declared war on Germany. Premier Badoglio told Eisenhower, "By this act all ties with the dreadful past are broken and my Government will be proud to be able to march with you on to the inevitable victory." Italians now fought on the Allied side as "cobelligerents."

■ American II and III Corps forces broke across the Volturno River. Bridgeheads were established on several points on the north side despite sharp resistance. The Germans began pulling back to the Winter Line, along the Garigliano and Sangro rivers about 75 miles south of Rome.

Oct. 14 Red Army forces concluded the recapture of the industrial center of the Ukraine by occupying Zaporodzhye.

■ The Philippines was declared an independent republic under Japanese tutelage.

Oct. 14–15 U.S. B-17s bombed the German ball-bearing manufacturing center at Schweinfurt, but the raid was extremely costly and for a time ended daylight attacks deep in Germany. Of the

291 aircraft which took off, 288 reached their targets. Sixty of them were shot down by German fighters.

This B-17 was sent into a fatal plunge to earth when a bomb from another U.S. bomber flying directly above it sheared off one of its tail fins.

Oct. 15 More troops crossed the Volturno River and began pushing northward before being blocked near Villa and Liberi.

Oct. 16 Preceeded by a massive two-hour artillery barrage, Russian forces launched a major offensive from the bridgeheads on the Dnieper.

Oct. 17 The German raider *Michel* was sunk by an American submarine off the coast of Japan. It was the last of the ten armed merchantmen which the German navy employed during the war. Beginning in February 1940, when the first one put to sea, they were a scourge to Allied merchant vessels. Each was equipped with six to eight powerful guns and torpedo tubes. Some even had one or two of their own reconnaissance

aircraft. Raiders only attacked ships operating alone. With the exception of one raider captain, Helmuth von Ruckteschell (who was later tried as a war criminal), the officers commanding these ships always operated within the rules of warfare and international law. In all, the raiders accounted for a total of 133 ships (830,000 tons).

■ Russian forces crossed the Dnieper south of Gomel.

Oct. 18 Montgomery's Eighth Army launched a fresh offensive and pushed toward the Trigno River.

■ Bougainville in ths Solomons came under heavy air attack as a prelude to an Allied landing.

■ The first trainloads of Jews left Rome for the Auschwitz concentration camp.

Oct. 19–30 Molotov, Eden, and Hull conducted a series of foreign minister conferences in the Russian capital which led to important plans and disclosures. The Russians were guaranteed that D-Day would be staged in May 1944, and the Soviets indicated for the first time that they would enter the war against Japan once Germany had been vanquished. To allay Russian fears, Britain and the U.S. agreed that Germany would have to surrender unconditionally and no separate armistice would be concluded. Russia indicated its willingness to join in an "international organization for peace."

Oct. 19 The third London protocol was signed with the U.S. and Britain pledging to provide the Soviet Union with 5,100,000 tons of supplies through June of 1944.

■ Allied aircraft began a five-day series of attacks on transportation targets in Italy to impede German logistics.

Oct. 20 Britain, Russia, and the U.S. agreed to establish a U.N. commission to investigate war crimes, establishing the basis for the Nürnberg war crimes trials.

■ Lord Wavell was installed as viceroy of India.

Oct. 21 Subhas Chandra Bose announced a pro-Axis provisional government of Free India (*Azad Hind*) in Singapore. The proclamation said its aim was to "bring about the expulsion of the British and their allies from India."

Oct. 22 The British 78th Division began crossing

Meet the best fed fighters in the world—
the U.S. Soldier, Sailor and Marine!

Typical dinners served the Army, week of Oct. 4th ...and our Sailors and Marines fared equally well.

Not one man in ten ate as nourishing, well balanced meals at home as he does in the U.S. Armed Forces today.

You could be proud to serve meals like these on company occasions—but the Army gets them for dinner every day. They show what care Uncle Sam takes of a son, husband or friend in the service today.

Because meat is as important as fighting weapons to a soldier's stamina and morale, the U.S. Quartermaster Corps sees that every man gets a pound of meat every day.

That means Armour and Company and other packers are shipping millions of pounds of meat *every day* to the Army alone! Besides Armour is supplying tons of meats and dairy products daily for our allies through lend-lease.

That's why you may find temporary shortages in certain meats at home—but our boys in service haven't felt any delays or shortages. The 3 billion dollar plants of the meat industry went to work for Uncle Sam the day war struck. We are glad that Armour and Company, manufacturers of Star Meats and Cloverbloom dairy products, is big enough to help this vital program in an important way.

SUNDAY

ROAST CHICKEN with brown gravy for Sunday dinner! Served with noodle soup, candied sweet potatoes, broccoli and raw carrot strips, buttered Parker House rolls. Ice cream for dessert. Cocoa. Each soldier's portion averaged a full pound of roast chicken.

MONDAY

FRANKFURTERS with Spanish Sauce. A ½ pound portion served each man, with potato cakes and buttered string beans. Orange-grapefruit salad. Bread, butter and coffee. Rice raisin pudding for dessert. The Army's menus are balanced by expert dietitians.

TUESDAY

BARBECUED SPARERIBS and sauerkraut. ½ pound of spareribs for each soldier, topped off with mashed potatoes. Mixed vegetable salad. Bread, butter and tea. Butterscotch meringue pie. Armour supplies a big share of the Army's prime quality pork.

WEDNESDAY

BAKED CORNED BEEF with horse-radish sauce, a generous ¼ pound portion for each man. Also potatoes au gratin, buttered peas, celery. Bread, butter and coffee. Peach cobbler. Soldiers can have second helpings of everything in these Army menus.

THURSDAY

SWISS STEAK with gravy—and each soldier's portion averaged 3.5 of a pound. Baked browned potatoes, buttered carrots, pepper hash. Bread, butter and cocoa. For dessert, apple turnovers with sweet sauce! Steak is a big favorite with men in the Army.

FRIDAY

BAKED FISH with tartar sauce—a generous ½ pound serving for each soldier. Balance of dinner includes parsley potatoes, buttered peas, cole slaw. Bread, butter and tea. And chocolate layer cake for dessert. Pastries are "home made" by Army cooks.

SATURDAY

ROAST BEEF with brown gravy. Also split pea soup, parsley potatoes, stewed tomatoes. String bean salad. Pumpkin pie, coffee. For this war the Quartermaster Corps and packers have developed a new *boneless* beef that is easier to handle and keep.

© ARMOUR AND COMPANY

Armour and Company

FREE ILLUSTRATED BOOKLET, "Food for Freedom"—shows why our fighting forces are the best fed, best equipped fighting men in the world. Send today for your copy free. Write Armour and Company, Department 30, Chicago, Illinois.

An advertisement appeared in Liberty *magazine detailing dinners served U.S. military forces in a typical week.*

the Trigno River as part of the planned assault on Rome.

Oct. 23 The provisional government of India of Subhas Chandra Bose declared war on Britain and the U.S.

Oct. 25 Dnepropetrovsk and Dneprodzerzhinsk were recaptured by the Russians.

■ Allied forces in Italy were directed to press offensive actions and engage a maximum number of Germans who might be massing for a counteroffensive.

Oct. 27 Germany blocked the Skagerrak to Sweden.

■ Heavy rain forced delays in expanding the Trigno bridgehead in Italy. Bad weather continued to hamper operations.

■ New Zealand forces landed on Stirling and Mono islands in the Treasury Islands as part of the Bougainville preinvasion plans.

Oct. 29 U.S. submarines began mining the waters off French Indochina. *Grenadier* placed 32 mines outside Haiphong. (Within a few days Hainan Strait and the approaches to Saigon were sown with mines.)

Oct. 31 The Italian 1st Motorized Group was incorporated into the U.S. Fifth Army, the first Italian unit to enter the war as an Allied cobelligerent.

Nov. 1 All German land communications to the Crimea were cut off by the Russians who landed at the eastern end of the Kerch Peninsula.

■ U.S. Marines invaded Bougainville, landing at Cape Torokina on the west coast. The 3rd Marine Division encountered heavy resistance on the ground and was subjected to constant aerial attack.

Nov. 2 The Japanese cruiser *Sendai* and a destroyer were sunk in the Battle of Empress Augusta Bay as the Japanese attempted to shore up Bougainville. No Japanese reinforcements reached the area.

■ British Eighth Army troops began their main assault across the Trigno River in Italy.

■ U.S. Fifth Air Force aircraft encountered their stiffest opposition of the entire war in attacks on Rabaul.

■ Chinese forces suffered heavy losses in attacking Japanese positions along the Tarung River in Burma.

Nov. 3 In the heaviest daylight raid yet by U.S. Eighth Air Force bombers, 500 planes attacked Wilhelmshaven.

■ Russian forces launched a major drive to recapture Kiev. Marshal Nicholas Vatutin's army group (40 infantry and armored divisions) crossed the Dnieper in a drive for the city.

■ With the advance of the Red Army, the Germans killed the 17,000 remaining Jews in the Maidanek concentration camp.

A U.S. Navy officer scrambles to assist a pilot struggling to escape his burning plane aboard the carrier Enterprise. *The pilot survived, suffering only minor injuries.*

Nov. 5 The Vatican was bombed by Allied aircraft.

■ In a massive attack on Rabaul by U.S. naval and air units, the Japanese suffered heavy losses. The Japanese had beefed up Rabaul with a powerful naval force which threatened the Bougainville beachhead, but the raid destroyed its effectiveness.

Nov. 6 Russian forces recaptured Kiev, the capital of the Ukraine, after the Germans withdrew. Under German occupation since Sept. 19, 1941, the third largest city of the Soviet Union had been almost totally ruined during the fighting.

Nov. 7 Japanese reinforcements were landed near Bougainville and the Marines underwent the first major Japanese counterattack, yielding some ground.

■ Russia's ambassador in Mexico City stated that Moscow regarded Polish territory occupied in 1939 as belonging to the Soviet Union.

■ Free France denied Lebanon's independence which had been granted by the Vichy government.

Nov. 8 Strong German counterattacks were repulsed along the Winter line below Rome on which the Germans planned to make their major stand. British patrols reached the Sangro River.

Rabaul harbor in New Britain is set afire as a low-flying U.S. B-25 completes its bombing run on the Japanese base.

Nov. 9 Churchill predicted the war would reach a climax in 1944.

Nov. 10 The Allied Control Commission for Italy was formed to integrate the Italian economy into the Allied war effort.

Nov. 11 French marines arrested the president and premier of Lebanon. They and other officials were interned in the mountain fortress of Rechayya. A strike was called by the Lebanese in support of the "national government."

■ German forces went on the offensive southwest of Kiev.

■ A heavy air offensive was launched against Rabaul. Marines on Bougainville were reinforced. At least 500 Japanese had been killed in the campaign thus far.

Nov. 12 Admiral Dönitz recorded in his diary the plight of the German U-boat fleet, which was losing the battle of the North Atlantic: "The enemy holds every trump card, covering all areas with long-range air patrols and using location methods against which we still have no warning. . . . The enemy knows all our secrets and we know none of his." What Dönitz did not know was that Ultra—the decoding of intercepted German radio messages—gave the Allies precise knowledge of German submarine locations and plans.

■ Leros in the Aegean was invaded by the Germans. The Allied garrison surrendered the next day.

■ Lebanon was placed under martial law while the Gaullist government in Algiers said the actions taken in Beirut did not have its approval. The U.S. government deplored Lebanese developments.

■ Japanese aircraft were withdrawn from Rabaul, ending the threat from that once powerful base.

■ Allied planes began daily raids on Japanese positions in the Gilbert and Marshall islands.

Nov. 14 German troops launched a counteroffensive to recapture Zhitomir.

THE NEAR-DISASTROUS TORPEDO ATTACK

At midafternoon on Nov. 14, 1943, a torpedo was fired at the U.S. battleship *Iowa* while it was steaming 350 miles east of Bermuda. Aboard *Iowa* were President Roosevelt and the highest ranking officers of the U.S. military (including generals Marshall and Arnold and admirals Leahy and King), all en route to the Tehran conference with Churchill and Stalin. As recorded in the President's Log: "Had that torpedo hit the *Iowa* in the right spot with her passenger list of distinguished statesmen, military, naval, and aerial strategists and planners, it could have had untold effect on the outcome of the war and the destiny of the country." The torpedo did not hit *Iowa*. It exploded in the battleship's wake, 1,200 yards astern. The torpedo which almost caused incalculable loss was fired by a U.S. destroyer, *William D. Porter,* one of three warships escorting *Iowa* and its high-level passengers. *Porter* was engaging in torpedo drill and was aiming at *Iowa*'s No. 2 magazine to add realism when its third tube shot out the live, fully armed torpedo. The weapon had been left unnoticed from *Porter*'s previous combat patrol. When the incident was over, the commanding general of the Air Force, General Arnold, could not resist asking Admiral King, commander of the U.S. Fleet, "Tell me, Ernest, does this happen often in your Navy?"

(RIGHT) *The U.S.S.* Saratoga *at dawn as the crew prepares to launch air strikes against Rabaul.*

A U.S. Navy SBD dive bomber leaves a U.S. carrier force en route to an attack on the Gilbert Islands.

Nov. 15 Alexander ordered Allied forces to halt operations in Italy and to regroup and prepare for an assault on the German Winter Line, held by the Tenth Army under General Heinrich von Vietinghoff.

■ The German XLVIII Panzer Corps, consisting of seven divisions, counterattacked toward Kiev.

Nov. 16 American B-17 bombers attacked the heavy-water production facility at Vemork, Norway. A total of 175 tons of explosives were dropped, but the results were disappointing, leaving production untouched. In the end, though, the raid achieved a basic Allied goal. The Germans decided it would be impractical to continue production at the site, effectively blocking the German effort to build an atomic bomb.

Nov. 17 Australia's 9th Division launched a powerful offensive to take Sattelberg on New Guinea.

Nov. 18 RAF bombers attacked Berlin in the heaviest air strike to date, dropping 350 two-ton bombs in 30 minutes.

■ Russian forces fell back near Zhitomir in the face of heavy German attacks.

Nov. 19 Faced with encirclement, the Russians abandoned Zhitomir.

■ U.S. Army troops were landed at Bougainville.

■ Two 3,000-ton freighters, the British *Penolver* and the American *De Lisle*, sank within 17 minutes of each other after striking mines off St. John's, Newfoundland. Fourteen crewmen of the British ship were picked up by the U.S. vessel and then rescued again, establishing a dubious record of having survived two ship sinkings within half an hour.

Nov. 20 U.S. 2nd Division Marines landed on Tarawa and Makin in the Gilbert Islands, the first of the central Pacific operations aimed at the ultimate invasion of Japan. Despite a heavy pre-assault air and naval bombardment, the landings were met with fierce resistance, compounded by communications confusion on the beaches of Tarawa.

Nov. 21 The Marines on Tarawa made little progress against violent opposition.

Nov. 21-22 In one of the heaviest strikes by any force against a single city, 775 RAF bombers attacked Berlin.

U.S. soldiers on Makin Island in the Gilberts take aim by the body of a slain Japanese defender.

U.S. soldiers land at Butaritari, Makin Atoll, under Japanese machine-gun fire.

Bodies of U.S. Marines, killed in the attack on Tarawa, lie sprawled on the beach.

Nov. 22–26 Chiang Kai-shek participated directly in Allied war planning for the first time with Roosevelt and Churchill in the Cairo conference. General plans were made for offensive operations in Burma including an increase in the number of Chinese troops to be involved. It was also agreed that B-29s would be based in the CBI theater for strikes against Japan proper. Churchill and the British were again turned down in their arguments to launch a large-scale military operation in the Balkans.

Nov. 22 The president of Lebanon and his minis-

ters were released after the French decided to discuss the question of Lebanese independence.

■ Makin was declared secure. U.S. losses in taking the island were 64 killed and 150 wounded.

■ U.S. Marines captured the western portion of Tarawa, effectively ending all Japanese resistance.

■ The Free French decided to reinstate the Lebanese government and in fact recognize the measure of independence previously granted by Vichy.

Nov. 24 The American escort carrier *Liscombe Bay* was sunk by a Japanese aerial torpedo off Makin. It went down 23 minutes after being hit, taking the lives of 644 men, including Rear Admiral Henry A. Mullinix.

■ British forces in Italy advanced north of the Sangro River, firmly establishing the bridgehead.

Nov. 25 Formosa was attacked for the first time as China-based U.S. Fourteenth Air Force bombers destroyed 42 Japanese planes on the ground.

■ Rangoon came under Allied air attack.

■ Japanese forces occupied Changteh in Hunan Province of China.

■ Sattelberg on New Guinea was captured by the Australians.

■ Five U.S. destroyers scored a one-sided victory in the Battle of Cape St. George, New Ireland. They intercepted a force of five Japanese destroyers bringing reinforcements to Buka and suffered no damage while sinking three of the Japanese ships. It was the last of the nighttime naval clashes in the Solomons area.

■ Russian forces threatened the Germans at Gomel while advancing on a broad front. Gomel was a key communications and transportation point on the central front.

Nov. 26 Gomel was abandoned by the Germans.

■ The U.S. Eighth Air Force employed 633 aircraft in raids on Germany, the greatest number of planes used by the command thus far.

Nov. 28–Dec. 1 Stalin met for the first time with Churchill and Roosevelt at the Tehran conference. It was agreed that the invasion of France (Operations OVERLORD and ANVIL) would receive highest U.S. and British priority. Stalin restated Russia's intention to fight against Japan once Germany surrendered.

Roosevelt, Stalin, and Churchill—the first meeting of the Big Three leaders, at Tehran.

POLAND: EASTERN FRONTIER

LEGEND

National boundaries

Line of Russian occupation, June 1941

Boundaries of the Ukraine and White Russia

Voivodship boundaries

Curzon Line

Railroads

Line "A"
Line "B"
Line "C"
Line "D"
Line "E"
Line "F"
Scale 1:3,700,000

This map was used by Stalin, Churchill, and Roosevelt at the Tehran conference. The red lines trace those made by Stalin to designate the postwar Soviet-Polish frontier demanded by the Russian leader.

Nov. 28 Tarawa was completely secured. The small atoll was the scene of the most bitter, intense fighting in the Pacific war. In a little more than a week, 4,630 Japanese were killed. Only 17 Japanese and 125 Koreans were taken prisoner. U.S. casualties were 1,115 killed or presumed killed and 2,292 wounded.

■ In Italy the Battle of the Sangro began as Indian and New Zealand forces led the attack to break northward.

■ The Red Army suffered a sharp setback. Russian forces were destroyed in the Korosten pocket.

Nov. 29 British armor units breached the Winter Line in Italy, and began clearing the Sangro ridge.

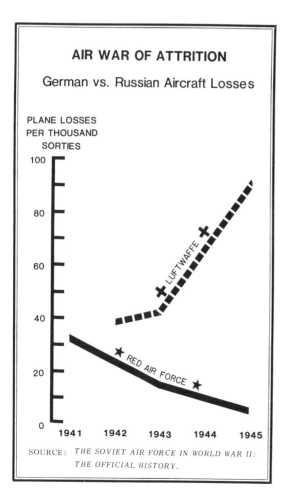

AIR WAR OF ATTRITION

German vs. Russian Aircraft Losses

PLANE LOSSES
PER THOUSAND
SORTIES

SOURCE: *THE SOVIET AIR FORCE IN WORLD WAR II: THE OFFICIAL HISTORY.*

■ Australian troops seized the Japanese supply base at Bonga in New Guinea and continued marching up the Huon Peninsula.

Nov. 30 The U.S. Fifth Army began diversionary attacks as a prelude to assaulting the Winter Line in the Camino Hills.

Dec. In negotiations with Albert Speer, head of German war production, Vichy France was able to arrange an exemption for the workers in 3,301 French factories (employing 723,124 people) freeing them from being drafted into the slave labor force for Germany.

Dec. 1 U.S. II and X Corps forces began assaulting German positions in the Camino Hills.

■ According to Moscow, partisans in Byelorussia had killed 282,000 German troops since the beginning of the war and had destroyed 812 tanks and 5,758 trains.

Dec. 2 In a raid of devastating consequences, 30 German bombers attacked crowded Bari Harbor. Two ammunition ships were hit, and the resulting explosions resulted in the loss of 17 other vessels. The Italian port was rendered useless for three weeks.

■ Hitler called on younger Germans to enlist in the military, with the minimum age eventually reduced to 15.

Dec. 3–7 U.S. and British delegates resumed their meetings in Cairo after concluding the Tehran conference. Further Pacific action was agreed upon, but an amphibious operation in the Bay of Bengal was canceled because of the need for landing craft in the projected invasion of southern France.

Dec. 3 Russian troops scored successes northwest of Gomel, capturing the highway junction of Dovsk.

■ U.S. and British troops made broad progress penetrating the Winter Line in Italy.

■ Göring issued orders to the commander of German bomber forces to launch a new round of bombing against Britain: "To avenge the terror attacks of the enemy, I have decided to intensify the air war over the British Isles by means of

The Russian Air Force gained in experience and numbers during the war, while the eastern front saw Luftwaffe losses climbing dramatically.

concentrated attacks on cities, especially industrial centers and ports."

Dec. 4 A provisional Yugoslav government under Tito was announced by the Partisans.

■ In an effort to divert the Chinese in Yunnan Province, the Japanese Eleventh Army climaxed an offensive in central China by capturing the rice center of Changteh.

■ German forces counterattacked on the Winter Line.

Dec. 5 Indian forces crossed the Moro River in Italy in a move to capture the harbor of Ortona.

■ Japanese planes attacked Calcutta, inflicting heavy damage in the dock area.

■ P-51s began escorting U.S. bombers in raids on targets in Europe.

Dec. 7 German forces resisted a British attack on Ortona. The U.S. Fifth Army began the second phase of its assault on the Winter Line.

Dec. 8 Heavy fighting continued along the Winter Line. Italian troops on the Allied side made limited progress. It was the first active combat for the Italians since switching sides.

■ Australian troops captured Wareo on New Guinea.

Dec. 9 Allied forces completed clearing the Camino Hills with the capture of Rocca d'Evandro.

■ The rail junction of Znamenka fell to the Russians.

■ Planes began operating out of the Torokina airstrip on Bougainville, only 200 miles from Rabaul.

■ Chiang Kai-shek called on Roosevelt to provide the Chinese with increased aid and to build up air strength in China.

Dec. 10 Russian troops launched a new offensive in the Ukraine.

Dec. 12 Rommel was appointed commander of German forces deployed along the coastal areas for defense against the anticipated Allied cross-Channel assault.

Dec. 13 Kiel was attacked by 710 radar-directed U.S. Eighth Air Force bombers with P-51 fighter escorts.

Dec. 14 Russia launched its winter offensive. Red Army forces reached the outskirts of Vitebsk and captured Cherkassy. The Germans, however, recaptured Radomyshl, south of Malin.

Generals Marshall and MacArthur in their only meeting of the war, on Goodenough Island off the coast of New Guinea.

Dec. 15 Trials began in Kharkov of German prisoners charged with having committed atrocities.

■ U.S. Sixth Army units landed on the west coast of the Arawe Peninsula of New Britain, 280 miles west of Rabaul, encountering only scattered opposition. Subsequent Japanese air attacks on the positions were costly to the Americans.

Dec. 17 U.S. troops captured San Pietro, while the Germans began pulling back at several sectors of the Italian front.

Dec. 18 Japanese planes raided Kunming in China in a move to lessen the threat to its forces from

Burma who would shortly launch a drive against India.

Dec. 20 Plans for an Allied amphibious assault on the west coast of Italy were canceled because of a lack of landing craft and an inability to overcome the German defenses along the Winter line.

■ The Arawe Peninsula on New Britain was cleared of all Japanese forces.

■ Roosevelt and Chiang Kai-shek exchanged messages which showed strong disagreement over future offensive operations in Burma. Roosevelt hedged on further economic aid to the Chinese.

Dec. 21 A German bridgehead over the Dnieper at Kherson was wiped out by the Russians.

Dec. 22 Berlin threatened reprisals on British and American prisoners in retaliation for the Russian atrocity trials at Kharkov.

■ Heavy fighting developed for Ortona with the 1st Canadian Division encountering stiff German resistance. Ortona was the best port on the Adriatic coast south of Pescara.

■ Kunming in China was again bombed by the Japanese.

Dec. 23 General Jean-Marie de Lattre de Tassigny arrived in Algiers after escaping from Riom prison and being flown to Britain. He was imprisoned by the Nazis after protesting violations of the armistice terms in the unoccupied territories of France. De Lattre took command of the French First Army when he arrived in Algeria.

Dec. 24 Eisenhower was appointed Supreme Commander, Allied Expeditionary Force (SCAEF); General Sir Henry Maitland Wilson, Supreme Allied Commander, Mediterranean Theater; General Sir Harold Alexander, Commander, Allied armies in Italy; General Bernard Montgomery, Commander, Allied ground forces under Eisenhower; and General Carl A. Spaatz, Commander, U.S. Strategic Air Forces in Europe.

■ U.S. bombers launched a major effort to knock out German secret weapons sites with attacks involving more than 1,300 planes. A record number of about 3,000 Allied planes were involved in missions against cities and military targets in Europe, including an RAF raid which dropped 1,120 tons on Berlin.

Dec. 25 Russian Baltic Army units cut the rail line between Vitebsk and Polotsk, halting shipments on the key east-west supply route.

■ Allied military leaders, meeting in Tunis, agreed to revive the plan for an amphibious landing south of Rome to break the Italian impasse.

Dec. 26 In the last classic duel between capital ships, *Scharnhorst* was sunk while attempting to intercept an Allied convoy to Murmansk. The German ship was first hit by four torpedoes launched by British and Norwegian destroyers. Badly damaged, *Scharnhorst* was then attacked by the British battleship *Duke of York*, three cruisers, and six destroyers. Within minutes, it rolled over to starboard and sank. The crew sang "Over a Seaman's Grave No Roses Bloom" as it was going under, and there were only 36 survivors of the 1,900-man crew. *Scharnhorst*'s destruction ended effective German efforts to block the Murmansk convoys. For the rest of the war the Allied loss rate was only four percent for each convoy.

■ Red Army forces pressed forward in the Kiev area.

■ U.S. Marines of the 1st Division landed east and west of Cape Gloucester on New Britain. While there was little initial opposition, the Marines were hampered by the uncharted swamps on the landing beach.

Dec. 27 Ortona fell to the Allies after two weeks of house-to-house fighting in the Italian city.

■ The Marines at Cape Gloucester advanced three miles toward the airfield.

■ Russian forces cut the rail line out of Vitebsk.

Dec. 28 After prolonged bitter fighting, Ortona was finally captured by the British Eighth Army.

■ British talks with the Turks were held to bring Turkey into the war.

Dec. 29 The Russian First Ukrainian Front, under Marshal Vatutin, began a spectacular breakthrough along a 185-mile front west of Kiev. Twenty-two German divisions were hurled back toward the Polish border.

■ The airfield at Cape Gloucester on New Britain was taken by U.S. Marines who suffered few casualties. Counterattacks on the Arawe Peninsula were repulsed.

■ Chinese 38th Division forces made progress in advancing toward the Tarung River in Burma, dispersing the Japanese at a key strongpoint.

A low-flying U.S. B-25 strafes a Japanese antiair-craft position at Rabaul.

U.S. Marines unload Coast Guard LSTs at Cape Gloucester, New Britain.

U.S. Marines, wading through three feet of surf, take a beachhead at Cape Gloucester, New Britain.

Dec. 30 An airstrip at Piva on Bougainville was activated by the U.S.

■ Cape Gloucester was cleared, giving the Allies control of western New Britain.

Dec. 31 Red Army units captured Zhitomir, leaving Vitebsk virtually isolated. German resistance at this time became fierce.

■ Ten British civilians were killed in air raids during the month. For the three months the total was 247 killed and 561 wounded.

(OPPOSITE, TOP) *U.S. forces land on Omaha Beach on D-Day, June 6, 1944, and draw sweeping German fire.*

(OPPOSITE, BOTTOM) *After the Germans withdrew from Roncy, France, an elderly French woman returned to search for her home and possessions.*

1944

Europe's liberation begins with a Channel crossing.

Jan. 1 Rommel was appointed to command Army Group B, covering the expected invasion front from Brittany to the Netherlands.

Jan. 2 Russian forces advanced to within 18 miles of the original Polish-Russian frontier.

■ U.S. Army troops were landed at Saidor, New Guinea. The action isolated 12,000 Japanese troops at Sio.

Jan. 3 Russian units drove across the prewar border into Poland, cutting the rail line to Warsaw.

Jan. 4 German school children were mobilized for war-related duty.

■ U.S. aircraft began transporting supplies to partisan units in western Europe in preparation for eventual disruptive action behind German lines.

■ Yugoslav Partisans captured Banja Luka.

■ British 46th Division forces crossed the Peccia River in Italy but only after overcoming stiff opposition.

Jan. 5 The U.S. Fifth Army launched the final assault on the German Winter line. British troops pulled back from the Peccia River bridgehead because tanks were unable to cross.

■ Australian and U.S. forces were within 60 miles of reaching a juncture in New Guinea as the Australians reached Kelanoa.

■ Berdichev, a rail junction southwest of Kiev, was taken by the Russians.

Jan. 6 San Vittore fell to U.S. forces in Italy.

Jan. 7 Russian troops advanced along a 60-mile front. Kirovograd, transportation center in the Dnieper bend, was virtually surrounded.

Jan. 8 Count Ciano and other Italian Fascist leaders were placed on trial in Verona.

■ German troops began falling back to positions to block Allied advances to Rome through the Liri valley.

■ The Russians captured Kirovograd.

■ U.S. Navy ships bombarded the Shortland Islands in the Solomons.

Jan. 9 Churchill and de Gaulle met in Marrakech, Morocco. The main issues were the role of the Free French forces in the forthcoming invasion of the continent and the degree of authority to be assumed by the French Committee in civil affairs inside France after the invasion.

■ Countess Ciano escaped to Switzerland.

■ New assaults were made on Cervaro and Monte Trocchio, the last points on the Winter Line held by the Germans.

■ British troops captured Maungdaw on the Arakan front in Burma.

Jan. 10 In a joint announcement Roosevelt and Churchill revealed that merchant shipping losses to U-boats were 60 percent less than a year ago.

■ German defenders offered strong resistance on the Winter Line's remaining positions.

■ The rail line between Smela and Kristinovka in the Ukraine was cut by the Russians. A large German force trapped north of Kirovograd was annihilated.

■ RAF aircraft began mining the mouths of the Salween near Moulmein, Burma. (The Japanese closed Moulmein to all shipping in March because of the mines.)

Jan. 11 Allied bombers launched Operation POINTBLANK, designed to cripple the German aircraft industry and render the Luftwaffe ineffective before the cross-Channel invasion. The initial attack caused heavy damage to the targeted factories but 60 of the 663 heavy bombers were lost.

■ Moscow announced that the Soviet-Polish border established by the 1939 Russian-German partition would remain. Russia thus reclaimed permanent possession of the western Ukraine and western Byelorussia.

Jan. 12 German troops counterattacked at Vinnitsa, southwest of Kiev. The Russians captured Sarny, in prewar Poland, enveloping it from the rear.

■ U.S. Fifth Army troops took Cervaro. Other strategic hills in the area were seized, opening up a clear route to the Rapido River.

Jan. 13 The Chinese 38th Division completed securing the Tarung River line in Burma.

■ U.S. forces mopped up opposition remnants north of Cervaro in preparation for an attack on the German positions along the Rapido.

Jan. 14 Russian forces began mass attacks against the Germans in the Baltic states. The Soviet Second Shock Army and the Forty-second and Forty-ninth armies moved against German Army Group North and prepared a pincers movement to recapture Novgorod.

■ French forces under General Alphonse Juin gave up their attempt to take heavily defended Monte Santa Croce.

■ Roosevelt wrote to Chiang to win a commitment of additional Chinese forces. He threatened to cut lend-lease aid if they were not sent.

Jan. 15 All Germans were cleared south of the Rapido River. U.S. forces captured Monte Trocchio, completing reduction of the Winter Line. Allied forces were now confronted by the Gustav Line, anchored by Cassino.

■ Russian forces launched major offensives to lift the siege of Leningrad and recapture Novgorod.

■ Sofia was attacked by Allied bombers, the beginning of a series of raids on Balkan cities.

■ Australian units reached Sio, on the north coast of the Huon Peninsula in New Guinea.

■ A British cabinet committee headed by Clement Attlee recommended the partition of Germany after the war.

Jan. 16 Eisenhower assumed command of the Allied Expeditionary Force.

■ The U.S. II Corps was ordered to drive toward Anzio.

■ Allied forces turned back the final Japanese counterattack on New Britain and moved to oust the Japanese from their last positions near Arawe.

■ Chiang countered Roosevelt's threat on an aid cutoff by saying China would no longer supply U.S. troops there if the U.S. did not grant a one billion dollar loan.

Jan. 17 The official Soviet newspaper *Pravda* charged that Britain was planning to negotiate a separate peace with Germany. London denied the charge.

■ British X Corps troops crossed the Garigliano River on the western hinge of the Gustav Line.

■ U.S. and French Expeditionary Corps forces began attacking the Gustav Line along the Rapido.

■ All Japanese resistance ended at Arawe on New Britain.

Jan. 19 In a speech to the House of Commons Eden warned the Spanish government against continued aid to Germany by maintaining Spanish troops on the Russian front.

■ British forces expanded the Garigliano beachhead.

■ Novgorod was retaken by the Russians.

Jan. 20 Russian forces blocked off the German corridor to the Gulf of Finland.

■ U.S. 36th Division forces reached the Rapido River but faced heavy fire when they attempted a crossing. The Americans suffered heavy casualties and abandoned the effort.

■ The rail junction of Mega, southeast of Leningrad, was retaken by the Russians.

Jan. 22 An Allied force invaded the coastal area around Anzio, 35 miles south of Rome. The first of three assaults began at 2:00 A.M., catching the Germans by surprise. More than 37,000 British and American troops were put ashore, protected by massive air and naval cover. By nightfall, the beachheads were consolidated and the U.S. VI Corps had moved seven miles inland. The port facilities of Anzio and Nettuno were captured intact. In outflanking the Germans and gaining a position just south of Rome, the Allies had secured a great advantage in breaking open the Italian campaign. (But the gain was nullified when the American Major General John P. Lucas failed to press forward and trap the Germans to the south. Instead, the Hermann Göring Panzer Division was moved in to attack the bridgehead and other large units were moved down from northern Italy to engage the Allies before the trap could be sprung.)

■ The U.S. 36th Division suffered heavy losses and finally abandoned its bridgehead across the Rapido.

Jan. 23 The Anzio beachhead was consolidated as German resistance was almost negligible, but Field Marshal Kesselring correctly determined that "the danger of a large-scale expansion of the beachhead was no longer imminent." The imminent threat to the Allies came from the Luftwaffe which attacked the new positions. German planes also attacked two British hospital ships off the Anzio coast, sinking *St. David* and damaging *Leinster*. The attacks were made at dusk with the ships fully lighted and identified.

■ Moscow announced that heavy rains had halted the offensive around Vitebsk where a German force was virtually encircled.

Jan. 24 U.S. troops on Anzio were halted to await reinforcements.

■ The Germans formed stiff lines of resistance on the main Italian front. Hitler ordered the Gustav Line to be held at all costs. The 34th Division moved to establish a new bridgehead across the Rapido.

■ Russian forces occupied Pushkin and Pavlovsk.

Jan. 25 An Allied raid on Rabaul resulted in heavy Japanese losses, including the destruction of 83 planes.

■ Three battalions of the 36th Division pushed across the Rapido.

■ Red Army troops captured the rail junction of Krasnogvardeisk (Gatchina) southwest of Leningrad.

Jan. 26 Moscow published its report on the Katyn massacre, blaming the Germans.

■ An Allied assault on Regabil failed.

■ Liberia declared war on Germany and Japan.

■ Argentina broke off diplomatic relations with Germany and Japan.

Jan. 27 Moscow announced the relief of Leningrad.

■ The U.S. military issued a report on atrocities committed by the Japanese on U.S. and Filipino military personnel after the fall of Bataan in 1942.

■ Fighting was heavy all along the Italian front. Allied pressures were countered by unexpectedly strong German resistance.

Jan. 29 U.S. Eighth Air Force radar-equipped bombers conducted their heaviest raid to date. More than 800 planes attacked Frankfurt am Main, killing 736 people.

■ German bombers raided Britain. Losses on this

U.S. Fifth Army troops land at Anzio, Italy.

FEB. 6 **1944**

and a raid of the 21st were 57 aircraft, cutting sharply into available Luftwaffe resources.

■ The rail line between Moscow and Leningrad was cleared of all Germans. To the south, a massive Red Army force opened up an offensive aimed at eliminating the German Eighth Army in the Ukraine.

■ U.S. naval planes began nine consecutive days of raids in the Marshall Islands to knock out Japanese air power and shipping.

Jan. 30 U.S. Rangers in the Anzio beachhead were ambushed and two battalions were almost entirely eliminated in a drive to capture Cisterna.

■ Future action by the Luftwaffe in Italy was sharply limited when U.S. Fifteenth Air Force planes attacked German air facilities in the Po valley.

■ The Chinese 22nd Division established complete control over the Taro plain in Burma.

Jan. 31 U.S. forces invaded Kwajalein and other islands in the Marshalls. Casualties were extremely light. The islands were the first of Japan's prewar territories to fall.

■ Australia formed a commission to investigate Japanese war crimes.

Feb. 1 The Gestapo chief in Poland was assassinated.

■ Kwajalein operations continued with virtually no Japanese resistance as U.S. Marines secured all their initial objectives.

■ The U.S. 3rd Division in the Anzio beachhead abandoned efforts to take Cisterna and began preparing for German counterattacks. British efforts to expand the Garigliano bridgeheads continued in the face of determined German resistance.

Feb. 2 Russian forces crossed the Estonian border and captured Vanakula. The Ukrainian front saw the Russians advancing on a 60-mile front west of the Dnieper.

■ Stalin agreed to permit American planes to use six Russian bases while involved in shuttle bombing operations.

Feb. 3 U.S. warships shelled Paramushiru Island in northern Japan, the first Allied naval attack on the Japanese homeland.

■ Ten German divisions of the Eighth Army were encircled by the Russians south of Korsun. Attempts to relieve the units forced the Germans to curtail offensive actions elsewhere.

■ German troops launched a counteroffensive at Anzio, directed against the Campoleone salient which was held by the British 1st Division.

Feb. 4 Japan launched a major offensive in Burma on the Arakan front in an effort to force the British back to India.

■ Kwajalein was declared secure. Japanese losses were 4,938 killed and 206 captured. U.S. casualties were 142 killed.

■ U.S. troops were forced back at Cassino. British forces yielded ground at Anzio.

U.S. soldiers prepare to bury fallen comrades near Anzio.

■ Moscow announced the Gulf of Finland and the Novgorod-Leningrad railway were totally secure.

■ China launched an attack in the Hukawng valley, in northern Burma.

■ Argentina broke diplomatic relations with Hungary, Bulgaria, Rumania, and Vichy France.

Feb. 5 British Chindits pushed forward toward Indaw from Ledo, an operation to divert the Japanese from the Salween area where new Chinese troops were being introduced into Burma from Yunnan Province.

■ Air and naval resupply efforts for the Allied forces at Anzio were further restricted by fresh German attacks.

Feb. 6 Allied troops along the Cassino front and in the Anzio pocket were forced to pull back in the face of heavy German counterattacks.

303

■ Five German divisions were trapped near Nikopol when the Russians captured Apostolovo, the rail junction which served as an outlet to the west.

■ British forces began pulling back on the Arakan front after being threatened by Japanese movements to drive a wedge between them.

Feb. 7 German troops attacked Anzio in their biggest counterattack yet, accompanied by heavy air and artillery support.

■ Russian troops reached the outskirts of Nikopol.

■ The first of the German *Schnorkel* submarines began operating in the North Atlantic.

■ A British force was encircled on the Arakan front.

Feb. 8 A six-ton bomb, heaviest used in the war to date, was dropped by an RAF bomber on the Gnome-et-Rhone factory at Limoges, France.

■ The Germans trapped at Nikopol refused to surrender to Red Army troops who pressed their encirclement to win total control of the important manganese center.

Feb. 9 Allied forces at Anzio suffered more setbacks despite heavy naval and air support to keep the Germans from driving the Allies into the sea.

■ Roosevelt requested Chiang's permission to send a U.S. military mission to the Chinese Communist base area and headquarters in Shensi Province.

Feb. 10 The pro-Allied Italian government was given administrative control over southern Italy, Sicily, and Sardinia.

■ Hungary's ambassador in Lisbon was instructed to inform the Western Allies that Budapest wished to surrender unconditionally, but not to the Russians.

■ The Japanese abandoned Truk as a major naval base.

■ Australian forces completed their occupation of the Huon Peninsula on New Guinea.

Feb. 10–11 Russian bombers attempted to bomb the *Tirpitz* in Kaafiord, Norway. Fifteen aircraft started out on the raid, but only four found the battleship. A one-ton bomb scored a near miss, but *Tirpitz* escaped major damage.

Feb. 11 Allied forces were repulsed in their efforts to stem the German pressures at Anzio.

■ New efforts were begun to break through the Gustav Line at Cassino.

Feb. 12 Germans forced Allied troops on the Anzio beachhead to fall back to the final defense line.

■ The first Allied assault on Monte Cassino in Italy was repulsed.

■ Allied planners set May for the cross-Channel invasion of France.

■ U.S. Marines occupied Rooke (Umboi) Island, at the western end of New Britain. Arno Atoll in the Marshalls was taken by Marines, the beginning of mopping-up operations to clear the many islands and atolls in the area.

■ The entire east bank of Lake Peipus in the Soviet Union was cleared of German troops. Russian units reached a point within forty-five miles of Pskov. The city controlled the approaches to Latvia.

Feb. 15 The abbey atop Monte Cassino was heavily bombed by Allied air and artillery. Roosevelt said such monuments could not be spared when American lives were at stake. Destruction of the heavily fortified abbey, it was assumed, would deny German defenders their commanding position over the countryside. Even though the abbey was virtually leveled, the Allies still could not take it. Indian and New Zealand forces

A battlefield truce on Mount Castellone in Italy to bury the dead resulted in this pictorial record of an American and a German sharing each other's cigarettes at the height of the fighting.

were repulsed in a frontal assault after the bombardment.

■ The London-based Polish government said it would refuse to accept the Curzon Line as the postwar frontier between Poland and Russia.

Feb. 15–16 RAF bombers dropped 2,642 tons of explosives on Berlin in 39 minutes. It was the heaviest raid of the war on the German capital. Forty-two of the 806 aircraft were downed.

Feb. 15–20 Japanese forces in the Solomons were completely cut off as Green Island was taken by New Zealand forces. Capture of the island also provided the Allies with an air base only 117 miles from Rabaul.

Feb. 16 German forces launched their major attack on the Anzio beachhead. The Fourteenth Army—aided by the Luftwaffe which was more active than ever before in attacking the pocket— hoped to drive the Allies into the sea. The Germans made limited gains against the U.S. 3rd Division positions but suffered heavy personnel and tank losses.

■ U.S. Army and Marine units converged at the Itni River, effectively securing all of the western part of New Britain.

Feb. 16–17 U.S. warships (led by six battleships) and planes (from nine carriers) attacked the Japanese base at Truk in the Carolines. Most of the airstrips were destroyed and two cruisers, three destroyers, and 200,000 tons of merchant shipping were sunk. Because of the damage inflicted and the inability of the Japanese to use Truk as a forward base, the Allies were able to bypass the island and neutralize it by keeping it isolated. (The attacks on Truk and another important Japanese base, Palau, during February and March had a critical effect on the war. About a third of all the tankers assigned to the combined fleet of Japan were sunk, which was to impair future fleet operations of the ship-poor Imperial Navy.)

Feb. 17 Soviet forces completed the "liquidation" of ten German divisions trapped in the Ukraine. Moscow announced that 55,000 Germans were killed and 18,200 taken prisoner in the Kanyew pocket.

■ American forces invaded Eniwetok Atoll without opposition.

■ More than 1,000 tons of bombs were dropped by Allied planes as part of a massive bombardment to prevent a German breakthrough to the sea at Anzio. Naval gunfire and artillery barrages helped contain the Germans who had driven a wedge into the center of the U.S. 45th Division line.

Feb. 18 German forces made their deepest penetration into the Anzio beachhead, driving the U.S. 179th Infantry Regiment back to its final line. The U.S. military regarded this as the crucial day of the Anzio operation.

■ Little ground was taken in assaults on Monte Cassino. Both sides began regrouping along the Gustav Line.

■ German Army Group North began withdrawing from the Russian Narva-Newel front. Russian troops captured Staraya Russa.

■ London was subjected to a new wave of bombing in the "Little Blitz."

■ British and New Zealand aircraft bombed Amiens prison in France, breaching the walls, and permitting about 70 Resistance internees to escape. The prisoners had been scheduled to be executed.

■ Allied destroyers bombarded Rabaul and Kavieng.

Feb. 19 The Anzio battle turned in favor of the Allies. German reserve strength was sapped by costly actions to clear the beachhead. U.S. troops and tanks of the 6th Armored Infantry, backed by air and artillery, advanced more than a mile.

■ U.S. Army and Marine units landed on Engebi Island, Eniwetok Atoll, in the Marshall Islands. Enemy resistance slowed the advance inland.

Exhausted U.S. Marines returned to their transports after capturing Eniwetok in the Marshall Islands in two days and nights of battle.

Feb. 20 Allied forces drove a wedge into the middle of the German line at Anzio and inflicted heavy losses, but the Germans were already preparing another offensive.

■ More than 1,000 U.S. bombers struck German aircraft factories centered in the Brunswick and Leipzig areas.

■ British patrol aircraft caught a nest of German U-boats in the Strait of Gibraltar, sinking three and damaging several others.

■ The southern part of Eniwetok was secured.

■ Norwegian Lieutenant Knut Haukelid, working with the British, sank the ferry *Hydro* in Lake Tinnsjö which was carrying rail tank cars loaded with heavy water from the Norsk Hydro facility at Vemork. The material was being shipped to Germany for atomic research purposes. Haukelid planted explosives with a time charge set to go off when the ferry reached the deepest part of the lake. The vessel went down in 1,300 feet of water, making it impossible to recover most of the heavy-water containers. Of the passengers, guards, and crew, 26 were drowned and 27 rescued.

Feb. 21 Eniwetok was totally cleared except for scattered mopping-up operations. (It was soon used by U.S. forces as a major advance base for forthcoming advances in the Pacific.)

■ Russian forces pressed forward in the Lake Ilmen area.

■ Tojo took direct command of the Japanese Army by becoming chief of the general staff.

■ Washington called on the Republic of Ireland to expel all Axis diplomats, who were charged with engaging in espionage activities.

Feb. 22 Krivoy Rog fell to the Red Army, returning control of the whole Ukrainian industrial area to the Russians.

■ U.S. Fifteenth Air Force bombers from Italy joined in the attacks on German aircraft factories.

■ Japanese aircraft attacked U.S. Naval Task Force 58 approaching the Marianas but suffered heavy casualties. Allied ships operating around Rabaul and Kavieng encountered no Japanese aircraft, a further measure of Tokyo's thinly stretched resources.

Feb. 23 U.S. VI Corps Major General John P. Lucas was replaced by Major General Lucian K. Truscott. Lucas was seen as too conservative at

Anzio, having failed to expand the beachhead and break out before the German Fourteenth Army could be organized to negate the great initial advantages.

■ Japanese forces at Sinzweya, Burma, began withdrawing after failing to oust the 7th Indian Division. It was the first time the British had defeated the Japanese in battle.

■ Heavy carrier-based air strikes were conducted against Japanese positions in the Marianas, the first attacks of the war against the islands. Saipan, Tinian, Rota, and Guam were bombed.

A torpedo strikes and sinks the Japanese liner Teiko Maru *(the captured French ship* D'Atagnan*), as photographed through the periscope of the U.S. submarine* Puffer *in the China Sea.*

Feb. 24 German fighters staged fierce attacks on Allied aircraft from Britain and Italy attempting to bomb Schweinfurt and other strategic target areas in Germany and Austria.

■ Indian forces in Burma cleared the Ngakyedauk Pass, while U.S. and Chinese units began their drive to capture Myitkyina.

Feb. 25 About 20 percent of the bombers of the U.S. Fifteenth Air Force attacking Regensburg aircraft factories were shot down.

■ The West African 81st Division occupied Kyauktaw in the Kaladan valley of Burma.

Feb. 26 The rail line between Dno and Novosokolniki was cleared by the Russians.

Feb. 29 German troops again assaulted the Anzio beachhead. The main attack was directed against the Allied right flank which was held by the U.S. 3rd Division. Some ground was lost but part of it was recovered by evening.

■ A thousand-man force from the U.S. 1st Infantry Division invaded the Admiralty Islands, several hundred miles inside the line of Japanese control in the southwest Pacific. The air base on Los Negros was taken after the Japanese offered only token resistance, but the force withdrew because it was not large enough to retain possession. A light nighttime counterattack on the beachhead was repulsed. MacArthur, who was on the beachhead, ordered it defended at all costs. The Admiralties were considered important in efforts to isolate the important Japanese base at Rabaul.

■ Moscow confirmed the Finns had offered to discuss peace terms.

■ Marshal Vatutin, commander of the First Ukrainian Front and one of the ablest Russian military leaders, was ambushed and fatally wounded by Ukrainian nationalist rebels.

■ In the first two months of the year British civilian air raid casualties were 1,068 killed and 1,972 injured.

March 1 Anzio defenders continued to beat back German attacks.

■ U.S. forces on Los Negros stopped Japanese assaults on the defense perimeter.

■ Red Army forces drove across the Narva River.

■ German slave labor chief Fritz Sauckel said there were five million foreign workers in Germany, 200,000 of them voluntarily.

March 2 With transportation in turmoil in Italy, hundreds of Italians jumped aboard a freight train in the mountains near Salerno. When it stalled, most of the crowded flatcars were in a tunnel. Toxic fumes from the engine's low-grade fuel blew into the tunnel and at least 426 people died of carbon monoxide poisoning.

■ More than 350 sorties were flown by U.S. bombers in support of the Anzio forces. The pounding of the German positions disrupted a planned counteroffensive.

■ U.S. Army troops seized the Momote airstrip on Los Negros.

March 3 The Anzio beachhead was secured as the Germans tried for the last time to mount offensive action. The U.S. 3rd Division held off the

attack, counterattacked, and gained some ground.

■ U.S. Army troops halted the major Japanese thrust to push the Americans off the Los Negros beachhead. Japanese losses were heavy, restricting their future actions.

■ Roosevelt announced that the Italian fleet would be divided equally between the U.S., Britain, and the Soviet Union under an agreement reached when Italy surrendered.

March 4 U.S. Eighth Air Force planes attacked Berlin for the first time.

■ A lull developed at Anzio. German troops were told to hold their positions and prepare for defensive action.

■ Under the command of General Stilwell, the First Chinese Army and Merrill's Marauders (special U.S. infiltration units names after Major General Frank Merrill) began the Battle of Walawbum in northern Burma. It was the first phase of a combined offensive with the British Chindits aimed at cutting the communications of the Japanese 18th "Chrysanthemum" Division, taking the rail and road center of Myitkyina, and reopening the Burma Road into China.

■ U.S. ships began bombarding the Admiralty Islands.

Polish Corps machine gunners man positions in Italy. Mount Marrone is in the distance.

U.S. Infantrymen comb the shell-torn jungle of Bougainville in a search to clear the largest of the Solomon Islands.

March 5 Russia launched its offensive to drive the Germans out of the Dnieper bend in the Ukraine. Red Army forces under Marshal Zhukov advanced 31 miles.

■ Three brigades of Chindits were dropped behind Japanese lines northeast of Indaw in central Burma. Their primary mission was to cut the communications of the Japanese 18th Division facing Stilwell.

March 6 Round-the-clock bombing operations against Germany began with a U.S. 800-plane daylight raid against Berlin in which 2,000 tons of bombs were dropped.

■ About 400 Japanese were killed in an unsuccessful bid to cross the Tanai River in Burma.

■ Red Army troops advanced along a 100-mile front in the Ukraine.

■ U.S. Marines landed near Talasea on New Britain and established a 2,000-yard-deep bridgehead.

March 7 Moscow said it considered the Curzon line unacceptable as the postwar border between Russia and Poland, holding that the frontier should be further west.

■ The 33rd Division of Lieutenant General Renya Mutaguchi's Fifteenth Army launched Operation U-GO, a major Japanese offensive aimed at capturing the Imphal plain and smashing the British IV Corps.

March 8 Japanese forces in Burma opened a strong drive toward Imphal.

■ Allied positions on Bougainville came under heavy Japanese artillery fire. Four aircraft were lost, and the undamaged planes were withdrawn to New Georgia.

■ Russian forces were within 60 miles of Rumania.

■ U.S. bombers resumed heavy raids on German targets. Accompanied by longer-range fighters which provided protection to and over targets, 590 Eighth Air Force planes attacked the Erkner ball-bearing factory in Berlin, inflicting damage which caused production slowdowns. Thirty-seven of the American planes were lost.

March 9 Red Army troops advanced to Tarnopol where house-to-house fighting developed.

■ The Talasea airstrip on New Britain was taken by U.S. Marines without opposition.

■ The First Chinese Army and Merrill's Marauders captured Walawbum in Burma, giving them full control of the Hukawng Valley.

March 10 Russian troops occupied the German air base at Uman.

■ Ireland refused to oust Axis diplomats, as requested by the U.S.

March 11 Russian forces occupied Berslav in their drive down the Dnieper.

■ The former minister of the interior in the government of Vichy France, Pierre Pucheau, was found guilty and sentenced to death by a military court in Algiers. He was the first of the collaborators to be so tried.

March 12 The Czech government in London called for an armed civilian uprising in Czechoslovakia.

■ British troops made advances on the Arakan front in Burma, taking Razabil.

■London ordered a halt to all travel between the Irish Republic and Great Britain because the Irish refused to order German and Japanese diplomats out of the country.

March 13 Kherson was recaptured by Russians who crossed the lower Dnieper.

■The Japanese 33rd and 15th divisions advancing toward the Imphal plain in Operation U-GO took the British by surprise and threatened to cut off the retreating 17th and 20th Indian divisions.

■In an outflanking amphibious operation, British west African troops landed on the Arakan coast.

March 14 Russian troops closed the trap around the Germans at Nikolayev.

■Indian forces attempting to pull back from the Imphal front found their path had been blocked by the Japanese.

March 15 Allied bombers again bombed Monte Cassino, dropping 1,200 tons on the German-held fortress. Indian and New Zealand forces followed with a direct assault, which was repulsed.

■Russian forces broke through German defenses on the Bug River and advanced along a broad front.

■German troops massed along the Hungarian border, preparing to occupy the territory of their shaky ally.

■Manus Island in the Admiralties was invaded by the U.S. 8th Cavalry Regiment.

March 16 New Zealand forces made only limited progress in their attacks at Cassino.

March 17 New Zealand units reached the rail station at Cassino.

■Dubno, the Ukrainian rail and road junction, was retaken by the Russians.

■Finland rejected Russia's terms for an armistice.

March 18 Russian troops reached the Rumanian border, capturing Yampol on the east bank of the Dniester.

■In the heaviest air raid of the war so far, RAF aircraft dropped more than 3,000 tons of bombs on Frankfurt am Main.

■An armored attack on the abbey of Monte Cassino by New Zealanders was turned back with heavy losses.

■After the Hungarian regent Admiral Miklos Horthy refused to sign a document requesting direct intervention, Hitler ordered German troops into Hungary.

March 19 Russian troops of the Second Ukrainian Front swept into northern Rumania after crossing the Dniester at several points.

■German paratroopers occupied the airfields of Hungary, while other units began crossing the frontier to take control of the country.

March 20 Germany completed its occupation of Hungary.

■The road and rail junction of Vinnitsa fell to the Russians.

■U.S. 4th Division Marines occupied Emirau Island in the Bismarck Archipelago. It was to be

Cassino was completely destroyed by Allied aircraft in an effort to open the route to Rome.

used as a naval and air base in the reduction of Rabaul.

March 21 The U.S. 34th Division arrived as reinforcements at Anzio.

■ American cavalrymen began a drive to secure Los Negros.

March 22 Japan advanced its large-scale offensive into India from Burma. Units of the Eighteenth Army reached a point 30 miles east of Imphal in the mountainous area of Manipur.

■ Tojo informed the Japanese Diet the war situation was grave.

■ Alexander halted frontal assaults at Cassino.

■ Frankfurt am Main was attacked in one of the deadliest bomber raids of the war against the city. One thousand and one people were killed.

March 23 New Zealand forces broke off their costly attempt to take Monte Cassino.

■ Russian troops broke through German positions on the central front and encircled Tarnopol, the Wehrmacht stronghold and operational base.

■ Japanese troops made small advances on Bougainville after U.S. artillery halted the assaults.

March 24 Los Negros was nominally secured when U.S. forces took over commanding high ground positions. Only small scale fighting followed.

■ Japanese forces were routed in a Bougainville counterattack. (It was the last major fight in the Solomons although some sporadic engagements were fought through May.)

■ British Major General Orde Wingate was killed when his plane crashed in Burma. The eccentric but effective Wingate had organized the Chindits and was a leading proponent of irregular warfare. (Because most of the other victims of the air crash were Americans—and no bodies could be identified—Wingate is buried in a common grave at Arlington National Cemetery near Washington, D.C.)

March 25 Organized Japanese resistance ended on Manus Island.

March 26 Red Army troops reached the Prut River in the Ukraine on a 53-mile front.

■ In one of the more bizarre and tragic incidents of the war the U.S. submarine *Tullibee* apparently torpedoed and sank itself. Operating north of Palau in the Carolines, the surfaced sub fired two torpedoes at a Japanese transport. Shortly thereafter *Tullibee* exploded and sank. The only survi-

vor, a gunner's mate on the bridge, said one of the torpedoes, equipped with a contact exploder, made a circular run and hit the sub.

March 27 Polish underground units were directed to make contact with the Russian army in Poland.

March 28 Nikolayev was retaken by the Russians.

■ The Allies conceded the campaign to take Monte Cassino was a "temporary failure."

March 29 Japanese troops cut the road between Imphal and Kohima. Chinese troops occupied Shaduzup as part of an effort in northeast Burma to divert the Japanese forces from their main goal of moving into India.

March 30–April 2 U.S. Naval Task Force 58 aircraft hammered Japanese targets in the western Carolines, including Palau, Yap, and Ulithi. The raids, which resulted in the destruction of 150 Japanese planes, 6 combat ships, and 104,000 tons of miscellaneous shipping, were designed to deny Japan a quick response to the projected invasion of Hollandia, New Guinea. A total of 20 U.S. planes were lost.

March 30 Russian forces were positioned 30 miles from the Ruthenian border.

■ U.S. bombers based in the Mediterranean began a series of heavy raids on the Balkans.

March 30–31 In a costly raid 795 RAF planes attacked Nürnberg but 95 were lost and 71 severely damaged. Long-range area raids were suspended as a result.

March 31 Admiral Mineichi Koga, commander-in-chief of the Japanese Combined Fleet, disappeared and was presumed killed while flying from Palau to Davao, in the Philippines, during a violent storm. (Tokyo did not announce his death until May. Admiral Soemu Toyodo was named to succeed Koga.)

■ Ochakov on the Black Sea was partially occupied by the Russians.

■ British civilian air raid casualties for March were 279 killed and 633 injured.

April 1 A German force of 40,000 was trapped by the Russians at Skala, in the Ukraine.

April 2 Units of the Second Ukrainian Front crossed into Rumania over the Prut River and occupied Gertza. Hitler continued to profess his belief in ultimate victory: "The Russians have exhausted and divided their forces."

Japanese ships burn in Palau harbor during a U.S carrier-based air attack in the western Carolines.

The giant German battleship Tirpitz *is camouflaged in a Norwegian fjord to avoid Allied air attacks.*

April 3 British naval aircraft attacked the German battleship *Tirpitz* in Norway's Altenfjord, causing limited damage.

■ U.S. and RAF bombers began bombing Budapest and other Hungarian cities, ending the August 1943 agreement to refrain from such attacks in exchange for free and safe access over Hungary. Germans, not Hungarians, now manned aerial defenses in Hungary.

■ U.S. bombers attacked Hollandia in the heaviest attack yet on the New Guinea base. (During the next four days more than 300 Japanese planes were destroyed, most of them on the ground. U.S. air superiority over Hollandia was established by these raids.)

April 4 De Gaulle was named commander of all Free French forces.

■ In a display of precision bombing six RAF Mosquitos bombed a Gestapo building in The Hague which contained the files on Dutchmen earmarked for deportation. In the center of a civilian area only the target building was destroyed in the low-level attack.

■ Japanese troops began their direct assault on Kohima. Indian troops from the Dimapur area were rushed to the front to help block the Japanese.

■ Moscow called on all Rumanians to abandon the Germans and cease fighting or face destruction.

April 5 U.S. planes launched the first in a new series of strikes against Axis oil targets. The first raid was directed at Ploesti in Rumania as 588 tons of bombs were dropped on rail facilities around the refining and production center.

Allied bombers suffered heavy losses in attacking Berlin. This B-17 managed to hold formation and drop its bombs on the German capital even with one wing aflame.

■ Tarnopol was captured by the Russians.

April 6 Japanese troops advanced within Kohima.

■ Only 25 Japanese planes were left in service at Hollandia.

April 7 Counterattacking German forces made some advances in the Crimea but suffered heavy casualties.

■ Kohima's water supply was cut off by the Japanese.

April 8 Russia launched its final drive to oust the Germans from the Crimea. Red Army troops on the central front were approaching the Czech border.

■ Stalin was told the date of the Normandy invasion. Almost simultaneously, the Japanese told the Soviets they were willing to mediate a peace between Germany and Russia. The initiative was Tokyo's, not Berlin's, and the Russians rejected the offer.

■ B-24s knocked out two spans of the Sittang bridge, regarded as the most critical target of the rail system in Burma. Its partial destruction

halted most Japanese rail shipments to Myitkyina for nearly two months.

April 9 Large units of the British Fourteenth Army were surrounded at Kohima as the Japanese blocked the final escape route. Air resupply was essential, but the onset of the monsoon rains made the task difficult.

April 10 The Black Sea port of Odessa was recaptured by Soviet forces. It had been under German occupation since October 1941. Kleist's Army Group A fell back beyond the Dniester River into Rumania.

■ German officers gave up their plans for another attack on Anzio.

■ General Slim ordered his forces in the Imphal-Kohima battle to take the offensive.

April 11 The German Seventeenth Army fell back to Sevastopol as the Red Army took Kerch in a new offensive to retake the Crimea.

April 13 In one of the heaviest air strikes of the war 3,000 Allied aircraft operating from bases in Britain and Italy struck at strategic targets in Germany, Hungary, and Yugoslavia.

■ Allied aircraft began a series of attacks on German coast artillery units in Normandy.

■ Soviet troops reoccupied Simferopol in the Crimea and captured 20,000 Germans.

This 17-year-old German was captured in his one-man torpedo submarine off the Anzio beachhead in Italy.

April 14–17 The German defense line in the Ukraine was split in two in a series of fierce battles.

April 14 In a step to prevent any word leaking out on Allied plans for the invasion of France, Britain sharply restricted diplomatic privileges. Communications were censored. No code traffic was permitted. Pouches had to be inspected. Only U.S., Russian, and British Dominion offices were exempt.

■ The first Jews from Greece began being transported from Athens to the Auschwitz concentration camp.

■ Two enormous explosions in the dock area of Bombay, India, killed as many as 940 people. The freighter *Fort Stikene*, carrying 1,300 tons of TNT, caught fire. As water was poured on the ship to contain the blaze, the munitions exploded. Another larger explosion occurred minutes later, obliterating the *Fort Stikene* and 19 other ships. Damage was estimated at $80 million. Forty thousand tons of food were lost in the explosions, leading to semifamine conditions in India later.

April 16 Yalta in the Crimea was recaptured by the Russians.

April 17 Japan launched what was to be its last major offensive in China. A division struck over the Yellow River in Honan Province in the first move of the campaign to seize Allied air bases and decimate Chinese ground forces.

April 18 Russian marines recaptured Balaklava in the Crimea.

■ Marshal Badoglio resigned as head of the Italian government, but the king requested he remain with a reconstituted cabinet.

April 19 Two Japanese divisions launched a southward thrust along the Peking–Hankow railroad in Honan Province, China.

April 20 British 2nd Division forces reached the besieged garrison at Kohima, but the Japanese continued to hold the vital road to Imphal.

April 22 U.S. Army amphibious forces landed near Hollandia, New Guinea.

■ Fighting ended on New Britain.

■ Russia concluded peace talks with Finland.

■ Yugoslav Partisans occupied the German-held island of Korcula in the Adriatic.

April 23 Sensitive to growing criticism of the heavy Allied bombing of Germany, Britain

defended the raids as essential to the liberation of the peoples of western Europe.

FLYING CASUALTIES

A U.S. Army Air Force heavy bomber combat crewman flying in the European theater was extremely lucky to come out of a tour of duty alive and uninjured. The odds were only a little more than nine to one. These were the casualty rates per 1,000 for the period from January through June 1944:

	Killed or Missing	Wounded	Total Casualties
Heavy bomber crewmen	712	175	887
Fighter pilots	484	39	523
Medium bomber crewmen	238	112	350

TOURS OF DUTY

In June 1944 U.S. Eighth Air Force tours of duty were as follows:

> Heavy bomber crews, 30 missions
> Medium bomber crews, 50 missions°
> Light bomber crews, 60 missions°
> Fighter pilots, 300 hours of combat flying

°These were approximate mission figures since definite numbers were never clearly defined but depended upon each crew's record.

April 24 The Strategy Section of the U.S. War Department's Operations Division determined that "the collapse of Japan can be assured only by the invasion of Japan proper."

■ Australian troops occupied Madang in New Guinea. P-40s of the Royal Australian Air Force began using the Tadji airstrip.

April 25 The Japanese intensified offensive operations in Honan Province in China with heavy attacks directed toward Chenghsien (Chengchow).

April 26 Alexishafen on New Guinea was occupied by Australian forces. U.S. troops gained control of the airfield at Hollandia.

Troops of the all-black U.S. 93rd Infantry Division patrol the Numa-Numa Trail on Bougainville.

April 27 Heavy fighting developed near Imphal as the Japanese tried to break through before heavy rains rendered further action impossible.

April 28 Japanese forces made broad gains in Honan Province. U.S. planes were concentrated in attacks on the Yellow River bridges to slow up the Japanese offensive.

■ U.S. and Chinese troops advanced up the Mogaung valley toward Myitkyina.

■ Pétain announced that France was threatened by civil war.

April 29–30 U.S. Naval Task Force 59 ships and planes returned to Truk for raids against the key Japanese base. About 120 Japanese aircraft were destroyed, plus large amounts of arms and petroleum supplies.

April 30 For the first time Stalin himself publicly acknowledged that the Soviet Union was receiving American and British aid.

■ U.S. and RAF bombers dropped 80,000 tons of explosives in western Europe during the month.

■ British civilian air raid casualties for April were 146 killed and 226 injured.

May Allied aircraft began to mine the sea approaches to Bangkok and Rangoon. A total of 560 of the delayed-action type weapons were laid. Together with aerial raids on the ports, shipping was sharply restricted. The Japanese were forced to keep virtually all merchants out of the Bay of Bengal and rely on smaller coastal ships and less accessible ports for resupply.

May 1 A Yugoslav Partisan military mission arrived in London for talks on forthcoming joint actions and the distribution of supplies.

■ U.S. battleships and carrier aircraft bombed Ponape Island in the Carolines.

May 3 Allied agreements were concluded with Spain which provided for a cutback in Spanish shipments of tungsten to Germany in exchange for Allied oil from the Americas.

May 4 U.S. reinforcements landed on New Guinea. In the Aitape area, 525 Japanese were killed in the previous two weeks to the loss of 19 Americans.

■ Chinese troops captured Inkangahtawng on the approaches to Kamaing in Burma.

May 5 Alexander ordered Allied units in Italy to break through the Gustav Line and take Rome.

■ Indian leader Gandhi was released from British custody because of ill health. He had been imprisoned since August 1942.

May 7 Russian forces launched their decisive attack on Sevastopol.

Chinese armored units advance into Burma in support of the Allied offensive.

May 8 Eisenhower designated D-Day, the cross-Channel invasion, as June 5. It had originally been set for an unspecified day in May.

May 9 Soviet forces recaptured Sevastopol after a 24-day siege.

■ Allied air units commenced a series of intensive raids on Luftwaffe bases in France to neutralize the German air threats on D-Day.

■ Japanese troops captured Lushan in China, completely cutting the Peking–Hankow rail line.

May 10 Chinese forces launched a major offensive aimed at retaking northern Burma. They crossed the Salween River and moved forward along a 100-mile front.

■ The Free French announced there were 175,000 resistance fighters in France.

May 11 A major offensive was launched by Allied forces in central Italy. The U.S. Fifth and British Eighth armies planned to break through the Gustav Line. Operations began after dark with heavy air and artillery bombardment preceding a frontal ground assault.

May 12 Allied forces in Italy advanced on a broad front, crossing the Rapido River. German resistance was fierce.

■ The last of the German troops in the Crimea were evacuated.

■ Japanese forces gained full control of the Peking–Hankow railroad in China.

■ In a joint statement, the U.S., Britain, and the Soviet Union called upon the Axis satellites of Hungary, Rumania, and Bulgaria to withdraw from the war or face the consequences of rigorous peace terms.

■ French Admiral Edmond Derrien was given a life sentence after having been found guilty of collaborationist activity by a French court in Algiers.

■ More than 800 U.S. bombers, with American and RAF fighter escorts, attacked synthetic oil plants in Germany, knocking several out of production temporarily. Luftwaffe losses were heavy, nearly 200 planes were downed, while the Allies lost 46 bombers and 10 fighters.

May 13 French colonial troops captured three key positions in the Abruzzi Mountains and smashed through the Gustav Line. The dramatic breakthrough opened the way for the Allies to move northward. German losses were heavy. More than 1,000 Germans were captured.

■ One of the few Japanese submarines to operate in the Western Hemisphere, the *Ro-501*, was sunk in the mid-Atlantic by an American destroyer escort.

May 14 German opposition was stiff in Italy, but the Allies continued their northward advance. The Rapido bridgehead was strengthened and expanded.

May 15 The Ausonia defile was cleared in Italy,

Smoke pours from an oil refinery in Ploesti, Rumania, as U.S. B-24s complete their run against the installation, May 1944.

and other key points on the Gustav line fell to the Allies, led by French Moroccan troops.

■ British and Indian units finally broke the Japanese defenses at Kohima. Other Allied forces reached a point 15 miles from Myitkyina in Burma.

■ The first groups of 380,000 Hungarian Jews were deported to concentration camps, mostly to Auschwitz. (A total of 250,000 of them were to be gassed.)

May 16 Allied forces smashed the last Gustav Line defenses on its eastern hinge.

■ All Japanese resistance ceased on the Kohima ridge, ending the siege there.

May 17 Kesselring ordered German troops out of the Cassino area. Allied troops were already attacking the next German defense positions, the Hitler Line. The British Eighth Army began a general offensive on the flank.

■ Myitkyina's airport was taken in a surprise attack by U.S. Marauders.

■ Street fighting broke out in Loyang, China, between Chinese and Japanese forces.

■ U.S. and British planes attacked Surabaja, Java, and sank 10 Japanese ships.

May 18 Monte Cassino fell to the Allies. At 9:30 A.M., Poles of the 3rd Carpathian Division raised their regimental flag over Monte Cassino, ending the bitter four-month struggle for the Benedictine monastery. The improvised Polish flag was hastily sewn, with pieces of it coming from a Red Cross flag and soldiers' handkerchiefs. Men from 15 nations participated in the battle. About 20,000 were killed. Another 100,000 were wounded.

POLISH TROOPS AT MONTE CASSINO

Polish II Corps casualties in the two-week fight for Monte Cassino were more than 1,200 dead and 2,500 wounded. The Polish cemetery carries the following epitaph for the fallen:

We Polish soldiers
For our freedom and yours
Have given our souls to God
Our bodies to the soil of Italy
And our hearts to Poland.

FROM THE DIARY OF A JAPANESE INFANTRYMAN

Military intelligence acquired a great deal of valuable material from the diaries of Japanese soldiers during the Pacific campaigns. Some revealed more than enemy troop data and plans. This is the excerpt from a diary kept by an unidentified Japanese noncommissioned officer of the 80th Infantry Brigade who was fighting in New Guinea. The date is May 18th, but the year has not been verified, though it was probably 1944.

"We finally departed in the evening for the other side of the river to attack the enemy. To begin with, we moved toward the Ramu River crossing point. At 9:20 we arrived at the Ramu River bank. I was first to cross the river under the guidance of a Waimeriba chief. Presently, I am crossing the comparatively swift Ramu River. Will I be able to return safely later?

"After searching Waimeriba without seeing any sight of the enemy, we headed for Waisha. While crossing a river, I felt a slight chill. Could it be that is the reason I feel a little feverish? Or is it the curse of the Ramu? At 1:20 we reached the barracks site where Tokuhisa recently attacked. This feeling! How can one describe the thrill? This is the first night combat for a long time.

"We are probably the first of the many men in the division to participate in night combat in New Guinea. Passing the plantation, we suddenly came out in front of a barracks. Slowly we approached the first and second houses, but there was no sign of the enemy. We surrounded the chief of Wesa and learned of the enemy situation. He informed us that the enemy was sleeping in Keneudei village. Pushing along on a mountain road, we proceeded to the next village. We crossed at the junction of the Wesa River. We are to attack from the village flank. Upon entering the village, we searched each house. There was no sign of the enemy except for a wireless set, a generator, and various equipment. Tonight's attack finally ended in failure. Reluctantly, we ate our breakfast. After breakfast, many natives from Wesa came to inform us that an American soldier was sleeping in a hut beyond the hill. With a determination to not let him escape this time, we advanced toward the hill.

"En route, we crossed a branch of the Wesa River. Since landing in New Guinea, this has been the first time I've seen such beautiful clear water. I washed my face with the water. We had a native from a Hoedei village guide us to where the American soldier was. By climbing up a steep hill and cautiously peering over it, a small roof could be seen. Stretching my neck a little further, I saw a mosquito net and a rifle. At that moment, a native police boy got a glimpse of me and scurried away. Immediately the American soldier threw the mosquito net aside and began to flee like a bird. Just when I thought he had got away Miike fired one shot, which hit the mark. We searched through the dead soldier's belongings and found a Bible, a diary, and a photo of his mother. Apparently he had malaria and was asleep. His mother is a woman with a very kind face. I don't know if he is her only son. How grieved she would be if she were to hear that her son was killed! Nevertheless, this is fate. A moment ago, he was probably reading his Bible or thinking about his home. With one shot of the rifle which echoed through the Bismarck Range, he had gone to heaven. For many years he has been our enemy, but now that he has become a departed soul, we forgave him for the resentment we held and buried him. We arrived at the Keneudi village. At 13:00 we left the village. We are returning to Waimeriba. Almost everyone in the platoon has injured his feet, except Miike and myself. When we arrived at Waimeriba it was 7:00 in the evening."

■ The campaign in the Admiralty Islands ended. U.S. losses were 326, while 3,280 Japanese were killed.

■ An attempt to seize Myitkyina was turned back by the Japanese, but the rail station fell to Chinese forces.

May 19 It was publicly revealed that 47 RAF officers had been executed by the Germans when they were recaptured after escaping from a POW camp.

■ British Eighth Army troops failed to breach the Hitler Line at Pontecorvo and Aquino. Gaeta was abandoned by the Germans who retreated north of the Liri River.

■ The Japanese at Myitkyina were partially surrounded.

■ U.S. forces landed on Wakde Island off the coast of New Guinea.

American 41st Division troops landing on Wakde Island, off Dutch New Guinea, May 18, 1944. Note fallen grenade in foreground.

A dead American soldier, felled in the invasion of Wakde Island, May 18, 1944.

May 20 Allied troops occupied the Gaeta peninsula in Italy.

■ Japanese-held Marcus Island was attacked by U.S. naval aircraft.

■ Insoemoar Island off New Guinea was secured by U.S. forces, who suffered 43 losses to 759 Japanese killed.

May 21 Allied fighters launched operational strikes against Axis rail transport in France and Germany.

■ Wakde Island was secured by U.S. forces, giving the Allied air forces a base to cover landing units in the projected invasion of Mindanao in the Philippines.

May 22 A referendum was approved in Iceland to break away from Denmark and to declare the island an independent republic.

May 23 A large-scale American and British offensive was begun to break out of Anzio. The U.S. 45th Division attacked the German positions at Cisterna while the 3rd Division smashed at the center. Among the units involved in the Anzio breakout was the 100th Japanese Infantry Battalion, made up of Americans of Japanese descent. About 1,500 Germans were captured in the day's action. Canadian I Corps troops penetrated the Hitler Line to the east.

■ Chinese forces went on the offensive in Honan Province.

May 24 Fighting was heavy at Anzio in seesaw encounters.

■ Wake Island was attacked by U.S. naval aircraft.

■ Six hundred German paratroopers made a surprise assault on Yugoslav Partisan headquarters near Drvar. Tito and Randolph Churchill, son of the prime minister, barely escaped.

May 25 Units from Anzio linked up with patrols from the U.S. Fifth Army at Terracina, breaking the pressing encirclement of the Anzio units which had been put ashore four months before. The Germans were pulling back in the face of the advancing ground forces and incessant Allied air attacks. More than 2,600 Germans were captured by noon.

May 26 The Allied offensive toward Rome was slowed down, primarily because of terrain and continuing stiff German resistance.

■ Japanese forces pushed U.S. Marauders back near Myitkyina.

May 27 The U.S. 41st Division landed on Biak Island in the Schoutens group, 900 miles from the Philippines. It met only token resistance.

■ U.S. Marauders were badly mauled around Myitkyina.

■ Two Japanese divisions advanced east of the Hsiang (Siang) River to press the campaign to overrun Allied air bases in China.

■ The entire coastline between Anzio and Terracina was under Allied control.

May 28 The entire Chinese Seventy-first Army was committed to the Burma battle south of the Salween River.

May 29 The U.S. 1st Armored and 34th divisions suffered heavy losses on the approaches to Rome.

■ Göring admitted to Hitler that the Allies had achieved total air superiority on the Italian front: ". . . at the moment the situation in Italy is such that not a single Luftwaffe aircraft dares show itself."

■ Tanks fought each other for the first time in the southwest Pacific area on Biak. The Japanese used armor in an effort to dislodge the Americans

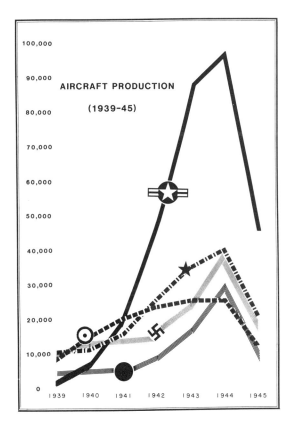

AIRCRAFT PRODUCTION

(1939-45)

While Allied air production soared, the surprising fact is that ouput by the Germans and the Japanese continued to climb in the face of limited resources and devastation of their homelands.

east of Parai. More than 500 Japanese were killed before the attack was halted.

■ The U.S. Navy escort carrier *Block Island* was torpedoed and sunk by a German U-boat off the Azores. It was the only American carrier sunk in the Atlantic during the war.

May 31 Allied troops began boarding ships for the Normandy invasion.

■ Powerful counterattacks were launched by the Germans north of Iasi (Jassy), in Rumania.

■ Intensive Allied bombing prior to the Normandy invasion resulted in a month's toll of 900 locomotives and 16,000 freight cars destroyed in Nazi-occupied western Europe.

■ For the first time in nearly four years there were no British civilian air raid victims during a monthly reporting period.

June 1 Allied forces took the offensive along a broad front south of Rome in an effort to knock out the German Fourteenth Army. Heavy resistance was encountered.

■ Monsoon rains stalled operations in Burma.

June 2 Alexander called on the people of Rome to save the Eternal City from destruction.

■ Pope Pius made an appeal to the Axis and Allied armies to save Rome.

■ German troops began withdrawing all along the Italian front.

■ Chinese forces surrounded Myitkyina in Burma and started tunneling into the town.

■ Japanese units won all their objectives in Honan Province and halted their offensive actions.

June 3 Hitler authorized Kesselring to withdraw his forces from Rome.

■ The battle for Kohima ended in a British victory, but U.S. and Chinese casualties at Myitkyina forced the Allies to halt offensive operations until the Allied forces could regroup.

June 4 The U.S. Fifth Army entered Rome. While the Germans fought some rear-guard actions, the city was spared the devastation of combat. By nightfall, Allied units were converging on Rome from all sectors. Germans withdrawing northward from Rome were hit steadily by Allied aircraft. Rome's population greeted the Allies enthusiastically after a lengthy period in which the Germans defended southern Italy with incredible determination to delay the inevitable capture of the first Axis capital to fall. Hitler ordered the Italian capital evacuated, according to Radio Berlin, to avoid putting the city "under

U.S. troops enter Rome.

the peril of destruction." With the exception of rail yards bombed by the Allies, Rome escaped the war relatively unscathed.

■ Because of bad weather, Eisenhower ordered a 24-hour postponement of D-Day until June 6.

■ An American Navy antisubmarine force captured a German submarine (*U-505*) 150 miles off the coast of Río de Oro (Spanish Sahara), Africa. It was the first enemy ship captured by a U.S. naval boarding party since 1814. The submarine surfaced when attacked, but the crew abandoned it when it started to sink. American seamen boarded and salvaged it, and the submarine was towed to the U.S.

June 5 American and British airborne troops began taking off for France. Their main mission was to seize vital ground behind the German forces on both flanks of the Normandy invasion

U.S. Navy Captain Daniel V. Gallery in the conning tower of the German submarine U-505 which was captured in the Atlantic by Gallery's ship, the U.S.S. Guadalcanal.

front and block German reinforcements from reaching the beachhead.

■ Alexander ordered the U.S. Fifth and British Eighth armies to advance to the Rimini-Pisa Line in Italy.

■ King Victor Emmanuel III of Italy transferred all royal powers to Crown Prince Umberto who was designated "Lieutenant General of the Realm."

■ Twenty thousand Chinese troops crossed to the west bank of the Salween River.

■ The U.S. XX Bomber Command flew its first missions, attacking Bangkok.

June 6 The greatest amphibious operation in military history was launched as Allied forces under the command of Eisenhower began landing on the northern coast of France between Cherbourg and Le Havre. H-Hour for the Americans was 6:30 A.M., later for the British units because of the tide. Within 24 hours, 176,000 troops were put ashore from 4,000 ships. They were protected by 9,500 aircraft and 600 warships. U.S. First Army forces quickly secured Utah Beach. The British Second Army overcame most resistance rapidly and drove toward Caen. Only at Omaha Beach were the forces almost totally stymied, but the U.S. V Corps established a firm beachhead by evening.

ALLIED D-DAY SUPPORT FORCE

Aircraft

5,409 fighters	1,645 light and medium
3,467 heavy bombers	bombers
	2,316 transports

These aircraft flew 14,674 sorties on D-Day. The bombers dropped 11,912 tons of explosives. Antiaircraft accounted for most of the 113 planes which were downed. The Germans had 319 aircraft in the area, only a hundred of them fighters.

Naval Craft

6 battleships	122 destroyers
23 cruisers	360 PT boats

Hundreds of frigates, sloops, and other small combat craft and 6,480 transports, landing craft, and special-purpose vessels.

■ U.S. 1st Armored Division units advanced 25 miles north of Rome.

■ U.S. planners set Oct. 1, 1945, as the date for invading Japan.

June 7 Halting progress was made in Normandy. Bayeux was attacked and main units hooked up

U.S. mechanized units land on the Normandy beachhead, June 6, 1944, under the protection of barrage balloons.

U.S. glider pilots who ferried assault paratroopers to their D-Day destinations are picked up at the beachhead.

ly Biak Island were turned back by Allied ships and planes. One of the destroyers was sunk.

June 9 The German garrison at Azeville surrendered to U.S. forces who pressed toward Cherbourg.

■ Allied aircraft began operating from bases in France.

THE INTERNATIONAL ROYAL AIR FORCE

By D-Day the RAF was made up of 487 squadrons under its command. It was international in character, as the following breakdown demonstrates:

British	330	New Zealand	6
Canadian	42	Czechoslovak	4
South African	27	Norwegian	4
French	27	Greek	3
Australian	16	Dutch	3
Polish	13	Belgian	2
Indian	9	Yugoslav	1

with paratroopers who had landed inland. Eisenhower went to the front to take direct command. Artificial harbors and protected anchorages (code-named MULBERRY) had been constructed from sunken ships and concrete caissons, greatly facilitating the transport of additional men and material to the front.

■ U.S. forces reached points 40 miles north of Rome. Civitavecchia was taken, permitting Allied use of the important transport facilities there once repaired.

■ King Leopold III of Belgium was taken to Germany.

June 8 A linkup was effected between the U.S. First and British Eighth armies near Port-en-Bessin. Bayeux, five miles from the landing beaches, was occupied. The rail link from the invasion area to Cherbourg was cut.

■ German forces abandoned positions along the Adriatic in central Italy.

■ Badoglio and his government arrived in Rome.

■ Five Japanese destroyers attempting to resupp-

■ The Soviets launched an attack on the Karelian Isthmus. The Red Army began assaulting the Mannerheim Line between Lake Ladoga and the Gulf of Finland after artillery pounded the area for three hours.

■ Badoglio resigned as Italy's premier and was succeeded by Ivanoe Bonomi, a premier before Mussolini assumed power.

June 10 In one of the most savage actions of the war, a company of the SS *Das Reich* Division killed all the inhabitants of the French village of Oradour-sur-Glâne, near Limoges. About 600 people, including the women and children, were executed on the spot or burned alive in the village church. They had committed no crimes but were the helpless victims of the SS which had been unable to find one of its commanders kidnapped by the French Maquis. The SS division had also been harassed by French Resistance fighters in their move to the Normandy front from Toulouse.

■ Indian troops captured Pescara on the Italian east coast.

■ The American and Chinese attacks on Myitkyina and Kamaing resumed in Burma.

A monument to fallen French World War I soldiers was reduced to a lifelike statue surveying the destruction of Isigny shortly after the D-Day landings.

■ Five Japanese divisions moved into position to attack Changsha in China.

June 11 U.S. forces surrounded Carentan which had already been abandoned by the Germans. The town had been pounded by U.S. battleships,

standing off the Normandy coast ten miles from Carentan. British troops captured Tilly-sur-Seulles but were driven out by nightfall.

■ The U.S. 36th Division advanced to a point 65 miles north of Rome.

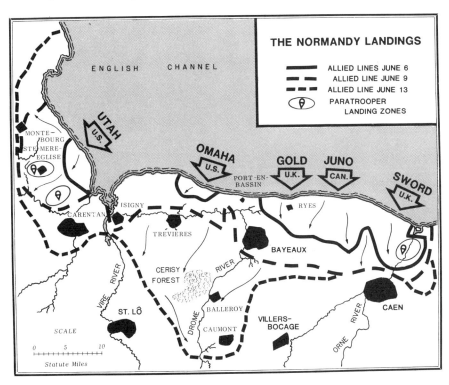

The Allied landings on the beaches of Normandy, June 6, 1944, constituted the greatest amphibious operation in history.

Lord Louis Mountbatten, Supreme Allied Commander, Southeast Asia, talks to an American fighter pilot, Lieutenant Charles Christmer.

(ABOVE) *A V-1 bomb falls on London.*

(BELOW) *London firefighters fight blaze at Regency Place and Rutherford Street after the area was hit by a V-1 bomb.*

■ Russian troops pushed 15 miles into Finland through the Mannerheim line.

■ U.S. naval and air forces attacked Guam, Saipan, and Tinian in the Marianas. Twelve U.S. planes were lost, but more than 200 Japanese aircraft were destroyed or seriously damaged.

■ American bombers shuttled to Russia bombed Focsani in Rumania before returning to their bases in Italy.

June 12 All beachheads on Normandy were linked, with the Allies established on a 50-mile-wide front.

■ Chinese Communist leader Mao Tse-tung announced his support of Chiang Kai-shek in the war against Japan.

June 13 Germany began launching V-1 rocket bombs against England. The missiles (*Vergeltungswaffe-1*, or Reprisal Weapon-1) marked a new phase of warfare, unmanned weapons capable of flying a maximum of 155 miles as instruments of terror. (Eight thousand V-1s were fired at England. A total of 2,300 reached London. They had a profound psychological effect on the civilian population. Defense was initially difficult, and the distinctive buzzing followed by its crashing descent was terrifying. The V-1 was 25 feet long and carried a one-ton warhead. Hitler's first "secret weapon" wrought a great toll, killing 5,479, injuring 15,934, destroying or damaging 1,104,000 houses, 149 schools, 11 churches and 95 hospitals.)

Hungerford Bridge near Charing Cross in London after being hit by a V-1 bomb.

■ U.S. VII Corps units drove to cut the Cotentin Peninsula and take Cherbourg.

■ Japanese units gained ground in bitter fighting at Myitkyina.

June 14 Japanese forces captured Liu-yang, increasing the threat to Changsha in China.

■ After an absence of four years, de Gaulle made a triumphal return to France.

June 15 Saipan in the Marianas was invaded by U.S. Marines. The 2nd and 4th Marine divisions were put ashore against a Japanese force of 17,600 men. The landing areas were bombarded by an awesome force of 7 battleships, 11 cruisers, and 26 destroyers. Saipan, together with Guam and Tinian, were regarded as essential bases for B-29 attacks on Japan. Resistance on Saipan was fierce, but the Marines secured a five-mile-wide beachhead on the first day. A furious counterattack by the Japanese 136th Infantry Regiment was hurled back by the 6th Marine Regiment. In eight hours of relentless combat, 700 Japanese were killed.

■ B-29s made their first raids on Japan from China, dropping 221 tons on the Yawata iron and steel plant on Kyushu. This was the first attack on the home islands since the Doolittle raid more than two years before.

■ U.S. troops gained control of the port of Quiné-

ville and occupied Gourbesville, but action in Normandy was indecisive.

■ Iwo Jima and the Bonin Islands were attacked by U.S. naval aircraft.

June 16 King George VI visited the Normandy front. Under U.S. VII Corps pressure, German forces began pulling back east of the Douve River.

■ Fierce fighting continued on Saipan as U.S. Marines threw back a strong Japanese counterattack.

■ Changsha in China came under direct Japanese attack.

June 17 The U.S. 9th Division sealed off the Cotentin Peninsula by reaching its west coast. Cherbourg was now isolated.

■ Colonial infantry division troops under French command landed on the isle of Elba.

■ Since the fighting on the Imphal plain began on March 4, British forces suffered 2,669 killed and nearly 10,000 wounded. Japanese casualties totaled 30,000.

■ Chinese forces fell back from the city of Changsha, which the Japanese began to occupy. The third Battle of Changsha, as it came to be known, was significant in that the Chinese won the first two battles in 1939 and 1941 and Changsha came to represent a point beyond which the Japanese could not penetrate. That they did indicated the determination of the Japanese to seize Hunan Province.

June 18 Russian forces breached the Mannerheim line in Finland.

■ Aslito airfield on Saipan was taken by the Marines.

June 19–20 The Battle of the Philippine Sea, decisive in the future course of the Pacific war, was fought in a giant clash of aircraft, surface ships, and submarines. Japan had planned to destroy the U.S. fleet operating in the Marianas by attacking with carrier aircraft. Two Japanese carriers, *Shokaku* and *Taiho*, were sunk by U.S. submarines before the battle began, crippling the Japanese strike force en route to its interception point and foredooming the operation. American planes were able to take the offensive instead, first attacking and sinking the carrier, *Hiyo*. Two U.S. battleships, two carriers, and a heavy cruiser were damaged, but the effect was negligible compared to Japanese losses, especially of aircraft. In two days of fighting, 476 Japanese

A U.S. Navy F6F pilot gets final target instructions (note blackboard under propeller) before taking off from the U.S.S. Yorktown *to engage in the Marianas "Turkey Shoot."*

planes were destroyed (some on suicide missions). A total of 130 U.S. aircraft were lost (80 percent of them because they ran out of fuel or could not find their carriers in the dark). The Japanese fleet pulled back to Okinawa. Its naval air arm was never again a factor in the Pacific war. The Japanese High Command, apprised of the battle losses, abandoned whatever hope was left that Japan could possibly win the war.

THE VERACITY OF CLAIMED DESTRUCTION

Most military units (of all nations) tend to exaggerate the damage inflicted on the enemy, either because they overstate their own destructiveness or can't visualize survival by their victims. There is also propaganda-inspired inflation by higher commands. A Japanese government official, Toshikazu Kase of the foreign ministry, candidly said "it was customary for GHQ (in Tokyo) to make false announcements of victory in utter disregard of facts, and for the elated and complacent public to believe in them." This example makes the point.

The Battle of the Philippine Sea
June 19–20, 1944

Japanese Claims at the Time:

U.S. naval forces lost "more than five aircraft carriers sunk or damaged, one battleship sunk, and more than 100 planes shot down." A great victory was claimed.

Actual U.S. Losses:

Two carriers, two battleships, and a cruiser were damaged. The Japanese underestimated plane destruction, however, since 130 U.S. aircraft were downed. As for the victory claim, three Japanese aircraft carriers were sunk and 426 of their 473 operational aircraft were lost. The Japanese High Command "thoroughly understood that the war was lost" after the battle, according to the U.S. naval history of the war.

June 19 Three U.S. divisions advanced toward Cherbourg.
■ U.S. forces opened a drive to capture the sole airfield on New Guinea remaining in Japanese hands.
June 20 U.S. Army units reached the outskirts of

Cherbourg, advancing to within four miles of the port itself.

■ The British Eighth Army entered Perugia, which the Germans had abandoned.

■ Viipuri (Vyborg) in Finland was occupied by the Red Army. The Gulf of Finland was now opened to Russian ships, insuring Leningrad's security.

June 21 In a massive raid on Berlin 1,000 Allied bombers, escorted by 1,200 fighters, inflicted heavy damage on the German capital and nearby areas. Of the force, 184 American planes continued on to Poltava in the Soviet Union. Later that night the Germans attacked the Poltava airstrip and inflicted heavy damage.

■ Red Army troops pushed into Finland on both sides of Lake Onega.

■ An ultimatum was issued to the commander of the German garrison at Cherbourg to surrender by 9:00 A.M. on the 22nd.

June 22 Cherbourg was hit by 1,000 Allied bombers as ground forces prepared to assault the key port city. No reply to the ultimatum was received.

■ Russian troops opened their summer offensive along a 300-mile front. The Red Army massed 146 infantry divisions and 43 tank brigades in the

drive initially aimed at Vitebsk. The action ended a comparative lull while the opposing forces regrouped and permitted their exhausted forces to prepare for this new round of fighting.

■ Imphal in India was relieved as British Fourteenth Army troops opened the road to Kohima. The starving and diseased Japanese began withdrawing through monsoon rain and mud. This marked the end of Mutaguchi's attempt to invade India.

■ Finnish officials began seeking formal peace terms from Russia while the Germans pressed to keep Finland in the war.

■ The GI Bill of Rights was signed into law, granting U.S. veterans educational and other special benefits for their eventual readjustment to civilian life.

June 23 The U.S. and Britain resumed diplomatic relations with Bolivia.

June 24 Russian troops reached the Dvina River on the Baltic front.

June 25 Emperor Hirohito summoned Japan's field marshals and fleet admirals to Tokyo to discuss the worsening military situation. He was advised that holding Saipan and other key islands would be extremely difficult and emphasis must

This is believed to be the only known picture taken of the German air attack on the U.S. shuttle base at Poltava in the Soviet Union in which 47 B-17s were destroyed and 19 heavily damaged.

be placed on establishing an "Inner Perimeter" around the home islands.

■ Street fighting developed within Cherbourg as U.S. troops pressed in on the German force. U.S. warships began bombarding German shore batteries and coastal defenses around the city.

■ Five German divisions were trapped as Russian troops cut the road between Smolensk and Minsk by encircling Vitebsk. German Army Group Center under General Ernst Busch broke under the assault.

June 26 The U.S. airbase at Hengyang in China was taken by the Japanese.

■ U.S. aircraft, taking off in Russia, bombed the oil installations at Drogobych (Drohobycz) and went on to Italy. Yak fighters escorted the American planes to the targets.

■ Vitebsk fell to the Russians. Eighty thousand Germans were captured. Stalin ordered salvos from Moscow's 224 guns to mark the first major victory of the summer offensive.

June 27 Russian troops crossed the Dnieper River.

■ All German resistance ended at Cherbourg, and the city was taken over by the U.S. 4th Division.

■ Fighting intensified on Saipan. Nafutan Point was cleared, with 550 Japanese killed.

June 28 British Second Army units crossed the Odon River in France as Montgomery's forces opened their drive for Caen.

■ Chinese forces began to stiffen their resistance around Hengyang in east China.

■ The British government agreed to establish a homeland for war refugees in one of the former Italian colonies of Africa.

■ Vichy Information Minister Philippe Henriot was assassinated by French underground commandos.

June 29 British forces expanded their Odon River bridgehead but broke off the offensive in view of German concentrations of armor.

June 30 Russian forces under Rokossovsky captured Bobruysk, the last German stronghold on the Fatherland line, opening up the way to Warsaw. Rokossovsky was promoted to marshal.

■ All German resistance ended on the Cotentin Peninsula.

■ Allied forces in Italy held a line from Lake Trasimeno, west of Perugia, to Pescara on the east coast.

■ As a result of the day and night V-1 flying

American M-10 tank destroyers lay down a barrage in an Italian mountain pass.

A London double-decker bus and a section of Waterloo were destroyed by a V-1 bomb.

bomb attacks on London, British civilian air raid casualties for the month soared to 1,935 killed and 5,906 wounded.

■ The U.S. broke diplomatic relations with Finland.

July 1 British Second Army forces beat back strong German counterattacks between Caen and Tilly-sur-Seulles, inflicting heavy tank losses. The Cherbourg peninsula was fully secured when the U.S. 9th Division reached Cap de la Hague.

■ Russian troops crossed the Berezina River and captured Borisov.

■ Copenhagen was placed under martial law.

■ The Bretton Woods International Monetary Conference was convened.

■ Admiral Nagumo, who commanded the Pearl Harbor attack force and led Japanese naval and air units in southeast Asia and the Indian Ocean to their successes in the early months of the Pacific war, shot and killed himself on Saipan. Nagumo's defeat in the Battle of Midway apparently left him demoralized, and he was demoted to command of a small flotilla operating in the Marianas.

July 2 Rundstedt was relieved as German commander in chief, west, and replaced by Field Marshal Hans Günther von Kluge.

■ Soviet forces cut the Vilna-Minsk railway and closed in on Minsk.

■ Japanese forces fell back to their final defense lines in northern Saipan.

July 3 The Battle of the Hedgerows began as the U.S. VIII Corps launched a general offensive down the west coast of the Cotentin Peninsula. Heavy rain precluded air support.

■ Minsk was recaptured by the Russians, which Moscow heralded as "one of the decisive victories of the war."

■ Siena was taken by Algerian forces, but the Germans stiffened their opposition southeast of Leghorn.

■ Iwo Jima and the Bonin Islands were subjected to intense bombardment by U.S. naval ships and aircraft. Two Japanese transports were sunk.

Navy attack aircraft return to their carrier after bombing Chichi Jima, in the Bonins.

July 4 Canadian troops took Carpiquet, west of Caen. U.S. 82nd Airborne Division forces made slow progress but were forced to withdraw outside La Haye-du-Puits.

■ Marines on Saipan fought their way to Garapan and Flores Point.

July 5 British Eighth Army units ran into stiffening German resistance in Italy south of Arezzo after making rapid advances to Tuoro and Umbertide.

July 6 Churchill revealed that 2,752 people had been killed by V-1 bombs, 2,754 of which had struck the London area.

■ De Gaulle arrived in Washington for meetings with Roosevelt.

■ German one-man *Biber* (Beaver) submarines attacked Allied ships off Normandy. Together with their raids on the 8th, the 29-foot-long craft sank three minesweepers and damaged the Polish cruiser *Dragon*. Seven of the mini-subs were sunk. (In addition to the above, *Bibers* were known to have sunk at least 12 merchant ships, 3 warships, and 3 patrol craft in all waters.)

July 7 RAF bombers dropped 2,602 tons of explosives to prepare the way for an all-out assault on Caen by the British Second Army.

■ B-29s bombed naval targets at Sasebo on the Japanese home island of Kyushu.

■ About 3,000 Japanese made a suicidal attack on U.S. Marine units on Saipan, inflicting heavy casualties, before being stopped.

■ Finnish troops began pulling back from the eastern portion of the Karelian front.

July 8 The British Second Army assaulted Caen. U.S. forces occupied La Haye-du-Puits.

■ With the commander of the Japanese Southern Army, Field Marshal Count Hisaichi Terauchi, having sanctioned the abandonment of the Imphal operation, the Japanese Fifteenth Army was ordered to retreat across the Chindwin. It was the final acceptance of defeat by Mutaguchi in the battle of Imphal-Kohima in which the Japanese lost 53,000 men out of the 85,000 committed.

■ Guam was bombarded by U.S. Navy warships, the beginning of daily attacks on the Mariana island, until it was invaded on the 21st.

July 9 Saipan's last defenses fell as U.S. forces secured the island. U.S. casualties were 3,674 Army and 10,437 Marines (including 3,126 dead), but the Japanese garrison of about 27,000 was almost completely eliminated. U.S. military intelligence felt, however, that Saipan represented a turning point in Japanese surrender attitudes. For the first time, large numbers were willing to lay down their arms. Although measured in hundreds, more POW's were taken on Saipan than any previous Pacific battle.

■ Caen was taken by Canadian and British forces. Stiff German opposition and the hedgerows slowed the drive of the U.S. VII Corps.

Japanese bodies line Tanapag Harbor after a counterattack was repulsed by U.S. forces on Saipan.

Japanese and Korean prisoners are evacuated from Saipan. Saipan was the first engagement in which large numbers of Japanese surrendered.

FEAR IN COMBAT

The U.S. Army told its soldiers fear in combat was normal. Recruits were instructed: "You'll be scared. Sure you'll be scared. Before you go into battle, you'll be frightened at the uncertainty, at the thought of being killed. Will it hurt? Will you know what to do? If you say you're not scared, you'll be a cocky fool. Don't let anyone tell you you're a coward if you admit being scared." (War Department pamphlet 21–13, 1944, p. 159.) Unique research by the U.S. Army during the war sustained the premise. In a sampling of wounded combat veterans, for example, 65 percent admitted being so filled with fear during combat that they could not function properly. The Army's Research Branch also found out *how* men felt in combat, the manifestations of fear. Four infantry divisions were selected, and combat veterans of the South and central Pacific responded with these figures showing the percentage reporting the occurrence of specific symptoms:

	Division A (2,095 men)	Division B (1,983 men)	Division C (1,299 men)	Division D (643 men)
Violent pounding of heart	84	78	74	68
Sinking stomach feeling	69	66	60	57
Shaking or trembling	61	54	53	39
Sick stomach	55	50	46	39
Cold sweat	56	45	43	39
Feeling faint or weak	49	46	36	34
Feeling of stiffness	45	44	43	31
Vomiting	27	21	18	8
Losing control of bowels	21	12	9	4
Urinating in pants	10	9	6	3

SOURCE: Samuel A. Stouffer, et al., *The American Soldier, Combat and Its Aftermath.*

■ Red Army troops crossed the Vuoksi River in Finland.

July 10 Hitler refused to permit the withdrawal of Army Group North behind the Dvina River, as recommended by Field Marshal Walther Model. The German Ninth and Fourth armies had been virtually annihilated already.

■ U.S. Vice President Henry Wallace—having concluded a visit to China—wrote a report scathingly critical of Chiang Kai-shek. Among other things, he proposed Roosevelt assign someone to mediate differences between the Chinese Nationalists and Communists.

■ Japanese troops launched a counterattack on New Guinea near Aitape.

July 11 St.-Lô came under U.S. attack.

■ Russian forces began attacking the German Panther defense line. Red Army units crossed into Latvia and penetrated 40 miles into Lithuania.

■ The U.S. recognized the French provisional government.

July 12 U.S. forces were blocked northeast and west of St.-Lô.

■ Allied war planes struck at the Po River bridges in Italy to impede German resupply efforts.

■ An attempt to capture Myitkyina failed, in part because Allied planes accidentally bombed their own troops.

July 13 Russian troops captured Vilna after five days of intensive street fighting. The way was opened for drives throughout the Baltic states. Red Army elements in Poland, after capturing Kaunas and Grodno, were now within 100 miles of the German frontier.

July 14 Pinsk was abandoned to the Russians. It was the last major German stronghold in the Pripet Marshes. Five Russian armies were now concentrated in the drive toward Warsaw. For the first time the Russians clearly dominated the skies, employing thousands of aircraft in support of their ground forces.

July 15 British and New Zealand units assaulted Arezzo, and the Germans began pulling out after dark.

■ The Russian advance into Finland was temporarily halted.

■ The commander of the German LXXXIV Corps in Normandy, General Dietrich von Choltitz, a veteran of extensive combat including Russia, reported on the fighting west of St.-Lô: "The

whole battle is one tremendous blood bath such as I have never seen in eleven years of war."

U.S. COMBAT WEAPONS RANKED FAILURES BY COMBAT TROOPS

M4 Sherman Tank. **Without significant exception, this tank received a bad rating. Armored troops didn't like the T-34 launcher which the Shermans carried as a mount. When the launcher was jettisoned, as was frequently the case, the Sherman lost its firepower. Battalion commanders of the 3rd Armored Division regarded the tanks as "deathtraps."**

Bazooka. **The 2.36-inch rocket and launcher was first used as an antitank weapon in the spring of 1943 during the Tunisian campaign, and its deficiencies were immediately apparent. It was designed to be the infantrymen's main weapon against enemy tanks, but it couldn't knock out either the German Panthers or Tigers at practical ranges. The German equivalent of the American bazooka—the *Panzerfaust*—was an example of an imitation being superior to the original. General Eisenhower said that, with the exception of German tanks, "only the German bazooka may be considered superior to an item of ours."**

Rocket Artillery. **The most widely used U.S. rocket was the 4.5-inch launcher which used fin-stabilized rockets. GI's didn't like them because they were inaccurate and gave away their positions, leading to the "shoot and scoot" method of deployment.**

SOURCE: Official U.S. Army History, Lida Mayo, *The Ordnance Department: On Beachhead and Battlefront.*

■ Japanese losses at Myitkyina thus far were 790 dead and 1,180 wounded, and the commander considered withdrawing even though the intensity of the Allied attacks had diminished.

July 16 British Eighth Army troops reached the Arno River in Italy and captured Arezzo. The Germans fought a strong delaying action, giving them time to build up their Gothic line defenses.

■ Russian troops captured Grodno, a key transportation center leading to East Prussia.

July 17 Russian forces swept into Poland, crossing the Bug River. German units in the Baltic states were ordered not to yield.

■ British troops advanced from their Arno River positions toward Florence. The Polish II Corps attacked Ancona.

■ Rommel was seriously wounded in Normandy when his car was attacked by a strafing aircraft.

■ Japanese Navy Minister Shigetaro Shimada resigned.

■ Two ammunition ships exploded in Port Chicago, California, killing 322 people and injuring hundreds more.

July 18 Hideki Tojo was removed as Japanese premier, war minister, and army chief of staff, the three positions he had held concurrently since the early part of the year. His fall from power was primarily the result of Japan's military setbacks in the Pacific, and the fall of Saipan was the final straw which set the rest of the cabinet and Japan's ruling elders against him. Tojo had called the loss of Saipan a "great disaster." A new cabinet was formed by Kuniaki Koiso, and Tojo's military responsibilities were assumed by Yoshiji-ro Umezu, who had been the army's ranking officer in China.

■ St.-Lô was captured by the U.S. XIX Corps, ending the Battle of the Hedgerows. British forces resumed their offensive in the Caen area, which was actually a diversion to draw German strength away from the U.S. sector. Allied aircraft dropped 7,700 tons of bombs around Caen on this day alone.

■ Russian forces were stopped on the East Prussian border at Augustow, but the Germans withdrew on the Baltic and Ukrainian fronts.

■ The U.S. 34th Division began its final assault on Leghorn. Ancona was taken by the Poles.

July 19 Five German divisions were trapped west of Brody in the Ukraine.

■ Russian troops crossed into Latvia near Dvinsk (Daugavpils).

■ Leghorn fell, but the Germans destroyed much of the town and port facilities with demolitions before withdrawing.

■ The 2nd British Division in Normandy cleared several towns on both banks of the Orne River.

July 20 Anti-Nazis in the army made a vain attempt to kill Hitler. Colonel Count Claus von

The French city of St.-Lô was reduced to rubble by German shelling and Allied bombing.

Stauffenberg was the only member of the Wehrmacht's anti-Hitler circle to attend top-level staff meetings. He had tried to kill Hitler on several occasions during the past seven months. On the first three occasions, at Berchtesgaden, Stauffenberg did not arm the bombs because Hitler did not appear or other Nazi leaders were absent. On this day, Stauffenberg placed two explosives under Hitler's map table at the Rastenburg "Wolf's Lair." The bombs went off as planned and Stauffenberg, who left the room on the pretext of having to make a telephone call, assumed his mission was accomplished. Hitler, dazed and slightly injured, survived the blast when the explosive force was spent through the open windows and in collapsing the flimsy wooden building. In the confined shelter, where the meeting was originally scheduled, Hitler certainly would have died. Of the 24 people in the room, four were killed. Stauffenberg and five collaborators, including generals Ludwig Beck and Erich Hoepner, paid with their lives for their roles in the plot. Stauffenberg's last words before being executed were "Long live our sacred Germany."

■ The Russian-supported Polish Committee of National Liberation was formed.

■ Red Army troops reached the Bug River on a 40-mile front.

July 21 U.S. 3rd Marine and 77th Army Division troops landed on Guam. Opposition was moderate and bridgeheads a mile inland were established by nightfall north and south of the Orote Peninsula.

■ Red Army troops raced toward Brest-Litovsk and Lublin.

July 22 Russian troops reached the 1940 Finnish-Russian border.

■ German forces in the Brody pocket were annihilated.

■ St. Gingolph was destroyed by the SS.

■ Japanese forces on Guam counterattacked but were repulsed. U.S. beachheads were expanded.

July 23 The last Soviet prewar city held by the

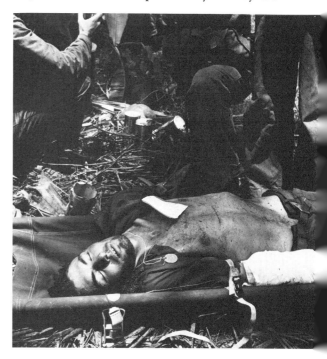

(ABOVE) *A wounded American awaits evacuation after being wounded on Guam.*

(LEFT) *U.S. Marines dodge Japanese defensive fire in the invasion of Guam.*

Germans, Pskov, was recaptured by the Third Baltic Army.

July 24 Two U.S. Marine divisions landed on Tinian Island. The Japanese garrison (essentially the 5th Infantry Regiment) fought for nine days until all were killed.

■ Russian troops reached the Maidanek concentration camp. Lublin was occupied.

■ The Polish government in London called the pro-Russian Polish organization a "handful of unknown Communists."

■ German army troops were ordered to give the "Hitler salutes" for the first time.

July 25 The U.S. First Army launched a major breakout in the St.-Lô area. About 3,000 Allied planes assisted the ground units as the weather cleared. Carpet bombing was employed for the first time. The aircraft dropped 5,000 tons of bombs, plus napalm. Many of the explosives fell on American troops by mistake, killing more than a hundred men of the 30th Division. Another victim was Lieutenant General Lesley J. McNair, chief of the Army Ground Forces, who was an observer.

■ U.S. Marine and Army units were four miles apart from linking up on Guam as the Japanese offered stubborn resistance.

■ Goebbels was named Reich minister for total war.

July 26 U.S. First Army forces crossed the Sèves and Ay rivers in their drive to St.-Lô.

■ Russian forces advanced to the Vistula River east of Radom. Narva in Estonia was captured by the Red Army.

■ Marines turned back a strong Japanese counterattack on Guam.

■ Roosevelt arrived in Honolulu to confer with his top Pacific commanders, MacArthur and Nimitz. Of immediate importance was whether the next major amphibious landing would be made in the Philippines or Formosa. Roosevelt opted for the MacArthur proposal, which was to reoccupy the Philippines (and to make good the general's promise that "I shall return.")

July 27 The U.S. First Army broke through German defenses south and west of St.-Lô.

■ Red Army troops rolled through what was once Poland, capturing Lwow (Lvov) and Stanislawow (Ivano-Frankovsk).

■ Hitler organized a new mobilization effort "to adapt in every respect the entire public life to the necessities of total warfare." Göring was named director of mobilization, Goebbels as his assistant, and Himmler as "dictator of the home front."

■ U.S. Marines cleared the northern part of Tinian and the airfield was undergoing repairs to make it operational at the earliest time.

July 28 U.S. forces made rapid progress in Normandy as German defenses began collapsing.

■ Brest-Litovsk, and Jaroslaw and Przemysl in Poland, fell to the Russians.

July 29 The first jet to be used in combat, the German Me-163 fighter, entered action.

■ German armored units suffered heavy losses while withdrawing from Roncey in Normandy.

■ Marines captured the Orote airstrip on Guam after overcoming fierce Japanese resistance.

July 30 The U.S. 4th Armored Division reached Avranches. Allied aircraft dropped 2,227 tons of bombs in advance of a new offensive by the British Second Army.

■ The Japanese commander at Myitkyina ordered his troops to withdraw and then commited hara-kiri.

■ Red Army troops crossed the Vistula River.

■ U.S. infantrymen of the 6th Division landed on the Vogelkop Peninsula on the northwest coast of New Guinea and the nearby islands of Amsterdam and Middleburg.

■ The Japanese held but five square miles at the southern tip of Tinian.

July 31 Russian troops reached positions within ten miles of Warsaw as street fighting developed inside the city. Marshal Konstantin Rokossovsky's First Byelorussian Front halted its drive toward Warsaw. The Russians feared a German counterattack from the south and decided not to extend their bridgeheads over the Vistula. By now, too, the Germans had rushed the SS *Viking* and the SS *Totenkopf* divisions, plus elements of the Hermann Göring and 19th Panzer divisions, to the Warsaw defense line. The Red Army reached the former capital of Lithuania, Kaunas. German Army Group North was almost cut off when Russian forces advanced toward the Gulf of Riga.

■ Allied forces advanced 50 miles along the Italian front during the month of July.

■ During the month, German V-2 rockets killed 2,441 British civilians; 7,107 were injured.

■ The British Second Army crossed the Soulevre River.

Aug. 1 East Prussia was isolated from the Baltic states by the Russians, who reached the Gulf of Riga 25 miles west of Riga. Kaunas fell.

■ The Russian Eighth Guards Army under General Vasili Chuikov crossed the Vistula at Magnuszew.

■ The Polish underground army in Warsaw, led by "General Bor" (the nom de guerre of General Tadeusz Komorovski) began full-scale military operations against the Germans, anticipating the imminent arrival of the Russians who were only a few miles outside the city.

■ U.S. forces entered Brittany from Normandy.

■ Tinian was declared secure. The Japanese lost about 5,000 men in the fight for the island. U.S. Marine and Navy losses were 389 killed.

■ An anti-Japanese Burmese government-in-exile was formed in India.

Aug. 2 The newly formed U.S. Third Army, under General George S. Patton, began advancing to complete Allied control of Brittany. Power-packed with armor, the force pushed through from the Avranches breach.

■ German human torpedoes led a series of concentrated attacks on Allied shipping in the English Channel.

■ Hitler ordered a counteroffensive in Brittany.

■ Turkey severed diplomatic and economic relations with Germany, but refused to declare war, as requested by the Allies.

■ Marshal Mannerheim succeeded Risto Ryti as president of Finland.

Aug. 3 Myitkyina in Burma was captured. Allied losses were heavy in fighting for the city, 972 Chinese and 272 Americans killed, 3,189 Chinese and 955 Americans wounded. Its occupation, however, permitted a route into China, from which offensive operations against Japanese positions throughout the western Pacific could be launched.

Aug. 4 The U.S. Third Army liberated Rennes but encountered strong opposition at St.-Malo, which was then bypassed. Montgomery ordered the British Second Army to attack Falaise and cut off the Germans to the west. Allied forces were 150 miles from Paris.

■ British forces reached the outskirts of Florence, advancing to the Arno River. The retreating Germans had destroyed all the bridges in the city except the celebrated 14th century Ponte Vecchio.

■ U.S. Army and Marine units hooked up on Guam, closing a gap which the Japanese might have exploited.

Aug. 5 The U.S. Third Army pushed a three-point attack, advancing toward Brest.

Aug. 6 German troops on the Brittany Peninsula were cut off by Patton's Third Army. Four German divisions were isolated. U.S. forces reached the German outer defense perimeter around Brest. Nantes was occupied.

■ The oil facilities around Drogobych (Drohobycz) were taken by the Russians.

■ Twenty-seven thousand Jews being held in camps east of the Vistula River were transported to Germany.

■ U.S. Fifteenth Air Force planes returned to Italy, completing shuttle bombing missions against targets in Rumania after refueling and rearming in Russia. Eighth Air Force B-17s at the same time bombed the German aircraft factory at Gdynia in Poland and proceeded to their Russian base.

Aug. 7 The Russian summer offensive stalled because of overextended supply lines. In three months the Red Army had advanced from the Dnieper to the Vistula, a distance of more than 400 miles. German counterattacks had pushed the Red Army back about 60 miles northeast of Warsaw. The Russian III Tank Corps had run out of fuel at Wolomin and was badly mauled.

■ German units in France counterattacked toward Avranches with massed armor. Their plan was to establish an anchor on the west for a new static defense line which would prevent a new round of mobile maneuvering by the Allies. They penetrated several miles and took Mortain before being halted with the help of Allied airpower.

Aug. 8 Canadian and British units advanced south from Caen toward Falaise. They were aided by 1,000 Allied aircraft which dropped 5,200 tons of bombs on German positions. The attack by the First Canadian Army threatened to cut off the German forces moving toward Avranches.

■ The British Eighth Army reached the Arno River at Florence and halted.

■ Eight German officers were hanged for their part in the Hitler bomb plot.

■ Hengyang city in China was occupied by the Japanese.

The Germans were forced out of France in Allied drives from across the English Channel (the Normandy landings) and from the Mediterranean.

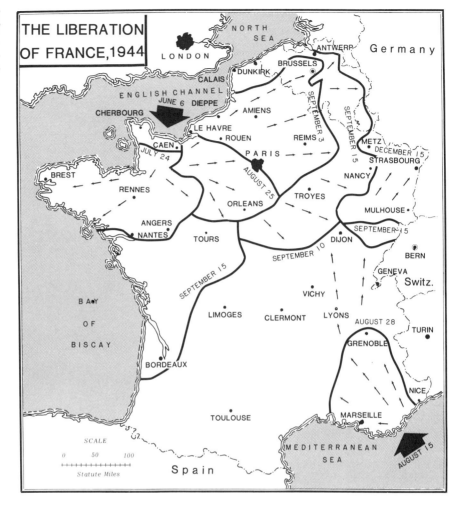

THE LIBERATION OF FRANCE, 1944

Aug. 9 Canadian First Army units were bogged down eight miles north of Falaise.

■ U.S. First Army forces wheeled to the northeast toward Argentan to join up with the Canadian troops in an attempt to close the Falaise gap. American XV Corps units reached Le Mans, 110 miles from Paris.

■ Eisenhower moved his headquarters from England to France.

■ As a result of the military setbacks suffered in eastern China by Nationalist forces, pro-Allied warlords informed the U.S. they would seek Chiang Kai-shek's resignation and prosecute the war vigorously.

■ An ordinance was issued by the Free French in Algiers declaring the Vichy government null and void.

Aug. 10 The U.S. VIII Corps continued hammering St.-Malo with limited success.

■ Japanese resistance ended on Guam, completing the U.S. conquest of the Marianas. In addition to gaining bases for the B-29s to bomb Japan, the Americans inflicted heavy losses on the Japanese in the Marianas campaign. The fight for Guam left at least 10,000 Japanese dead. U.S. casualties were about 5,000, including 1,400 killed in action.

Aug. 11 The Falaise gap was narrowed to 20 miles.

■ Pétain authorized Admiral Paul Auphan to

American B-29s pass Mount Fuji while on a bombing mission against Japanese targets.

British troops of the Eighth Army pass the famed Cathedral of Santa Maria del Fiore during the occupation of Florence.

represent Vichy in negotiations proposed to be held with Free French representatives on the future of France. De Gaulle refused any communication with Vichy.

Aug. 12 An oil pipeline from the Isle of Wight to Cherbourg went into operation, greatly facilitating fuel supply deliveries to Allied forces in France.

■ U.S. XV Corps troops occupied Alençon and proceeded to attack Argentan.

■ The German offensive toward Avranches was completely stymied by the U.S. First Army.

■ German units began withdrawing from Florence.

■ Churchill and Tito met in Italy.

Aug. 13 German troops started pulling out through the Falaise gap. The escape corridor was held open by fierce German resistance. U.S. and Canadian units began sweeping around the Falaise-Argentan outlet to close it.

■ An Allied airlift of arms and ammunition from Italy was started to aid the Warsaw underground army.

■ Indian troops crossed the Ponte Vecchio in Florence to help Italians clear the city of Germans.

Aug. 14 Red Army troops resumed their offensive toward Warsaw.

■ The Canadian II Corps began outflanking the Germans on the Caen-Falaise road, with its 2nd Division advancing to within four miles of Falaise. RAF planes dropped 3,723 tons of bombs on German positions.

■ U.S. 7th Armored Division and 5th Infantry Division units spearheaded an offensive toward Chartres.

Aug. 15 U.S. and French forces under Lieutenant General Alexander M. Patch landed in southern France in the Cannes-Toulon area. Heavy air and naval support facilitated the operation, which was designed to extend the Germans further. They were already trying to cope with

Free French and colonial troops march forward in the virtually unopposed landings in southern France.

numerically superior Allied forces in northern France, and removal of units from Italy bogged down German defense efforts there as well.

■ German defenders blocked the Russians attempting to break through the Carpathian mountain passes.

Aug. 16 Canadian forces virtually completed the encirclement of Falaise, but the German force was pulling out before the trap could be entirely closed. The British I Corps began pushing toward the Seine River.

Aug. 17 Falaise was captured. St.-Malo's defenders surrendered. Patton's tanks advanced to within 40 miles of Paris.

■ Field Marshal Model replaced Kluge as German commander, west. Kluge was suspected of being involved in the bomb plot to kill Hitler (of which he had practically no knowledge, but he had been involved with the Allies on armistice negotiations. Kluge killed himself while returning to Berlin on the 19th).

■ Red Army units reached the East Prussian border along the Sesupe River, bringing the ground war to prewar German soil for the first time. The Germans launched a counterattack in Lithuania to reopen lines to their Baltic forces.

■ Bulgaria announced it wished to stop fighting.

■ U.S. and French troops in southern France established a 50-mile-wide bridgehead.

■ All remaining Japanese forces were cleared from India.

Aug. 18 Plans were announced for the Allied occupation of Germany.

■ Allied forces began to seal the Falaise gap, leaving the Germans with only a small area northwest of Elbeuf to cross the lower Seine.

■ French resistance fighters seized control of Haute-Savoie. U.S. and Algerian troops began their drive toward Marseilles, having cleared the coast from Cannes to Toulon.

■ Polish and Italian forces began attacking the German Gothic Line on the Adriatic flank.

■ Roosevelt named Partick J. Hurley, a former secretary of war, as his special envoy to China. He was to effect an understanding between the Nationalists and Communists.

Aug. 19 A five-day cease-fire was declared in the Paris area to permit German evacuation of their forces from the French capital. One of the reasons for the German request was an uprising by French resistance fighters in Paris. American troops reached the Seine River.

■ Russian forces launched their major offensive to clear the Balkans.

■ Canadian and U.S. units completely closed the Falaise gap, trapping most of the German Seventh and parts of the Fifth Panzer armies. A total of 50,000 men were captured. At least 10,000 Germans were killed in the fighting to escape the trap. Reports vary on the number who escaped, ranging from 20,000 to 40,000.

■ Allied forces in southern France fanned out in all directions, meeting limited opposition.

■ Pétain and other officials of the Vichy government were forcibly moved to Belfort by the Germans.

Aug. 20 A bridgehead across the Seine was established by the U.S. 79th Division near Mantes-Gassicourt (Mantes-la-Jolie), trapping the German forces remaining in Normandy.

■ Free French forces reached the hills overlooking Toulon.

■ Red Army troops crossed the Danube into Rumania. It was a massive undertaking, involving 939,000 Red Army troops, 1,400 tanks, and 1,700 aircraft. At the same time the Rumanians turned on the Germans, seizing the bridges over the Danube and Prut rivers, effectively trapping 16 German divisions.

■ Allied planes began dropping limited supplies to the Polish Home Army in Warsaw.

■ U.S. forces secured the Biak area of New Guinea. In three months of fighting, 4,700 Japanese were killed, 220 captured. American casualties were 400 killed, 2,000 wounded.

Aug. 21 Canadian and Polish forces were left to reduce the Falaise gap while the main body of the Canadian II Corps pushed eastward toward Rouen.

■ French and U.S. forces occupied Aix-en-Provence which was abandoned by the Germans.

■ Field Marshal Model, commander in chief, west, informed Berlin the German Seventh Army was no longer an effective fighting force. The Seventh, as well as the Fifth Panzer and Fifteenth armies, had adhered to Hitler's orders to stand and fight. Instead of withdrawing and regrouping, the Germans suffered enormous losses while obeying Hitler and exposed the entire western front.

■ German troops advanced to within 35 miles of Riga in their Baltic counteroffensive.

■ The Dumbarton Oaks International Peace and Security Conference opened in Washington, D.C.

Aug. 22 The U.S. 5th Division advanced toward Fontainebleau. Orders were issued for the attack to take Paris.

■ French, American, and Algerian forces began their final assault on Marseilles.

■ Polish forces cleared all Germans south of the Metauro River in Italy.

■ Iasi (Jassy) fell as the Russians resumed their Rumanian offensive.

Aug. 23 Rumania's King Michael accepted Soviet surrender terms and ordered all forces to stop fighting. He had Antonescu arrested.

■ French resistance forces began taking over the administration of Paris with the cease-fire period completed. U.S. and French troops were blocked in their advance toward Paris in the Versailles area. The U.S. 5th Division took Fontainebleau.

■ Deauville on the Channel coast was taken by the Allies, led by Belgian troops.

Aug. 24 Rumanian troops battled German forces who attempted to seize control of Bucharest.

■ U.S. XX Corps units crossed the Seine at Melun and Montereau.

■ Bordeaux and Cannes were occupied. Allied troops pushed on to Antibes. U.S. forces had advanced 140 miles inland from the Mediterranean.

■ New mobilization measures were issued by Goebbels to put Germany on a "total war" footing. Laborers were ordered to go on a 60-hour workweek. All holidays were abolished. All schools and theaters were closed. Within the military, headquarters staffs were purged of what Hitler termed "rear area swine," who were assigned to combat units.

Aug. 25 Paris was liberated as tanks of the French 2nd Armored Division began rolling into the French capital from the southwest at 7 A.M. U.S. forces marched in from the south shortly afterwards. The German commander in Paris, General Choltitz, surrendered to French Brigadier General Jaques Philippe Leclerc at 3:15 P.M. Jubilant Parisians paused long enough to join in the house-to-house clearing of sizable German pockets remaining. Since D-Day the Germans had suffered 200,000 dead and wounded in the fighting for France. Another 200,000 had been captured.

■ American forces began an all-out effort to take Brest.

■ British Eighth Army forces launched their all-out offensive against the Gothic Line in Italy.

■ The Aitape operation in New Guinea was completed, with 8,821 Japanese killed and 98 captured. Allied losses were 440 killed.

■ Rumania declared war on Germany.

Aug. 26 Bulgaria proclaimed its neutrality and announced it was ordering an end to all fighting and would disarm German troops in the country.

Sniper fire scattered Parisians who had gathered at the Place de la Concorde to celebrate the liberation of Paris.

■ Allied forces began streaming across the Seine south of Rouen and pressed eastward.
■ An attempt was made on de Gaulle's life in Paris.

General de Gaulle led services at the Notre Dame Cathedral in Paris after liberation. Collaborationists and German soldiers in civilian clothes began firing from the balcony, wounding many participants.

■ Soviet forces reached the Danube near Galati in Rumania, opening up a clear path through the Balkans.
■ Hitler ordered the withdrawal of all German troops from Greece.
■ British, Canadian, and Polish troops established bridgeheads across the Metauro River in Italy.
Aug. 27 Allied forces in France were beginning to experience extreme supply shortages, although few units were actually stalled.
■ Galati, Rumania's third largest city and main port on the Danube, was occupied by the Russians.
Aug. 28 Russian troops entered Transylvania through the Oituz Pass in the Carpathians.
■ U.S. Third Army units crossed the Marne and took Château-Thierry.
■ Marseilles was occupied by French and American troops as the last German forces surrendered. All resistance ended in Toulon. Most of the German Nineteenth Army escaped a trap which was to be sprung at Montélimar by fleeing northwards. The route up the Rhône valley was now open.
Aug. 29 Russian troops occupied Constanta on the Rumanian Black Sea coast and then pushed

French women collaborators, shorn of hair and partially stripped, are led through Paris in disgrace.

south into Bulgaria, ignoring Sofia's self-proclaimed neutrality.

■ An armed uprising against the Germans began in Slovakia.

■ Soissons fell to U.S. forces.

■ Eleven Japanese divisions began a drive from Hengyang toward the U.S. air bases at Kweilin and Liuchow in China.

Aug. 30 Ploesti and its oil facilities fell to the Russians.

■ Bucharest was occupied by the Third Ukrainian Army.

■ German troops were withdrawn from Bulgaria.

■ The U.S. 5th Armored Division began a drive toward Compiègne. Canadian and British forces under Lieutenant General Miles Dempsey were in control of the Seine west of Paris and began moving north toward Gournay.

Aug. 31 British Second Army troops reached Amiens and began crossing the Somme. U.S. forces reached the Maginot Line and took Reims.

■ The U.S. VI Corps raced up the Rhône valley toward Lyon.

■ Since D-Day, German losses were staggering. In a three-month period total losses on the eastern and western fronts were 1,200,000 dead, wounded, and missing. Fifty divisions were destroyed in the east, 28 in the west. In addition, 230,000 German troops were surrounded in pockets in France. Together with the defection of two Rumanian armies and the Bulgarians to the Russians, the German High Command faced its bleakest outlook of the war. Berlin was further vexed by the presence of 555 Soviet divisions advancing from the east.

■ British civilian air raid casualties for the month were 1,103 killed and 2,921 wounded.

Sept. 1 British Eighth Army troops broke through the German Gothic defense line in Italy. U.S. Fifth Army forces crossed the Arno River.

■ Nice fell to General de Tassigny's First French Army.

This former rifle range in the French ministry of aviation building in Paris was used by the Germans to execute French Resistance fighters.

■ Dieppe was liberated by the 2nd British Division.

Sept. 2 Finland accepted Russia's armistice terms.

■ Red Army troops reached the Bulgarian border.

■ German units were evacuated from the Aegean Islands.

■ U.S. First Army units crossed into Belgium.

■ Lyon was liberated by Free French forces.

■ Eisenhower ordered a halt to the drives of the U.S. First and Third armies because of a lack of fuel. They were to remain in place until gasoline supplies could be replenished. Each army needed about 400,000 gallons a day. The Third was down to 25,000. The U.S. 3rd Cavalry Group was one of the few units still attacking, but with captured gasoline. Germany used this pause to build up its defenses along the Siegfried line.

Sept. 3 Brussels was liberated by the British 21st Army Group.

■ U.S. naval units attacked Japanese positions on Wake Island.

Sept. 4 Finland ordered its forces to cease firing, bringing the Russian-Finnish war to an end.

■ Rundstedt was reinstated as German commander in chief, west.

■ British forces entered Antwerp. U.S. units in the south were 40 miles beyond Lyon.

Sept. 5 The American 9th and 3rd Armored divisions crossed the Meuse, near Sedan and Dinant. Stiff German resistance halted the U.S. XII Corps at the Moselle (Mosel) River.

■ Ghent was liberated by the British 7th Armored Division.

■ On this the ninetieth day since the Normandy landings, the Allies had 2,086,000 men ashore in France. They had been supplied with 3,446,000 tons of goods.

■ Russia declared war on Bulgaria, which surrendered in 20 hours.

■ Moscow broadcasts called on Poles in Warsaw to stage an uprising: "Fight the Germans. No doubt Warsaw already hears the guns of the battle which is soon to bring her liberation . . . , join battle with the Germans, this time for the decisive action."

■ Under heavy U.S. pressure, Argentina announced all war criminals would be denied asylum.

Sept. 6 Russian troops crossed the Yugoslav border from Rumania at Turnu-Severin near the Iron Gate (gorge) on the Danube.

■ The U.S. 7th Armored Division began a drive to cross the Moselle River.

■ Britain ended the blackout, permitting indoor lighting without curtains, shades, or drapes. Training for the Home Guard was suspended.

■ Sixteen U.S. carriers launched air strikes against Yap, Ulithi, and the Palau islands, the first phase of a three-day operation against Japanese positions in the western Carolines.

■ Chinese forces from Burma and western Yunnan in China linked up at the Kaolingkung Pass, the first opening of a land route between the two countries since 1942.

A Chinese soldier uses a flame thrower in attacking Japanese positions in the city of Tengchung, replaced in Sept.

Sept. 7 The British Guards Armored Division reached the Albert Canal in Belgium but found all bridges destroyed.

■ U.S. troops crossed the Moselle River north of Metz. Besançon was taken by the 3rd Division.

■ Dieppe was opened to Allied shipping.

■ The first elements of the French provisional government arrived in Paris to begin administrating the country.

■ Hungary and Rumania began fighting each other for control of Transylvania.

■ Bulgaria declared war on Germany as Russian troops of the Third Ukrainian Front began marching into Bulgaria across the Danube. The Bulgars offered no resistance.

■ Allied forces began mopping up Japanese remnants around Sung Shan on the Salween front. The Chinese cleared this area to open the Burma Road, suffering 7,675 killed. Most of the 2,000-man Japanese force was eliminated.

Sept. 8 The first V-2 rocket bombs landed in England, in west London.

The Germans began directing V-2 rockets against Allied targets in Sept. 1944.

■ German troops moved to put down the Slovak uprising.

■ Liège fell to the U.S. First Army.

■ The 2nd Canadian Division began attacking Dunkirk. An all-out assault was launched on Brest by the U.S. 2nd, 8th, and 29th divisions. The German 106th Panzer Brigade was decimated in a futile counterattack between Landres and Mairy, northwest of Metz, losing 30 tanks and 60 halftracks.

■ Two Japanese divisions and a brigade from Canton joined in the drive on Kweilin and Liuchow.

Sept. 9 U.S. cavalrymen entered the Netherlands near Maastricht.

■ Russia ended hostilities in Bulgaria. A pro-Communist government was established in Sofia.

Sept. 10 Le Havre was assaulted by the 49th and 51st British divisions after 5,000 tons of bombs were dropped on German positions by Allied aircraft. The French II Corps reached Dijon and linked up with Allied forces which had been landed at Normandy.

■ Warsaw's mayor appealed for immediate Allied aid. Stalin approved the use of Russian airfields for British and U.S. planes to drop supplies to the Polish forces in Warsaw. Red Army units also resumed their offensive in the Warsaw sector, attacking the suburb of Praga.

■ The British Eighth and the U.S. Fifth armies began attacks to break through the rugged Apennine Mountains into the Po valley. The long battle, made difficult by bad weather, was one of the most difficult of the Italian campaign.

■ Russia and Finland signed an armistice agreement, ending their three-year war.

Sept. 11 Advance units of the U.S. First Army crossed into Germany near Stalzenburg. The 85th Reconnaissance Squadron of the 5th Armored Division made its way across the frontier at 6:05 P.M. and met no opposition.

SUBMARINE SINKINGS OF POW TRANSPORT SHIPS

One of the great tragedies of the war took place on Sept. 11, 1944, when three American submarines sank two Japanese transports carrying 2,218 British, Australian, and U.S. prisoners of war (all of whom had survived the infamous building of the bridge over the River Kwai) from Singapore to Formosa. A total of 1,274 of the Allies lost their lives when the subs torpedoed the *Rakuyo Maru* and the *Kachidoki Maru.* Both Japanese vessels went down almost immediately. Other Japanese ships rescued 792 of the men (of whom 606 survived the war after being reimprisoned). U.S. submarines picked up 159, but seven died shortly thereafter.

SOURCE: CINCPAC Summary of Operations in the Pacific War Areas, Sept. 1944; Joan and Clay Blair, *Return from the River Kwai.*

■ U.S. First Army forces liberated the capital city of Luxembourg.

Sept. 12–16 The second Québec conference (OCTAGON) was held to concentrate on Pacific strategy now that Germany's defeat seemed near. U.S. and British planners agreed on the invasion of Japan, to be launched in October 1945 with troops landing on Kyushu. It was also decided to recapture Burma as soon as possible.

Churchill and Roosevelt in Québec for the OCTA-GON conference plan for the final phases of the war.

Sept. 12 British Second Army forces crossed into the Netherlands.

■ U.S. First Army troops advanced five miles into Germany near Trier. Units of the 3rd Division pushed to within 1,000 yards of the Siegfried line. Bridgeheads across the Moselle were established by the U.S. XII Corps north and south of Nancy.

■ Le Havre was occupied as the German garrison of 12,000 surrendered.

■ A German force of 20,000 men under Major General Erich Elster formally surrendered to the U.S. 83rd Infantry Division at the Beaugency bridge on the Loire. Elster originally suggested a face-saving mock battle which the Americans would "win." The U.S. commander—Robert C. Macon—turned him down, and the Germans laid down their arms without incident.

■ British bombers dropped 400,000 incendiary bombs on Frankfurt am Main.

■ Red Army forces broke through the Negotin gap in Yugoslavia, opening the way to the Dalmatian coast.

■ Britain, the U.S., and Russia signed an armistice agreement with Rumania. Rumania agreed to join in the war against Germany and Hungary. Russia promised to return Transylvania to Rumania.

Sept. 13 Eisenhower ordered the capture of the Ruhr basin and a deep-water port, either Antwerp or Rotterdam, to facilitate the flow of supplies.

■ Canadian 4th Armored Division elements crossed the Leopold Canal near Bruges.

■ The besieged German garrison at Brest refused to surrender.

■ Shuttle bombing by U.S. planes involving Russian bases ended because Red Army advances placed the bases too far from the front.

■ Soviet aircraft began limited airdrops to Polish resistance forces in Warsaw, regarded by the Poles as too little, too late.

Sept. 13–14 A hurricane off the American east coast was responsible for the sinking of a U.S. destroyer, *Warrington,* and two Coast Guard cutters, *Cudloe* and *Jackson.*

Sept. 14 Russian troops reached the Warsaw suburb of Praga. The Eighth Soviet Guards Army had a firm foothold on the Vistula bridgehead. Other Russian units in the south advanced to the Czech frontier.

An English mother and her two children survey their destroyed home in the Kew area of London.

U.S. Marines of the 1st Division inch forward after landing on Peleliu Island, Sept. 1944.

■ Germany was pounded by 5,000 Allied aircraft in raids on targets from the Siegfried line to Berlin.

■ The newly appointed commander of German forces in the west, *Generalfeldmarschall* Gerd von Rundstedt, told Hitler "the Battle for the West Wall" had begun. The West Wall (or Siegfried Line) had been largely dismantled since 1940, but it still represented a formidable barrier between the Allies and the Rhine River.

■ Japanese units ended their counteroffensive on the Salween front.

Sept. 15 U.S. Marines began landing on Peleliu Island of the Palau group, about 450 miles east of Mindanao in the Philippines. For three days before the assault, U.S. ships had pounded the island with 6,000 tons of explosives. The 1st Marine Division established a shallow beachhead but approached the airstrip in the first day of intense fighting. (Peleliu turned into a bitter month-long battle, one of the roughest of the Pacific war. Progress was measured in yards. The Japanese hid in caves and fought suicidally. Pillboxes covered all positions.)

■ U.S. forces began assaulting the Siegfried line in Germany. Nancy fell.

■ The Channel coast was basically cleared as far north as Zeebrugge in Belgium.

U.S. landing craft blast the assault beach on one of the Palau Islands before landing Marines.

■ RAF aircraft dropped 12,000-pound bombs on the *Tirpitz*.

■ The Polish First Army—operating under the Russians—began assaulting Germans along the Vistula at Czerniakow. (The Poles were unsuccessful and lost 2,000 men in the next four days.)

■ U.S. 31st Division troops landed on Morotai Island in the Moluccas group.

■ Brazilian troops went into the line in Italy, deploying along the Serchio River valley. (A full division eventually went into combat, the first Brazilians ever to fight in Europe.)

Sept. 16 Sofia, Bulgaria's capital, was occupied by Russian troops. Red Army units opened an offensive toward the Baltic with Tallinn and Riga as immediate objectives.

■ A general anti-German strike was launched in Denmark.

■ Hitler outlined a plan for a massive counteroffensive in the Ardennes Forest to his generals. He told Keitel, Jodl, and Guderian: "I have just made a momentous decision. I shall go over to the counterattack, that is to say, here (pointing to a map)—out of the Ardennes, with the objective Antwerp." At the time, Germany had 55 divisions on the Western Front, facing 96 Allied divisions in place and another dozen in Britain.

■ A German force of 20,000 men from the Biscay Bay area surrendered to the U.S. 83rd Division southwest of Orléans.

■ U.S. First Army units reached points three miles inside Germany near Aachen.

Sept. 17 Twenty thousand Allied airborne forces landed behind German lines between Eindhoven and Arnhem in the Netherlands. Their task was to take three bridges over the Maas (Meuse), Waal, and Lower Rhine respectively. Ground forces, meanwhile, drove northward from the Meuse-Escaut (Scheldt) Canal. The purpose of Operation MARKET GARDEN was to outflank the Siegfried line and drive to the Ruhr basin.

■ Canadian troops of the 3rd Division launched the decisive attack on Boulogne, defended by about 10,000 Germans.

■ Russian forces entered Estonia.

■ Allied Commandos and Tito Partisans occupied the Dalmatian Islands off the Yugoslav coast.

■ Kweilin in China was abandoned as a base for the U.S. Fourteenth Air Force.

Sept. 18 German units counterattacked around Arnhem. Allied reinforcements were late in arriving. The Fifth Panzer Army counterattacked to eliminate the U.S. bridgeheads over the Moselle but were rebuffed with the loss of 50 tanks.

■ All organized German resistance ended in Brest.

■ British aircraft attacked Bremerhaven with 420,000 incendiaries.

■ U.S. planes flew massive amounts of supplies to Warsaw's underground army but Stalin refused further missions of this kind. The Soviet air force also stopped airlifts to the Polish garrison in Warsaw (but they were resumed three days later).

Sept. 18–21 As the German army was abandon-

Yugoslav Partisans pose with villagers near the Dalmatian coast. Holding a rifle and kneeling in right foreground is an Italian soldier who joined the Partisans.

Heavy flak bursts were encountered by American B-17s bombing Ludwigshafen, Germany.

ing Tallinn, Estonian civilians rose up and proclaimed an independent government. The Estonians, under Otto Tief, battled the retreating Germans until the 21st when Russian armor swept into the city.

Sept. 19 Russia and Finland signed an armistice agreement, restoring the 1940 border although Petsamo and the Porkkala headland came under Russian control in exchange for Finnish rights to Hangö.

■ Allied troops were trapped at Arnhem as all breakthrough attempts and reinforcement efforts failed, mostly because of bad weather and strong German resistance.

■ One hundred German bombers attacked Eindhoven, the only time long-range Luftwaffe aircraft were used in the fight for western Europe.

■ Brittany was cleared as the U.S. VIII Corps occupied the Crozon peninsula.

Sept. 20 The British 1st Airborne Division suffered heavy casualties at Arnhem. Three hundred of its wounded were surrendered to the Germans. Allied forces faced a critical situation even though small advances were made at Nijmegen.

■ U.S. Marines took heavy losses on Peleliu. It

became apparent the island could not be taken easily.

■ Angaur Island in the Palaus was secured by U.S. forces.

Sept. 21 A Polish paratrooper force of 750 men was landed at Arnhem. The British Guards Armored Division was stopped three miles outside of Nijmegen in its effort to reach Arnhem.

■ In Italy British Eighth Army units captured Rimini on the Adriatic coast.

■ The general strike in Denmark was crushed by the Germans.

■ Aircraft from 12 U.S. carriers began a two-day attack on Luzon, sinking several Japanese ships.

Sept. 22 Boulogne's besieged German garrison surrendered after a long and costly defense.

■ Eisenhower ordered Patton's Third Army to halt its offensive from the Moselle because of the growing supply shortage.

■ Marine planes began operating from Peleliu.

■ A U.S. regimental combat team landed unopposed on Ulithi Atoll in the western Carolines, giving the Allies a valuable base for Pacific operations. The Japanese had abandoned Ulithi a month earlier.

Sept. 23 The U.S. 34th Division passed through the Gothic Line in Italy.

■ Russian units reached the Gulf of Riga at Parnu. To the south, Red Army forces crossed the prewar Hungarian border.

■ RAF bombers breached the Dortmund-Ems canal in a night precision raid. Twelve-thousand-pound Tall Boy bombs were used on the raid. Of the 141 aircraft involved, 14 were lost.

■ A unit of the U.S. Army's 81st Division arrived on Peleliu to aid the Marines.

Sept. 24 Japanese forces counterattacked on Peleliu, but U.S. positions were held.

■ Red Army forces penetrated 20 miles into Czechoslovakia from Poland. Soviet naval units began occupying Estonian ports on the Baltic.

■ San Marino declared war on Germany.

Sept. 25 Canadian units launched an assault on isolated Calais.

■ Survivors at Arnhem started to be evacuated.

■ British Eighth Army units crossed the Uso River in force.

■ The *Volkssturm* (People's Militia) was formed in Germany. Men up to 65 were pressed into the last-ditch defense force.

Yugoslav Partisans capture a schooner used by the Germans to supply their forces on the Dalmatian coast.

Sept. 26 Allied withdrawals continued from Arnhem, with the operation a costly failure.

■ Estonia was completely occupied by the Russians.

Sept. 27 German planes tried but failed to destroy the Nijmegen bridges.

■ Sweden closed its port to all foreigners.

Sept. 28 Canadian 3rd Division troops fought their way into Calais.

■ German troops launched a strong counterattack at Arnhem to retake the Nijmegen bridge.

Sept. 29 A truce was called at Calais to evacuate civilians.

■ The Russians flew their last missions to drop supplies for the Poles in Warsaw. In ten nights of airlift operations, the Red Air Force had flown 2,500 sorties in support of the Warsaw garrison and delivered 50 tons of munitions and food.

■ The U.S. submarine *Narwhal* rescued 81 Allied prisoners of war who had survived the sinking of the Japanese freighter *Shinyo Maru*. Hundreds of the prisoners were being transported from Mindanao when the ship was torpedoed by another American submarine. The survivors found their way to Sindangan Bay in Mindanao, where Filipino guerrillas radioed for aid, bringing in *Narwhal*.

Sept. 30 More Russian forces crossed the Danube into Yugoslavia from Rumania and raced for Belgrade.

■ British civilian air raid casualties for the month were 190 killed and 360 wounded.

Oct. 1 The U.S. First Army plan to attack the Siegfried Line on this date was frustrated by bad weather. For the rest of the month the Americans were confined to reducing the perimeter around Aachen. The Calais garrison of 5,000 Germans surrendered to the Canadians.

■ Brazilian troops went on the offensive in Italy, aiming toward Bologna.

■ Finnish army units attacked German forces in Finland.

■ Hungarian officials secretly arrived in Moscow to conclude an armistice agreement.

Oct. 2 The Warsaw uprising was crushed by the Germans. An estimated quarter-million Poles

Underground factories were used by the Germans to keep war production going even under incessant Allied air attacks. This machine shop was located two miles underground in occupied France.

were killed in two months of fierce fighting. Poles insisted the Russians purposely delayed their advance into Warsaw so the Germans could annihilate the anti-Communist Polish Home Army, which they did. The pro-Moscow Lublin government denounced the "futile uprising which cost thousands of lives."

■ German troops began withdrawing from Athens.

■ The U.S. Army's 30th Division attacked the Siegfried line between Aachen and Geilenkirchen. It made its way to Übach-Palenberg.

■ Russian troops launched an offensive to clear German troops from northern Finland. Finnish forces attacked the Germans at Kemi, near the Swedish border.

Oct. 3 U.S. 2nd Armored Division forces crossed the shallow Würm River at Marienberg and established a bridgehead beyond the Siegfried Line.

■ German forces seized control of communications facilities in Hungary after learning of secret peace talks in Moscow.

Oct. 4 British troops began landing in Greece.

■ Russian units advanced to within 10 miles of Belgrade.

Oct. 5 British forces landed in Albania and the Greek islands.

Oct. 6 Russian forces crossed into Czechoslovakia over the Tisza River from Hungary.

■ Canadian troops in Belgium established a bridgehead over the Leopold Canal north of Maldegem.

Oct. 8 U.S. forces broke out of the Hürtgen Forest and advanced toward Schmidt.

Oct. 9–18 The Moscow conference of the three powers, with Churchill, Stalin, and Ambassador Harriman (representing Roosevelt) was convened to consider Poland and the Balkans. No progress was made on the composition of a Polish government, but ratios of "interests" were established, with Britain to have 100 percent in Greece, the Russians and Britain 50 percent each in Yugoslavia, and the Russians with 75 or 80 percent in Bulgaria, Rumania, and Hungary.

Oct. 9 The U.S. XX Corps broke off its attacks against Fort Driant near Metz, which had been a seemingly impenetrable obstacle.

■ Allied ships began hauling supplies through Le Havre.

■ Marcus Island in the Pacific was bombarded by U.S. cruisers and destroyers.

■ The Dumbarton Oaks conference ended and plans were concluded for collective security measures to be organized by the United Nations.

Oct. 10 Russian troops reached the Baltic Sea near Memel, Lithuania, cutting off the Germans in Latvia. Advance elements in Hungary were within 45 miles of Budapest.

■ Corinth in Greece was taken by British and Greek forces.

■ German troops at Aachen were given 24 hours to surrender.

■ Okinawa and other islands in the Ryukyus were attacked by U.S. naval aircraft from 17 carriers, with Japan's air capability reduced still further.

Oct. 12 British paratroopers and engineers landed near Athens.

■ Aachen came under air and artillery attack.

Free French Air Force Spitfires began using the field at Luxeuil-les-Bains, France, after it was retaken by Allied ground forces.

■ Soviet troops cut the Belgrade-Budapest rail line at Subotica in Yugoslavia.

■ V-weapons were launched against Antwerp. The Germans had promised to demolish Antwerp with waves of bombers if the port were opened to the Allies (which it was at the end of November) but the V-weapons began falling without warning. (Both V-1s and V-2s were used, a total of 1,214 until the terror bombing ended in March. About 3,000 died, mostly civilians, and as many as 15,000 people were wounded as a result of the V-weapons.)

Oct. 13 American forces occupied Aachen.

■ British advance units entered Athens.

■ Riga, the Latvian capital on the Baltic, was captured by Soviet troops, trapping a large German force in western Latvia.

Oct. 14 For his suspected association in the anti-Hitler plot, Field Marshal Rommel was given the choice of suicide or the ignominy of a military trial and certain execution. He swallowed a poison capsule, thoughtfully provided by Hitler's representatives. Although he was once Hitler's "favorite general," Rommel was genuinely respected among the Allies as a brilliant tactician and strategist. Berlin claimed he died of wounds suffered in combat.

■ Athens was cleared of all German troops. British troops were landed on Corfu.

■ Belgrade was surrounded by the Russians.

■ Russian troops crossed into Norway in its northernmost province of Finnmark.

■ Duisburg was raided by the RAF and hit with 10,000 tons of bombs.

■ U.S. Navy aircraft completed a three-day sweep of Formosa, destroying 280 Japanese planes.

■ Peleliu was declared secure, although scattered resistance continued through the end of November. An estimated 10,700 Japanese were killed in the month-long fighting. U.S. Marine losses were 1,124 killed and 117 missing.

Oct. 15 Petsamo in Finland was cleared of all Germans.

■ Hungary publicly announced it was seeking an armistice. Admiral Horthy broadcast a request for terms from the Allies. Three hours after the broadcast Horthy was ousted by the Germans who installed a Hungarian Nazi, Ferenc Szalasi, as regent.

■ A Chinese offensive was launched from northern Burma to open the supply route to China.

Oct. 16 Horthy and all top officials of the Hungarian government were arrested by the Germans and removed to Germany. Hitler determined that Hungary would be held at all costs because of its oil, manganese, and bauxite.

■ An all-out attack on East Prussia was begun by the Third White Russian Front.

■ U.S. Fifth Army forces launched the decisive drive toward Bologna.

■ Nimitz announced that in the past week U.S. naval forces in the Pacific had destroyed 73 Japanese ships and 670 planes.

Oct. 17 U.S. Rangers began landing on the islands off Leyte Gulf in the Philippines.

Oct. 18 Tokyo issued orders for Operation SHO ("VICTORY"), a series of "decisive battles" to be

British artillery fires on German positions at San Benedetto, Italy.

Japanese artist Susuki Makoto's painting of Tokyo civilians being directed to air raid shelters as the U.S. bomber offensive intensified.

initiated by the Japanese to end the threat to the home islands.

■ General Stilwell was relieved of his command in China, having reached a point of poisoned relations with Chiang Kai-shek.

■ All German males between 16 and 60 were registered for the *Volkssturm*.

■ Russian troops swept into Czechoslovakia through the Carpathian passes from Poland.

■ The Greek government returned to Athens.

■ Franco wrote a letter to Churchill proposing a Spanish-British alliance to combat what he called "the insidious power of Bolshevism." Churchill dismissed the notion immediately.

Oct. 19 Hitler ordered Warsaw destroyed.

■ Spain closed its frontier with France.

■ Belgrade was evacuated by the Germans.

■ British forces captured the abandoned Japanese supply base of Mohnyin in Burma.

Oct. 20 After two-and-a-half years U.S. troops returned to the Philippines. The Sixth Army under Lieutenant General Walter Krueger was put ashore near Tacloban and Dulag on the east coast of Leyte. There was light opposition and the the two beachheads were expanded and separated by only a ten-mile gap. By nightfall, 132,400 men and 200,000 tons of equipment and supplies were ashore. Four hours after the first landing, General MacArthur waded ashore and broadcast his famous "I have returned" address to the Filipinos. (MacArthur was to be filmed three more times wading ashore at other beaches

during the next few days, leading to the persistent stories of eyewitnesses who stated correctly but misleadingly that they saw the general landing a long time after the initial landing.)

■ Belgrade and Dubrovnik were liberated by Russian troops and Tito's Yugoslav army.

Oct. 21 Aachen was surrendered by the Germans after bitter fighting. The defense of the city seriously damaged Germany's ability to contest the Allies, having drained Berlin's reserve strength to perilous levels.

A shaken Hitler surveys a bombed-out German village.

■ Russian forces reached the Danube south of Budapest.

■ Japanese units counterattacked on Leyte after choosing to make a strong defense rather than fight a delaying action.

Oct. 22 Russian troops reached positions all along the Norwegian border. The Red Army drive in East Prussia was halted, and the front there was to remain static until Janaury. Other forces reached the Danube at Baja in Hungary.

■ Yugoslav Partisans entered Belgrade.

■ U.S. troops made minor gains on Leyte, encountering strong Japanese resistance and difficult terrain.

Oct. 23–26 In the greatest battle in the history of naval warfare American naval ships and planes inflicted staggering losses on the Japanese in the Battle of Leyte Gulf. The Imperial Navy lost 34 ships, inluding 3 battleships (*Musashi*, *Fuso*, and *Yamashiro*), 4 carriers (*Zuikaku*, *Chiyoda*, *Zuiho*, and *Chitose*), 10 cruisers (*Atago*, *Mayo*, *Chokai*, *Suzuya*, *Chikuma*, *Mogami*, *Tama*, *Kimu*, *Abukuma*, and *Noshiro*), 13 destroyers, and 5 submarines. U.S. losses were the light carrier *Princeton*, 2 escort carriers, 2 destroyers, and a destroyer escort. Leyte Gulf marked the deepest decline of the Japanese navy as an effective fighting force. Loss of the super battleship *Musashi* was a particularly difficult loss for the Japanese. The supposedly indestructible dreadnought took 20 torpedoes and 17 bomb hits, and then rolled over taking nearly half of the 2,200-man crew with her.

Oct. 23 MacArthur restored the Philippines civil

(TOP, LEFT) *The U.S. escort carrier* St. Lo *explodes after a hit by a Japanese kamikaze in the Battle of Leyte Gulf.*

(TOP, RIGHT) *Crewmen aboard Japanese carrier* Zuikaku *salute as ship sinks during the Battle of Cape Engano.*

(RIGHT) *The ward room of the U.S. escort carrier* Suwannee *is converted into an emergency sick bay after the ship was attacked by the Japanese off Leyte Gulf in the Philippines.*

Filipino guerrillas and U.S. troops rest on Leyte between operations. The Filipinos are carrying captured Japanese rifles.

■ What remained of the Japanese fleet was split between the Inland Sea of Japan and the waters near Singapore.

Oct. 27 Kamikaze attacks were launched on ships of U.S. Task Force 38 off the Philippines.

■ German forces launched a counterattack in the Netherlands but their penetration was contained by the U.S. 7th Armored Division.

■ A new offensive was launched by the Russians in Latvia.

■ The stalled Japanese offensive in east China was resumed, again aimed at the U.S. air bases at Kweilin and Liuchow.

Oct. 28 Russia and Bulgaria signed a formal armistice agreement in Moscow. The Bulgarian military was placed under Soviet control.

■ German troops began evacuating Albania.

■ Russian forces advanced to within 40 miles of Budapest.

■ The first Japanese Kamikaze hit was scored when a suicide plane damaged the U.S. cruiser *Denver* off Leyte.

■ Eisenhower issued orders for Allied troops to cross the Rhine and drive into the German heartland.

■ Stilwell was replaced by Major General Albert C. Wedemeyer in the China theater.

government under President Sergio Osmeña at ceremonies at Tacloban, the temporary capital. U.S. forces pressed forward in several-pronged attacks to consolidate their gains on Leyte.

Oct. 24 U.S. cavalrymen secured San Juanico Strait on Leyte.

Oct. 25 Britain, Russia, and the U.S. reestablished formal relations with Italy.

■ Russian forces crossed into Norway from Finland along a broad front.

Oct. 26 Heavy rains and flooding restricted movement in the Italian fighting.

U.S. Rangers patrol through a village on Dinagat Island in the Philippines.

A daily report on prisoners held at the Natzviller concentration camp, dividing the inmates by age and by the following categories: Aryans, professors, homosexuals, soldiers, priests, Spaniards, foreign civil workers, Jews, socialists, criminals, anarchists, Gypsies, and prisoners of war.

Oct. 29 The *Tirpitz* was attacked by RAF Lancasters using 12,000-pound bombs.

■ The Chinese Expeditionary Force in Burma began a drive toward Lung-ling.

Oct. 30 The last gassings took place at Auschwitz.

■ German thrusts in the Peel Marshes of Holland were turned back.

Oct. 31 Eighteen Mosquitos with British, Canadian, Australian, and New Zealand crews destroyed the Gestapo headquarters at Aarhus, Denmark, with precision bombing. There were two hospitals less than 100 yards away, but the 48 500-pound bombs dropped resulted in nothing but superficial damage to them.

■ Russian troops in Hungary crossed the Tisza River and broadened the advance toward Budapest.

■ British civilian air raid casualties for the month were 172 killed and 416 wounded.

Nov. 1 Germany moved to complete its withdrawal from Greece with only rear-guard units left to cover the retreat from Salonika and Florina.

Unterteilung in Altersstufen

der im Konzentrationslager *etzweiler

einsitzenden Häftlinge nach dem Stande vom 31. Oktober 194 4

männliche Häftlinge

Häftlingsart	insgesamt	—20	20—30	30—40	40—50	50—60	60—70	70—80	über 80
Schutzhäftlinge arisch	11867	1587	4878	3472	1765	146	19	-	-
Bibelforscher	5	-	1	-	3	1	-	-	
Homosexuelle	13	-	1	6	4	2	-	-	-
aus der Wehrmacht	18	-	14	4	-	-	-		
Geistliche	7	-	-	3	3	1	-		
Rotspanier	6	-	1	3	2	-	-	-	
Ausl. Zivilarbeiter	1988	444	953	437	152	1	1	-	-
Juden	3720	508	1258	1334	565	49	6	-	-
Asoziale	211	39	68	52	41	8	3	-	
Berufsverbrecher	342	7	127	103	93	17	5		
Sich.-Verw.	28	2	9	14	3	-	-	-	
Zigeuner	74	3	21	35	14	1	-	-	-
Kriegsgefangene	207	5	105	87	9	1	-	-	-
Gesamtstärke	18486	2595	7436	5550	2644	227	34	-	-

The U.S. carrier Franklin *lies crippled after being hit by a kamikaze off Samar in the Philippines.*

■ Japanese reinforcements were landed on Leyte.

Nov. 2 Leyte valley was cleared of all Japanese forces.

■ Russian tanks reached the outskirts of Budapest, but they pulled back.

Nov. 3 Canadians of the 3rd Division cleared the Breskens pocket in Holland, netting about 12,500 prisoners.

■ Lung-ling along the China-Burma border was retaken by the Chinese, ending a seesaw battle which extended for months.

Royal Scotch Fusiliers, in Burma, advance from Myitkyina to Mandalay to bagpipe accompaniment.

JAPANESE BALLOON ATTACKS ON THE U.S.

Japan began an explosive balloon campaign against the United States and Canada on November 3, 1944. The Japanese army's Special Balloon Regiment based at Otsu in Ibaraki Prefecture launched about 9,300 hydrogen-filled paper or rubberized-silk balloons during the next five months. Taking advantage of constant westerly winds, the Japanese hoped to disturb Americans in an inexpensive psychological warfare campaign by attaching incendiary material and bombs to the balloons. The large devices (32 feet in diameter) carried a container of magnesium flash powder and 33-pound antipersonnel bombs. Altogether, about 285 of the balloons reached North America. Most of the balloons apparently self-destructed before reaching earth. Six Americans were killed on May 5, 1945, in the Gearhart Mountains, about 65 miles from Klamath Falls, Oregon. A minister's wife and five children aged 11 to 13 were among a group which had located one of the devices when the bomb exploded. They were the only known victims of the campaign. Two brush fires were reported, one of which incredibly delayed work on the production of material for an atomic bomb which was later dropped on Japan. A power failure at the Hanford, Washington, atomic processing facility resulted when the incendiary triggered a safety mechanism which forced a shutdown of the reactor.

SOURCE: Robert C. Mikesh, *Japan's World War II Balloon Bomb Attacks on North America.*

■ Japanese planes began attacks on Saipan and Tinian in the Marianas to disrupt missions from the islands directed against the Japanese home islands.

■ U.S. aircraft attacked Japanese positions in the Ormoc valley of Leyte.

Nov. 4 A German counterattack drove U.S. units out of Kommerscheidt.

■ The Russians advanced along the rail line to Budapest but rain and troop exhaustion slowed down the drive.

Nov. 5 German advances continued in the Netherlands against positions of the U.S. V Corps.

■ U.S. B-29s bombed Singapore.

Nov. 6 A regiment of the Chinese 22nd Division crossed the Irrawaddy River and advanced to Shwegugale.

■ Stalin accused the Japanese of aggression. This belated recognition was important only in that it foretold Russian actions in Asia.

Nov. 7 Roosevelt was elected for a fourth term as U.S. president.

■ Russia refused to renew diplomatic relations with Switzerland because of the Swiss ban on the Communist party and Swiss-German trade. Part of that trade was in military equipment which the isolated Swiss had to provide under virtual duress. (Not until March of 1945 did the Swiss agree to end arms exports to Germany. By then the Allies were able to provide some consumer goods.)

■ Shwegu in Burma was taken by the Chinese.

■ U.S. X Corps troops on Leyte started the drive for Ormoc, encountering heavy resistance.

■ Master Soviet spy Richard Sorge was executed in Tokyo.

Nov. 8 U.S. Third Army forces in France crossed the Seille River and began a broad offensive toward the Saar River.

■ The Canadian First Army secured the approaches to Antwerp by clearing Walcheren Island and taking 8,000 prisoners.

■ Another Japanese division was landed at Ormoc on Leyte.

■ Germany began transferring 38,000 Jews from Budapest to concentration camps in Germany.

Nov. 9 U.S. Third Army troops broke across the Moselle in an offensive aimed at taking Metz.

■ More Japanese landed at Ormoc, but the ships pulled out before ammunition and supplies could be unloaded and were eventually sunk by U.S. aircraft.

Nov. 10 Heavy fighting developed as the Germans offered strong resistance to the offensive of the U.S. XX Corps around the Moselle.

■ Japanese units captured the U.S. airbases at Kweilin and Liuchow.

■ Chinese forces skirted Japanese defenders and moved into the Bhamo plain of Burma.

■ Wang Ching-wei, head of the pro-Japanese

Nanking government of China, died and was succeeded by Chen Kiung-po.

Nov. 11 The giant aircraft carrier *Shinano* joined the Japanese fleet. *Shinano* was considered unsinkable, with a special steel deck (30 centimeters thick) over a layer of concrete considered capable of withstanding any kind of bombing attack. She carried 70 planes and was rightly considered a major boost to Japan's fading naval strength in the Pacific. (*Shinano* was torpedoed 17 days later by the U.S. submarine *Archerfish* in the Kumano Sea. She sank on the morning of the 29th, with a loss of 500 men among the crew of 1,400. *Shinano*'s record was the shortest of any major man-of-war during the conflict.)

A U.S. PT boat picks a Japanese survivor in the Surigao Strait, the Phillippines.

A Japanese cruiser in Manila Bay attempts to evade U.S. aircraft.

■ German civilians were evacuated from Metz.

Nov. 12 Allied forces finally succeeded in sinking the *Tirpitz*. The German battleship was always a potential threat during the war. As an actual weapon of war *Tirpitz* contributed almost nothing. Only once—in the bombardment of the island of Spitzbergen, Norway, in September of 1943—did she ever fire her mammoth guns against an enemy target. Still, the British felt they had to get rid of the threat. By now the *Tirpitz* had been forced to hole up in Altenfjord in Norway. Efforts to destroy her by air failed, mostly because of bad weather, heavy defenses, and effective use of smoke screens. Finally, however, 32 RAF Lancasters flying at 14,000 feet caught the *Tirpitz* under perfect bombing conditions on this date and scored hits with three 12,000-pound bombs. The *Tirpitz* turned completely over, taking about 1,200 crewmen to their deaths. Only 76 survived. If further proof was needed that the battleship was obsolete, the death of *Tirpitz* provided it.

■ The bitter fighting for the approaches to Antwerp ended as Allied forces cleared the Dutch islands at the mouth of the Scheldt River.

Nov. 13 Fierce German resistance continued as the U.S. Third Army was either stalled or thrown back in the Moselle area.

Nov. 14 Yugoslav forces took Skoplje, the staging point for the German forces withdrawn from Greece.

■ An offensive against the Belfort gap along the Doubs River was launched by the French First Army.

Nov. 16 In the heaviest aerial attack of the war in support of a ground operation, 2,807 U.S. and British planes dropped more than 10,000 tons of bombs on German defensive positions near Aachen. The bombing was a prelude to an offensive by the U.S. First and Ninth armies to drive to the Roer (Rur) River. The towns of Düren, Jülich, and Heinsburg were obliterated.

■ The U.S. VII Corps opened its drive toward Cologne.

Nov. 17 Belgian resistance forces were asked by the Allies to lay down their arms and let regular combat troops continue the fighting.

■ German resistance ended in Tirana, the capital of Albania.

■ The U.S. 10th Armored Division pursued the retreating Germans to the Saar River. Troops of the U.S. 5th Division reached the suburbs of Metz.

■ Japanese forces began an offensive to take Kweiyang, which would open the way to Kunming and Chungking.

Nov. 18 U.S. Third Army units fought their way into Metz. Geilenkirchen was surrounded on three sides by British and American troops. The French First Army drove seven miles through the Belfort gap between the Rhine-Rhône Canal and the Swiss border.

Nov. 18–19 The first in a series of 16 more raids was conducted by the RAF against Berlin. In this initial attack 402 British bombers inflicted extensive destruction. German defenses were unable to cope with the waves of attacking aircraft. Only nine bombers were downed.

A line of U.S. warships steams through the waters of the western Pacific.

Nov. 19 Geilenkirchen was taken. Moroccan troops reached Belfort's suburbs and encountered stiff resistance. The French 5th Armored Division became the first Allied group to reach the Rhine when it advanced to Rosenau. Seppois became the first Alsace village recovered.

■ Metz was entered by U.S. troops.

■ German troops being withdrawn from Yugoslavia were subjected to attacks by Partisans and British troops.

■ Indian troops began crossing the Chindwin

River in Burma as part of Mountbatten's and Slim's offensive strategy of pursuing the Japanese through the monsoon and retaking central Burma.

■ U.S. troops landed on Asia Island off the northwest coast of New Guinea.

Nov. 20 The U.S. 4th Division was stalled in the Hürtgen Forest, gaining only a little more than a mile in five days of hard fighting with heavy losses. The French 2nd Armored Division crossed the Saar River. Heavy fighting broke out in Belfort as French and Moroccan troops entered the city.

Nov. 21 Fierce fighting continued within Metz. A strong German counterattack threatened French forces at Mulhouse.

■ Albanian communist guerrillas seized control of Tirana and Durazzo.

■ Chinese 38th Division units closed in on Bhamo.

Nov. 22 British 53rd Division troops reached the Maas River, with other units advancing toward Venlo. The Germans beefed up their defenses behind the Roer River and generally stiffened to hold back the U.S. Ninth Army. German resistance ended in Metz, and the U.S. Army pushed on to the Saar River. Mulhouse was secured by the French First Army.

Nov. 23 The French 2nd Armored Division cleared Strasbourg. With the Rhine now occupied this far in the north and the French in control from Mulhouse to the Swiss border, a large area known as the Colmar pocket of Alsace was the only area in this part of France still held by the Germans.

■ After weeks of seesaw fighting, the Russians gained control of the Hungarian rail junction of Cop (Csap).

■ British Eighth Army units crossed the Cosina River in Italy.

■ German forces withdrew from Finnish Lapland.

■ Macedonia in Greece was evacuated by the Germans.

■ Canada's Parliament, in special session, approved sending 16,000 draftees overseas to fill the depleted ranks of the Canadian army. Until now, only volunteers were sent abroad, and the French Canadians particularly opposed being drafted for combat service.

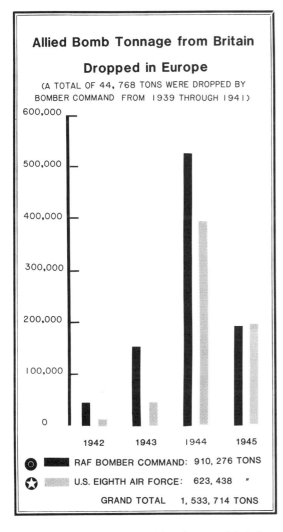

Allied Bomb Tonnage from Britain

Dropped in Europe

(A TOTAL OF 44,768 TONS WERE DROPPED BY BOMBER COMMAND FROM 1939 THROUGH 1941)

RAF BOMBER COMMAND: 910,276 TONS

U.S. EIGHTH AIR FORCE: 623,438 "

GRAND TOTAL 1,533,714 TONS

Britain as a base for Allied bombers enabled thousands of aircraft to pound the Axis mercilessly.

French soldiers blast German positions in the Chateau du Belfort (center, far distance) with 57-mm antitank fire.

Nov. 24 U.S. B-29s began attacking Japan from bases on Saipan in the Marianas. The first strike was against Tokyo with 111 bombers.

■ Eisenhower issued orders to clear areas west of the Rhine, before attempting to cross it. French armored units in Strasbourg urgently called for infantry help to hold the city.

■ Japanese forces captured Nanning in China in an effort to link up with units from Indochina.

Nov. 25 Japanese kamikaze planes began attacking Allied ships in force off Luzon and in Leyte Gulf. The U.S. carriers *Essex, Intrepid, Hancock,* and *Cabot* were all damaged.

■ In the deadliest strike by a V-2 rocket 164 people were killed when one of the German weapons hit a Woolworth store in south London.

■ Alexander was promoted to field marshal.

■ Russian troops cleared Csepel Island in the Danube, just south of Budapest.

■ Japanese troops were ordered to fall back in central Burma.

(TOP) *Japanese kamikaze pilots prepare to take off on suicide missions from Mito airfield, in Japan, as portrayed by artist Ihara Usaburo.*

(LEFT) *Crewmen of the U.S.S. Lexington killed during a kamikaze attack are buried at sea.*

Nov. 26 U.S. troops began breaking out of the Hürtgen Forest.

■ Himmler ordered destruction of the crematoria at Auschwitz.

Nov. 27 U.S. Secretary of State Hull resigned after nearly 12 years in office and was succeeded by Edward R. Stettinius.

■ U.S. B-29s raided Tokyo and Bangkok.

■ All fighting on Peleliu and the adjacent Palau Islands ended. About 13,600 Japanese were killed; 400 were captured. U.S. Army and Marine casualties were 1,792 killed and 8,006 wounded.

■ Chiang Kai-shek refused to permit U.S. munitions to be shipped to Chinese Communist forces, as proposed by General Wedemeyer.

■ The port of Antwerp was opened to Allied shipping. V-bomb attacks were intensified, falling at a rate of one every 12½ minutes at the height of the raids. Despite the V-weapons, the Allies were able to move 25,000 tons through Antwerp daily.

Nov. 28 Disobeying orders from Tokyo, the Japanese Eleventh Army crossed the Kwangsi-Kweichow provincial border in southern China.

■ U.S. Third Army units broke into the Saar basin.

Nov. 29 German counterattacks were repulsed by the U.S. 95th Division at the Saar heights commanding Saarlautern (Saarlouis).

■ Red Army troops crossed the Danube north of the Drava River, near the Yugoslav-Hungarian border.

■ Northern Finland was secured by the Russians.

Nov. 30 Chiang Kai-shek ordered the return of the Chinese 22nd and 38th divisions to China from Burma to defend Kunming, which was imperiled by the Japanese advances.

(TOP) *A main intersection in Antwerp, Belgium, moments after a V-2 rocket fell.*

(RIGHT) *Nine Belgians were killed on this Antwerp street, victims of a German V-2 bomb.*

A burial is held in the Burmese jungle, final rites for a British infantryman killed by a sniper.

■ Russian troops occupied Eger, 60 miles northeast of Budapest.

■ Canadian forces broke into Germany from positions around Nijmegen.

■ The U.S. drive for Limon on Leyte was stalled further by strong Japanese opposition.

■ British civilian air raid casualties for the month were 716 killed and 1,511 wounded.

Dec. 1 U.S. 4th Division troops still could not push clear of the Hürtgen Forest, gaining only 1,000 yards in three days of heavy fighting.

■ German forces on Crete were withdrawn to Suda Bay and other coastal embarkation points.

■ Soviet troops crossed the Ondava River in eastern Czechoslovakia and pushed on to Budapest from the north and northeast.

■ Japanese troops on Leyte ran out of food supplies. There was no way for the Japanese to be replenished except by occasional submarine deliveries.

Dec. 2 U.S. forces reached Saarlautern and were engaged in house-to-house fighting.

■ British Eighth Army units began probing actions before an all-out offensive in Italy.

■ East African troops of the British Fourteenth

Army advanced to the Chindwin River in Burma.

■ De Gaulle arrived in Moscow for meetings with Stalin.

Dec. 3 The British Eighth Army went on the offensive to take Bologna, as British, Canadian, and Polish units advanced abreast.

■ The U.S. Ninth Army reached the Roer River, capturing Flossdorf. The British Second Army had cleared the west bank of the Meuse. U.S. 95th Division troops surprised the Germans defending the last bridge over the Saar near Saarlautern. The span was captured intact, permitting the 379th Regiment to break across the river. The unit went on to capture the first bunkers of the Siegfried line. As a result Hitler dismissed General Otto von Knobelsdorff, commander of the First Army, blaming him for the penetration of the West Wall.

■ East African and Indian troops of the British Fourteenth Army broke across the Chindwin.

■ Civil war erupted in Greece as pro- and anti-communist forces refused to lay down their arms as demanded by the British.

■ The British Home Guard was demobilized.

More than 8,000 prisoners were cremated in this oven at the Struthof concentration camp, near Natzviller.

A U.S. soldier and a French partisan inspect a cremation oven at the liberated Struthof concentration camp.

■ The Japanese Eleventh Army ran out of supplies and had to halt its unauthorized advance toward Kweiyang in China's Kweichow Province.

Dec. 4 American Third Army forces advanced to and began to penetrate German defenses along the Siegfried line.

■ Canadian troops took Ravenna in Italy.

■ General Wedemeyer requested that all B-29s be removed from their China bases because of the difficulty of supplying them by air over the Hump.

■ The U.S. Sixth Army was ordered to eliminate Japanese defenses at Ormoc on Leyte.

Dec. 5 U.S. forces of the Seventh Army pressed into Germany on a 30-mile front. The 45th Division reached Mertzwiller where it faced determined German resistance. Saarlautern fell to the U.S. Third Army, but the city was now virtually destroyed.

■ Russian advances were made on a broad front in Hungary with forward units reaching Lake Balaton.

■ The Allied offensive in Italy was stalled by stiff defenses.

Dec. 6 U.S. 90th Division forces broke across the Saar in assault boats and secured a small bridgehead.

■ Rumanian troops joined the Russians in clearing northeast Hungary.

■ Despite intense hardships Japanese forces on Leyte refused to yield without inflicting losses and even counterattacked in one sector.

Dec. 7 Intense fighting took place at the Saarlautern bridgehead as the U.S. Third Army attempted to break through German fortified positions.

■ French troops began to reduce the Colmar pocket.

■ Russian troops cleared the entire southern shore of Lake Balaton. Yugoslav forces began crossing the Danube in force.

■ Thirteen Japanese ships attempting to resupply forces on Leyte were sunk by U.S. aircraft. U.S. forces were put ashore on the eastern shore of Ormoc Bay in a flanking movement. The beachhead was attacked by about 50 Japanese planes but 36 were believed to have been shot down.

Dec. 8 Pillbox-to-pillbox fighting developed as

Royal Air Force DC-3s drop supplies to British troops across the Chindwin River from Kalewa in Burma.

the U.S. 95th Division penetrated the Siegfried Line beyond Saarlautern.

■ U.S. bombers and naval ships began the systematic bombing of Iwo Jima as a prelude to amphibious attack. The island came under attack for the next 72 days.

Dec. 9 Budapest was about two-thirds encircled as Russian troops tightened their control around the Hungarian capital.

■ Serbia and Macedonia were cleared of all German troops.

■ The British Eighth Army suspended its Italian offensive, too weakened even to exploit the advantages of beating off counterattacks which had been extremely costly to the Germans.

Dec. 10 France and Russia signed a 20-year mutual assistance pact in Moscow.

■ German troops launched savage counterattacks against the U.S. Third Army around Saarlautern but were contained.

■ British 36th Division patrols advanced into Indaw and Katha in Burma.

■ Ormoc on Leyte was occupied by the U.S. 77th Division.

Dec. 11 British troops in Italy crossed the Lamone River but tanks were unable to make it to the bridgehead.

■ Ormoc Bay on Leyte was completely secured by U.S. forces. The Japanese were cut in two. More importantly, Ormoc yielded vast stockpiles of munitions which were the supply mainstays of the Japanese Thirty-fifth Army. Leyte was now lost to the Japanese, whose force on the island was reduced to 35,000 men.

Dec. 12 German forces pulled back across the Roer River. Maginot Line defenses blocked the U.S. Seventh Army advances.

■ British Eighth Army units crossed the Naviglio Canal and attacked Faenza on the Italian front.

■ A V-2 hit the Rex Cinema in Antwerp killing 492 people and seriously injuring about 500 others.

Dec. 13 The area west of the Roer River was almost totally cleared by the U.S. VII Corps. In northern Alsace units of the XV Corps occupied Seltz and Niederroedern.

■ German counterattacks were launched against the British bridgehead across the Naviglio Canal.

■ Chinese 38th Division troops entered Bhamo in Burma.

Dec. 14 Polish and British forces launched a new offensive in Italy.

Dec. 15 Mindoro in the Philippines was invaded by U.S. Army forces. Japanese suicide planes attacked the landing convoy, causing heavy damage and sinking two LST's. There was no opposition on the beaches and elements moved inland quickly.

■ Bhamo was captured by the Chinese.

■ Russian troops crossed into Czechoslovakia at Sahy on the Ipel' River.

Dec. 16 In a carefully coordinated counteroffensive the Germans launched a massive attack on the U.S. First and Ninth armies along a 40-mile front in the Ardennes Forest in Luxembourg. It became famous as the Battle of the Bulge. Rundstedt employed the German Fifth and Sixth Panzer armies (about 300,000 men) in a mighty blow which caught the Americans by surprise. German paratroopers were landed behind the American lines, causing havoc and breaking

Tense crewmen aboard U.S. Navy cruiser attempt to identify aircraft during the American invasion of Mindoro in the Philippines.

Dec. 17–18 A mighty typhoon about 500 miles east of the Philippines inflicted heavy losses and damage on the U.S. Third Fleet. Three destroyers capsized and 769 lives were lost. Severe damage was suffered by eight carriers, a light cruiser, seven destroyers, and a variety of auxiliaries. Nearly 150 planes were lost off carrier decks or damaged beyond repair. Nature thus inflicted greater losses on the U.S. Navy than they were to suffer in any single battle in the Pacific war.

■ In the Battle of the Bulge two regiments of the U.S. 106th Division near Schönberg failed to break out of their trapped positions. The 7th Armored Division was heavily engaged at St.-Vith. The 28th Division was badly mauled. German units advanced to points outside Bastogne and Houffalize.

A German infantryman during the Ardennes offensive (the Battle of the Bulge), Dec. 1944.

communications. Rundstedt intended to advance to the Meuse River and the Albert Canal and eventually to retake Antwerp.

Dec. 17 Allied reinforcements were rushed to the Ardennes. The U.S. 82nd and 101st Airborne divisions moved to defend key road junctions. The Germans made small gains in the direction of Malmédy. In this Belgian city about 90 American POW's were killed in what became known as the "Malmédy Massacre." Caught by surprise in the swift German advance, approximately 170 U.S. soldiers were taken prisoner and rounded up on a farm field. What happened next is disputed. Some evidence indicates another German unit came upon them and started shooting without realizing the Americans were disarmed POW's. Others suggest it was a deliberate massacre.

■ Kientzheim in Alsace, near Colmar, was taken by the French First Army.

■ Russian main force units were within five miles of Budapest.

A German infantryman commands an advance in the Ardennes offensive.

Dec. 18 Russian troops crossed the Hungarian-Czech border on a 70-mile front north of Miskolc.

■ Hangkow in China, a Japanese major supply base, was attacked by U.S. Fourteenth Air Force planes, including 77 B-29s. Previously the Superforts were directed against targets in Japan, but the deteriorating ground situation in China demanded an interruption of the Japanese logistical lines.

Dec. 19 All Allied offensive actions against the Rhine were halted because of the German Ardennes offensive. Montgomery was given command of all Allied forces north of the Bulge, Bradley all forces to the south. Bastogne was almost surrounded as the 101st Airborne Division arrived in the village.

■ A U.S. naval attack on Luzon was postponed because of a typhoon. The Japanese Thirty-fifth Army on Leyte was told it could expect no further reinforcements or supplies.

Dec. 20 German troops advanced to Stavelot and Noville and continued applying great pressure on U.S. forces at St.-Vith.

■ Kawlin in Burma was captured by the 19th Indian Division.

Dec. 21 Bastogne came under siege. U.S. ammunition and food supplies were running low. U.S. units beat back the German drive to take Stavelot.

■ U.S. Sixth Army forces completed securing the Ormoc valley on Leyte.

■ A provisional Hungarian government was formed at Debrecen.

Dec. 22 German forces launched their final drive to reach the Meuse River. U.S. forces within the Bastogne pocket kept retreating or were attempting to avoid fatal entrapment. Brigadier General Anthony C. McAuliffe, acting commander of the trapped 101st Airborne Division, was issued an ultimatum by the Germans at Bastogne: Surrender honorably or face "annihilation." His famous reply was, "Nuts." The U.S. Third Army was by now beginning to attack the Germans in the Ardennes salient from the south, having shifted from an offensive across the Saar, a brilliant maneuver by Patton.

German troops, who caught American forces by surprise in the Ardennes offensive, pause to savor captured cigars.

■ The Vietnamese Liberation Army under Vo Nguyen Giap was formed in Indochina.

Dec. 23 Clearing weather permitted Allied aircraft to come to the aid of the besieged Bastogne garrison. Supplies were dropped by air and German positions were bombed.

Dec. 24 U.S. forces began to push the Germans back on some sectors of the Ardennes front as reinforcements began arriving.

■ The Colmar pocket was cleared by the U.S. 3rd Division.

■ Only a 20-mile-wide escape corridor was left to the Germans in Budapest as the Russians continued to close the circle around the city.

Dec. 25 The Bastogne perimeter held against strong German pressure from all sides. German tanks advanced to within four miles of the Meuse, where the crossings were now covered by British troops.

■ Only a rail exit to the west in a nine-mile-wide corridor remained open to the Germans in Budapest.

■ Churchill and Eden arrived in Athens in an effort to end the Greek civil war.

Dec. 26 Bastogne's siege was lifted as tanks of the U.S. 4th Armored Division broke the German encirclement. Only the tanks were able to penetrate initially as the Germans contested any advance through the corridor. Thus ended the Ardennes offensive, a tactical victory for the Germans. But it was so costly that the German army was never able to recover from its staggering losses, including 220,000 men (half of them as prisoners) and more than 1,400 tanks and heavy assault guns. The net effect of the final German

A German army medical corpsman surrenders to an Allied tank at Humain, Belgium.

offensive was to delay the Allies by six weeks.

■ The Akyab peninsula in Burma was cleared after the Japanese decided to withdraw.

■ Japanese naval ships attacked U.S. beachhead positions on Mindoro in the Philippines.

Dec. 27 A secure corridor out of Bastogne was cleared as trucks and ambulances sped in to assist the trapped Americans.

A gilded Buddha miraculously survived destruction of a temple in Mangshih (Lushi), China.

■ Budapest was totally blocked as Russian forces sealed the city on all sides. Fighting broke out in the eastern and western suburbs.

■ U.S. B-29s launched their fifth attack on Tokyo.

Dec. 28 The projected advance toward Bologna by the U.S. Fifth Army was postponed because of the losses sustained in the Serchio valley fighting. But the Germans were already beginning to withdraw from the valley.

Dec. 29 Door-to-door fighting broke out in central Budapest. The provisional Hungarian government declared war on Germany.

Dec. 30 German units sought to close the Bastogne corridor, forcing the Americans to abandon an attack on Houffalize.

Dec. 31 The U.S. 77th Division, in 11 days of fighting on Leyte, killed 5,779 Japanese while losing 17 Americans.

■ RAF Mosquitos attacked the Gestapo headquarters in Oslo.

■ By gaining some lost ground in the Serchio valley of Italy, the U.S. Fifth Army was able to restore the lines of last October.

■ British civilian air raid casualties for the month were 367 killed and 847 wounded.

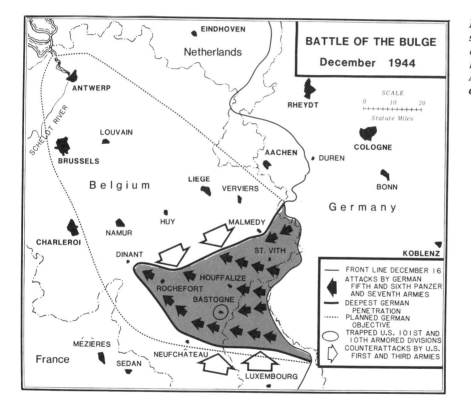

Hitler's surprise last offensive, in the Ardennes Forest, caused heavy Allied casualties, particularly American, but the German drive eventually failed.

(OPPOSITE, TOP) *The Potsdam conference, with two new leaders, Britain's Prime Minister Clement Attlee and U.S. President Harry Truman, joining Stalin, July–Aug. 1945.*

(OPPOSITE, BOTTOM) *The Allied fleet steams into Tokyo Bay to accept the Japanese surrender.*

1945 Peace returns—for a while.

Jan. 1 Admiral Sir Bertram Ramsay, naval commander of the Allied Expeditionary Force, was killed when his plane crashed while taking off from his headquarters outside Paris.

■ Operation NORDWIND, a German counterattack, was launched in the Esztergom-Bicske area of Hungary, which was occupied by the Russians who were using it as a base to attack Budapest.

■ U.S. Eighth Army units began a campaign which lasted through May to clear Leyte in the Philippines. A series of deception operations was initiated, but the Japanese did not fall for the several feints.

■ The communist Lublin committee declared itself the legitimate government of Poland.

Jan. 1–2 In its last major operation of the war, the Luftwaffe sent about 800 planes against Allied air bases and ports in France and the Low Countries. The results were disastrous for the Germans as 364 of the aircraft were downed. About 125 Allied planes were lost, but operations continued from the target fields.

Jan. 2 The corridor into Bastogne was expanded by the U.S. 4th Armored Division.

■ Danish underground forces destroyed a factory in Copenhagen producing V-2 parts.

German bombers blasted a Paris railroad station, leaving only its shell, Dec. 1944.

■ Japanese kamikazes attacked the American fleet leaving Leyte Gulf for Luzon.

Jan. 3 German units penetrated Aachen in their counterattack against the U.S. Seventh Army but were thrown back. Rundstedt began pulling out some of his troops and armored forces.

■ Akyab on the Arakan front in Burma was captured by British and Indian forces.

■ American Third Fleet units attacked Japanese units around Formosa, Okinawa, and the Pescadores. Despite bad weather, the two-day operation netted 12 ships sunk and 110 planes destroyed for the loss of 18 U.S. planes.

■ Wanting was recaptured by the Chinese, but the Japanese drove the Chinese out of the Sino-Burmese border town by nightfall.

■ Turkey broke diplomatic relations with Japan.

■ The first Canadian draftees to be sent abroad sailed for Europe from Halifax. Except for service in Kiska, conscripts had not been sent abroad. Of the 60,000 men in this category, many seemed intent on not going into combat areas. Prior to this first overseas departure, 7,800 had gone absent without leave and 6,300 were still absent at sailing time. As some boarded the ship, they dropped their rifles into the water from the gangplank. Most of the resistance came from French Canadians but Canadians of central European origin were also among the objectors. In all, 13,000 draftees eventually did go to Europe.

Jan. 4 The U.S. invasion force approaching Lingayen Gulf in the Philippines was subjected to heavy Japanese air attack. The escort carrier *Ommaney Bay* had to be sunk by other U.S. ships after being hit by a kamikaze.

■ The occupation of Akyab was completed.

■ German troops attempted but failed to fight their way out of Budapest.

Jan. 5 German forces recrossed the Rhine and recaptured Offendorf, Herlisheim, and Rohrweiler in Alsace.

■ London and Washington refused to accept the Lublin committee as the government of Poland.

Jan. 6 U.S. Seventh Army forces halted the German counterattack on the Rhine.

■ The Japanese air force on Luzon was reduced to 35 planes, from a total of 150 only a week before.

Jan. 7 German forces, trying to break through to Budapest and relieve the hard-pressed garrison, captured Esztergom, northwest of the capital.

■ Montgomery reported the Allies were on the offensive in the Ardennes.

Jan. 8 Hitler agreed to the withdrawal of German forces to Houffalize, which was already under Allied attack.

■ Heavy fighting broke out in central Budapest.

■ Frankfurt was attacked by 1,000 U.S. bombers.

Jan. 9 U.S. Sixth Army forces landed at Lingayen Gulf in Luzon, 100 miles north of Manila. Most units advanced without encountering serious opposition, but I Corps could only establish a narrow beachhead. By nightfall, 68,000 U.S. troops were ashore.

U.S. battleships Pennsylvania *and* Colorado *followed by cruisers* Louisville, Portland, *and* Columbia *form a battle line entering Lingayen Gulf in the Philippines prior to the American landing at Luzon.*

Two members of Hitler's Youth Division, the 12th SS Panzer, after surrendering to U.S. forces.

■ U.S. Seventh Army units failed to dislodge the Germans from their positions on the west bank of the Rhine.

Jan. 10 The U.S. First Army opened an offensive toward St.-Vith through Houffalize. German units counterattacked around Strasbourg.

■ Hitler decreed that anyone diverting clothing and equipment intended for use by the military would be executed.

■ U.S. Sixth Army units on Luzon pushed forward on most sectors of the front.

Jan. 11 German forces began pulling back southeast of Bastogne.

■ Serious fuel shortages began to affect German armored units. Allied bombing of transport cut supplies drastically. The Panzer Lehr division alone abandoned 53 tanks during the next four days because of a lack of gasoline.

■ A truce was effected between Greek communist guerrillas and British troops.

FOREIGNERS IN HITLER'S SERVICE

Hitler's loyal *Waffen* SS was by 1945 mostly made up of non-Germans. Of the 40 *Waffen* SS divisions, 27 were essentially filled by about a half-million foreigners, mostly European (but some Asians and Americans as well), who were attracted to the ideological militancy of these elite units. These numbers of western Europeans reflected the widespread appeal:

Dutch	50,000	Danish	6,000
Flemish	22,000	Swiss	800
French	20,000	Swedish	300
Walloon	20,000	Others	280
Norwegian	6,000		

The largest number of non-German *Waffen* SS troops came from the Soviet Union. They were largely Ukrainians, about 100,000 of whom had volunteered while being held as prisoners of war. Other large numbers came from Croatia, Latvia, Lithuania, Estonia, Finland, and Albania.

Jan. 12 Russian forces, under Zhukov and Marshal Ivan S. Konev, launched their greatest offensive of the war from Poland and East Prussia. A total of 1,350,000 Russians went into action, attacking a German force one-sixth their size. Stalin advanced the start of the offensive at the request of Churchill to relieve the pressure on the western front. The central eastern front was vulnerable, with the Germans isolated in the north in Latvia and in southern Hungary, incapable of being moved to the area of the major advance.

■ U.S. Task Force 38 aircraft sank about 40 Japanese ships off the Indochinese coast.

Jan. 13 The 51st British Division advanced to the Ourthe River and hooked up with the U.S. 87th Division. U.S. 30th Division elements reached the Amblève River in driving south for Malmédy. The Houffalize-St.-Vith road was cut.

■ Japan's depleted air defense forces launched their final strike against U.S. positions at Lingayen Gulf.

Jan. 14 U.S. First Army forces made broad advances, establishing several bridgeheads across the Amblève.

■ The Red Army widened its offensive with forces pushing forward from positions north and south of Warsaw.

■ Indian troops of the British Fourteenth Army established a bridgehead across the Irawaddy at Thabeikkyin, but the Japanese counterattacked in force and touched off a month-long battle for control of the area.

Jan. 15 Russian forces in Poland wheeled south

British 36th Division troops move through Tigyaing in the reoccupation of Burma.

to the Carpathians southwest of Krakow, capturing Kielce. Hitler refused Army Group Center permission to withdraw from the Warsaw area.

■ The British 7th Armored Division captured Bakenhoven in the Netherlands as the Second Army moved to clear the German salient between the Meuse and the Roer and Würm rivers.

■ U.S. elements reached Houffalize.

■ In China Japanese troops began their drive to capture the U.S. air base at Suichuan, in western Kiangsi Province.

■ The U.S. beachhead on Luzon was widened to 45 miles.

■ A British commercial ship left London for France, the first nonmilitary vessel to cross the channel since May 1940.

Jan. 16 The U.S. First and Third armies hooked up at Houffalize and eliminated the German Ardennes salient. British 7th Armored Division units drove northeast, capturing Dieteren in the Netherlands.

■ Norwegian resistance forces gained control of the northern part of their country.

■ Russian forces captured Radom in Poland.

■ Hitler moved his headquarters in East Prussia

to the bunker under the Reich Chancellery in Berlin. There he spent the remainder of his life.

■ Hitler pulled the Sixth Panzer Army out of the western front and sent it to Hungary.

■ Hong Kong was attacked by U.S. naval planes, which found Japanese air defenses almost nonexistent.

Jan. 17 Warsaw was taken by forces of the First White Russian Front under Marshal Zhukov and units of the Lublin Polish army. Ukrainian units occupied Czestochowa.

■ MacArthur ordered the U.S. Sixth Army to speed up its drive to take Manila and Clark Field.

Jan. 18 Russian forces advanced rapidly toward German Silesia. Modlin in Poland was captured.

■ All German forces were cleared from the east side of the Danube in Budapest.

■ The Communist Lublin committee arrived in Warsaw to assume control over liberated Poland.

■ Two Japanese raiding parties attempted to destroy U.S. aircraft and arms dumps on Peleliu but were unsuccessful.

A Japanese ship sinks after being torpedoed by the U.S. submarine Aspro.

■ The Japanese government directed the military to "concentrate converting all armament production to special attack weapons of a few major types." This meant Japan's limited facilities were to be concentrated on suicide planes, human torpedoes, and high-speed small attack boats.

Jan. 19 Krakow, Lodz, and Tarnow in Poland were occupied by the Russians. German forces were in full retreat along a 500-mile front.

■ Japanese troops in China began occupying bridges and tunnels along the Canton–Hankow rail line.

Jan. 20 U.S. XXI Corps and French First Army forces launched attacks in southern Alsace to clear the Colmar pocket and the west bank of the Rhine.

■ East Prussia was almost encircled by Red Army forces advancing from the south and east. Tilsit (Sovetsk) fell.

■ Trapped German troops in Budapest attempted to break out of the city toward the Danube.

■ The first small U.S. convoy reached Kunming, China, over the Burma Road and a hastily repaired branch route. It took 16 days to drive from Myitkyina in Burma.

■ Roosevelt was inaugurated for a fourth term as U.S. president.

Jan. 21 First Ukrainian Front troops crossed into German Silesia. Several towns fell as Russian units reached points 10 miles from the Oder River. Tannenberg (Stebark) in East Prussia was taken by units of the White Russian front.

■ A V-1 rocket hit Antwerp, killing 76 and wounding 57.

■ U.S. naval aircraft destroyed about 100 Japa-

The Burmese city of Namhkam is occupied by the Chinese 30th Division.

"Some of our aircraft is missing" might have been the apt comment of the crewmen of this C-47 which escaped an attack by a Japanese fighter. The Japanese pilot first expended his ammunition in trying to shoot it down and then rammed the American transport, which somehow still managed to make it back to base.

nese planes on the ground at air bases on Okinawa and Formosa.

■ Tarlac on Luzon in the Philippines was taken by the U.S. 40th Division which then pushed on to San Miguel.

Jan. 22 The Burma Road was declared open, but Japanese activity along the Sino-Burmese border precluded a free flow of traffic.

■ U.S. forces advanced to the outskirts of St.-Vith.

■ Corregidor was bombed by Allied aircraft.

■ The German XXVIII Army Corps began pulling out of Memel.

Jan. 23 St.-Vith was taken by the U.S. 7th Armored Division.

■ German forces regained control of Berg on the Rhine in a powerful armor-infantry counterattack.

■ Red Army troops advanced to the Oder River 24 miles west of Breslau (Wroclaw). Several Czechoslovak towns and villages fell to the Russians.

Jan. 24 The American air base at Suichuan in China was abandoned.

■ Russian forces resumed their offensive in Latvia.

Jan. 25 Tokyo directed its China Expeditionary Force to discontinue offensive operations in the interior and to concentrate its efforts in defending the coast and north China.

■ U.S. B-29s dropped 366 mines in the approaches to Singapore. Other aircraft mined the waters off Saigon, Camranh Bay, and Penang. It was the largest mining operation of the war.

Jan. 26 Russian troops reached the Auschwitz concentration camp, freeing 2,819 inmates. Red Army units reached a point 120 miles from Berlin.

■ East Prussia was sealed off as Red Army units reached the Gulf of Danzig northeast of Elbing (Elblag).

■ U.S. 37th Division troops reached the edge of Clark Field on Luzon.

■ Thirteen V-2 rockets hit London.

Jan. 27 The Masurian Lakes region of East Prussia was overrun, tightening the Red Army encirclement of Königsberg (Kaliningrad). Poznan (Posen) and Torun (Thorn) in Poland were surrounded.

■ U.S. Third Army units reached the border between Germany and Luxembourg.

■ Two Japanese cargo ships (totaling 3,200 tons) were sunk far up the Yangtze River after striking mines laid by U.S. Fourteenth Air Force B-24s operating out of India.

■ The U.S. invasion force for Iwo Jima left Hawaii.

Jan. 28 The last Germans were eliminated from the Ardennes bulge, and the line was restored to the original German starting point of Dec. 16. The German offensive inflicted 75,000 casualties on 29 U.S. and 4 British divisions. In turn, the Germans suffered 100,000 dead and wounded, and lost 800 tanks and about 1,000 planes.

■ Memel was occupied, completing the occupation of Lithuania by the Russians.

■ Captured Red Army General Andrei A. Vlasov took over command of the anti-Stalin Russian army fighting with the German *Waffen* SS.

■ A trickle of supplies began reaching China over the Burma Road, which Chiang Kai-shek renamed the Stilwell Road.

■ Mindoro was secured by U.S. forces.

Jan. 29 Russian forces crossed into Pomerania in Germany, capturing Schönlanke and Woldenberg, 95 miles from Berlin.

This pagoda in Burma was used by Japanese snipers before being attacked and left burning in Allied mopping up operations.

■ In a further move to isolate Japanese units on Luzon, the U.S. 11th Airborne Division landed at the south entrance to Manila Bay.

■ French and U.S. forces reached the outskirts of Colmar.

■ A small force of Germans continued to fight in the western part of Budapest.

■ The U.S. Sixth Army began its final drive toward Manila.

■ China was sliced in half as the Japanese captured Kukong (Shaokuan), the last Chinese strongpoint on the Hankow railroad.

Feb. 1 The U.S. Seventh Army halted its offensive actions, establishing defensive positions generally along the Moder River in northern Alsace.

■ Berlin was subjected to heavy Allied bombing, which continued on an almost round-the-clock basis.

■ The communications center of Torun on the Vistula in Poland was surrendered to the Red Army. Soviet armor units pressed to within 43 miles of Berlin on the Oder River.

■ U.S. forces advanced rapidly in their southward drive to recapture Manila.

Feb. 2 Roosevelt and Churchill met on Malta before proceeding to Yalta in the Crimea for conferences with Stalin. It was Churchill's last—and again—unsuccessful attempt to win American support for a push into the Balkans.

■ The U.S. 1st Infantry and 82nd Airborne divisions assaulted the Siegfried Line, breaching the West Wall and taking Udenbreth and Neuhof.

■ All combat operations ended on Leyte.

Feb. 3 U.S. 1st Cavalry Division units reached the northeast suburbs of Manila.

■ French forces liberated Colmar.

■ The U.S. 82nd Airborne Division turned back sharp German counterattacks along the Siegfried Line.

■ Japanese troops occupied Namyung (Nanhsiung) in northern Kwantung Province, China.

Feb. 4–9 In the last international war conference in which Roosevelt and Churchill would participate, the U.S. and British leaders and Stalin met at Yalta and agreed on the next phase of the war.

■ Chinese protecting the Stilwell Road 80 miles from Lashio were attacked by the Japanese, but it was the last effort to block the key overland route into China.

■ U.S. Army units were landed northwest of Subic Bay near San Antonio on Luzon. They were deployed eastward to cut off the Japanese on the Bataan Peninsula.

Jan. 30 Hitler marked the 12th anniversary of his accession to power in a speech still filled with defiance. It was his last radio broadcast. Russian forces reached a point 70 miles from Berlin.

Jan. 30–31 The 25,000-ton German transport *Wilhelm Gustloff* was torpedoed and sunk while evacuating soldiers and civilians from East Prussia. Only 900 of the 6,000 aboard survived.

Jan. 31 The U.S. XVIII Corps advanced through the Bucholz Forest into German territory at Neuhof.

Believing Germany would collapse around July 1, they planned a program to weaken Japan before actually invading the home islands. As a reward for its forthcoming entry into the war against Japan, Russia was to receive parts of Manchuria (a fact not disclosed to the Chinese until later).

Feb. 4 A regiment of the U.S. 9th Infantry Division reached the first of the dams on the Roer River in Germany.

■ The first full convoy from Ledo reached Kunming, China.

■ U.S. Eighth Army units began their push into Manila from the south.

Feb. 5 Soviet troops under Zhukov reached the Oder River at Küstrin (Kostrzyn), only 50 miles from Berlin.

■ Moroccan and U.S. forces linked up at Rouffach, cutting the Colmar pocket in two.

■ Australian forces landed on New Britain.

■ American forces drove into Manila from the north.

Feb. 6 The Vosges Mountains were secured as organized German resistance ended. All roads

Churchill arriving at Livadia Palace, site of the Yalta conference, Feb. 1945.

Stalin, Roosevelt, Churchill, and Molotov dine with their aides at Livadia Palace during the Yalta conference.

leading out of the region were blocked by Allied troops.

■ German defenses stiffened as the U.S. Third Army continued its assault on the Siegfried Line, but the fortifications were penetrated and Habscheid fell.

■ Most of Manila was cleared north of the Pasig River. Four thousand Americans were released from Manila prisons.

Feb. 7 The Germans blew up the floodgates of the Schwammenauel Dam in an effort to halt the Allied advance.

■ The Belgian government resigned.

■ Japanese troops captured the Allied air base at Kanchow in China.

Feb. 8 The British XXX Corps launched an offensive to clear the area between the Meuse and Rhine rivers, opening the battle of the Reichswald.

■ The Colmar pocket was reduced to four villages west of the Rhine.

■ Paraguay declared war on Germany and Japan.

■ British civilian war casualties from the start of the war through this date were 57,468 killed and 79,178 injured.

Feb. 9 British and Canadian forces cracked the Siegfried line and reached the Rhine. U.S. 78th Division units reached the north end of the Schwammenauel Dam and seized the control house.

■ The Colmar pocket was closed, with the German Nineteenth Army eliminated as a fighting force. It had lost about 25,000 men in the Alsace fighting. Allied forces now held the west bank of the Rhine from Strasbourg to the Swiss border.

■ Intense fighting continued in and around Manila. U.S. units on the outer defenses of Nichols Field encountered intense opposition.

■ Ramree Island off the coast of Burma was secured by British Commonwealth forces.

Feb. 9–10 A Soviet submarine sank the German transport *General von Steuben* in the Baltic. Of the 3,000 injured soldiers and civilian evacuees from East Prussia aboard, 300 survived.

Feb. 10 A severe earthquake rocked Tokyo, followed almost immediately by a devastating raid by 90 B-29 bombers.

■ Germans flooded the Roer River valley, which was to frustrate the U.S. Ninth Army's planned

offensive toward Düsseldorf. German forces were able to concentrate on defending positions between the Rhine and Meuse.

■ The East Prussian port of Elbing was taken by the Russians.

Feb. 11 The German garrison in Budapest was reduced still further as the Russians occupied 45 city blocks. More than 15,000 Germans were killed trying to escape. Breslau was threatened with encirclement, posing a menace to Dresden 80 miles to the west. All German resistance ended inside besieged Poznan.

Feb. 11–12 Record raids were launched against Essen and Dortmund as 1,079 and 1,108 heavy bombers raided the cities with 5,000 and 5,487 tons of bombs, respectively.

Feb. 12 The 20th Indian Division crossed the Irrawaddy west of Mandalay, Burma.

■ The U.S. submarine *Batfish* sank its third Japanese submarine in four days off the Philippine coast.

■ Japanese troops inside Manila were totally isolated.

■ German women were pressed into *Volkssturm* service. All women between 16 and 60 were declared eligible.

Feb. 13–14 In the most intense incendiary attacks of the war, RAF and U.S. planes devastated the German city of Dresden in raids which have become synonymous with the term "terror bombing." At least 35,000 people were killed in the firestorms (which were most vividly described by a POW witness, Kurt Vonnegut, Jr., in his novel *Slaughterhouse Five*). General George C. Marshall said the raids were in response to a Russian request to "paralyze" Dresden in support of their drive from Breslau. Churchill said, "The destruction of Dresden remains a serious query against the conduct of Allied bombing."

■ General Slim launched a new drive toward Meiktila to cut off Lieutenant General Heitaro Kimura's forces in the Mandalay area. The 7th Indian Division began the operation by crossing the Irrawaddy at Nyaungu.

Feb. 13 Budapest fell after a 45-day fight. About 35,000 Germans were captured. Breslau's 150,000-man garrison was threatened by encirclement.

■ Organized German opposition ended in the Reichswald. Prüm was captured after Allied units established bridgeheads, across the Our and Sauer rivers.

■ Summary courts were established by Germany in the combat area for Wehrmacht and *Waffen SS* troops, with death sentences to be carried out "normally by a firing squad, but in the case of particularly base scoundrels by hanging."

■ Nichols Field near Manila was secured by the 11th Airborne Division.

Feb. 14 The U.S. XII Corps established a solid bridgehead beyond the Siegfried line.

■ U.S. Sixth Army forces reached the Bataan Peninsula. American PT boats entered Manila Bay for night reconnaissance, the first U.S. naval units to operate in those waters since May 1942.

■ Chile declared war on Japan.

Feb. 15 Martial law was proclaimed in Germany with the establishment of summary courts. Death sentences were ordered for anyone found guilty of attempting to "undermine German resolution or striking power."

■ Ukrainian Front troops reached Brandenburg Province.

■ The 7th Indian Division consolidated its bridgehead over the Irrawaddy at Pagan in Burma.

■ U.S. 38th Division elements landed on Mariveles, on the southern tip of Bataan.

Feb. 16 American paratroopers landed on Corregidor Island, followed by boat-borne 34th Division infantrymen two hours later, completely surprising the Japanese. (A total of 4,215 Japanese died defending the island, to the loss of 136 Americans.)

■ An Indian brigade landed on the Arakan coast 62 miles south of Akyab to cut off the Japanese retreating toward Prome.

■ Breslau was totally surrounded by the Red Army.

Feb. 17 U.S. forces began operations to retake the Bataan Peninsula.

■ Tokyo area aircraft plants and airfields were attacked by U.S. naval planes.

■ In a disastrous attempt to clear beach defenses on Iwo Jima, 170 U.S. Navy frogmen were killed.

Feb. 18 U.S. Third Army troops launched another drive to break through the Siegfried Line.

■ Russian General I. D. Chernyakhovsky, commander of the Third White Russian Front, died of wounds received in a battle outside Königsberg. Only 39 when he died, Chernyakhovsky was one of the youngest and best generals in the Red Army. Troops under his command fought at Kursk, captured Minsk, Vilna, and Kaunas, and battled their way into East Prussia.

Feb. 19 U.S. Marines invaded Iwo Jima. The island was known as the "unsinkable airfield," 775 miles from the main Japanese home island of Honshu. It was used by Japanese fighters to inter-

U.S. landing craft assault Iwo Jima. Mount Suribachi rises in the background.

cept U.S. bombers attacking the home islands. The 30,000-man invasion force was not sure of what to expect because Iwo had been pounded by ships and planes for 72 days before the amphibious assault. Despite the merciless preinvasion raids, the Japanese were stubborn defenders, and the next month of fighting was to exact one of the highest casualty tolls of the Pacific war.

■ U.S. Army troops were put ashore on Samar and Capul islands, which, with the occupation of Biri Island the next day, gave the U.S. control of the San Bernadino Strait in the Philippines.

■ Units of the U.S. 80th Division began encircling German troops trapped within the Siegfried Line.

■ Himmler made his first peace overtures to Swedish Count Folke Bernadotte of the Red Cross.

■ The U.S. government requested all public amusements to observe midnight curfew.

Feb. 20 Allied units broke through the Siegfried line along a broad front.

■ Japanese units on Mount Suribachi on Iwo Jima pounded the Marines, whose units suffered 20 to 30 percent casualties in the first two days of combat.

■ The White House in announcing Roosevelt's meetings in Africa with Haile Selassie and Kings Farouk and Ibn Saud, said pointedly that de Gaulle had refused to meet with the President.

Feb. 21 Troops of the U.S. Third Army pushed forward toward the Saar-Moselle triangle.

■ Bataan, except for a small Japanese pocket around Mount Natib, was retaken by U.S. forces, who suffered a total of only 50 casualties in regaining an area which was contested four years before at a cost of thousands of lives.

■ U.S. Marines on Iwo Jima had now lost half their tanks while making progress measured in yards.

Feb. 22 The Allies launched Operation CLARION, a massive bombing attack by 10,000 aircraft from Britain, France, Italy, Holland, and Belgium to cut transportation lines in central Germany and isolate the western front. Two hundred individual targets were bombed, with the heavy bombers coming in as low as 5,000 feet instead of the normal bombing altitude of 25,000. The raids are credited with marking the end of large-scale mobility of the German armed forces.

■ German resistance began to disintegrate along the Siegfried line. U.S. Third Army forces crossed the Saar River.

■ General Eisenhower announced that 900,000 German prisoners were now being held by the Allies.

Feb. 23 Mount Suribachi on Iwo Jima was taken by the Marines.

■ Poznan was taken by the Russians after a

U.S. Marines receive medical care on the beachhead at Iwo Jima.

(RIGHT) *The U.S. flag is raised atop Mount Suribachi on Iwo Jima.*

THE CONTROVERSIAL IWO JIMA PICTURE

Associated Press photographer Joe Rosenthal took what is probably the best-known picture of the war, the raising of the U.S. flag over Mount Suribachi on Iwo Jima. It is also among the most controversial. People have claimed it was posed or otherwise a misrepresentation. The following is the most authoritative account of what actually happened, based on the research of *Washington Star* reporter Jeremiah O'Leary, himself a Marine combat correspondent during the war.

A less dramatic shot of the actual first flag raising was taken about 10:15 on the morning of Feb. 23, 1945, by Marine combat photographer Louis R. Lowrey. The Stars and Stripes (54 by 28 inches) was attached to an iron pipe and jammed into the volcanic surface. Lowrey returned to the beachhead to be treated for minor cuts and bruises after being thrown by the concussion of a Japanese grenade shortly after the picture was taken. He met Rosenthal and told him: "Joe, you ought to get up on top of Suribachi. There are some great shots of the whole island from up there." Rosenthal did climb to the top, arriving there just as a larger flag (96 by 56 inches) had been brought up from an LST. First Lieutenant Harold G. Schrier, who had been responsible for the initial flag raising, decided to replace the smaller flag with the larger one. Rosenthal was 35 feet away from the flag when he took his famous photograph, one of 18 he took at the summit.

SOURCE: *Washington Star*, Feb. 23, 1979.

month-long siege. A German force of 23,000 men surrendered. Red Army units fought their way into Breslau from the south.
■ The U.S. Ninth and First armies smashed across the Roer River, the flood waters having subsided.
■ U.S. forces liberated prisoners at the Los Baños internment camp in the Philippines. Heavy fighting took place in the center of Manila.

■ Turkey and Uruguay declared war on Germany and Japan.
Feb. 24 Except for a few small pockets of resistance, U.S. forces established control over Manila. Most of Corregidor was cleared, with the Japanese clinging to a two-mile pocket at the eastern end of the island.
■ U.S. and Brazilian forces made limited advances in Italy, breaking what had been a virtual stalemate.
■ Egyptian Prime Minister Ahmed Maher Pasha was assassinated. He had just read a royal decree declaring war on Germany and Japan.
Feb. 25 Three U.S. Marine divisions abreast attempted to advance northward the width of Iwo Jima, but Japanese resistance remained fierce.
■ U.S. B-29s were directed to begin night fire raids on large Japanese cities instead of daylight precision raids against industrial centers. In the

first of the fire raids on Tokyo, 334 B-29s dropped 1,667 tons of incendiaries. The attack destroyed 15 square miles of the Japanese capital. Naval aircraft continued attacking aircraft production plants and airfields around Tokyo.

■ Sharp street fighting developed in Breslau.

Feb. 26 The 19th Indian Division began a major southward advance toward Mandalay as part of Slim's plan to distract the Japanese from his main thrust from Pagan, on the opposite side of the Irrawaddy front.

■ Red Army troops in Pomerania reached the Baltic.

Feb. 27 U.S. VII Corps forces advanced rapidly towards Cologne but ran into determined resistance outside the city.

■ Canadian divisions broke through to the Hochwald Forest and reached Grieth on the Rhine.

■ Stricter rationing was ordered for German civilians.

■ Russia established a pro-Soviet government in Rumania.

■ Lebanon declared war on Germany and Japan.

Feb. 28 Remnants of the Japanese force in Manila were contained in two government buildings. U.S. Army units went ashore at Puerto Princesa on the east coast of Palawan Island in the Philippines. The landing was the beginning of operations in the southern Philippines, with the Eighth Army under Lieutenant General Robert L. Eichelberger directed to take the area and cut off the Japanese in the East Indies.

■ Russian troops captured the transport centers of Neustettin (Szczecinek) and Prechlau in Pomerania.

■ Elements of the U.S. Ninth Army advanced to within 16 miles of Cologne.

ICE CREAM GOES TO WAR

The most unusual ship of the war was an American ice cream barge. Constructed of concrete, the ship's only responsibility was to produce ice cream for U.S. sailors in the South Pacific. The crew pumped out 5,100 gallons of ice cream every hour.

■ British civilian air raid casualties for the month were 483 killed and 1,152 wounded.

March The central Pacific was effectively cleared of all Japanese submarines. Only a few reconnaissance patrols were undertaken by the Japanese, but Allied shipping was free from any serious underwater threat until the end of the war. The only major submarine base outside Japan's home waters now was Penang. Both Japanese and German submarines continued operations out of the Malayan base, the German U-boats even after Germany's surrender.

March 1 U.S. Ninth Army and First Canadian Army troops continued their swift pursuit through Germany and Holland, capturing 20 towns and villages. The Panzer Lehr Division was forced out of Mönchengladbach. Thus far in the three weeks of the offensive toward the Rhine, 66,000 Germans had been taken prisoner.

■ Orders were issued that no German staff officer could cross to the east bank of the Rhine.

■ A limited Allied offensive in Italy was postponed because of extremely bad weather.

■ The Ryukyu Islands were attacked by U.S. ships and planes.

■ Saudi Arabia declared war on Germany and Japan. Iran declared war on Japan.

March 2 U.S. 10th Armored Division forces occupied Trier. Allied units had now reached the Rhine north and south of Düsseldorf.

■ Soviet forces cut the road between Stettin (Szczecin) and Danzig, isolating East Pomerania and West Prussia.

■ MacArthur returned to Corregidor shortly after all Japanese resistance ended. The Japanese lost about 5,200 men defending the island. Total U.S. casualties were more than 1,000.

■ Two-thirds of Iwo Jima was now in Marine hands. The first of the island's airfields was opened to U.S. transports.

March 3 Manila was declared totally secure.

■ German 15-year-olds were ordered to front-line duty.

■ Allied prisoners at the Fobach POW camp in northeast France were liberated by advancing American troops.

■ German forces remaining on the west bank of the Rhine began to withdraw.

■ Finland declared war on Germany.

March 4 The Ninth U.S. and Canadian First

Allied strategic bombing proved decisive only when the raids were directed against the German synthetic fuels industry, such as this one against the hydrogenation plant at Magdeburg.

armies hooked up in the area of Geldern, in Germany.

■ U.S. First Army troops advanced toward Cologne after crossing the Erft River.

■ The 2nd and 3rd Canadian divisions cleared the Hochwald and Balberger forests.

■ The U.S. 10th Mountain Division made broad advances in Italy.

■ The 17th Indian Division captured Meiktila in Burma, cutting the communications of the Japanese in central Burma and opening a large-scale battle.

■ German bombers, for the first time in seven months, attacked Britain.

■ Synthetic oil facilities in Hamburg and Gelsenkirchen were pounded by 2,000 Allied bombers.

March 5 U.S. troops reached Cologne, which was largely in ruins.

■ German demolition teams began destroying those bridges left standing over the Rhine.

■ East Anglia in England was bombed by 12 Luftwaffe planes.

March 6 U.S. Ninth Army forces completed clearing the area from the Roer to the Rhine rivers.

■ Cologne was largely cleared of German troops.

■ German forces counterattacked around Lake Balaton in Hungary.

■ U.S. Air Force fighters began operating out of Iwo Jima.

■ Allied units crossed the Irrawaddy 30 miles from Mandalay.

March 7 The Rhine River was crossed at Remagen by the U.S. 9th Armored Division. The historic crossing of the final natural barrier to the German heartland came when the Ludendorff rail bridge was found intact. The 9th and 78th divisions were quickly moved into position to exploit the major breakthrough. German artillery failed to destroy the bridge as U.S. troops and equipment poured over the Rhine.

■ All German resistance north of the Moselle River began collapsing.

■ The Jewish Brigade entered action in Italy, crossing the Montone River in its first encounter.

■ Japanese 7th Division troops counterattacked in an effort to recapture Meiktila in Burma. The 17th Indian Division was trapped as the Japanese captured Taungtha. Lashio fell to the Chinese 37th Division.

■ The Allies declared Goebbels and Ribbentrop to be war criminals.

March 8 U.S. troops pushed into Bonn.

■ British and Canadian units reached the Rhine at Xanten.

■ Remnants of two German army corps retreated across the Rhine, giving the Allies full control of the area west of the river.

■ Thirty thousand Germans surrendered in the former Polish Corridor.

The bridge at Remagen, captured by the U.S. 9th Armored Division, was the rail span over the Rhine which opened the Allied drive into the German heartland.

■ Secret talks began between Allen Dulles, OSS (Office of Strategic Services) intelligence chief in Bern, and Karl Wolff, SS commander in northern Italy, on ending the war in Italy. Field Marshal Kesselring was willing to stop the fighting if the forces under his command could be repatriated and fight with the Allies in Germany against Russia. Stalin, when he learned of the talks, accused Britain and the U.S. of duplicity.

■ Hitler decreed: "Anyone captured without being wounded or without having fought to the limit of his powers has forfeited his honor. He is expelled from the fellowship of decent and brave soldiers. His dependents will be held responsible."

March 9 The main body of the U.S. Third Army reached the Rhine.

■ Japanese troops began attacking French garrisons in Indochina and removing all vestiges of Vichy rule. (The Japanese feared Allied amphibious operations involving Free French troops and assumed the French garrisons around Hanoi and Haiphong would join the fight against the occupiers.)

■ Units of the 19th Indian Division broke into Mandalay which was bitterly defended by the Japanese. (The fighting continued inside the city for nearly two weeks.)

■ The 3rd Marine Division reached the northern coast of Iwo Jima, splitting the Japanese defenders.

■ B-29s firebombed Japanese cities, hitting Tokyo hardest. More than 83,000 were killed and 40,000 wounded in the Japanese capital. It was one of the most destructive air attacks in history. About 16 square miles of Tokyo were obliterated. A total of 279 Superforts hit the city from altitudes of 7,000 feet.

THE DEADLIEST AIR RAID IN THE WAR AGAINST JAPAN

Tokyo—not Hiroshima or Nagasaki—was the target of the deadliest air raid of the Pacific war. Incendiary bombs were the strike weapons.

On the night of March 9–10, 1945, waves of American B-29s (a total of 279) delivered unequaled destruction of a population center—Tokyo. The Superforts dropped 1,665 tons of delay-fuzed napalm-filled bombs which on impact spewed adhering fire as far as a hundred feet.

In only 30 minutes the incendiaries created an inferno which killed 83,793 Japanese. The actual causes of death were direct incineration, suffocation, or scalding, primarily of those forced into boiling canals and rivers. Another 41,000 victims were injured. More than a million people lost their lives in the 1944–1945 Allied air attacks as 15.8 square miles of central Tokyo were completely destroyed.

Japanese 1945 Air Raid Deaths

Tokyo, March 9–10
    incendiary raid   83,793 deaths
Hiroshima, Aug. 6
    atomic bomb attack   70,000 deaths
Nagasaki, Aug. 8
    atomic bomb attack   20,000 deaths

March 10 The U.S. First and Second armies linked up at the Rhine, trapping large numbers of Germans west of the river.

■ Rundstedt was relieved as German commander in chief, west, and replaced by Kesselring.

■ Transylvania was restored to Rumania by the Soviet Union.

■ In another fire raid on Tokyo, 170 B-29s destroyed a square mile of the city and 27,970 buildings. Premier Koiso expressed sympathy to the Japanese people for their suffering at the hands of the "most cruel and barbaric" Americans.

■ U.S. 41st Division forces landed at Zamboanga, at the southwest tip of Mindanao in the Philippines. The operation was designed to deny the Japanese passage from the Sulu to the Celebes Sea. The U.S. units occupied Zamboanga city and two airfields in the initial day's advances.

March 11 Allied forces now controlled the west bank of the Rhine from Nijmegen in the Netherlands to Koblenz, where it meets the Moselle.

■ U.S. 78th Division units moved to cut the Autobahn between Cologne and Frankfurt but were slowed by fierce resistance. Positions on the east bank of the Rhine were extended and strengthened. U.S. Navy landing craft went into operation at Remagen and ferried troops and supplies over the Rhine for the rest of the month.

■ In a Berlin speech commemorating Heroes' Day, Hitler urged Germans to fight on: "We know what the fate of Germany would be otherwise. Our enemies, drunk with victory, have made it clearly known: extermination of the German nation."

■ Red Army forces began attacking Danzig and Gdynia, both of which were encircled.

■ Dortmund was struck by 5,000 tons of RAF bombs.

■ Emperor Bao Dai proclaimed Vietnam's independence from the French, but the Japanese remained in firm control.

March 12 Russian troops captured Küstrin, a German strongpoint on the eastern approaches to Berlin.

■ The U.S. VIII Corps completed mopping up operations west of the Rhine.

■ The RAF "earthquake" bomb was dropped for the first time. The 10-ton weapon was used to knock out the Bielefeld viaduct.

March 13 A Japanese force was sealed inside Mandalay.

■ Congress voted 354 to 28 to extend the Lend-Lease act for one more year, but with the restric-

Searchlights punctuate Tokyo's skies, presenting this view to the bomber leading a nighttime raid on the Japanese capital.

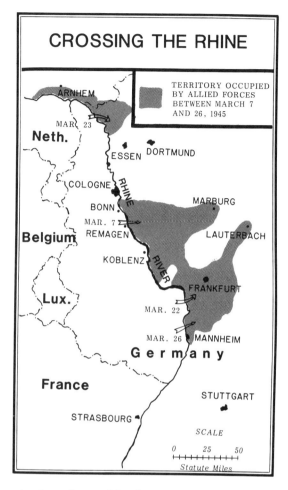

CROSSING THE RHINE

TERRITORY OCCUPIED BY ALLIED FORCES BETWEEN MARCH 7 AND 26, 1945

ARNHEM
MAR. 23
Neth.
ESSEN DORTMUND
COLOGNE
RHINE
BONN
MARBURG
MAR. 7
REMAGEN
Belgium
LAUTERBACH
KOBLENZ
RIVER
Lux.
FRANKFURT
MAR. 22
MAR. 26 MANNHEIM
G e r m a n y
France
STUTTGART
STRASBOURG
SCALE
0 25 50
Statute Miles

The crossing of the Rhine at Remagen opened the way for Allied forces to pour into the heartland of Germany.

March 14–15 U.S. bombers raided Osaka, inflicting 13,000 casualties.

March 15 The U.S. Seventh Army began an offensive to clear the Saar-Palatinate triangle, within the Rhine, Moselle, and Lauter-Saar rivers.

■ Russian troops broke through to the Baltic southwest of Königsberg.

■ The isolated 17th Indian Division at Meiktila continued to hold out as other Fourteenth Army units fought to clear the road.

March 16 The British Foreign Office confirmed there had been German peace feelers through its legation in Stockholm.

■ Units of the U.S. 87th Division began attacks to cross the Moselle near Winningen and Kolberg and reached the outskirts of Koblenz. To the south tanks of the U.S. 4th Armored Division pierced 32 miles to the Nahe River and captured two bridges south of Bad Kreuznach. All resistance south of the Moselle now collapsed.

■ Soviet forces launched an offensive to take Vienna from bases in Hungary.

■ Iwo Jima was declared secure.

March 16–17 Kobe was bombed by B-52s, resulting in 15,000 casualties.

March 17 The U.S. 87th Division entered Koblenz.

■ Eisenhower called on civilians in Frankfurt and Mannheim to evacuate the cities.

■ The Ludendorff bridge at Remagen finally collapsed, but Allied forces were already firmly entrenched east of the Rhine. U.S. engineers had by now been able to construct bridges rapidly, completing one span in 10 hours and 11 minutes under battlefield conditions.

■ Japanese forces on Iwo Jima were reduced to a pocket less than one-half square mile in size.

■ The 2nd British Division captured Ava on the Irrawaddy south of Mandalay.

March 18 A U.S. regiment landed on Panay in the Philippines and pushed toward Iloilo.

■ The port of Kolberg (Kolobrzeg) was taken by the Russians, ending all German pockets on the

tion it not be used for "postwar relief, rehabilitation or reconstruction."

March 14 U.S. 11th Armored and 90th Infantry Division units crossed the Moselle River southwest of Koblenz. First Army troops advanced to within two miles of the Autobahn linking Frankfurt and the Ruhr.

■ A total of 372 Luftwaffe planes attacked the Rhine River bridges during the past week. Allied antiaircraft shot down 80.

■ Adolf Eichmann declared he could go to his grave happy knowing he had helped kill six million Jews.

■ Only Fort Dufferin in Mandalay remained in Japanese hands.

■ A few Japanese pockets remained on Iwo Jima as U.S. Marines began mop-up operations.

Baltic between the Polish Corridor and the mouth of the Oder River.

■ Massive air attacks were launched against Berlin and Frankfurt. More than 1,000 people were killed in Frankfurt. (The city suffered 5,559 dead as a result of Allied air raids during the war.) The attack on Berlin was the heaviest launched by the U.S. Eighth Air Force, involving 1,250 bombers. They were attacked in force by German jets for the first time. The ME-262s and other interceptors, plus heavy antiaircraft fire, accounted for the loss of 24 bombers and 5 fighters. Another 600 planes were damaged.

■ All Japanese schools were ordered closed for one year beginning April 1.

March 19 Hitler ordered the destruction of industrial, communications, and transportation facilities threatened by Allied capture, the so-called "Nero Decree." U.S. 70th Division units began crossing the Saar River near Saarbrücken.

■ Germany canceled all army leaves, ordered the registration of all refugees, and commanded civilians to inform the police of all army and Labor Corps deserters.

■ Soviet troops recaptured all Hungarian territory lost to the Germans since their counterattack was launched two weeks before.

■ U.S. Navy units attacked the Kobe-Kure area of Japan.

■ Lieutenant Commander Joseph T. O'Callahan won the Congressional Medal of Honor for heroism aboard the carrier *Franklin* when it was attacked by kamikazes off Kobe, Japan. He was the first naval chaplain ever to be so honored. A total of 772 men aboard *Franklin* were killed. The ship was severely crippled but it was able to make the 12,000-mile voyage to the Brooklyn Navy Yard for repairs.

■ Japanese forces on Panay began withdrawing to the mountains.

■ The last surviving ship of a 21-vessel Japanese convoy was sunk off Singapore. The tanker *Sarawak Maru* ended up like the others, picked off one by one over a ten-week period as the convoy attempted to bring supplies from Japan to forces in southeast Asia. Some were sunk in daylight attacks by carrier planes and in nighttime attacks by submarines in the China seas; others were hit by mines strewn along their path in the Singapore Strait; eventually all were lost, testament to the effectiveness of the Allied blockade.

March 20 Nagoya was hit by B-29 incendiaries.

■ Japanese forces were found to have withdrawn from Fort Dufferin in Mandalay, leaving the Burmese city totally under Allied control. This marked the consummation of Slim's victory over General Kimura's Burma Area Army, which now retreated towards Rangoon with losses of up to a third of its strength.

■ Iloilo was taken by units of the U.S. 40th Division.

■ The U.S. 70th Division captured Saarbrücken.

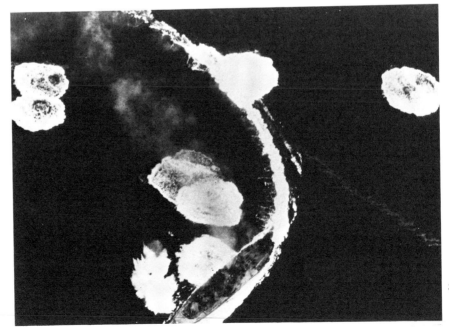

A Japanese battleship takes evasive action while under attack from a U.S. carrier-based aircraft in Kure Bay, Japan.

■ Hitler made his last public appearance, decorating children who had distinguished themselves in combat.

THE GERMAN KAMIKAZES

In March 1945 a request went out to Luftwaffe pilots to volunteer for *Sonderkommando* units. They were asked to fly virtual suicide missions against Allied bombers. About 300 men joined. They were given a special 10-day training course at the Stendal air base near Magdeburg. The pilots were instructed in fighter-ramming techniques (coming out of the sun, firing throughout, and a final ramming dive aimed at a point just forward of the bomber's tail), but the main effort was psychological motivation through lectures and films. Unlike the Japanese, they were given a chance to bail out, if possible. About 210 of the pilots were assigned to four groups known as *Sonderkommando Elbe* in units names for winged attackers like *Falken* (falcon) or *Raubvogel* (bird of prey). The remaining 90 were sent to Prague. The *Elbe* pilots went into action on April 7, with patriotic music and words of exhortation fed into their headsets (radio transmitters were removed so the pilots could not talk to each other or their bases). It is not clear how many were killed, but 169 German fighters were downed that day by U.S. Eighth Air Force aircraft. Twenty-two out of 1,300 bombers were lost.

March 21–24 In a major effort to draw off German planes from the Rhine area, U.S. and RAF planes attacked Berlin and other targets. During this period, Allied aircraft from Britain, France, and Italy flew 42,000 sorties.

March 21 Japanese forces opened their drive to take the Laohokow air base in China.

■ Japanese piloted bombs made their first known appearance of the war while futilely attempting to attack the U.S. naval fast carrier task force whose planes were striking targets on Honshu and Kyushu.

■ The 2nd British Division opened the road to Mandalay from Ava.

■ A flight of 18 RAF Mosquitos bombed the Gestapo headquarters building in Copenhagen. While the building was hit (35 were killed, including 9 Danish prisoners) greater damage was done to a nearby Catholic grade school, killing 86 children and 17 adults.

■ Churchill told Britons food supplies were short in Britain because of the pressing need to feed liberated parts of the continent.

March 22 U.S. 90th Division forces cleared Mainz. Other U.S. units achieved total surprise in establishing a late night crossing of the Rhine at Oppenheim, south of Mainz.

■ U.S. aircraft completed a week-long campaign in support of Allied ground forces in which bombers flew 21,692 missions throughout Europe.

■ Danzig and Gdynia came under Russian siege. Heavy fighting developed between Lake Balaton and the Danube in Hungary. Other Red Army units began an offensive directed at Vienna and Bratislava.

■ During the last five days U.S. Naval Task Force 58 accounted for 528 Japanese aircraft in battles around Okinawa and the home islands.

March 23 U.S. First Army troops broke out of the Remagen bridgehead and advanced to the Sieg River.

■ British and Canadian troops began assaulting German positions on the Rhine north of the Ruhr. Wesel came under attack after the river was crossed by the British 1st Commando Brigade. U.S. units to the south continued breaching the Rhine fortifications on a broad front. The German First Parachute Army could offer only slight opposition to the advancing Allies.

■ A carrier task force of the British Pacific Fleet joined the U.S. in operations against the Japanese islands.

■ Russian units cut through to the Gulf of Danzig, cutting a wedge between the ports of Gdynia and Danzig.

■ De Gaulle announced that Indochina would be given a limited form of self-government after the war. He added, however, that Vietnam, Cambodia, and Laos would remain within the French Union.

March 24 Russian troops southwest of Budapest advanced 44 miles and occupied large numbers of towns and villages.

■ The Japanese pocket on Iwo Jima was reduced to 50 square yards.

■ British 6th and U.S. 17th Airborne Division paratroopers were dropped north and northeast of Wesel. They soon made contact with British infantry units advancing from the west. It was the largest airborne operation of the war, involving 5,051 aircraft and 40,000 men.

March 25 U.S. Third Army units began their attack across the Rhine, after a preliminary bombardment by 1,250 guns. The 6th Armored Division broke through and started driving toward Frankfurt along the Autobahn. The Remagen bridgehead was expanded to a 30-mile-long front, 10 miles deep. American forces moved into Darmstadt. All organized resistance west of the Rhine had ended.

■ All installations at the Laohokow air base in China were blown up before U.S. Fourteenth Air Force personnel withdrew. This was the last of the American air bases to fall to the Japanese.

March 26 The U.S. Seventh Army crossed the Rhine near Worms and made contact with the Third Army which had reached the Main near Offenbach. The Rhine-Main airport was captured and Frankfurt was penetrated.

■ Red Army units made substantial advances through Hungary and Czechoslovakia.

■ The U.S. Americal Division landed on Cebu in the Philippines, to the west of Cebu City.

■ A final attack was made by the Japanese on Iwo Jima. About 200 of the trapped troops staged a suicidal assault from their tiny pocket. At least 196 were killed.

March 27 The U.S. Third and First armies linked up near the Lahn River. About 20 towns were taken in the advance which carried the Allies to within 200 miles of Berlin. British XVII Corps forces advanced five miles through the Wesel Forest.

■ House-to-house fighting took place in Danzig and Gdynia.

■ Russian troops were 60 miles from Vienna.

■ Sixteen prominent anti-communist Poles, including the deputy premier of the government-in-exile, were invited to a conference with Russian officials on political matters. When they arrived, all were arrested. The Poles were sent to Moscow and imprisoned, eliminating the last vestiges of anti-communist leadership remaining within Poland.

■ Cebu City fell to the Americal Division.

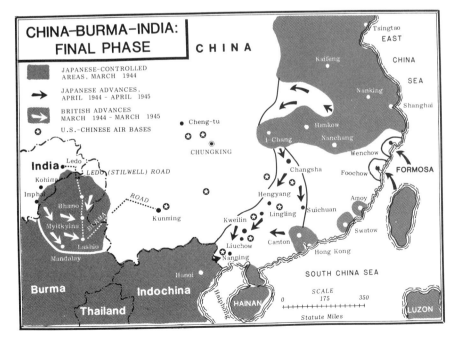

The Allied effort to clear the Burma Road to China was matched by Japan's moves to capture U.S. air bases which threatened the Japanese home islands.

■ B-29s began night missions to mine the waters around Japan, eventually establishing a total blockade. (More than 1,000 tons of mines were dropped into Shimonoseki Strait alone within the next four days.)

■ The last V-2 rocket bomb fell on Britain. In all, the 1,115 V-2s launched against England killed 2,855 people and seriously injured 6,268.

■ Argentina, under U.S. pressure, declared war on Germany and Japan.

March 28 Hitler dismissed Guderian as chief of the Army General Staff after a violent quarrel in the Reich Chancellery.

■ Russian units reached the Austrian border. Gdynia was occupied in the north.

■ British Second Army forces began an offensive to reach the Elbe. U.S. troops began occupying Frankfurt. Mannheim's burgomaster sought to surrender the city. The American 4th Armored Division found a bridge over the Main intact. First Army units reached Marburg and Giessen, advancing up to 40 miles a day.

■ Eisenhower confirmed plans for the final campaign to knock Germany out of the war, choosing Leipzig instead of Berlin as the ultimate objective. Russia was to occupy the German capital. The decision had wide-ranging political implications. Churchill futilely tried to change the thrust of the final Allied push, continuing to express his concern over Russian political gains after their military conquests.

■ Soldiers of the Burma National Army revolted against the Japanese in central and southern Burma and joined forces with the Allies.

March 29 U.S. 5th Division forces completed the capture of Frankfurt. Mannheim was abandoned by the Germans.

■ French forces crossed the Rhine near Germersheim.

■ U.S. 3rd Armored Division units pursued disorganized German forces 50 miles northward toward Paderborn.

■ Fighting continued in the eastern section of Danzig.

■ The Kerama Islands in the Ryukyus were secured by the U.S. 77th Division, clearing the approaches to projected landing beaches on Okinawa.

■ Goebbels said, "The Germans must stay on their feet no matter how, just stay on their feet, and then the moral and historical superiority of the German people can manifest itself."

March 30 The Russian Third Ukrainian Front crossed into Austria from Hungary near Köszeg. Danzig fell. Bulgarian and Soviet units advanced to the Drava River boundary between Hungary and Yugoslavia. The capital of Slovakia, Bratislava, was threatened as the Russian Second Ukrainian Front pressed westward across the Hron and Nitra rivers.

■ The British 6th Airborne and 11th Armored divisions reached the Ems River.

Members of the Jewish Brigade receive matzos at a Passover service on the Italian front.

U.S. infantrymen take cover behind a sea wall in the face of Japanese fire on Zamami Shima in the Ryukyus campaign.

■ Tanks of the U.S. 6th Armored Division broke through German defenses north of Frankfurt and dashed toward Kassel. Heidelberg fell.

■ U.S. Air Force bombers sank ten German submarines in raids on naval facilities in the Bremen-Hamburg area.

March 31 German troops began withdrawing from the Netherlands.

■ U.S. forces discovered 350 suicide boats in the Kerama Islands, which had been positioned for attacks on Allied shipping during the expected invasion of Okinawa.

■ British civilian air raid casualties for March were 792 killed and 1,426 injured.

April 1 In what was to become the last—and the bloodiest—major amphibious operation of the Pacific war, the U.S. Tenth Army invaded the island of Okinawa, 360 miles south of Japan. Two Army and two Marine divisions, a force of about 60,000 men, came ashore after intensive air and naval bombardment. At first there was little Japanese opposition, except for the kamikaze attacks on the invasion fleet. Kadena airfield was taken at once, and the beachheads were firmly established, but the defenses stiffened to a level probably unmatched in the Pacific war.

■ French II Corps units established contact with the U.S. Seventh Army south of Heidelberg after crossing the Rhine near Germersheim.

■ The Ruhr was completely encircled as the U.S.

U.S. Navy rocket-launching ships hit invasion beaches during the Okinawa invasion.

First and Ninth armies linked up at Lippstadt, 20 miles west of Paderborn, trapping German Army Group B and two corps of Army Group H. It was one of the largest envelopments in history, with 325,000 Germans eventually captured. In numbers, it was a loss greater than Stalingrad.

■ Soviet forces advanced to within 13 miles of Bratislava.

■ *Radio Werwolf* began broadcasting. The radio station was created by Goebbels to rally Germans to suicidal resistance. Its repeated theme was *besser tot als rot* ("better dead than red").

April 2 Resistance on Okinawa remained light.

■ The 49th Canadian Division advanced toward Arnhem from its Nijmegen bridgehead. U.S. troops pushed into Münster. German troops offered strong opposition around Kassel. Martin Bormann issued a proclamation, which called for "victory or death."

■ British Royal Marines and Commandos

launched an offensive between the Comacchio lagoon and the Adriatic Sea.

■ Russian forces crashed through to within 50 miles of Berlin, but swifter progress was made toward Vienna.

April 3 The British Guards Armored Division reached the Dortmund-Ems Canal near Lingen. Münster was completely secured by the U.S. 17th Airborne Division. A hard-fought battle ended when the Germans at Aschaffenburg surrendered.

■ Russian troops occupied the Austrian manufacturing center of Wiener Neustadt.

April 4 Hungary was cleared of all German troops, who retreated into Yugoslavia. Bratislava in Slovakia fell. Red Army troops moved westward along the Polish-Czech border toward the Moravian gap.

■ The U.S. Ninth Army reached the Weser River but found the bridges destroyed. Patton's tanks were within 70 miles of Leipzig. French First Army units occupied Karlsruhe. Troops of the U.S. 90th Division occupied Merkers and found vast hoards of gold and art treasures buried by the Nazis in a salt mine.

■ The U.S. 4th Armored Division liberated the concentration camp outside Ohrdruf, the first of the infamous prisons reached by the Allies from the west. General Patton (who vomited on visiting the site) rounded up townspeople to witness the horrors which had been perpetrated in their immediate area. Many victims were still lying where they had been shot by the retreating Nazis. Ohrdruf's burgomaster and his wife were among those brought to the camp by Patton. When they returned home, they hanged themselves.

■ For the first time since landing, U.S. forces on Okinawa encountered significant Japanese resistance.

April 5 Moscow denounced the Russian-Japanese neutrality pact which had been signed on April 13, 1941, and was to run for five years.

■ The Japanese cabinet resigned because of the Soviet action. Admiral Kantaro Suzuki replaced General Kuniaki Koiso as premier.

■ In an unmistakable order for mass suicide, the

U.S. Tenth Army soldiers move inland after landing on Okinawa.

The Japanese super battle-ship Yamato *sinks in the East China Sea off the coast of Kyushu, destroyed by U.S. aircraft while on a suicide mission.*

Japanese Imperial Navy commanded its remaining men-of-war to engage the Americans in a final banzai: "Second Fleet is to charge the enemy anchorage of Kadena off Okinawa Island at daybreak of 8 April. Fuel for only a one-way passage will be supplied."
■ A bridgehead across the Weser was established by the U.S. 2nd Armored Division. The U.S. First Army cleared a broad area within the Ruhr pocket. Units of the U.S. 6th Armored Division occupied Mulhouse. French units began attacking German fortified positions at the north end of the Black Forest.
■ *Schwarze Korps*, official organ of the Gestapo, admitted that Germany was "only days or perhaps weeks from absolute collapse."
April 6 The first of the concentrated kamikaze attacks off Okinawa sank two U.S. destroyers, *Bush* and *Calhoun*, and four auxiliaries. Only 24 of the 355 suicide planes from Kyushu actually hit targets, but they caused great destruction. The furious fighting also resulted in many U.S. ships hitting each other. A battleship (*North Carolina*), a cruiser (*Pasadena*), two transports, a sub-chaser, a cargo ship, and two LST's were all damaged by friendly fire.
■ U.S. 84th and 2nd Armored Division forces broke across the Weser River near Minden. The

U.S. XVIII Airborne Corps began a major offensive across the Sieg River.
■ The German POW camp at Hammelburg was liberated, but all the prisoners except the seriously wounded had been evacuated.
■ The Germans moved 15,000 Jewish prisoners out of Buchenwald concentration camp.
■ Red Army forces advanced to the suburbs of Vienna.
■ Yugoslav Partisans gained control of Sarajevo.
■ The British 56th Division moved in force across the Reno River in Italy.
April 7 Russian units crossed the Danube and smashed into Vienna. Street fighting commenced.
■ Göttingen was taken by U.S. troops.
■ Japanese air and naval units suffered a disastrous setback in the battle of the East China Sea. Task Force 58 planes intercepted the Japanese Second Fleet heading for Okinawa. The 72,200-ton battleship *Yamato* was subjected to three hours of bombing and torpedo attacks and finally capsized with only 269 survivors from the 3,292-man crew. It was the largest single loss involving a warship in history. Other casualties of the battle included the cruiser *Yahagi*, 4 destroyers, and 54 aircraft. Ten U.S. planes were downed, of the 900 which were involved in the attacks.

JAPAN'S GIANT SHIPS

Japan had the biggest and most powerful warships of the war. In 1937 the Imperial Navy ordered two giant battleships, the *Yamato* and the *Musashi*, in total violation of the Washington and London naval treaties because of their size and armament. Each ship was 862 feet long. Carrying crews up to 2,500 men strong, the ships had a range of 7,200 miles and could hit a top speed of 27 knots.

Above all, the guns on the *Yamato* and the *Musashi* made the ships unique. They possessed 18.1 inch guns. Nothing afloat was comparably equipped. The ships had nine of the giant guns apiece, each of which could hurl a shell 35 miles and pierce 16 inches of steel plate. A single hit was deemed sufficient to knock out a carrier, and it was assumed one 18.1 inch shell could kill a concentrated battalion of ground soldiers.

For all this, the ships were flops. They were already obsolete when commissioned. Of the two others in the class, one was converted to a carrier (*Shinano*) after the Battle of Midway. Construction of the other (No. 111) was simply halted.

The *Yamato*'s record illustrates the point. Although it saw considerable action (the Battles of Midway, Philippine Sea, and Leyte Gulf), it is believed to have sunk only one ship, the destroyer *Hoel* in the Battle of Samar. But in this action, the *Yamato*'s smaller, conventional guns provided the kill, not the 18.1 inchers. While it carried 1,080 giant shells, it fired only 81 and probably none of them hit anything. And this was the *only* time the *Yamato* ever fired the big guns. U.S. aircraft finally sank the *Yamato* on April 7, 1945.

The *Musashi*'s record was even less impressive, having been sunk in the 1944 Battle of Leyte Gulf. Their contribution to the Japanese war effort was practically nil.

- Iwo Jima-based U.S. aircraft made their first attacks on Japan. Fighters began arriving on Okinawa.
- British Fourteenth Army forces isolated a large Japanese force between Mandalay and Meiktila.

April 8 Russian troops began an all-out assault on Königsberg in East Prussia. Red Army units started driving toward Linz and Graz in Austria.

- The British Guards Division broke for Bremen after overwhelming German defenders east of Lingen. U.S. 42nd Division forces reached the outskirts of Schweinfurt.

April 9 British bombers sank the German cruisers *Admiral Scheer* and *Hipper* at Kiel.

- The Allied Fifteenth Army Group opened its final offensive in Italy, smashing across the Senio River. In perhaps the broadest employment of an integrated international force in history, troops from Britain, the U.S., France, New Zealand, South Africa, Poland, India, Senegal, Brazil, Italy, Greece, Morocco, Algeria, plus the Jewish Brigade were involved in the final phase of the Italian campaign.
- The fortress at Königsberg fell to the Third White Russian Front, virtually ending all German resistance in East Prussia. The fight for the city left 42,000 Germans dead. Another 92,000 were captured.
- A U.S. Liberty Ship loaded with aerial bombs exploded in Bari, Italy. The blast and resulting fire killed 360 people and injured 1,730.
- The island of Jolo in the Sulu Sea was occupied by U.S. forces.
- British Pacific Fleet planes attacked Japanese airfields on Formosa which were used to launch raids on U.S. ships off Okinawa.

April 10 Thirty of 50 German Me-262 jet fighters were shot down by U.S. bombers and their P-51 escorts in the Berlin area. The attacking force of 1,232 B-17s and B-24s was able to beat off the largest jet effort of the war. Only ten of the bombers were lost.

- Hannover in Lower Saxony was taken by the U.S. 84th Division while the 5th Armored Division opened the final assault toward the Elbe River. Former Chancellor Papen was captured by U.S. troops in the Ruhr.
- British Royal Marines swept around the Senio River lines by assault boats, threatening the German rear defenses in Italy.
- Indian and British troops took Pyawbwe, a key point on the Mandalay–Rangoon rail line in Burma.
- Churchill announced that total Commonwealth

By the time Germany surrendered, its cities had been laid waste.

DESTRUCTION OF GERMANY

PERCENTAGE OF CITIES DESTROYED
BY ALLIED AIR ATTACKS

KIEL 69%
ROSTOCK 32%
LÜBECK 30%
BREMERHAVEN 79%
HAMBURG 75%
EMDEN 56%
BREMEN 60%
STETTIN 53%
HANOVER 60%
BERLIN 33%
MÜNSTER 65%
BRUNSWICK 47%
MAGDEBURG 44%
AACHEN 59%
(SEE BOX INSET)
LEIPZIG 20%
KASSEL 69%
DRESDEN 59%
BONN 83%
CHEMNITZ 41%
FRANKFURT 52%
KOBLENZ 58%
SCHWEINFURT 43%
MAINZ 61%
NÜRNBERG 51%
SAARBRÜCKEN 48%
STUTTGART 46%
KARLSRUHE 32%
ULM 28%
FREIBURG 37%
MUNICH 42%

DORTMUND 54%
DUISBURG 48%
BOCHUM 83%
ESSEN 50%
HAGEN 67%
DÜSSELDORF 64%
MÖNCHENGLADBACH 54%
COLOGNE 61%

and Empire casualties thus far were 1,126,802 military and 34,161 merchant marine. In addition, British civilian casualties were 144,542.

■ Lieutenant General Sosaku Suzuki, commander of the Thirty-fifth Army, was lost at sea during the withdrawal of Japanese forces from Cebu.

April 11 Allied forces occupied Coburg. Survivors of the Buchenwald concentration camp were liberated: 5,000 French, 3,500 Poles and Polish Jews, 2,200 Germans, 2,000 Russians, 2,000 Czechs, 2,000 Ukrainians, 600 Yugoslavs, 400 Dutch, 500 Austrians, 200 Italians, 200 Spaniards, and 300 of other nationalities. The POW camp at Bad Sulza was overrun.

■ American Seventh Army forces drove into Bavaria.

■ U.S. Ninth Army units reached the Elbe near Magdeburg. More than 300,000 Germans were taken prisoner during the past two weeks of fighting.

■ The U.S. 92nd Division captured Carrara in Italy.

■ Spain broke diplomatic relations with Japan.

■ U.S. 38th Division forces counted 5,500 Japanese dead in the fighting to clear the area west of Clark Field in the Philippines.

■ Reserve elements of the Americal Division landed on Bohol Island in the Philippines.

■ Japanese suicide planes continued to strike U.S. naval ships off Okinawa, disabling the carrier *Enterprise* and damaging the battleship *Missouri*.

■ The 5th Indian Division drove south from Pyawbwe, spearheading Slim's drive to capture Rangoon, now only 300 miles away, before the arrival of the monsoon rains which were expected to begin in a month.

April 12 Franklin Delano Roosevelt, president of the U.S. longer than anyone, died of a massive stroke at the winter White House in Warm Springs, Georgia. Harry S. Truman became the 33rd president.

■ U.S. 2nd and 5th Armored Division forces reached the Elbe at Wittenberge, Werben, and

U.S. forces return to Fort Drum in Manila Bay in the reoccupation of the Philippines, April 1945.

■ U.S. Fifth Army units pushed off on an offensive to clear the Po River valley from positions in the Apennines south and southwest of Bologna.

■ The Japanese High Command ordered the expeditionary force in China to pull four divisions back to central and northern China, leading to a withdrawal from the Hunan-Kwangsi railroad which linked the former Allied air bases recently captured by the Japanese.

■ A fierce Japanese counteroffensive was turned back on Okinawa.

April 14–15 A group of Japanese army officers attempted to seize control of the government in Tokyo. Fearing an imminent capitulation to the Allies, the officers won some support from the Imperial Guards Division and occupied part of the palace. There they searched futilely for the emperor's surrender speech which had been recorded. General Takeshi Mori was killed when he refused to give the dissidents control of the army. The uprising was quelled, and its leader, Major Kenji Hatanaka, committed suicide.

Sandau. Units established a small bridgehead on the east side of the river.

■ Canadian I Corps units began attacking Arnhem.

■ A U.S. Fifth Army offensive in Italy was delayed because of unfavorable weather. German positions along the Santerno River collapsed before the British Eighth Army.

■ The U.S. destroyer *Manner L. Abele* was sunk by a Japanese *baka*, or piloted bomb, off Okinawa. The *baka* was a more lethal kamikaze. A total of 151 Japanese planes were downed.

■ Japanese nighttime counterattacks penetrated positions held by the 96th Division on Okinawa, but the American line held. Charges against U.S. positions during the day left 1,594 Japanese dead.

April 13 Russian troops of the Second and the Third Ukrainian fronts completed the capture of Vienna.

■ Taungdwingyi in Burma was taken by the 20th Indian Division.

■ Chinese forces launched a general offensive in Honan and Hupei provinces. The Japanese opened a drive to take Chinchiang.

April 14 The U.S. First and Ninth armies linked up in the Ruhr, splitting the pocket in two. Several high-ranking German generals were captured. Bayreuth was occupied.

FIRST HELICOPTER RESCUE IN HISTORY

Captain James L. Green, United States Army Air Force, was the first person in history to owe his life to a helicopter. As a spotter-liaison pilot in April 1945 operating out of Shinbwiyang airfield in Burma, Green was searching for the crew of a transport forced to parachute into the tortuous Naga Hills while flying a mission over the Hump. At Green's side was a Naga chieftain who was acting as a guide. The light plane ran out of fuel and crash-landed in the high jungle. A search team, called in by radio, reached the crash site a week later, by which time the chieftain was dead and Green was barely alive. To subject the badly injured man to the ordeal of being carried out of the mountains would have meant certain death. A small Sikorsky YR-4 helicopter was available at Shinbwiyang, but the crash site was out of its element. Still, Lieutenant R.F. Murdock decided to try a rescue even if the underpowered craft might have difficulty in climbing to the mountainous levels. He did, barely, and carried Green to safety. Never before had a helicopter been involved in rescue work, but the pattern was set for the years ahead. In general, however, the helicopter was not fully developed during World War II, and it did not come into its own until the Korean conflict.

SOURCE: Lt. Col. Carroll V. Glines, Jr., *Helicopter Rescues.*

April 15 Arnhem was totally occupied by the 49th Canadian Division while the 5th Armored pushed off from there toward the Zuider Zee (Ijsselmeer).

■ The French First Army crossed the Rhine, occupied Kehl and continued clearing the Black Forest. U.S. forces overran the large I.G. Farben chemical plant at Leverkusen.

■ British troops freed 40,000 prisoners at the Belsen concentration camp and found 10,000 unburied dead bodies.

■ Marines of the 6th Division were subjected to intense artillery barrages delivered from Japanese hill positions on the Motobu Peninsula of Okinawa. Heavy casualties were suffered by the Marines in attempting to seize the heights.

April 16 Hitler ordered that "he who gives the order to retreat is to be shot on the spot." Since the first of the month Allied forces on the western front captured 755,573 German troops.

■ In the greatest maritime loss in history, about 6,500 Germans were drowned while being evacuated from Danzig. Their ship, the overloaded 5,230-ton merchantman *Goya*, was torpedoed in the Baltic near Cape Rixhöft (Rozewie) and quickly sank. (A total of 18,000 Germans were lost when the refugee ships in the Baltic were subjected to constant Allied air and naval attack. Sixteen such vessels were sunk between January and May.)

■ General Carl A. Spaatz, commander of U.S. Strategic Air Forces in Europe, announced that all strategic operations had ceased and air units would henceforth merely engage in mopping-up action against Germany.

■ A huge Russian force began its drive for Berlin along the Oder and Neisse rivers, attacking the German Ninth and Fourth Panzer armies.

■ Russian and RAF fighter planes joined together from the east and west for the first time while attacking a train near Dresden.

■ German units began pulling back along a broad front in Italy.

■ The German pocket battleship *Lützow* was sunk by RAF bombers during a daylight attack on Swinemünde (Swinoujscie).

■ Indian troops seized Shwemyo in Burma.

■ Ie Shima, off Okinawa, was invaded by the U.S. 77th Division.

■ Japanese troops began pulling out of Cebu City.

April 17 The U.S. promised the Soviet Union an additional 5,700,000 tons of supplies.

■ Red Army forces began establishing bridgeheads across the Oder and Neisse rivers in their drive for Berlin.

■ The American Seventh Army began closing in on Nürnberg, symbolic center of the Nazi state. U.S. 30th Division units captured most of Magdeburg. German resistance was ferocious in the fighting around Nürnberg. The U.S. VI Corps raced to the Swiss border to block the German escape route from the Black Forest. French troops split the German Nineteenth Army in two by taking Freudenstadt.

■ The U.S. X Corps landed on Mindanao in the Philippines and met little resistance. The force was concentrated at Malabang on Moro Gulf. It was the last major amphibious operation necessary to regain the Philippines.

■ Japanese troops suffered heavy casualties as U.S. Marines finished taking the Motobu Peninsula on Okinawa.

April 18 All resistance in the Ruhr pocket ended with the surrender of 325,000 German troops under the command of Field Marshal Model. Except for the Russian surrender around Kiev in September 1941, this was the single largest capitulation of the war.

■ The Canadian 5th Armored Division reached the Zuider Zee, completing the last offensive action of the Canadian First Army in the war.

■ All road outlets out of Nürnberg were blocked.

■ A patrol of the U.S. 90th Division crossed into Czechoslovakia.

■ British Eighth Army units gained control of the Argenta gap, over the key route to the Po valley.

■ American war correspondent Ernie Pyle was killed by a sniper on Okinawa.

■ U.S. 24th Division troops began their assault on Fort Pikit on Mindanao, a key junction on the road to Kabacan.

EFFECTS OF MASS BOMBING ON GERMANY

Excerpts from the U.S. Strategic Bombing Survey:

• After two-and-a-half years of RAF and U.S. strategic bombing of war production targets, "Germany's military output in aircraft weapons and ammunition was raised more than threefold, in tanks nearly sixfold."

• "As to the effects of bomb damage on the civilian economy, there is no evidence that shortages of civilian goods ever reached a point where the German authorities were forced to transfer resources from war production in order to prevent disintegration on the home front."

• "Their [the German civilian population] morale, their belief in ultimate victory or satisfactory compromise and their confidence in their leaders declined, but they continued to work efficiently as long as the physical means of production remained." [Industrial facilities,

according to the survey, remained sufficient to the very end of the war.]

• "The attack on transportation was the decisive blow that completely disorganized the German economy."

• "Transport proved to be the weakest link in the [German] logistic chain. Its failure was the immediate cause of the breakdown of the supply system and consequently was a decisive factor in the collapse of the German Army."

SOURCE: "The Effect of Strategic Bombing on the German Economy. The Impact of the Allied Air Effort on German Logistics." U.S. Strategic Bombing Survey.

April 19 British Second Army forces began assaulting Bremen. The British 11th Armored Division reached the Elbe. The U.S. XV Corps broke into the walled city within Nürnberg. Leipzig fell to the U.S. 2nd and 69th divisions.

■ On Ie Shima, Japanese resistance was stiff around the town of Ie and the heights which became known as Bloody Ridge.

■ Under tremendous naval and air support, U.S. Army forces launched a general offensive to break Japanese defenses on Okinawa. The heaviest fighting was on Kakazu Ridge.

■ Indian forces occupied Magwe and Myingun on the Irrawaddy in Burma.

April 20 Three U.S. divisions finally cleared Nürnberg. Rothenburg was taken by the Second Polish Army. French troops entered Stuttgart.

■ U.S. Fifth Army columns broke out of the Apennine Mountains and into the Po plain.

Fighting reduced much of Nürnberg, Germany, to rubble by the time U.S. 3rd Infantry Division troops entered the city.

Infantrymen of the U.S. 3rd Division clear snipers from Nürnberg.

■ Japanese in the Mount Popa area of Burma were trapped by British 2nd Division and Indian 268th Brigade forces.

■ Bohol Island in the Philippines was cleared of all Japanese.

April 21 The Russian Eighth Guards Army under General Chuikov penetrated to the suburbs of Berlin. The Germans counterattacked the advancing Red Army but failed to forestall a pincers movement developing around the German capital.

■ American and Polish troops occupied Bologna, an elusive objective for months. French troops took Stuttgart.

■ Field Marshal Model committed suicide.

■ Ie Shima was secured. In six days of fighting on the small island, 4,706 Japanese were killed and 149 captured.

■ Fort Pikit on Mindanao was occupied by U.S. troops after the Japanese withdrew.

■ British Fourteenth Army units advanced to within 200 miles of Rangoon.

April 22 Hitler refused to leave Berlin although its encirclement was imminent. Units of the First White Russian Front continued to advance in the eastern suburbs.

■ The French First Army reached Lake Constance. U.S. Seventh Army forces swept to the Danube. Field Marshal Alexander said German units in northern Italy had "no hope of escaping." Allied planes hammered at the Alpine escape passes.

■ Mindanao's Japanese force was split in two as the U.S. X Corps landed as a blocking force.

■ Palawan was declared secure.

■ Indian troops of the Fourteenth Army recaptured the Yenangyaung oil fields, the largest in Burma. Most Japanese forces were ordered to withdraw from Rangoon and move back to Pegu and Moulmein.

April 23 Hitler stripped Göring of authority because of Göring's apparent assumption of power.

■ Fighting developed in Berlin proper, with the Russians penetrating from the east and south.

■ British troops entered Bremen.

■ The central Philippines campaign ended with Cebu under complete control of the U.S. Eighth Army.

■ Allied bridgeheads were established over the Po River.

April 23–24 SS Chief Himmler offered to surrender to Britain and the U.S. but not the Soviet Union. The offer was made through Count Bernadotte.

FATE OF THE GERMAN GENERALS

A total of 3,363 Germans achieved the rank of general during the war. One of four did not survive, an unusually high mortality rate among officers supposedly directing troop movements from a secure rear echelon. Of the 819 German generals who were no longer alive at the time of the surrender, 352 were killed in action or missing and presumed dead in combat. Another 49 met accidental deaths. Natural deaths claimed 310. A total of 101 committed suicide (including Rommel, who chose suicide over certain execution). After the war, another 57 received death sentences from Allied war crime courts, 25 from German courts.

April 24 Hitler ordered Göring arrested.

■ Elements of the First White Russian and First Ukrainian fronts linked up inside Berlin. Potsdam was occupied.

■ Ulm fell to U.S. 1st Armored Division columns. U.S. Seventh Army units crossed the Danube at Dillingen.

■ U.S. and British forces in Italy, began pouring across the Po River, with the German Gothic line almost totally eliminated.

April 25 U.S. 69th Division and Russian 59th Guards Division patrols made contact on the Elbe near Torgau, the first linkup of ground forces from east and west. Eisenhower ordered Allied forces not to advance beyond the Elbe and Mulde rivers.

■ Berlin was completely encircled by the Russians.

■ RAF planes bombed Berchtesgaden. The last strategic attacks in the European theater were flown against Pilsen, Wangerooge, Kiel, and Munich.

■ The naval base at La Spezia on the Ligurian coast was captured by the Allies.

■ The U.S. Seventh Army crossed the Danube on a broad front.

■ Yugoslav troops attacked Fiume (Rijeka).

■ Germans trapped in the Black Forest made a desperate bid to break out toward the Bavarian Alps.

■ The United Nations Conference on International Organization opened in San Francisco.

■ Japanese units routed the Chinese 58th Division at Wukang.

April 26 Pétain was arrested.

■ U.S. troops were firmly established across the Danube. Bremen was taken by the British Second Army. (Except for a small area at the Ems estuary, all of northeast Holland was cleared of Germans.)

■ Russian units captured Stettin and Brno (in Czechoslovakia).

■ Italian partisans seized control of Genoa and fighting broke out around Milan. Verona, Reggio nell' Emilia, and Parma fell to Allied troops.

■ U.S. troops on Okinawa met furious Japanese resistance on the Maeda escarpment.

April 27 Count Bernadotte informed Himmler the U.S. and Britain would not accept German armistice talks without the Russians.

■ Soviet troops controlled three-fourths of Berlin.

■ U.S. 11th Armored Division units crossed into Czechoslovakia north of Bischofsreut.

■ French troops crossed the border into Italy. Genoa was occupied by the U.S. Fifth Army.

■ Hitler sent what turned out to be his final message to Mussolini: "The struggle for our survival is at its height. Employing great masses and materials, Bolshevism and the armies of Jewry allied themselves to join their malignant forces in Europe in order to precipitate chaos in our continent."

■ De Gaulle refused to turn over control of Stuttgart to U.S. or U.K. troops.

■ A U.S.-Australian force of cruisers and destroyers began a four-day bombardment operation against Tarakan Island, the oil producing facility off the northeast coast of Borneo.

■ U.S. troops occupied Baguio on Luzon. Columns of the 33rd and 37th divisions entered the hill city.

■ The Japanese port of Nagoya was closed to all shipping, the first major facility to cease operations because of the U.S. blockade.

April 28 Benito Mussolini was shot and killed after being caught by Italian partisans as he was attempting to flee Italy. As the Allied forces pressed closer to the area, Mussolini and his mistress, Clara Petacci, headed first for Milan where

Men and women of Nürnberg were forced to bury Nazi concentration camp murder victims after the area was taken by Patton's Third Army.

fruitless discussions took place on a surrender, then for the Swiss border. When the partisans at Dongo found Mussolini he was wearing a German noncommissioned officer's overcoat. A quick execution—from a submachine gun—was followed the next day by the exhibition of their bodies, hung upside down, in the Piazza Loreto in Milan. Toward the end of his megalomaniacal life, Mussolini had said, "I made a mistake and I shall pay for it, if my life can still serve as payment." Hitler learned of Mussolini's death in a Radio Stockholm broadcast.

■ U.S. troops advanced to Venice.

■ American units of the Seventh Army reached the Austrian border near Füssen and occupied Augsburg.

■ The Red Army took 27,000 prisoners around Berlin.

GERMANY'S CIVILIAN LOSSES

It is estimated that 500,000 German civilians and foreign forced-labor workers perished in the Allied air attacks on Germany. At least 1,600,000 civilians were wounded in the raids or through involvement in ground combat clashes. The war left 1,200,000 German widows and 60,000 orphans. In the postwar realignment of the German borders, 12,300,000 Germans were expelled from East Prussia, Silesia, Pomerania, and the Sudetenland.

April 29 Hitler designated Dönitz as his successor and was married to Eva Braun in his Berlin bunker. The Reich Chancellery came under Russian artillery fire.

■ An unconditional surrender was signed at Caserta by German Army Group Southwest commander in Italy, General Vietinghoff. The fighting was to end on May 2. Allied forces reached Genoa and Padua, which had been pre-

viously taken over by partisans. Milan was under partisan control.

■ U.S. Seventh Army units reached Munich.

■ More than 250 RAF aircraft dropped emergency food supplies in the Netherlands on prearranged areas. The German Twenty-fifth Army was still holding out in large pockets of the Netherlands, and the plight of the civilians was becoming desperate. Churchill estimated three million were starving. He had written on the 10th: "We believe that large numbers are dying daily, and the situation must deteriorate rapidly now that communications between Germany and Holland are virtually cut. I fear we may soon be in the presence of a great tragedy." *Reichskommissar* for the Netherlands Seyss-Inquart had agreed to the food relief flights.

■ Heavy losses in the fighting for the Maeda escarpment on Okinawa forced relief of the badly mauled U.S. 96th Division.

April 30 Hitler committed suicide. Dressed in a new Nazi uniform and modestly bemedaled, Hitler took a cyanide capsule while seated on a couch in the Reich Chancellery in Berlin. So ended the "Thousand Year Reich." His new wife,

Eva Braun, also took poison. Their bodies were doused in gasoline and burned. Only the Russians saw their remains, and it is still not known what became of the final evidence of Hitler's death. Goebbels and his wife killed themselves and their six children at the same time. Most of the world rejoiced at the news of Hitler's death, but it was by no means a universal feeling. In neutral Portugal, for example, the government ordered two days of national mourning and flags were flown at half-staff.

■ Marshal Graziani was executed by Italian partisans.

■ U.S. First Army units hooked up with Russian troops at Eilenburg. Munich was occupied. More than 110,000 Allied POW's were liberated. U.S. and French troops met on the French-Italian border. Turin was occupied by the U.S. Fifth Army. Dachau concentration camp was liberated and 32,000 prisoners were released.

■ Yugoslav Partisans entered Trieste.

■ Units of the 17th Indian Division advanced to Pegu in Burma.

■ Japanese assaults on U.S. ships off Okinawa intensified. During the month 20 were sunk and 157 were damaged, 90 by kamikazes. U.S. naval forces during this period destroyed 1,100 Japanese planes.

■ U.S. forces advanced to within four miles of Davao on Mindanao.

■ There were no civilian air raid casualties in Britain during the month. A total of 60,585 were killed and 86,175 seriously wounded since Sept. 1939.

May 1 The "Flensburg government" of Germany under Admiral Dönitz was announced.

■ U.S. Third Army forces advanced into Czechoslovakia on a 100-mile-wide front southeast of Ascha.

■ Field Marshal Rundstedt was captured by U.S. 141st Regiment troops at Bad Tölz, south of Munich.

■ Eight tons of emergency food supplies were dropped to the civilian population in the Netherlands by U.S. aircraft. (The special flights continued through the 8th, with German cooperation.)

■ British paratroopers landed south of Rangoon.

■ A brigade of the 9th Australian Division landed on Tarakan, which had been in Japanese hands since January 1942.

■ British Eighth Army troops advancing on Trieste made contact with Yugoslav Partisans at Monfalcone.

May 2 All fighting in Italy ended as the unconditional surrender of one million German troops there took effect, ending what the Allies called the "slow and bitter" campaign. Allied troops completed the occupation of Turin and Milan.

■ Berlin was completely under the control of Russian forces.

■ Ireland's Prime Minister Eamon de Valera called at the German legation in Dublin to express condolences for Hitler's death.

■ British Second Army units reached the Baltic, sealing off Denmark and Schleswig-Holstein.

■ RAF Mosquitos attacked Kiel, the last Allied bombing raid of the European war.

■ Rangoon was found to have been abandoned by the Japanese.

■ The 20th and 17th Indian divisions occupied Prome and Pegu in Burma.

■ U.S. 1st Division Marines suffered heavy losses

Members of the 50th Gurkha Parachute Regiment check equipment before taking off from Akyab (Sittwe) for air assault on Rangoon.

while making only negligible advances around the Asa River in Okinawa.

May 3 German forces in Hamburg surrendered. U.S. Seventh Army units reached the Brenner Pass after taking Innsbruck. The 2nd Armored Division was ordered to take Berchtesgaden.

■ A civilian uprising began in Prague.

■ New Zealand troops advanced into Trieste and were confronted by Yugoslav Partisans, and the two sides faced each other in a potentially ugly showdown.

■ A brigade of the 26th Indian Division entered Rangoon. Allied paratroopers and amphibious forces converged on the city. The war in Burma was effectively ended with the recapture of Rangoon. The campaign to retake Burma cost 4,115 British and Indian dead, 13,764 wounded, in addition to smaller numbers of U.S. and Chinese casualties. Japanese losses in the campaign were about 100,000.

■ Davao, on Mindanao in the Philippines, which was literally in ruins, was cleared by U.S. forces.

■ Japanese troops on Okinawa began their only major offensive of the Ryukyus campaign. An amphibious force tried to land behind U.S. lines on both coasts. As many as 800 Japanese were killed, and those who did land were soon killed or captured.

May 4 About one million German troops surren-dered in the Netherlands, Denmark, and north-west Germany. The terms were to become effec-tive at 8 A.M. the next day. Salzburg surrendered as officers of the German Nineteenth Army began negotiating an end to the fighting in Ba-varia.

May 5 German representatives arrived at Supreme Headquarters, Allied Expeditionary Force (SHAEF), a school building in Reims, to discuss final surrender terms. British airborne troops landed in Copenhagen after street fighting broke out between Danish civilians and the Ger-mans. Prague resistance forces battled the Ger-mans inside the city.

■ All fighting ended in Bavaria with the surren-der of the German First and Nineteenth armies. The U.S. Fifth Army from Italy linked up with the U.S. Seventh Army from Germany at the Brenner Pass.

■ Former French Premiers Daladier, Blum, and Reynaud, Generals Gamelin and Weygand, Rev-erend Martin Niemöller, and former Austrian Chancellor Schuschnigg were liberated in Austria by U.S. troops.

■ Hans Frank, governor general of German-occupied Poland, was taken prisoner by U.S. troops.

■ U.S. Third Army units occupied Linz in Aus-tria.

■ Japanese kamikazes sank 17 U.S. ships off Oki-

This pitiful scene at the Wöbbelin concentra-tion camp shows the emo-tional reaction of one of the liberated inmates who has just been told he would have to wait for evacuation until the more serious cases were treated.

nawa in a 24-hour period. A total of 131 Japanese planes were destroyed.

■ The 26th Indian Division entered Rangoon.

■ British ships bombarded the airfields on the Sakishima Islands in the southern Ryukyus.

May 6 The campaign in Burma was declared over by Admiral Mountbatten, although fighting actually continued in many sectors for several weeks.

■ U.S. Third Army units captured Pilsen, 65 miles from Prague.

■ The SS-sponsored Russian army of POW's under General Vlasov joined in the fight against the Germans for Prague. American tanks penetrated to the suburbs. The Soviets requested the U.S. Third Army to withdraw at this point, which it did, falling back 60 miles from Prague.

■ German Army Group G, comprising all units in Austria, surrendered unconditionally to the U.S. Sixth Army Group.

May 7 The German High Command surrendered unconditionally. General Jodl signed the instru-

Hitler's retreat at Berchtesgaden, in ruins at war's end, is surveyed by a U.S. soldier.

A P-47 fighter plane flies over Hitler's destroyed compound at Berchtesgaden.

ment of surrender at SHAEF headquarters. The fighting was to end at 11:01 P.M. on May 9. Associated Press correspondent Edward Kennedy scooped the world by flashing the story, but he was ordered expelled from the European theater for premature release of the news.

■ Seyss-Inquart was arrested in Hamburg.
■ Breslau in Silesia fell to the Red Army.
■ The Vlasov army was rejected by the Czechs. Vlasov fled Prague to reach U.S. lines

May 8 The war in Europe was declared ended. Churchill and Truman proclaimed V-E Day. All

Supreme Allied Commander Dwight Eisenhower and his deputy, Air Chief Marshal Sir Arthur Tedder, at their headquarters in Reims, France, announce the end of the war in Europe.

The war in Europe ended on May 7, 1945, with the signing of an unconditional surrender document in the War Room of the Allied headquarters, Reims, France. Colonel General Alfred Jodl, with back to camera and flanked by two aides, signed the document for Germany.

resistance ended in Latvia. The German Sixteenth and Eighteenth armies surrendered along the Leningrad front.

■ Göring surrendered near Fischhorn in Austria.

■ Prince Olaf and British representatives accepted the surrender of German troops in Norway.

■ Rain brought a respite to the fierce fighting on Okinawa.

May 9 All fighting was officially ended in Europe. The surrender was ratified by a ceremony in Berlin, with Zhukov and Keitel signing the document.

■ Russian forces under Marshal Konev occupied Prague, the last of the European capitals to be liberated.

■ Quisling surrendered to Norwegian police in Oslo. (He was executed by a firing squad Oct. 24.)

■ The German garrison surrendered the Channel Islands, the only British home territory occupied by the Germans during the war. Forty miles from Cherbourg and 80 miles south of the English coast, the nine islands had been under German control since June 30, 1940.

THE *PRINZ EUGEN*

Only one of Germany's major warships survived the war. The heavy cruiser *Prinz Eugen*, launched in 1938, saw as much action as any in the fleet. It was bombed, hit by a submarine-launched torpedo, struck a mine, saw action in which the *Bismarck* was sunk, made the Channel dash in Feb. 1942, and was involved in Baltic evacuation operations until the end of the war. It was surrendered in Copenhagen on May 9, 1945. The *Prinz Eugen*'s career finally ended when it was used as a target ship in the U.S. A-bomb tests at Bikini.

A chalk-scrawled postscript to the war in the Charlottenburg district of Berlin: "It took Hitler 12 years to build this."

May 10 All German forces in Czechoslovakia capitulated although some isolated units continued to fight.

■ The U.S. announced that 3,100,000 American troops would be withdrawn from Europe.

■ British Fourteenth Army units from Arakan linked up with Allied forces west of the Irrawaddy.

■ The U.S. Marine 5th Division attacked across the Asa estuary on Okinawa, establishing a mile-wide beachhead.

May 11 An attack by two corps of the U.S. Tenth Army was launched on Okinawa. Some elements advanced to positions commanding the island's capital of Naha. Japanese aircraft staged heavy attacks on U.S. ships in the area, damaging the carrier *Bunker Hill* and two destroyers.

■ Wewak on New Guinea was occupied by the 6th Australian Division.

■ German forces on the Aegean Islands surrendered. Soviet troops began mopping-up operations in Austria and Czechoslovakia.

May 12 German troops on Crete surrendered.

■ The German Baltic Army laid down its arms.

■ SS General "Sepp" Dietrich was captured.

■ Tito's Partisan army claimed the destruction of six German divisions.

May 13 Most German resistance ended in Czechoslovakia. Red Army troops concluded all offensive operations.

■ The Balete Pass on Luzon was cleared by U.S. Army units opening up the Cagayan valley.

May 14 An Austrian republic was reestablished in Vienna.

May 15 U.S. Eighth Army forces launched new attacks on Mindanao and Negros in the Philippines.

■ British ships and planes attacked Japanese positions on the Andaman Islands.

■ Naha, on Okinawa, was captured.

■ Recalcitrant German units in eastern Germany and northern Czechoslovakia ended all resistance.

May 16 U.S. planes began one of the most intensive napalm bombing operations of the war, against Japanese units defending the Ipo Dam, east of Manila, which provided the main source of water for the capital of the Philippines. Fifth Fighter Command dropped 110,000 gallons of napalm on the well-entrenched Japanese in a three-day period, and the U.S. 43rd Division was able to take control of the dam when the bombing had destroyed most of the defending positions.

■ U.S. 6th Division Marines were badly mauled in attacking Sugar Loaf hill on Okinawa.

May 17 Five British destroyers sank the Japanese heavy cruiser *Haguro* in the Malacca Strait. It was the last surface naval battle of the war.

■ Dutch troops landed on Tarakan Island, reinforcing the Australians who had encountered stiff opposition from the Japanese defenders.

May 18 Sugar Loaf on Okinawa was taken by U.S. Marines. In 10 days of intense fighting for the hill, the 6th Division suffered 2,662 casualties. A further indication of the level of combat was that 1,289 Marines were victims of combat fatigue.

■ Chinese troops reoccupied the port of Foochow in Fukien Province.

May 19 The U.S. 77th Division suffered heavy casualties in fighting for the Ishimmi ridge on Okinawa and had to be withdrawn.

■ The arrival of French troops touched off demonstrations in Syria and Lebanon.

■ Dr. Alfred Rosenberg, the unofficial "philosopher" of the Nazi party, was arrested in Flensburg.

■ Stalin denied the Polish leaders in Moscow were arrested for political reasons.

■ Ipo on Mindanao was cleared by the U.S. 45th Division.

May 20 Japanese troops began pulling out of Kwangsi Province in China to return to Japan for defense of the home islands.

■ Negotiations broke down between French officials and the Syrians and Lebanese.

May 21 The British coalition ended as the Labor party rejected Churchill's proposal to continue the alliance with the Conservatives. Churchill was forced to call for general elections, Britain's first in ten years.

■ Himmler was arrested in Bremervörde by a British patrol.

■ Japanese units at Shuri on Okinawa began withdrawing.

■ The Japanese supply base at Malaybalay in Mindanao was captured by U.S. 31st Division units.

May 22 Heavy rains began pounding Okinawa, hampering operations for almost two weeks.

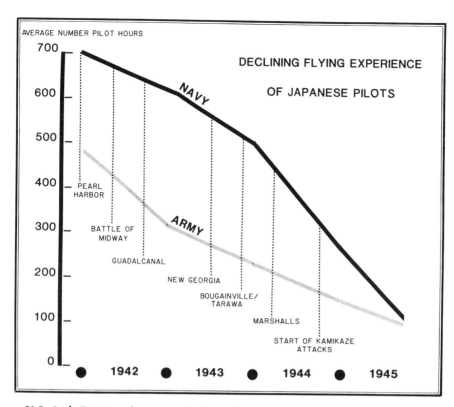

AVERAGE NUMBER PILOT HOURS

DECLINING FLYING EXPERIENCE

OF JAPANESE PILOTS

700

600

NAVY

500

400 — PEARL
HARBOR

300 — BATTLE OF
MIDWAY

ARMY

GUADALCANAL

200 —

NEW GEORGIA

BOUGAINVILLE/
TARAWA

MARSHALLS

100 —

START OF KAMIKAZE
ATTACKS

0 —

● 1942 ● 1943 ● 1944 ● 1945

Japan's fortunes declined in direct proportion to the diminishing skills of its pilots. In the end young Japanese Kamikaze pilots, with virtually no training, needed only to reach any available target and plunge to their death.

■ U.S. 24th Division forces reached Tambongan on Mindanao.

May 23 Heinrich Himmler committed suicide while being held by the British at Lüneburg, swallowing poison from a concealed vial.

■ Julius Streicher, the notorious Jew baiter, was captured in Bavaria by a Jewish officer from New York. Ostracized during most of the war and hated by even his fellow Nazis, Streicher had turned to farming in his final years and pursued his hobby, collecting pornography.

■ Senior surviving members of the Nazi government and the German High Command were imprisoned at Flensburg.

■ Japan's largest port, Yokohama, stopped functioning because of Allied air and sea attacks.

May 24 General Robert Ritter von Greim, who succeeded Göring as head of the Luftwaffe, committed suicide.

■ Japanese forces attacked U.S. air bases on Okinawa and Ie Shima and offshore shipping. Paratroopers were landed on the Yontan airfield on Okinawa, but the Japanese force was eliminated

after several U.S. planes were destroyed. The aerial attacks against the fleet, which continued through the next day, caused heavy damage but no ships were lost.

May 25 The U.S. Chiefs of Staff set Nov. 1 as the date for the invasion of Japan.

■ Bassein, 87 miles west of Rangoon, was occupied by Allied forces.

May 26–27 Chinese troops occupied Nanning, the capital of Kwangsi Province, cutting off the land outlet from Indochina for the Japanese. As many as 200,000 Japanese were stranded.

May 27 Japanese aircraft launched a heavy two-day series of strikes against U.S. ships around Okinawa. More than a hundred Japanese planes were destroyed in the attacks. The U.S. destroyer *Drexler* was sunk.

■ Tokyo was closed to all maritime shipping, its facilities destroyed.

■ U.S. 25th Division units took Santa Fe on Luzon.

■ Australian positions on Tarakan were attacked by Japanese aircraft. Most of Borneo was cleared.

KAMIKAZES

From their first flights on Oct. 25, 1944, until the end of the war a total of 1,228 Japanese kamikaze corps pilots plunged to their deaths in suicide missions. This unprecedented planned program of human sacrifice was Japan's final act of desperation to halt the overwhelming U.S. naval force which was pounding its way inexorably toward the home islands. The kamikazes took a frightful toll in American lives, but they did not stop the onrushing fleet nor delay the inevitable defeat of the empire. Still, the destruction was awesome, as the following attests.

U.S. Navy Ships Hit by Kamikazes

Sunk		Damaged
0	Fleet carriers	16
0	Light carriers	3
3	Escort carriers	17
0	Battleships	15
0	Heavy cruisers	5
0	Light cruisers	10
13	Destroyers	87
1	Destroyer escorts	24
0	Submarines	1
2	High-speed minelayers	15
0	Light minelayers	13
5	Landing ships - tanks	11
1	Mine sweepers	10
9	Auxiliaries and small craft	61
34 Total		Total 288

Total Australian casualties in the campaign were 436 killed and 1,460 wounded.

May 28 The British and American navies issued a joint announcement to all merchant ships in the Atlantic, Arctic, and Indian oceans that convoys were abolished and that they should now "burn navigation lights at full brilliancy and need not darken ship." War conditions continued to apply only in the Pacific.

■ William Joyce ("Lord Haw Haw") was captured in Flensburg. Joyce was a British fascist who became a radio propagandist for the Nazis during the war. (Convicted of treason, he was eventually executed.)

■ Queen Wilhelmina returned to the Netherlands.

■ More than 100 Japanese planes were shot down in attacks off Okinawa. This was Japan's final effort to turn the Okinawan campaign around. One U.S. destroyer was sunk, but the air strikes were not successful.

■ Open fighting broke out between the French and Arabs in Syria and Lebanon.

May 29 French forces shelled Damascus and Hama in Syria, and the Syrians asked the British for help.

■ Belgian Socialists called on King Leopold III to abdicate. The monarch had always been held in low regard by the government-in-exile and by many Belgians for his independent policies immediately preceding the war and his capitulation to the Germans in 1940 without reference to the French and British who were aiding in Belgium's defense.

May 30 Two battalions of U.S. Marines reached the southeast edge of Naha on Okinawa.

■ Damascus was again bombed by the French.

■ Tehran asked Britain, the U.S., and Russia to remove their troops from Iran.

May 31 Organized resistance ended on Negros Island in the Philippines.

■ A regiment of the 37th Division began moving northward from Santa Fe through the Cagayan valley on Luzon.

■ Japanese forces pulled out of Shuri on Okinawa.

■ More fighting broke out in Syria. London informed de Gaulle that orders had been issued for British troops to intervene.

■ Chiang Kai-shek gave up his title as premier but remained president of China.

June 1 Japanese resistance on Luzon was reduced to rear-guard delaying actions.

June 2 De Gaulle criticized British intervention in Syria and Lebanon.

June 3 French troops were withdrawn from Beirut and Damascus.

June 4 U.S. Marines landed on the Oroku Peninsula on Okinawa. About half the Naha airfield was cleared.

June 5 Nature hurled a typhoon almost as destructive as the kamikazes against the U.S. ships around Okinawa. Severe damage was inflicted on 4 battleships, 8 carriers, 7 cruisers, 11 destroyers, and a host of auxiliaries.

■ Japanese units fought desperately on Okinawa's Oroku Peninsula. The severe rains subsided but land transport was extremely difficult because of the mud.

■ Aritao on Luzon was captured.

June 6 The Naha airfield on the Oroku Peninsula was cleared by the U.S. Marine 6th Division.

■ Brazil declared war on Japan.

June 7 Chinese forces reached Paoching, having driven the Japanese back to the starting point of their spring offensive.

June 8 U.S. 37th Division patrols reached the Magat River on Luzon.

June 9 Japanese forces on Okinawa's Oroku Peninsula were trapped when the 4th and 22nd Marine regiments were linked.

■ All Japanese escape routes from the Cagayan valley in Luzon were blocked

■ Mandog on Mindanao was captured by the U.S. 24th Division, eliminating the final Japanese defense position on the island.

June 10 The 9th Australian Division landed unopposed on Borneo at Brunei Bay and assaulted the nearby islands of Labuan and Muara.

■ Chinese forces captured the port of Wenchow, 450 miles west of Okinawa.

■ The Japanese pocket on the Oroku Peninsula was reduced to an area 1,000 yards by 2,000 yards.

■ British Pacific Fleet units left Manus Island to begin operations against Truk in the Carolines.

June 11 Ishan in Kwangsi Province was retaken by the Japanese.

■ The Japanese on Oroku were forced into a 1,000-yard square but fought tenaciously.

June 12 Japanese troops on Oroku began committing mass suicide or surrendering.

■ U.S. forces started clearing the Orioung Pass on Luzon.

■ All resistance ended in the Visayan Islands. U.S. dead in the campaign were 835 and 2,300 were wounded. Japanese losses were estimated at 10,000 dead.

■ Yugoslav forces withdrew from Trieste after urging New Zealand and Indian troops to pull out of the disputed city.

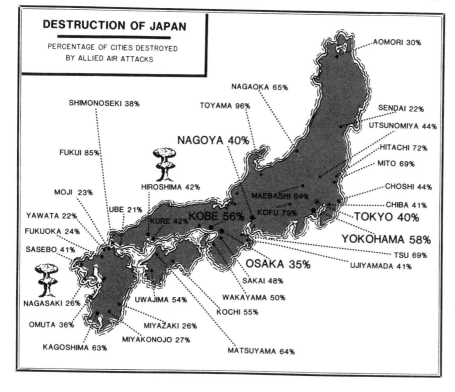

DESTRUCTION OF JAPAN

PERCENTAGE OF CITIES DESTROYED
BY ALLIED AIR ATTACKS

AOMORI 30%
NAGAOKA 65%
TOYAMA 96%
SHIMONOSEKI 38%
SENDAI 22%
UTSUNOMIYA 44%
NAGOYA 40%
FUKUI 85%
HITACHI 72%
MITO 69%
HIROSHIMA 42%
MOJI 23%
MAEBASHI 64%
CHOSHI 44%
UBE 21%
CHIBA 41%
YAWATA 22%
KURE 42%
KOBE 56%
KOFU 79%
TOKYO 40%
FUKUOKA 24%
YOKOHAMA 58%
SASEBO 41%
TSU 69%
OSAKA 35%
UJIYAMADA 41%
SAKAI 48%
NAGASAKI 26%
UWAJIMA 54%
WAKAYAMA 50%
KOCHI 55%
OMUTA 36%
MIYAZAKI 26%
KAGOSHIMA 63%
MIYAKONOJO 27%
MATSUYAMA 64%

Atomic bombs dropped on Hiroshima and Nagasaki brought the Pacific war to an end, but Japan's devastation extended to other cities as well.

June 13 All resistance ended on the Oroku Peninsula. A total of 159 Japanese were captured. About 200 bodies were found.

■ Australian troops captured Brunei City (Bandar Seri Begawan) on Borneo.

June 14 Ribbentrop was arrested by British troops in a Hamburg boardinghouse.

■ A five-day seesaw battle at Ishan in China ended with the Chinese finally establishing possession of the city.

■ The U.S. Joint Chiefs of Staff issued directives to the top military leaders in the Pacific to prepare plans for the occupation of Japan in the event Tokyo suddenly capitulated.

June 15 Chinese forces advanced along a broad front in Kwangsi Province.

■ U.S. OSS units finished clearing the Shan Hills of Burma.

■ Australian forces completed clearing the islands of Labuan and Muara, off Borneo.

June 16 British naval units bombarded the Japanese base at Truk in the Carolines.

■ Belgian Premier Achille van Acker and his cabinet resigned in protest against the contemplated return of King Leopold III.

June 17 U.S. Army forces pierced the final defense line of the Japanese Thirty-second Army on Okinawa. The commander of the Japanese naval base on Okinawa, Admiral Minoru Ota, was found dead, having committed hara-kiri.

■ The U.S. 37th Division began crossing the Cagayan River.

■ All Japanese troops in south China began withdrawing northwards in five long columns between the Yellow and Yangtze rivers.

June 18 Organized Japanese resistance ended on Mindanao.

■ Lieutenant General Simon Bolivar Buckner, Jr., U.S. Tenth Army commander, was killed by a Japanese shell on Okinawa.

■ Australian units reached Tutong in Brunei.

■ U.S. aircraft began a series of raids on Japan's secondary cities.

■ Eisenhower addressed a joint meeting of the U.S. Congress as he began a series of victory celebrations in his honor.

June 19 British and Indian forces invaded Thailand from Burma.

■ King Leopold III refused to abdicate the Belgian throne. (He was to remain until 1951 when his wartime role finally forced him to step down.)

■ Spain was barred from UN membership as long as the Franco regime remained in power. (Spain was admitted in 1955, however, while Franco still ruled.)

■ Four million New Yorkers turned out to cheer Eisenhower in a 35-mile motorcade through the city.

June 20 Japanese civilians and troops on Okinawa began surrendering in greater numbers. Nearly a thousand soldiers laid down their arms, an unprecedented action by Imperial Army forces.

■ Japanese air attacks on U.S. ships off Okinawa had so far killed 2,658 men.

■ All the islands of the southern Philippines were declared secure.

■ More Australian troops landed unopposed at Lutong in Sarawak, 82 miles from Brunei Bay.

■ Polish leaders in London denied the legal right of the Russians to try the Polish ministers who had flown to Moscow.

June 21 Twelve of the 16 Poles on trial in Moscow were found guilty of engaging in "underground activities."

June 22 Okinawa was declared captured by U.S. forces. The commanding general of the Japanese defenders, Lieutenant General Mitsuru Ushijima, committed suicide. Thus ended the 81-day campaign in which the Americans suffered their heaviest losses of the Pacific war. In securing the island considered essential for the invasion of Japan proper, 12,520 U.S. soldiers and marines were killed, and 36,631 wounded. About 110,000 Japanese were killed (90 percent of the number involved) and 7,400 were captured. Okinawan action virtually eliminated Japanese home air defenses as 7,830 planes were destroyed or lost in kamikaze attacks. Eight hundred Allied planes were downed. The U.S. Navy lost 4,907 men and 36 ships—none larger than a destroyer. About 180 Japanese vessels—including the largest battleship in the world, *Yamato*—were sunk. U.S. officials were alarmed by the ferocity of the Japanese on Okinawa and feared even greater resistance on the Japanese home islands. Okinawa was a key consideration, as a result, in the decision to use the atomic bomb against Japan.

■ U.S. planes dropped 3,000 tons of bombs on

Japanese munitions plants in Kobe, Osaka, Nagoya, and Okayama.

■ All resistance ended on Tarakan Island. Australian units captured Sarawak.

■ Liuchow was set afire by retreating Japanese forces in China.

June 23 U.S. paratroopers and glider forces linked up with a large Filipino guerrilla force on Luzon and began closing a trap around the Japanese.

June 25 The Miri oil fields in Sarawak were captured by Australian forces.

■ Seven villages south of Prome were cleared of Japanese units.

June 26 The United Nations Charter was signed at the San Francisco UN Conference on International Organization (it was ratified Oct. 24).

■ Liuchow airfield was taken by the Chinese.

■ U.S. B-29s began nighttime attacks on Japanese oil refineries.

June 27 The campaign on Luzon effectively ended as U.S. 37th Division forces advanced to Aparri.

■ A kamikaze hit the U.S. carrier *Bunker Hill* off Okinawa, killing 373 men.

June 28 Australian units captured Kuala Belait.

■ A new Polish government was formed in Warsaw.

June 29 Ruthenia was formally ceded to the Soviet Union by Czechoslovakia. Russia had thus acquired since 1939 a total of 300,000 square miles of new territory in Europe, land greater in size than the state of Texas.

June 30 The Luzon campaign was declared officially ended, but 11,000 Japanese were still in the Sierra Madre Mountains and 12,000 in the Ifugao-Bontoc area. (The Japanese lost 317,000 men in the Philippines campaign. Another 7,236 were captured. U.S. dead, wounded and missing totaled 60,228.)

■ Chungchin on the Indochinese border fell to the Chinese, and the Chinese forces continued their advance into Indochina itself.

COMBAT AND SUPPORT TROOP RATIOS U.S. ARMY
(Based on Troop Deployments June 30, 1945)

Theater of Operation	Percent of Combat Troops	Percent of Support Troops
European	37.5	62.5
Mediterranean	41.9	58.1
Southwest Pacific	39.5	60.5
Central Pacific°	26.5	73.5

°Central Pacific figures are misleading since the Army supported six Marine divisions which are not included in combat troop totals.

July 1 The 7th Australian Division invaded Balikpapan, Borneo, one of the richest oil-producing areas in Asia. Resistance was light initially, but gradually stiffened.

Australian 18th Brigade machine gunners close in on Japanese positions at Balikpapan, Borneo.

July 2 The Okinawan campaign was declared officially ended.

■ Only 200,000 people remained in Tokyo. All others were evacuated to safer areas. Japan said five million people had been killed or wounded in the American air raids.

■ Balikpapan's oil facilities were seized by the Australians.

■ The U.S. submarine *Barb* became the first American underwater craft to fire rockets in shore bombardment, hitting Kaihyo Island off the east coast of Karafuto (Sakhalin) Island.

July 3 The Allies took over their zones of occupation in Berlin.

July 4 U.S. and Filipino guerrilla units began clearing out Japanese pockets of resistance around Sarangani Bay on Mindanao.

July 5 MacArthur announced the liberation of the Philippines.

■ General elections were held in Britain. Because of the large number of military absentee ballots, the outcome was not determined until the 26th.

■ Australian Prime Minister John Curtin died. He had headed the government since 1941.

■ The procommunist government of Poland was recognized by Washington and London.

■ Australian units landed at Penadjim Point, across Balikpapan Bay in Borneo.

July 9 Dutch troops landed north of Balikpapan, completing encirclement of the bay.

■ Chinese forces recaptured the Tanchuk air base.

July 10 More than 1,000 U.S. and British aircraft bombed the Tokyo area, concentrating on airfields and industrial facilities. It was the greatest assault yet on the Japanese capital.

July 12 Japan requested Moscow to serve as mediator to bring about a cease-fire with the western Allies.

■ The Japanese home islands of Shikoku and Honshu were heavily bombed.

July 13 Berlin's municipal council confiscated all property held by members of the Nazi party.

■ Italy declared war on Japan.

July 14 A thousand naval aircraft raided Hokkaido and the port of Kamaishi. The latter was also bombarded by U.S. battleships, cruisers, and destroyers, the first naval gunfire directed against the Japanese home islands.

July 15 U.S. naval ships bombarded Muroran on Hokkaido.

■ Ten large Japanese cities were devastated by U.S. bombers.

■ Australian troops captured Mount Batochampar in Borneo which had been a key Japanese defense position.

The important oil facility at Balikpapan on the east coast of Borneo was recaptured by Australian forces after it had been operated by the Japanese since early 1942.

THE LEAGUE OF NATIONS AT WAR

Unknown to most people, the League of Nations functioned throughout the war. It did nothing constructive, but it had done nothing more in prior years to prevent the conflict. A one-time Irish journalist, Sean Lester, functioned as acting secretary-general. With a staff of 30 professionals and 70 clerical and maintenance personnel, Lester kept the League going from a few rooms of the cavernous Palais des Nations in Geneva's Ariana Park. Papers on health, education, and trade were written, but read by no one. Few funds were left, and even the host Swiss cut off their modest contribution. The League radio station was ordered shut down. The Swiss bent their neutrality to appease the Germans, even banning postage stamps bearing pictures of League buildings. When the League's successor came into being as the United Nations, Lester and a small League delegation attended the sessions at the San Francisco Opera House. But lest the memory of the League darken the prospects of the world's new hope, they were given seats in the very last row of the gallery. Pointedly ignored and unwanted, Lester and the others returned to Geneva, a final Assembly was held, and the League passed out of existence on April 19, 1946.

SOURCE: Elmer Bendiner, *A Time for Angels.*

July 16–Aug 2 Leaders of the Big Three met in the final conference of the war, appropriately code named TERMINAL, in Potsdam, Germany. Stalin, Truman, and Churchill—initially—drew up terms for the surrender of Japan. The thrust of the conference was political, however, with the first indications of suspicion and mistrust manifesting themselves. In a real sense, Potsdam was the termination of World War II and the onset of the Cold War.

July 16 The first atomic bomb was exploded at the U.S. Test facility at Alamogordo, New Mexico. Truman was advised of the successful test at Potsdam in a terse coded message, "Babies satisfactorily born."

■ A force of 500 B-29s bombed targets on Honshu and Kyushu. Altogether, more than 1,500 American planes pounded Japan.

■ Japanese units began pulling out of Amoy, in southern China.

July 17 Allied aircraft and Third Fleet ships attacked Tokyo and other key areas and encountered no defending planes or opposition of any kind. Battleships alone fired 2,000 tons of bombs on their targets. A British fast carrier task force, commanded by Vice Admiral H.B. Rawlings, joined in attacks on Japan this date as part of the Third Fleet, the first joint U.S.-British naval operation in the Pacific.

July 18 The battleship *Nagato*, which was reduced to service as a floating antiaircraft battery, was damaged by U.S. planes at Yokosuka.

■ Australian patrols found the Sambodja oil fields on Borneo totally evacuated by the Japanese.

■ The Belgian Senate voted to forbid the return of Leopold III.

July 19 Japanese units in Burma began an all-out effort to break out of their encircled positions.

July 21 Heavy fighting took place along the Sittang River as the Japanese continued their counterthrusts.

■ U.S. radio broadcasts called on Japan to surrender or face destruction.

July 23–24 In a series of almost unopposed sea and air attacks, U.S. and British units pounded Japanese military positions on Shikoku and Kyushu. More than 100 ships were sunk.

July 24 An air armada of 1,600 planes attacked the Japanese airfields, the naval base at Kure and ships in the Inland Sea. The battleships *Hyuga*, *Ise*, and *Haruna* were sunk.

■ Six hundred B-29s bombed the Osaka-Nagoya area, Japan's second largest population center.

■ Truman told Stalin the atomic bomb would be used against the Japanese.

July 24–26 British naval and air units launched attacks on Japanese troop positions and transportation targets on the west coast of Malaya.

July 25 In a statement from Potsdam the Allied leaders called on Japan to surrender or face "utter destruction." Radio Tokyo indicated Japan would accept peace terms but not unconditional surrender.

■ Japanese forces pulled out of Taunggyi in the Shan states of Burma.

July 26 Winston Churchill was ousted as British prime minister as the Labor party was swept into power. Labor garnered 393 seats to 213 for the Conservatives (31 went to minor parties), while the popular vote was 47.8 percent Labor to 39.8 Conservative.

July 27 Clement Attlee, leader of the Labor party and deputy prime minister in the Churchill coalition cabinet, was named head of the British government. Attlee immediately flew to Potsdam to join Stalin and Truman in the Big Three conference.

■ Leaflets were dropped on Japan's major cities, warning of their destruction if the Japanese did not surrender.

■ Chinese forces fought their way back into Kweilin.

July 28 Two thousand Allied planes bombed Kure, Kobe, and targets on the Inland Sea. The U.S. destroyer *Callaghan* was sunk by a suicide plane off Okinawa, the last ship to be destroyed by the kamikazes.

July 29 U.S. warships pounded naval and air facilities at Hamamatsu on Honshu.

July 30 Tokyo rejected the Potsdam ultimatum.

■ Food shortages became so acute in Japan the government called on the civilian population to collect 2.5 million bushels of acorns to be converted into eating material. The average Japanese had to survive on a daily intake of 1,680 calories, or 78 percent of what was considered the minimum necessary to survive.

■ Two British midget submarines entered Singapore harbor and sank the Japanese heavy cruiser *Takao* by attaching limpet mines to its bottom. (Midget submarines also were used to disrupt communication cables linking Singapore, Saigon, and Hong Kong.)

July 31 Pierre Laval was flown from Spain (where he had been given asylum) to Linz, Austria, aboard Franco's personal plane. He surrendered to U.S. authorities who turned him over to the French army. Laval felt he should return to France to justify his role in the Vichy government and to avoid being made the scapegoat for that dismal period when France was under Nazi rule. Laval was subsequently executed (by a firing squad after failing in an attempt to commit suicide with cyanide pills he had secreted in his overcoat ever since he thought the Nazis might try to kill him).

■ Japan was told eight of its cities would be leveled if it did not surrender.

Aug. 1 Allied forces completely sealed off Japanese troops at Buin, at the southern tip of Bougainville.

■ Traffic on the Yangtze River in China was totally disrupted. The Japanese had now lost 36 ships (with 11 others damaged, for a total loss of 35,000 tons) as a result of Allied aerial mines.

Aug. 2 B-29s dropped 6,600 tons of bombs on five Japanese cities. Most of Toyama was obliterated.

Aug. 3 Japan was totally blockaded.

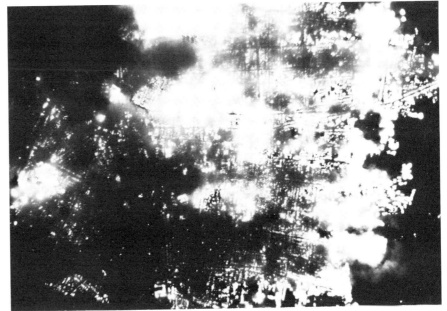

Toyama, Japan, burns during a destructive nighttime incendiary raid by American B-29s.

■ The last of the organized Japanese troops in Burma were either killed or captured. In the "Battle of the Breakthrough" 10,000 Japanese under Major General T. Koba in the Pegu Yoma (mountain range) were mauled, with 8,300 killed.

Aug. 5 In Manchuria the Chinese 58th Division took Hsinking (Changchun).

Aug. 6 A 9,000-pound atomic bomb with destructive power previously unimagined was dropped by the U.S. B-29 *Enola Gay* on Hiroshima at 8:15 A.M. It scared the center of the city for a fraction of a second with a heat of 300,000° centigrade. It is still not clear how many people died. Official U.S. estimates of the dead were placed as high as 78,000. Japanese sources place

the figure as high as 240,000 (about half the people in Hiroshima at the time).

Aug. 7 Marshal Tito barred the return of King Peter II to Yugoslavia.

Aug. 8 Russia declared war on Japan, effective the next day.

Aug. 9 The second atomic bomb was dropped on Nagasaki. Casualties were estimated at 35,000.

■ Red Army troops invaded Manchuria, attacking from the Maritime Province. Another force attacked a thousand miles west from Transbaikalia, north of Mongolia.

■ Chinese paratroopers were dropped on the Canton-Hankow rail line.

Aug. 9–10 In an effort to destroy Japanese aircraft which had been moved to northern Honshu,

Hiroshima is destroyed by the atomic bomb.

Scores of U.S. aircraft overfly the Pacific fleet in the final days of the war.

U.S. and British carrier-based planes attacked airfields in continuous waves. Thirty-four of the Allied planes were downed, but 397 Japanese aircraft were destroyed and 320 damaged.

Aug. 10 Tokyo announced the Japanese were willing to surrender but only if the status of the emperor remained unchanged.

■ U.S. and British battleships pounded the Japanese coastal city of Kamaishi, concentrating on the steel mills.

OPERATION *STARVATION*

Operation STARVATION was code-named to leave no room for ambiguity. Its purpose was to starve the Japanese into submission. It was a U.S. Air Force and Navy effort to complete the blockade of Japan by mining the country's inner waters and harbors. From March 27 until Aug. 15, 1945, B-29s, the principal aircraft used in the operation, dropped 12,135 mines in Japan's home waters. A known total of 670 ships of all sizes (for a combined total of 1,400,000 tons) were sunk or put out of commission. The effect was devastating. Industrial production was slashed to almost nothing. Food shortages developed and stricter rationing was imposed on the already hard-pressed Japanese civilian population. Experts had warned government leaders that if the war continued through the spring of 1946 about seven million people might be expected to die of starvation. Japan, which only three years before had ruled an empire extending over several million square miles in the Pacific and Asia, was reduced to a position of not being able to transport even the basics of life to its people.

Aug. 11 The Allies responded to the conditional peace terms of the Japanese by declaring that the emperor would be subject to Allied authority.

Aug. 12 Soviet troops advanced into northern Korea and invaded southern Sakhalin Island (Karafuto).

Aug. 13 In one of the most concentrated raids of the war, 1,600 aircraft attacked Tokyo.

■ Millions of copies of Japanese translations of the

Potsdam Declaration were dropped on Japan's cities. The document called on the Japanese "to follow the path of reason" or face "utter devastation."

■ The Mongolian People's Republic declared war on Japan.

Aug. 14 Japan agreed to surrender unconditionally.

■ In the final raid of the war, B-29s attacked Kumagaya, Isesaki, and Akita.

Aug. 15 V-J Day was proclaimed by the Allies. All offensive actions were ended. MacArthur was informed he would become Supreme Commander for the Allied Powers (SCAP).

■ Emperor Hirohito went on radio for the first time to order all Japanese to lay down their arms.

■ The rationing of gasoline and canned goods ended in the United States. This was fortunate since many Americans celebrated V-J Day by joyously tearing up their ration coupons. Unfortunately, many also destroyed coupons for items which continued to be rationed.

JAPANESE MILITARY CASUALTIES (1937–1945)

Total killed in action, all theaters		1,140,429
Actions against U.S. forces	485,717	
Actions against British and Dutch forces	208,026	
China	202,958	
Actions in Australian battle zones	199,511	
French Indochina	2,803	
Manchuria and U.S.S.R.	7,483	
Other overseas	23,388	
Japan proper	10,543	
Total wounded		295,247
Missing in action		240,000°

° In Oct. 1955 a total of 61,200 "detainees" were held in the Soviet Union, North Korea, and the People's Republic of China.

SOURCE: *Japan Statistical Year Book, 1949.*

Aug. 16 General Prince Toshihiko Higashikuni, an uncle-in-law of the emperor, became prime minister and formed a Japanese cabinet to arrange for surrender.

Aug. 17 Indonesian nationalists proclaimed the independence of the Dutch East Indies.

Aug. 18 Subhas Chandra Bose was killed when his Japanese aircraft crashed off Formosa while en route to Tokyo.

Aug. 19 A Japanese delegation arrived in Manila from Tokyo to receive instructions on the plans for the occupation of Japan and the signing of the surrender documents.

■ MacArthur ordered a halt on all amphibious landing operations.

■ Russian units linked up with Chinese Communist forces.

Aug. 20 Russian troops occupied Harbin and Mukden.

■ The Japanese delegation in Manila returned to Tokyo.

Aug. 21 Japanese forces in Manchuria were told

Japanese surrender negotiators arrive at U.S.-held Ie Shima, off Okinawa, en route to Manila to begin talks on ending the war in the Pacific.

Allied prisoners marked their POW camp in the Tokyo-Yokohama area to signal their location to U.S. airmen. Rooftop sign at lower right informs them that Gregory "Pappy" Boyington, Marine Corps ace, is in the camp.

by their officers to surrender. The Kwantung Army surrendered at Hsinking (Changchun).

Aug. 22 For the first time in the war a Japanese force surrendered en masse. The garrison on Mili Atoll in the Marshall Islands capitulated in a ceremony on an American destroyer escort.

Aug. 23 Stalin announced that Soviet forces had occupied Manchuria, southern Sakhalin, Shimushiru, and Paramushiro in the Kuriles.

■ A U.S. Air Force B-24 crashed into a crowded school building in Freckelton, England, killing 76 children and the entire crew.

■ All lend-lease shipments were halted by Truman.

Aug. 25 Radio Tokyo reported "groups are committing hara-kiri before the Imperial Palace in large numbers."

■ General Yamashita informed the commander of the U.S. 32nd Division that he had ordered all Japanese troops in the Philippines to lay down their arms.

Aug. 27 Victorious U.S. Navy ships steamed into Tokyo's Sugami Bay. Admiral Halsey, Third Fleet commander, led the force which was probably the greatest display of naval might in history. It included 23 aircraft carriers, 12 battleships, 26 cruisers, 116 destroyers and escorts, 12 submarines, and 185 other smaller ships.

Aug. 28 Japanese forces in Burma formally surrendered in Rangoon.

■ Southern Sakhalin was taken by the Russians.

■ U.S. Air Force technicians arrived at Atsugi air base, near Tokyo, the first Allied personnel to arrive in Japan.

Aug. 29 The final report of the official inquiry into the 1941 attack on Pearl Harbor was released by Truman. Former Secretary of State Hull, General Marshall, and Admiral Stark were censured. Truman objected to the findings on Hull and Marshall.

Aug. 30 The Allied occupation of Japan began with the arrival of units of the U.S. 1st Marine Division at the Yokosuka naval base and the Army's 11th Airborne Division at the Atsugi air base.

■ British naval forces under Rear Admiral C.H.J. Harcourt reoccupied Hong Kong.

Sept. 1 Iva Toguri d'Aquino, who was known throughout the Pacific from her propaganda broadcasts as "Tokyo Rose," was located by two American newsmen in Tokyo. The American nisei graduate of UCLA was eventually arrested, tried, and convicted on charges of treason.

Sept. 2 Japan surrendered. Foreign Minister Mamoru Shigemitsu signed the formal instrument of surrender for Japan in Tokyo Bay aboard the U.S.S. *Missouri*. General of the Army Douglas MacArthur signed for the Allied powers, Fleet Admiral Chester W. Nimitz for the United States, General Hsu Yung-chang for China,

U.S. Ambassador to China Patrick J. Hurley confers at the Communist headquarters in Yenan with Mao Tse-tung (second from left) and Chou En-lai (extreme right).

Admiral Sir Bruce Fraser for the United Kingdom, Lieutenant General K. Derevyanko for the Soviet Union, General Sir Thomas Blamey for Australia, Colonel L. Moore-Gosgrove for Canada, General Jacques Leclerc for France, Admiral C. E. L. Helfrich for the Netherlands and Air Vice-Marshal Sir L. M. Isitt for New Zealand. World War II ended.

Japanese envoys arrive aboard the U.S.S. Missouri *for surrender ceremonies.*

General MacArthur, as Supreme Commander of Allied Forces, signs the surrender document aboard the U.S.S. Missouri. *Generals Wainwright and Percival, former prisoners of the Japanese, stand behind, Sept. 2, 1945.*

Men and Arms

MEN

COSTS BY INDIVIDUAL NATIONS DIRECTLY RELATED TO THE WAR
(in U.S. Dollars)

U.S.	$288,000,000,000
Germany	212,336,000,000
France	111,272,000,000
U.S.S.R.	93,012,000,000
U.K.	49,786,000,000
China	49,072,000,000
Japan	41,272,000,000
Italy	21,072,000,000
Canada	20,104,000,000
Australia	10,036,000,000
Netherlands	9,624,000,000
Belgium	6,324,000,000
India	4,804,000,000
New Zealand	2,560,000,000
Sweden°	2,344,000,000
South Africa	2,152,000,000
Turkey	1,924,000,000
Switzerland°	1,752,000,000
Norway	992,000,000
Portugal	320,000,000

PEAK STRENGTH OF ARMED FORCES DURING WORLD WAR II

U.S.S.R.	12,500,000	Netherlands	500,000
U.S.	12,364,000	Sweden°	500,000
Germany	10,000,000	Bulgaria	450,000
(including Austria)		Hungary	350,000
Japan	6,095,000	Finland	250,000
France	5,000,000	Brazil	200,000
China		Czechoslovakia	180,000
Nationalist	3,800,000	New Zealand	157,000
Communist	1,200,000	Greece	150,000
U.K.	4,683,000	South Africa	140,000
Italy	4,500,000	Thailand	126,500
India	2,150,000	Iran	120,000
Poland	1,000,000	Portugal°	110,000
Spain°	850,000	Argentina	100,000
Turkey	850,000	Afghanistan°	92,000
Belgium	800,000	Mexico	60,000
Canada	780,000	Egypt	54,000
Australia	680,000	Iraq	47,000
Switzerland°	650,000	Ethiopia	38,000
Rumania	600,000	Peru	30,000
Philippines	500,000	Albania	25,000
Yugoslavia	500,000	Norway	25,000

°Neutral throughout war

SOURCE: Arthur Guy Enoch, *This War Business.*

PEAK STRENGTH OF ARMED FORCES DURING WORLD WAR II (*Cont.*)

Chile	25,000	Guatemala	5,000
Cuba	20,000	Dominican	
Colombia	15,000	Republic	4,000
Denmark	15,000	Haiti	3,500
Venezuela	11,000	Nicaragua	3,000
Ecuador	9,000	El Salvador	3,000
Bolivia	8,000	Honduras	3,000
Paraguay	8,000	Liberia	1,000
Uruguay	8,000	Costa Rica	400
Saudi Arabia°	8,000		

° Neutral

SOURCE: Office of the U.S. Army Adjutant General

U.S. ACTIVE MILITARY PERSONNEL (1939–1945) (Enlisted and Officers)

	Army	Navy	Marines	Total
1939	189,839	125,202	19,432	334,473
1940	269,023	160,997	28,345	458,365
1941	1,462,315	284,427	54,359	1,801,101
1942	3,075,608	640,570	142,613	3,858,791
1943	6,994,472	1,741,750	308,523	9,044,745
1944	7,994,750	2,981,365	475,604	11,451,719
1945	8,267,958	3,380,817	474,680	12,123,455

PROFILE OF U.S. SERVICEMEN (1941–1945)

• 38.8 percent (6,332,000) of U.S. servicemen and women were volunteers.

• 61.2 percent (11,535,000) were draftees. Of the 17,955,000 men examined for induction, 35.8 percent (6,420,000) were rejected as physically or mentally unfit.

• Average duration of service: 33 months.

• Overseas Service: 73 percent served overseas, with an average of 16.2 months abroad.

• Combat Survivability (out of 1,000): 8.6 were killed in action, 3 died from other causes, and 17.7 received nonmortal combat wounds.

• Noncombat Jobs: 38.8 percent of the enlisted personnel had rear echelon assignments—administrative, technical, support, or manual labor.

• Average Base Pay: Enlisted: $71.33 per month; Officer: $203.50 per month.

U.S. CIVILIAN POPULATION AND MILITARY STRENGTH

	Civilian Population	Armed Forces	
		Total	Overseas
July 1940	131,658,000	464,000	168,000
July 1941	131,595,000	1,807,000	281,000
July 1942	130,942,000	3,918,000	940,000
July 1943	127,499,000	9,240,000	2,494,000
July 1944	126,708,000	11,689,000	5,512,000
July 1945	127,573,000	12,355,000	7,447,000
Jan. 1946	133,782,000	6,907,000	3,462,000
July 1946	138,385,000	3,004,000	1,335,000

SOURCE: U.S. Bureau of the Census.

LEADING FIGHTER ACES BY NATIONALITIES (With Number of Enemy Planes Downed in Combat)

Australian
Group Captain C.R. Caldwell	28½

British
Group Captain J.E. Johnson	38
Wing Commander J.R.D. Graham	29
Wing Commander R.R.S. Tuck	29
Squadron Leader J.H. Lacey	28
Flight Lieutenant E.S. Lock	26
Wing Commander B. Drake	24½
Squadron Leader W. Vale	24
Flight Lieutenant G. Allard	23
Wing Commander D.R.S. Bader	23

Canadian
Flight Lieutenant G.F. Beurling	31⅓
Squadron Leader V.C. Woodward	21⅞
Squadron Leader H.W. McLeod	21

Czech
Sergeant J. Frantisek	28

French
Squadron Leader P.H. Clostermann (with RAF)	33
Captain Marcel Albert (with Russian Air Force)	23
Wing Commander J.E.F. Demozay (with RAF)	21
Captain Edmond Marin la Meslée	15
Captain Michel Dorance	14
Sous Lieutenant Camille Plubeau	14

Finnish
Captain Hans H. Wind	75

German

Major Erich Hartmann	352
Major Gerhard Barkhorn	301
Major Günther Rall	275
Oberstleutnant Otto Kittel	267
Major Walther Nowotny	255
Major Wilhelm Batz	237
Major Erich Rudorffer	222
Oberstleutnant Heinrich Bär	220
Oberst Hermann Graf	211
Major Heinrich Ehrler	209

(Twenty-five other Luftwaffe pilots scored 150 or more victories. Most of these high figures were achieved in action against the Soviet Union. The leading aces in action in the West were Hauptmann Hans-Joachim Marseille, 158; Bär, 124; Oberstleutnant Kurt Bühligen, 112; and General Adolf Galland, 103.)

Irish

Wing Commander B. Finucane (with RAF)	32

Japanese

Hiroyishi Nishizawa	87
Shoichi Sugita	80
Saburo Sakai	64
Hiromichi Shinohara	58
Waturo Nakamichi	55
Takeo Okumura	54
Naoshi Kanno	52
Satoshi Anabuki	51
Yasuhiko Kuroe	51

New Zealand

Wing Commander C.F. Gray	27½
Wing Commander A.C. Deere	22
Wing Commander E.D. Mackie	22
Wing Commander W.V. Crawford-Compton	21½
Flight Lieutenant R.B. Hessely	21½

Polish

Wing Commander W. Urbanowicz (17 with RAF, 3 with USAAF)	20

Russian

Ivan Kozhedub	62
Aleksandr Pokryshkin	59
Grigorii Rechkalov	58
Nikolai Gulaev	57
Kirill Yevstigneev	52
Dimitrii Glinka	50
Aleksandr Klubov	50
Ivan Pilipenko	48
Arsenii Vorozheikin	46
Vasilii Kubarev	46
Nikolai Skomorokhov	46

(The Soviets also produced the only women of the war credited with downing five or more enemy aircraft: Lieutenant Lily Litvak, 7, and Lieutenant Katya Budanova, 6.)

South African

Squadron Leader M.T. St. J. Pattle	41
Group Captain A.G. Malan	35
Squadron Leader J.J. Le Roux	23½
Wing Commander P.H. Hugo	22

U.S. Army Air Force

Major Richard I. Bong	(P)40
Major Thomas B. McGuire	(P)38
Colonel Frances S. Gabreski	(E)31
Lieutenant Colonel Robert S. Johnson	(E)28
Colonel Charles H. MacDonald	(P)27
Major George E. Preddy	(E)26
Colonel John C. Meyer	(E)24
Captain Ray S. Whetmore	(E)22½
Colonel David C. Schilling	(E)22½
Lieutenant Colonel Gerald R. Johnson	(P)22
Major Neel E. Kearby	(P)22
Lieutenant Colonel Jay T. Robbins	(P)22

(P)*Pacific* (E)*Europe*

U.S. Navy

Captain David McCampbell	34
Lieutenant Cecil E. Harris	24
Commander Eugeane A. Valencia	23

U.S. Marine Corps

Lieutenant Colonel Gregory Boyington (including six as a Flying Tiger)	28
Major Joseph J. Foss	26
First Lieutenant Robert M. Hanson	25
Major Kenneth A. Walsh	21
Captain Donald M. Aldrich	20

THE VICTORIA CROSS

Few awards, if any, carry the esteem of Britain's Victoria Cross. Instituted by Queen Victoria in 1856 to honor those who were brave in her cause, the medal has been awarded 1,351 times. Unlike other medals, however, it has become ever rarer to win. In World War II only 182 Victoria crosses were awarded, 88 of them posthumously. Enlisted men received 85 of the medals. The following indicates how Britain chose to honor the select few "For Valour."

THE VICTORIA CROSS (Cont.)

By Nationality		By Combat Area	
British	109	Burma	31
Australian	19	North Africa	27
Indian	17	Air missions	26
Canadian	13	Naval missions	24
Nepalese (Gurkha)	10	Northwest Europe	
New Zealand	8	(1944–1945)	22
South African	3	Italy	20
Rhodesian	1	Pacific	11
Fijian	1	France-Belgium	
Dane	1	(1940)	6
		St.-Nazaire raid	5
		East Africa	4
		Dieppe raid	3
		Syria	2
		Crete	1

THE ORDER OF THE IRON CROSS

Germany's highest military award came in eight different classes. From highest to lowest:
1. Great Cross of the Iron Cross (only one was awarded, to Hermann Göring).
2. Knight's Cross to the Iron Cross with Golden Oak Leaves and Swords and Diamonds (only one was awarded, to Hans-Ulrich Rudel, the famed Stuka pilot who flew 2,530 combat missions, believed to be the greatest number ever flown by anyone).
3. Knight's Cross to the Iron Cross with Oak Leaves and Swords and Diamonds (only 27 were awarded).
4. Knight's Cross to the Iron Cross with Oak Leaves and Swords (154 were awarded).
5. Knight's Cross to the Iron Cross with Oak Leaves (860 were awarded).
6. Knight's Cross to the Iron Cross (about 7,500 awarded).
7. Iron Cross, 1st Class.
8. Iron Cross, 2nd Class.

MILITARY FORMATIONS

With few exceptions, almost all armies of the world organize their forces in the same way. The following is a rough guide to the components of armies with normal complements.

	Composition	Commander
Army Group (Soviet equivalent is Army Front)	2 or more armies	Field marshal or general
Army	2 or more corps	General
Corps	2 or more divisions	Lieutenant general
Division	2 or more brigades	Major general
Brigade	2 or more regiments	Brigadier general
Regiment	2 or more battalions	Colonel
Battalion	2 or more companies	Lieutenant colonel or major
Company	2 or more platoons	Captain
Platoon	2 or more squads	Lieutenant
Squad	8 to 12 men	Sergeant

Infantry Divisions

U.S. Army Infantry Division: Basically made of three regiments, each made up of three 900-men battalions, thus 8,100 combat personnel, plus an additional 6,000 in a variety of support roles.

British Infantry Division: By 1944, units were made up of three brigades, each consisting of three 900-men battalions, plus a reconnaissance regiment, a machine-gun battalion, and support units for a total of 18,000 officers and men.

Russian Rifle Division: Full strength unit was 14,000 men.

Chinese Division: Twelve thousand officers and men but often only half that number, equipped with poor equipment.

German Infantry Division: Originally made up of three regiments each made up of three battalions, but by 1944 each regiment was reduced to two-battalion strength, or a total of 12,500.

Japanese Field Division: Ideally, 18,000 officers and men but lesser numbers as war progressed.

Italian Division: The normal complement was about 14,000 men, but in North Africa in 1942 their five infantry and two mechanized divisions were reduced to an average of only 3,200 each.

Armored Divisions

British: Consisted of an armored reconnaissance regiment and an armored brigade, which consisted of three armored regiments and a motor battalion, plus a three-battalion infantry brigade, a machine-gun company, and four artillery regiments. Full complement consisted of 15,000 officers and men who operated 246 heavy tanks, 44 light tanks, 1,398 machine guns, 468 mortars and bazookas, 48 field guns, 78 antitank guns, and 141 antiaircraft guns.

U.S.: Generally made up of about 11,000 officers and men equipped with 270 tanks and 36 field guns.

German: A typical panzer division in 1944 consisted of two armored and four infantry battalions totaling

14,750 officers and men, manning between 160 and 180 tanks, and more than 200 field guns. SS panzer divisions had about the same number of tanks but were larger because of two additional infantry battalions.

Russian: A Red Army tank corps had three tank brigades and a motorized rifle brigade. It was normally equipped with 230 tanks and other armored vehicles, including antitank self-propelled guns. A Red Army mechanized corps had three motorized brigades and a single tank brigade, with the same advantage in self-propelled guns over tanks that a corps had in tanks over such guns.

Miscellaneous Formations

German: Panzer grenadier divisions had 45 self-propelled guns and about 2,800 other motorized vehicles, but no tanks. Fully manned, such a division had a normal complement of 14,750 officers and men.

The German airborne corps used in the 1941 invasion of Crete (the last time such a large formation was used by the Germans) consisted of 13,000 men, organized into an assault regiment and three parachute regiments, each made up of three parachute battalions, plus support units and elements of a mountain division flown into the combat area by transports.

British: A British airborne division was made of two parachute brigades and a single transported brigade, each made up of three battalions, plus airborne reconnaissance regiments and artillery, engineering, and support units. A total of 12,000 officers and men manned more than 1,700 vehicles and a wide range of infantry and artillery weapons.

U.S.: American airborne divisions were structurally the same as a similar British unit but had fewer than 9,000 men.

ORGANIZATION OF TYPICAL JAPANESE AND CHINESE DIVISIONS (1937)

	Japanese	Chinese°
Personnel	21,945	10,923
Horses	5,849	—
Small arms and rifles	9,476	3,821
Light machine guns	541	274
Heavy machine guns	104	54
Grenade launchers	576	243
Howitzers	64	16
Heavy artillery	44	30
Tanks	24	—
Small vehicles	262	—
Trucks	266	—
Horse-drawn carts	555	—

° The Chinese figures were based on the 10 divisions which were reorganized in 1937. Most of the other divisions had only half the manpower and material figures cited above.

SOURCE: Hsu Long-hsuen and Chang Ming-kai, *History of the Sino-Japanese War (1937–45)*.

ESTIMATED COSTS OF WORLD WAR II

Battle deaths	14,904,000
Battle wounded	25,218,000
Civilian deaths	38,573,000
Direct economic costs	$1,600,000,000,000

SOURCE: R. Ernest Dupuy, *World War II: A Compact History*

THE TOLL OF WAR BY NATIONS (1939–1945)

Australia

Military personnel	680,000
Military killed and missing	29,395
Military wounded	39,803
Prisoners of war	26,363

Austria

Military personnel	800,000
Military killed and missing	380,000
Military wounded	350,117
Civilian dead°	145,000

°including 60,000 murdered Jews

Belgium

Military personnel	800,000
Military killed	9,561
Military wounded	14,500
Civilian dead°	75,000

°including 25,000 murdered Jews

Brazil

Military personnel°	200,000
Military killed°°	943
Military wounded	4,222

Britain

Military personnel	4,683,000
Military killed and missing	271,311
Army dead	144,079

°40,334 in combat status
°°including 457 Brazilian Expeditionary Force and 8 Brazilian Air Force personnel killed in Italy

THE TOLL OF WAR BY NATIONS
(1939–1945) (*Cont.*)

Britain

RAF dead	69,606
Royal Navy dead	50,758
Women's Auxiliary Services	624
Unaccounted for	6,244
Merchant navy killed	30,248
Merchant navy missing	4,654
Military wounded	277,077
Army	239,575
RAF	22,839
Royal Navy	14,663
Women's Auxiliary Services	744
Merchant navy wounded	4,707
Military prisoners of war°	172,592
Army	152,076
RAF	13,115
Royal Navy	7,401
Women's Auxiliary Services	20
Merchant navy prisoners of war°	5,720
Private homes destroyed	456,000
Private homes damaged	4,073,000

°Of POW's, 7,310 died while in German captivity and 12,443 died while in Japanese captivity.

British colonies

Military killed and missing	21,805
Military wounded	6,972
Prisoners of war	8,115

Bulgaria

Military personnel	450,000
Military killed and missing	18,500
Military wounded	21,878

Canada

Military personnel	780,000
Military killed and missing	39,319
Military wounded	53,174
Prisoners of war	9,045

China (1937–1945)

Military personnel	5,000,000
Nationalist	3,800,000
Communist	1,200,000
Military killed	1,324,516
Military wounded	1,762,006
Civilians killed	°

°Variously estimated from 700,000 to 10,000,000

Czechoslovakia

Military personnel	180,000
Military killed	6,683
Military wounded	8,017
Civilian dead°	310,000

°including 250,000 murdered Jews

Denmark

Military personnel	15,000
Military killed	4,339

Estonia

Civilian dead	140,000

Finland

Military personnel	250,000
Military killed	79,047
Military wounded	50,000

France

Military personnel	5,000,000
Military killed	205,707
Presurrender	125,310
Free French	80,397
Military wounded	390,000
Civilian dead°	173,260
Private homes destroyed	255,500
Private homes damaged	1,051,000

°including 65,000 murdered Jews

Germany

Military personnel	10,000,000
Military killed and missing	3,300,000
Civilian dead°	2,300,000
Civilians killed in Allied Air Raids°°	593,000
Private homes destroyed	270,000
Private homes damaged	1,300,000

°*plus* approximately 170,000 murdered Jews
°°includes 56,000 foreign civilians in Germany

Greece

Military personnel	150,000
Military killed	16,357
Military wounded	49,933
Civilian dead°	155,300

°including 60,000 murdered Jews and 30,000 other civilians who were executed.

Hungary

Military personnel	350,000
Military killed	147,435
Military wounded	89,313
Civilian dead°	280,000

°including 200,000 murdered Jews

India
Military personnel	2,393,891
Military killed and missing	36,092
Military wounded	64,354
Prisoners of war	79,489

Italy
Military personnel	4,500,000
Military killed°	262,420
Army	220,775
Navy	28,837
Air Force	12,808
Military wounded	120,000
Civilian dead°°	93,000

°An additional 17,400 Italian military personnel were killed in action against Germany after Italy became an Allied cobelligerent in 1943.

°°including 8,000 murdered Jews

Japan (1937–1945)
Total killed in action, all theaters	1,140,429
Actions against U.S. forces	485,717
Actions against British and Dutch forces	208,026
China	202,958
Actions in Australian battle zones	199,511
French Indochina	2,803
Manchuria and U.S.S.R.	7,483
Other overseas	23,388
Japan proper	10,543
Total wounded	295,247
Missing in action°	240,000
Civilians killed while attached to the military	285,000
Japanese killed in air raids on home islands	668,000
Private homes destroyed	2,251,928
Private homes damaged	1,270,000

Heaviest hit cities:
Tokyo homes destroyed or severely damaged	709,906
Osaka homes destroyed	328,237
Nagoya homes destroyed	136,557
Kobe homes destroyed	131,528

°In Oct. 1955 a total of 61,200 "detainees" were held in the Soviet Union, North Korea, and the People's Republic of China.

Latvia
Civilian dead	120,000

Lithuania
Civilian dead	170,000

Netherlands
Military personnel	500,000
Military killed	13,700
Military wounded	2,860
Civilian dead°	236,300
Private homes destroyed	82,530
Private homes damaged	427,620
Schools destroyed	250
Schools damaged	1,700

°Including 104,000 Jews. Of the non-Jewish Dutch civilian dead, 2,700 were killed as hostages, 21,000 in bombing and shelling incidents, and 15,000 as a result of famine.

New Zealand
Military personnel	157,000
Military killed	12,162
Military wounded	19,314
Prisoners of war	8,453

Norway
Military personnel	25,000
Military dead°	4,780
Civilian dead°°	5,417

°including 3,638 merchant seamen
°°including 2,091 resistance fighters and 689 Norwegians serving in the German army

Poland
Military personnel	1,000,000
Military killed	320,000
Military wounded	530,000
Civilian dead°	6,028,000
Private homes destroyed	516,000
Private homes severely damaged	1,300,000
Schools destroyed	6,152

°including 3,200,000 murdered Jews

Rumania
Military personnel	600,000
Military casualties	519,822
Against Russians	350,000
Against Germans	169,822
Civilian dead°	465,000

°including 425,000 murdered Jews

South Africa
Military personnel	140,000
Military killed and missing	8,681
Military wounded	14,363
Prisoners of war	14,589

THE TOLL OF WAR BY NATIONS (1939–1945) (Cont.)

Soviet Union

Military personnel	20,000,000
Military dead°	13,600,000
Military wounded	5,000, 000
Civilian dead°°	7,720,000

°Includes 3,000,000 Russians who were captured and either were killed or died in captivity. The total consists of 1,000,000 who were believed to have died in occupied Russia, another 1,000,000 in POW camps in Germany and Poland, 500,000 who died in transit, and 500,000 who were executed.
°°Includes 1,720,000 Russian, Lithuanian, and Latvian Jews. It is estimated that 1,000,000 civilians died in the siege of Leningrad.

U.S.A.

Military personnel		16,353,659
Military killed		292,131
Army and Air Force	234,874	
Navy	36,950	
Marines	19,733	
Coast Guard	574	
Military wounded		671,278
Army and Air Force	565,861	
Navy	37,778	
Marines	67,207	
Coast Guard	432	
Merchant Marine dead		5,662
Killed at sea	845	
Died as POWs	37	
Missing and presumed dead	4,780	

Yugoslavia

Military personnel	3,741,000
Military dead	305,000
Military wounded	425,000
Civilian dead°	1,355,000

°Including 55,000 murdered Jews

CAUSES OF BRITISH CIVILIAN CASUALTIES

	Killed	Seriously Wounded	Total
Aircraft bombs	51,509	61,423	112,932
Flying bombs	6,184	17,981	24,165
Long-range rockets	2,754	6,523	9,277
Cross-Channel bombardment	148	255	403
Totals	60,595	86,182	146,777

SOURCE: Terence Henry O'Brien, *History of the Second World War, Civil Defense.*

PRISONERS OF WAR

Prisoners held by the Allies (excluding those in the Soviet Union):

German	630,000
Italian	430,000
Japanese	11,600

Prisoners held by Germany:

French	765,000
Italian	550,000
British Commonwealth	200,000
Yugoslav	125,000
American	90,000

Prisoners held by Japan:

British Commonwealth	108,000
Dutch	22,000
American	15,000

ESTIMATED NUMBER OF JEWS KILLED UNDER NAZI RULE

	Original Jewish Population	Number Killed	Percent Surviving
Baltic States (Estonia, Latvia, and Lithuania)	253,000	228,000	10
Belgium	65,000	40,000	40
Bulgaria	65,000	14,000	78
Czech Protectorate (Bohemia and Moravia)	90,000	80,000	11
France	350,000	90,000	74
Germany/ Austria	240,000	210,000	10
Greece	70,000	54,000	23
Hungary	650,000	450,000	30
Italy	40,000	8,000	80
Luxembourg	5,000	1,000	80
Netherlands	140,000	105,000	25
Norway	1,800	900	50
Poland	3,300,000	3,000,000	10
Rumania	600,000	300,000	50
Slovakia	90,000	75,000	17
Soviet Union (areas under German control)	2,850,000	1,252,000	56
Yugoslavia	43,000	26,000	40
Total	8,851,800	5,933,900	33

SOURCE: Lucy S. Dawidowicz, *The War Against the Jews (1933–1945).*

GERMAN AND ITALIAN CASUALTIES SUFFERED AGAINST U.S., BRITISH, AND FRENCH UNITS IN EUROPE AND NORTH AFRICA

	Battle Dead	Permanently Disabled	Captured	Total
North Africa	19,600	19,000	130,000	160,600
Sicily	5,000	2,000	7,100	14,100
Italy	86,000	15,000	357,089	458,089
Western front	230,000	49,000	7,614,794°	7,926,794°
Total	373,600	85,000	8,108,983°	8,567,583°

°Includes 3,404,949 disarmed enemy forces.

SOURCE: Biennial Report of the Chief of Staff of the U.S. Army to the Secretary of War, July 1,1943, to June 30, 1945 (Sept. 1, 1945).

BRITISH CIVILIAN CASUALTIES
(All Causes)

		Killed			Seriously Wounded	
1939–40	London	Rest of Britain	Total	London	Rest of Britain	Total
1941	13,596	10,171	23,767	18,378	12,151	30,529
1942	6,487	13,431	19,918	7,641	13,524	21,165
1943	27	3,209	3,236	52	4,096	4,148
1944	542	1,830	2,372	989	2,461	3,450
1945	7,533	942	8,475	19,611	2,378	21,989
	1,705	155	1,860	3,836	387	4,223
Totals	29,890	30,705	60,595°	50,507	35,675	86,182°

°Includes 967 people killed and 678 wounded in Northern Ireland not listed in annual totals.

WEEKLY RATIONS FOR PRISONERS IN CLASS II NAZI CONCENTRATION CAMPS°
(1940–1945)

	Aug. 1940–May 1942	May 1942–April 1944	April 1944–Feb. 1945	March 1945
Meat and processed meat	14.1 ozs.	9.9 ozs.	7.0 ozs.	8.7 ozs.
Fat (margarine, lard, etc.)	7.0 ozs.	6.0 ozs.	6.4 ozs.	2.9 ozs.
Cottage or skim milk cheese	5.1 ozs.	5.1 ozs.	3.5 ozs.	1.4 ozs.
Bread	6 lbs.	5 lbs. 6 ozs.	5 lbs. 12 ozs.	3 lbs. 14 ozs.
Sugar	2.8 ozs.	2.8 ozs.	2.8 ozs.	—
Marmalade	3.5 ozs.	3.5 ozs.	3.5 ozs.	8.5 ozs.
Cereals	5.1 ozs.	5.1 ozs.	8.8 ozs.	—
Flour	7.9 ozs.	4.4 ozs.	4.4 ozs.	—
Skim milk	—	—	1¾ qts.	1¾ qts.
Coffee substitute	2.7 ozs.	2.2 ozs.	2.2 ozs.	1.1 ozs.
Potatoes	7 lbs.12 ozs.	5 lbs.12 ozs.	8 lbs.13 ozs.	7 lbs.12 ozs.
Fresh vegetables	6 lbs.3 ozs.	5 lbs.12 ozs.	8 lbs.13 ozs.	13.2 ozs.

Supplementary Diet for Heavy-Duty Workers

Meat and processed meat	14.1 ozs.	9.9 ozs.	9.9 ozs.	13.3 ozs.
Fat	3.5 ozs.	3.5 ozs.	3.5 ozs.	1.9 ozs.
Bread	3 lbs.	3 lbs.	3 lbs.	2 lbs. 7 ozs.

°Class II camps were more rigorous than the Class I labor camps but less severe than the Class III death camps.

SOURCE: Eugen Kogon, *The Theory and Practice of Hell.*

TABLE OF COMPARATIVE RANKS
Table of Equivalent Officer Ranks

	U.S. Army and Air Force	U.S. Navy (and Coast Guard)	U.S. Marine Corps
1.	-	-	-
2.	General of the Army	Fleet Admiral	-
3.	-	-	-
4.	-	-	-
5.	General	Admiral	General
6.	Lieutenant General	Vice Admiral	Lieutenant General
7.	Major General	Rear Admiral	Major General
8.	Brigadier General	-	Brigadier General
9.	-	-	-
10.	Colonel	Captain	Colonel
11.	Lieutenant Colonel	Commander	Lieutenant Colonel
12.	Major	Lieutenant Commander	Major
13.	Captain	Lieutenant	Captain
14.	-	-	-
15.	First Lieutenant	Lieutenant (Junior Grade)	First Lieutenant
16.	-	-	-
17.	Second Lieutenant	Ensign	Second Lieutenant

Table of Equivalent Enlisted Ranks

	U.S. Army and Air Force	U.S. Navy (and Coast Guard)	U.S. Marine Corps
1.	Master Sergeant	Chief Petty Officer	Sergeant Major (or Master Gunnery Sergeant)
2.	First Sergeant	-	First Sergeant (or Master Sergeant)
3.	Technical Sergeant	Petty Officer 1st Class	Gunnery Sergeant
4.	Staff Sergeant (Technician 3rd Grade)	Petty Officer 2nd Class	Staff Sergeant
5.	Sergeant (Technician 4th Grade)	Petty Officer 3rd Class	Sergeant
6.	-	-	-
7.	Corporal (Technician 5th Grade)	Seaman 1st Class	Corporal
8.	Lance Corporal	-	Lance Corporal
9.	-	-	-
10.	Private 1st Class	Seaman 2nd Class	Private First Class
11.	-	-	-
12.	Private	Apprentice Seaman	Private

TABLE OF COMPARATIVE RANKS

Table of Equivalent Officer Ranks

	Belgium	British Army	Britain, RAF	Britain, Royal Navy
1.	-	-	-	-
2.	-	Field Marshal	Marshal of the RAF	Admiral of the Fleet
3.	-	-	-	-
4.	-	-	-	-
5.	Lieutenant General	General	Air Chief Marshal	Admiral
6.	Major General	Lieutenant General	Air Marshal	Vice Admiral
7.	Colonel-Brigadier	Major General	Air Vice-Marshal	Rear Admiral
8.	-	Brigadier	Air Commodore	Commodore
9.	-	-	-	-
10.	Colonel	Colonel	Group Captain	Captain
11.	Lieutenant Colonel	Lieutenant Colonel	Wing Commander	Commander
12.	Major	Major	Squadron Leader	Lieutenant Commander
13.	Captain Commandant	Captain	Flight Lieutenant	Lieutenant
14.	Captain	-	-	-
15.	Lieutenant	Lieutenant	Flying Officer	Sub-Lieutenant
16.	-	-	-	-
17.	Second Lieutenant	Second Lieutenant	Pilot Officer	-

Table of Equivalent Enlisted Ranks

	Belgium	British Army	Britain, RAF	Britain, Royal Navy
1.	Sergeant Major	Regimental Sergeant Major	Master Technician	Chief Petty Officer
2.	First Sergeant	Sergeant Major	Flight Sergeant, Chief Technician	Petty Officer
3.	-	Quartermaster Sergeant	-	-
4.	-	Staff Sergeant	-	-
5.	Sergeant	Sergeant	Sergeant, Senior Technician	-
6.	-	-	-	-
7.	Corporal	Corporal	Corporal	Leading Seaman
8.	-	Lance Corporal	-	-
9.	Private 1st Class	-	Junior Technician	-
10.	-	Senior Private	-	-
11.	Private	-	-	-
12.	-	Private	Private	Seaman

TABLE OF COMPARATIVE RANKS (*Cont.*)

Table of Equivalent Officer Ranks

	Bulgaria	China	Czechoslovakia	Denmark	Finland
1.	-	Generalissimo*	-	-	-
2.	-	-	-	-	Marshal of Finland
3.	-	-	-	-	-
4.	-	-	-	-	-
5.	General of Army	General	General of Army	General	General
6.	Lieutenant General	Lieutenant General	-	Lieutenant General	Lieutenant General
7.	Major General	Major General	General of Division	Major General	Major General
8.	-	-	General of Brigade	-	-
9.	-	-	-	-	-
10.	Colonel	Colonel	Colonel	Colonel	Colonel
11.	Lieutenant Colonel	Lieutenant Colonel	Lieutenant Colonel	Lieutenant Colonel	Lieutenant Colonel
12.	Major	Major	Major	-	Major
13.	Captain	Captain	Staff Captain	Captain	Captain
14.	-	-	Captain	Captain Lieutenant	-
15.	First Lieutenant	First Lieutenant	Senior Lieutenant	First Lieutenant	Lieutenant
16.	-	-	Lieutenant	-	-
17.	Second Lieutenant	Second Lieutenant	Junior Lieutenant	Second Lieutenant	Second Lieutenant

Table of Equivalent Enlisted Ranks

	Bulgaria	China	Czechoslovakia	Denmark	Finland
1.	Sergeant Major	First Sergeant	Staff Sergeant	Sergeant Major	Sergeant Major
2.	-	-	-	-	-
3.	-	-	Sergeant	-	Senior Sergeant
4.	-	-	Senior Platoon Sergeant	-	-
5.	Sergeant	Sergeant	Platoon Sergeant	Sergeant	Sergeant
6.	Candidate Sergeant	-	-	-	Junior Sergeant
7.	Corporal	Corporal	Corporal	Corporal	Corporal
8.	-	-	-	Lance Corporal	-
9.	-	-	-	-	-
10.	-	Private 1st Class	-	-	-
11.	-	Private 2nd Class	-	-	-
12.	Private	Private 3rd Class	Private	Private	Private

*Held only by Chiang Kai-shek.

TABLE OF COMPARATIVE RANKS

Table of Equivalent Officer Ranks

	France, Army	France, Navy	German Army and Luftwaffe	German SS
1.	-		Reichsmarschall°	-
2.	Marshal of France	Admiral	Generalfeldmarschall	Reichsführer-SS°°
3.	-		-	-
4.	-	Vice Admiral D'escadre		SS-Oberstgruppenführer
5.	General of Army	Vice Admiral	Generaloberst	SS-Obergruppenführer
6.	General of Army Corps		General der Infanterie, der Flieger, etc.	SS-Gruppenführer
7.	General of Division	Rear Admiral	Generalleutnant	SS-Brigadeführer
8.	-		Generalmajor	SS-Oberführer
9.	-			SS-Standartenführer
10.	Colonel	Captain	Oberst	SS-Obersturmbannführer
11.	Lieutenant Colonel	Commander	Oberstleutnant	SS-Sturmbannführer
12.	Major	Lieutenant Commander	Major	SS-Hauptsturmführer
13.	Captain	Lieutenant	Hauptmann (Rittmeister in Cavalry)	
14.	-			SS-Obersturmführer
15.	Lieutenant	Lieutenant (Junior Grade)	Leutnant	
16.	-			SS-Untersturmführer
17.	Second Lieutenant	Ensign	Unterleutnant	

Table of Equivalent Enlisted Ranks

	France, Army	France, Navy	German Army and Luftwaffe	German SS
1.	Chief Sergeant	-	Oberfeldwebel	SS-Sturmscharführer
2.	-	-	Feldwebel	SS-Hauptscharführer
3.	-	Petty Officer 1st Class	Fähnrich	SS-Oberscharführer
4.	-	Petty Officer 2nd Class	Unterfeldwebel	-
5.	Sergeant	Petty Officer 3rd Class	Unteroffizier	SS-Scharführer
6.	Chief Corporal		Stabsgefreiter and Hauptgefreiter	SS-Unterscharführer
7.	Corporal	Leading Seaman Class I	Obergefreiter	SS-Rottenführer
8.	-		Gefreiter	-
9.	Private 1st Class	Leading Seaman	-	SS-Sturmmann
10.	-	Able Seaman	Oberschütze	Obermann
11.	-		-	SS-Mann
12.	Private	Seaman	Mannschaften	SS-Anwärter
13.	-			

° Conferred upon Hermann Göring in July 1940 and held exclusively by him.

°° Held exclusively by Heinrich Himmler.

433

TABLE OF COMPARATIVE RANKS (*Cont.*)

Table of Equivalent Officer Ranks

#	Imperial Japanese Army	Imperial Japanese Navy	Indian Army (British)	Indian National Army (Japanese)
1.	-	-		
2.	-	-		
3.	-	-		
4.	-	-		
5.	General	Admiral		General
6.	Lieutenant General	Vice Admiral		Lieutenant General
7.	Major General	Rear Admiral		Major General
8.	-	-		
9.	-	-		
10.	Colonel	Captain		Colonel
11.	Lieutenant Colonel	Commander		Lieutenant Colonel
12.	Major	Lieutenant Commander		Major
13.	Captain	Lieutenant, Senior Grade		Captain
14.	-	-		
15.	Lieutenant	Lieutenant	Risaldar/Subadar	First Lieutenant
16.	-	-		
17.	Second Lieutenant	-	Jemadar	Second Lieutenant

Table of Equivalent Enlisted Ranks

#	Imperial Japanese Army	Imperial Japanese Navy	Indian Army (British)	Indian National Army (Japanese)
1.	Sergeant Major	Senior Petty Officer	Risaldar/Havildar-Major	Sub-Officer
2.	-	-		
3.	-	-		
4.	-	Petty Officer 1st Class		
5.	Sergeant	Petty Officer 2nd Class	Dafadar/Havildar	Havildar
6.	-	-		
7.	Corporal	Leading Seaman	Naik/Amaldar	Naik
8.	Leading Private	Senior Seaman	Lance Naik	Lance Naik
9.	Superior Private	-		
10.	Private 1st Class	Seaman 1st Class		
11.	Private 2nd Class	Seaman	Rifleman/Sepoy	
12.	Recruit	Recruit	Recruit	Recruit

TABLE OF COMPARATIVE RANKS
Table of Equivalent Officer Ranks

	Italy	Italy (Regia Aeronautica)	Netherlands	Poland (Army)	Poland (Navy)
1.	First Marshal of the Empire	Air Marshal	-	-	-
2.	Marshal of Italy	-	-	Marshal of Poland	-
3.	-	-	-	-	-
4.	General of Army	General of Air Army	General	General of Army	-
5.	Commanding General of Army	General of Air Squad	Lieutenant General	-	-
6.	General of Army Corps	General of Air Division	Major General	-	-
7.	General of Division	General of Air Brigade	-	General of Division	Vice Admiral
8.	General of Brigade	-	-	General of Brigade	Rear Admiral
9.	-	-	-	-	-
10.	Colonel	Colonel	Colonel	Colonel	Commander
11.	Lieutenant Colonel	Lieutenant Colonel	Lieutenant Colonel	Lieutenant Colonel	Lieutenant Commander
12.	Major	Major	Major	Major	Sub-Lieutenant Commander
13.	First Captain	Captain	Captain	Captain	Captain
14.	Captain	-	-	-	Lieutenant
15.	First Lieutenant	Lieutenant	First Lieutenant	Lieutenant	-
16.	Lieutenant	-	-	-	-
17.	Lieutenant	Second Lieutenant	Second Lieutenant	Sub-Lieutenant	Sub-Lieutenant

Table of Equivalent Enlisted Ranks

	Italy	Italy (Regia Aeronautica)	Netherlands	Poland (Army)	Poland (Navy)
1.	Sergeant Major	Sergeant Major	Sergeant Major	Senior Sergeant	Senior Boatswain
2.	-	-	Sergeant 1st Class	-	-
3.	-	-	-	-	-
4.	-	-	-	-	-
5.	Sergeant	Sergeant	Sergeant	Sergeant	Boatswain
6.	Corporal Major	-	-	Lance Sergeant	Boatswains Mate
7.	Corporal	Leading Airman	Corporal	Corporal	Mate
8.	-	-	-	-	-
9.	-	-	-	-	-
10.	-	-	Private 1st Class	Senior Private	Senior Seaman
11.	-	-	-	-	-
12.	Private	Airman	Private	Private	Seaman

TABLE OF COMPARATIVE RANKS (*Cont.*)

Table of Equivalent Officer Ranks

Soviet Union	Soviet Union Political Commissars	Yugoslavia
1. Generalissimo°	-	-
2. Marshal of the Soviet Union	-	Field Marshal
3. Marshal (Senior)	-	-
4. Marshal	-	-
5. General (Commander of Army, 1st Rank)	Commissar of Army (1st and 2nd Rank)	General of Army
6. General (Commander of Army, 2nd Rank)	Commissar of Army Corps	-
7. Lieutenant General	Commissar of Division	General of Division
8. Major General	Commissar of Brigade	General of Brigade
9. -	-	-
10. Colonel	Commissar of Regiment	Colonel
11. Lieutenant Colonel	-	Lieutenant Colonel
12. Major	Commissar of Battalion	Major
13. Captain	Senior Politruk	First Captain
14. -	-	Captain
15. Senior Lieutenant	Politruk	Lieutenant
16. Lieutenant	-	-
17. Junior Lieutenant	Politruk	Second Lieutenant

Table of Equivalent Enlisted Ranks

Soviet Union	Yugoslavia
1. Sergeant Major (Starshina)	First Sergeant
2. -	-
3. -	-
4. Senior Sergeant (Starshina Serzhant)	Sergeant
5. Sergeant (Serzhant)	
6. Junior Sergeant (Mladshiy Serzhant)	
7. Corporal	Corporal
8. -	
9. -	
10. Private First Class (Ye Freitor)	
11. -	
12. Private (Ryadovoi)	Private

°Conferred upon Stalin in 1945 and held exclusively by him.

ARMS

TANKS

	Weight (in tons)	Length	Speed (mph)	Range (in miles)	Armament	Crew	No. Built
British							
Mark IIA "Matilda"	29.7	18'5''	15	160	1 Mark IX mg	4	2,987
Mark III "Valentine"	17.9	17'9''	15	90	1 2-pounder	3	8,275
Mark IV "Churchill"	43.1	24'5''	15	120	1 6-pounder	5	5,640
Mark VI "Crusader"	22.1	19'7''	27	200	1 2-pounder	5	5,300
Mark VIA	5.7	13'2''	35	131	1 mg	3	1,000 plus
Mark VIII "Cromwell"	30.8	20'10''	38	174	1 75-mm	5	
German							
PzKpfw II	9.35	15'9''	25	118	1 20-mm 1 mg	3	650
PzKpfw III	24.5	17'9''	25	160	1 50-mm 2 mg	5	5,650
PzKpfw IV	19.7	19'4''	26	125	1 75-mm 2 mg	5	6,000
PzKpfw V	49.3	29'	24	124	1 75-mm	5	3,740
PzKpfw VI "Tiger I"	62.7	27'9''	23	73	1 88-mm 2 mg	5	1,350
PzKpfw VI "Tiger II"	74.8	33'9''	26	106	1 88-mm 2 mg	5	485
PzKpfw "Elephant"	74.8	22'3''	22	49	1 88-mm	6	90
PzKpfw "Chaser"	17.6	20'7''	26	130	1 75-mm	4	1,577
PzKpfw "Panther"	50	33'1''	28	100	1 88-mm	5	384
Italian							
L 3	3.4	10'5''	26	75	2 mg (also flame-thrower versions)	2	2,500
L 11/39	10.8	15'6''	21	124	1 37-mm 2 mg	2	100
Mi3/40	15.4	16'2''	20	124	1 47-mm 1 mg		2,000
Japanese							
Type 89B "Chi-Ro"	12.8	18'1''	15.5	100	1 57-mm 2 mg	4	
Type 95 "Ha-Go"	7.5	14'4''	28	155	1 37-mm	3	2,464
Type 97 "Chi-Ha"	15.6	18'1''	24	130	1 47-mm 2 mg	5	
Russian							
JSII "Joseph Stalin"	45.3	32'2''	23	150	1 122-mm 4 mg	4	
KV1A "Kliment Voroshilov"	52	22'	25	208	1 76.2-mm 2 mg	5	10,000
SU85	32.4	26'8''	34	186	1 85-mm	5	
T26	10.1	15'3''	16.8	215	1 45-mm 2 mg	3	4,500

TANKS (*Cont.*)

Russian

	Weight	Length	Speed (mph)	Range (in miles)	Armament	Crew	No. Built
T34/76	29.7	21'7''	32		1 76-mm	4	40,000 (all models)
T34/85	34.4	20'2''	32	250	1 85-mm 2 mg	5	

U.S.

	Weight	Length	Speed (mph)	Range (in miles)	Armament	Crew	No. Built
M3 "Lee" and "Grant"	31	18'6''	22	146	1 75-mm 1 37-mm 4 mg	6	4,924
M3A1 "Stuart"	14.3	14'10''	36	60	1 37-mm	4	4,621
M4A3 "Sherman"	37.1	19'3''	30	120	1 76-mm 3 mg	5	49,000
M26 "Pershing"	41.1	28'10''	20	92	1 90-mm 2 mg	5	2,428

MILITARY AIRCRAFT PRODUCTION
(Includes All Types)

	1939	1940	1941	1942	1943	1944	1945°
Britain	7,940	15,049	20,094	23,672	26,263	26,461	12,070
Soviet Union	10,382	10,565	15,735	25,436	34,900	40,300	20,900
U.S.	2,141	6,086	19,433	47,836	85,898	96,318	46,001
Germany	8,295	10,826	12,401	15,409	24,807	40,593	7,540
Japan	4,467	4,768	5,088	8,861	16,693	28,180	8,263

°through end of war

EUROPEAN STRATEGIC BOMBING TARGETS OF ALLIED AIR FORCES
RAF Bomber Command and U.S. Eighth and Fifteenth Air Forces
(in Tons)

	Area Bombing	Rail Facilities	Oil and Chemical Plants	Aircraft Factories	Miscellaneous	Total
Jan. 1940–Dec. 1942	55,000	11,000	—	—	32,000	98,000
Jan. 1943–March 1944	177,000	31,000	°	16,000	77,000	301,000
April 1944–April 1945	376,000	488,000	216,000	22,000	355,000	1,457,000
Total Strategic	608,000	530,000	216,000	38,000	464,000	1,856,000
Total Nonstrategic Military						844,000

°Less than 500 tons

SOURCE: Basic data from *U.S. Strategic Bombing Survey: Europe.*

COMBAT AIRCRAFT OF WORLD WAR II

The following is a performance summary of the principal combat aircraft flown by the major participants. They are divided by type: fighters, bombers, and attack aircraft, the last being a definition for the planes which generally served dual or multipurpose roles. Performance characteristics are typical for the model designated, but each aircraft went through several, if not dozens, of modifications and improvements. The figures are intended to give the reader a basic knowledge of the aircraft for purposes of comparison. The column "No. Built" indicates all models of the particular aircraft, not just the model indicated.

British Fighters

	Max. Speed (mph)	Service Ceiling (feet)	Max. Range (miles)	Armament	No. Built
Beaufighter I F	325	27,000	1,540	6 x .303	5,928
				4 x 20-mm	
Blenheim IV F	266	26,500	1,950	7 x .303	3,297
Defiant	303	30,500	500	4 x .303	1,064
Gladiator	245	32,500	440	4 x .303	767
Hurricane II C	339	35,600	460	4 x 20-mm	14,231
Spitfire I	355	34,000	395	8 x .303	20,334
Spitfire XIV	448	43,500	460	2 x 20-mm	
				4 x .303	
Tempest VI	438	37,000	740	4 x .20-mm	942
Typhoon	412	35,200	510	4 x .20-mm	3,300

French Fighters

	Max. Speed	Service Ceiling	Max. Range	Armament	No. Built
Dewoitine D520	327	36,090	777	1 x 20-mm	740
				6 x 7.5-mm	
Morane-Saulnier MS-406	302	30,840	497	1 x 20-mm	1,081
				2 x .75-mm	

German Fighters

	Max. Speed	Service Ceiling	Max. Range	Armament	No. Built
Focke-Wulf FW-190D	435	39,000	560	2 x 20-mm	20,001
				2 x 30-mm	
Heinkel He-219	416	41,660	1,243	2 x 20-mm	587
				1 x 30-mm	
Messerschmitt Me-109G	400	39,750	460	2 x 7.9-13-mm-	30,480
				3 x .20-mm	
Messerschmitt Me-110G	368	36,800		6 x 7.9-mm	
				4 x 20-mm	
				1 x 37-mm	
Messerschmitt Me-163 Komet (Jet)	596	54,000	65	2 x 30-mm	370
Messerschmitt Me-262 (Jet)	560	40,000	650	4 x 30-mm	1,294
				3 x 20-mm	

Italian Fighters

	Max. Speed	Service Ceiling	Max. Range	Armament	No. Built
Fiat G-50 Freccia	385	42,650	994	2 x 12.7-mm	590
				1 x 20-mm	
Macchi C-200 Saetta	312	29,200	354	2 x 12.7-mm	
				2 x 7.7-mm	
Macchi C-202 Folgore	370	36,000		2 x 7.7-mm	1,500

COMBAT AIRCRAFT OF WORLD WAR II (Cont.)

Japanese Fighters

	Max. Speed (mph)	Service Ceiling (feet)	Max. Range (miles)	Armament	No. Built
Kawanishi Shiden, "George"	369	35,400	989	2 x 7.7-mm 4 x 20-mm	1,440
Kawasaki Hien, "Tony"	367	37,700	1,243	2 x 20-mm 2 x 7.7-mm	2,654
Mitsubishi A5M, "Claude"	273	32,800	460	2 x 7.7-mm	782
Mitsubishi Zero-Sen, "Zeke"	360	39,370	1,940	3 x 13.2-mm	10,937
Mitsubishi Raiden, "Jack"	382	38,800	1,580	4 x 20-mm	480
Nakajima Ki-27, "Nate"	286	34,000	389	2 x 7.7-mm	3,399
Nakajima Ki-43, "Oscar"	363	36,800	1,060	2 x 20-mm	5,919
Nakajima Ki-44 "Tojo"	376	36,700	560	2 x 12.7-mm 2 x 40-mm	1,233
Nakajima Ki-84, "Frank"	388	34,450	1,025	2 x 20-mm 2 x 30-mm	3,514

Russian Fighters

	Max. Speed (mph)	Service Ceiling (feet)	Max. Range (miles)	Armament	No. Built
Lavochkin La-7	423	34,448	392	3 x 20-mm	
Lavochkin La-11	460	36,100	466	4 x 23-mm	
Mikoyan Mig-3	398	39,370	776	1 x 12.7-mm 2 x 7.62-mm	
Petlyakov Pe-3	336	28,870	746	1 x 12.7-mm 2 x 7.62-mm	11,400
Polikarpov I-16	288	29,500	500	2 x 7.62-mm	7,000
Yakovlev Yak-1	373	32,800	582	1 x 20-mm 2 x 12.7-mm	37,000
Yakovlev Yak-3	447	35,450	506	1 x 20-mm 2 x 12.7-mm	
Yakovlev Yak-9	370	33,135	565	1 x 20-mm 1 x 12.7-mm	

U.S. Fighters

	Max. Speed (mph)	Service Ceiling (feet)	Max. Range (miles)	Armament	No. Built
F4F Wildcat	318	35,000	900	4 x .50	
F4U Corsair	415	37,000	1,015	6 x .50	12,571
F6F Hellcat	376	37,500	1,090	6 x .50	12,272
P-38L Lightning	414	44,000	460	1 x 20-mm 4 x .50	9,942
P-39D Airacobra	335	29,500	600	1 x .37 2 x .50 2 x .30	4,900
P-40F Kittyhawk	364	30,000	610	6 x .50	13,738
P-47D Thunderbolt	428	40,000	1,000	8 x .50	15,579
P-51D Mustang	437	41,900	2,300	6 x .50	14,490
P-61B Black Widow	366	33,100	3,000	4 x .50	976
P-63A Kingcobra	36±	43,000	2,200	1 x .37 3 x .50	332

British Bombers

	Max. Speed (mph)	Service Ceiling (feet)	Max. Range (miles)	Bomb Load (pounds)	Crew	No. Built
Halifax III	280	20,000	1,985	7,000	7	6,176
Hampden	254	19,000	1,100	4,000	4	1,430
Lancaster III	280	20,000	2,250	10,000	7	7,377
Stirling III	270	17,000	2,010	2,500	7/8	2,221
Wellington X	255	18,250	1,885	1,500	6	11,461
Whitley V	222	21,000	1,650	3,000	5	1,737

German Bombers

	Max. Speed (mph)	Service Ceiling (feet)	Max. Range (miles)	Bomb Load (pounds)	Crew	No. Built
Dornier Do-217E	305	21,500	1,170	4,400	4	1,730
Heinkel He-111	240	26,000	1,510	2,200	4/5	5,656
Junkers Ju-885	370	35,000	700	1,980	2/6	14,980
Junkers Ju-188	325	33,000	1,200	4,400	5	1,100

Italian Bombers

	Max. Speed (mph)	Service Ceiling (feet)	Max. Range (miles)	Bomb Load (pounds)	Crew	No. Built
Savoia-Marchetti SM-79	270	23,000	1,240	2,200	4/5	1,300

Japanese Bombers

	Max. Speed (mph)	Service Ceiling (feet)	Max. Range (miles)	Bomb Load (pounds)	Crew	No. Built
Mitsubishi G4M, "Betty"	283	30,000	2,262	2,200		2,479
Mitsubishi 7 Ki-21, "Sally"	294	30,500	1,635	2,200	7	2,064
Mitsubishi Ki-67, "Peggy"	346	30,100	1,840	1,875		727
Nakajima-100, "Helen"	312	30,500	1,600	2,200	8	1,233

Russian Bombers

	Max. Speed (mph)	Service Ceiling (feet)	Max. Range (miles)	Bomb Load (pounds)	Crew	No. Built
Ilyushin II-4	255	32,800	1,616	2,205	4	6,800

U.S. Bombers

	Max. Speed (mph)	Service Ceiling (feet)	Max. Range (miles)	Bomb Load (pounds)	Crew	No. Built
B-17 E (Boeing)	317	35,000	1,100	6,000	6/10	12,731
B-24J (Consolidated Vultee)	290	28,000	2,200	5,000	10	19,203
B-25J (North American)	275	24,000	1,500	4,000	4/6	9,816
B-26E (Martin)	310	23,000	1,150	3,000	5/7	5,157
B-29 (Boeing)	357	36,000	3,250	10,000	10/14	3,000

British Attack Aircraft

	Max. Speed (mph)	Service Ceiling (feet)	Max. Range (miles)	Bomb Load (pounds)	Crew	No. Built
Beaufort	260	16,500	1,600	2,000	4	2,080
Blenheim V	260	31,500	1,950	1,000	3	3,297
Mosquito IX	400	37,000	1,860	1,000	2	7,781

French Attack Aircraft

	Max. Speed (mph)	Service Ceiling (feet)	Max. Range (miles)	Bomb Load (pounds)	Crew	No. Built
Potez	633	26,250	810	1,323	2/3	900

German Attack Aircraft

	Max. Speed (mph)	Service Ceiling (feet)	Max. Range (miles)	Bomb Load (pounds)	Crew	No. Built
Arado Ar 234 Butz (Jet)	461	32,800	684	3,300	1	210
Dornier Do-215	280	31,170	932	2,200	4	535
Focke-Wulf FW-189	217	23,950	416	440	3	846
Henschel Hs-129	253	29,530	547	220	1	
Junkers Ju-87	250	24,000	620	1,500	2	4,881

COMBAT AIRCRAFT OF WORLD WAR II (*Cont.*)

Japanese Attack Aircraft

	Max. Speed (mph)	Service Ceiling (feet)	Max. Range (miles)	Bomb Load (pounds)	Crew	No. Built
Aichi D3A, "Val"	281	31,170	1,131	380	2	1,294
Kawasaki Ki-48, "Lily"	314	33,135	1,491	1,764	4	1,977
Nakajima B6N, "Jill"	299	29,659	1,084	1,320	3	
Nakajima Ki-44, "Tojo"	376	36,745	560	440	1	1,233
Yokosuka D4Y, "Judy"	360	34,500	749	680	2	2,038

Russian Attack Aircraft

Ilyushin 11-2 Stormovik	311	21,325	373	1,323	1/2	42,330
Sukhoi Su-2	283	28,870	746	882	2	1,500 (plus)
Tupolev SB-2	280	35,000	990	1,100	3	6,000
Tupolev Tu-2	342	31,168	1,553	3,300	4	1,000

U.S. Attack Aircraft

A-20 Boston, Havoc (Douglas)	351	25,000	1,000	4,000	2/3	7,385
A-26 Invader (Douglas)	355	22,100	1,400	8,000	3	1,355
A-29 Hudson (Lockheed)	261	24,500	2,160	750	4	2,584
A-30 Baltimore (Martin)	320	24,000	1,060	1,000	4	1,975
SBD Dauntless (Douglas)	252	24,300	456	1,000	2	5,936
SB2C Helldiver (Curtiss)	281	24,700	1,100	1,000	2	7,200
TBM Avenger (Grumman)	267	30,100	2,530	2,000	3	9,839

SELECTED WEAPONS AND WAR ITEMS PRODUCED BY ALL NATIONS (1939–1945)

Aircraft	443,031
Guns (from rifles to artillery pieces)	49,319,462
Ammunition (from bullets to heavy bombs)	82,352,314,472
Ships (naval and merchant)	79,000,000 tons
Vehicles (jeeps through tanks)	5,157,458

SOURCE: Arthur Guy Enoch, *This War Business.*

MILITARY AIRCRAFT LOSSES (1939–1945)

Germany	95,000	Canada	2,389
U.S.	59,296	France	2,100
Japan	49,485	New Zealand	684
Britain	33,090	India	527
Australia	7,160	Sweden°	272
Italy	4,000	Denmark	154

°Neutral

(Russian losses were extremely high, but they were undisclosed by the Soviet government.)

SOURCE: Arthur Guy Enoch, *This War Business.*

U.S. AIRCRAFT PRODUCED IN GREATEST NUMBERS (July 1940–Aug 1945)

B-24	18,188	F6F	12,210
P-47	15,579	C-47	10,247
P-51	14,490	TBM-TBF	9,812
P-40	13,700	P-39	9,585
B-17	12,677	P-38	9,535

BRITISH AND U.S. AIRCRAFT DELIVERIES TO RUSSIA

Hurricanes	2,000
Spitfires	
MK VB	143
LF 9s	1,186
P-39 Airacobras	4,746
P-63 Kingcobras	2,400
P-47 Thunderbolts	195
B-25 Mitchells	862
C-47s	700
All others	6,633
Total	18,865
Lost in transit	638

(The Soviets produced 158,218 of their own aircraft between 1939 and the conclusion of the war in 1945.)

GERMAN AIRCRAFT PRODUCTION
(Sept. 1939–May 1945)
Most Produced Planes

Aircraft	Numbers	Aircraft	Numbers
Me-109	30,480	Ju-87	4,881
FW-190	20,001	Ju-52	2,804
Ju-88	15,000	Do-217	1,730
Me-110	5,762	He-177	1,446
He-111	5,656	Me-262	1,294

Total of 10 most produced planes   89,054

All Planes Produced by Type

Fighters	53,729	Transports	3,079
Bombers	18,235	Liaison	2,549
Ground attack	12,539	Jet aircraft	
Trainers	10,942	and rockets	1,988
Reconnaissance	6,299	Naval	1,190
Gliders	3,145	Total	113,515

Aircraft Production by Year

1939	2,518	1943	24,807
1940	10,247	1944	40,593
1941	12,401	1945	7,540
1942	15,409		

WEAPONS AND MUNITIONS DELIVERED TO U.S. ARMY AND AIR FORCE (1942–1945)

Combat aircraft	129,255
Support aircraft	80,930
240-mm howitzers	315
155-mm field guns	6,389
8-inch field guns	1,193
105-mm howitzers	18,269
90-mm guns	4,853
76-mm guns	14,952
75-mm guns	58,342
3-inch guns	9,325
57-mm guns	16,999
37-mm guns	62,397
Antiaircraft artillery pieces	49,100
Rocket launchers	476,628
Aircraft machine guns	1,575,114
Ground machine guns	945,989
Antiaircraft machine guns	72,777
Rifles	6,174,363
Carbines	6,117,822
Submachine guns	1,790,847

WEAPONS AND MUNITIONS DELIVERED TO U.S. ARMY AND AIR FORCE (1942–1945) (Cont.)

Ammunition	
240-mm and 8-inch	3,126,000
155-mm	27,340,000
105-mm	93,081,000
90-mm	16,386,000
75-mm	75,244,000
37-mm	100,500,000
Mortar	97,174,000
Bombs (all types)	37,701,000
Tanks	
Heavy	2,464
Medium	55,560
Light	26,003
Jeeps	631,873

LOSSES SUFFERED BY RAF BOMBER COMMAND ON DAY AND NIGHT MISSIONS (1939–1945)

	Number of Missions	Aircraft Losses	Pct. Loss
	1939		
Day	163	29	17.8
Night	170	4	2.3
Day	3,316	152	4.6
Night	17,493	342	2.0
Day	3,507	213	6.1
Night	27,101	701	2.6
Day	2,313	109	4.7
Night	32,737	1,291	3.9
Day	1,792	59	3.3
Night	62,736	2,255	3.6
Day	35,096	224	0.6
Night	113,352	2,349	2.1
Day	20,664	90	0.4
Night	44,074	507	1.2

SOURCE: Sir Charles Webster and Nobel Franklin, *The Strategic Air Offensive Against Germany, 1939–45*, Vol. IV.

THE NAMING OF WARSHIPS

	Japan	United States
Battleships	Ancient provinces	States
Heavy cruisers	Mountains	Cities (Late in the war heavier models named after territories or possessions)
Light cruisers	Rivers	Cities
Carriers	Mythical flying objects, animals, or large birds	Famous early ships or battles of the Revolutionary War
Destroyers	Poetic description of weather (e.g., *Shigure*, "Drizzling autumn rain")	Distinguished U.S. naval personnel
Submarines	Prefixed by I, Ro, or Ha, corresponding to A, B, and C, with consecutive numbers	Fish

MAJOR COMBAT SHIPS

British Battleships

	Displacement (full load tons)	Length (feet)	Beam (feet)	Maximum Side Armor (inches)	Service Speed (knots)	Cruising Range (statute miles)	Guns	Crew
Hood	46,200	860	105	12	28.8	6,000	4 x 4''	1,421
King George V (also *Prince of Wales*, *Duke of York*, *Anson*, and *Howe*)	44,780	754	103	15	29.5	14,000	10 x 14''	1,644
Nelson (also *Rodney*)	38,000	710	106	14	24	16,500	9 x 16'' 12 x 6''	1,314
Queen Elizabeth (also *Barham* and *Valiant*)	37,400	640	104	13	23.5	13,500	8 x 15''	1,124

French Battleships

	Displacement	Length	Beam	Maximum Side Armor	Service Speed	Cruising Range	Guns	Crew
Dunkerque (also *Strasbourg*)	36,500	704	102	9.75	30.5	8,900	8 x 13''	1,381
Richelieu (also *Jean Bart*)	47,500	812	108	15.7	32	10,110	8 x 15''	1,670

German Battleships

	Displacement	Length	Beam	Maximum Side Armor	Service Speed	Cruising Range	Guns	Crew
Bismarck (also *Tirpitz*)	50,153	823	118	12.75	30	11,038	8 x 15'' 12 x 5.9'' 16 x 4.1''	2,092

Italian Battleships

	Displacement	Length	Beam	Maximum Side Armor	Service Speed	Cruising Range	Guns	Crew
Andrea Doria (also *Caio Duilio*)	28,928	612	91.8	9.8	27	4,250	12 x 5.3'' 10 x 3.5''	1,485

Japanese Battleships

	Displacement	Length	Beam	Maximum Side Armor	Service Speed	Cruising Range (statute miles)	Guns	Crew
	(full load tons)	(feet)	(feet)	(inches)	(knots)			
Ise (also Hyuga)	38,700	720.5	111	12	33	11,240	8 x 14'' 16 x 5''	1,463
Kongo (also Hiei, Haruna, and Kirishima)	36,610	723	95	8	30	11,660	8 x 14'' 8 x 6''	1,437
Mikasa	15,179	432	76.2	9	18	5,300	14 x 16'' 8 x 8''	830
Nagato (also Mutsu)	42,785	725.3	113	11.8	25	10,300	18 x 5.5'' 8 x 5''	
Yamato (also Musashi and Shinano)	72,809	862	127.6	16.1	27	7,200	9 x 18.1'' 6 x 6/1'' 24 x 5''	2,200

Russian Battleships

	Displacement	Length	Beam	Maximum Side Armor	Service Speed	Cruising Range	Guns	Crew
Marat (also Sevastopol and Oktyabrskaya Revolutsia)	26,170	606.5	88.25	8.9	23.4	1,120	12 x 12'' 16 x 4.7''	1,286

U.S. Battleships

	Displacement	Length	Beam	Maximum Side Armor	Service Speed	Cruising Range	Guns	Crew
Iowa (also New Jersey, Missouri, and Wisconsin)	55,710	887	108	12.1	33	20,727	9 x 16'' 20 x 5''	2,270
North Carolina (also Washington)	44,800	729	108	12	28	—	9 x 16'' 20 x 5''	2,339
Tennessee (also California)	40,500	624	114	14	21	10,000	12 x 14'' 16 x 5''	2,375
Texas (also New York)	32,000	573	106	12	21	10,000	10 x 14'' 6 x 5''	1,530

British Cruisers

	Displacement	Length	Beam	Maximum Side Armor	Service Speed	Cruising Range	Guns	Crew
County class (13 built)	14,450	630	68.5	5.5	31.5	12,370	1 x 5.2'' 1 x 2.5''	700
Dido (15 others)	6,700	512	50.5	3	32	3,480	10 x 5.25''	480
Town class (15 built)	11,470	591	61.75	4	32.5	8,330	12 x 6'' 8 x 4''	700
York (also Exeter)	9,500	575	57	3	32	10,000	6 x 8'' 4 x 4''	630

Dutch Cruisers

	Displacement	Length	Beam	Maximum Side Armor	Service Speed	Cruising Range	Guns	Crew
De Ruyter	7,548	561	51.5	2	32	8,100	7 x 5.9''	435

MAJOR COMBAT SHIPS (*Cont.*)
German Cruisers

	Displacement	Length	Beam	Maximum Side Armor	Service Speed	Cruising Range	Guns	Crew
	(full load tons)	*(feet)*	*(feet)*	*(inches)*	*(knots)*	*(statute miles)*		
Graf Spee (also *Deutschland* and *Scheer*)	16,200	610	69.9	3.1	28	9,000	6 x 11″ 8 x 5.9″ 6 x 4.1″	1,150
Hipper (also *Blücher* and *Prinz Eugen*)	18,400	677	69.9	3.1	32	6,540	8 x 8″ 12 x 4.1″	1,600
Königsberg (also *Köln* and *Karlsruhe*)	8,350	569.9	54.4	2.8	32	6,780	9 x 5.9″ 4 x 3.5″	820

Italian Cruisers

Garibaldi (19 others)	11,262	612	61.9	5.1	34	4,500	10 x 6″ 8 x 3.9″	640
Zara (also *Fiume, Pola,* and *Gorizia*)	14,350	599	66.6	5.9	34	5,360	8 x 8″ 12 x 3.9″	830

Japanese Cruisers

Kuma (also *Tama, Kitatami, Kiso,* and *Oi*)	5,380	534	46.6	1.97	36	9,000	4 x 5.5″	
Mogami (also *Mikuma, Kumano,* and *Suzuya*)	12,400	646	66.3	—	34.5	—	6 x 7.9″ 8 x 5″	850

U.S. Cruisers

Alaska (also *Guam*)	34,250	808	90.75	9	33	—	9 x 12″ 12 x 5″	2,251
Baltimore (13 others)	17,070	675	70.9	6	33	—	9 x 8″ 12 x 5″	1,700
Brooklyn (8 others)	12,700	608	61.75	4	32.5	17,840	15 x 6″ 8 x 5″	868
Cleveland (26 others)	13,755	610	66.5	5	33	—	12 x 6″ 12 x 5″	1,200
Portland (also *Indianapolis*)	12,575	610	66.1	4	32	—	9 x 8″ 8 x 5″	952

British Aircraft Carriers

	Displacement	Length	Beam	Service Speed	Cruising Range	Planes	Crew
	(full load tons)	*(feet)*	*(feet)*	*(knots)*	*(statute miles)*		
Ark Royal	27,720	721	96	31	8,775	72	1,636
Eagle	27,500	667	105	24	3,570	21	950
Furious	28,500	786	107.8	29.5	—	33	1,200
Hermes	13,000	600	70	25	—	20	850
Illustrious (also *Formidable, Victorious, Indomitable, Implacable,* and *Indefatigable*)	28,619	743	95.75	30.5	11,000	36	1,500

Japanese Aircraft Carriers

	Displacement (full load tons)	Length (feet)	Beam (feet)	Service Speed (knots)	Cruising Range (statute miles)	Planes	Crew
Hosho	8,500	552	74.5	25	8,680	21	550
Soryu (also Hiryu)	18,800	746	85.3	34.5	7,680	71	1,101
Taiho	37,270	855	98	33	10,000	74	1,751

U.S. Aircraft Carriers

Essex (23 others)	39,800	899	93	33	18,000	80	3,448
Hornet (also Yorktown and Enterprise)	29,100	827	114	33		85	2,900
Independence (8 others)	15,100	622	71	32	11,000	45	1,109
Lexington (also Saratoga)	49,500	874	105.5	33.25		80	3,300

ALL TONNAGE SUNK BY AXIS OPERATIONS

	U-boats	Aircraft	Mines	Warships and Raiders	Unknown	Total
1939 (from Sept.)	421,156	2,949	262,697	61,337	7,253	755,392
1940	2,186,158	580,074	509,889	511,615	203,905	3,991,641
1941	2,171,070	1,017,411	230,842	487,204	421,336	4,328,558
1942	6,266,215	700,020	104,588	396,242	323,632	7,790,697
1943	804,277	309,729	41,347	43,345	19,520	1,218,219
1944	358,609	52,175	81,503	17,348	20,875	530,510
1945 (through Aug.)	281,716	44,351	93,663	10,222	7,063	437,015
Totals	12,489,201	2,706,720	1,324,529	1,527,313	1,003,584	19,052,032*

*There is a discrepancy of 685 tons higher tonnage by yearly total than by the total of operational categories, apparently due to the inability to reconcile conflicting data on causes of losses.

SOURCE: S.W. Roskill, *War at Sea*, Vol. IV.

ALL TONNAGE SUNK DUE TO AXIS OPERATIONS BY GEOGRAPHICAL LOCATION (as Percentage of Total)

	Atlantic	Pacific, Mediterranean, and Other Areas
1939	99.1	0.1
1940	91.6	8.4
1941	76.1	23.9
1942	79.0	21.0
1943	37.2	62.8
1944	63.9	36.1
1945	83.9	16.1

SOURCE: S.W. Roskill, *War at Sea*, Vol. IV.

TOTAL ALLIED SHIPPING LOSSES BY CAUSES (1939–1945)

How	Ships Lost	Tonnage
Submarines	2,828	14,687,231
Aircraft	820	2,889,883
Mines	534	1,406,037
Merchant raiders	133	829,644
Warship raiders	104	498,447
E-boats	99	229,676
Other (including scuttling, capture, unknown, etc.)	632	1,029,802

SOURCE: S.W. Roskill, *White Ensign: the British Navy at War, 1939–1945.*

MERCHANT MARINE SHIPPING LOSSES
(1939–1945)
(by Registration)

	Number of Ships	Tonnage
Argentine	2	8,289
Australian	19	42,274
Belgian	86	263,198
Brazilian	30	122,896
Canadian	68	330,254
Chilean	1	1,858
Chinese	4	13,348
Colombian	3	184
Cuban	5	10,134
Danish	27	65,239
Dominican Republic	4	3,755
Dutch	286	1,195,204
Egyptian	30	36,093
Estonian	12	21,630
Faeroes Islands	14	2,434
Finnish	27	62,471
French	90	334,140
German	1,595	7,088,779
Greek	262	883,200
Honduran	10	24,498
Hungarian	1	4,295
Icelandic	5	5,024
Italian	13	50,368
(before June 1940)		
Italian	467	1,155,080
Japanese	2	16,453
(before Dec. 1941)		
Japanese	2,346	8,618,109
Latvian	9	31,640
Lebanese	4	302
Lithuanian	1	1,566
Mexican	6	29,942
New Zealand	8	44,510
Nicaraguan	3	4,850
Norwegian	427	1,728,531
Palestinian	8	1,065
Panamanian	107	542,772
Polish	11	40,864
Portuguese	11	18,449
Russian	43	162,441
Spanish	28	49,851
Swedish	204	481,864
Swiss	2	3,225
Syrian	7	312
Turkish	21	17,179
U.K.	4,786	21,194,000

	Number of Ships	Tonnage
U.S.	578	3,524,983
Uruguayan	2	11,070
Venezuelan	1	2,650
Yugoslav	24	79,368
Total	11,700	48,330,641

SOURCE: Arthur Guy Enoch, *This War Business.*

HOW AXIS SUBMARINES WERE SUNK
(1939–1945)

How	German	Italian	Japanese	Total
Ships	246	37	70	353
Shore-based aircraft	245	9	4	258
Ship-borne aircraft	43	1	8	52
Ships and aircraft	50	5	9	64
Submarines	21	19	25	65
Bombing raids	62	3	–	65
Aircraft-laid mines	16	–	3	19
Ship-laid mines	9	–	1	10
Other	64	3	5	72
Unknown	29	8	5	42
Total	785	85	130	1,000

SOURCE: "German, Italian, and Japanese U-boat Casualties During the War—Particulars of Destruction," First Lord of the Admiralty, June 1946.

FATE OF THE JAPANESE OCEAN-GOING MARITIME FLEET

Tonnage, Dec. 1941	5,900,000 tons	
Built during war	4,100,000	
Total	10,000,000 tons	
Sunk during war	8,617,000 tons	
Heavily damaged	937,000	
Total	9,554,000 tons	

Cause of Losses

Submarines	54.7 percent (63 percent of the numerical sinkings)
Air attacks	30.9 percent
Mines and other	14.4 percent

SOURCE: Masanori Ito, *The End of the Imperial Japanese Navy.*

NAVAL LOSSES (1939–1945)

Number of Ships				By Tonnage			
U.S.	19,034	Canada	32	U.S.	5,457,100	Australia	39,660
Britain	2,831	Australia	30	Britain	2,294,367	Canada	23,811
Germany	1,069	Denmark	30	Japan	1,965,646	Denmark	16,300
Japan	686	Iceland	15	Germany	1,084,650	Iceland	8,300
Italy	376	Sweden°	7	France	455,000	India	5,047
France	239	India	5	Italy	357,853	Sweden°	2,400
Netherlands	105	New Zealand	4	Netherlands	171,760	New Zealand	1,287
Norway	79			Norway	45,712		

° Neutral

SOURCE: Arthur Guy Enoch, *This War Business.*

NAVAL SHIP LOSSES
U.S. Battleships

	Location	Agent	Date
Arizona	Pearl Harbor	Aircraft	Dec. 7, 1941
Oklahoma	Pearl Harbor	Aircraft	Dec. 7, 1941

U.S. Aircraft Carriers

Hornet	Off Solomon Islands	Aircraft	Oct. 26, 1942
Lexington	Coral Sea	Aircraft	May 8, 1942
Princeton	Off Philippines	Aircraft	Oct. 24, 1944
Wasp	Off Espiritu Santo	Submarine	Sept. 15, 1942
Yorktown	Off Midway	Aircraft	June 7, 1942

U.S. Escort Carriers

Bismarck Sea	Off Iwo Jima	Kamikaze	Feb. 21, 1945
Block Island	Off Madeira Islands	Submarine	May 29, 1944
Gambier Bay	Off Timor Island	Surface Ships	Oct. 25, 1944
Liscome Bay	Off Tarawa	Submarine	Nov. 24, 1943
Ommaney Bay	Off Panay, Philippines	Kamikaze	Jan. 4, 1945
St. Lo	Off Leyte, Philippines	Kamikaze	Oct. 25, 1944

U.S. Heavy Cruisers

Astoria	Off Savo, Solomons	Surface ships	Aug. 9, 1942
Chicago	Off Guadalcanal	Surface ships	Jan. 30, 1943
Houston	Off Java	Surface ships	March 1, 1942
Indianapolis	Off Leyte, Philippines	Submarine	July 29, 1945
Northampton	Off Savo, Solomons	Surface ships	Nov. 30, 1942
Quincy	Off Savo, Solomons	Surface ships	Aug. 9, 1942
Vincennes	Off Savo, Solomons	Surface ships	Aug. 9, 1942

U.S. Light Cruisers

Atlanta	Off Guadalcanal	Surface ships	Nov. 13, 1942
Helena	Kula Gulf, Solomons	Surface ships	July 6, 1943
Juneau	Off Guadalcanal	Surface ships	Nov. 13, 1942

NAVAL SHIP LOSSES (Cont.)

Other U.S. Naval Ship Losses

Destroyers	71	Coast Guard vessels	15	Landing craft-support (LCS)	6
Destroyer escorts	11	Seaplane tenders	3	Tugs	10
Submarines	52	Motor torpedo boats	68	Tankers	27
Minelayers	3	Landing ships-tank (LST)	40	District patrol craft (YP)	36
Mine sweepers	24	Landing ships-medium (LSM)	9	Miscellaneous district craft	179
Submarine chasers	18	Landing craft-tank (LCT)	67		
Gunboats	12	Landing craft-infantry (LCI)	22		

Royal Navy Battleships

	Location	Agent	Date
Barham	Off Libya	Submarine	Nov. 25, 1941
Prince of Wales	Off Malaya	Aircraft	Dec. 10, 1941
Queen Elizabeth°	Alexandria	Frogmen	Dec. 17, 1941
Royal Oak	Scapa Flow	Submarine	Oct. 14, 1939

°Restored, but never returned to service

Royal Navy Battle Cruisers

Repulse	Off Malaya	Aircraft	Dec. 10, 1941
Hood	North Atlantic	Surface ship	May 24, 1941

Royal Navy Aircraft Carriers

Ark Royal	East of Gibraltar	Submarine	Nov. 13, 1941
Audacity	North Atlantic	Submarine	Dec. 21, 1941
Avenger	Off Algerian coast	Submarine	Nov. 15, 1942
Courageous	Off British coast	Submarine	Sept. 17, 1939
Eagle	East of Gibraltar	Submarine	Aug. 11, 1942
Glorious	Norwegian Sea	Surface ships	June 8, 1942
Hermes	Off Ceylon	Aircraft	April 9, 1942

Royal Navy Cruisers

Bonaventure	North Atlantic	Submarine	March 31, 1941
Cairo	Off Tunisia	Submarine	Aug. 12, 1942
Calcutta	Off Crete	Aircraft	May 30, 1941
Calypso	Mediterranean	Submarine	June 10, 1940
Charybdis		Torpedo boats	Oct. 23, 1943
Cornwall	Off Ceylon	Aircraft	April 5, 1942
Coventry	Off Tobruk	Aircraft	Sept. 13, 1941
Curaçao	Off Ireland	Rammed	Oct. 2, 1942
Curlew	Narvik	Surface ship	May 26, 1940
Dorsetshire	Off Ceylon	Aircraft	April 5, 1942
Dunedin	Central Atlantic	Submarine	November 1941
Edinburgh	Arctic	Submarines and surface ships	May 2, 1942
Effingham	Norway	wrecked	May 17, 1940
Exeter	Java Sea	Surface ships	March 1, 1942
Fiji	Off Crete	Aircraft	May 22, 1941
Galatea	Off Alexandria	Submarine	Dec. 15, 1941
Gloucester	Off Crete	Aircraft	May 22, 1941

Royal Navy Cruisers (*Cont.*)

Hermione	Eastern Mediterranean	Submarine	June 16, 1942
Manchester	Off Tunisia	Torpedo boats	Aug. 13, 1942
Naiad	Mediterranean	Submarine	March 11, 1942
Neptune	Off Malta	Mines	Dec. 19, 1941
Penelope	Off Anzio	Submarine	Feb. 18, 1944
Rawalpindi	Iceland-Faeroes Passage	Surface ships	Nov. 23, 1939
Southampton	Mediterranean	Aircraft	Jan. 11, 1941
Spartan	Anzio	Glider bomb	Jan. 29, 1944
Trinidad	Arctic	Aircraft	April 1942
York	Suda Bay, Crete	Torpedo boats	March 26, 1941

Other Royal Navy Losses

Destroyers	132	Submarines	74	Monitors	1
Sloops	10	Cutters	3	Frigates	10
Corvettes	22	Fleet minesweepers	32	Fast minelayers	3
Other minelayers	5	Hospital ships	2	Armed merchant cruisers	15
Antiaircraft ships	2	Fighter catapult ships	2	Submarine and destroyer tenders	2

Royal Australian Navy Cruisers

	Location	Agent	Date
Canberra	Off Guadalcanal	Surface ships	Aug. 9, 1942
Perth	Java Sea	Surface ships	Feb. 28, 1942
Sydney	Off Western Australia	Raider	Nov. 19, 1941

Other Australian Ships

Destroyers 4   Sloops 2   Fleet Mine sweepers 3

Royal Canadian Navy Ship Losses

Destroyers	6
Frigates	1
Corvettes	10
Fleet mine sweepers	4

Royal Indian Navy Ship Losses

Sloops	1
Corvettes	1

British Ships Manned by Allied Navies

Destroyers	7
Submarines	3
Corvettes	5

Russian Battleship

	Location	Agent	Date
Marat	Kronshlot	Aircraft	Sept. 1941

Russian Cruiser

Kirov	Kronshlot	Aircraft	Sept. 1941

Other Russian Ships

Destroyers 36   Submarines 50

Greek Battleships

Kilkis°	Piraeus	Aircraft	April 23, 1941
Lemnos°°	Piraeus	Aircraft	April 23, 1942

°The former U.S.S. *Mississippi*
°°The former U.S.S. *Idaho*

NAVAL SHIP LOSSES (*Cont.*)

Greek Cruisers

	Location	Agent	Date
Helle	Tenos	Submarine	Aug. 15, 1940

Other Greek Ships

Destroyers	4	Submarines	4	Minelayers	4	Miscellaneous	28
Destroyer Escorts	10	Hospital ships	1	Mine Sweepers	4		

German Battleships

Bismarck	West of Brest	Surface ships	May 27, 1941
Schlesien°	Swinemünde	Mine	
Schleswig-Holstein°	Gdynia	Aircraft	Dec. 18, 1944
Tirpitz	Norway	Aircraft	Nov. 12, 1944

German Battle Cruisers

Gneisenau	Gdynia	Scuttled	March 29, 1945
Scharnhorst	Barents Sea	Surface ships	Dec. 26, 1943

German Pocket Battleships

Graf Spee	Montevideo, Uruguay	Scuttled	Dec. 17, 1939
Lützow	Swinemünde	Aircraft	April 16, 1945
Scheer	Kiel	Aircraft	April 9, 1945

German Cruisers

Blücher	Oslo Fjord	Shore fire and surface ships	April 9, 1940
Emden	Kiel	Aircraft	April 9, 1945
Hipper	Kiel	Scuttled	May 3, 1945
Karlsruhe	Off Kristiansand, Norway	Submarine	April 9, 1940
Köln	Wilhelmshaven	Aircraft	April 30, 1945
Königsberg°°	Off Bergen, Norway	Aircraft	April 10, 1940
Seydlitz	Königsberg	Scuttled	April 10, 1945

Other German Ships

Destroyers and torpedo boats	101	S-Boats (equivalent of U.S. P.T.'s or British M.T.B.'s)	146
Mine Sweepers (M- and R-boats)	282	Submarines	785
Armed merchant cruisers	7	Hospital ships	2
Mine detector ships (*Sperrbrecher*)	64	Corvettes	25
Minelayers	23	Miscellaneous	860

Dutch Cruisers

De Ruyter	Java Sea	Surface ships	Feb. 27, 1942
Java	Java Sea	Surface ships	Feb. 27, 1942

° Both the *Schlesien* and *Schleswig-Holstein* were relegated to noncombat status before being sunk.

°° Salvaged and sunk again Sept. 22, 1944

Japanese Battleships

	Location	Agent	Date
Fuso	Surigao Strait, Philippines	Surface ships	Oct. 25, 1944
Haruna	Kure, Japan	Aircraft	July 28,1945
Hiei	Off Savo, Solomons	Ships and aircraft	Nov. 13, 1942
Hyuga	Kure, Japan	Aircraft	July 28, 1945
Ise	Kure, Japan	Aircraft	July 28, 1945
Kirishima	Off Savo, Solomons	Surface ships	Nov. 15, 1944
Kongo	Off Foochow, China	Submarine	Nov. 21, 1944
Musashi	Sibuyan Sea, Philippines	Aircraft	Oct. 25, 1944
Mutsu	Hiroshima Bay	Accident	June 8, 1943
Yamashiro	Surigao Strait, Philippines	Surface ships	Oct. 25, 1944
Yamato	Off Kyushu, Japan	Aircraft	April 7, 1945

Japanese Carriers

	Location	Agent	Date
Akagi	Off Midway	Aircraft	June 4,1942
Chitose	Off Luzon, Philippines	Aircraft	Oct. 25, 1944
Chiyoda	Off Luzon, Philippines	Ships and aircraft	Oct. 25, 1944
Hiryu	Off Midway	Aircraft	June 5, 1942
Hiyo	Philippine Sea	Aircraft	June 20, 1944
Kaga	Off Midway	Aircraft	June 4, 1942
Ryujo	Off Malaita Island, Solomons	Aircraft	Aug. 24, 1942
Shinano	Off Honshu	Submarine	Nov. 29, 1944
Shoho	Coral Sea	Aircraft	May 7, 1942
Shokaku	Off Yap Island	Submarine	June 19, 1944
Soryu	Off Midway	Aircraft and submarine	June 4, 1942
Taiho	Off Yap Island	Submarine	June 19, 1944
Unryu	East China Sea	Submarine	Dec. 19, 1944
Zuiho	Off Luzon, Philippines	Aircraft	Oct. 25, 1944
Zuikaku	Off Luzon, Philippines	Aircraft	Oct. 25, 1944

Japanese Escort Carriers

	Location	Agent	Date
Chuyo	Off Honshu, Japan	Submarine	Dec. 4, 1943
Kaiyo	Beppu Bay, Japan	Aircraft	July 24, 1945
Jinyo	Yellow Sea	Submarine	Nov. 17, 1944
Otaka	Off Luzon, Philippines	Submarine	Aug. 18, 1944
Unyo	South China Sea	Submarine	Sept. 16, 1944

Japanese Heavy Cruisers

	Location	Agent	Date
Aoba	Kure, Japan	Aircraft	July 28, 1945
Ashigara	Off Singapore	Submarine	June 8, 1945
Atago	Off Palawan, Philippines	Submarine	Oct. 23, 1944
Chikuma	Off Samar, Philippines	Ships and aircraft	Oct. 25, 1944
Chokai	Sibuyan Sea, Philippines	Aircraft	Oct. 24, 1944
Kurutaka	Off Savo, Solomons	Surface ships	Oct. 11, 1942
Haguro	Off Penang, Malaya	Ships and aircraft	May 16, 1945
Kako	Off New Ireland	Submarine	Aug. 10, 1942
Kinugasa	Off Savo, Solomons	Aircraft	Nov. 14, 1942
Kumano	Off western Luzon	Aircraft	Nov. 25, 1944

NAVAL SHIP LOSSES (*Cont.*)

Japanese Heavy Cruisers

	Location	Agent	Date
Maya	Off Palawan, Philippines	Submarine	Oct. 23, 1944
Mikuma	Off Midway	Aircraft	June 6, 1942
Mogami	Mindanao Sea, Philippines	Ships and aircraft	Oct. 25, 1944
Nachi	Manila Bay	Aircraft	Nov. 5, 1944
Suzuya	Off Samar, Philippines	Aircraft	Oct. 25, 1944
Tone	Kure, Japan	Aircraft	July 28, 1945

Japanese Light Cruisers

Abukuma	Off Negros, Philippines	Ships and aircraft	Oct. 26, 1944
Agano	Off Truk	Submarine	Feb. 16, 1944
Isuzu	Off Soembawa, East Indies	Submarine	April 7, 1945
Jintsu	Off Kolombangara, Solomons	Surface ships	July 13, 1943
Kinu	Off Masbate, Philippines	Aircraft	Oct. 26, 1944
Kiso	Manila Bay	Aircraft	Nov. 13, 1944
Kuma	Off Penang, Malaya	Submarine	Jan. 11, 1944
Nagara	Off Kyushu, Japan	Submarine	Aug. 7, 1944
Naka	Off Truk	Aircraft	Feb. 17, 1944
Natori	Off Samar, Philippines	Submarine	Aug. 18, 1944
Noshiro	Off Panay, Philippines	Aircraft	Oct. 26, 1944
Oi	South China Sea	Submarine	July 19, 1944
Oyodo	Kure, Japan	Aircraft	July 28, 1945
Sendai	Off Bougainville, Solomons	Surface ships	Nov. 2, 1943
Tama	Off Luzon, Philippines	Submarine	Oct. 25, 1944
Tatsuta	Off Yokohama	Submarine	March 14, 1944
Tenryu	Bismarck Sea	Submarine	Dec. 18, 1942
Yahagi	Off Kyushu, Japan	Aircraft	April 7, 1945
Yubari	Off Palau	Submarine	April 27, 1944
Yura	Off Santa Isabel, Solomons	Aircraft	Oct. 25, 1942

Training Cruisers

Kashii	South China Sea	Aircraft	Jan. 12, 1945
Katori	Truk	Ships and aircraft	Feb. 17, 1944

Other Japanese Naval Losses

Destroyers 133   Submarines 129

Italian Battleships
(As Axis Member and Allied Cobelligerent)

Cavour	Taranto	Aircraft	Nov. 11, 1940
Roma	Mediterranean	Aircraft	Sept. 9, 1943

Italian Cruisers

Attendolo	Naples	Aircraft	Dec. 4, 1942
Bande Nere	Off Stromboli	Submarine	April 1, 1942
Barbiano	Off Tunisia	Surface ships	Dec. 13, 1941

NAVAL SHIP LOSSES (*Cont.*)

Bolzano	La Spezia	Guided torpedo	June 22, 1944
Colleoni	Off Crete	Surface ship	July 19, 1940
Diaz	Off Libya	Submarine	Feb. 24, 1941
Fiume	South of Crete	Surface ships	March 28, 1941
Giussano	Off Tunisia	Surface ships	Dec. 13, 1941
Gorizia°	La Spezia	Scuttled	Sept. 8, 1943
Pola	South of Crete	Aircraft	March 28, 1941
San Giorgio	Tobruk	Scuttled	Jan. 22, 1940
Trento	Off Libya	Aircraft and submarine	June 16, 1942
Trieste	Maddalena, Italy	Aircraft	April 10, 1943
Zara	South of Crete	Surface ships	March 29, 1941

Other Italian Naval Losses

Destroyers	55	Mine sweepers	35	(5 by aerial bombing,	
Destroyer escorts	65	Minelayers	3	2 by mines,	
Corvettes	7	S-Boats	110	1 by submarine)	
Submarines	107	Hospital ships	8	Miscellaneous	346

°Salvaged and sunk again June 26, 1944, by frogmen.

Bibliography

The official military and diplomatic histories of the war prepared by the Allied governments are unexcelled in depth and objectivity. They are more than mere accounts of each victor's participation, providing perspectives which equal any scholar's. Official records of all participants were researched exhaustively and treated fairly.

The United Kingdom Military Series *History of the Second World War* (edited by Sir James Butler) covers grand strategy (6 volumes), campaigns (22 volumes), and civil affairs (4 volumes). Augmenting this series is the projected 5-volume *British Foreign Policy in the Second World War*. Not all are available but lists of both series in print can be obtained from Her Majesty's Stationery Office (HMSO), P6c, Atlantic House, Holborn Viaduct, London EC1P 1BN.

About 75 volumes will be published in the series *United States Army in World War II* (Office of the Chief of Military History). Most have been issued and many can still be purchased through the Superintendent of Documents, Government Printing Office (GPO), Washington, D.C. 20402.

U.S. Army records covering World War II weigh 17,000 tons, and the other services are as vast. The Air Force, Navy, and Marine Corps histories are exhaustive. Seven volumes edited by Wesley Frank Craven and James Lea Cate, Office of Air Force History, *The Army Air Forces in World War II* (University of Chicago Press), the 15-volume series *History of United States Naval Operations in World War II* by Samuel Eliot Morison (Little, Brown and Company), and the 5-volume *History of U.S. Marine Corps Operations in World War II* (Historical Branch, Headquarters, U.S. Marine Corps) and the 15 monographs on individual campaigns are excellent as well as comprehensive.

Diplomatic material of inestimable value is contained in the special series of *Foreign Relations* on the war published by the Historical Office, U.S. Department of State. Particularly valuable are those volumes covering the conferences at Casablanca, Québec, Cairo, Tehran, Yalta, and Potsdam.

Canada's contribution is the *Official History of the Canadian Army in the Second World War* (Historical Section, Canadian General Staff), Queen's Printer, Ottawa. Other official histories from other countries have been published, and continue to be published, and these works from Australia, New Zealand, South Africa, India, Pakistan, and the Netherlands should be consulted.

German, Italian, and Japanese material to a large extent is embodied in the Allied histories, but individual accounts are important. They are listed in the memoirs and specialized sections below.

The biggest gap in the war is the absence of official Soviet military and diplomatic history. Much of what has been made available is useful, but the total output lacks credibility. It has been subjected to political rewriting and revisionism.

For this publication I relied heavily on a particular group of books which helped in compiling a chronology: *Events Leading Up to World War II: Chronological History, 1931–1944* (Committee on Foreign Affairs, U.S. House of Representatives, GPO, 1944); *The War Reports of General George C. Marshall, General H. H. Arnold, and Admiral Ernest J. King*

(J. B. Lippincott, 1947); *U.S. Army in World War II: Chronology, 1941–1945* (GPO, 1960); *U.S. Naval Chronology, World War II* (GPO, 1955); *Voices of History* (annual editions) (Grammercy Publishing); *History of the Second World War*, weekly publication (London: Marshall Cavendish); and *Encyclopedia of World War II*, edited by Thomas Parrish (Simon and Schuster, 1978). Frequently consulted and valuable in the preparation of the maps were *The West Point Atlas of American Wars*, Volume II, edited by Colonel Vincent J. Esposito (Frederick A. Praeger, 1959) and *Atlas of the Second World War*, edited by Brigadier Peter Young, cartography by Richard Natkiel (Berkley Publishing, 1974).

GENERAL HISTORIES

Adams, Henry H. *1942: The Year That Doomed the Axis.* Paperback Library, 1969.

Arnold-Forster, Mark. *The World at War.* Stein and Day, 1973.

Baldwin, Hanson. *Battles Lost and Won: Great Campaigns of World War II.* Harper and Row, 1966.

———. *Great Mistakes of the War.* Harper and Brothers, 1950.

Calvocoressi, Peter, and **Wint, Guy.** *Total War.* Pantheon, 1972.

Collier, Basil. *The Second World War: A Military History.* William Morrow, 1967.

Davis, Kenneth. *Experience of War.* Doubleday, 1965.

Dollinger, Hans. *The Decline and Fall of Nazi Germany and Imperial Japan* (translated from the German by Arnold Pomerans). Bonanza Books, 1968.

Dupuy, R. Ernest. *World War II: A Compact History.* Hawthorn, 1969.

Elliott, J.G. *Unfading Honor: The Story of the Indian Army, 1939–1945.* A.S. Barnes, 1965.

Enock, Arthur Guy. *This War Business.* Bodley Head, 1951.

Esposito, Vincent J., ed. *A Concise History of World War II.* Frederick A. Praeger, 1964.

Flower, Desmond, and **Reeves, James, eds.** *The Taste of Courage: The War, 1939–1945.* Harper and Brothers, 1960.

Freiden, Seymour, and **Richardson, William, eds.** *The Fatal Decisions.* William Sloane Associates, 1956.

Fuller, John F.C. *The Second World War, 1939–1945: A Strategical and Tactical History.* Duell, Sloan and Pearce, 1949.

Heiferman, Ronald. *World War II.* Octopus Books, 1975.

Hoyle, Martha Byrd. *A World in Flames: A History of World War II.* Atheneum, 1969.

International Military Tribunal. *Trial of the Major Criminals Before the International Military Tribunal.* 42 Vols. 1947.

Irving, David. *Hitler's War.* Viking Press, 1977.

Jones, James. *WWII. A Chronical of Soldiering.* Ballantine Books, 1976.

Keegan, John, ed. *The Rand McNally Encyclopedia of World War II.* Rand McNally, 1977.

Liddell Hart, B.H. *History of the Second World War.* G.P. Putnam's Sons, 1970.

———. *The Other Side of the Hill.* Cassell and Co., 1948. (Published in U.S. as *The German Generals Talk.* William Morrow, 1948.)

Michel, Henri. *The Second World War.* Frederick A. Praeger, 1975.

Miller, Francis Trevelyan. *History of World War II.* Winston, 1945.

Shugg, Roger W., and **DeWeerd, H.A.** *World War II: A Concise History.* Infantry Journal Press, 1946.

Snyder, Louis. *The War: A Concise History.* Julian Messner, 1960.

Stouffer, Samuel A., et al. *The American Soldier: Combat and Its Aftermath* (2 vols.). Princeton University Press, 1949.

Strawson, John. *Hitler's Battles for Europe.* Charles Scribner's Sons, 1971.

Sulzberger, C.L. *World War II.* American Heritage Press, 1970.

Taylor, A.J.P., ed. *History of World War II.* Octopus Books, 1974.

Toland, John. *The Last 100 Days.* Doubleday, 1959.

Trevor-Roper, H. R., ed. *Blitzkrieg to Defeat.* Holt, Rinehart and Winston, 1965.

U.S. Chief of Counsel (Nuremberg). *Nazi Conspiracy and Aggression* (8 vols.). GPO, 1946–48.

MEMOIRS AND DIARIES

Alexander, Field Marshal Earl. *The Alexander Memoirs, 1940–1945* (edited by John North). McGraw-Hill, 1963.

Anders, Wladyslaw. *An Army in Exile.* Macmillan, 1949.

Arnold, Henry H. *Global Mission.* Harper and Brothers, 1949.

Badoglio, Pietro. *Italy in the Second World War.* Oxford University Press, 1948.

Bradley, Omar N. *A Soldier's Story.* Henry Holt, 1951.

Brereton, Lewis H. *Brereton Diaries.* William Morrow, 1946.

Bryant, Arthur. *The Turn of the Tide.* Doubleday, 1950.

———. *Triumph in the West.* Doubleday, 1959.

Butcher, Harold. *My Three Years with Eisenhower.* Simon and Schuster, 1946.

Chennault, Claire L. *Way of a Fighter*. G. P. Putnam's Sons, 1949.

Churchill, Winston. *The Second World War* (6 vols.: *The Gathering Storm, Their Finest Hour, The Grand Alliance, The Hinge of Fate, Closing the Ring, Triumph and Tragedy*). Houghton Mifflin, 1948–53.

Ciano, Count Galeazzo. *The Ciano Diaries* (edited by Hugh Gibson). Doubleday, 1946.

Clark, Mark. *Calculated Risk*. Harper and Brothers, 1950.

Cunningham, Andrew B. *A Sailor's Odyssey: The Autobiography of Admiral of the Fleet Viscount Cunningham of Hyndhope*. E. P. Dutton, 1951.

De Gaulle, Charles. *The War Memoirs of Charles de Gaulle* (3 vols.). Simon and Schuster, 1958–60.

Eden, Anthony. *The Reckoning: The Memoirs of Anthony Eden, Earl of Avon*. Houghton Mifflin, 1965.

Eichelberger, Robert L., and Mackaye, Milton. *Our Jungle Road to Tokyo*. Viking Press, 1950.

Eisenhower, Dwight D. *Crusade in Europe*. Doubleday, 1948.

———. *The Papers of Dwight D. Eisenhower: The War Years* (5 vols.) (edited by Alfred D. Chandler, Jr., and Stephen E. Ambrose). Johns Hopkins University Press, 1970.

———. *Report by the Supreme Commander to the Combined Chiefs of Staff on the Operations in Europe of the Allied Expeditionary Force, 6 June 1944–8 May 1945*. GPO, 1946.

Galland, Adolf. *The First and the Last*. Henry Holt, 1954.

Gehlen, Reinhard. *The Service: The Memoirs of General Reinhard Gehlen*. World Publishing, 1972.

Goebbels, Joseph. *The Goebbels Diaries (1942–43)* (edited and translated by Louis P. Lochner). Doubleday, 1948.

———. *Final Entries, 1945: The Diaries of Joseph Goebbels* (edited by Hugh Trevor-Roper). G.P. Putnam's Sons, 1978.

Grew, Joseph C. *Turbulent Era: A Diplomatic Record of Forty Years, 1904–1945* (2 vols.). Houghton Mifflin, 1952.

Groves, Leslie R. *Now It Can Be Told*. Harper and Brothers, 1962.

Guderian, Heinz. *Panzer Leader* (translated from the German by Constantine FitzGibbon). E.P. Dutton, 1952.

Guingand, Sir Francis de. *Operation Victory*. Charles Scribner's Sons, 1947.

Halifax, Lord. *Fullness of Days*. Dodd, Mead, 1957.

Halsey, William F., and Bryan III, J. *Admiral Halsey's Story*. McGraw-Hill, 1947.

Harriman, W. Averell, and Abel, Elie. *Special Envoy to Churchill and Stalin, 1941–1946*. Random House, 1975.

Hassell, Ulrich von. *The von Hassell Diaries, 1938–1944*. Doubleday, 1947.

Hitler, Adolf. *Mein Kampf*. Various editions. (Unexpurgated English translation from the German by James Murphy.) Houghton Mifflin, 1943.

Hull, Cordell. *The Memoirs of Cordell Hull* (2 vols.). Macmillan, 1948.

Infield, Glenn B. *The Poltava Affair*. Macmillan, 1973.

Ismay, General Lord. *The Memoirs of General Lord Ismay*. Viking Press, 1960.

Kase, Toshikazu. *Journey to the Missouri*. Yale University Press, 1950.

Keitel, Wilhelm. *The Memoirs of Field-Marshal Keitel* (edited by Walter Görlitz; translated from the German by David Irving). Stein and Day, 1966.

Kennedy, Sir John. *The Business of War*. William Morrow, 1958.

Kenney, George C. *General Kenney Reports: A Personal History of the Pacific War*. Duell, Sloan and Pearce, 1949.

Kesselring, Albert. *Kesselring: A Soldier's Record*. William Morrow, 1954.

King, Ernest J., and Whitehill, Walter M. *Fleet Admiral King, A Naval Record*. W.W. Norton, 1952.

Krueger, Walter. *From Down Under to Nippon*. Combat Forces Press, 1953.

Leahy, William D. *I Was There*. McGraw-Hill, 1950.

Liddell Hart, B.H., ed. *The Rommel Papers*. Harcourt, Brace, 1956.

MacArthur, Douglas. *Reminiscences*. McGraw-Hill, 1964.

Macmillan, Harold. *The Blast of War*. Harper and Row, 1967.

Mannerheim, Carl G.E. von. *Memoirs of Marshal Mannerheim*. E.P. Dutton, 1954.

Manstein, Erich von. *Lost Victories*. Henry Regnery, 1958.

Mellenthin, F.W. von. *Panzer Battles*. University of Oklahoma Press, 1956.

Montgomery, Bernard L. *Memoirs*. World Publishing, 1958.

Moran, Lord. *Churchill: Taken From the Diaries of Lord Moran*. Houghton Mifflin, 1966.

Murphy, Robert. *Diplomat Among Warriors*. Doubleday, 1964.

Nicolson, Harold. *The Diaries and Letters of Harold Nicolson: The War Years, 1939–1945*. Atheneum, 1967.

Papen, Franz von. *Memoirs*. E.P. Dutton, 1953.

Patton, George S. *War As I Knew It*. Houghton Mifflin, 1947.

Reynaud, Paul. *In the Thick of the Fight, 1930–1945*. Simon and Schuster, 1955.

Ridgway, Matthew B. *Soldier: The Memoirs of Matthew B. Ridgway.* Harper and Brothers, 1956.

Skorzeny, Otto. *Skorzeny's Secret Missions.* E.P. Dutton, 1951.

Smith, Holland, and Finch, Percy. *Coral and Brass.* Charles Scribner's Sons, 1949.

Speer, Albert. *Inside the Third Reich.* Macmillan, 1970.

Stilwell, Joseph, and White, Theodore. *The Stilwell Papers.* William Sloane Associates, 1948.

Stimson, Henry L., and Bundy, McGeorge. *On Active Service in Peace and War.* Harper and Brothers, 1947.

Tedder, Lord Arthur. *With Prejudice.* Little, Brown, 1966.

Truman, Harry S. *Year of Decisions, 1945.* Doubleday, 1955.

Warlimont, Walter. *Inside Hitler's Headquarters, 1939–1945.* Frederick A. Praeger, 1965.

Wedemeyer, Albert C. *Wedemeyer Reports.* Henry Holt, 1958.

Weizsäcker, Ernst von. *The Memoirs of Ernst von Weizsäcker.* Henry Regnery, 1951.

Weygand, Maxine. *Recalled to Service.* Doubleday, 1952.

Zhukov, Georgi K. *Memoirs.* Delacorte Press, 1971.

BIOGRAPHIES

Blumentritt, Guenther. *Von Runstedt.* Odhams Press, 1952.

Browne, Courtney. *Tojo: The Last Banzai.* Holt, Rinehart and Winston, 1967.

Bullock, Alan. *Hitler: A Study in Tyranny.* Harper and Brothers, 1962.

Burns, James MacGregor. *Roosevelt: The Soldier of Freedom.* Harcourt Brace Jovanovich, 1970.

Chaney, Otto. *Zhukov.* University of Oklahoma Press, 1971.

Deakin, F.W. *The Brutal Friendship: Mussolini, Hitler and the Fall of Italian Fascism,* Harper and Row, 1962.

Dietrich, Otto. *Hitler* (translated from the German by Richard and Clara Winston). Henry Regnery, 1955.

Ellis, William Donohue, and Cunningham, Thomas J. *Clarke of St. Vith.* Dillon/Liederbach, 1974.

Essame, Hubert. *Patton: A Study in Command.* Charles Scribner's Sons, 1974.

Farago, Ladislas. *Patton: Ordeal and Triumph.* Obolensky, 1964.

Fest, Joachim C. *Hitler.* Harcourt Brace Jovanovich, 1974.

Gilbert, Felix, ed. *Hitler Directs His War.* Oxford University Press, 1950.

Halder, Franz. *Hitler as War Lord* (translated from the German by Paul Findlay). G.P. Putnam's Sons, 1950.

Hassett, William D. *Off the Record with F.D.R., 1942–1945.* Rutgers University Press, 1958.

Hibbert, Christopher. *Il Duce: The Life of Benito Mussolini.* Little, Brown, 1962.

Hutton, J. Bernard. *Hess.* Macmillan, 1971.

Irving, David. *The Trail of the Fox.* Weidenfeld and Nicholson, 1977.

James, D. Clayton. *The Years of MacArthur, 1941–1945,* Vol. II. Houghton Mifflin, 1975.

Kirkpatrick, Sir Ivone. *Mussolini: A Study in Power.* Hawthorne, 1964.

Lewin, Ronald. *Rommel as Military Commander.* Ballantine Books, 1970.

Lohbeck, Don. *Patrick J. Hurley.* Henry Regnery, 1956.

Mosley, Leonard. *Hirohito, Emperor of Japan.* Prentice-Hall, 1966.

———. *The Reich Marshal: A Biography of Hermann Goering.* Doubleday, 1974.

Payne, Robert. *The Life and Death of Adolf Hitler.* Frederick A. Praeger, 1973.

———. *The Rise and Fall of Stalin.* Simon and Schuster, 1964.

Pogue, Forest C. *George C. Marshall: Ordeal and Hope.* Viking Press, 1966.

———. *George C. Marshall: Organizer of Victory.* Viking Press, 1973.

Potter, E.B. *Nimitz.* U.S. Naval Institute, 1976.

Potter, John Deane *The Life and Death of a Japanese General* (General Tomoyuki Yamashita). Signet, 1962.

———. *Yamamoto.* Viking Press, 1965.

Reiman, Viktor. *Goebbels: The Man Who Created Hitler* (translated from the German by Stephen Wendt). Doubleday, 1976.

Seaton, Albert. *Stalin as Military Commander.* Frederick A. Praeger, 1976.

Sherwood, Robert E. *Roosevelt and Hopkins.* Harper and Brothers, 1948.

Shiroyama, Saburo. *War Criminal: The Life and Death of Hirota Koki* (translated from the Japanese by John Bester). Kodansha International, 1977.

Strawson, John. *Hitler As Military Commander.* B.T. Batsford, 1971.

Sykes, Christopher. *Orde Wingate: A Biography.* World, 1959.

Taylor, Robert Lewis. *Winston Churchill.* Doubleday, 1952.

Toland, John. *Adolf Hitler.* Doubleday, 1976.

Toye, Hugh. *The Springing Tiger: A Study of Subhas Chandra Bose.* Cassell, 1959.

Trevor-Roper, H.R. *The Last Days of Hitler.* St. Martin's Press, 1947.

Willoughby, Charles A., and **Chamberlain, John.** *MacArthur, 1941–1951.* McGraw-Hill, 1954.

Woodward, C. Vann. *The Battle for Leyte Gulf.* Macmillan, 1947.

Young, Desmond. *Rommel, The Desert Fox.* Harper and Brothers, 1950.

DIPLOMATIC AND POLITICAL RELATIONS

Ambrose, Stephen E. *Eisenhower and Berlin: The Decision to Halt at the Elbe.* W.W. Norton, 1967.

Armstrong, Anne. *Unconditional Surrender: The Impact of the Casablanca Policy Upon World War II.* Rutgers University Press, 1961.

Baumont, Maurice. *The Origins of the Second World War* (translated from the French by Simone de Couvreur Ferguson). Yale University Press, 1978.

Beard, Charles A. *President Roosevelt and the Coming of the War, 1941.* Yale University Press, 1948.

Beitzell, Robert. *The Uneasy Alliance: America, Britain, and Russia, 1941–1943.* Alfred A. Knopf, 1972.

Clemens, Diane S. *Yalta.* Oxford University Press, 1970.

Cole, Wayne S. *Charles A. Lindbergh and the Battle Against American Intervention in World War II.* Harcourt Brace Jovanovich, 1974.

Deane, John R. *The Strange Alliance.* Viking Press, 1947.

Feis, Herbert. *Churchill, Roosevelt and Stalin.* Princeton University Press, 1957.

———. *The Road to Pearl Harbor.* Princeton University Press, 1950.

Friedlander, Saul. *Pius XII and the Third Reich.* Alfred A. Knopf, 1968.

Higgins, Trumbull. *Soft Underbelly.* Macmillan, 1968.

Jonas, Manfred. *Isolationism in America, 1935–1941.* Cornell University Press, 1966.

Kolko, Gabriel. *The Politics of War: The World and United States Foreign Policy, 1943–1945.* Random House, 1968.

Kubek, Anthony. *How the Far East Was Lost.* Henry Regnery, 1963.

Loewenheim, Francis L.; Langley, Harold D.; and **Jonas, Manfred, eds.** *Roosevelt and Churchill, Their Secret Wartime Correspondence.* E.P. Dutton, 1975.

Louis, William Roger. *Imperialism at Bay: The United States and the Decolonization of the British Empire, 1941–1945.* Oxford University Press, 1978.

McSherry, James E. *Stalin, Hitler, and Europe, 1933–1939: The Origins of World War II* (Vol. 1); *1939–1941: The Imbalance of Power* (Vol. 2). World Publishing, 1968 and 1970.

Mee, Jr., Charles L. *Meeting at Potsdam.* Evans, 1975.

O'Connor, Raymond. *Diplomacy for Victory: FDR and Unconditional Surrender.* W.W. Norton, 1971.

Renouvin, Pierre. *World War II and Its Origins.* Harper and Brothers, 1969.

Rowse, A.L. *Appeasement: A Study in Political Decline, 1933–39.* W.W. Norton, 1961.

Smith, Gaddis. *American Diplomacy During the Second World War, 1941–1945.* John Wiley and Sons, 1965.

Snell, John L. *Illusion and Necessity: The Diplomacy of Global War, 1939–1945.* Houghton Mifflin, 1963.

Tansill, Charles Callan. *Back Door to War: Roosevelt Foreign Policy, 1933–1941.* Henry Regnery, 1952.

Taylor, A.J.P. *The Origins of the Second World War.* Atheneum, 1962.

Taylor, Telford. *Munich: The Price of Peace.* Doubleday, 1979.

Thorne, Christopher. *Allies of a Kind: The United States, Britain, and the War Against Japan, 1941–1945.* Oxford University Press, 1978.

U.S. Department of Defense. *The "Magic" Background of Pearl Harbor* (8 vols.). GPO, 1977.

Welles, Sumner. *Seven Decisions That Shaped History.* Harper and Brothers, 1951.

Woodward, Sir Ernest L. *British Foreign Policy in the Second World War.* HMSO, 1962.

THE PREWAR WARS

Brome, Vincent. *The International Brigades: Spain, 1936–1939.* Heinemann, 1965.

Coffey, Thomas M. *Lion by the Tail: The Story of the Italo-Ethiopian War.* Viking Press, 1974.

Colodny, Robert Garland. *The Struggle for Madrid.* Paine, 1958.

Del Boca, Angelo. *The Ethiopian War, 1935–1941* (translated from the Italian by P.D. Cummins). University of Chicago Press, 1969.

Dorn, Frank. *The Sino-Japanese War, 1937–41.* Macmillan, 1974.

Dugan, James, and **Lafore, Laurence.** *Days of Emperor and Clown: The Italo-Ethiopian War 1935–1936.* Doubleday, 1973.

Jackson, Gabriel. *The Spanish Republic and the Civil War, 1931–1939.* Princeton University Press, 1967.

Quigley, Harold S. *Far Eastern War, 1937–1941.* World Peace Foundation, 1942.

Steer, George. *Caesar in Abyssinia.* Little, Brown, 1937.

Thomas, Hugh. *The Spanish Civil War.* Harper and Brothers, 1961.

WESTERN EUROPE

Adleman, Robert H., and **Walton, George.** *The Devil's Brigade.* Chilton Book, 1966.

Barker, A.J. *Dunkirk: The Great Escape.* David McKay, 1977.

Buckley, Christopher. *Norway; The Commandos; Dieppe.* HMSO, 1952.

Carell, Paul. *Invasion—They're Coming* (translated from the German by Ewald Osers). Bantam Books, 1973.

Carter, Ross. *Those Devils in Baggy Pants.* Signet, 1951.

Eisenhower, John S.D. *The Bitter Woods.* G.P. Putnam's Sons, 1969.

Essame, Hubert. *The Battle for Germany.* Charles Scribner's Sons, 1969.

Fleming, Peter. *Operation Sea Lion.* Simon and Schuster, 1957.

Hechler, Ken. *The Bridge at Remagen.* Ballantine Books, 1957.

Historical Division, U.S. War Department. *American Forces in Action* (8-volume series on U.S. Army operations in Europe). U.S. War Department, 1945.

Howarth, David. *D-Day, The Sixth of June, 1944.* McGraw-Hill, 1959.

Leasor, James. *Green Beach.* Heinemann, 1975.

Liebling, A.J. *The Road Back to Paris.* Doubleday, 1944.

MacDonald, Charles B. *Company Commander.* Infantry Journal Press, 1947.

————. *The Mighty Endeavor: American Armed Forces in the European Theater in World War II.* Oxford University Press, 1969.

Majdalany, Fred. *The Fall of Fortress Europe.* Doubleday, 1968.

Marshall, S.L.A. *Bastogne.* Infantry Journal Press, 1946.

————. *Night Drop.* Atlantic-Little, Brown, 1962.

Merriam, Robert L. *Dark December* (the Battle of the Bulge). Ziff-Davis Publishing, 1947.

Montgomery, Bernard L. *Normandy to the Baltic.* Houghton Mifflin, 1948.

Moulton, J.S. *Battle for Antwerp.* Hippocrene Books, 1978.

Petrow, Richard. *The Bitter Years: The Invasion and Occupation of Denmark and Norway, April, 1940–May, 1945.* Morrow Quill Paperbacks, 1979.

Ryan, Cornelius. *A Bridge Too Far.* Simon and Schuster, 1974.

————. *The Last Battle.* Simon and Schuster, 1966.

————. *The Longest Day.* Simon and Schuster, 1959.

Saunders, Hilary St. George. *Combined Operations: The Official Story of the Commandos.* Macmillan, 1943.

Spears, Sir Edward. *Assignment to Catastrophe* (2 vols.). A.A. Wyn, 1954–55.

Speidel, Hans. *Invasion 1944.* Henry Regnery, 1950.

Stafford, David. *Britain and European Resistance, 1940–1945.* Macmillan, 1980.

Taylor, Telford. *The March of Conquest, The German Victories in Western Europe, 1940.* Simon and Schuster, 1958.

Toland, John. *Battle: The Story of the Bulge.* Random House, 1959.

Westphal, Siegfried. *The German Army in the West.* Cassell, 1951.

Wheatley, Ronald. *Operation Sea Lion.* Oxford University Press, 1958.

Wilmot, Chester. *The Struggle for Europe.* Harper and Brothers, 1952.

EASTERN EUROPE

Bethell, Nicholas. *The War Hitler Won: The Fall of Poland, September, 1939.* Holt, Rinehart and Winston, 1972.

Caidin, Martin. *The Tigers are Burning.* Hawthorn Books, 1974.

Carell, Paul. *Hitler Moves East* (translated from the German by Ewald Osers). Little, Brown, 1965.

————. *Scorched Earth: Hitler's War on Russia* (translated from the German by Ewald Osers). Harrap, 1970.

Cecil, Robert. *Hitler's Decision to Invade Russia, 1941.* David McKay, 1976.

Chuikov, Vasili I. *The Beginning of the Road: Battle for Stalingrad* (translated from the Russian by Harold Salver). Holt, Rinehart and Winston, 1964.

————. *The Fall of Berlin* (translated from the Russian by Ruth Kisch). Rinehart and Winston, 1968.

Clark, Alan. *Barbarossa: The Russian-German Conflict, 1941–45.* William Morrow, 1965.

Craig, William. *Enemy at the Gates: The Battle for Stalingrad.* Readers Digest Press, 1973.

Engle, Eloise, and **Paananen, Lauri.** *The Winter War: The Russo-Finnish Conflict, 1939–40.* St. Martin's Press, 1962.

Erickson, John. *The Soviet High Command: A Military-Political History, 1918–41.* St. Martin's Press, 1962.

Kennedy, Robert M. *The German Campaign in Poland (1939).* GPO, 1955.

Korwin-Rhodes, Marta. *The Mask of Warriors: The Siege of Warsaw, September, 1939.* Libra, 1964.

Langdon-Davies, John. *Invasion in the Snow, The Soviet-Finnish War.* Houghton Mifflin, 1941.

Lukacs, John A. *The Great Powers and Eastern Europe.* Henry Regnery, 1953.

Pavlov, Dimitri V. *Leningrad 1941: The Blockade* (translated from the Russian by John Clinton Adams). University of Chicago Press, 1965.

Salisbury, Harrison E. *The 900 Days: The Siege of Leningrad.* Harper and Row, 1969.

————. *The Unknown War*. Bantam Books, 1978.

Schröter, Heinz. *Stalingrad*. E.P. Dutton, 1958.

Seaton, Albert. *The Russo-German War, 1941–45*. Frederick A. Praeger, 1971.

Thorwald, Jürgen. *The Illusion: Soviet Soldiers in Hitler's Armies* (translated from the German by Richard and Clara Winston). Harcourt Brace Jovanovich, 1975.

Werth, Alexander. *Russia at War, 1941–45*. E.P. Dutton, 1964.

Zawodny, Janusz K. *Death in the Forest*. University of Notre Dame Press, 1962.

Zhukov, Georgi. *Marshal Zhukov's Greatest Battles* (edited by Harrison Salisbury; translated from the Russian by Theodore Shabad). Harper and Row, 1969.

Ziemke, Earl F. *Stalingrad to Berlin*. GPO, 1968.

FRANCE

Barber, Noel. *The Week France Fell*. Stein and Day, 1976.

Chapman, Guy. *Why France Fell*. Rinehart and Winston, 1968.

Collins, Larry, and **Lapierre, Dominique.** *Is Paris Burning?* Simon and Schuster, 1965.

Dank, Milton. *The French Against the French: Collaboration and Resistance*. J.B. Lippincott, 1974.

Langer, William L. *Our Vichy Gamble*. Alfred A. Knopf, 1947.

Lattre de Tassigny, Jean de. *The History of the French First Army*. Allen and Unwin, 1952.

Shiber, Etta. *Paris—Underground*. Charles Scribner's Sons, 1943.

Shirer, William L. *The Collapse of the Third Republic*. Simon and Schuster, 1969.

Warner, Geoffrey. *Pierre Laval and the Eclipse of France*. Macmillan, 1969.

GERMANY

Borkin, Joseph. *The Crime and Punishment of I. G. Farben*. Free Press, 1978.

Cooper, Matthew. *The German Army, 1933–1945*. Stein and Day, 1978.

Delarue, Jaques. *The Gestapo: A History of Horror* (translated from the French by Mervyn Savill). Dell Publishing, 1965.

Downing, David. *The Devil's Virtuosos: German Generals at War, 1940–5*. New English Library, 1978.

Gordon, Harold J. *Hitler and the Beer Hall Putsch*. Princeton University Press, 1972.

Grunberger, Richard. *The Twelve-Year Reich: A Social History of Germany, 1933–45*. Holt, Rinehart and Winston, 1971.

Höhne, Heinz. *The Order of the Death's Head: The Story of Hitler's S.S.* (translated from the German by Richard Barry). Coward-McCann, 1970.

Irving, David. *The War Path: Hitler's Germany, 1933–1939*. Viking Press, 1978.

Mayer, Milton. *They Thought They Were Free: The Germans, 1933–45*. University of Chicago Press, 1955.

Oechsner, Frederick, et al. *This Is the Enemy*. Curtis Publishing, 1942.

Rothfels, Hans. *The German Opposition to Hitler* (translated from the German by Lawrence Wilson). Henry Regnery, 1962.

Shirer, William L. *Berlin Diary*. Alfred A. Knopf, 1941.

————. *The Rise and Fall of the Third Reich*. Simon and Schuster, 1960.

Steiner, John M. *Power Politics and Social Change in National Socialist Germany*. Humanities Press, 1976.

Steinert, Marles. *23 Days: The Final Collapse of Nazi Germany*. Walker, 1969.

Vogt, Hannah. *The Burden of Guilt: A Short History of Germany, 1914–45* (translated from the German by Herbert Strauss). Oxford University Press, 1964.

Wheaton, Eliot Barculo. *Prelude to Calamity: The Nazi Revolution, 1933–1935*. Doubleday, 1968.

Whiting, Charles. *Hitler's Werewolves: The Story of the Nazi Resistance Movement, 1944–1945*. Bantam Books, 1973.

ITALY

Adleman, Robert H., and **Walton, George.** *Rome Fell Today*. Little, Brown, 1968.

Kurzman, Dan. *The Race for Rome*. Doubleday, 1975.

Linklater, Eric. *The Campaign in Italy*. HMSO, 1951.

Majdalany, Fred. *The Battle of Cassino*. Houghton Mifflin, 1957.

Smith, E.D. *The Battle of Cassino*. Charles Scribner's Sons, 1975.

Vaughan-Thomas, Wynford. *Anzio: The Massacre at the Beachhead*. Holt, Rinehart and Winston, 1961.

NORTH AFRICA, MIDDLE EAST AND THE MEDITERRANEAN

Barnett, Correlli. *The Battle of El Alamein: Decision in the Desert*. Macmillan, 1964.

————. *The Desert Generals*. Viking Press, 1961.

Bergot, Erwan. *The Afrika Korps*. Charter Books, 1975.

Buckley, Christopher. *Five Ventures* (Iraq, Syria, Persia, Madagascar, and the Dodecanese). HMSO, 1957.

————. *Greece and Crete, 1941*. HMSO, 1952.

Carell, Paul. *The Foxes of the Desert* (translated from the German by Mervyn Savill). E.P. Dutton, 1960.

Clark, Alan. *The Fall of Crete.* William Morrow, 1962.

Cowles, Virginia. *The Phantom Major.* Harper and Brothers, 1958.

Crisp, Robert. *Brazen Chariots.* W.W. Norton, 1960.

Jackson, W.G.F. *The Battle for North Africa, 1940–43.* Mason, 1975.

Majdalany, Fred. *The Battle of El Alamein.* J.B. Lippincott, 1965.

Montgomery, Bernard L. *El Alamein to the River Sangro.* E.P. Dutton, 1948.

Schmidt, Heinz W. *With Rommel in the Desert.* George G. Harrup, 1951.

Strawson, John. *The Battle for North Africa.* Charles Scribner's Sons, 1979.

JAPAN

Bergamini, David. *Japan's Imperial Conspiracy: How Emperor Hirohito Led Japan into War Against the West.* William Morrow, 1971.

Butow, Robert J.C. *Japan's Decision to Surrender.* Stanford University Press, 1974.

———. *Tojo and the Coming of the War.* Princeton University Press, 1961.

Coffey, Thomas M. *Imperial Tragedy.* World Publishing, 1970.

Craig, William. *The Fall of Japan.* Dial Press, 1967.

Feis, Herbert. *Japan Subdued: The Atomic Bomb and the End of The War in the Pacific.* Princeton University Press, 1961.

Hayashi, Saburo, and Cook, Alvin D. *Kogun: The Japanese Army in the Pacific War.* Marine Corps Association, 1959.

Ienaga, Saburo. *The Pacific War: World War II and the Japanese, 1931–1945* (translated from the Japanese by Frank Baldwin). Pantheon Books, 1978.

Maki, John M. *Japanese Militarism.* Alfred A. Knopf, 1945.

CHINA

Feis, Herbert. *The China Tangle.* Princeton University Press, 1953

Hsu, Long-hsuen, and Ming-kai, Chang. *History of the Sino-Japanese War (1937–1945)* (translated from the Chinese by Wen Ha-hsuing). Chung Wu Publishing Co., Taipei, 1971.

Liang, Chin-tung. *General Stilwell in China, 1942–1944: The Full Story.* St. John's University Press, 1972.

Liu, F.F. *A Military History of Modern China.* Princeton University Press, 1956.

Perry, Hamilton Darby. *The Panay Incident.* Macmillan, 1969.

Schaller, Michael. *The U.S. Crusade in China, 1938–1945.* Columbia University Press, 1979.

Tsou, Tang. *America's Failure in China 1941–50.* University of Chicago Press, 1963.

Tuchman, Barbara W. *Stilwell and the American Experience in China, 1911–1945.* Macmillan, 1970.

Utley, Freda. *China at War.* Faber and Faber, 1939.

White, Theodore H., and Jacoby, Annalee. *Thunder Out of China.* William Sloane Associates, 1946.

Young, Arthur N. *China and the Helping Hand, 1937–1945.* Harvard University Press, 1963.

PACIFIC THEATER

Asada, Teruhiko. *The Night of a Thousand Suicides* (translated from the Japanese by Ray Cowan). St. Martin's Press, 1970.

Belote, James H. and William M. *Corregidor: The Saga of a Fortress.* Harper and Row, 1967

Collier, Basil. *The War in the Far East.* William Morrow, 1968.

Garfield, Brian. *The Thousand-Mile War: World War II in Alaska and the Aleutians.* Ballantine Books, 1969.

Hough, Frank O. *The Island War: The United States Marine Corps in the Pacific.* J.B. Lippincott, 1947.

Leckie, Robert. *Challenge for the Pacific.* Doubleday, 1965.

———. *Helmet for My Pillow.* Bantam Books, 1958.

Lord, Walter. *Day of Infamy.* Henry Holt, 1957.

———. *Lonely Vigil: Coastwatchers of the Solomons.* Viking Press, 1977.

O'Sheel, Patrick, and Cook, Gene, eds. *Semper Fidelis: The U.S. Marines in the Pacific—1942–1945.* William Sloane Associates, 1947.

Pratt, Fletcher. *The Marine's War.* William Sloane Associates, 1948.

Russ, Martin. *Line of Departure: Tarawa.* Zebra Books, 1978.

Sakai, Saburo, and Caidin, Martin. *Samurai!* E.P. Dutton, 1958.

Smith, S.E., ed. *The United States Marine Corps in World War II.* Random House, 1969.

Toland, John. *But Not in Shame.* Random House, 1961.

———. *The Rising Sun.* Doubleday, 1970.

Tregaskis, Richard. *Guadalcanal Diary.* Random House, 1943.

SOUTHEAST ASIA

Belden, Jack. *Retreat with Stilwell.* Alfred A. Knopf, 1943.

Bonham, Frank. *Burma Rifles.* Berkley Publishing, 1965.

BIBLIOGRAPHY

Campbell, Arthur. *The Siege : A Story from Kohima.* Macmillan, 1956.

Dorn, Frank. *Walkout with Stilwell in Burma.* Thomas Y. Crowell, 1971.

Eldridge, Fred. *Wrath in Burma.* Doubleday, 1946.

Evans, Sir Geoffrey C., and Brett-James, Anthony. *Imphal, A Flower on Lofty Heights.* St. Martin's Press, 1962.

Fellowes-Gordon, Ian. *The Magic War: The Battle for North Burma.* Charles Scribner's Sons, 1971.

Leasor, James. *Boarding Party: The Last Action of the Calcutta Light Horse.* Houghton Mifflin, 1979.

————. *Singapore, the Battle That Changed the World.* Doubleday, 1968.

Masters, John. *Bugles and a Tiger.* Viking Press, 1956.

————. *The Road Past Mandalay.* Harper and Brothers, 1961.

Mountbatten, The Earl of Burma. *Report to the Combined Chiefs of Staff by the Supreme Allied Commander Southeast Asia, 1943–1944.* HMSO, 1951.

Ogburn, Charlton, *The Marauders.* Harper and Brothers, 1959.

Percival, A.E. *The War in Malaya.* Eyre and Spottiswoode, 1949.

Slim, Sir William. *Defeat Into Victory.* Cassell, 1956.

AIR WAR

Bekker, Cajus. *The Luftwaffe War Diaries.* Doubleday, 1968.

Coffey, Thomas M. *Decision Over Schweinfurt: The U.S. 8th Air Force Battle for Daylight Bombing.* David McKay, 1977.

Collier, Basil. *The Battle of Britain.* Macmillan, 1962.

DeChant, John A. *Devilbirds: The Story of Marine Corps Aviation in World War II.* Harper and Brothers, 1947.

Deighton, Len. *Fighter: The True Story of the Battle of Britain.* Alfred A. Knopf, 1977.

Fitzgibbon, Constantine. *The Blitz.* Wingate, 1957.

Glines, Lt. Col. Carroll V., Jr. *Helicopter Rescues.* Scholastic Book Services, 1971.

Guedalla, Philip. *Middle East, 1940–1942: A Study in Air Power.* Hodder and Stoughton, 1944.

Gunston, Bill. *The Illustrated Encyclopedia of Combat Aircraft of World War II.* Bookthrift Publications, 1978.

Harris, Sir Arthur. *Bomber Offensive.* Macmillan, 1947.

Hastings, Max. *Bomber Command: The Myths and Reality of the Strategic Bombing Offensive, 1939–45.* Dial Press, 1979.

Infield, Glenn. *Big Week!* Pinnacle Books, 1974.

Inokuchi, Rikichei, and Nakajima, Tadashi. *The Divine Wind.* U.S. Naval Institute, 1958.

Jablonski, Edward. *Airwar* (published in one, two and four vols.). Doubleday, 1971–72.

Jackson, Robert. *The Red Falcons: The Soviet Air Force in Action, 1919–1969.* Clifton Books, 1970.

Killen, John. *A History of the Luftwaffe.* Doubleday, 1968.

Longmate, Norman. *Air Raid: The Bombing of Coventry, 1940.* David McKay, 1978.

Lyall, Gavin, ed. *The War in the Air: The Royal Air Force in World War II.* William Morrow, 1969.

Mason, Herbert Molloy, Jr. *The Rise of the Luftwaffe, 1918–1940.* Dial Press, 1973.

Middlebrook, Martin. *The Nuremberg Raid.* William Morrow, 1974.

Mikesh, Robert C. *Japan's World War II Balloon Bomb Attacks on North America.* Smithsonian Institution Press, 1973.

Ministry of Defense of the U.S.S.R. *The Soviet Air Force in World War II* (translated from the Russian by Leland Fetzer; edited by Ray Wagner). Doubleday, 1973.

Okumiya, Masatake, and Horikoshi, Jiro. *Zero.* E.P. Dutton, 1956.

Richard, Denis, and Saunders, Hilary St. G. *Royal Air Force, 1939–45* (3 vols.), HMSO, *The Fight at Odds* (1953), *The Fight Avails* (1954), and *The Fight Is Won* (1954); all published in paperback edition. HMSO, 1975.

Sherman, Frederick, *Combat Command: The American Aircraft Carriers in the Pacific War.* E.P. Dutton, 1950.

Sherrod, Robert. *History of Marine Corps Aviation in World War II.* Combat Forces Press, 1952.

Shores, Christopher, and Ring, Hans. *Fighters Over the Desert: The Air Battles in the Western Desert, June, 1940 to December, 1942.* Arco Publishing, 1969.

Townsend, Peter. *Duel of Eagles.* Simon and Schuster, 1970.

Verrier, Anthony. *Bomber Offensive.* Macmillan, 1968.

Weal, Elke C., ed. *Combat Aircraft of World War Two.* Gage Trade Publishing, 1977.

Whelan, R. *The Flying Tigers.* Doubleday, 1944.

NAVAL WARFARE

Auphan, Paul, and Mordal, Jacques. *The French Navy in World War II.* U.S. Naval Institute, 1959.

Bekker, C.D. *Swastika at Sea: The Struggle and Destruction of the German Navy, 1939–1945.* Kimber, 1953.

Bennett, Geoffrey. *Naval Battles of World War II.* David McKay, 1975.

464

Blair, Clay, Jr. *Silent Victory: The U.S. Submarine War Against Japan* (2 vols). J.B. Lippincott, 1975.

Bragadin, Marc A. *The Italian Navy in World War II.* U.S. Naval Institute, 1957.

Buchheim, Lothar-Günther. *U-Boat War* (translated from the German by Gudie Lawaetz). Bantam Books, 1979.

Bulkley, Robert J., Jr. *At Close Quarters: PT Boats in the United States Navy.* GPO, 1962.

Busch, Harold. *U-Boats at War* (translated from the German by L.P.R. Wilson). Ballantine Books, 1955.

Cocchia, Aldo. *The Hunters and the Hunted: Adventures of Italian Naval Forces* (translated from the Italian by Margaret Gwyer). U.S. Naval Institute, 1958.

Dull, Paul S. *The Imperial Japanese Navy (1941–1945).* U.S. Naval Institute, 1978.

Farago, Ladislas. *The Tenth Fleet.* Paperback Library, 1964.

Frank, Wolfgang. *The Sea Wolves.* Rinehart, 1955.

Fuchida, Mitsuo, and **Okumiya, Masatake.** *Midway: The Battle That Doomed Japan.* U.S. Naval Institute, 1955.

Hough, Richard. *Death of the Battleship.* Macmillan, 1963.

Hoyt, Edwin P. *The Battle of Leyte Gulf.* Pinnacle Books, 1973.

————. *Blue Skies and Blood: The Battle of the Coral Sea.* Paul S. Eriksson, 1975.

Hughes, Terry, and **Costello, John.** *The Battle of the Atlantic.* Dial Press, 1977.

Ito, Masanori. *The End of the Imperial Japanese Navy* (translated from the Japanese by Andrew Y. Kuroda and Roger Pineau). W.W. Norton, 1962.

Karig, Walter, et al. *Battle Report* (5 vols.) Rinehart, 1946–49.

Kemp, P.K. *Key to Victory.* Little, Brown, 1957.

Kennedy, Ludovic. *The Chase and Sinking of the Battleship "Bismarck."* Viking Press, 1974.

Lord, Walter. *Incredible Victory.* Pocket Books, 1968.

Lott, Arnold S. *Most Dangerous Sea: U.S. Navy in Mine Warfare.* U.S. Naval Institute, 1959.

MacIntyre, Donald. *The Naval War Against Hitler.* Charles Scribner's Sons, 1971.

Martienssen, Anthony K. *Hitler and His Admirals.* E.P. Dutton, 1949.

Morison, Samuel Eliot. *The Two-Ocean War: A Short History of the United States Navy in the Second World War.* Little, Brown, 1963.

Padfield, Peter. *The Battleship Era.* Pan Books, 1972.

Peillard, Leonce. *Sink the Tirpitz.* G.P. Putnam's Sons, 1968.

Riesenberg, Felix. *Sea War: The Story of the U.S. Merchant Marine in World War II.* Rinehart, 1956.

Robertson, Terence. *Channel Dash.* E.P. Dutton, 1958.

Roscoe, Theodore. *United States Submarine Operations in World War II.* U.S. Naval Institute, 1949.

Roskill, S.W. *White Ensign: The British Navy at War, 1939–1945.* U.S. Naval Institute, 1960.

Ruge, Friedrich, *Der Seekrieg, the German Navy's Story, 1939–1945.* U.S. Naval Institute, 1957.

Schofield, Brian B. *The Russian Convoys.* Batsford, 1964.

Thomas, David. *Battle of the Java Sea.* Pan Books, 1971.

Vonder Porten, Edward P. *The German Navy in World War Two.* Thomas Y. Crowell, 1969.

Watts, Anthony J., and **Gordon, Brian.** *The Imperial Japanese Navy.* Doubleday, 1971.

Werner, H.A. *Iron Coffins.* Holt, Rinehart and Winston, 1969.

Winton, John (pseud.), ed. *The War at Sea, 1939–45.* William Morrow, 1968.

THE HOLOCAUST

Dawidowicz, Lucy S. *The War Against the Jews, 1933–1945.* Holt, Rinehart and Winston, 1975.

Hilberg, Raul. *The Destruction of the European Jews.* Quadrangle Books, 1961.

————ed. *Documents of Destruction: Germany and Jewry, (1933–1945).* W.H. Allen, 1972.

Kogon, Eugen. *The Theory and Practice of Hell.* Farrar and Strauss, 1950.

Levin, Nora. *The Holocaust: The Destruction of European Jewry, 1933–1945.* Thomas Y. Crowell, 1968.

Nyiszli, Miklos. *Auschwitz.* Fell, 1970.

Zeiger, Henry A., ed. *The Case Against Adolf Eichmann.* Signet, 1960.

THE HOME FRONTS

Blum, John Morton. *V Was For Victory: Politics and American Culture During World War II.* Harcourt Brace Jovanovich, 1976.

Cantril, Hadley. *Public Opinion, 1935–1946.* Princeton University Press, 1951.

Collier, Richard. *The City That Would Not Die: The Bombing of London, May 10–11, 1941.* E.P. Dutton, 1960.

Lingeman, Richard R. *Don't You Know There's a War On? The American Home Front, 1941–1945.* G.P. Putnam's Sons, 1970.

McLaine, Ian. *Ministry of Morale.* Allen and Unwin, 1979.

Marwick, Arthur. *The Home Front: The British and the Second World War.* Thames and Hudson, 1976.

Mosley, Leonard. *Backs to the Wall: The Heroic*

Story of the People of London During World War II. Random House, 1971.

Perrett, Geoffrey. *Days of Sadness, Years of Triumph: The American People, 1939–1945.* Coward, McCann and Geoghegan, 1973.

Polenberg, Richard. *War and Society: The United States, 1941–1945.* J.B. Lippincott, 1972.

Schoenbaum, David. *Hitler's Social Revolution: Class and Status in Nazi Germany, 1933–1939.* Doubleday, 1966.

ESPIONAGE AND INTELLIGENCE

Accoce, Pierre, and **Quet, Pierre.** *A Man Called Lucy.* Coward-McCann, 1966.

Bazna, Elyesa. *I Was Cicero.* Harper and Brothers, 1962.

Cave Brown, Anthony. *Bodyguard of Lies.* Harper and Row, 1975.

———, ed. *The Secret War Report of the OSS.* Berkley Publishing, 1976.

Deacon, Richard. *A History of the British Secret Service.* Taplinger, 1969.

Deakin, F. W., and **Storry, G.R.** *The Case of Richard Sorge.* Harper and Row, 1966.

Dulles, Allen. *Great True Spy Stories.* Harper and Row, 1968.

———. *The Secret Surrender.* Harper and Row, 1966.

Farago, Ladislas. *The Broken Seal: The Story of Operation Magic and the Pearl Harbor Disaster.* Random House, 1967.

———. *Burn After Reading.* Pinnacle Books, 1972.

———. *The Game of the Foxes.* David McKay, 1971.

Garlinski, Jozef. *The Enigma War.* Charles Scribner's Sons, 1980.

Ind, Allison. *Allied Intelligence Bureau: Our Secret Weapon in the War Against Japan.* Curtis Books, 1958.

Jones, R.V. *Most Secret War.* Coronet Books, 1979.

Kahn, David. *The Code-Breakers.* Macmillan, 1967.

———. *Hitler's Spies: German Military Intelligence in World War II.* Macmillan, 1978.

Lewin, Ronald. *Ultra Goes to War.* McGraw-Hill, 1978.

Manvell, Roger, and **Fraenkel, Heinrich.** *The Canaris Conspiracy.* David McKay, 1969.

Masterman, J.C. *The Double-Cross System in the War of 1939 to 1945.* Yale University Press, 1972.

Meissner, Hans-Otto. *The Man with Three Faces* (Sorge). Evans, 1955.

Montagu, Ewen. *Beyond Top Secret Ultra.* Coward, McCann & Geoghegan, 1978.

Pawle, Gerald. *The Secret War.* William Sloane Associates, 1957.

Perrault, Gilles. *The Red Orchestra.* Simon and Schuster, 1969.

Reader's Digest. *Secrets and Spies: Behind the Scenes Stories of World War II.* Reader's Digest Association, 1964.

Roosevelt, Kermit. *War Report of the O.S.S.* (2 vols.). Walker, 1976.

Smith, R. Harris. *O.S.S.: The Secret History of America's First Central Intelligence Agency.* University of California Press, 1972.

Stevenson, William. *A Man Called Intrepid: The Secret War.* Harcourt Brace Jovanovich, 1976.

Winterbotham, F.W. *The Ultra Secret.* Harper and Row, 1974.

Zacharias, Ellis M. *Secret Missions: The Story of an Intelligence Officer.* G. P. Putnam's Sons, 1946.

Index

NOTE: References to countries (and cities) are to military operations on their soil. References to illustrations are in *italics*.

Aachen: **1944**: 347, 349–52, 358; **1945**: 371
Abadan: **1941**, 171, 172
Abe, Gen. Nobuyuki, 89
ABIGAIL, Operation (1940), 142
Acker, Achille van, 411
Addis Ababa: **1941**, 52
ADLER (EAGLE), Operation (1940), 129
Admiralty Islands: **1942**: 211; **1944**: 307, 317
Agedabia: **1941**: 194; **1942**: 197, 198
"Air Raid Precautions Bill" (British; 1937), 57
Air war: **1932**: 10; **1937**: 52, 60; **1939**: 95; **1940**: 112–14, 119, 123, 125–42; **1941**: 144, 149, 151, 162, 176, 188; **1942**: 205, 206, 210, 212–14, 219, 223, 227, 230, 234, 250; **1943**: 263, 272, 280, 283, 288, 292, 294–96, 298; incendiaries, 273–74; **1944**: 301–3, 307, 310, 312–15, 318, 329, 334, 342, 355, 362, 368; V-1 and V-2 rockets, 351, *361*, 364, 374; **1945**: 370, 374–75, 382, 383, 386, 388, 391, 394, 414, 417; German suicide missions, 388; total British

casualties, 402; V-2 rockets, 390; *See also* Naval war; *specific countries and cities*
Albania: **1939**: 76, 79, 81–83; **1941**: 144–55; **1944**: 354, 358
Aleutian Islands: **1942**: 218, 220, 227, 231, 233, 236, 240; **1943**: 253, 262, 264–67, 270, 274, 275, 277, 278
Alexander, Field Marshal Sir Harold: **1942**: operations under, 207, 214, 227–30; **1943**: operations under, 272, 282, 290, 296; **1944**: operations under, 310, 314, 319, 321; promoted, 360; **1945**: operations under, 399
Alexander I (King of Yugoslavia), 29, 30
Alexandria: **1942**, 211
Alfonso XIII (King of Spain), 45
Algeria, *see* North African campaigns
Algiers: **1942**, 242
Alien Restoration Act (U.S.; 1940), 124
Alliance treaty (1942), British-Russian-Iranian, 200
Amiens: **1940**: 114, 115; **1944**: 305, 342
Anan, Gen. Tadaki, 175
Andaman Islands: **1942**: 206, 208–10; **1945**: 407
Anders, Gen. Wladyslaw, 170
Andrews, Gen. Frank M., 265

Anglo-Iraqi treaty (1930), 155
Anschluss (1937–1938), 56, 62–66
Anti-Comintern Pact (1936), 48, 57, 74, 79, 81, 82, 88, 182, 183
Antigua: **1941**, 151
Anti-Semitism, *see* Jews
Antonescu, Gen. Ion, 130, 145, 203, 234, 340
Antwerp: **1944**, 343, 345, 351, 357, 358, *361*, 364, 365, 374
ANVIL, Operation (1944), 292
Anzio: **1944**, 301, *302*, *303*, 304–7, 310, *312*, 318, 319
Aosta, Amadeus, Duke of, 128, 157
Araki, Gen. Sadao, 2
ARCADIA conference (1941), 192–93, 198
Arens, Joseph, 109
Argentan: **1944**, 337, 338
Arita, Hachiro, 75, 76, 105, 110, 124
Armed forces, 1939 world, 89
Armistice, *see* Surrender and armistices
Arnhem: **1944**: 347–49; **1945**: 392, 396, 397
Arnim, Gen. Jürgen von, 254, 260, 265–66
Arnold, Gen. Henry, 288–89
Arras: **1940**: 115; **1942**: 212
Aryan (Civil Service) Law (German; 1933), 20
Athens: **1941**: 156; **1944**: 350, 351

Atlantic Charter (1941), 170
"Atlantic Directive, Battle of the" (British; 1941), 149
Atomic bombs: **1940**: French and German interest in, 105; **1941** and **1942**: U.S. development of, 179–80, 186, 246; **1943**: Germans abandon effort, 290; **1944**: German research on, 306; **1945**: first U.S. test of, 414; German ship in testing, 406; over Hiroshima, 384, 385, *410*, *416*; over Nagasaki, 384, 385, *410*, 416; U.S. decision to use, 411
Atrocities and repression: **1933**: book burning in Germany, 21; in consolidating Hitler's power, 18–22; Göring on, 20; **1934**: Nazi blood purge, 28; **1937**: purge of Russian military, 52–53; **1939**: in Czechoslovakia, 100; in Poland, 99, 102; **1941**: in Croatia, 162; executions for partisan activity, 175; in France, 171, 173, 179; Serbians murdered, 179; **1942**: in Czechoslovakia, 196, 219, 220; in France, 214, 225, 233, 236; Japanese, 201, 214; as war crimes, 198, 230, 236; **1943**: trials for, in Kharkov, 295; as war crimes, 264, 278, 285; **1944**: executed British officers, 317; report on Bataan, 302; war crimes commission and, 303; and war criminals in Argentina, 343; *See also* Jews
Attlee, Clement, 266, 301, *369*, 415
Auchinleck, Gen. Sir Claude, 164, 182, 190, 197, 204, 222–27, 229, 268
Aung San, 189
Auphan, Adm. Paul, 337–38
Australia: **1942**: 200, 204, 209, 214; **1943**: 264, 265, 268
Austria: **1937–1938**: Anschluss, 56, 62–66; **1941**: 152; **1942**: 231; **1943**: 276; **1945**: 386, 388–90, 392–94, 396, 403, 404, 407
Austro-German agreement (1936), 45
"Autumn offensive" (1941), 181
Avranches (France): **1944**, 335, 336, 338
Axis: 1939 creation of, 84
Azaña, Manuel, 43, 45, 79
Azores: **1941**: 161, 162; **1943**: 278, 284

Ba Maw, 274

Badoglio, Marshal Pietro, 38–40, 44, 141, 273, 275, 279, 280, 283, 284, 313, 322
Baghdad: **1941**, 158, 162
Bahamas: **1941**, 151
Bahrain: **1940**, 134
Balbo, Italo, 124
Baldwin, Stanley, 28, 34, 37–38, 44, 52
Bali: **1942**, 204, 205
Balkan Entente, 69, 105
Balkan Pact (1934), 27
Bangkok: **1944**, 314, 321, 361
Bao Dai (Vietnamese emperor), 385
Barcelona: **1939**, 78, 79
Bardia: **1941**: 144, 153, 155, 194; **1942**: 196, 243
Bari: **1943**: 294; **1945**: 394
Barré, Gen. Georges, 244
Barthou, Louis, 27, 29
Basra: **1941**, 156, 517
Bastogne: **1944**: 365–68; **1945**: 370
Bataan: **1941**: 192, 194; **1942**: 197–99, 202–3, 210, *211*; **1945**: 376, 379, 380
"Bataan Death March" (1942), *195*, 211, *217*
Batavia: **1942**, 207
BATTLEAXE, Operation (1941), 163
Baudouin, Paul, 125
Bayeux: **1944**, 321–22
Beaverbrook, Lord, 176
Beck, Gen. Ludwig, 67, 79, 334
Beda Fomm, Battle of (1941), 146
Beirut: **1941**: 168; **1945**: 409
Belfort: **1940**: 121; **1944**: 358, 359, *360*
Belgium: **1940**: 112, 114; **1942**: 228; **1944**: 343–45, 351, 357, 358, 361, 364, 365, 374; **1945**: 378
Belgorod: **1943**: 257, 259, 262, 275
Belgrade: **1941**: 153–54; **1944**: 349, 351–53
Benes, Eduard, 65, 72, 73
Benevento: **1943**, 284
Benghazi: **1941**: 146, 148, 152, 158, 192; **1942**: 200, 209, 232, 234, 245
Bennett, Sgt. Paul, 274
Berchtesgaden: **1945**, 400, 403, *404*
Beria, Lavrenti, 165
Berlin: **1940**: 117, 129, 130; **1941**: 150, 153, 155, 170, 173; **1942**: 231; **1943**: 254, 256, 260, 290, 296, 297; partial evacuation of, 276; **1944**: 305, 307, 308, *312*,

358; **1945**: 376, 377, 385, 387, 390, 397, 399–402, 413; Charlottenburg district, *406*
Bermuda: **1941**, 130, 151
Bernadotte, Count Folke, 380, 399, 400
Béthouart, General, 116
Biddle, Anthony J. Drexel, Jr., 93
Biddle, Francis, 236
Bilbao: **1937**, 51, 53
Bismarck Archipelago: **1942**: 196, 200, 205, 248; **1943**: 269, 284, 287–89, *297*; **1944**: 301, 302, 304–6, 308–10, 313; **1945**: 377
Bismarck Sea, Battle of the (1943), 260
Bizerte: **1943**, 264, 265
"Black May" (1943), 265
Blamey, Gen. Sir Thomas, 420
Blitzkrieg, 90
Blockades: **1937**: of China, by Japanese, 55; of Spain, 58; **1939**: of Britain, 93; of Germany, 91, 93; **1940**: of Britain, 129; of Italy, 119; **1941**: of Britain, 151; of Germany, 170; **1942**: of Germany, 236; of Japan, 390, 400, 415, 417
Blomberg, Gen. Werner von, 63
Blum, Léon, 38, 44, 45, 53, 62, 65, 66, 403
Bock, Field Marshal Fedor von, 169
Bohol Island: **1945**, 395, 399
Bologna: **1944**: 349, 351, 362, 368; **1945**: 396, 399
Bombing: camouflage of cities (1940), 130; *See also specific cities*
Bonin Islands: **1944**: 325, 329, 364; **1945**: 375, *379*, *380*, *381*, 382–84, 386, 389, 394
Bonnet, George, 70, 71
Bonomi, Ivanoe, 322
Borghese, Prince, 192
Boris III (King of Bulgaria), 149, 191, 278
Borisov: **1944**, 329, 348
Bormann, Martin, 159, 204, 392
Borneo: **1941**: 191, 192; **1942**: 197, 199, 200, 203; **1945**: 400, 408–10, *412*, *413*, 414, 416
Bose, Subhas Chandra, 268, 269, 285, 286, 417
Bougainville: **1943**: 285, 287; **1944**: *308*, *314*
Boulogne: **1940**: 115; **1944**: 347
Boyington, Gregory (Pappy), 418
Bradley, Gen. Omar, 263, 366

Bratislava: **1945**, 388, 390, 392

Brauchitsch, Field Marshal Walther von, 81, 191–92

Braun, Eva, 401–2

"Breakthrough, Battle of the" (1945), 416

Bremen: **1941**: 142, 144; **1942**: 223; **1943**: 268; **1944**: 347; **1945**: 394, 398–400

Breslau: **1942**: 231; **1944**: 308; **1945**: 375, 378, 379, 381, 382, 405

Brest: **1941**: 162; **1944**: 336, 340, 344, 345, 347

Brest-Litovsk: **1939**: 94, 95; **1941**: 165; **1944**: 334, 335

Brett, Gen. George H., 213

Bretton Woods International Monetary Conference (1944), 329

Britain, Battle of: **1937**: decision on fighter aircraft and, 60; **1940**: 128–42

British-Egyptian alliance (1936), 46

British Guiana: **1941**, 151, 167

British-Hungarian agreement (1943), 276

British-Italian agreement (1938), 66

Brody: **1944**, 333, 334

Brooke, Gen. Sir Alan, 119

Browder, Earl, 218

Brüning, Heinrich, 8, 11–14

Brussels: **1944**, 343

Brussels conference (1937), 56–58

Bryansk: **1941**: 174, 176–78; **1943**: 283

Bucharest: **1942**: 231; **1944**: 340, 342

Buckner, Gen. Simon Bolivar, Jr., 411

Budapest: **1942**: 231; **1944**: 311, 353, 355, 356, 364, 365, 367, 368; **1945**: 350, 370, 371, 373, 374, 376, 378

Budenny, Marshal Semyon, 168

Bulgaria: **1941**: 149, 152, 155; **1944**: 301, 315, 340, 342–44, 347, 350

Bulge, Battle of the (1944), 364, *365*, *366*, 367, 368, 375

Burma: **1941**: 189–91, 193; **1942**: 196, 198–201, 203, 204, 206–10, 212–14, 217, 232, 233, 238, 248–50; **1943**: 252, 256, 257, 259, 261–63, 266, 274, 287, 291, 295–96; **1944**: 300, 301, 303, 304, 306–9, 351, 352, 355, 357, 359, 360, *362*, 366, 367; **1945**: 371, 372, *374*, *376*, 378, 379, 383, 386,

388, 390, 396–99, 402, 403, 407, 408, 411, 414, 419

Burma Road (Stilwell Road): **1940**: 126, 135; **1941**: 181; **1942**: 207, 214; **1944**: 307, 344; **1945**: 374–76, 389

Busch, Gen. Ernst, *105*, 328

Byrnes, James F., 277

Caballero, Largo, 46, 52

Cabenallas, Gen. Miguel, 45

Caen: **1944**, 321, 328, 330, 333

Cairo: **1942**, 227

Calais: **1940**: 116; **1944**: 348, 349

Calcutta: **1943**, 295

Calinescu, Armand, 95

Camacho, Manuel Avila, 264

Cambodia: **1941**, 144, 165

Canada: **1942**, 222

Canaris, Adm. Wilhelm, 141

Cannes: **1944**, 339, 340

Canterbury: **1942**, 240

Canton: **1937**: 56; **1938**: 74; **1942**: 227, 229

Cape Esperance, Battle of (1942), 236–37

Cape Matapan, Battle of (1941), 151

Cape St. George, Battle of (1943), 292

Cape Verde Islands: **1941**, 162

Capuzzo, Fort: **1940**: 120; **1941**: 155, 182

Carlson, Col. Evans E., 229

Carol II (King of Rumania), 60, 63, 64, 122, 125, 130, 140

Caroline Islands: **1944**: 304, 305, 310, 314, 343, *346*, 348, 351, 361; **1945**: 373, 410, 411

CARTWHEEL, Operation (1943), 269

Casablanca: **1942**, 242, 243

Casablanca conference (1943), 253, 279–80

Castellano, Gen. Giuseppe, 277, 279

Castle, William, 4

Catroux, Gen. Georges, 132

Cavagnari, Adm. Domenico, 141

Cavallero, Gen. Ugo, 141, 145

Cebu Island: **1942**: 212, 213; **1945**: 389, 395, 399

Celebes: **1942**, 198, 203

Cervaro: **1944**, 300, 301

Chamberlain, Neville: **1937**: endorses "Quarantine" speech, 56; on Germany's restraint, 53; as prime minister, 52; **1938**: Czech situation and, 70–73; defense

strategy and, 66; and foreign policy, 64, 65, 76; Godesberg meeting with Hitler, 71, 72; Roosevelt message to, 62; Sudeten problem and, 69; **1939**: abandons appeasement, 79–81; army placed on war footing by, 82; and Czech situation, 80; guarantees made to Poland by, 82, 88; Hitler on, 87; and Mussolini meeting, 78; and rearmament, 83; on repeal of U.S. embargo, 99; satisfying Japanese demands, 86; warns Germany, 98; **1940**: 125; British pledge to Belgium, 105; death of, 138; on lack of aid to Finland, 108; resigns, 112

Chang Hsueh-liang, 48

Changchun: **1945**, 416, 419

Changsha: **1939**: 97; **1941**: 175–76; **1942**: 196; **1944**: 323, 325

Changsha, Second Battle of (1941), 175–76

Changsha, Third Battle of (1944), 325

Changteh: **1943**, 255, 292

Channel Islands: **1940**: 124, 126; **1945**: 406

Chautemps, Camille, 53, 62

Chen Kiung-po, 357

Chennault, Col. Claire L., 190, 236

Cherbourg: **1942**: 212; **1944**: 321, 322, 325–29, 338

Chernyakhovsky, Gen. I. D., 379

Chiang Kai-shek: **1931**: resignation of, 5; **1932**: returns to government, 12, 14; **1935**: head of Nanking government, 39; Mao's united front, 34; **1936**: establishes control over Kwangtung Province, 45; kidnapped, 48; strengthens control over country, 46; **1937**: combined forces to fight Japan under, 50; **1938**: 66; and blowing up Yellow River dikes, 67–68; Japanese refuse contacts with, 62; on Japanese rulers, 76; **1939**: victory under, 97; **1940**: and renewed Japanese operations, 111; U.S. loan to government of, 132; **1941**: and aid to Burma, 193; and cooperation with Communists, 153; on non-compromise with Japan, 149; offers aid for Burma campaign, 192; Russians propose alliance with, 165; and U.S. aid, 156; U.S. freezes all Chinese assets, 169;

Chiang Kai-shek (Continued)
1942: and aid to Burma, 211; and aid to China, 219; in command of China theater, 196; on Doolittle raid, 214; Stilwell and, 201; visits India, 203, 205; **1943**: and aid for China, 295; and Allied conferences, 278; and Burma operations, 296; in Cairo conference, 291, *292*; code names for, 277; named president of China, 281; and Stilwell, 292; and use of Communist troops, 280; **1944**: Mao Tse-tung and, 324; and munitions to Communist forces, 361; and Roosevelt on additional Chinese forces, 301; Roosevelt and, and contact with Communists, 304; seeking removal of, 332, 337; Stilwell and, 352; **1945**: gives up premiership, 409; renames Burma Road, 375

Chiang Kai-shek, Madame, 259, *292*

China-Burma-India theater, *see* Burma; India; Sino-Japanese war

Chinchow: **1931**, 3–5

Choltitz, Gen. Dietrich von, 332, 340

Chou En-lai, 48, *419*

Christian X (King of Denmark), 278

Christmer, Lt. Charles, *324*

Chuguyev: **1943**, 257, 276

Chuikov, Gen. Vasili, 336, 399

Chungking: **1938–1941**: 62; **1943**: 278

Churchill, Randolph, 318

Churchill, Sir Winston: **1933**: view of events in Asia, 19; **1934**: warns of German arms buildup, 30; **1938**: and Czech situation, 73; **1939**: appointed Lord of Admiralty, 91; calls for alliance with Soviet Union, 85; on Russian invasion of Poland, 96; **1940**: *113*; and air war, 113, 130; appeals to Roosevelt for ships, 120–21; becomes prime minister, 112; broadcast double of, 116–17; claims on enemy losses, 107; and Coventry bombing, 139; defense of Britain in hands of, 108; on French fleet, 125; and French request for separate peace, 119; granted absolute power for war effort, 115; Hitler offers peace to, 124, 126–27;

leasing British bases, 129; message to Roosevelt, 114, 134; message to Stalin, 124; on resolve to defeat Hitler, 135; speech on "finest hour," 122; war goals of, 113; warns neutrals, 104; **1941**: and aid to invaded Russia, 164; asked for troops by Stalin, 174; "Battle of the Atlantic Directive," 149; condemns reprisal killings, 179; and Japanese attack on Thailand, 185; lend-lease and, 150; message to Stalin, 167; message to Young, 192; and naval losses, 165; pleas for arms, 147; policy on war with Japan, 180; Roosevelt Asia proposals and, 182; and Roosevelt map war strategy, 192–93; and Roosevelt meeting, 170; seeks bases in Turkey, 146; and U.S. supplies for North Africa, 155; wins vote of confidence, 158; **1942**: 238; and attack through Balkans, 243; on bombing Italian cities, 246; on British successes in Egypt, 243; on German use of poison gas, 217; and India situation, 208, 232; on Madagascar fighting, 216; message to Stalin on shipping, 225; on Rommel, 197; and Roosevelt, on second front, 222; Roosevelt and, establish unified southwest Pacific command, 196; and second front, 218, 222, 229; on victory, 209; visits Egyptian front, 227; vote of confidence in, 200, 223; **1943**: *253*; address to Italian people, 272; addresses U.S. Congress, 267; and Balkans invasion from west, 265, 267, 291; in Cairo conference, 291, *292*; code name for, 277; predicts climax of war in 1944, 288; and Roosevelt meetings, 265, 267, 276–77, 288, 292, *293*; and surrender of Italian ships, 284; in Tehran conference, 288, 292, *293*; **1944**: and de Gaulle, 300; Franco message to, 352; and Greek civil war, 367; in Moscow conference, 350; on people killed by V-1 bombs, 330; in second Quebec conference, *345*; and Tito meeting, 338; **1945**: and Balkans invasion from west, 376, *377*; coalition under, ended, 407; on Dresden bombing, 378; on food shortages, 388;

ousted, 415; in Potsdam conference, 414; and Russian offensive (January), 372; and starving Dutch, 401; and thrust of final drive into Germany, 390; on total Commonwealth casualties, 394–95; V-E Day, 405; in Yalta conference, 376

Chvalkovsky, Frantisek, 79

Ciano, Count Galeazzo, 47, 79, 84, 86, 102, 127, 257, 300

Ciano, Countess, 300

Cisterna: **1944**, 303, 318

CITADEL, Operation (1943), 267

CLARION, Operation (1945), 380

Clark, Gen. Mark, 237

Clark Field: **1941**: 188; **1945**: 373, 375, 395

Clowes, Gen. Cyril A., 230

Codes: Enigma, 28, 129, 132, 158; Japanese, broken, 132, 157; Ultra intercepts of Enigma, 139, 158, 180, 221, 240, 254, 264, 265, 288

Codreanu, Corneliu, 66, 76

Colmar: **1944**: 363, 367; **1945**: 374, 376–78

Cologne: **1942**: 211, 218–19; **1945**: 382, 383, 385

Commercial treaties: **1911**, U.S.-Japanese, 86, 105; *See also* Trade agreements

Concentration camps: **1942**, U.S., 191, 210; *See also* Jews

Conciliation pacts: **1932**, Estonian-Russian, 14; Latvian-Russian, 14; Russian-Finnish, 13

Concordat (1933), 22–23

Coningham, Air Marshal Arthur, 237

Constanta: **1944**, 341–42

Consultation pacts: **1934**: French–Russian, 30; **1935**: Austro-Hungarian, 36

Cooper, Alfred Duff, 73

Cooperation and coordination treaty (1934), Estonia, Latvia and Lithuania, 29

Copenhagen: **1944**: 329; **1945**: 370, 388

Coral Sea, Battle of the (1942), *215*

Coral Sea, Battle of the (1943), 255

Corfu Island: **1943**: 283; **1944**: 351

Corinth: **1941**: 156; **1944**: 350

Corregidor Island: **1941**: 194; **1942**: 196, 209, 214–16; **1945**: 375, 379, 381, 382

Corsica: **1943**, 280, 284
Coulondre, Robert, 76, 85
Coventry: **1940**, 139
Crete: **1940**: 137; **1941**: 156, 159–60, 162; **1943**: 270, 274; **1944**: 362; **1945**: 407
Criaova, Treaty of (1940), 131
Cripps, Sir Stafford, 124, 152, 163, 165, 208, 210, 212, 226
CRUSADER, Operation (1941), 181
"Crystal Night" ("Night of Glass"; 1938), 74–75
Cunningham, Gen. Sir Alan, 147–48, 284
Currier, Col. D. E., 275
Curtin, John, 264, 268, 413
Cvetkovich, Dragisla, 79
Czechoslovakia: **1938**: 64–74; **1939**: 79–81; **1944**: 308, 312, 342, 344, 348, 350, 352, 362, 364, 366; **1945**: 389, 398, 400, 407, 412
Czestochowa: **1943**: 269; **1945**: 373

Dakar: **1940**: 132; **1942**: 245
Daladier, Edouard, 66, 71, 72, 88, 107, 108, 117, 403
Damascus: **1941**: 164; **1945**: 409
Dan, Baron Takuma, 11
Danzig: **1933**: 21–23; **1937**: 56; **1938**: 74–76; **1939**: 81–86, 88, 90; **1942**: 231; **1945**: 382, 385, 388–90, 397
Darlan, Adm. Jean, 123, 125, 148, 155, 158–59, 161, 238, 243–46, 249
Darré, Walther, 79
Darwin: **1942**: 204, 209; **1943**: 265
Davao: **1945**, 402, 403
de Gaulle, see Gaulle, Gen. Charles de
Debuchi, Katsuji, 3
Delbos, Yvon, 58
Delmer, Sefton, 19
Dempsey, Gen. Miles, 342
Denmark: **1940**: 107–9; **1943**: 278–79; **1944**: 329, 347, 348, 355; **1945**: 370, 388, 402, 403
Derevyanko, Gen. K., 420
Derna: **1941**: 146, 152, 192; **1942**: 209
Derrien, Adm. Edmond, 315
Devers, Gen. Jacob L., 265, 283
DeWitt, Gen. John L., 189, 191
Dieppe: **1942**: 229; **1944**: 343, 344
Dietrich, Gen. Josef (Sepp), 260, 407
Dill, Sir John, 148
Dinagat Island: **1944**, 354

Dinant: **1940**: 114; **1944**: 343
Dixon, Lt. Commander Robert, 215
Dnepropetrovsk: **1941**: 171; **1943**: 286
Dollfuss, Engelbert, 23, 27, 28
Dönitz, Adm. Karl, 250, 256, 263, 265, 283, 288, 401, 402
Doolittle, Gen. James B., 212, *213*, 214, 217, 325
Dorogobuzh: **1942**: 205; **1943**: 279
Dortmund: **1945**, 378, 385
Doumer, Paul, 13
Dresden: **1945**, 379, 397
Drogobych: **1944**, 328, 336
Duca, Ion, 24
Dulles, Allen, 384
Dumbarton Oaks International Peace and Security Conference (1944), 340, 350
Dunkirk: **1940**: 115–16, *117*; **1944**: 344
Durazzo: **1934**: 28; **1944**: 359
Düsseldorf: **1940**: 142; **1942**: 227, 232; **1945**: 378

Earhart, Amelia, 53
Early, Stephen T., 185
East China Sea, battle of the (1945), 393
East Indies: **1941**: 163, 179, 186; **1942**: 198, 201, 204, 206, 207, 216
Economic agreements, see Trade agreements
Eden, Sir Anthony: **1935**: becomes foreign secretary, 39; **1936**: and Rhineland situation, 43; on sanctions against Italy, 44; **1937**: on sanctions against Japan, 60; **1938**: and German moves in Austria, 63; **1940**: as foreign secretary, 142; **1941**: British postwar aims, 162; and Greek situation, 148, 149; **1942**: on extermination of Jews, 248; **1943**: code name for, 277; **1943**: in meeting on conduct of war, 285; and Greek civil war, 367; warning to Spanish government, 301
Edward VIII (King of England), 42, 48; *See also* Windsor, Duke of
Egypt, see North African campaigns
Eichelberger, Gen. Robert L., 382
Eichmann, Adolf, 386
Eindhoven: **1944**, 347, 348
Eisenhower, Gen. Dwight D.: **1942**:

abandons attack on Tunis, 249; command under, 223, 232; **1942**: Darlan and, 243; in North African campaign, 240, 241; **1943**: appointed Supreme Commander, 296; Badoglio and, 284; code name for, 277; in command in North Africa, 257; and invasion of Italy, 278; and invasion of southern France, 276; and Italian surrender, 280, 283; reprimands Patton, 275; **1944**: and clearing west Rhine area, 360; command given, 301, 321, 322, 337; halts armies, 343; orders drive into Germany, 354; Patton halted by, 348; postpones D-Day, 320; and Ruhr, 345; sets date for cross-Channel invasion, 315; **1945**: announces end to war, 405; calls for civilian evacuation, 386; on German prisoners, 380; plans for final campaign, 390; sets limits on advance, 400; in victory celebration, 411
Einstein, Albert, 14, 16, 19–20, 86
El Agheila: **1941**: 147, 150–51; **1942**: 248
El Alamein: **1942**, 221, 223, 225, 227, 231, 232, 236–41
"11 percent Naval Expansion Act" (1940; U.S.), 120
Elizabeth (Queen to George VI), 69, 238
Ellice Islands: **1943**, 278
Elster, Gen. Erich, 345
Emden: **1941**: 151; **1943**: 283
Emergency Powers Act (British; 1940), 115
Emmons, Gen. Delos C., 191
Empress Augusta Bay, Battle of (1943), 287
Enabling Act (German; 1933), 20
Enigma code (German), 28, 129, 133, 158; Ultra intercepts of, 139, 158, 180, 221, 240, 254, 264, 265, 288
Epp, Gen. Ritter von, 46
Essen: **1940**: 138; **1942**: 212, 219; **1943**: 260, 270; **1945**: 378
Estonia: **1940**: 127, 129; **1944**: 347–49
Ethiopian-Italian war: **1935**: 91; **1936**: 42–44, 48, 55, 56; **1938**: 66, 67, 75; **1941**: 145–48, 150, 151, 157
Evian Conference on Refugees (1938), 68–69
Faid Pass: **1942**: 247; **1943**: 256, 258, 263

Falaise: **1944**, 336–40
Farouk (King of Egypt), 202, 380
Fehn, Gen. Gustav, 266
Feodosiya: **1941**: 194; **1942**: 199, 201, 217
Fermi, Enrico, 246
Fiji Islands: **1942**, 200
Finland, *see* Russo-Finnish fighting
Finland, Gulf of (1944), 301, 303
Fletcher, Adm. Jack, 230
Florence: **1944**, 333, 336, *338*
Fonck, Col. René, 128
Foochow: **1941**: 156; **1945**: 407
Forbes, W. Cameron, 9
Formosa: **1942**: 229; **1943**: 292; **1944**: 351, 371; **1945**: 394
Forster, Albert, 88
Four-Power Pact (1933), 22
France: **1940**: 107, 112–23; the fleet and, 117, 118, 123–25; **1941**: 162; **1942**: 207, 212, 217, 229, 232–33; fleet scuttled, 245, 246; Germans complete occupation of, 243; second front and, 206, 209, 210, 218, 222, 225, 226, 229, 234, 235; Vichy army dissolved, 245; Vichy protests to U.S., 212; **1943**: date for invasion set, 267, 285; fleet and, 267; provisional government formed, 267, 278; second front and, 253, 276; Vichy drafting laborers, 258; Vichy evacuation of children in shore towns, 263; Vichy exemption of workers, 294; **1944**: 304, 305, 312, 313, 315, 319–22, *323*, 324–25, 328–42, 347, 352, 358–60; Free French landings, 338, *339*; and provisional government, 344; Vichy government declared null and void, 337
Franco, Gen. Francisco: **1936**: begins civil war, 45; government of, recognized by Germany and Italy, 48; named caudillo, 47; **1937**: blockades Spanish coast, 58; counteroffensive against, 59; turns from Madrid to Bilbao, 51; victories of, 56; **1938**: drive on Catalonia, 76; gains of, 66; recognition of regime of, 62, 67; **1939**: 81; assumes total power, 86; Catalonia taken by, 79; supports Axis cause, 92; U.S. recognizes, 82; **1940**: and Hitler meeting, 135, *136*, 141; and world war, 129, 141, 142, 149, 168; **1943**: offers to mediate in world

war, 266; **1944**: message to Churchill, 352; **1945**: Laval and, 415; and UN membership, 411
Franco-Belgian military alliance (1921), 47
Franco-Czech alliance (1934), 27
Franco-Italian treaty (1935), 32
Franco-Lebanese treaty (1936), 48
François-Poncet, André, 72
Frank, Hans, 20, 99, 403
Frankfurt am Main: **1943**: 284; **1944**: 302, 309, 310, 345; **1945**: 371, 385–87, 389, 390
Fraser, Adm. Bruce, 420
French Guiana: **1943**, 261
Freyberg, Gen. Bernard, 162
Frick, Wilhelm, 58
Friedman, Col. William, 132
Friendship treaties: **1937**: Bulgarian-Yugoslav, 40; Sino-Russian, 55; **1938**: British-Turkish, 67; Franco-German, 76; Greek-Turkish, 66; Italian-Manchukuo, 68; **1939**: Russian-German, 96; Spanish-German, 100; **1940**: Hungarian-Yugoslav, 141; Japanese-Thai, 141; **1941**: German-Turkish, 163, 268; Yugoslav-Russian, 152
Fritsch, Gen. Werner von, 63
Fuller, Gen. J. F. C., 113
Furanghi, Ali, 172
Fushimi, Prince Hiroyasu, 153

Gailani, Rashid Ali, *see* Rashid Ali
Galápagos Islands: **1942**, 232
Gallery, Capt. Daniel V., *320*
Gamelin, Gen. Maurice, 43, 84, 114, 403
Gandhi, Mohandas K., 198, 214, 226, 227, 236, 314
Gaulle, Gen. Charles de: **1940**: calls for continuation of war, 122; Chad loyal to, 129–30; enters government, 117; Free French government under, 124, 136; Laon attack under, 114; ousted, 122; Vichy government on, 125; **1941**: exile government under, 175; **1942**: Darlan and, 244; and North African invasion 242; **1943**: arrives in Algiers, 267; Caribbean Islands and, 270; Giraud and, 253; as head of provisional government, 274; **1944**: as commander of Free French forces, 311; and invasion of France, 300; and Stalin meeting,

362; triumphal return to France, 325, *341*; Vichy and, 338; **1945**: and limited self-government in Indochina, 388; and Roosevelt, 380; and Stuttgart, 400; and Syria situation, 409
Gauthier, Pierre, 203
Gazala: **1941**: 188, 191
Gdynia: **1944**: 336; **1945**: 385, 388–90
Geilenkirchen: **1944**, 350, 358, 359
Geldern: **1940**: 112; **1945**: 382–83
Geneva Disarmament Conference (1932), 10–11, 14–16, 18, 23, 24, 28
Geneva Protocol (1925), on use of poison gas, 91
Genoa: **1941**: 147; **1945**: 400, 401
Gentlemen's agreement (1936), Austro-German, 45
George II (King of Greece), 156
George V (King of England), 42
George VI (King of England), 48, 69, 212, 230, 238, 268, 325
German rearmament: **1932**: 11, 14; **1933**: 24; **1933–1939**: 78; **1934**: 26, 27, 29; **1935**: 32–35; **1936**: 43, 44, 46; **1937**: 52; **1938**: 67, 69; **1939**: 82; **1942**: 232; **1943**: 256
German-Russian pact (1939), 82–87
Germany: **1940–1945**: bombing of, *see specific cities*; **1944**: 339, 346, 348, *349*, 351–53, 356, 358, 362; *Volkssturm* formed, 348, 352; **1945**: 374–407; civilian losses, 401; effects of mass bombing on, 398; fate of German generals, 400; summary courts established in, 379; *Volkssturm*, women eligible for, 378; youths ordered to front, 382
Gertsdorff, Col. Rudolf von, 262
Gestapo (German secret state police): **1933**: leaders of, *17*; **1936**: assume control over internal security, 42; **1941**: arrests Jews in Paris, 159
Ghormley, Adm. Robert L., 238
Giap, Vo Nguyen, 367
Gilbert Islands: **1941**: 189; **1942**: 201, 229; **1943**: 277, 288, 289, *290*, *291*, 292
Giral, José, 45, 46
Giraud, Gen. Henri, 214, 240, 241 244, 249, 253, 274, 277
Godfroy, Adm. René, 267
Goebbels, Joseph, 42, 46, 265, 268,

273, 275, 335, 340, 383, 390, 392, 402

Goebbels, Mrs. Joseph, 402

Goga, Octavian, 60, 63

Gomel: **1941**: 171, 172; **1943**: 285, 292, 294

Göring, Hermann: **1932**: *13*; elected president of Reichstag, 14; **1933**: *17*; establishes auxiliary police force, 19; mission to Rome, 21; orders buildup of German air force, 22; on repression, 20; **1937**: orders halt to heavy-bomber production, 52; **1938**: *61*; and "Crystal Night," 75; and war in the east, 76; **1939**: and bombing attacks, 93; on Jewish problem, 79; **1940**: and air war, 129, 135; war production under, 104; **1941**: on elimination of Jews, 169; goaded into bombing Moscow, 168; Hess and, 158; **1942**: 204; on Allied blockade, 236; **1943**: Jeschonnek and, 278; orders bombing of Britain, 294–95; **1944**: on air superiority in Italy, 319; as director of mobili-
̵ʳ̵ᵗⁱᵒⁿ, ³³⁵ rest of, ̵ʳᵘthor-
him-

̵ʳtter von,

ʲ1, 145–46, 169,

ʲ42, 230, 235, 240
̵szpan, Herschel, 74

̵Guadalcanal: **1942**: 225, 227, 229–40, 243–46, 248, 250; **1943**: 253, 255, 257, 258, 263, 267, 268

Guam: **1941**: 179, 183, 189; **1944**: 306, 324, 325, 330, 334, 335–37

Guderian, Gen. Heinz: **1940**: operations under, 113–16, 119; **1941**: operations under, 165, 168, 170,

173, 174; **1943**: Hitler and, 267; **1944**: Ardennes counteroffensive and, 347; **1945**: dismissed, 390

Guernica: **1937**, 52

Guernsey Island: **1940**, 124, 126

GYMNAST, Operation (1942), 198

Haakon VII (King of Norway), 109–11

Habbaniyah: **1941**, 156, 157, 159

Habicht, Theo, 22

Hacha, Emil, 76, 80

Haile Selassie (Emperor of Ethiopia), 30, 42, 44–45, 157, 380

Halder, Gen. Franz, 126, 166, 180–81

Halfaya Pass: **1941**: 156, 159, 162; **1942**: 196, 198

Halifax, Lord, 63, 67, 70, 78, 86, 98, 127, 142

Halsey, Adm. William F., 238, 419

Hamburg: **1941**: 157; **1942**: 226; **1943**: 256, 273–75; **1945**: 383, 403

Hamilton, Duke of, 158

Hammerstein, Gen. Kurt von, 24

Hangö: **1939**: 98; **1940**: 108; **1944**: 348

Hankow: **1936**: 47, 67, 68, 74; **1942**: 229

Harbin: **1932**: 9–11; **1945**: 418

̵Harcourt, Adm. C. H. J., 419

̵armon, Leonard Roy, 273

̵arriman, Averell, 176, 234, 350

̵ashimoto, Col. Kingoro, 59

̵ta, Gen. Shunroku, 126

̵atanaka, Maj. Kenji, 396

̵aukelid, Lt. Knut, 306

̵Hawaii: **1942**, 207

Hayashi, Gen. Senjuro, 51, 52

Hedgerows, Battle of the (1944), 329, 332, 333

Helfrich, Adm. C. E. L., 420

Henderson, Nevile, 52, 69, 70

Hengyang: **1944**, 328, 336, 342

Henlein, Konrad, 58, 65–67, 70

Henriot, Philippe, 328

Hess, Rudolf, *17*, 158–59, 204, 237

Heydrich, Reinhard, 79, 80, 169, 175, 199, 218, 220

Higashikuni, Gen. Prince Toshihiko, 417

Himmler, Heinrich: **1936**: control over internal security given to, 42; **1940**: orders construction of Auschwitz, 111; **1941**: on educa-

tional policies in the east, 157; **1942**: and order in Denmark, Norway, Belgium and Holland, 229; as minister of interior, 278; **1943**: orders Polish ghettoes liquidated, 268; orders Russian ghettoes liquidated, 268; **1944**: as dictator of home front, 335; orders Auschwitz crematoria destroyed, 361; **1945**: arrested, 407; suicide of, 408; surrender sought by, 380, 399, 400

Hindenburg, Paul von, 3–4, 12–16, 18, 19, *21*, 28

Hiranuma, Baron Kiichiro, 78

Hirohito (Emperor of Japan), 8, *9*, 173, 184–86, 266, 327–28, 417

Hiroshima: **1945**: 384, 385, *410*, *416*

Hirota, Koki, 26, 27, 32, 38, 43, 46, 50, 52, 55

Hitler, Adolf: **1931**: 3; von Hindenburg receives, 3–4; **1932**: and ban on Storm Troopers, 14; becomes German citizen, 11; chancellorship and, 15, 16; in election, 12; **1933**: *17*, *21*; demands revision of Versailles Treaty, 21–22; disarmament of others as goal of, 20–21; gains control of army, 23, 24; granted dictatorial powers, 20; named chancellor, 18; renounces war except against Bolshevism, 23; repression consolidating power of, 18–22; retires generals, 23; torpedoes disarmament conference, 23, 24; **1934**: 25; becomes president of Reich, 28; blood purge by, 28; British ambassador on, 26–27; military oath of allegiance to, 28–29; Mussolini and, *see under* Mussolini, Benito; and Polish pact, 26; **1935**: *31*; charges against Lithuania, 36; defends renunciation of Versailles, 34; Hoare-Laval agreement and, 39; and relations with Russia, 33; **1936**: aid to Franco, 45; Rhineland reoccupation under, 43–44; and Rome-Berlin Axis, 47; speech on Nazi rule over Urals and Ukraine, 46; **1937**: and bomber production, 52; course to war set by, 57; Halifax and, 58; and living space, 55, 58; and neutrality of Belgium, Netherlands and Switzerland, 51; policy state-

Hitler, Adolf *(Continued)*
ment by, 50–51; **1938**: *61, 69*;
Anschluss, 62–66; invasion of
Czechoslovakia set by, 70; re-
places advisers and leaders, 63;
tours western fortifications, 70;
1939: 81, *90*; agreement with
Russians, 82–88; assassination attempt on, 99; on concluding war,
95; Danzig sought by, 78; decision to invade Poland made by,
79; fall of Poland, 55, 96, 97; and
first submarine attack, 91; on
goals, 87; and Italian non-readi-
ness for war, 86; on Jews, 79,
102; on naval warfare, 93; and
Norway invasion, 101–2; offensive west under, 96, 97, 99; peace
overtures by, 97, 98; and Polish
problem, 81–83, 86–90; and Russo-Finnish war, 98; Teleki message to, 85–86; visits Polish front,
92; **1940**: and air war, 129, 130,
132, 138; arms deliveries to Russians and, 108; Churchill on
resolve to defeat, 135; and Denmark invasion, 109; dividing
spoils, 122; Dunkirk and, 115,
116; and Franco meeting, 135,
136, 141; and French bases in
North Africa, 126; French surrender and, 122; and Greek situation, 140; Iceland and, 112; and
invasion of Britain, 125; and
invasion of Russia, 142; and invasion of west, 105, 118; and Laval
meeting, *135*; and Molotov talks,
139, *139*; and Norway invasion,
106, 109; offers peace to Britain,
126–27; and Pétain meeting,
136; reincorporates Eupen, Malmédy and Moresnet, 114; Stalin
on intentions of, 124; urges move
on Suez Canal, 123–24; **1941**:
143, 173; aid to Libya by, 145;
aims in invasion of Russia, 164;
assumes command of German
army, 191–92; and attack on
Yugoslavia, 152–54; on Balkan
campaign, 157; bars military
effort in Iraq, 161; Crete and,
156, 160; and Darlan meeting,
158–59; goads Göring into
bombing Moscow, 168; halts
drive on Moscow, 168–70, 175;
Hess and, 158; and Japanese
attacks in Pacific, 185; and
Leningrad siege, 165; and Matsuoka meeting, 152; on naval

war, 148; "Night and Fog
Decree," 188; and Ribbentrop
meeting, *180*; Roosevelt pledges
to defeat, 172; on Russia as broken, 177, 180; and Russian
recapture of Rostov, 183; on seizure of Crimea, 171; urges
greater Japanese participation in
war, 149; and U.S. war plans,
185; and Yugoslav situation,
149–51; **1942**: and Allies in
North Africa, 243; and Antonescu meeting, 203; approves withdrawal from Caucasus, 250; and
Bormann, 204; calls off Malta
invasion, 218; and German casualties, 204–5; given absolute
power, 214; height of rule of,
228; and Lidice, 220; and Mannerheim meeting, 219; Middle
East objectives of, 223; and naval
war, 250; and occupation of
France, 243; orders operations
halt, 237; predicts destruction of
Russian army (March), 209; Reichenau and, 198; and Rommel,
222; on Stalingrad, 235, 242, 245,
248; and use of poison gas, 217;
Vichy army dissolved by, 245;
and von Leeb, 213; **1943**:
attempts on life of, 261, 262;
Balkans and, 273; bombing during anniversary ceremonies for,
256; Guderian and, 267; and
invasion of Sicily, 272; Jeschonnek and, 278; Kharkov and, 258;
lowering enlistment age, 294;
and naval war, 283; on Paulus,
256; and redeployment in Italy,
276; and Stalingrad, 254, 255,
262; on uprising in Jewish ghetto, 264; and withdrawal from
Ukraine, 280; **1944**: *352*; and air
superiority in Italy, 319; Ardennes offensive under, 368;
attempt on life of, 333–34; and
"Battle for the West Wall," 346;
belief in ultimate victory (April),
310; counteroffensive outlined
by, 347; and Hungary, 351; and
invasion of Italy, 302; and loss of
Seventh Army, 340; new mobilization effort under, 335; on
"rear area swine," 340; officers
killed for attempts on life of,
336; orders counteroffensive in
Brittany, 336; orders Warsaw
destroyed, 352; orders withdrawal from Greece, 341; refuses any

withdrawal, 332; Rome withdrawal ordered by, 319–20; and
Rommel's death, 351; and V-1
bombs, 324; and West Wall penetration, 362; **1945**: foreigners in
service to, 372; and Guderian,
390; on honor, 384; last public
appearance of, 388; last radio
broadcast of, 376; on material
diverted from military, 372;
moves into bunker, 373; "Nero
Decree" of, 387; no retreat order
of, 397; orders Göring arrested,
400; refuses to leave Berlin, 399;
strips Göring of authority, 399;
suicide of, 401–2; urges continued fight (March), 385; Valera
expression of condolences for
death of, 402; and withdrawal
from Warsaw area, 373
Hoare, Sir Samuel, 34, 36, 39
Hoare-Laval agreement (1935), 39
Hodza, Milan, 64–66
Hoepner, Gen. Erich, 334
Hoffman (German non-commis-
sioned officer), 173
Hokkaido: **1945**, 413
Homma, Gen. Masaharu, 192, 202–
03
Hong Kong: **1938**: 74; **1940**: 126;
1941: 181, 188, 190–93; **1945**:
419
Honshu Island: **1945**, 413–17
Hoover, Herbert, 18, 158
Hopkins, Harry, 169
Hore-Belisha, Leslie, 104
Horinouchi, Kensuke, 134
Horthy, Adm. Miklos, *69, 173*, 309,
351
Hoth, Gen. Hermann, 165, 168,
170
Houffalize: **1944**: 365, 368; **1945**:
372, 373
Hseuh Yuan, Gen., 175
Hsu Hung-chang, 419
Hsueh-liang, Marshal, 8
Hull, Cordell: **1933**: predicts war,
24; **1935**: protests Japanese
moves in north China, 39; **1936**:
and hands off policy on Spain,
46; **1937**: on foreign policy, 54;
1938: and Asian situation, 71;
denounces isolationism, 68; on
increasing fleet size, 63; on neutrality, 67; **1939**: urges Neutrality Act revision, 84; **1940**: on
effect on England of U.S. entry
into war, 134; and Japan, 105,
130, 131; on way to avoid war,

128; **1941**: compensation for *Robin Moore*, 179; reconstruction plan of, 159; and Roosevelt-Konoye meeting, 176; and war with Japan, 180, 182, 183; **1942**: Martinique and West Indies U.S. occupation, 245; **1943**: code name for, 277; in meeting on conduct of war, 285; **1944**: resigns, 361; **1945**: Pearl Harbor and, 419

Hungary: **1941**: 151, 152; **1944**: 304, 309, 311, 315, 344, 348–51, 353, 363, 366, 368; **1945**: 370, 372, 373, 383, 387–89, 392

Hurley, Patrick J., 339, *419*

Iasi: **1944**, 319, 340

Ibn Saud (King of Saudi Arabia), 380

Iceland: **1940**: 112; **1941**: 159, 167; **1942**: 227; **1944**: 318

Ichang: **1940**, 119, 121

Iloilo: **1945**, 386, 387

Imrédy, Bela, 67, 79

India: **1942**: 210, 227, 229, 231, 232, 236; U.S. forces in, 214; **1943**: Bose government and, 285–86; famine in, 279; **1944**: 310–13, *314*, 315–19, 321, 322, 325, 327, 330, 339, 344–46

Indochina: **1940**: 130, 132; **1941**: 150, 168–70, 184–86; **1942**: 225; **1943**: 287; **1945**: 384, 388, 412

Indonesia (former Dutch East Indies): **1945**, 418

Inonu, Ismet, 209

Inouye, Junnosuke, 11

Inskip, Sir Thomas, 60

Inter-Allied Conference (London; 1942), 198

Inter-American Conference (1940), 127

International Disarmament Conference (1931), 4–5

Inukai, Tsuyoshi, 5, 13

Ionian Islands: **1943**, 280

Iran: **1941**: 171, 172, 174; **1942**: 248; **1945**: 409

Iraq: **1941**: 155–59, 161, 162; **1942**: 248

Ishan: **1945**, 410, 411

Isigny: **1944**, 323

Isitt, Air-Vice Marshal Sir L. M., 420

Italo-Yugoslav treaty (1937), 51

Italy: **1943**: 274–88, 294–96; invasion of Sicily, 263, 266–77, 283; **1944**: 300–7, *309*, 310, 312, 314–

22, 332, 333, 336, *338*, 339–42, 344, 347–50, 354, 359, 362–64, 368; bombing of, *see specific cities*; **1945**: 381–84, 390, 392–403

Iwo Jima: **1944**: 325, 329, 364; **1945**: 375, *379*, *380*, *381*, 382–84, 386, 389, 394

Jamaica: **1941**, 151

Japan: **1943** and **1945**: bombing of, *see specific cities*; **1944**: invasion needed to collapse, 313; planned invasion of, 312, 345; **1945**: invasion preparations, 388, 408; military casualties of (1937–1945), 417; occupation of, 411, 419; surrender, *369*, 413–15, 417, *418*, 419, *420*; weapons for defense of, 373–74; Yalta conference and, 377

Java: **1942**: 204–7, 209; **1944**: 316

Java Sea, Battle of the (1942), *206*

Jersey Island: **1940**, 125

Jeschonnek, Gen. Hans, 278

Jews: **1930s**: anti-Semitic demonstrations in central Europe, 7; **1933**: in Germany, 19–20; **1935**: Nürnberg Laws, *36*; **1938**: Austrian anti-Semitism, 65; "Crystal Night" in Germany, 74–75; Danzigen anti-Semitism, 76; deportation of Polish, from Germany, 74; emigration problem for, 68–69; German anti-Semitism, 66; Hungarian anti-Semitism, 67; Italian laws and, 69; **1939**: Austrian and Czech, deported to Poland, 98; German, 81; Hitler on, 79, 102; immigration to Palestine, 84; Star of David badges for Polish, 100; **1940**: Auschwitz concentration camp ordered constructed, 111; deported from Alsace-Lorraine and Rhineland, 135; Mussolini and, 127; Polish ghettoes, 111, 139; **1941**: Babi Yar massacre, 176; final solution for, 169; Gestapo arrest, in Paris, 159; killed in Baltic states, 192; killed and injured in Baghdad, 162; and martial law in north Holland, 149; murdered in Lwow, 166; murdered in Riga, 189; murdered in Vilna, 192; pogrom in Kaunas, 165; Polish, transferred to Warsaw ghetto, 146; remaining in Germany, 157; Star of David for, in Greater

Reich, 174; Star of David ordered for Balkan, 167; synagogue destruction in Paris, 176; U.S., as war party, 174; in Vichy France, 163; **1942**: barred from public transport in Germany, 214; in Bir Hacheim defense, 220; concentration camp sites, *202*; Eden on extermination of, 248; Hitler on ridding Europe of, 201; Oberg on, 215; Parisian, sent to Auschwitz, 210; resettlement from Warsaw, 226; Star of David for, in France and Holland, 219; UN and crimes against, 249; Wannsee Conference on final solution, 199; **1943**: Berlin free of, 268; Czestochowa ghetto uprising, 269; liquidation in German occupied Russia, 268; liquidation of all Polish ghettoes, 268; murdered in Maidanek, 287; resistance in Warsaw ghetto, 254, 264; of Rome, bound for Auschwitz, 285; **1944**: of Budapest transferred to German camps, 357; and destruction of Auschwitz crematoria, 361; in eastern camps, moved west, 336; Greek, sent to Auschwitz, 313; of Hungary sent to Auschwitz, 316; last gassings at Auschwitz (October), 355; Natzviller, 355; Struthof, *362*; **1945**: in Belsen concentration camp, 397; in Buchenwald, 393, 395; and concentration camp outside Ohrdruf, 392; in Dachau concentration camp, 402; Eichmann on, 386; in Hitler's final message, 400; Jewish Brigade, 383, *390*, 394; in Nürnberg camps, *401*; Russians liberate, in Auschwitz, 375; Russians liberate, in Maidanek, 335; and Wöbbelin concentration camp, *403*

Jodl, Gen. Alfred, 71, 122, 185, 347, 404, *405*

Johnson, Nelson T., 156

Johore: **1942**, 197, 198

Jolo Island: **1941**: 192; **1945**: 394

Jones, Charles S., 205

Joyce, William (Lord Haw Haw), 409

Juin, Gen. Alphonse, 301

Kaifeng: **1938**, *68*

Kalinin, Mikhail I., 98

Kalinin: **1941**, 177–78, 191

Kaluga: **1941**, 177, 194

Kamaishi: **1945**, 413, 417

Kamensk: **1942**: 225; **1943**: 254

Kant, Immanuel, 14

Karafuto Island: **1945**, 413, 417

Kase, Toshikazu, 326

Kassel: **1945**, 391, 392

Kasserine Pass: **1943**, 259, 260

Katsuki, Gen. Kiyoshi, 54–55

Katyn massacre (1940), 115, 263, 264, 302

Kaunas: **1941**: 164; **1944**: 332, 335, 336

Kavieng: **1942**: 200; **1944**: 305, 306

Keitel, Field Marshal Wilhelm, 81, 132, 175, 280, 347, 406

Kellogg-Briand Pact (Pact of Paris; 1928), 4, 8, 11, 12, 55, 102

Kelly, Capt. Colin, 189

Kennedy, Edward, 405

Kennedy, John F., 275

Kennedy, Joseph, 74, 125, 132

Kent, Duke of, 230

Kenya: **1941**, 147–48, 150

Kerama Islands: **1945**, 391

Keren: **1941**, 146, 150, 151

Kerrl, Hans, 37

Kesselring, Field Marshal Albert, 139, 280, 281, 302, 316, 319, 384, 385

Kharkov: **1941**: 179; **1942**: 215–18; **1943**: 257–59, 261, 275, 276, 278

Kherson: **1943**: 296; **1944**: 309

Khlopov (attaché), 161

Kidd, Adm. Isaac C., 187

Kido, Marquis Koichi, 266

Kiel: **1940**: 124; **1943**: 295; **1945**: 365

Kielce: **1939**: 92; **1945**: 372–73

Kiev: **1941**: 164, 167, 171, 173–75, 309; **1943**: 287, 290, 296

Kimmel, Adm. Husband E., 200, 206

Kimura, Gen. Heitaro, 379, 387

King, Gen. Edward P., Jr., 211

King, Adm. Ernest J., 146, 155, 210, 289

Kiosseivanov, George, 76

Kirov, Serge, 30

Kirovograd: **1944**, 300, 301

Kleist, Field Marshal Ewald von, 115, 119, 173, 174, 182, 252, 258, 312

Klopper, Gen. H. B., 222

Kluge, Field Marshal Hans Günther von, 261, 262, 329, 339

Knobelsdorff, Gen. Otto von, 362

Koba, Gen. T., 416

Kobe: **1942**: 212; **1945**: 386, 387, 411–12, 415

Koblenz: **1945**, 385, 386

Koga, Adm. Mineichi, 310

Koiso, Gen. Kuniaki, 333, 385, 392

Kolberg: **1945**, 386–87

Komorovski, Gen. Tadeusz (General Bor), 336

Konev, Marshal Ivan S., 372, 406

Konigsburg: **1942**: 231; **1945**: 375, 379, 386, 394

Konosuke, Tamura, 257

Konoye, Prince: **1937**: becomes premier, 52; and Sino-Japanese war, 53; **1938**: on China policy, 62–63, 76; **1939**: resigns, 78; **1940**: becomes prime minister, 126; new cabinet under, 122; on war with U.S., 134; **1941**: 173; new government under, 168; proposed meeting with Roosevelt, 170, 172, 175, 176; resigns, 178

Koo, Wellington, 55–56, 58

Kopets, Gen., 164

Korea: **1945**, 417

Korizis, Alexander, 155

Krakow: **1939**: 92; **1945**: 374

Krasnodar: **1942**, 227, 229

Krofta, Kamil, 52, 67

Krueger, Gen. Walter, 352

Krymsk: **1942**: 230; **1943**: 265

Kuala Lumpur: **1942**, 197, 198

Kube, Wilhelm, 13–14

Kuhl, Sgt. Charles H., 274–75

Kula Gulf, Battle of (1943), 270

Kunming: **1943**: 295–96; **1944**: 361; **1945**: 374, 377

Kure: **1945**, 387, 415

Kursk: **1941**: 179; **1942**: 215, 223; **1943**: 257, 267, 270–71, 273

Kurusu, Saburo, 40

Küstrin: **1945**, 377, 385

Kweilin: **1944**: 342, 344, 347, 354, 357; **1945**: 415

Kweiyang: **1944**, 358, 363

Kyushu: **1944**: 325; **1945**: 414

La Spezia: **1941**: 147; **1943**: 268; **1945**: 400

"*Laconia* Order" (1942), 232

Lampson, Sir Miles, 202

Langsdorff, Capt. Hans, 101

Lattre de Tassigny, Gen. Jean de, 296, 342

Latvia: **1940**: 127, 129; **1941**: 164; **1944**: 340, 351, 354; **1945**: 373, 375, 405–6

Lausanne Convention (1932), 14

Laval, Pierre: **1934**: becomes foreign minister, 29; **1935**: named premier, 34; treaty with Italy, 32; **1936**: Popular Front opposed by, 44; **1940**: and Hitler meeting, 135; hopes for defeat of British, 127; named foreign minister, 137; named vice premier, 122; ousted, 142; and plots against Britain, 128; and war with Britain, 125; **1941**: attempt on life of, 172; **1942**: as chief of government, 212; and Hitler and Mussolini meeting, 243; hopes for German victory, 222, 229; and laborers called to work in Germany, 237; named premier, 209; protests bombing, 232; total authority of, 244; vows collaboration, 245; warns of danger of Russian victory, 213; **1943**: code name for, 277; and fleet at Alexandria, 267; **1945**: surrenders, 415

Le Havre: **1942**: 231, 232; **1944**: 321, 345, 350

Le Mans: **1944**, 337, 344

League Covenant, 4, 10–12, 37, 55, 102

League of Nations: **1931**: Sino-Japanese conflict, 2–5; **1932**: Lytton Report to, 15, 16; Sino-Japanese conflict and, 8, 10–13; **1933**: China situation, 18–20; condemns German action on Jews, 22; German withdrawal, 23, 24; Japanese withdrawal, 20, 74; **1934**: Soviet Union enters, 29; **1935**: accepts use of embargo, 38; Ethiopian situation, 32, 33, 35–37; German rearmament, 34; sanctions against Italy, 38, 39; **1936**: Ethiopian situation, 42, 43; Haile Selassie addresses, 44–45; Italy withdraws, 44; lost German colonies and, 46; Loyalists appeal to, 48; and poison gas in Ethiopia, 44; Rhineland reoccupation and, 43; sanctions against Italy abandoned, 44; **1937**: Germany withdraws from, 59; Italy withdraws from, 59; Sino-Japanese war, 55, 56; Spanish civil war and, 52; **1938**: call for action against Germany in, 71; Sino-Japanese war and, 63, 66, 71–74; **1939**: Hungary withdraws from, 82; and Polish problem, 85; and Russo-Finnish war, 100, 101; and Sino-Japanese war, 78; Soviet Union expelled from, 102; **1939–1946**: functions of, 414; **1940**: Denmark withdraws from, 127; Rumania withdraws from, 126; **1941**: Vichy France withdraws from, 155; **1946**: dissolved, 414

Leahy, Adm. William D., 209, 215–16, 288–89

Leary, Adm. Herbert F., 213

Lebanon: **1941**: 163, 164, 167, 168, 183; **1943**: 287, 288, 291–92; **1945**: 407, 409

Lebrun, Albert, 121

Leclerc, Gen. Philippe, 340, 420

Ledo Road, 277

Leeb, Field Marshal Ritter von, 213

Left, the: **1931**: Chinese, 4; **1932**: Austrian, 7; Chinese, 13; German, 12, 15; **1933**: Austrian, 20; German, 19–22, 24; Rumanian, 24; **1934**: Austrian, 27; Chinese, 29; French, 26, 27; Spanish, 29; **1935**: Chinese, 38; French, 35, 38; **1936**: Spanish, 43; **1937**: Chinese, 40; **1938**: Czech, 74; **1939**: French, 96

Leipzig: **1944**: 306; **1945**: 390, 392, 398

Lend-lease: **1941**: 144, 145, 147, 148, 150, 151, 179, 180, 182; **1942**: 220, 231; **1944**: 301; **1945**: 385–86, 419

Lenin, V. I., 178

Leningrad: **1941**: 164, 165, 167, 172–75, 180, 181, *184*, 188, 193; **1942**: 211, 213, 230; **1943**: 253–55; **1944**: 301, 302; **1945**: 406

Leopold III (King of Belgium), 116, 322, 409, 411

Ley, Robert, *61*

Leyte: **1944**: 268, 352, 353, *354*, 356, 357, 362–64, 366; **1945**: 370, 376

Leyte Gulf, Battle of (1944), *353*

Liberia: **1942**, 216

Libya, *see* North African campaigns

Lidice: **1942**, 220

Liège: **1940**: 113; **1944**: 344

Lille: **1940**: 116; **1942**: 236

Lin Piao, Gen., 56

Lindbergh, Charles A., 156, 174

Linz: **1945**, 394, 403

Lithuania: **1940**: 120, 127; **1941**: 164; **1944**: 332; **1945**: 375

Little Entente: **1932**: renews defensive alliance, 13; **1933**: new German threat and, 18; **1934**: and murder of Alexander I, 29; Rome Protocols and, 27; **1936**: Austrian conscription protested, 44; **1937**: Austria seeks support of, against Germany, 52; **1938**: and Anschluss, 65; Bulgaria and, 69

Litvinow, M. M., 83

Liuchow: **1944**: 343, 344, 354, 357; **1945**: 412

Liverpool: **1940**: 140; **1941**: 157

Locarno treaty (1925), 43, 52, 71

London: **1940**: 128, 131, 132, *141*, 142; **1941**: 155, 158, 169; **1944**: *346*; "Little Blitz," 305; V-1 bombing, *324*, *325*, 328, *329*, 330; V-2 bombing, 360; **1945**: V-2 rocket bombing, 344, 375

London Naval Agreement (1936), 43, 47

London Naval Conference (1936), 42

London Naval Treaty (1931), 48

London protocol (1943), 285

Long, Breckinridge, 36

Lowrey, Louis R., 381

Lublin: **1944**, 334, 335

Lucas, Gen. John P., 302, 306

Luther, Hans, 24

Luxembourg: **1940**: 112, 128; **1944**: 345, 364; **1945**: 375

Luxeuil-les-Bains: **1944**, *350*

Luzon: **1941**: 188, 189, 192; **1942**: 202, 203; **1944**: 348, 366; **1945**: *371*, 372–73, 375, 376, 395, 400, 407–10, 412

Lwow: **1939**: 95; **1941**: 165, 166; **1943**: 268; **1944**: 335

Lyon: **1940**: 122; **1944**: 342, 343

Lytton, Earl of, 5

Lytton Report (1932), 15, 16, 19

Ma Chan-shan, Gen., 4

MacArthur, Gen. Douglas: **1932**: war views of, 15; **1941**: returned to active duty, 169; stand at Bataan, 192; **1942**: command under, 205, 209, 213; leaves Corregidor, 207; operations under, 209, 232, 240; **1943**: and Marshall, 295; **1944**: Philippines op-

erations and, 352–54; in strategy meeting, 335; **1945**: halts operations, 418; Japan surrenders to, 419, *420*; Philippines operations and, 373, 382, 413; as supreme commander, 417

McAuliffe, Gen. Anthony C., 366

MacDonald, Ramsay, 4, 34

McNair, Gen. Lesley J., 335

Macon, Gen. Robert C., 345

Madagascar: **1942**, 215, 232–35, 237, 240

Madrid: **1936**: 46, 47; **1939**: 81–82

Magdeburg: **1945**, *383*, 395, 397

Maher Pasha, Ahmed, 381

Mahir Pasha, Ali, 202

Maikop: **1942**: 225; **1943**: 256

Mainz: **1942**: 229; **1945**: 388

Maisky, Ivan, 277

Makassar Strait, Battle of (1942), 200, 203

Makoto, Susuki, 352

Malaya: **1941**: 185, 186, 188, 190–93; **1942**: 196–97, 199, 200; **1945**: 414

Maleme: **1941**, 160, 161

Malenkov, Georgi, 165

Malgobek: **1942**: 236; **1943**: 252

Malmédy: **1944**: 365; **1945**: 372

"Malmédy Massacre" (1944), 365

Malta: **1941**: 155; **1942**: 209, 216, 218; **1943**: 270

Malta conference (1945), 376

Manchurian incident (1931), 2, 3, 6; *See also* Sino-Japanese war

Mandalay: **1942**: 204, 206, 210, 214, 232; **1944**: 356; **1945**: 378, 383–88, 394

Mangshih: **1944**, *367*

Manila: **1941**: 193, 194; **1942**: 196; **1945**: 373, 376–82, 407

Manly, Chester, 185

Mann, Thomas, 19–20

Mannerheim, Field Marshal Carl Gustav, 108, 165, 219, 336

Mannheim: **1940**: 142; **1945**: 386, 390

Manstein, Field Marshal Fritz Erich von, 165, 217–18, 261

Mao Tse-tung, 4, 13, 18, 34, 48, 324, 419

"Marco Polo Bridge Incident" (1937), 53

Marcus Island: **1942**: 207; **1943**: 279; **1944**: 318, 350

Marianas Islands: **1941**: 179, 183, 189; **1944**: 306, 310, 324–30, *331*, 333, *334*, 335–37, 356, 360

MARKET GARDEN, Operation (1944), 347

Marseilles: **1944**, 339–41

Marshall, Gen. George C.: **1942**: 210, 240; **1943**: 276, 277, 288–89, *295*; **1945**: 378, 419

Marshall Islands: **1942**: 201; **1943**: 277, 288; **1944**: 303, 304, *305*; **1945**: 419

Masaryk, Jan, 27, 29

Matsuoka, Yosuke: **1932**: 16; **1940**: 127, 128, 134–35, 141; **1941**: in Axis meeting, 151; and decision not to attack Russia, 165–66; and Hitler meeting, 152; on Japanese domination of western Pacific, 146; on Oceania, 148; and pact with Russia, 154–55; on policy in Asia, 145; and resignation of government, 168

Maung Saw, U, 181, 199

Mechili: **1941**, 153, 192

Medjez el Bab: **1942**, 244, 245, 248

Medvezhyegorsk: **1941**, 186, 190

Memel: **1944**: 350; **1945**: 375

Menzies, Robert G., 159

Mercader, Ramón, 129

Merrill, Gen. Frank, 307

Mersa Matruh: **1940**: 131; **1942**: 223

Messe, Gen. Giovanni, 260

Messina: **1943**, 269, 271, 274, 277

Metaxas, Gen. John, 33, 34, 134–36, 146

Metz: **1944**, 344, 350, 357–59

Miaja, Gen. José, 79–80

Michael (King of Rumania), 130, 140

Midway, Battle of (1942), 219, 329

Midway Island: **1941**: 197; **1942**: 200, 215, 218

Mikawa, Adm. Gunichi, 187

Milan: **1940**: 129; **1942**: 234; **1945**: 400–2

Milch, Erhard, 52

Military convention (1942), Italo-Germano-Japanese, 198

Mindanao: **1942**: 207; **1944**: 318; **1945**: 385, 397–99, 403, 407–8, 411, 413

Mindoro: **1944**: 364, *365*, 367; **1945**: 375

Minsk: **1941**: 165, 167; **1944**: 329

Mitscher, Adm. Marc A., *213*

Model, Field Marshal Walther, 339, 340, 397, 399

Mogadishu: **1941**, 148–49

Mohammed Reza Pahlevi (Shah of Iran), 175

Molotov, Vyacheslav M.: **1935**: policy statement of, 32; **1936**: hopes for improved Soviet-German relations, 42; **1939**: becomes foreign minister, 83; on concessions from Finland, 99; and fall of Warsaw, 93; on foreign policy, 85; and German-Soviet pact, 86–88; and pact with Britain and France, 84; on Russian invasion of Poland, 94–95; **1940**: confers with Germans, 134, *138*; congratulates Germans, 122; declares neutrality in coming war, 108; and Hitler talks, 138, *139*; on invasion of Norway and Denmark, 109; policy statement of, 128; protests award of Transylvania to Hungary, 130; **1941**: rejects reports of imminent German attack, 163; **1942**: and second front, 218; **1943**: code name of, 277; in meeting on conduct of war, 285; **1945**: at Yalta conference, 377

Moluccas Islands: **1944**, 347

Monarchy: **1935**: Austrian and Greek, 35, 37, 38; **1937**: Austrian, 51; **1938**: Italian, 66; Rumanian, 66; **1945**: Belgian, 409, 411; Yugoslav, 416

Mönchengladbach: **1940**: 113; **1945**: 382

Monroe Doctrine, 124–25

Monte Cassino: **1944**, 301, 303–5, *309*, 310, 316

Monte Trocchio: **1944**, 300, 301

Montgomery, Field Marshal Bernard: **1942**: North African campaign of, 227, 229, 236, *237*, 238–41, 296; **1943**: Italian campaign of, 230, 263, 266, 273, 285, 328, 336, 366, 371

Moore-Gosgrove, Col. I., 420

Mori, Gen. Takeshi, 396

Morocco, *see* North African campaigns

Morrison, Herbert, 73

Moscicki, Ignace, 88, 96

Moscow: **1941**, 164, 168, 169, 171, 175, 177–81, 183–86, 194

Moscow conference (1944), 350

Moser (German cadet), 171

Mount Castellone: **1944**, *304*

Mountbatten, Adm. Lord Louis, 209, 278, *324*, 359, 404

Mukden: **1931**: 2; **1945**: 418

MULBERRY (artificial harbors; 1944), 322

Mulhouse: **1944**: 359; **1945**: 393

Müller, Heinrich, 74–75

Mullinix, Adm. Henry A., 292

Mulugeta, Ras, 43

Munich: **1940**: 138, 139; **1945**: 400–2

Munich meeting (1938), 72, 73

Münster: **1941**: 166–67; **1945**: 392

Murdock, Lt. R. F., 397

Murmansk: **1940**: 130; **1941**: 165; **1942**: 207, 210

Murphy, Robert D., 127

Muselier, Adm. Emile, 193

Mussert, Anton, 248

Mussolini, Benito: **1932**: expected years of rule under, 15; **1933**: and nonaggression treaty with Russia, 23; undercutting League of Nations, 22; **1934**: and German moves in Austria, 28; orders conquest of Ethiopia, 30; rapport with Hitler, 28; **1935**: *31*; and Ethiopian conflict, 32, 35–37; to Hitler on League sanctions, 39; reinvigorating armed forces, 38; views on world affairs, 32; **1936**: on German-Austrian agreement, 45; and how "Axis" got its name, 47; victory celebration of, 44; **1937**: bids for Islamic support, 51; intervenes in Spain, 50; Schuschnigg and, 52; **1938**: and annexation of Albania, 76; Anschluss and, 64, 65; and Czechoslovak situation, 72; rapport with Hitler, 66; recognition of empire under, 75; **1939**: Albania situation and, 79, 82; British meet with, 78; and German-Soviet pact, 88; Hitler on, 87; and Italo-German frontier, 83; and nonreadiness for war, 86, 88; Pact of Steel and, 84; pledges neutrality, 95; Roosevelt message to, 83; Teleki message to, 85–86; on war, 84; **1940**: and division of spoils, 122; enters war, 108, 112, 114, 116, 118; Franco message to, 129; on Germany as undefeatable, 111; Hitler to, on Franco, 142; to Hitler, on living space, 104; Hitler bringing, into war, 108; and Hitler conferences, 128, 134, 145; on invasion of Greece, 139; Roosevelt appeals to, 114; Rumanians meet with, 127; urged to move on Suez

Canal, 123–24, 128; **1941**: Hitler to, on invasion of Russia, 164; and Hitler meetings, 145, 162, 171; on victory and policy, 148; on war and U.S., 151; **1942**: and assumed Axis victory in Africa, 223, 225; and Hitler meeting, 214; Laval and, 243; **1943**: diary of, 280; and Hitler meetings, 263, 280, 281; and invasion of Italy, 272; as minister of foreign affairs, 257; overthrown, 273; rescued, 281; and Ribbentrop, 260; on Russia after Stalingrad, 262; and Saló Republic, 283; **1944**: 322; **1945**: Hitler learns death of, 401; Hitler's final message to, 400; killed, 400–1

Mutaguchi, Gen. Renya, 308, 327

Mutual assistance treaties (pacts): **1935**: Franco-Russian, 34; Russo-Czech, 34; **1936**: Russo-Mongolian, 44; **1939**: Franco-Turkish, 85; Franco-Turkish-British, 99; Latvian - Lithuanian - Estonian - Russian, 96; Latvian-Russian, 97; Lithuanian-Russian, 97–98; Polish-British, 88; **1941**: Anglo-Russian, 167; **1942**: Anglo-Russian, 218; Anglo-Russian-U.S., 220; **1944**: Franco-Russian, 364

Nagano, Adm. Osami, 153

Nagasaki: **1945**: 384, 385, *410*, 416

Nagoya: **1942**: 212; **1945**: 387, 406, 411–12, 414

Nagumo, Adm. Chuichi, 183, 187, 327

Nancy: **1944**, 345, 346

Nanking: **1932**: 10; **1937**: 56, 60

Nankow: **1937**, 54–55

Nanning: **1944**: 360; **1945**: 408

Naples: **1942**: 247; **1943**: 277, 284

Napoleon I (Emperor of the French), 205

Narvik: **1940**, 109, 112, 116–18

Narvik, First Battle of (1940), 109

Narvik, Second Battle of (1940), 110

National Mobilization Bill (Japanese; 1938), 65

Naujocks, Alfred, 90

Naval agreements: **1935**: German-British, 34, 83; **1937**: German-British, 68; Germano-Russian-British, 54; **1938**: Russian-British, 68

Naval conference (1935), 39

Naval Expansion Act (U.S., 1940), 127

Naval war: **1939**: 96–98, 100; **1940**: 106, 108–10, 117–20, 125, 127, 129, 131, 137, 138, 141; **1941**: 144–60, *161*, 162–65, 169–75, 178–82, 185, 189, 191, 192; **1942**: 198, 199, 202–8, 210, 211, 214–35, 237, 241–43, 247–50; **1943**: 252, 256, 258, 260, 261, 265–67, 270, 276, 281, 283–85, 290, 292, 296; **1944**: 302, 304, 305, *306*, 310, 311, 315, 319, 320, 322, 329, 330, 336, 344–45, 347, 354, 355, 357, 358, *360*, 363–65; **1945**: 371, 372, 375, 376, 378, *387*, 388, 391–92, 394, 396, 397, 402–4, 407, *408*, 409–12, 414, *415*; *See also* Air war; *and specific battles*

Neame, Gen. Sir Philip, 152

Nedic, Milan, 172

Negrín, Juan, 52, 79

Nehru, Jawaharlal, 198, 203

"Nero Decree" (1945), 387

Netherlands: **1940**: 112, 114, 115; **1942**: 224, 228; **1944**: 344–49, 354–56; **1945**: 373, 382, 391, 392, 396, 397, 400–3

Neurath, Konstantin von, 62, 80, 175

Neutrality Act (U.S.; 1935), 35, 37, 43, 52, 84, 95, 97, 99, 112, 119, 150, 177, 180, 181

Neutrality treaties (pacts): **1933**: Germano-Russian, 21; **1941**: Russo-Japanese, 154, 392; Russo-Turkish, 150

New Britain: **1942**: 200; **1943**: 295–96, *297*, *298*

New Caledonia: **1942**, 243

New Guinea: **1942**: 199, 200, 205, 207, 210, 226, 229–35, 237, 240, 243–49; **1943**: 252, 254, 255, 259, 269, 272, 280, 283, 284, 290, 292, 294, 295; **1944**: 300, 301, 304, 310, 312–14, 317, *318*, 332, 335, 340, 359; **1945**: 407

New Hebrides: **1942**, 218, 243

New Zealand: **1942**, 222

Newfoundland: **1940**: 130; **1941**: 151

Nichols Field: **1945**, 378, 379

Nicholson, James B., 128

Niemöller, Martin, 52, 403

"Night and Fog Decree" (German; 1941), 188

Nijmegen: **1944**: 348, 349, 362; **1945**: 385

Nikolayev: **1944**, 309, 310

Nimitz, Adm. Chester W., 191, 219, 225, 335, 351, 419

Nine-Power Treaty (1922), 8, 11, 54, 56, 57, 74

Nishino, Kizo, 205

Noboyoshi, Gen. Muto, 15

Noguès, Gen. Auguste, 122

Nomonhan Incident (1939), 83–84

Nomura, Adm. Kichisaburo, 148, 158, 160, 168, 170

Nonaggression treaties: **1932**: Estonian-Russian, 13; Finnish-Russian, 9, 100; Latvian-Russian, 11; Polish-Russian, 14, 16, 76; **1933**: Italo-Russian, 23; **1934**: Germano-Polish, 26, 83; Polish-Russian, 27; Russian-Estonian-Latvian-Lithuanian, 27; **1935**: German willingness to join, with eastern neighbors, 33; **1937**: Sino-Russian, 55; **1938**: Balkan Entente, 69; Polish-Russian, 75; **1939**: Germano-Danish, 85; Germano-Latvian-Estonian, 85; Spanish-Portuguese, 81; **1940**: Japanese-Thai, 119; Turkish-Bulgarian, 148

Nonintervention Committee on Spain, 46–48, 50, 51

Nonintervention patrols (1937), 53, 54

Nonintervention policy in Spanish Civil War (1936), 45, 46

Nonrecognition, Doctrine of (1932), 8, 11–12

NORDWIND, Operation (1943), 370

North African campaigns: **1940**: 106, 120, 123–24, 128, 131, 137, 141, 142; **1941**: 144–53, 156, 158, 159, 162, 163, 181, 192–94, 197; Afrika Korps, 146; **1942**: 194, 196–98, 200, 203, 209, 211, 218–29, 231–34, 237–49; **1943**: 254–66

North Atlantic, Battle of the, *see* Naval war

Norway: **1939**: 101–2; **1940**: 106–12, 116; **1941**: 174; **1942**: 244–45; **1944**: 351, 353; **1945**: 373, 406

Novgorod: **1941**: 170; **1943**: 254, 301

Novorossiysk: **1942**: 231; **1943**: 282

Nürnberg: **1944**: 310; **1945**: 397, *398*, *399*, *401*

Nürnberg rally (1938), *61*

Oberg, Karl, 215, 225

O'Callahan, Lt. Commander Joseph T., 387
O'Connor, Gen. Sir Richard, 141, 152
OCTAGON conference (1944), 345
Odessa: **1941**: 170, 171, 178; **1944**: 312
Ogura, Musatsume, 153
O'Hare, Lt. Edward (Butch), 205
Okada, Adm. Keisuke, 28, 43
Okayama: **1945**, 411–12
Okinawa: **1944**: 350; **1945**: 371, 390, *391, 392,* 393–403, 406–11, 413
Olaf, Prince (Norway), 406
Omaha Beach: **1944**, *299*
Omori, Sentaro, 187
Open Door policy, 5, 8, 75
Oradour-sur-Glâne: **1944**, 322
Oran: **1942**, 242, 243
Orel: **1941**: 176–77; **1942**: 212· **1943**: 271, 273, 275, 280
Ortona: **1943**, 295, 296
Osaka: **1945**, 386, 411–12, 414
Oshima, Baron Hiroshi, 148, 150
Oslo: **1940**: 109; **1944**: 368
Osmeña, Sergio, 354
Osmoc: **1944**, 357, 363, 364, 366
Ota, Adm. Minoru, 411
Oumansky, Constantine A., 150
OVERLORD, Operation (1944), 292
Ozawa, Adm. Jisaburo, 211

Pacelli, Eugenio Cardinal (later Pius XII), 22; *See also* Pius XII
"Pact of Steel" (1939), 84
Paderborn: **1945**, 390, 392
Pakhoi: **1936**, 47, 48
Palawau Island: **1945**, 382, 399
Palermo: **1943**, 273
Palestine problem: **1938**: 69, 74; **1939**: 84
"Palm Sunday Massacre" (1943), 263
Palmyra: **1941**, 159, 164, 166
Panay: **1942**: 212; **1945**: 386, 387
Pantelleria Island: **1943**, 266–68
Papagos, Gen. Alexander, 136–37
Papen, Franz von, 13, 15, 16, 31, 45, 394
Paramushiru Island: **1944**: 303; **1945**: 419
Paris: **1940**: 116, 119, *120*; **1941**: 176; **1942**: 207; **1944**: 339, 340, *341, 342,* 370
Paris protocols, 162

Patch, Gen. Alexander M., 338
Patton, Gen. George S., Jr.: **1943**: *251;* in North African campaign, 260; operations under, 261, 263, 272, 273; soldier slapped by, 274–75; **1944**: operations under, 336, 339, 348, 366; **1945**: operations under, 392, 401
Paul, Prince (regent of Yugoslavia), 148, 149
Paulus, Field Marshal Friedrich von, 229, 252, 253, 255, 256
"Pavlov, Gen. D. G.," 47
Pearl Harbor: **1941**: *143*, 145–46, 179–84, *186, 188;* **1942**: 200, 206, 207, 263; **1945**: 419
Peel, Sir Robert, 53
Peking: **1935**: 34; **1937**: 54
Pelelin Island: **1944**: *346*, 348, 351, 361; **1945**: 373
Percival, Gen. A. E., 202, 203, *204, 420*
Permet: **1940**, 140–41
Pescadores: **1954**, 371
Petacci, Clara, 400–1
Pétain, Marshal Philippe: **1940**: 133; armistice call by, 119; assumes dictatorial powers, 126; assures U.S. on fleet, 137; becomes premier, 121; breaks relations with Britain, 125; and government remaining in France, 123; and Hitler meeting, *136;* named vice premier, 114; on ouster of Laval, 142; **1941**: 193; collaboration policy of, 159, 170; warned on collaboration, 160–61; **1942**: as chief of state, 212; Darlan and, 244; and dissolution of Vichy army, 245; and German occupation of unoccupied zone in France, 243; on Madagascar conflict, 215; message of, to Roosevelt, 242; names Laval as premier, 209; **1943**: plans to kidnap, 281; Robert and, 270; **1944**: and Free French representatives, 338; removed to Belfort, 340; sees threat of civil war, 314; **1945**: arrested, 400
Peter II (King of Yugoslavia), 151, 416
Petsamo: **1944**, 348, 351
Philippine Sea, Battle of the (1944), 325–36
Philippines: **1935**: commonwealth status under U.S. rule, 39; **1941**: 156, 179, 183, 186, 189, 191–94; **1942**: defenses, 197–98, 207, 209,

210, 220; **1943**, 277, 284; **1944**: 318, 357, 362–64, *365,* 366–68; **1945**: 370, 375, 376, 380, 381, 385–87, *396,* 397–99, 403, 307–9, 411–13, 419
Phillips, Adm. Sir Tom, 189
Phillips, William, 111
Picasso, Pablo, 52
Pikit, Fort: **1945**, 398, 399
Pilsen, **1945**, 400, 404
Pilsudski, Marshal Josef, 34
Pittman, Key, 120
Pius XII, 22, 73, 80, 105, 151, 267, 319
Platt, Gen. Sir William, 145
Ploesti: **1940**: 138; **1942**: 220; **1943**: 274; **1944**: 311, *315,* 342
POINTBLANK, Operation (1944), 301
Poison gas: British and, 96, 98; in China, 220; in Ethiopian-Italian war, 39–40, 42–43, 91; Germans warned against use of, 217; in Pacific war, 91–92, 220; against Russian POWs in Auschwitz, 172
Poland: **1939**: 76, 79, 82–97; **1940**: Katyn massacre, 115, 263, 264, 302; **1944**: 300, 305, 308, 310, 332–36, 350; **1945**: 370–75, 385, 388–90, 411, 413
Polish-Rumanian alliance, 48
Poltava: **1943**: 283; **1944**: *327*
Port Moresby: **1942**, 201, 226, 227, 230–33, 235
Potsdam conference (1945), *369,* 400, 414, 415
Potsdam Declaration (1945), 417
Pound, Sir Dudley, 284
Poznan: **1945**, 375, 378, 380–81
Praga: **1944**, 344, 345
Prague: **1945**, 403, 404, 406
Prien, Lt. Günther, 98
Prüm: **1945**, 378–79
Pskov: **1944**, 304, 334–35
Pucheau, Pierre, 308
Purple code, 157
Pu-yi, Henry, 11, 27
Pyle, Ernie, 398

QUADRANT conference (1943), 276–77
Quezon, Manuel L., 192
Quisling, Vidkin, 101–2, 109–11, 132, 201, 406

Rabaul: **1942**: 196, 200, 205, 248; **1943**: 269, 284, 287–89, *297;*

1944: 302, 305, 306, 309–10

"Racial Violence" decrees (German; 1937), 53

Radom: **1939**: 93; **1944**: 335; **1945**: 373

Raeder, Adm. Erich, *31*, 93, 102, 107, 150, 250, 256

Ramsay, Adm. Sir Bertram, 370

Rangoon: **1941**: 192; **1942**: 198, 204–6, 211, 232; **1944**: 314; **1945**: 395, 399, *402*, 403, 404, 419

"Rape of Nanking" (1937), 60

Rashid Ali, 151–52, 156, 159, 162

Rath, E. von, 74, 75

Rauschning, Hermann, 29

Rawlings, Adm. H. B., 414

Rearmament and remobilization: **1933**: Belgian, 20; Chinese, 20; **1934**: British, 28; Japanese, 30; **1935**: Austrian, 33; British, 38; Ethiopian, 37; French, 33; Italian, 33, 35, 37, 38; Russian, 33; **1936**: Austrian, 44; British, 43, 46; embargo of arms to Spain, 45, 46; Italian, 47; Japanese, 42; Russian and embargo on arms shipment to Spain, 47; Spanish, 46–48; **1937**: British, 60; Chinese, 53, 54; Italian, 51; Japanese, 53, 54; **1938**: British, 67, 68, 72; Bulgarian, 69; French, 64, 67, 68, 70, 72; Hungarian, 74; Italian, 62; Japanese, 63, 66, 68; Polish mobilization, 75; Russian troops mass in Ukraine, 71; U.S., 63, 67, 68; **1939**: British, 83, 88–90, 100–1; French, 90; Polish, 88, 89; Russian, 90; U.S., 78, 85, 93; **1940**: Belgian, 104; British, 131, 133; Dutch, 112; Rumanian, 117; U.S., 107, 114, 116, 119–22, 126–32, 135; U.S., cost of tanks and planes (1940–1980), 177; U.S. naval, 145, 162, 176; and U.S. strikes, 159; **1942**: Australian, 203; Canadian conscription, 203, 204, 225; U.S. draft, 283; **1944**: Canadian draft, 359, 371; *See also* German rearmament

Regensburg: **1943**: 277; **1944**: 306

Reggio di Calabria: **1943**, 280

Reichenau, Field Marshal Walther von, 198

Reichstag fire (1933), 19

Reims: **1940**: 119; **1944**: 342

Reinhardt, Gen. Georg-Hans, 113–14

Remagen: **1945**, 383, *384*, 386, 388, 389

Reparations payments: **1932**: 8, 11, 14; **1937**: 50

Reynaud, Paul, 108, 117, 119, 121, 405

Reza Khan (Shah of Iran), 175

Rhineland reoccupation (1936), *41*, 43–44

Ribbentrop, Joachim von: **1937**: and German colonies, 51; **1938**: as foreign affairs minister, 63, 67, *69*; and Polish situation, 74; and war in the east, 76; **1939**: and partition of Poland, 93; on policy, 79; and Polish problem, 79, 90; Russo-German pact and, 86, 88; **1940**: and Duke of Windsor, 134; message of, to Stalin, 134; **1941**: and Hitler meeting, *180*; Japan advised to enter war against Britain by, 148; **1943**: Mussolini and, 260; **1945**: arrested, 411; declared war criminal, 383

Riccardi, Adm. Arturo, 141

Riga: **1941**: 165; **1944**: 340, 347, 351

Right, the: **1931**: Central European, 6; French, 5; German, 3; **1932**: German, *12*, 13–17, 19–21; Japanese, 13; **1933**: Austrian, 20, 21; British, 19; in Danzig, 23; German, 18–23; Rumanian, 24; **1934**: Austrian, 28; Bulgarian, 27; French, 26, 27; **1935**: Austrian, 34; Czech, 34; Estonian, 33; **1936**: French, 45; Rumanian, 46; **1937**: Austrian, 50, 51, 56; Chinese, 50; in Danzig, 52; and plot against Szalasi, 51; Rumanian, 60; **1938**: Austrian, 62–64; Bulgarian, 66; Czech, 65–67, 70; Lithuanian, 76; Rumanian, 63, 66, 76; **1939**: Czech, 79; in Danzig, 84; Hungarian, 79; Rumanian, 95; **1940**: Dutch, 112; French, 114; Norwegian, 132; Rumanian, 111, 125, 130, 140; Swiss, 139–40; Uruguayan, 132; Yugoslav, 111; **1941**: Rumanian, 145

Rios, Juan Antonio, 237

Ritchie, Gen. Sir Neil, 183, 221, 223

River Platte, Battle of the (1939), 101

Robert, Adm. Georges, 217, 270

Roberts, Owen J., 200

Robinson, Bernard, 222

Röhm, Ernest, 28

Rokossovsky, Gen. Konstantin K., 252, 328, 335

Rome: **1943**: 272, 276, 281, 285–88; **1944**: 300, 314, 318, 319

Rome agreement (1935), 32

Rome-Berlin Axis (1936), 47

Rome protocols (1934), 27

Rommel, Field Marshal Erwin: **1940**: in invasion of France, 113, 115; **1941**: assumes African command, 146, 148; attempt on life of, 181; operations under, 148, 150–53, 155–57, 159, 182, 191; **1942**: Farouk and, 202; as legend, 197; made field marshal, 223; operations under, 198–200, 218–27, 231, 232, 240; **1943**: in command in Greece, 273; and cross-Channel invasion, 295; operations under, 259, 260, 274; **1944**: command given to, 300; suicide of, 351, 400; wounded, 333

Rommel, Gen. Juliusz, 94

Roosevelt, Eleanor, 238

Roosevelt, Franklin Delano: **1932**: elected, 15; **1933**: becomes president, 20; opening way for U.S. recognition of Russia, 23; **1935**: appeals to Mussolini, 35; arms embargo on Ethiopia and Italy, 37; on foreign policy, 38; isolationists and, 35; **1936**: call to the Americas, 48; election of, 47; signs amended Neutrality Act, 43; **1937**: bans transport of munitions to Japan or China, 55; "Quarantine" speech of, 56; signs Neutrality Act, 52; **1938**: Czech situation and, 70, 73; message of, to Chamberlain, 62; rearmament called for by, 63; **1939**: cables Hitler, 88; Einstein message to, on atomic bomb, 86; Finno-Russian conflict and, 98; limited emergency proclaimed by, 93; message of, to Hitler and Mussolini, 83; and neutrality, 78, 81; and rearmament, 78; repeals arms embargo act, 95; and sale of aircraft to Spain, 79; on sending U.S. boys to fight, 99; **1940**: appeals to Italy not to enter war, 111; Churchill and, *see under* Churchill, Sir Winston; declares national emergency, 124; on defense and Italy's entry into war, 119; on direct aid to Britain, 142; given power over exports,

Roosevelt, Franklin Delano (Continued)
125; increased budget requested by, 126; and lease of British bases, 129; and limited embargo against Japan, 125; Mussolini appealed to by, 114; and national defense budget, 104; naval expansion and, 120; promises not to go to war, 137; and rearmament, 116, 134; Reynaud appeals to, 119; signs Naval Expansion Act, 127; Welles sent to report on Europe, 105–6; **1941**: and aid for invaded Russia, 164, 165; on arming merchant ships, 177; Azores and, 161, 162; begins third term, 145; condemns reprisal killings, 179; criticizes Lindbergh, 156; criticizes Vichy, 159; in deadlock with Japan, 181–82; denounces German sinkings, 164; Indochina neutrality and, 168, 169; and Japanese invasion of Indochina, 184–86; lend-lease program under, 144, 150; on liberty ships, 176; on naval war, 174; 1942 budget requests of, 144; and opening of Red Sea, 153; pledges to defeat Hitler, 172; and proposed meeting with Konoye, 170, 172, 175, 176; on repealing Neutrality Act, 180, 181; Ribbentrop on, 148; unlimited emergency proclaimed by, 161–62; and U.S. supplies for North Africa, 155; views of, on relations between nations, 155; and Yugoslav situation, 148; **1942**: and aid to China, 202; antiinflation program of, 232; and Browder's release, 218; draft age and, 237; Japan threatened with use of gas by, 91; Leahy and, 225–26; orders MacArthur to leave Philippines, 205; Pétain's message to, 242; recalls Leahy, 209; and seizure of patents, 213–14; tax bill signed by, 237; and U.S. economy placed on war footing, 214; on U.S. military strength, 226; and Vichy neutrality, 203, 205–6; and war crimes, 230, 236; on war declarations and Japanese use of gas, 220; on war strategy, 197; Willkie as representative of, 234; **1943**: 253; addresses Canadian Parliament, 278; addresses

Italian people, 272; budget requests of, 253; and Burma operations, 296; at Cairo conference, 291, *292*; Camacho and, 264; Chiang Kai-shek and, 295; code name for, 277; and recall of Stilwell, 282; and surrender terms for Italy, 274; at Tehran conference, 292, *293*; in torpedo attack, 288–89; and war crimes, 264; **1944**: Chiang Kai-shek and, 301, 304; election of, 356; inaugurated, 374; and Italian fleet, 307; on monuments, 304; and Moscow conference, 350; and naval war, 300; at second Quebec conference, *345*; special envoy sent to China, 339; and war in Pacific, 335; **1945**: death of, 395; de Gaulle and, 380; at Yalta conference, 376, *377*
Rosenberg, Alfred, 101, 407
Rosenthal, Joe, 381
Rostov: **1941**: 179, 181–83; **1942**: 225, 226, 250; **1943**: 252, 257, 258
Rostow, Eugene V., 191
Rotterdam: **1940**: 114; **1944**: 345
Rouen: **1940**: 118, 119; **1942**: 229, 230, 232; **1944**: 340
Ruckteschell, Capt. Helmuth von, 285
Ruhr: **1940**: 114; **1943**: 260, 266, 268–69; **1944**: 347; **1945**: 391–93, 396, 397
Rumania: **1940**: 134; **1941**: 145, 152; **1944**: 310, 311, 315, 319, 320, 324, 340–42, 344, 345, 350; **1945**: 382, 385
Runciman, Lord, 69
Rundstedt, Field Marshal Gerd von, 183, 329, 343, 346, 364–65, 371, 385, 402
Russo-Finnish fighting: **1939**: 97–102; **1940**: 104–7; **1941**: 163, 165, 167, 171, 173–75, 177, 180, 183, 184, 190; **1943**: 257; **1944**: 307, 309, 313, 324, 325, 330, 332, 334, 343, 344, 348–50, 359, 361
Russo-Japanese fighting: **1905**: 6; **1938**: 69; **1939**: 83–85, 87, 97; **1941**: 178; **1942**: 212; **1945**: 416–19
Rutba: **1941**, 157, 158
Ryti, Risto, 336
Ryukyu Islands: **1945**: 382, 390, *391*, 398, 399, 404, 407; *See also* Okinawa
Rzhev: **1942**: 230, 245, 246; **1943**: 260

Saar plebiscite (1935), 30, 32
Saarlautern: **1944**, 361–64
St. Germain, Treaty of (1919), 33
St.-Lô: **1944**, 332, *333*, 335
St.-Malo: **1944**, 336, 337, 339
St.-Vith: **1944**: 365, 366; **1945**: 372, 375
Saipan: **1944**, 306, 325, 327–30, *331*, 333, 356, 360
Saito, Adm. Viscount Makoto, 13, 43
Sakishima Islands: **1945**, 404
Salamana: **1942**, 199, 200, 207
Salazar, Antonio, 264
Salerno: **1943**, 281, 282
Salonika: **1941**: 153; **1944**: 355
San Benedetto: **1944**, *351*
Sandau: **1945**, 395–96
Sangro, Battle of the (1943), 294
Santa Cruz, Battle of (1942), 238, 239
Sapieha, Stefan Cardinal, 139
Sarawak: **1942**: 196, 197; **1945**: 411, 412
Sardinia: **1943**: 281, 282; **1944**: 304
Sauckel, Fritz, 307
Saudi Arabia: **1940**, 134
Savo Island, Battle of (1942), 227
Schacht, Hjalmar, 78
Schellenburg, Walter, 134
Schleicher, Kurt von, 14, 16, 18
Schouten Islands: **1944**, 318
Schrader, Commander A. E., 142
Schrier, Lt. Harold G., 381
Schuschnigg, Kurt von, 28, 34, 51, 52, 56, 62–64, 403
Schweinfurt: **1943**: 277, 285; **1944**: 306; **1945**: 394
SEALION (invasion of Britain), 132
Sedan: **1940**: 114; **1944**: 343
Selective Training and Service Act (U.S.; 1940), 132
Seuss, Hans, 105
Sevastopol: **1941**: 179, 193, 194; **1942**: 197, 218–20, 222, 223; **1944**: 312, 314, 315
Seyss-Inquart, Arthur, 63, 64, 115, 248, 401, 405
Shang Chen, Gen., 67
Shanghai: **1932**: 9, 13; **1937**: 54, 55, 57, 58; **1940**: 123; **1941**: 188
Shanghai incidents (1932), 8–13
Shelley, Norman, 116–17
Shigemitsu, Mamoru, 266, 419
Shigeru, Gen. Honjo, 2
Shikoku Island: **1945**, 413, 414
Shimada, Shigetaro, 333

Shiozawa, Adm. Kiochi, 9
SHO, Operation (VICTORY; 1944), 351–52
Shori, Arai, 262
Short, Gen. Walter C., 200, 206
Sidi Barrani: **1940**: 131, 132, 141; **1942**: 222
Sidi Rezegh: **1941**: 181; **1942**: 222
Sihanouk, Norodom (King of Cambodia), 208
Sikorski, Gen. Wladislaw, 96, 270
Simon, Sir John, 70
Simovich, Gen. Dusan, 151
Simpson, Wallis W., 48, 134
Singapore: **1938**: 63; **1941**: 148, 150, 156, 159, 188, 189; **1942**: 196, 198, 200–4; **1944**: 356; **1945**: 375, 387, 415
Sino-Japanese war: **1931**: 2–6; **1932**: 8–15; **1933**: 18–23; **1935**: 33, 34, 38–39; **1936**: 42, 46, 48; **1937**: 51, 53–60; **1938**: 62–74, 76; **1939**: 78, 79, 82–84, 91, 96–97; **1940**: 104, 111, 119–21, 123, 128, 140; **1941**: 156, 170, 175–76, 181–82, 189, 190, 192; **1942**: 202, 203, 208–9, 211, 217, 218, 224, 225, 226, 235–37; **1943**: 253, 260, 261, 266–67, 284, 292, 295–96; **1944**: 313–15, 318, 342–44, 354, 357, 361, 363, 366; **1945**: 373–75, 396, 407, 410, 411, 413–16, 418–19
Sirovy, Gen. Jan, 71
Skoplje: **1941**: 152; **1944**: 358
Skorzeny, Col. Otto, 281
Slim, Gen. William, 209, 312, 359, 378, 382, 387, 395
Slutsky, Mikhail, 268
Smigly-Ridz, Marshal Edward, 85–87
Smith, Capt. Fred M., 264
Smolensk: **1941**: 170; **1942**: 211; **1943**: 281, 283
Smuts, Gen. Jan Christian, 58, 92
Soddu, Gen. Ubaldo, 138, 145
Sofia: **1941**: 151, 155; **1944**: 301, 347
Sollum: **1940**: 131, 142; **1941**: 156; **1942**: 198
Solomon Islands: **1942**: 200, 214, 218, 227, 230, 250; **1943**: 259, 269, 270, 272, 276–78, 281–85, 287, 288, 290, 295, 298; **1944**: 300, 305, 308, 310, 314
Somaliland: **1940**: 128, 129; **1941**: 147–51; **1942**: 246, 249
Soong, T. V., 278
Sorge, Richard, 160, 178, 357

Soviet-German alliance (1939), 82–87
Soviet Union: **1940**: 127, 129, 140, 142; **1941**: 160, 162, 164–83, 184, 185–86, 188, 193, 194; Crimea, 175, 179, 180, 193, 194; moving industry to rear, 167, 177; warned of invasion, 150, 152, 156–58, 160, 161, 163; **1942**: 199–201, 204–6, 209, 210, 215–18, 222–30, 233–36, 240, 249, 250; Crimea, 196, 207, 211–12, 216, 224; **1943**: 252, 254–62, 265, 267, 268, 270–79, 283, 285, 287, 290, 292, 294–96; **1944**: 300–15, 328, 329, 332–36, 339, 347–51, 354; *See also* Russo-Finnish fighting; Russo-Japanese fighting
Spaak, Paul-Henri, 52
Spaatz, Gen. Carl A., 296, 397
Spanish civil war: **1936**: 41; the Left and the Right in, 45; Popular Front winning elections and, 43; Loyalist government flees to Valencia, 48; nonintervention in, 45, 46; **1937**: ban on arms and volunteers in, 50, 51; Catalonia under Loyalist rule in, 55; German and Italian intervention in, 50, 52, 53; Loyalist government moves to Barcelona, 57; Loyalists counterattack in, 59, 60; Nationalist victories in, 56; **1938**: Italians withdrawing from, 73; Nationalist gains in, 66, 76; repatriation of volunteers in, 68; **1939**: end of, 78–82; Italian and German volunteers in, 82
Speer, Albert, 273, 294
Spoleto, Duke of (Tomislav I), 159
Spratly Islands: **1939**, 82
SS (Schutzstaffel; Black Shirts): **1933**: occupy trade union headquarters, 21; in police forces, 18, 19; purpose of, 24; **1934**: in blood purge, 28
Stalin, Joseph: **1934**: trigger to great purges under, 30; **1939**: demands made on Finland by, 98; Hitler cable to, 87; orders war on Finland, 100; and pact with Germany, 87; policy statement by, 80; **1940**: on Hitler's intentions, 124; Hitler's and Mussolini's view of, 134; Katyn massacre and, 115; Ribbentrop's message to, 134; **1941**: accepts conference with Allies, 170; asks for British troops, 174; assumes

position of commander-in-chief, 167; assumes premiership, 158; calls for second front, 168; Churchill's message to, 167; on defense committee, 165; and Kiev defense, 175; "Mother Russia" speech by, 180; and pact with Japan, 154–55; and reconstituted Polish army, 184–85; remains in Moscow, 178; scorched earth policy of, 166; warned of invasion, 150, 152, 156–58, 160, 161, 163; **1942**: on Allied aid, 235; Churchill to, on shipping, 225; and convoys to Russia, 224; orders January offensive, 196; prohibits retreat, 226–27; on Russian losses in Crimea, 218; second front called for by, 23, 241; on war turning against Germany (February), 205; Willkie and, 234; **1943**: on halt of Murmansk convoys, 263; at Tehran conference, 288, 292, 293; **1944**: accuses Japan of aggression, 356; acknowledges Allied aid, 314; and date of Normandy invasion, 312; and meeting with de Gaulle, 362; in Moscow conference, 350; orders victory salvos, 328; and supplying Warsaw, 347; and U.S. bombing runs, 303; **1945**: and arrest of Polish leaders, 407; offensive into Poland and East Prussia and, 372; at Potsdam conference, 369, 414, 415; on Soviet occupation in Asia, 419; and surrender of Italy, 384; Truman tells, of atomic bomb, 414; at Yalta conference, 376, 377
Stalingrad: **1942**: 227–45, 248, 250; **1943**: 252–58, 262
Stalino: **1941**: 178; **1943**: 280
Standley, Adm. William, 260
Stanley, Oliver, 104
Staraya Russa: **1942**: 205, 207, 209, 210; **1944**: 305
Stark, Adm. Harold R., 210, 419
STARVATION, Operation (1945), 417
Stauffenberg, Col. Count Claus von, 333–34
Stavisky affair (France; 1934), 26
Stettin: **1942**: 231; **1945**: 400
Stettinius, Edward R., 361
Stilwell, Gen. Joseph W., 201, 209, 218, 277, 280, 282, 307, 308, 352, 354

Stimson, Henry L.: **1931**: Manchurian situation and, 3, 4; **1932**: concerned by events in China, 9; on crisis in Manchuria, 15; and Doctrine of Nonrecognition, 8, 11; **1940**: calls for conscription, 127; **1941**: and naval war, 157–58

Storm Troopers (SA; *Sturmabteilung*), 19; **1932**: 12, 14; **1933**: 18, 19, 21, 24; **1934**: purge of, 28

Stoyadinovich, Milan, 79, 150

Strasbourg: **1944**: 359, 360; **1945**: 372, 378

Streicher, Julius, 408

"Strengthening of German Manhood Decree" (German; 1939), 97

Stresa conference (1935), 33, 63

Stuttgart: **1945**, 398–400

Sudetenland, 34, 56, 58, 63–73

Suetsugu, Adm. N., 182–83

Sugiyama, Gen. Hajime, 54

Suichuan: **1945**, 373, 375

Sumatra: **1942**, 203, 208, 209

Suñer, Rámon Serrano, 214, 231

SUPERCHARGE, Operation (1942), 240

Surrender and armistices: **1932**: Sino-Japanese armistice, 13; **1941**: Iranian surrender, 174; Syrian-Lebanese armistice, 167; Thai and French Indochinese, 158; **1943**: Italian surrender, 274, 275, 279, 280, 283; Sino-Japanese armistice, 266; unconditional surrender policy set, 253; **1944**: Bulgarian surrender, 339, 354; Finnish surrender, 307, 309, 313; Hungarian surrender, 304, 349, 351; Rumanian surrender, 345; **1945**: German surrender, 380, 384, 386, 399, 403–7; Japanese surrender, *369*, 413–15, 417, *418*, 418–19, *420*

Sushinsky, Vladimir, 268

Suzuki, Adm. Kantaro, 392

Suzuki, Gen. Sosaku, 395

Suzuki, Gen. Teichi, 153, 189

Sweden: **1943**: 275, 287; **1944**: 349

Switzerland: **1944**, 356–57

Syracuse: **1941**: 171; **1943**: 271

Syria: **1941**: 158, 159, 162–64, 167, 175, 176; **1945**: 407, 409

Szalazi, Ferenc, 51, 351

Taclobau: **1944**, 352, 354

Tallinn: **1944**, 347–48

Tananarive: **1942**, 233, 234

Tangku, Truce of (1933), 22

Tani, Masayuki, 234

Tarakar Island: **1945**, 400, 408, 412

Taranto: **1940**: 138; **1943**: 281

Tarawa: **1941**: 189; **1943**: 282, 290, *291*, 292, 294

Tarnopol: **1944**, 308, 310, 312

Taruc, Luis, 210

Tassafaronga Point battle (1942), 246

Tavs, Leopold, 63

Tedder, Air Chief Marshal Sir Arthur, *405*

Tehran conference (1943), 292, *293*

Teleki, Count Paul, 85–86, 151

Tengah: **1942**, 202, 203

Tengchung: **1944**, *343*

Terauchi, Field Marshal Count Hisaichi, 330

Terboven, Josef, 201

TERMINAL conference (1945), 414

Terracina: **1944**, 318, 319

Teruel: **1937**: 60; **1938**: 63

Teschen: **1938**, 71–73

Thailand: **1941**: 179, 185, 186, 188–91; **1942**: 200; **1945**: 411

Thälmann, Ernst, 12

Thoma, Gen. Ritter von, 240

Tief, Otto, 348

Tientsin: **1937**: 54; **1939**: 85

Tikhvin: **1941**, 180, 188

Timor: **1942**, 204, 205, 209

Timoshenko, Marshal Semën, 106–7, 112, 165, 167, 199

Tinian Island: **1944**, 306, 324, 325, 335, 336, 356

Tirana: **1944**, 358, 359

Tiso, Father Joseph, 76, 80, 89

Tito, Marshal (Josip Broz): **1941**: partisan movement under, 166; **1943**: British aid to, 267; plans to kidnap, 281; provisional government under, 295; **1944**: and Churchill meeting, 338; and German paratrooper attack, 318; operations under, 347, 352; **1945**: bars return of king, 416; operations under, 407

Titulescu, Nicolae, 46

Tobruk: **1941**: 145, 153, 155, 157, 171, 179, 189; **1942**: 201, 220–22, 232, 233, 243

Togo, Shigenori, 181, 231

Tojo, Gen. Hideki: **1940**: as war minister, 122; **1941**: *178*; government under, 178; policy statement by, 183; war policy of, 183–84; warns of long war, 191; **1942**: assumes foreign minister post, 231; calls on Australia to surrender, 226; and India, 208, 218; Russian neutrality and, 225; **1943**: Bose and, 268; expanded power of, 284; Shigemitsu and, 266; **1944**: assumes command of army, 306; removed from power, 333; on situation (March), 310

Tokushiro, Kobayakawa, 206

Tokyo: **1944**: 352, 360, 361, 368; **1945**: 378, 379, 382, 384, 385, 408, 413, 414, 417, 419

Tokyo Express: **1942**, 239–40

Tokyo Rose (Toguri d'Aquino), 419

TORCH, Operation (1942), 231, 232

Torun: **1945**, 375, 376

Toulon: **1942**: 245, 246; **1944**: 339, 340

Toungoo: **1942**, 209, 210

Toyama: **1945**, *415*

Toyoda, Adm. Teijiro, 153, 169

Toyodo, Adm. Soemu, 310

Trade agreements: **1931**: U.S.-Japanese, 86, 105; **1932**: British-Russian, not renewed, 15; **1935**: Russo-German, 33; **1936**: Austro-Czech, 44; Sino-Russian, 45; **1939**: Polish-Russian, 79; Rumanian-German, 102; Sino-Russian, 85; **1940**: Franco-Italian, 107; Germano-Italian, 107; Germano-Rumanian, 111, 116; Germano-Russian, 106; **1941**: Germano-Russian, 145; Germano-Turkish, 177; Russian-Japanese, 163; Russian-U.S.-British, 176; **1942**: Germano-Turkish, 235; Rumanian-Turkish, 233; **1943**: Germano-Turkish, 264

Treasury Islands: **1943**, 287

Tresckow, Gen. Henning von, 261

Trevelyan, George Macaulay, 46

TRIDENT conference (1943), 267

Trier: **1944**: 345; **1945**: 382

Trieste: **1945**, 402, 403, 410

Trinidad: **1941**, 151, 167

Tripartite Pact (1940), 132–34, 140, 151, 176, 177, 182, 196

Tripoli: **1941**: 148, 155; **1942**: 199, 245; **1943**: 254, 255

Trondheim: **1940**, 109, 111

Trotsky, Leon, 129

Truk: **1944**: 304, 305, 314; **1945**: 410, 411
Truman, Harry S., *369*, 395, 405, 414, 415, 419
Truscott, Gen. Lucian K., 306
Tsingtao: **1936**: 48; **1937**: 60
Tsouderos, Emmanuel, 156
Tukachevsky, Gen. Mikhail, 33
Tulagi: **1942**, 214, 218, 227
Tunis: **1942**: 245, 246, 248; **1943**: 264–66
Tunisia, *see* North African campaigns
Turin: **1940**: 128; **1942**: 238, 245; **1945**: 402
Tyranowski, Jan, 139

Uchida, Count Yusuya, 14
Udet, Gen. Ernst, 181
U-GO, Operation (1944), 308, 309
Ultra (German code intercepts), 139, 158, 180, 221, 240, 254, 264, 265, 288
Uman: **1941**: 170; **1944**: 308
Umberto, Prince, 321
Umezu, Yoshijiro, 333
United Nations: **1942**: crimes against Jews, 249; Ethiopia joins, 236; signatories of, 196; **1943**: and war crimes, 285; **1945**: Spain barred from, 411
United Nations Conference on International Organization (1945), 400, 412
United States: **1942**: 222, 232; **1943**: 272; **1944**: 356
Ushijima, Gen. Mitsuru, 411

Valera, Eamon de, 402
Valuyki: **1942**: 225; **1943**: 254
Vatican: **1943**, 287
Vatutin, Marshal Nicholas, 287, 296, 307
Velikiye Luki: **1942**: 245, 246; **1943**: 252
Vella Gulf battle (1943), 276
Vemork: **1943**: 260; **1944**: 290, 306
Venezuela: **1942**, 204
Venice: **1945**, 401
Versailles, Treaty of (1919), 8, 11, 21–22, 27, 29, 33, 34, 43, 48, 50
Vian, Capt. Philip, 106
Victor Emmanuel III (King of Italy), 44, 82, 88, 127, 151, 273, 313, 321
Vienna: **1942**: 231, 276; **1945**: 386, 388, 389, 392, 393, 396

"Vienna Awards" (1938), 74
Vietinghoff, Gen. Heinrich von, 290, 401
Vilna: **1941**: 164; **1944**: 332
Vinnitsa: **1944**, 301, 309
Visconti-Prasca, Gen. Sebastiano, 136–38
Vitebsk: **1941**: 167; **1943**: 298; **1944**: 302, 327, 328
Vlasov, Gen. Andrei A., 375, 404, 405
Vonnegut, Kurt, Jr., 378
Voronezh: **1942**: 223, 224; **1943**: 254, 255
Voronstov, Captain, 158
Voroshilov, Marshal Kliment, 165, 171
Vyazma: **1941**: 173–74, 176–78; **1942**: 230

Wainwright, Gen. Jonathan, 209, 215–16, *420*
Wake Island: **1941**: 179, 189–90, 192; **1943**: 284; **1944**: 318, 343
Wallace, Henry, 332
Wang, C. T., 3
Wang Ching-wei, 66, 108, 140, 165, 357
Wannsee Conference (1942), 199
War declarations (and diplomatic ruptures): **1940**: 125; **1941**: 156, 164, 188, 190, 191; **1942**: 214, 217, 219–21, 225, 227, 230, 232, 237, 246, 249; **1943**: 253, 254, 260, 263, 264, 284, 287, 296; **1944**: 302, 303, 308, 309, 327, 329, 336, 340, 348, 368; **1945**: 371, 378, 379, 381, 382, 390, 395, 410, 413, 416, 417
Warsaw: **1939**: 92, 93, 95–97; **1942**: 231; **1944**: 332, 335, 344, 349, 352; uprising, 336, 338, 340, 343, 345, 347; **1945**: 372, 373
Washington Naval Treaty (1922), 30, 42
Wavell, Gen. Sir Archibald P., 164, 192, 196, 197, 203, 268, 285
Wedemeyer, Gen. Albert, 185, 354, 361, 363
WEISS (plan of war on Poland), 82
Weizsäcker, Ernst von, 85
Welles, Sumner, 85, 105–6, 133, 150, 157, 168
Werben: **1945**, 395–96
Wesel: **1940**: 112; **1945**: 388, 389
"West Wall, Battle for the" (1944), 346

Weygand, Gen. Maxime, 114, 117, 119, 122, 149, 168, 403
Wheeler, Burton K., 185
White, Byron R., 275
Wiener Neustadt: **1943**: 276; **1945**: 392
Wilhelm II (Kaiser of Germany), 162
Wilhelmina (Queen of Netherlands), 248, 409
Wilhelmshaven: **1939**: 92; **1941**: 167; **1943**: 256, 287
Willkie, Wendell, 234
Wilson, Gen. Sir Henry Maitland, 163, 296
Windsor, Duke of (formerly Edward VIII), 134; *See also* Edward VIII (King of England)
Wingate, Gen. Orde, 257, 259, 262, 310
Windelman, Gen. Henri, 114
Wittenberge: **1945**, 395–96
Wojtyla, Karol (future John Paul II), 139
Wolff, Karl, 384
Wu Pei-fu, Gen., 66

Yalta conference (1945), 376
Yamamoto, Adm. Isoroku, 179, 263
Yamashita, Gen. Tomoyuki, 203–4, 419
Yamschchikova, Olga, 234
Yang Fu-cheng, Gen., 48
Yefremov, Gen. Mikhail G., 212
Yin Ju-keng, 38, 39
Yokohama: **1942**: 212; **1945**: 408
Yonai, Adm. Mitsumasu, 104
Young, Sir Mark, 192, *193*
Yugoslavia: **1940**: 140; **1941**: 148, 150–57, 167, 169, 171, 172, 179, 184; **1942**: 215, 267, 281; **1944**: 300, 314, 343, 345, 347, *349*, 350–53, 358, 359, 363, 364; **1945**: 392, 400, 402, 403

Zeitzler, Gen. Kurt, 248
Zhdanov, Andrei, 47
Zhitomir: **1943**: 288, 290, 298
Zhukov, Marshal Georgi K.: **1939**: attacks Japanese, 87; **1941**: heads Moscow defenses, 179; Moscow offensive under, 186; **1944**: operations under, 308; **1945**: German surrender to, 406; operations under, 372, 373, 377
Zog (King of Albania), 81, 82
Zweig, Arnold, 19–20

KILROY WAS HERE